TERRORISM AND HOSTAGES
IN INTERNATIONAL LAW
— A COMMENTARY ON
THE HOSTAGES CONVENTION 1979

TERRORISM AND HOSTAGES IN INTERNATIONAL LAW

— A COMMENTARY ON THE HOSTAGES CONVENTION 1979

by

JOSEPH J. LAMBERT

A PUBLICATION OF
THE RESEARCH CENTRE FOR INTERNATIONAL LAW,
UNIVERSITY OF CAMBRIDGE

CAMBRIDGE
GROTIUS PUBLICATIONS LIMITED
1990

SALES &   GROTIUS PUBLICATIONS LTD.
ADMINISTRATION   PO BOX 115, CAMBRIDGE CB3 9BP, UK

British Library Cataloguing in Publication Data

Lambert, Joseph J.
  Terrorism and hostages in international law: a commentary on the Hostages Convention 1979.
  1. Taking as hostage — Treaties
  I. Title
  341. 7'7

ISBN 0-949009-46-6

JOSEPH J. LAMBERT
1990

All rights reserved. No part of this publication may be reproduced or transmitted in any form or by any means, including photocopying and recording, without the written permission of the copyright holder, application for which should be addressed to the publisher. Such written permission must also be obtained before any part of this publication is stored in a retrieval system of any nature.

Typeset and printed by
The Burlington Press (Cambridge) Limited, Foxton, Cambridge

To my father,

and to the memory of my mother

SUMMARY TABLE OF CONTENTS

Foreword	*xxvii*
Preface	*xxix*
Table of Cases	*xxxi*
Abbreviations	*xxxiii*
Introduction	1

PART I
THE PROBLEM OF INTERNATIONAL TERRORISM AND THE RESPONSE OF INTERNATIONAL ORGANIZATIONS — 11

1. The Meaning of Terrorism — 13
2. The Problem of Terrorism in Perspective — 23
3. The International Community and Efforts to Control Terrorism: a Lack of Consensus — 28
4. Achievements of the United Nations and the Specialized Agencies with Respect to Terrorism: the Five Conventions and Two Protocols Imposing the Obligation *aut dedere aut judicare* — 46
5. The Emergence of the Hostages Convention — 57

PART II
THE HOSTAGES CONVENTION: COMMENTARY — 69

Preamble — 71

Article 1: The Offences of Hostage-Taking, Attempt and Participation — 77

Article 2: Establishment of Penalties for Convention Offences — 93

Article 3: Easing the Situation of the Hostage — 109

Article 4:	Co-operation to Prevent Acts of Hostage-Taking	119
Article 5:	Establishment of Jurisdiction over the Offences	133
Article 6:	Matters Prior to Trial or Extradition	167
Article 7:	Notification of the Results of Prosecution	185
Article 8:	*Aut dedere aut judicare*	187
Article 9:	Discrimination Clause	209
Article 10:	Facilitation of the Extradition Option	227
Article 11:	Mutual Assistance in Criminal Proceedings	245
Article 12:	Relationship between the Convention and the Laws of Armed Conflict	263
Article 13:	Limitation of the Convention to International Acts of Hostage-Taking	299
Article 14:	Territorial Integrity and Political Independence	313
Article 15:	Preservation of the "Treaties on Asylum"	327
Articles 16-20:	Dispute Settlement and Final Articles	343
Conclusion		347
Appendix I:	International Convention Against the Taking of Hostages, 1979	357
Appendix II:	FRG Draft Convention	365
Index		371

FULL TABLE OF CONTENTS

Foreword	*xxvii*
Preface	*xxix*
Table of Cases	*xxxi*
Abbreviations	*xxxiii*
Introduction	1

PART I

THE PROBLEM OF INTERNATIONAL TERRORISM AND THE RESPONSE OF INTERNATIONAL ORGANIZATIONS — 11

1. The Meaning of Terrorism	13
(A) The lack of a generally accepted definition of the term "terrorism"	13
(B) Individual and State terrorism	14
(C) Two working definitions of terrorism	17
(D) State-sponsored terrorism	19
(E) The "international" nature of terrorism	22
2. The Problem of Terrorism in Perspective	23
3. The International Community and Efforts to Control Terrorism: a Lack of Consensus	28
(A) Pre-World War II efforts to control terrorism	28
(B) General Assembly deliberations	29
(i) 1972-1973	32
The *Ad Hoc* Committee on International Terrorism	36
(ii) 1976-1987	39

4. Achievements of the United Nations and the Specialized Agencies with Respect to Terrorism: the Five Conventions and Two Protocols Imposing the Obligation *aut dedere aut judicare*   46

   (A) Segmentation of the problem of terrorism   46

   (B) Offences covered by the anti-terrorism conventions and protocols   51

      (i) ICAO instruments   51

     (ii) IMO instruments   52

    (iii) UN Conventions   53

   (C) Characteristics of the anti-terrorism instruments   54

      (i) Common provisions   54

     (ii) Reliance on municipal law   55

    (iii) Shortcomings of the instruments   56

5. The Emergence of the Hostages Convention   57

   (A) Establishment of the *Ad Hoc* Committee on the Drafting of an International Convention Against the Taking of Hostages   57

   (B) The bypassing of the ILC and the Terrorism Committee   59

   (C) Procedural and substantive drafting progress of the Convention   61

   (D) The drafting records of the Hostages Convention   65

PART II

THE HOSTAGES CONVENTION: COMMENTARY — 69

PREAMBLE — 71

1. Introduction — 71
2. Interpretation — 72

ARTICLE 1

THE OFFENCES OF HOSTAGE-TAKING, ATTEMPT AND PARTICIPATION — 77

1. Introduction — 77
2. Interpretation — 79

   Paragraph 1: The definition of the offence of hostage-taking — 79

   "Any person who . . ." — 79

   ". . . seizes or detains . . ." — 80

   ". . . and threatens to kill, to injure or to continue to detain . . ." — 82

   The scope of liability for "threats" — 82

   ". . . another person . . ." — 84

   ". . . in order to compel . . ." — 84

   ". . . a third party, namely, a State, an international intergovernmental organization, a natural or juridical person, or a group of persons . . ." — 85

   ". . . to do or abstain from doing any act . . ." — 87

   ". . . as an explicit or implicit condition for the release of the hostage . . ." — 87

"... commits the offence of taking of hostages (hostage-taking) within the meaning of this Convention." 88

Paragraph 2: Attempt and participation as offences under the Convention 89

"Any person who: (a) attempts to commit an act of hostage-taking ..." 89

"... or (b) participates as an accomplice of anyone who commits or attempts to commit an act of hostage-taking ..." 90

ARTICLE 2

ESTABLISHMENT OF PENALTIES FOR CONVENTION OFFENCES 93

1. Introduction 93

   The role of municipal law in the suppression and punishment of hostage-taking and other "international crimes" 93

2. Interpretation 101

   "Each State Party shall make the offences set forth in article 1 punishable ..." 101

   "... by appropriate penalties which take into account the grave nature of those offences." 102

   The response of certain States Parties to the obligation set forth in this Article 103

   "Appropriate" penalties under this Convention compared to "severe" penalties under the ICAO Conventions 106

ARTICLE 3

EASING THE SITUATION OF THE HOSTAGE 109

1. Introduction 109

2. Interpretation 110

Paragraph 1: The obligation to ease the situation of the hostage ... 110

"The State Party in the territory of which the hostage is held by the offender . . ." ... 110

". . . shall take all measures it considers appropriate to ease the situation of the hostage, in particular, to secure his release . . ." ... 111

    The potential conflict between Article 3 and Article 8: A grant of immunity in return for the release of hostages ... 112

    The *Achille Lauro* incident ... 115

". . . and, after his release, to facilitate, when relevant, his departure." ... 116

Paragraph 2: The obligation to return objects to the hostage or third party ... 117

"If any object which the offender has obtained as a result of the taking of hostages comes into the custody of a State Party, that State Party shall return it as soon as possible to the hostage or the third party referred to in article 1, as the case may be, or to the appropriate authorities thereof." ... 117

ARTICLE 4

CO-OPERATION TO PREVENT ACTS OF HOSTAGE-TAKING ... 119

1. Introduction ... 119

    The need for, and obstacles to, international co-operation to prevent acts of hostage-taking ... 120

2. Interpretation ... 122

    "States Parties shall co-operate in the prevention of the offences set forth in article 1, particularly by:" ... 122

    Subparagraph (a) ... 122

"... taking all practicable measures to prevent preparations in their respective territories for the commission of those offences within or outside their territories . . ."   122

"... including measures to prohibit in their territories illegal activities of persons, groups and organizations that encourage, instigate, organize or engage in the perpetration of acts of taking of hostages;"   126

Subparagraph (b)   127

"... exchanging information and co-ordinating the taking of administrative and other measures as appropriate to prevent the commission of those offences."   127

    Co-operative measures implemented by States to prevent terrorism   129

ARTICLE 5

ESTABLISHMENT OF JURISDICTION OVER THE OFFENCES   133

1. Introduction   133

    The expansion of jurisdictional bases by multilateral conventions dealing with international offences   134

2. Interpretation   140

    Paragraph 1: Establishment of primary jurisdiction over the offences   140

        "Each State Party shall take such measures as may be necessary to establish its jurisdiction . . ."   142

        "... over any of the offences set forth in article 1 which are committed:"   143

        "... in its territory . . ."   143

        "... or on board a ship or aircraft registered in that State . . ."   147

        "... by any of its nationals . . ."   147

"... or, if that State considers it appropriate, by those stateless persons who have their habitual residence in its territory ..."	148
"... in order to compel that State to do or abstain from doing any act ..."	150
"... or ... with respect to a hostage who is a national of that State, if that State considers it appropriate."	152
Paragraph 2: Establishment of subsidiary jurisdiction over the offences	155
"Each State Party shall likewise take such measures as may be necessary to establish its jurisdiction over the offences set forth in article 1 in cases where the alleged offender is present in its territory ..."	155
"... and it does not extradite him to any of the States mentioned in paragraph 1 of this article."	156
The legal effect of the establishment of universal jurisdiction	157
Paragraph 3: Jurisdiction exercised in accordance with internal law	159
"This Convention does not exclude any criminal jurisdiction exercised in accordance with internal law."	159
3. Problems relevant to the establishment of jurisdiction under the Convention	159
A. Jurisdiction over crimes attendant to acts of hostage-taking	159
B. Priority of jurisdiction	163

ARTICLE 6

MATTERS PRIOR TO TRIAL OR EXTRADITION   167

1. Introduction   168

2. Interpretation ... 168

Paragraph 1: Taking measures to ensure the presence of the accused ... 168

"Upon being satisfied that the circumstances so warrant ..." ... 168

"... any State Party in the territory of which the alleged offender is present ..." ... 172

"... shall, in accordance with its laws, take him into custody or take other measures to ensure his presence for such time as is necessary to enable any criminal or extradition proceedings to be instituted." ... 173

"That State Party shall immediately make a preliminary inquiry into the facts." ... 174

Paragraph 2: Notification to other States of the measures taken ... 174

"The custody or other measures referred to in paragraph 1 of this article shall be notified without delay ..." ... 174

"... directly or through the Secretary-General of the United Nations ..." ... 175

"... to: ... the State where the offence was committed ... the State against which compulsion has been directed or attempted ... the State of which the natural or juridical person against whom compulsion has been directed or attempted is a national ... the State of which the hostage is a national or in the territory of which he has his habitual residence ... the State of which the alleged offender is a national, or, if he is a stateless person, in the territory of which he has his habitual residence ... the international intergovernmental organization against which compulsion has been directed or attempted ... all other States concerned." ... 176

Paragraph 3: Right of the accused to visitation and communication ... 177

CONTENTS   xvii

"Any person regarding whom the measures referred to
in paragraph 1 of this article are being taken shall be
entitled . . . to communicate without delay . . ."   178

". . . with the nearest appropriate representative of the
State of which he is a national or which is otherwise
entitled to establish such communication . . ."   178

". . . or, if he is a stateless person, the State in the
territory of which he has his habitual residence;"   179

". . . to be visited by a representative of that State."   180

Paragraph 4: Effective exercise of the rights in paragraph
              3 guaranteed   181

"The rights referred to in paragraph 3 of this article shall
be exercised in conformity with the laws and regulations
of the State in the territory of which the alleged offender is
present subject to the proviso, however, that the said laws
and regulations must enable full effect to be given to the
purposes for which the rights accorded under paragraph
3 of this article are intended."   181

Paragraph 5: Protection by the International Committee of
              the Red Cross   181

"The provisions of paragraphs 3 and 4 of this article
shall be without prejudice to the right of any State Party
having a claim to jurisdiction in accordance with paragraph
1(b) of article 5 to invite the International Committee of
the Red Cross to communicate with and visit the alleged
offender."   181

Paragraph 6: Notification of the findings of the preliminary
              inquiry   183

"The State which makes the preliminary inquiry contemplated in paragraph 1 of this article shall promptly
report its findings to the States or organization referred
to in paragraph 2 of this article and indicate whether it
intends to exercise jurisdiction."   183

ARTICLE 7

NOTIFICATION OF THE RESULTS OF PROSECUTION — 185

1. Introduction — 185

2. Interpretation — 186

ARTICLE 8

AUT DEDERE AUT JUDICARE — 187

1. Introduction — 187

   The principle *aut dedere aut judicare* and its use in multilateral treaties — 188

2. Interpretation — 193

   Paragraph 1: Submission of the case for the purpose of prosecution when extradition does not occur — 193

   "The State Party in the territory of which the alleged offender is found . . ." — 194

   ". . . shall, if it does not extradite him . . ." — 194

   ". . . be obliged, without exception whatsoever . . ." — 194

   The obligation to prosecute when no request for extradition is made — 196

   ". . . and whether or not the offence was committed in its territory . . ." — 198

   ". . . to submit the case to its competent authorities for the purpose of prosecution . . ." — 198

   ". . . through proceedings in accordance with the laws of that State." — 200

CONTENTS   xix

"Those authorities shall take their decision in the same
manner as in the case of any ordinary offence of a grave
nature under the law of that State."   201

Paragraph 2: Fair treatment of the offender   204

"Any person regarding whom proceedings are being
carried out in connexion with any of the offences set
forth in article 1 shall be guaranteed fair treatment . . ."   204

". . . at all stages of the proceedings . . ."   206

". . . including enjoyment of all the rights and guarantees
provided by the law of the State in the territory of
which he is present."   207

    The inclusion of human rights provisions in
    anti-terrorism conventions   207

ARTICLE 9

DISCRIMINATION CLAUSE   209

1. Introduction   209

    The role of "discrimination clauses" in the law of extradition   210

    The inclusion of a discrimination clause in this Convention   213

2. Interpretation   215

Paragraph 1: Obligation not to extradite when persecution
                  or prejudice would result   215

"A request for the extradition of an alleged offender,
pursuant to this Convention, shall not be granted . . ."   215

". . . if the requested State Party has substantial grounds
for believing:"   218

". . . that the request for extradition for an offence set forth
in article 1 has been made for the purpose of prosecuting
or punishing a person on account of his race, religion,
nationality, ethnic origin or political opinion . . ."   219

CONTENTS

"... or ... that the person's position may be prejudiced: ... for any of the reasons mentioned in subparagraph (a) of this paragraph ..."   222

"... or ... for the reason that communication with him by the appropriate authorities of the State entitled to exercise rights of protection cannot be effected."   222

Paragraph 2: Modification of inconsistent treaties   223

"With respect to the offences as defined in this Convention, the provisions of all extradition treaties and arrangements applicable between States Parties are modified as between States Parties to the extent that they are incompatible with this Convention."   223

ARTICLE 10

FACILITATION OF THE EXTRADITION OPTION   227

1. Introduction   227

2. Interpretation   229

Paragraph 1: The offences included as extraditable offences in extradition treaties between States Parties   229

"The offences set forth in article 1 shall be deemed to be included as extraditable offences in any extradition treaty ..."   229

The meaning of "extraditable offence"   231

The effect of this Article on the political offence exception to extradition   233

"... existing between States Parties."   236

"States Parties undertake to include such offences as extraditable offences in every extradition treaty to be concluded between them."   237

Paragraph 2: The Hostages Convention as the legal basis for extradition   238

"If a State Party which makes extradition conditional
on the existence of a treaty receives a request for
extradition from another State Party with which it has
no extradition treaty . . ." 238

". . . the requested State may at its option consider this
Convention as the legal basis for extradition in respect of
the offences set forth in article 1." 238

"Extradition shall be subject to the other conditions
provided by the law of the requested State." 240

Paragraph 3: The offences as extraditable where the States
Parties do not require an extradition treaty 241

"States Parties which do not make extradition conditional
on the existence of a treaty shall recognize the offences set
forth in article 1 as extraditable offences between
themselves subject to the conditions provided by the
law of the requested State." 241

    The inequality of obligations created by this Article 242

Paragraph 4: The offences treated as having taken place
in the territories of the States with primary
jurisdiction 243

"The offences set forth in article 1 shall be treated, for
the purpose of extradition between States Parties, as if
they had been committed not only in the place in which
they occurred but also in the territories of the States
required to establish their jurisdiction in accordance with
paragraph 1 of article 5." 243

ARTICLE 11

MUTUAL ASSISTANCE IN CRIMINAL PROCEEDINGS 245

1. Introduction 245

    The existing state of mutual assistance in criminal matters
under international law 246

2. Interpretation	250
Paragraph 1: Rendering assistance in criminal proceedings	250
"States Parties shall afford one another . . ."	250
". . . the greatest measure of assistance . . ."	250
". . . in connexion with criminal proceedings brought in respect of the offences set forth in article 1 . . ."	257
". . . including the supply of all evidence at their disposal necessary for the proceedings."	258
Paragraph 2: Preservation of other obligations regarding mutual assistance	260
"The provisions of paragraph 1 of this article shall not affect obligations concerning mutual judicial assistance embodied in any other treaty."	260

ARTICLE 12

RELATIONSHIP BETWEEN THE CONVENTION AND THE LAWS OF ARMED CONFLICT   263

1. Introduction	263
Development of the Article	266
2. Interpretation	273
"In so far as the Geneva Conventions of 1949 for the protection of war victims or the Additional Protocols to those Conventions are applicable to a particular act of hostage-taking, and in so far as States Parties to this Convention are bound under those conventions to prosecute or hand over the hostage-taker, the present Convention shall not apply to an act of hostage-taking . . ."	273
". . . committed in the course of armed conflicts as defined in the Geneva Conventions of 1949 and the Protocols thereto . . ."	278

". . . including armed conflicts mentioned in article 1, paragraph 4, of Additional Protocol I of 1977, in which peoples are fighting against colonial domination and alien occupation and against racist régimes in the exercise of their right of self-determination . . ."	278
3. The Geneva instruments and the obligation to prosecute or hand over hostage-takers	279
A. Non-international armed conflicts	280
Common Article 3 of the four Geneva Conventions and Protocol II	280
Note on acts of hostage-taking which are strictly internal in nature	282
B. International armed conflicts	282
The four Geneva Conventions of 1949	282
C. Armed conflicts for "national liberation"	286
The Civilians Convention	286
The situation under traditional international law	286
The case reconsidered in light of modern developments in international law	288
1977 Additional Protocol I Relating to the Protection of Victims of International Armed Conflicts	293
The expansion of the obligation to extradite or prosecute hostage-takers under Protocol I	297

ARTICLE 13

LIMITATION OF THE CONVENTION TO INTERNATIONAL ACTS OF HOSTAGE-TAKING — 299

1. Introduction	299
2. Interpretation	301
"This Convention shall not apply . . ."	301

". . . where the offence is committed within a single State . . ."	301
Status of the Convention in an otherwise internal offence when the target of demands is a foreign State or a third party located in a foreign State	302
The elements of the offence of hostage-taking	303
Development of the Article	307
(i) where a foreign State is subjected to demands	308
(ii) where a third party who is not a national of the territorial State is subjected to demands	310
". . . the hostage and the alleged offender are nationals of that State . . ."	312
". . . and the alleged offender is found in the territory of that State."	312
The offences of participation and attempt	312

ARTICLE 14

TERRITORIAL INTEGRITY AND POLITICAL INDEPENDENCE — 313

1. Introduction	313
Development of the Article	313
The debate concerning the use of force to rescue hostages and other uses of force occasioned by terrorism	316
2. Interpretation	322
"Nothing in this Convention shall be construed as justifying the violation of the territorial integrity or political independence of a State in contravention of the Charter of the United Nations."	322

ARTICLE 15

PRESERVATION OF THE "TREATIES ON ASYLUM" — 327

1. Introduction	327

The nature of asylum	328
Development of the Article	330
2. Interpretation	334
"The provisions of this Convention shall not affect the application of the Treaties on Asylum . . ."	334
". . . in force at the date of the adoption of this Convention . . ."	340
". . . as between the States which are parties to those Treaties; but a State Party to this Convention may not invoke those Treaties with respect to another State Party to this Convention which is not a party to those Treaties."	340

ARTICLES 16-20

DISPUTE SETTLEMENT AND FINAL ARTICLES — 343

Conclusion		347
Appendix I:	International Convention Against the Taking of Hostages, 1979	357
Appendix II:	FRG Draft Convention	365
Index		371

FOREWORD

This book is important for two reasons: its subject and its method.

The taking of hostages is a regrettably prominent aspect of contemporary terrorism. Though the gap between the promise and the performance of the international community in reacting to this insidious and evil practice may be wide, the value of identifying with reasonable precision the manner in which States have committed themselves to dealing with the problem is self-evident. In this work Dr Lambert provides us with a detailed statement of the measures directed, if not at actually preventing hostage-taking, at least at reducing the chance that the terrorist will escape justice.

The development of the law relating to the consequences of hostage-taking is largely a matter of treaty. As the International Court of Justice has constantly recognized, and never more clearly than in its recent judgment regarding its jurisdiction in *Nicaragua* v. *Honduras* (ICJ *Reports* 1988, p. 69), the process of interpretation involves consideration of three elements: the actual words used; the preparatory work underlying the treaty; and the practice of the parties in applying it. This is the method used by Dr Lambert in this work. He has in a rigorous and exhaustive manner subjected every paragraph of every article of the Hostages Convention to this type of scrutiny. It is a time-consuming process that no practitioner or judge can pursue when confronted by the need to apply the Convention in urgent circumstances. Yet this kind of examination is an essential part of the intellectual process of extracting from the words of the Convention their correct legal meaning. This work is, therefore, bound to assume a prominent place in any future treatment of the subject.

The present study has been prepared under the auspices of the Research Centre for International Law of the University of Cambridge. One of the principal objectives of the Research Centre is to improve access to the raw materials of international law. Hence its commitment to the continuance and improvement of such fundamental research tools as the *International Law Reports*. In this same line of thought, the Research Centre also aims to generate a series containing close textual analyses of treaties of contemporary importance. We are therefore particularly pleased to have as the first of these Dr Lambert's lucid and comprehensive commentary on the Hostages Convention.

E. LAUTERPACHT
Director

Research Centre for International Law
University of Cambridge
November 1989

PREFACE

There can be few modern problems which are so elusive of effective regulation and which so challenge the efficacy of international law as that of international terrorism. The decision to prepare a commentary on the Hostages Convention was made in the autumn of 1985 when, in the aftermath of the *Achille Lauro* incident, it seemed important to examine in detail the international rules that had been laid down regarding international terrorism in general and hostage-taking in particular. Part I is essentially introductory in nature, examining such matters as the growth of the problem of international terrorism, the divergent views as to what "terrorism" is, the various efforts of the world community to deal with it and the general background to the Hostages Convention. Part I thus places the Convention in the larger context of the problems of "terrorism" and its suppression. Part II is an article-by-article commentary on the Convention itself. Because of the many points of similarity between this Convention and the other multilateral agreements regarding particular "terrorist" offences, this part is also, albeit to a much lesser extent, a commentary upon those other instruments. In general, it is hoped that this book will provide an insight into the precise nature of the rules laid down by international law regarding the suppression of terrorism and may help in assessing the effectiveness of those rules.

The book is the product of my work as a Research Scholar of the Research Centre for International Law in the University of Cambridge. It was initially presented in August 1988 as my thesis for the Ph.D. degree in that University, but I have since been able to update it in a number of respects to September 1989.

My thanks go first and foremost to the Research Centre and to its Director, Mr E. Lauterpacht, CBE, QC. Without the financial support of the former and the close guidance and constant encouragement of the latter, this work could not have been possible. I wish also to thank Professor D. W. Bowett, CBE, QC, my academic supervisor while at Cambridge, for his many helpful comments along the way. Finally I extend my gratitude to the Venerable Y. Zangmo, Mrs Diane Ilott, Mr John Adlam and Mr S. R. Pirrie, all of Grotius Publications Limited, for their valuable assistance in preparing the manuscript for publication, and to Miss Maureen MacGlashan, the Assistant Director of the Research Centre, for so kindly compiling the very full index.

JOSEPH J. LAMBERT

New York
October 1989

TABLE OF CASES

Acquisition of Polish Nationality, 149-50
Asylum Case, 328 n. 5
Burt, *In re*, 216 n. 33
Caroline, The, 318-19
Castioni, *In re*, 211 n. 9
Conditions of Admission of a State to Membership in the United Nations (Article 4 of Charter), 67 n. 255
Corfu Channel, 123 n. 15
Deportation to U., 212 n. 12
Eain *v.* Wilkes, 211 n. 9
Folkerts *v.* State-Secretary of Justice, 212 n. 13, 218 n. 43, 223 n. 61
Gallina *v.* Fraser, 216 n. 33
Gerstein *v.* Pugh, 170 n. 12
Greece *v.* United Kingdom, 112 n. 8
Interpretation of Minorities Treaty, 149-50
Interpretation of the Convention of 1919 concerning Employment of Women during the Night, 67 n. 255
Ireland *v.* United Kingdom, 112 n. 8
John Deere Ltd. *v.* Sperry Corp., 247 n. 10
Joyce *v.* Director of Public Prosecutions, 151 n. 70
Lawless Case, 112 n. 8
Legal Consequences for States of the Continued Presence of South Africa in Namibia (South West Africa), 310 n. 30
Lincoln, *In re*, 211 n. 9
List, *In re*, 78 n. 2
Lotus, The S.S., 152 n. 79
North Sea Continental Shelf Cases, 158 n. 103, 292 n. 90
Northern Cameroons, Case Concerning, 344 n. 4
Over the Top, 104 n. 43
R. *v.* Baxter, 304 n. 11
R. *v.* Casement, 148 n. 53
R. *v.* Martin, 148 n. 53
R. *v.* Owen, 304 n. 11
Rights of Nationals of the United States of America in Morocco, 345 n. 5
Schtraks, *In re*, 146 n. 48
Signe Tiedmann, The *v.* The Signe, *et al.*, 247 n. 7
T. *v.* Swiss Federal Prosecutor's Office, 218 n. 42
Treacy *v.* Director of Public Prosecutions, 304-6
United States Diplomatic and Consular Staff in Tehran, Case Concerning, 3 n. 12, 110 n. 3, 317 n. 23, 343 n. 3
U.S. *v.* Arjona, 123 n. 15

U.S. *v.* Bowman, 148 n. 53
U.S. *v.* Flores, 147 n. 49
U.S. *v.* Heng Awkak Roman, 89-90 n. 47
U.S. *v.* Jackson, 90 n. 47
U.S. *v.* Mandujano, 89-90 n. 47
Westinghouse Electric Corp. and Duquesne Light Co., *et al.*, *Re*, 247 n. 10

ABBREVIATIONS

AC	Appeals Cases
AJIL	American Journal of International Law
All ER	All England Reports
Am. U.L.R.	American University Law Review
ANC	African National Congress
Aust. YBIL	Australian Yearbook of International Law
BYIL	British Yearbook of International Law
Can. YBIL	Canadian Yearbook of International Law
Case W.R. J. Int'l L.	Case Western Reserve Journal of International Law
Cmnd	United Kingdom Command Papers
Colum. J. Trans. L.	Columbia Journal of Transnational Law
Cor. Int'l L.J.	Cornell International Law Journal
Crim. L.R.	Criminal Law Review
Dep't St. Bull.	Department of State Bulletin
DLR	Dominion Law Reports
Doc	Document
EEZ	Exclusive Economic Zone
F.	Federal Reporter
F. 2d	Federal Reporter, Second Series
FRG	Federal Republic of Germany
F. Supp.	Federal Supplement
First Report of the Hostages Committee	Report of the *Ad Hoc* Committee on the Drafting of an International Convention Against the Taking of Hostages, UN GAOR, 32nd Sess., Supp. 39, UN Doc A/32/39 (1977)
GA	United Nations General Assembly
Ger. YBIL	German Yearbook of International Law
Harv. Int'l L.J.	Harvard International Law Journal
H.C. Debs.	House of Commons Debates
H.L. Debs.	House of Lords Debates
Hostages Committee	*Ad Hoc* Committee on the Drafting of an International Convention Against the Taking of Hostages
IATA	International Air Transport Association
ICAO	International Civil Aviation Organization
ICJ	International Court of Justice
ICJ Rep.	International Court of Justice Reports
ICLQ	International and Comparative Law Quarterly
ICRC	International Committee of the Red Cross

ILA	International Law Association
ILC	International Law Commission
ILM	International Legal Materials
ILR	International Law Reports
IMO	International Maritime Organization
IRA	Irish Republican Army
Is.YBHR	Israel Yearbook of Human Rights
J. Crim. L. & Crim'y	Journal of Criminal Law and Criminology
J. Int'l L. & Econ.	Journal of International Law and Economics
KB	King's Bench
LN	League of Nations
LNTS	League of Nations Treaty Series
LQR	Law Quarterly Review
McDonald	McDonald, "The United Nations Convention against the Taking of Hostages: The Inside Story", 6 Terr. J. 545 (1982)
Misc.	United Kingdom Command Papers, Miscellaneous Series
OAS	Organization of American States
OPEC	Organization of Petroleum Exporting Countries
PAULTS	Pan-American Union Law and Treaty Series
PAUTS	Pan-American Union Treaty Series
PCIJ	Permanent Court of International Justice
PFLP	Popular Front for the Liberation of Palestine
PLO	Palestine Liberation Organization
Proc. ASIL	Proceedings of the American Society of International Law
QB	Queen's Bench
Res	Resolution
RC	*Recueil des cours de l'Academie de droit international*
Rev. int'l d. pén.	*Revue international droit pénal*
Rosenne	Rosenne, "The International Convention Against the Taking of Hostages 1979", 10 Is.YBHR 109 (1980)
Rosenstock	Rosenstock, "International Convention Against the Taking of Hostages: Another International Community Step Against Terrorism", 9 Denver Journal of International Law and Policy 169 (1980)
SC	United Nations Security Council
S.Ct.	Supreme Court Reporter

Second Report of the Hostages Committee	Report of the *Ad Hoc* Committee on the Drafting of an International Convention Against the Taking of Hostages, UN GAOR, 33rd Sess., Supp. 39, UN Doc A/33/39 (1978)
Shubber	Shubber, "The International Convention Against the Taking of Hostages", 52 BYIL 205 (1981)
StGB	*Strafgesetzbuch* (German Criminal Code)
StPO	*Strafprozessordnung* (German Code of Criminal Procedure)
Terrorism Committee	*Ad Hoc* Committee on International Terrorism
Terr. J.	Terrorism: An International Journal
Third Report of the Hostages Committee	Report of the *Ad Hoc* Committee on the Drafting of an International Convention Against the Taking of Hostages, UN GAOR, 34th Sess., Supp. 39, UN Doc A/34/39 (1979)
TIAS	United States Treaties and other International Acts Series
TS	United States Treaty Series
UN	United Nations
UN Chron	United Nations Chronicle
UN GAOR	United Nations General Assembly Official Records
UNHCR	United Nations High Commission for Refugees
UNITAR	United Nations Institute for Training and Research
UN SCOR	United Nations Security Council Official Records
UNTS	United Nations Treaty Series
UKTS	United Kingdom Treaty Series
Univ. Chi. L.R.	University of Chicago Law Review
US	United States Reports
USC	United States Code
Va. J. Int'l L.	Virginia Journal of International Law
Vand. J. Trans. L.	Vanderbilt Journal of Transnational Law
Verwey	Verwey, "The International Hostages Convention and National Liberation Movements", 75 AJIL 69 (1980)
White	White "The Hague Convention for the Suppression of Unlawful Seizure of Aircraft", 6 The Review of the International Commission of Jurists 38 (1971)
WLR	Weekly Law Reports
Wood	Wood, "The Convention on the Prevention and Punishment of Crimes Against Internationally Protected Persons, including Diplomatic Agents", 23 ICLQ 791 (1974)
YBILC	Yearbook of the International Law Commission

Introduction

As the phenomenon of international terrorism has proliferated since the 1960s, so has it received the increasing attention of governments, scholars, politicians, commentators and the general public. It has, moreover, been addressed at length by the world community in various fora, particularly the United Nations. However, serious differences in opinion over almost every aspect of terrorism — most fundamentally over the meaning of the term itself — have resulted in the failure of the international community to adopt a comprehensive and universally acceptable approach to combatting the problem. No single convention dealing with the suppression and punishment of terrorism as a whole has as yet entered into force,[1] and it seems unlikely that such an instrument will be adopted in the near future, if ever.

However, the international community, within the framework of the United Nations and the specialized agencies ICAO and IMO, has been able to fashion agreement on the suppression of certain manifestations of terrorism. Those bodies have so far promulgated a total of six conventions and two protocols dealing with many of the offences favoured by terrorist groups: the 1963 Tokyo Convention on Offences and Certain other Acts Committed on Board Aircraft;[2] the 1970 Hague Convention for the Suppression of Unlawful Seizure of Aircraft;[3] the 1971 Montreal Convention for the Suppression of Unlawful Acts Against the Safety of Civil Aviation[4] and 1988 Protocol thereto for the Suppression of Unlawful Acts of Violence at Airports Serving International Civil Aviation;[5] the 1973 New York Convention on the Prevention and Punishment of Crimes Against Internationally Protected Persons, including Diplomatic Agents;[6] the 1979 International Convention Against the Taking of Hostages;[7] and the 1988 Rome Convention for the Suppression of Unlawful Acts Against

---

[1] It may be noted that the League of Nations adopted a convention on the suppression of terrorism in the 1930s; however, that instrument — partially because of its ambitious scope — never came into force. See pp. 28-29 (notes 74-81 and accompanying text in Part I).

[2] 704 UNTS 219, *reprinted in* 2 ILM 1042 (1963).

[3] 860 UNTS 105, *reprinted in* 10 ILM 133 (1971).

[4] 974 UNTS 177, *reprinted in* 10 ILM 1151 (1971).

[5] ICAO Doc 9518 (1988).

[6] 1035 UNTS 167, *reprinted in* 13 ILM 41 (1974). The Convention is annexed to GA Res 3166 (XXVIII) of 14 December 1973, UN GAOR, 28th Sess., Supp. 10, p. 146, UN Doc A/9030 (1974).

[7] UKTS 81 (1983), Cmnd 9100, *reprinted in* 18 ILM 1456 (1979). The Convention is annexed to GA Res 34/146 of 17 December 1979, UN GAOR, 34th Sess., Supp. 46, p. 245, UN Doc A/34/46 (1980).

the Safety of Maritime Navigation[8] and Protocol thereto for the Suppression of Unlawful Acts Against the Safety of Fixed Platforms Located on the Continental Shelf.[9] With the exception of the Tokyo Convention, all of these instruments have as their central provision the obligation *aut dedere aut judicare*, i.e., that all offenders must either be extradited or submitted to the appropriate authorities of the State in which they are found for the purpose of prosecution.

It is with the Hostages Convention that this study is primarily concerned. The taking of hostages in an effort to compel a third party, most commonly a State, to do or abstain from doing a certain act or acts is a common type of terrorist crime. Incidents of hostage-taking, moreover, often overlap with crimes which are the subject of one or more of the other international anti-terrorism conventions, such as aerial hijacking and attacks on diplomats. However, the ways in which these abductions take place vary greatly, and the class of potential victims seems unlimited. Consider, for example, the following prominent incidents of hostage-taking:

1) The OPEC hostage-taking

On 21 December 1975, six men calling themselves the "Arm of the Arab Revolution", a name for the "Popular Front for the Liberation of Palestine", seized the Vienna headquarters of the Organization of Petroleum Exporting Countries, killing three persons and taking 60 hostages. The terrorists urged war on Israel, demanded a share of oil wealth for Palestinians and criticized Egypt for dealing with the United States. After a deal with the Austrian authorities, the hostage-takers left for Algeria, taking most of the hostages with them, including Sheik Amed Zaki Yamani of Saudi Arabia and officials of numerous other States. On 23 December, the terrorists released the hostages unharmed, reportedly after ransom was paid by Saudi Arabia and Iran. The terrorists were granted asylum by Algeria and subsequently went to Libya.[10]

2) The Entebbe incident

On 27 June 1976, an Air France civilian aircraft en route from Tel Aviv to Paris was hijacked by members of the "Popular Front for the Liberation of Palestine". The hijackers demanded that the aircraft be diverted to Entebbe airport in Uganda. After landing at Entebbe, the passengers were taken off the aircraft and held in an airport terminal. The hostage-takers demanded the release of 53 Arab prisoners, most

[8] IMO Doc SUA/CONF/15/Rev. 1 (1988).
[9] IMO Doc SUA/CONF/16/Rev. 2 (1988).
[10] See *New York Times*, Dec. 22, 1975, p. A1, Dec. 23, 1975, p. A10, Dec. 24, 1975, p. A4, Dec. 25, 1975, p. A8, Dec. 30, 1975, p. A4 & Dec. 31, 1975, p. A24.

of whom were held in Israel and the rest in various other countries. Some days after arriving at Entebbe, the hijackers released many of the passengers, but continued to hold the 98 Israeli and Jewish passengers, as well as the crew of the aircraft. The Ugandan authorities did not seem to take any steps to secure the release of the hostages; indeed, there was reason to believe that the Ugandan authorities actively assisted the hostage-takers. On 3 July 1976, an Israeli commando force landed at Entebbe airport and paratroopers stormed the airport building, freeing the hostages. Seven of the eight hijackers were killed, as were 20 Ugandan soldiers, three hostages and one Israeli commando. Another hostage, a dual national of the United Kingdom and Israel, who had been hospitalized prior to the Israeli action and, therefore, not rescued, was later killed, apparently on the orders of Idi Amin.[11]

3) The seizure of the American diplomatic and consular staff in Tehran

On 4 November 1979, the US embassy compound in Tehran was overrun and occupied by several hundred demonstrators, many of whom were militant students. The Americans present in the compound were held captive. 13 hostages were soon released; however, most of the remaining 52 hostages — 50 of whom were diplomatic and consular staff and two of whom were private citizens — were held for over a year. Despite calls from the Security Council, and a determination by the ICJ that Iran was in violation of various international obligations, the Iranian government made no effort to secure the release of the hostages; indeed, it was clear that the students were fully supported, and even controlled, by the Iranian regime. The hostage-takers initially demanded the return of the deposed Shah, but after his death some months later they sought the return of his wealth and a guarantee that the United States would not interfere in Iranian affairs. They also sought the release of Iranian assets in the United States, which had been frozen by the US government in response to the incident. The US broke off diplomatic relations with Iran, expelled Iranians from the US and imposed economic sanctions. The incident also resulted in a failed rescue operation by US forces. After 444 days, the hostages were released when agreement on terms was reached by Iran and the US, with the assistance of Algeria.[12]

---

[11] See XXII *Keesing's Contemporary Archives* 27888-91 (1976); Boyle, *World Politics and International Law* 77-78 (1975).

[12] See XXVI *Keesing's Contemporary Archives* 30150, 30205-12, 30524-38 (1980); XXVII *Keesing's Contemporary Archives* 31081-87 (1981). See also *Case Concerning the United States Diplomatic and Consular Staff in Tehran*, ICJ Rep. 1980, p. 3; SC Res 457, UN SCOR, 34th Sess., Resolutions & Decisions, UN Doc S/INF/35, *reprinted in* 18 ILM 1644 (1979).

4) The hijacking of the *Achille Lauro*

On 7 October 1985, the Italian cruise ship *Achille Lauro* was hijacked by members of the "Palestine Liberation Front" whilst off the coast of Egypt in international waters. The hijackers held the ship's approximately 400 passengers and crew hostage, and sought the release of 50 Palestinians held in Israeli jails. During the hostage-taking, an American Jew, Leon Klinghoffer, was shot by the terrorists and his body was thrown overboard. The Government of Egypt failed to hold the terrorists for prosecution or for extradition; instead it made a bargain by which, in return for the release of the ship and the hostages, the offenders were placed on an aircraft bound for Tunis. The United States employed F-14 jets to intercept the aircraft and divert it to Italy, where the hostage-takers were taken into Italian custody.[13]

5) The hostage-takings in Lebanon

The mid- and late-1980s have witnessed a spate of hostage-takings against foreigners, mainly Westerners, in Lebanon. The total number of hostages is constantly changing, as new victims are seized and old ones escape, are killed or are released. The victims have included businessmen, educators, diplomats, UN personnel, intelligence officials, media workers, relief workers, clergymen and a church envoy sent to seek the release of hostages. Although groups with various names have claimed responsibility for the abductions, it is widely believed that most of the hostages have been held by the groups "Islamic Jihad" and "Hezbollah", both of which have strong links with Iran and Syria. The hostage-takers have sought various concessions from States, including the release of prisoners held in connexion with bomb attacks in Kuwait, the payment of ransom and the cancelling of arms sales to Saudi Arabia. They have also demanded that States negotiate with them for the release of the hostages.[14] Although most of the States whose nationals have been seized assert a policy of "no deals" with the hostage-takers, some have attempted to obtain the release of their nationals by reaching accommodation with Iran whereby it would use its influence with the hostage-takers to that end. For example, in 1986, officials of the United States, in a largely unsuccessful effort,

---

[13] See *New York Times*, Oct. 8, 1985, p. A1, Oct. 9, 1985, p. A1, Oct. 10, 1985, p. A1 & Oct. 11, 1985, p. A1. For further facts regarding this incident, see p. 26 (note 65 in Part I); pp. 115-116 (notes 17-24 and accompanying text in the commentary on Article 3).

[14] See XXXI *Keesing's Contemporary Archives* 33684-85 (1985); XXXII *Keesing's Contemporary Archives* 34133, 34585-86 (1986); *Time*, Aug. 31, 1987, pp. 12-13 & Aug. 19, 1989, pp. 14-25; *International Herald Tribune*, Nov. 2, 1987, p. 1. As of August 1989, there were believed to be approximately 16 foreign hostages held in Lebanon, mostly American but also from Britain, France, Ireland, Italy and West Germany. See *The Economist*, Aug. 5, 1989, p. 37.

agreed to sell arms to Iran in return for its assistance in freeing American hostages.[15] In 1988, the French government obtained the release of its last three remaining nationals held as hostages in Lebanon, reportedly after agreeing, *inter alia*, to re-establish diplomatic relations with Iran and to repay an outstanding loan.[16]

Since 1949, international conventions have contained prohibitions on certain acts of hostage-taking committed during armed conflicts.[17] Moreover, pursuant to the New York Convention, States must suppress the kidnapping of diplomats and other internationally protected persons.[18] However, prior to the adoption of the Hostages Convention, no international convention contained a general prohibition on the taking of hostages, whether committed in peacetime or during war and regardless of the identity of the victims. The Hostages Convention thus fills in the gaps left by existing conventions. It was adopted in December 1979 by consensus in the General Assembly and, as of August 1989, had 56 States Parties.[19] The Hostages Convention imposes a number of obligations upon States Parties which are designed both to prevent acts of hostage-taking and, more particularly, to bring to justice those persons who commit such

---

[15] See XXXIII *Keesing's Contemporary Archives* 35182-87 (1987).

[16] See *Time*, May 16, 1988, p. 14 & May 30, 1988, p. 17. Although Iran at one point claimed that it could not help to secure the release of hostages in Lebanon, in 1986, its Deputy Foreign Minister stated that it played a role in the release of two other French hostages, and was able to do so because of "ideological links" with groups in Lebanon. He stated that it could also assist in the release of British hostages if "London should change its policy towards the Islamic Republic". XXXII *Keesing's Contemporary Archives* 34585-86 (1986). In 1987, the Speaker of the Iranian Parliament stated that Iran would intercede on behalf of all foreigners held in Lebanon if the US put pressure on Israel and Kuwait to release Lebanese Shiites held in connexion with attacks in those countries. See XXXIV *Keesing's Record of World Events* 35671 (1988). In July 1988, the Speaker again stated that Iran would use its influence in Lebanon to help free the hostages if the US released frozen Iranian assets and changed its hostile attitude towards Iran. See *International Herald Tribune*, July 27, 1988, p. 1; see also *Time*, Aug. 14, 1989, p. 14.

[17] See generally p. 283 (note 59 and accompanying text in the commentary on Article 12).

[18] See p. 53 (note 183 and accompanying text in Part I).

[19] The States Parties to the Convention are: Antigua, Austria, Bahamas, Barbados, Bhutan, Brunei, Bulgaria, Byelorussian SSR, Canada, Cameroon, Chile, Czechoslovakia, Denmark, Dominica, Ecuador, Egypt, El Salvador, Finland, Federal Republic of Germany, German Democratic Republic, Ghana, Greece, Guatemala, Honduras, Hungary, Iceland, Italy, Japan, Jordan, Kenya, Korea, Kuwait, Lesotho, Malawi, Mauritius, Mexico, New Zealand, Netherlands, Norway, Oman, Panama, Philippines, Portugal, Senegal, Spain, Surinam, Sweden, Switzerland, Togo, Trinidad, Ukrainian SSR, USSR, United Kingdom, United States, Venezuela and Yugoslavia. See Bowman & Harris, *Multilateral Treaties Index and Current Status* 448 (1984) & 6th Supp. (1989); 89 Dep't St. Bull., Nos. 2142, p. 50, 2144, p. 92 & 2146, p. 86 (1989); 88 Dep't St. Bull., Nos. 2134, p. 83, 2136, p. 76 & 2139, p. 84 (1988). The Convention also has an additional 12 signatories: Belgium, Bolivia, Dominican Republic, Gabon, Haiti, Iraq, Israel, Jamaica, Liberia, Luxembourg, Uganda and Zaire. Bowman & Harris, *supra*.

acts. This study consists primarily of a comprehensive analysis of the Convention, examining in detail both the language employed in the instrument and, within the framework of a treaty commentary, the legal issues relevant to the suppression of the offence. The Hostages Convention and the other anti-terrorism conventions have already been the subject of some examination in legal literature.[20] This study hopes to go beyond the existing works by examining in significantly greater detail the terms of each article in the context of the particular aspect of international law dealt with therein.[21]

There are two main reasons why this study is thought necessary. The first is that, while greater levels of co-operation have recently been reached on bilateral and regional levels,[22] the obligations contained in this Convention constitute the most significant measure of co-operation on the prevention and punishment of acts of international terrorism that the world community as a whole has so far been able to agree upon. Moreover, the level of co-operation obtained therein seems the best that the world community will be able to achieve for some years to come. Three of the anti-terrorism instruments — the Montreal Protocol and the Rome Convention and Protocol — were adopted in 1988, and there is every reason to believe that future attempts to deal with other aspects of the problem of terrorism on a universal basis will follow the pattern established in these instruments. Therefore, despite the flaws of the Hostages Convention (which are discussed in the appropriate places in the commentary), it, and others like it, remain the best hope for effective legal control of international terrorism. An understanding of the

---

[20] See, e.g., Rosenstock, "International Convention Against the Taking of Hostages: Another International Community Step Against Terrorism", 9 Denver J. Int'l L. & Policy 169 (1980); Rosenne, "The International Convention Against the Taking of Hostages 1979", 10 Is.YBHR 109 (1980); Shubber, "The International Convention Against the Taking of Hostages", 52 BYIL 205 (1981); White, "The Hague Convention for the Suppression of Unlawful Seizure of Aircraft", 6 The Review of the International Commission of Jurists 38 (1971); Wood, "The Convention on the Prevention and Punishment of Crimes Against Internationally Protected Persons, including Diplomatic Agents", 23 ICLQ 791 (1974); Bloomfield & Fitzgerald, *Crimes Against Internationally Protected Persons: Prevention and Punishment* (1975); Rozakis, "Terrorism and the Internationally Protected Persons in the Light of the ILC's Draft Articles", 23 ICLQ 32 (1974); Shubber, "Aircraft Hijacking under the Hague Convention 1970 — A New Regime?", 22 ICLQ 706 (1973); Verwey, "The International Hostages Convention and National Liberation Movements", 75 AJIL 69 (1981); Halberstam, "Terrorism on the High Seas: The *Achille Lauro*, Piracy and the IMO Convention on Maritime Safety", 82 AJIL 269 (1988).

[21] It must be acknowledged that the comments of many of the writers just mentioned proved helpful, mainly as points of departure for further discussion, and some of these works are referred to throughout this study. Particularly helpful were the articles prepared by those commentators who participated in the drafting of one or more of the conventions, in so far as they were able to provide some insights into the discussions, manoeuvring and decisions which were held off the record.

[22] See generally the commentary on Article 4 (pp. 119-131).

precise nature of the obligations imposed by the Convention is thus important. It is hoped that this study will shed some light on the meaning of the Convention as well as on its shortcomings.

This study focuses on the Hostages Convention, rather than on any of the other anti-terrorism instruments, for a number of reasons: the offence of hostage-taking is one of the most common forms of terrorism (both on its own and as it overlaps with such other offences as aircraft hijacking and assaults on diplomats); the Hostages Convention is broader in scope than the other instruments in the sense that it is not limited solely to offences on board aircraft or on board ships or against internationally protected persons; and the Convention has some provisions which are more innovative and controversial than those contained in the other instruments. But because of the extensive commonality of provisions in the anti-terrorism instruments (other than the Tokyo Convention), this study is to a large extent also a study of the Hague, Montreal, New York and Rome Conventions and Protocols. Throughout this study, therefore, references and comparisons are made to those other instruments (and, less often, to the two regional instruments on the subject, the 1977 European Convention on the Suppression of Terrorism[23] and the 1971 OAS Convention to Prevent and Punish the Acts of Terrorism taking the form of Crimes against Persons and Related Extortion that are of International Significance).[24]

The second broad justification for close examination of this Convention is that its preparation was a significant episode in the continuing process of the codification of international law, and its drafting history presents an interesting study of the dynamics of multilateral treaty making. The subject of terrorism is emotionally highly charged and political in nature. During the preparation of this Convention the draftsmen were sometimes very far apart indeed in their viewpoints and the debate was often conducted at cross-

---

[23] ETS 90. This Convention lists, in Article 1, numerous offences, including aerial hijacking and the taking of hostages, which may not be the subject of the political offence exception to extradition (although pursuant to Article 13, States Parties may make reservations to Article 1). When extradition is not granted, a State Party must submit the case to its authorities for the purpose of prosecution. For further details of the obligation *aut dedere aut judicare* as formulated in this instrument, see pp. 189 & 196 (notes 8 & 32 and accompanying text in the commentary on Article 8). As of 1 January 1989, the European Convention had 19 States Parties. See Bowman & Harris, note 19, *supra*, at p. 417 & 6th Supp.

[24] PAUTS 37. The OAS Convention seeks to suppress acts of violence directed against diplomats and other internationally protected persons. For further details of the obligation *aut dedere aut judicare* as formulated in this instrument, see p. 189 (note 7 and accompanying text in the commentary on Article 8). This Convention is not terribly important due to the subsequent adoption of the New York Convention dealing essentially with the identical subject matter.

purposes. On a number of occasions it seemed as if no further progress would be possible. However, after three years of preparation the draftsmen managed to agree upon a treaty which condemns unequivocally all acts of hostage-taking and requires that all perpetrators be brought to justice. At the same time, the obligations imposed therein are not so onerous as to be politically unacceptable to any civilized State.

It almost need not be said that the problem of international terrorism is not solely a legal one. Terrorism has political, sociological and economic aspects, and it is sometimes — but by no means always — the weapon of oppressed and desperate people who have no other outlet for their grievances. The suggestion has been made that international law has only a limited role to play in the eradication of terrorism and that, therefore, faith in its effectiveness in this regard is misplaced.[25] It is, of course, true that international law can no more completely solve the problem of international terrorism than municipal law can completely eradicate the problem of domestic crime. Indeed, it is by its nature bound to be less effective than most municipal law enforcement systems. Moreover, given the lack of consensus which exists amongst States regarding the various aspects of the problem, the challenges for international law are that much compounded.

However, there are ways in which international law can contribute to the alleviation of the problem of terrorism, many of which are dealt with in this Convention. This Convention imposes obligations upon States Parties with respect to: the establishment of jurisdiction over criminal offences; the enacting of domestic penal legislation; the extradition, granting of asylum and prosecution of offenders; mutual assistance in criminal matters; dealing with hostage situations in their territories; the establishment of co-operative preventative measures; dispute resolution; and the protection of human rights. In addition, the Convention deals with the interaction between international criminal law and the law of armed conflict. As a whole, the

---

[25] Laqueur, *The Age of Terrorism* 308 (1987). Noting the various notions amongst States with respect to the legitimacy of terrorism, Laqueur states that international law is "inadequate" to deal with the problem. He also states that "[i]nternational terrorism is an extra-legal activity and for this reason the contributions of legal experts are bound to be limited." The problems faced by the international community in attempting to take action on terrorism are discussed in Part I. However, the bulk of legal commentators believe that international law, whatever its mixed results to date regarding terrorism, is ultimately essential to controlling the problem. See, e.g., Sofaer, "Terrorism and the Law", 64 Foreign Affairs 901-923 (1986). As one commentator notes, there "seems to be a great need for more interaction between the international lawyer, the sociologist, the criminologist and the political scientist" in dealing with terrorism. DeSchutter, "Prospective Study of the Mechanisms to Repress Terrorism", in Centre de droit international, *Réflexions sur la définition et la répression du terrorisme* 254 (1973).

Convention imposes a comprehensive and far-reaching set of obligations upon States in the field of international criminal law.

This study is divided into two parts. Part I is essentially introductory in nature, dealing with such matters as: the lack of consensus amongst both scholars and States as to the meaning of the term "terrorism"; the "types" of terrorism (i.e., "individual terrorism", "State terrorism" and "State-sponsored terrorism"); the seriousness of the problem of terrorism; and the efforts of the United Nations to deal with it — both in a comprehensive fashion and, along with the specialized agencies, on a piecemeal basis. This part is designed to provide an overview of the problem of terrorism and to place the taking of hostages and the drafting of this Convention in the larger context of that problem. But also, by highlighting both the conceptual differences which exist with respect to the term "terrorism" and the attendant political obstacles to co-operation in combatting the phenomenon, Part I is intended to demonstrate that a comprehensive and universally acceptable approach to the elimination of terrorism will, at least in the near future, remain elusive. The only way to go forward in the search for international co-operation in the suppression of terrorism is in the piecemeal fashion already begun.[26]

Part II, the bulk of the study, is the detailed commentary on the Hostages Convention, the importance of which has already been discussed. The commentary on each article has both an introduction and an interpretation section. The introduction sections are designed to summarize briefly the obligations contained in the article, identify the place of the article within the framework of the Convention, highlight the areas of controversy, if any, surrounding its development and identify, where relevant, the corresponding provisions both in the other anti-terrorism conventions developed by the UN and the specialized agencies and in the original draft convention submitted by the FRG. Some introduction sections, where it was thought necessary

---

[26] It is unclear at the time of writing which, if any, aspect of international terrorism will next be the subject of an international convention, although the General Assembly has requested other agencies, such as the Universal Postal Union and the International Atomic Energy Agency, to consider measures against terrorism. See p. 43 (note 145 in Part I). It may be noted, however, that very often a particularly violent and disturbing incident serves as the catalyst for the drafting and adoption of a terrorism convention. This was the case with, *inter alia*, the ill-fated League of Nations Convention and the Hostages Convention. See pp. 28 & 57 (notes 74 & 196 and accompanying text in Part I). The drafting of the Rome Convention was proposed by the governments of Italy, Egypt and Austria in 1986, the year following the *Achille Lauro* incident. See IMO Docs C57/25 (1986) & C57/INF.3 (1986). Similarly, the Montreal Protocol resulted from a proposal by the Canadian government in October 1986, following terrorist attacks in the Rome and Vienna airports in December 1985 and bomb explosions in the Frankfurt and Tokyo airports in June 1985. See Faller, "Current Legal Activities of ICAO: Development of a Legal Instrument for the Suppression of Unlawful Acts of Violence at Airports Serving International Aviation", 36 *Zeitschrift für Luft- und Weltraumrecht* 219, 219-20 (1987).

or helpful, contain background discussions on the subject matter treated in the article. Moreover, while in general information from the *travaux préparatoires* is discussed at the relevant point in the interpretation sections, the introduction sections of the commentaries on some articles contain detailed discussions regarding the development of that article. This is done with respect to those articles, most of which are new to this Convention, where it was thought that an exposition of their development was particularly helpful for the subsequent interpretation. The interpretation sections constitute the main part of the commentary. Through examination of the language of the article, the *travaux préparatoires* and the applicable law, they are designed to identify the precise nature of the obligations imposed upon States Parties.

PART I

THE PROBLEM OF INTERNATIONAL TERRORISM AND THE RESPONSE OF INTERNATIONAL ORGANIZATIONS

1. THE MEANING OF TERRORISM

(A) *The lack of a generally accepted definition of the term "terrorism"*

The term "terrorism" is unsatisfactory. It is emotive, highly loaded politically and lacking a universally, or even generally, accepted definition. As Walter Laqueur has said, the term has been used as a synonym for "rebellion, street battles, civil strife, insurrection, rural guerilla war, *coups d'état* and a dozen other things."[1] The result is that it has "become almost meaningless, covering almost any, and not necessarily political, act of violence."[2] Even amongst scholars in the field a great many definitions have been promulgated: in a 1983 study Alex Schmid compiled 109 definitions of terrorism.[3] Although there seems to be general agreement that terrorism involves the threat or use of violence, that it seeks to create a climate of fear and that it often relies on publicity, differences in definition range from the semantic to the conceptual.[4] J. Bowyer Bell has charged that the academic response to terrorism has been inadequate, leading to a situation where there is no agreement on the bounds of terrorism, its basic causes or the best way to analyze it.[5]

As noted, the word terrorism is politically loaded. Some commentators have suggested that the labelling of a particular act as terroristic tells less about that act than it does about the labeller's political perspective, that it is more a formulation of a social judgment than a description of a set of phenomena.[6] Thus, the relativist adage is often heard that "one man's terrorist is another man's freedom

---

[1] Laqueur, "Terrorism — A Balance Sheet", *Harper's Magazine* (March and November 1976), *reprinted in* Laqueur (ed.), *The Terrorism Reader* 262 (1979).
[2] Laqueur, *The Age of Terrorism* 11 (1987). As Laqueur suggests, one of the many areas of disagreement regarding the concept of terrorism is whether it should be limited to political violence or whether it should also include violence by those not politically motivated. Bassiouni, for example, lists three types of terrorists: 1) psychopathological offenders; 2) common criminals; and 3) ideologically motivated persons. Bassiouni, "Methodological Options for International Legal Control of Terrorism", in Bassiouni (ed.), *International Terrorism and Political Crimes* 490-491 (1975). Others, however, would limit the concept of terrorism to political offences. See Gal-Or, *International Cooperation to Suppress Terrorism* 2 (1985).
[3] See Schmid, *Political Terrorism: A Research Guide to Concepts, Theories, Data Bases and Literature* 119-152 (1983). In an excellent and thorough work, Schmid examines the various definitions of terrorism and the relationships between terrorism and such other phenomena as guerilla warfare, political assassination, anarchism and "terror". *Id.* at pp. 20-71. For a definition formulated by Schmid, see pp. 17-18 (note 26 and accompanying text). Further to the problem of defining terrorism, see Wardlaw, *Political Terrorism* 3-17 (1982).
[4] See Schmid, note 3, *supra*; Laqueur, note 2, *supra*, at pp. 142-173.
[5] Bell, "Trends in Terror: The Analysis of Political Violence", 29 World Politics 447, 481 (1977).
[6] See, e.g., Rubenstein, *Alchemists of Revolution* 17-18 (1987); Bonanate, "Some Unanticipated Consequences of Terrorism", 16 J. Peace Research 197, 197 (1979).

fighter".[7] And while most writers appear to agree that terrorism is a term which can be applied to both sub-State and State violence, some have focused only on violence from below and have ignored terror conducted by States.[8] Some writers, moreover, have charged that the powerful Western States have limited their use of the term, on ideological grounds, to violence by those who oppose the established order, rather than allowing it to cover also the terror of States.[9] Conversely, as seen in greater detail below, many developing countries have tried to remove the actions of "national liberation movements" from the concept of terrorism, and have been eager to concentrate instead on State activity.[10]

Fortunately, the nature of this study does not require the formulation or identification of a precise definition of terrorism. We are concerned here with the interpretation of a multilateral treaty which clearly defines the international crime which is its subject matter, rather than with the subject of terrorism as a whole. Nevertheless, because this Convention is part of an attempt to deal with the larger problem of terrorism, and since there are frequent references to "terrorism" in this study, some discussion should be devoted to what is meant by that term.

(B) *Individual and State terrorism*

Approaching the concept of terrorism by reference to the actors in a situation, two basic types may be identified: "Individual" (or group) terrorism and "State" terrorism. Individual terrorism has many manifestations, and is used by groups large and small, nationalists, separatists, liberation fighters, etc.[11] Because of its many manifest-

---

[7] See, e.g., Bassiouni, note 2, *supra*, at p. 485; Rosie, *Directory of International Terrorism* 18 (1986).

[8] A majority in Schmid's survey of 109 definitions of terrorism would include State violence as well as insurgent and vigilante violence, although a significant minority is limited only to anti-State violence. See Schmid, note 3, *supra*, at pp. 103-104.

[9] See Chomsky & Hemen, *The Political Economy of Human Rights*, Vol. I, 85-87 (1979). See also the preamble to the self-styled "Geneva Declaration on Terrorism", signed by R. Boudabbous, F. Boyle, R. Charvin, R. Clark, R. Falk, H. Koechler, S. MacBride, W. Perdue, and T. Sono, in 37 International Practitioner's Notebook 9 (July 1987), wherein the authors assert that the public is encouraged to associate terrorism with those who fight for independence and freedom, rather than with those who oppose this struggle.

[10] See, e.g., pp. 30-31 (notes 87-91 and accompanying text).

[11] On the diversity of the phenomenon, Laqueur states:
Terrorism, interpreted here as the use of covert violence by a group for political ends, is usually directed against a government, but is also used against other ethnic groups, classes or parties. The aims may vary from the redress of specific grievances to the overthrow of a government and the seizure of power, or to the liberation of a country from foreign rule. Terrorists seek to cause political, social and economic disruption, and for this purpose frequently engage in planned or indiscriminate murder. Terrorism may appear in conjunction with a political campaign or with guerilla war, but it also has a 'pure' form. It has been waged by national and religious

ations, it is difficult to generalize on this aspect of terrorism without sacrificing accuracy, and it is enough to say for now that individual terrorism is terrorism "from below" rather than terrorism committed by organs of the State. The vast bulk of the literature on the subject of terrorism deals with individual terrorism,[12] and, in general, the use of the term "terrorism" in this study refers to this aspect of the problem.

In contrast to individual terrorism stands the concept of "State" terrorism. Traditionally, State terrorism refers to acts of terror, such as torture, killings, mass arrests, etc., which are conducted by the organs of the State against its own population, whether the entire population, a certain segment thereof (such as a minority community or political opposition), or the population of an occupied country.[13] While individual terrorism is usually anti-State, and, therefore, subversive, the purpose of State terrorism is to enforce the authority and power of the State. An early example of this type of terrorism is the Jacobin "Reign of Terror" in 18th century France, during which some 300,000 people were arrested, about 17,000 people were officially executed and many others died in prison or without a trial.[14] Indeed, although the term terrorism is now commonly used, in both academic discussion and common parlance, to refer to individual or anti-State violence, it seems that the term originated with the Jacobin era and was generally associated for many years with State terror.[15] Other examples of State terrorism are the activities of the Nazis, the Stalinist repression in the USSR, the rule of Pol Pot in Kampuchea in the 1970s and the treatment of the *desapiracidos* of Latin America.[16]

While the examples just mentioned fit neatly into the traditional view of State terrorism (i.e., they constituted violence in a domestic or occupied territory setting), in recent years a wider view of the concept

---

groups, by the left and the right, by nationalist as well as internationalist movements, and it has been state-sponsored . . . . Terrorist movements have frequently consisted of members of the educated middle classes, but there has also been agrarian terrorism, terror by the uprooted and the rejected, and trade union and working-class terror . . . . Terror has been directed against autocratic regimes as well as democracies; sometimes there has been an obvious link with social dislocation and economic crisis, at other times there has been no such connection.

Laqueur, note 2, *supra*, at pp. 72-73.

[12] However, there appears to be a growing literature on State terrorism. See, e.g., Stohl & Lopez (eds.), *The State as Terrorist* (1984); Berman & Clark, "State Terrorism: Disappearances", 13 Rutgers L.J. 531 (1982).

[13] See Laqueur, note 2, *supra*, at p. 145; Gal-Or, note 2, *supra*, at p. 2. Some writers, such as Gal-Or, use the term "terrorism" to refer to individual violence and the term "terror" to refer to such tactics by States. See *id.*; Schmid, note 3, *supra*, at p. 64. It may be noted that the use of terror by a State against its own population does not generally fit within the scope of "international" terrorism. See pp. 22-23 (notes 45-48 and accompanying text).

[14] See Schmid, note 3, *supra*, at p. 66.

[15] *Id.* at pp. 66-67.

[16] See Stohl & Lopez, note 12, *supra*, at p. 4; Laqueur, note 2, *supra*, at p. 145.

of State terrorism has been taken in some quarters, a view that includes State action on the international as well as on the domestic plane. For example, a United Nations document from the 1970s refers to a concept of State terrorism held by some States as:

> terror inflicted on a large scale and with the most modern means on whole populations for purposes of domination or interference in their internal affairs, armed attacks perpetrated under the pretext of reprisals or of preventative action by States against the sovereignty and integrity of third States, and the infiltration of terrorist groups or agents into the territory of other States.[17]

Some writers have similarly expanded the scope of State terrorism to include such activity as "coercive diplomacy", e.g., the US bombing of Hanoi in 1972 and nuclear deterrence,[18] while others have expanded it even further so as to include almost every type of objectionable act — or arguably objectionable act — that a State may take on the international level, including military manoeuvres and war games in the vicinity of another State which present a threat to that other State, the transport of nuclear weapons through the territory of other States and international waters and "the development, testing and deployment of nuclear and space-weapons systems".[19] These latter views expand the concept of "terrorism" to an unwarranted extent and are not generally held.[20]

Writers disagree, moreover, regarding the extent to which State terrorism and individual terrorism are similar phenomena and should be studied together. Laqueur, for example, allows that State terrorism is responsible for many more deaths and injuries each year than is individual terrorism and recognizes that it is a problem well worth study. However, he argues that State terrorism and individual terrorism are fundamentally different concepts and should be studied separately. Beyond the fact that both types of terrorism attempt to induce a state of fear, "there are no important similarities, as they fulfill different functions and manifest themselves in different ways". He adds that "a study of the functions and the techniques of the

---

[17] Report of the *Ad Hoc* Committee on International Terrorism, UN GAOR, 28th Sess., Supp. 28, para. 24, UN Doc A/9028 (1973).
[18] See, e.g., Stohl, "International Dimensions of State Terrorism", in Stohl & Lopez, note 12, *supra*, at pp. 44-45, who argues that the word terrorism — defined as a "purposeful act or threat of violence to create fear and/or compliant behavior in a victim and/or audience of the act or threat" — describes many of the uses and threats of force in the international system. Along with "coercive diplomacy", he adds "covert behavior" and "surrogate terrorism" (assistance to groups or States which improves their capacity for terrorism) to the categories of State terrorism.
[19] See "Geneva Declaration on Terrorism", note 9, *supra*, at pp. 9-10.
[20] See generally Stohl, note 18, *supra*, who admits that most scholars would not consider the type of behaviour he lists as terrorism.

Gestapo is important, but it will be of no more help in understanding the Baader-Meinhof gang than the study of Auschwitz or of Pol Pot would be for comprehending the IRA or Abu Nidal."[21] Michael Stohl and George Lopez suggest that the concepts are essentially similar and that study of the two should be tied together.[22] Paul Wilkinson suggests that the two concepts are complementary and that an understanding of individual or group terrorism requires an understanding of the use of terror and violence by States.[23] Moreover, as noted below, many developing countries maintain that State terrorism is the predominant cause of individual terrorism and should be dealt with as the first necessary step towards eliminating individual terrorism.[24]

(C) *Two working definitions of terrorism*

Despite all of the uncertainty and disagreement in this area, there are some definitions of terrorism which seem reasonable in so far as they, to a certain extent, bridge the gap between some of the various viewpoints (except as regards the widest notions of State terrorism). Drawing together the various common elements of the definitions included in his study, mentioned earlier,[25] and adding a few elements of his own, Schmid developed a lengthy definition. It is worth setting out this definition in full, not so much because it is of direct assistance in understanding the provisions of the Hostages Convention, but because it is of use both in this general discussion of terrorism and, more importantly, in the later discussion regarding the methodology of the UN and specialized agencies in dealing with the problem, which avoids definitions altogether and concentrates instead on the prohibition of specific acts. Schmid's definition is as follows:

> Terrorism is a method of combat in which random or symbolic victims serve as instrumental *targets of violence*. These instrumental victims share group or class characteristics which form the basis for their selection for victimization. Through previous use of violence or the credible threat of violence other members of that group or class are put in a *state of chronic fear (terror)*. This group or class, whose members' sense of security is purposively undermined, is the *target of terror*. The victimization of the target of violence is considered extranormal by most observers from the witnessing audience on the basis of its atrocity; the time (e.g., peacetime) or place (not a battlefield) of victimization or the disregard for rules of combat

---
[21] Laqueur, note 2, *supra*, at p. 146.
[22] Stohl & Lopez, note 12, *supra*, at pp. 6-7.
[23] Wilkinson, "Can a State be 'Terrorist'?", 57 International Affairs, p. 467 (1981).
[24] See p. 38 (note 128 and accompanying text).
[25] See p. 13 (note 3 and accompanying text).

accepted in conventional warfare. The norm violation creates an attentive audience beyond the target of terror; sectors of this audience might in turn form the main object of manipulation. The purpose of this indirect method of combat is either to immobilize the target of terror in order to produce disorientation and/or compliance, or to mobilize secondary *targets of demands* (e.g., a government) or *targets of attention* (e.g., public opinion) to changes of attitude or behaviour favouring the short or long-term interests of the users of this method of combat.[26]

This definition does not count as terrorism acts where there is no "target of terror", i.e., where the act of violence has a more immediate and direct purpose. Examples of acts excluded would be a hijacking where the perpetrator's only purpose is to get to a destination which is not the intended one of the aircraft (a situation which would be covered by the Hague Convention on hijacking)[27] and the assassination of a political figure which is intended only to eliminate that person.[28] It also excludes violence against things, as opposed to violence against people. Partly for these reasons, Schmid acknowledges that this definition is flawed.[29] However, it is a good definition in that it includes acts of violence committed both by individuals (or groups) and by State actors. The purpose can be either revolutionary or to enforce the authority of the State. In fact, the definition does not allow consideration of the motive behind the act or of the identity of the perpetrator. As Schmid states, "[w]hether the perpetrator is a 'lone wolf', a criminal, a vigilante, a psychopath, an insurgent or an agent of a regime should be irrelevant in assessing whether or not certain forms of violence should be defined as terroristic".[30]

A simpler definition of terrorism is proffered by the US Department of State: terrorism is "premeditated, politically motivated violence perpetrated against noncombatant targets by subnational groups or clandestine state agents, usually intended to influence an audience".[31] This definition requires a political motivation, but does not favour one political viewpoint over another. Similar to Schmid's definition, it does not allow for a relativist concept of terrorism, i.e., that "one man's terrorist is another man's freedom fighter". The

---

[26] Schmid, note 3, *supra*, at p. 111.
[27] See p. 52 (note 178 and accompanying text) for the description of the crime of hijacking as set forth in Article 1 of the Hague Convention.
[28] Schmid, note 3, *supra*, at p. 62.
[29] *Id*. at pp. 110-111. Schmid states that his definition is not a "true or correct" definition of terrorism since "[t]errorism is an abstract phenomenon of which there can be no real essence which can be discovered or described". He recognizes that some might find his definition to be too narrow.
[30] *Id*. at p. 106.
[31] US Department of State, *Patterns of Global Terrorism: 1988,* p. v (1989).

motives or causes of the actors are irrelevant, at least in theory (application of the definition to a certain set of circumstances, however, still involves a degree of subjectivity). The definition includes terror by the State, but only in so far as it involves "clandestine state agents". Its advantage over Schmid's definition is that it does not absolutely require a "target of terror" and could thus include, for example, hijackings and assassinations such as those excluded from Schmid's definition. It should be noted that neither of these definitions would seemingly be acceptable to some developing States which have argued, as noted in some detail below,[32] that the legitimate causes of certain groups, specifically national liberation movements, should take their actions outside the concept of terrorism.

(D) *State-sponsored terrorism*

Without regard to one's view of the extent to which certain State activities qualify as "State terrorism", the necessity for current concepts of terrorism, even if primarily concerned with individual or group terrorism, to include activity by State agents has become clear since the mid-1970s with the increase of another "type" of terrorism — "State-sponsored terrorism". This type of activity has emerged as a significant phenomenon on the world stage (Wilkinson estimates that 25% of international political terrorism is now State-sponsored or State-directed)[33] and it does not fit easily into the categories of individual terrorism or State terrorism. It is, as the name suggests, generally terrorism against one State which is "sponsored" by another State. The degree of sponsorship varies, and can consist, for example, of such things as the supply of financial assistance, training, arms and travel documents to terrorist groups which, to a greater or lesser degree, have their own agenda, or which, alternatively, are directly controlled by the sponsoring State (hence the alternative term "State-directed terrorism"). As can readily be appreciated, access to the resources of a State may greatly increase the destructive potential of a terrorist group, and, indeed, can change the nature of a terrorist campaign.[34] Experts in the field have thus concluded that this type of

---

[32] See, e.g., pp. 31 & 37 (notes 89 & 120 and accompanying text).

[33] Wilkinson, *Terrorism and the Liberal State* 275 (2nd ed. 1986). Laqueur notes that this type of terrorism existed in a minor form in the pre-World War II period, but became a permanent feature of international politics in the 1970s, characterized by "an almost impenetrable maze of linkages, intrigues, common and conflicting interests, including open and covert collaboration with foreign governments who preferred to stay in the shadows." Laqueur, note 2, *supra*, at pp. 268-269.

[34] For example, arms and ammunition, including Sam 7 missiles, believed to have been en route to Northern Ireland from Libya in January 1988 could have
(*continued on p. 20*)

terrorism has little in common with the terrorism of the past. It is, in fact, a form of surrogate warfare, allowing a State to strike at its enemies in a way that is relatively inexpensive financially and less risky militarily than conventional armed conflict.[35] Examples of State-sponsored terrorism are the Syrian involvement in the 1986 attempted sabotage of an El Al flight from Heathrow airport,[36] and the suspected Libyan supply of arms to the Irish Republican Army.[37] It is important to note that State sponsorship of terrorism in the territory of another State is specifically forbidden by the General Assembly's Declaration on Principles of International Law and its Resolution on Aggression.[38]

State-sponsored or State-directed terrorism has many forms. It does not always, for example, consist of the assisting or directing of pre-existing or autonomous or semi-autonomous groups. Nor are its

---

([34] *continued*)
"significantly alter[ed] the course of the terrorist war" in that region. See *The Sunday Times*, 24 Jan. 1988, p. 1. Although there seems to be general recognition that the growing phenomenon of State-sponsorship of, and involvement in, international terrorism has added a new dimension to the problem, there is some disagreement as to the extent to which this is so. Netanyahu, for example, states that international terrorism is "rooted in the political ambitions and designs of expansionist states" rather than frustration and social misery, and that international terrorism would be "impossible" without the support of such States as Syria, Libya, Iran and Iraq. Netanyahu, "Defining Terrorism", in Netanyahu (ed.), *Terrorism: How the West Can Win* 7 (1986). The US Secretary of State argued in 1984 that, while violent individuals and fanatics can exist anywhere, terrorism in many countries would have died out without significant support from other States. 84 Dep't St. Bull., No. 2093, p. 13 (1984). Rubenstein, while acknowledging the support that some groups get from outside, argues that much terrorism is rooted in legitimate social grievances, enjoys significant popular support and would exist even without State support. Rubenstein, note 6, *supra*, at pp. 50-64.

[35] See Wilkinson, note 33, *supra*, at p. 277. In 1975, one commentator predicted that this new type of low-level warfare would result in a situation wherein staying power is more important than firepower. See Jenkins, "International Terrorism: A New Mode of Conflict", in Carlton & Schaerf (eds.), *International Terrorism and World Security* 30-31 (1975).

[36] On 24 October 1986, Nezar Hindawi, a Palestinian of Jordanian nationality, was convicted in the United Kingdom of attempting to destroy the aircraft by means of explosives concealed in his girlfriend's luggage. There was evidence at the trial which indicated that Hindawi was acting under instructions from the Syrian intelligence service, that he had travelled to London under a false name on a Syrian diplomatic passport and had received support from the ambassador and staff of the Syrian embassy in London. The Foreign and Commonwealth Secretary subsequently announced that this evidence, coupled with additional evidence obtained by intelligence services, was "conclusive" proof of Syrian involvement in the incident, and the UK cut ties with Syria. See XXXII *Keesing's Contemporary Archives* 34771-72 (1986). It may be noted that a month after Hindawi's conviction, his brother, Ahmed Hasi, and another man were convicted in the FRG on charges stemming from the bombing of the German-Arab Friendship Society in West Berlin. Syria was implicated in that incident also, resulting in the expulsion of three Syrian diplomats from the FRG and in the issuing of an arrest warrant for the deputy chief of the intelligence unit of the Syrian Air Force. See *id*. at p. 34835.

[37] See note 34, *supra*.

[38] See pp. 29-30 (notes 83-85 and accompanying text).

victims always symbolic targets only. For example, some States, such as Libya and Iran, employ their own agents abroad to assassinate opponents of their regimes.[39] A person killed in this way can be both a direct and a symbolic victim in so far as the act may serve both to eliminate an enemy of the regime and to serve as a warning to others. This type of activity is similar to traditional State terrorism (in so far as it is directed against political opposition rather than against the security of another State), though it is conducted abroad. Moreover, it is not wholly new: for example, Stalin directed Soviet agents to liquidate Trotsky in Mexico.[40] States have employed their agents abroad in other types of terrorist attacks also. In 1985, French agents engaged in an act of terrorism in New Zealand territory by blowing up the *Rainbow Warrior*, a ship owned by the environmental group "Greenpeace" and involved in protesting French nuclear testing in the South Pacific. This act incidentally resulted in the death of a member of that group.[41] State-sponsored terrorism is not, however, always conducted abroad. Whatever may have been the role of the Iranian regime in the initial seizure and detention of the American diplomats and civilians in Tehran, it is clear that the subsequent holding of the hostages was approved of and controlled by the State.[42] Examples such as these sometimes blur the line between "individual terrorism" (since, for example, in the case of the embassy take-over, the original seizure of the hostages may have been solely at the initiative of the students), "State-terrorism" and "State-sponsored terrorism".[43]

---

[39] For example, in October 1987, an Iranian opposition figure, along with his son, was found shot dead in his home in London after reportedly ignoring warnings from Iranian agents to cease his anti-Khomeini activities. Also in 1987, attempts were made on the lives of a former Iranian cabinet member and a supporter of a former Iranian prime minister. See *The Sunday Times*, 4 Oct. 1987, p. 3. For other examples of such activity by Libya and Iran, see 88 Dep't St. Bull., No. 2130, pp. 44 & 51-53 (1988).
[40] See Parry, *Terrorism from Robespierre to Arafat* 184 (1976).
[41] In this case, France acknowledged its role in the incident. For the facts of this episode, see XXXI *Keesing's Contemporary Archives* 33852-53 (1985). The *Rainbow Warrior* incident, a clear example of terrorism, demonstrates that it is not only developing or Eastern-bloc States that resort to this type of combat.
[42] See p. 3 (note 12 and accompanying text in the Introduction).
[43] To underscore this point, it may be noted that there is sometimes inconsistency in terminology amongst commentators when referring to such acts of violence by States. With respect to the Iranian hostages situation, Stohl and Lopez have referred to it as State terrorism, while Wilkinson has called it State-sponsored terrorism. See Stohl & Lopez, note 12, *supra*, at pp. 5-6; Wilkinson, note 33, *supra*, at p. 280. With respect to the assassination of opponents abroad, Laqueur has called it State terrorism, while Wilkinson has referred to it as State-sponsored terrorism. See Laqueur, note 2, *supra*, at p. 145; Wilkinson, note 33, *supra*, at p. 276. One way of avoiding the use of the sometimes confusing or imprecise terms of "State" or "individual" or "State-sponsored" terrorism is to classify the act according to its purpose. Thornton, for example, suggests two categories of terrorism — "enforcement" and "agitational" — while Wilkinson suggests three — "revolutionary", "sub-revolutionary", and "repressive". See Thornton, "Terror as a Weapon of Political Agitation", in Eckstein (ed.), *Internal War* 72 (1964); Wilkinson, note 33, *supra*, at p. 57.

22   TERRORISM AND THE INTERNATIONAL RESPONSE

While the foregoing discussion may be helpful in attempting to understand what may be meant by the term "terrorism", it must be emphasized that the definitions listed above and any distinctions as to whether terrorism is "State terrorism" or "individual terrorism" or "State-sponsored terrorism" are to a large extent unimportant for the narrower exercise of studying the Hostages Convention and the other multilateral instruments on terrorism. These instruments simply require the outlawing of certain clearly defined acts no matter why or by whom committed. The Conventions are directed towards individual, rather than State, liability for the proscribed offences, but they are as applicable to those acting on behalf of a State as they are to persons acting in a private capacity.[44]

(E) *The "international" nature of terrorism*

It should be noted that terrorism can be domestic or international in nature. Domestic terrorism, as the name implies, involves the citizens and territory of one State and is directed against (or by) that State. For terrorism to be international, there must be an "internationalizing" element, and many definitions and criteria have been advanced for deciding when that element exists. The US State Department, for example, defines terrorism as international when it involves "citizens or territory of more than one country".[45] Laqueur observes that the term "international terrorism" can refer to State-sponsored terrorism against foreign countries, to co-operation between terrorist groups and to attacks against foreign nationals or property in the terrorist's own country or elsewhere.[46] Wilkinson suggests that terrorism is international when it is "directed against foreigners or foreign targets", when it is "concerted by the governments or factions of more than one state", or when it is "aimed at influencing the policies of a foreign government".[47] Another commentator notes, somewhat vaguely, that terrorism is international when "the interests of more than one state are involved".[48] It can readily be seen that there are no

---

[44] See pp. 79-80 (notes 8 & 9 and accompanying text in the commentary on Article 1).
[45] *Patterns of Global Terrorism*, note 31, *supra*.
[46] Laqueur, note 2, *supra*, at p. 266.
[47] Wilkinson, note 33, *supra*, at p. 182. The International Law Association states that terrorism is international, despite its having been committed "within the jurisdiction of one country", when it is committed "against any foreign government or international organization, or any representative thereof", or "against any national of a foreign country because he is a national of a foreign country", or "by a person who crosses an international frontier into another country from which his extradition is requested". See ILA, *Report of the Sixty-First Conference* 6-7 (1984).
[48] Mann, "Personnel and Property of Transnational Business Operations", in Evans & Murphy (eds.), *Legal Aspects of International Terrorism* 399 (1978).

contradictions between these various formulations, and that whenever the citizens, territory or entity of a second State are involved in a terrorist act, that act can be considered as international terrorism. In any event, for the purposes of the study of the Hostages Convention it may be noted that the instrument applies only to international acts of hostage-taking and that the criteria for whether or not such an act is international in nature are contained in Article 13.

2. THE PROBLEM OF TERRORISM IN PERSPECTIVE

The government of the United States, for one, has devoted a considerable amount of energy to the issue of international terrorism, establishing various preventative programmes, adopting legislation on the problem[49] and operating, within the State Department, an Office of Counter-Terrorism with an "Ambassador-at-large for Counter-Terrorism".[50] Terrorism has been the subject of numerous speeches and statements by the President and other officials,[51] and has led to the bombing of Tripoli by US armed forces due to the alleged involvement of Libya in international terrorist acts.[52] As noted in more detail below, other countries have also devoted considerable attention to the problem,[53] and it has been the subject of significant United Nations activity.[54] The academic literature on the subject is

---

[49] For example, in 1984, the US enacted legislation which authorizes the Attorney-General and Secretary of State to pay rewards to those who furnish information leading to the arrest or conviction of terrorists whose targets are Americans, urges the President to seek increased international co-operation to combat terrorism and allocates funds to increase the security of US missions abroad. See 1984 Act to Combat International Terrorism, Public Law No. 98-533, 98 Stat. 2706 (1984). See Leich, "Four Bills Proposed by President Reagan to Counter Terrorism", 78 AJIL 915 (1984). The US has also passed legislation allowing US courts to exercise jurisdiction over offences which are committed in terrorist attacks against Americans abroad. See p. 154 (note 87 and accompanying text in the commentary on Article 5). For a history of US legislation on the subject of terrorism, see Pearl, "Terrorism — Historical Perspective on United States Congressional Action", 10 Terr. J. 139 (1987). For details of US preventative programmes, see pp. 130-131 (notes 41-44 and accompanying text in the commentary on Article 4).

[50] See generally 84 Dep't St. Bull., No. 2092, p. 68 (1984); 87 Dep't St. Bull., No. 2120, p. 2 (1987).

[51] See, e.g., speech of the President on 8 July 1985, 85 Dep't St. Bull., No. 2101, pp. 7-10 (1985); speech of the Secretary of State on 25 October 1984, 84 Dep't St. Bull., No. 2093, pp. 12-17 (1984).

[52] For a brief outline of the facts of the Libyan incident, see p. 321 (notes 48-54 and accompanying text in the commentary on Article 14).

[53] See generally the commentary on Article 4 (pp. 119-131). The United Kingdom, for example, has enacted the Prevention of Terrorism Act 1984, which gives the government extraordinary powers, *inter alia*, to ban persons suspected of terrorism from the UK or from constituent parts thereof.

[54] This activity has related both to the treatment of the general topic of terrorism and to the drafting of specific conventions. See generally §§3-5, *infra*.

vast,[55] and it is the frequent subject of more popular literature and other media treatment.

Is it possible that the issue of international terrorism commands an undue amount of attention? It is surely the case that there are greater problems facing the international community than terrorism, such as world hunger and environmental damage. A larger number of casualties are caused each year by, for example, automobile accidents. And it does not seem that terrorism is an effective tool of revolution: no modern political systems — democratic (which because of their beliefs and openness are in many ways the most vulnerable to terrorism)[56] or otherwise — have fallen, or seem in danger of falling, due solely to the efforts of terrorist groups.[57] The mass media are often blamed for providing ready and perhaps undue coverage of terrorist incidents (and thereby promoting the phenomenon).[58] And some have argued that the problem of international terrorism is cynically overstated by politicians. One commentator, for example, has written:

> For elected officials seeking an issue that is relatively safe politically, terrorism makes an excellent target. It is an emotional issue that can arouse public sentiment, and it continues to generate considerable media attention. The highly visible nature of terrorism makes it an excellent topic which politicians can use to attract instant news coverage ... elected officials have found the issue of terrorism an excellent subject for political rallies and campaign rhetoric ... government officials, plagued by economic or social ills among the populace, may find terrorism an attractive issue to divert public sentiment from pressing social problems ... and solidify the public conscience against a common enemy.[59]

There is, therefore, disagreement as to the seriousness of the

---

[55] Books and articles exist which deal with such topics as the history of terrorism and its development as a modern phenomenon, explanations for its development, its moral justifications, ways in which it can be combatted, its legal aspects, the examination of the various groups which use it and the causes they espouse, the relationship between terrorism and liberal democracies, the effect of terrorism upon its victims, the phenomenon of State terrorism, the links between various terrorist groups and the financing of terrorism. There is also a considerable literature concerning the relationship between terrorism and the mass media. One bibliography lists 5,574 entries on terrorism. See Lakos, *International Terrorism: A Bibliography* (1986).

[56] Wilkinson, note 33, *supra*, at pp. 103-05, 287.

[57] Commentators seem to agree that terrorism is not an effective revolutionary strategy. See *id.* at p. 53; Rubenstein, note 6, *supra*, at pp. 168-69, 234-35; Laqueur, note 2, *supra*, at pp. 5-6, 303.

[58] See generally, Wardlaw, note 3, *supra*, at p. 77; Schorr, "The Encouragement of Violence", in Netanyahu, note 34, *supra*, at p. 114; Bassiouni, "Terrorism, Law Enforcement, and the Mass Media: Perspectives, Problems, Proposals", 72 J. Crim. L. & Crim'y 1-51 (1981).

[59] Smith, "Antiterrorism Legislation in the United States: Problems and Implications", 7 Terr. J. 213-215 (1984-85).

problem of terrorism.[60] But even if it is accepted that an inordinate amount of attention is paid to the issue of terrorism by the media, the public and politicians, it must also be recognized that the problem is real, it has taken on a new dimension in the last two decades,[61] and its effects are serious. Moreover, to say that there are more serious international problems than terrorism does not dispense with the need to deal with this issue. Terrorism leads to the death and injury of thousands of innocent persons each year.[62] It undermines the confidence of people in the international systems of transportation and communication and their confidence in the ability of their governments to protect them.[63] While the chance that a particular individual will be the direct victim of a terrorist attack is slight, few air travellers, for example, could have failed to contemplate the possibility of their flight being hijacked or sabotaged, or have not

---

[60] For example, one commentator has called terrorism the "cancer of the modern world". See Johnson, "The Cancer of Terrorism", in Netanyahu (ed.), note 34, *supra*, at p. 31. Others have stated that terrorism is "a growing threat to the maintenance of an orderly society". Alexander, Baum & Danzinger, "Terrorism: Future Threats and Responses", 7 Terr. J. 367 (1984-5). By way of contrast, compared with other problems of the modern world, another commentator has called terrorism a "side-show". See Laqueur, note 2, *supra*, at p. 298. Then Prime Minister Chirac of France expressed the view in 1986 that the US and UK overreact to Arab terrorism. See XXXII *Keesing's Contemporary Archives* 34772 (1986). See also Simon, "Misunderstanding Terrorism", 67 Foreign Policy 104 (1987).

[61] There is general agreement that the problem of terrorism has taken on a new dimension since the 1960s. This is due not only to increased State-sponsorship of such activity, but also to the advent of the technology which led to such developments as mass air travel and mass communications. See e.g., Laqueur, note 2, *supra*, at pp. 203-04; Wardlaw, note 3, *supra*, at p. 25; 88 Dep't St. Bull., No. 2130, p. 47 (1988).

[62] The US Department of State calculates that in the year 1988, 658 people were killed and 1,131 were wounded in 856 international terrorist attacks involving the citizens and property of 79 nations and occurring in 68 countries. The number of incidents in 1988 represents a 3% increase over 1987, when there were 832 international terrorist incidents, resulting in the loss of 633 lives and the wounding of 2,272 persons. See US Department of State, *Patterns of Global Terrorism: 1988* 1-4 (1989). Also according to the State Department, between 1976 and 1986, there were more than 6,000 international terrorist incidents, resulting in the death of nearly 5,000 people and the wounding of 8,000. See US Department of State publication entitled "Gist" on the subject of International Terrorism (May 1987). The number of actual incidents, moreover, does not tell the whole story: the State Department also calculates that in the year 1986 the United States and its allies foiled more than 120 planned international terrorist attacks. Whitehead, "Terrorism: The Challenge and the Response" in US Department of State, "Current Policy", No. 900, p. 2 (1986). The total number of international incidents each year does not inexorably rise from the past year's total. For example, the total for 1986 was lower than that for 1985. See 88 Dep't St. Bull., No. 2130, p. 40 (1988). However, the overall pattern is one of steady growth in the number of incidents. Between 1981 and 1985, the number of international terrorist incidents grew from some 500 per year to 800 per year. *Id.*

Statistics on terrorism will, of course, vary according to such factors as the definition of terrorism used and the thoroughness of the study concerned. See Laqueur, note 2, *supra*, at pp. 166, 334-35. No opinion is expressed on the State Department methodology or accuracy of figures; these particular statistics are included in this study simply to present a picture of the scope of the problem.

[63] See Laqueur, note 2, *supra*, at p. 9.

experienced the delays and inconvenience of airport security measures. Preventative measures, moreover, often involve some loss of individual freedom (which may in turn alienate people from their governments),[64] and security measures must ultimately be paid for. The hostage-takings in Lebanon and the attendant security risks to journalists must adversely affect news gathering and, thus, the ability of the public to obtain accurate news from that troubled area. Attacks against diplomats have a destabilizing effect on the international system.

Moreover, of utmost importance, international terrorism has a damaging effect both on international relations and on domestic politics. With respect to international relations, cases can easily be identified wherein the phenomenon of terrorism has caused a worsening of relations — temporary or otherwise — both as between States which are normally on good terms with each other and as between States which, if not overtly antagonistic to each other, are on somewhat less than friendly terms or have different political and/or social systems. As examples of the former, in the aftermath of the 1985 hijacking in the Mediterranean of the Italian cruise ship *Achille Lauro*, tensions arose between the United States and Italy due to the Italian government's refusal to hold Abu Abbas, the suspected mastermind of the operation, pending an extradition request;[65]

---

[64] See Wilkinson, note 33, *supra*, at p. 81.

[65] The *Achille Lauro* case highlights one of the difficulties inherent in bringing terrorists to justice — the lack of political will even on the part of Western democratic States. One of the men on board the Egyptian aircraft diverted to Italy (see p. 4 (note 13 and accompanying text in the Introduction)) was Abbas, the reported leader of the Palestine Liberation Front, who was accused by the United States of being the mastermind of the *Achille Lauro* incident, although he had not been on board the ship. After learning that Abbas was on the plane, the US issued a warrant for his arrest, along with warrants for the other terrorists, and asked Italy to detain him while it formulated an extradition request. Italy was not at that time a party to the Hostages Convention (although it was a signatory); however, the US-Italian bilateral extradition treaty, which was in force at that time, has an article concerning provisional arrest pending a formal request for extradition. See Art. XII, Treaty on Extradition, 13 October 1983, US-Italy, TIAS 10, 837, *reprinted in* 24 ILM 1527 (1985). Although it held the other terrorists, the Italian government released Abbas, despite being shown evidence of his participation in the hijacking. Italian officials justified their refusal, which provoked an angry response from the US, on the grounds of insufficient evidence; however, other officials indicated that the real reason for the failure to hold Abbas was fear that it would result in an outburst of Arab terrorism in Italy. *New York Times*, Oct. 13, 1985, p. A1 & p. A20 & Oct. 14, 1985, p. A1. Abbas went to Yugoslavia, which reportedly granted him diplomatic immunity (as an official of the PLO) and also refused to hold him for extradition. See *New York Times*, Oct. 14, 1985, p. A1 & p. A19. This was despite the fact that Yugoslavia was at that time party both to the Hostages Convention (see Bowman & Harris, *Multilateral Treaties Index and Current Status*, 4th Supp., p. 106 (1987)) and to a bilateral extradition treaty with the United States. See Treaty on Extradition, 25 October 1901, US-Yugoslavia, TS 406. It might be noted that prosecutors in Sicily subsequently issued arrest warrants for Abbas in connexion with the *Achille Lauro* incident. *New York Times*, Oct. 27, 1985, p. A10, Oct. 31, 1985, p. B8 & Nov. 20, 1985, p. A3. Abbas was tried and convicted *in absentia* for offences connected with the case. *New York Times*, July 11, 1986, p. A1.

tensions also arose between the United States and Egypt due to the American diversion to Italy of the Egyptian aircraft carrying the hijackers.[66] As examples of the latter, diplomatic relations between the United Kingdom and Syria were broken off as a result of Syrian involvement in the attempted sabotage of an El Al aircraft which was to embark from Heathrow airport in 1986;[67] suspected Libyan involvement in terrorism and the bombing of Tripoli by the United States in response thereto has created a great strain between those two nations.[68]

With respect to the detrimental effects that terrorism can have on domestic politics, it may be noted that in the aftermath of the *Achille Lauro* affair the coalition government of Italy fell temporarily as a result of one party's protest at the government's handling of the Abu Abbas extradition request.[69] And the Reagan administration's 1986 decision to sell arms to Iran in exchange for Iran's assistance in securing the release of US hostages held in Lebanon caused a general outcry in the United States (and abroad), led to numerous investigations, including those by the Congress and a special prosecutor, and seriously damaged the reputation and effectiveness of the President.[70]

It is thus not difficult to see the need for effective, legal and non-violent measures to combat terrorism. Given the ease and relative lack of resources with which many types of terrorist acts can be conducted, even with significant international co-operation the phenomenon in all likelihood cannot be eliminated.[71] Unfortunately, divisions in world opinion on the issue of terrorism has made elusive

---

[66] See p. 322 (note 56 and accompanying text in the commentary on Article 14). See also Oakley, "International Terrorism", 65 Foreign Affairs 611, 612 (1987).

[67] See note 36, *supra*.

[68] See generally Schumacher, "The United States and Libya", 65 Foreign Affairs 329 (1986-87). Moreover, the US action caused a temporary strain in US relations with its allies. Because of European disapproval of the bombing, 83% of Americans expressed a negative attitude to perceived European weakness in dealing with terrorism, and some Congressmen called for a reduction of US troops in Europe. See Oakley, note 66, *supra*, at p. 618. On the bombing of Tripoli, see p. 321 (notes 48-54 and accompanying text in the commentary on Article 14).

[69] See *New York Times*, Oct. 16, 1985, p. A12 & Oct. 17, 1985, p. A1.

[70] See XXXIII Keesing's *Record of World Events* 35182-87 (1987). See generally Oakley, note 66, *supra*.

[71] In addition, Bassiouni notes three reasons why groups will continue to resort to terrorism: 1) because conventional war has outlived its usefulness; 2) nuclear strategy is not yet "useful"; and 3) there exist no conflict resolution devices for the settlement of disputes arising out of ideological claims and human rights violations. Bassiouni, note 2, *supra*, at p. 490. Other commentators agree that terrorism will continue. Jenkins identifies a number of factors, such as modern air travel, mass media, the widespread availability of arms, the existence of a terrorist infrastructure and State-sponsorship of terrorism, which argue for the persistence of terrorism. See Jenkins, "Future Trends in International Terrorism", in Slater & Stohl (eds.), *Current Perspectives on International Terrorism* 247-249 (1988).

even such co-operative measures which are necessary to alleviate the problem.

3. THE INTERNATIONAL COMMUNITY AND EFFORTS TO CONTROL TERRORISM: A LACK OF CONSENSUS

Since before World War II, efforts have been made in various fora to deal with the problem of international terrorism on a more or less universal basis. Unquestionably, the greatest obstacle to controlling international terrorism has been the difficulty States have had in reaching any broad consensus on the issues involved, not only as to the best way of achieving such control, but even as to the necessity and desirability of doing so.

(A) *Pre-World War II efforts to control terrorism*

It hardly need be said that, although the problem of international terrorism has grown in importance since the 1960s with the advent of modern technology, particularly with regard to transportation and communication, terrorism is not a new phenomenon. Experts have traced examples back to antiquity, and, more recently, activities which have been characterized as terrorism were conducted in the late 19th and early 20th centuries by anarchists in parts of Europe and the United States, radical nationalists and separatists in various parts of the world and by Russian revolutionaries.[72]

Between the two World Wars a number of International Conferences for the Unification of Penal Law addressed the issue of terrorism but did not draft a convention or take any other binding steps to deal with the problem.[73] A more significant effort was made by the League of Nations in the 1930s. In the wake of the 1934 assassinations of King Alexander of Yugoslavia and French Foreign Minister Barthou, the League of Nations, at the behest of France, drafted and adopted in 1937 the Convention on the Prevention and Punishment of Terrorism[74] (and an accompanying Convention on the Establishment of an International Criminal Court).[75] The League's

---

[72] See generally Parry, note 40, *supra*, at pp. 39-130; Laqueur, note 2, *supra*, at pp. 12-21.
[73] See Study prepared by the Secretariat in accordance with the decision taken by the Sixth Committee at its 1314th meeting on 27 September 1972, UN Doc A/C.6/418/Rev. 1, paras. 22-26; Zlataric, "History of International Terrorism", in Bassiouni (ed.), *International Terrorism and Political Crimes* 478-480 (1975).
[74] LN Doc C.546(1).M.383(1).1937.V, *reprinted in* Hudson (ed.), *International Legislation*, Vol. VII, 862 (1941).
[75] LN Doc C.547(1).M.384(1).1937.V, *reprinted in* Hudson, note 74, *supra*, at p. 878.

Terrorism Convention was directed mainly at crimes against heads of State and other public officials; however, it contained a number of far-reaching obligations unrelated to such crimes. For example, the Convention required States Parties generally to prevent and punish acts of terrorism, defined as "criminal acts directed against a State and intended or calculated to create a state of terror in the minds of particular persons, or a group of persons, or the general public".[76] Moreover, States Parties were specifically obliged to enact criminal sanctions for certain acts if they constituted terrorism within the meaning of the foregoing definition. These acts included, *inter alia*, attacks on the lives and physical integrity of heads of State and other public officials, destruction of public property and acts calculated to endanger the lives of members of the public.[77] The Convention, moreover, recognized, but did not require in most instances, application of the principle *aut dedere aut judicare*.[78] Although the Convention had 24 signatories, it was ratified by only one State and never came into force.[79] It seems that the Convention was the victim of the tense international atmosphere extant on the eve of World War II, its overly-ambitious scope and lack of agreement on the definition of terrorism.[80] Moreover, while many governments were genuinely opposed to terrorism, it served the purposes of others which were, therefore, less inclined to take steps to curb the problem.[81]

(B) *General Assembly deliberations*

In the period since World War II, during which the phenomenon of international terrorism has become prevalent and its manifestations increasingly sophisticated, the difficulties in reaching agreement on steps to control the problem have become even more acute. One principle upon which agreement was reached fairly early on in the United Nations is that States have a responsibility not to conduct, support or encourage terrorist activity against other States.[82] Such prohibitions are contained in the 1974 resolution defining

---

[76] Art. 1, note 74, *supra*.
[77] *Id*. at Art. 2.
[78] *Id*. at Art. 10. See pp. 188-189 (note 3 and accompanying text in the commentary on Article 8).
[79] See generally Hudson, note 74, *supra*, at p. 862.
[80] See generally Wardlaw, note 3, *supra*, at p. 105; Zlataric, note 73, *supra*, at p. 482.
[81] See generally Laqueur, note 2, *supra*, at pp. 20-21.
[82] Agreement on this principle was also reached in the League of Nations. See Article 1 of the Terrorism Convention, note 74, *supra*. In addition to the presence of such a clause in the Terrorism Convention, the Council resolved in 1934 that States had the duty not to encourage or tolerate in their territory terrorist activity directed against other States. See 1934 League of Nations Official Journal 1839.

aggression,[83] the ILC's as-yet uncompleted "Draft Code of Offences Against the Peace and Security of Mankind",[84] and the 1970 Declaration on Principles of International Law.[85] The latter instrument provides that each State has the duty to refrain from encouraging the organization of armed bands, irregular forces and mercenaries for incursion into the territory of another State, and "the duty to refrain from organizing, instigating, assisting or participating in acts of civil strife or terrorist acts in another State or acquiescing in organized activities within its territory directed towards the commission of such acts".

Beyond this, however, there has been a constant struggle between Western States, on the one hand, and many developing States, supported to varying degrees by Eastern-bloc States, on the other, to reach consensus as to what types of acts constitute terrorism and what persons are terrorists. More fundamentally, this disagreement reflects an ideological split on the permissible uses of violence. This split has been particularly apparent since the early 1970s when Western States, in an attempt to stem the increasing number of terrorist incidents directed against civilians removed from the place of a conflict, took serious initiatives in the UN to deal with the issue. As chronicled in detail below, the West has proceeded from the premise that certain types of violence, for example, the hijacking of civil aircraft and the taking of hostages, etc., are always impermissible, regardless of the cause espoused by the perpetrators.[86] Many developing States, however, have been suspicious of these efforts, believing that they are designed to weaken those seeking to rid themselves of oppression.[87] Some of these States have won their own independence from colonial powers only after a long struggle, and are sympathetic to groups fighting for their own "national liberation". They have viewed as legitimate all or most types of revolutionary violence. These States, which by their sheer numbers can command a ready majority in the General Assembly of the UN, maintained that the legitimacy of violence could not be evaluated without reference to its motivation

---

[83] Art. 3(f) & (g), GA Res 3314 (XXIX) of 14 December 1974, UN GAOR, 29th Sess., Supp. 31, p. 142, UN Doc A/9631 (1975).
[84] See Art. 1(3)(4) & (5), 1951 YBILC, Vol. II, p. 58; Art. 11(3) & (4), 1986 YBILC, Vol. II, Part 2, p. 43 n. 105.
[85] Declaration on Principles of International Law concerning Friendly Relations and Cooperation among States in accordance with the Charter of the United Nations, GA Res 2625 (XXV) of 24 October 1970, UN GAOR, 25th Sess., Supp. 28, p. 121, UN Doc A/8028 (1971).
[86] See generally pp. 33, 35 & 37-38 (notes 99, 109 & 121-122 and accompanying text).
[87] See, e.g., the comments of the representative of China to the Sixth Committee to the effect that the attempt to focus upon acts such as hijacking and hostage-taking is a pretext to oppose national liberation. UN GAOR, 31st Sess., C.6 (58th mtg.), paras. 26-27, UN Doc A/C.6/31/SR.58 (1976).

and that, moreover, self-determination, a principle sanctioned by numerous General Assembly resolutions (including the Declaration on Principles, which also provides that States have the duty to promote self-determination, *inter alia*, by assisting the UN in eliminating colonialism),[88] is a legitimate justification for the use of force.[89] Moreover, since national liberation groups are generally poorer and less well-armed than their oppressors, they must be allowed to use the types of force which are available to them: the means used to achieve national liberation had to be measured in the context of the choices of means at their disposal.[90] Finally, some States seemed to resent the attempt by Western States to condemn revolutionary violence without at the same time condemning the violence used by colonial, occupying or racist powers.[91]

The result of all of this has not only been failure to come to a universally acceptable approach to the elimination of terrorism (or even to a generally agreed-upon working definition of terrorism), but arguably, at least until recent years, acceptance by the General Assembly of the use of certain types of violence, including terrorism, providing that the cause in which it was committed passed a certain litmus test of national liberation. As discussed in greater detail below, the resolutions of the General Assembly on the subject of terrorism throughout the 1970s contained very little condemnation of acts of individual or group terrorism. Instead, they consistently reaffirmed the legitimacy of self-determination and the struggle for national liberation, and condemned acts of "repression and terrorism by colonial, racist and alien régimes". Moreover, the titles of these resolutions refer to the "study of the underlying causes" of terrorism, i.e., "misery, frustration, grievance and despair".[92] These resolutions, along with debate in the General Assembly which indicated wide support for violence perpetrated by liberation groups, have led many

---

[88] See note 85, *supra*.

[89] For example, in 1972, the Cuban representative to the Sixth Committee stated that he rejected any draft which implies that national liberation movements are illegal by virtue of having used violence to achieve their noble ends. UN GAOR, 27th Sess., C.6 (1358th mtg.), para. 36, UN Doc A/C.6/SR.1358 (1972). The representative of Oman argued that those fighting for national liberation and self-determination should not be condemned; rather, they should be admired for their heroic struggles. UN GAOR, 27th Sess., C.6 (1370th mtg.), para. 46, UN Doc A/C.6/SR.1370 (1972).

[90] See, e.g., the comments of the representative of Yemen to the Sixth Committee wherein he stated that he "resolutely defends" the right of national liberation movements to use "all necessary means" to achieve their ends. UN GAOR, 31st Sess., C.6 (63rd mtg.), para. 1, UN Doc A/C.6/31/SR.63 (1976).

[91] See, e.g., the comments of the representative of Cuba, wherein he stated that such actions as the US bombing of Hanoi were true acts of terrorism and that the method of combat used by national liberation movements could not be declared illegal while the policy of terror by States against certain peoples "was declared legitimate". UN GAOR, 27th Sess., C.6 (1370th mtg.), para. 46, UN Doc A/C.6/SR.1370 (1972).

[92] See the resolutions cited in notes 114, 136, 138, 141, 143, 144 & 145, *infra*.

commentators to conclude that the General Assembly, far from outlawing or condemning terrorism, has legitimized it. One commentator, for example, has stated that the General Assembly has "tolerated and justified" terrorism,[93] and the Legal Adviser to the State Department has stated that: "Attributing acts of terrorism to injustice and frustration obviously tends to excuse, if not justify, those acts . . . especially . . . when the causes are all assumed to be sympathetic".[94]

A brief outline of General Assembly activity in dealing with the issue of terrorism in general (as opposed to dealing with it on a piecemeal, crime by crime basis) is instructive as to the divisions which exist with respect to the issue.

(i) *1972-1973*

In September 1972, immediately following the killing of 11 Israeli athletes at the 1972 Munich Olympic games by members of the "Black September" group,[95] and in the wake of other bloody and well-publicized terrorist acts,[96] the Secretary-General of the United Nations proposed that the issue of international terrorism be considered by the General Assembly during its 27th session. He expressed deep concern over the increasingly international nature of terrorism and over the fact that modern technology had added a formidable new dimension to this "ancient problem". As originally proposed the agenda item was entitled "measures to prevent terrorism and other forms of violence which endanger or take innocent human lives or jeopardize fundamental freedoms". Some days later the Secretary-General stated that it was "obviously" no good to consider the complex question of terrorism without considering the underlying situations which give rise to it, i.e., "misery, frustration, grievance and despair so deep that men were prepared to sacrifice human lives, including their own, in the attempt to effect radical change" (wording which would remain in the title of subsequent General Assembly resolutions on the topic). He also stated that he did not wish his proposal to affect the

---

[93] Gal-Or, note 2, *supra*, at pp. 86-87. Another commentator states that the UN has proved to be a "broken reed" on the subject of terrorism and that the split is so deep that a generally acceptable machinery to fight terrorism will remain beyond reach. Wilkinson, note 33, *supra*, at p. 284.

[94] Sofaer, "Terrorism and the Law", 64 Foreign Affairs 901, 904 (1986). He also states that the references to struggles for independence and liberation are implied justification for terrorist acts. Similarly, the Austrian representative to the Sixth Committee stated that the General Assembly resolutions on the subject "implied at least to a certain extent that the ends justified the means". UN GAOR, 31st Sess., C.6 (70th mtg.), para. 49, UN Doc A/C.6/31/SR.70 (1976).

[95] See XXIII *Keesing's Contemporary Archives* 25493 (1972).

[96] Including the murder and wounding of numerous persons at Lod Airport in Israel by Japanese terrorists in May 1972. On the facts of this incident, see Rosie, note 7, *supra*, at pp. 179-80.

principles of the General Assembly regarding "colonial and dependent peoples seeking independence and liberation".[97] The Secretary-General's later remarks were apparently made in deference to those developing States which protested that the issue of international terrorism could not be considered without an examination of its causes.[98]

Despite this attempt to assuage concerned States, however, there remained considerable opposition to including the item on the General Assembly agenda. While Western States strongly favoured its inclusion, many Arab, African and Eastern bloc States did not, asserting that it would adversely affect the right to self-determination and national liberation. It was at this point that the fundamental differences of opinion on the issue which would hamper UN efforts throughout the 1970s, and afterwards, became apparent. In short, Western States, while maintaining that they did not wish to impinge upon the right to self-determination, asserted that certain acts must be unlawful regardless of their underlying motivation.[99] However, many (but not all)[100] developing States asserted that actions committed in the name of national liberation could not be considered as terrorism. The representative of Mauritania, for example, stated that the UN could not go back on its commitments to peoples struggling for independence. The actions of such groups "were merely the logical and inevitable consequences of political situations ... [i]n the circumstances, such persons could not be blamed for committing desperate acts which in themselves were reprehensible; rather, the real culprits were those who were responsible for causing such desperation".[101] The representative of Syria stated that the real "terrorism" was colonialism, "which needed to be combatted by all available means". He added that "[t]here had never been a national liberation movement which had not employed all the means at its disposal".[102] The representative of Saudi Arabia, while not specifically

---

[97] See UN GAOR, 27th Sess., Annexes (Agenda item 92), pp. 1-2, UN Doc A/8791 & Add. 1 & Corr. 1 (1972). Prior to the Secretary-General's initiative, the International Law Commission, involved at that time in the drafting of the New York Convention, suggested in a report that the General Assembly consider the general problem of terrorism. See Study of Secretariat, note 73, *supra*, at para. 42.

[98] Sofaer, note 94, *supra*, at p. 903.

[99] See, e.g, the comments of the representative of the US, UN GAOR, 27th Sess., C.6 (1357th mtg.), para. 26, UN Doc A/C.6/SR.1357 (1972).

[100] See, e.g., the comments of the representative of Rwanda who stated that while national liberation is a legitimate end, it could not justify immoral means such as kidnappings and murder. In his view, one evil could not be used to justify another. UN GAOR, 27th Sess., C.Gen. (202nd mtg.), para. 27, UN Doc A/BUR/SR.202 (1972).

[101] *Id.* at para. 5. Such desperation, he continued, resulted from such factors as political systems based on inequality, barbarous acts, racist minority rule, and opposition to self-determination and independence.

[102] *Id.* at para. 11. He further asserted that the Secretary-General's proposal would justify colonialist efforts to crush national liberation movements. See also the comments of the representative of Guinea, *id.* at para. 9.

arguing that the UN should not address the issue of terrorism, argued that the issue should not be considered by the General Assembly in that session as proposed by the Secretary-General. Rather, it should be assigned to an *ex officio* Committee, set up for that purpose, which could make a "dispassionate and objective" study of the question. The issue could then be considered in the next session of the General Assembly "without undue haste or emotionalism". In apparent concern over the fact that the attempt to place the issue of terrorism on the agenda came immediately after the Munich massacre, he warned that if the issue was considered in that session the General Assembly would become a platform for "vilification, indiscrimination and acrimony".[103] Nevertheless, a majority of States in the General Committee favoured its inclusion on the agenda[104] and it was sent to the General Assembly where it was considered both in plenary and in the Sixth Committee.

When the matter was taken up by the Sixth Committee, the United States submitted a draft resolution and "Draft Convention for the Prevention and Punishment of Certain Acts of International Terrorism".[105] The US draft convention did not directly address State involvement in terrorist activity (other than in the preamble). Rather, in a manner similar to the then recently completed ICAO instruments, it was primarily concerned with the prevention and punishment of terrorist acts committed by individuals and groups. The draft convention was modest in scope in the sense that it neither attempted to define terrorism nor dealt with all acts which could be terroristic in nature. It simply listed three types of acts — unlawful killing, serious bodily injury, and kidnapping — with respect to which States Parties would be obliged, *inter alia*, to establish their jurisdiction, establish penalties under their domestic laws and comply with the obligation *aut dedere aut judicare*.[106] However, these obligations would only obtain if the offences were international in nature according to criteria set down in the draft and committed in order to "damage the interests of or obtain concessions from a State or an

---

[103] UN GAOR, 27th Sess., C.Gen. (201st mtg.), para. 43, UN Doc A/BUR/SR.201 (1972).

[104] The vote was 15 in favour and 7 against, with 2 abstentions. UN GAOR, 27th Sess., C. Gen. (202nd mtg.), para. 55, UN Doc A/BUR/SR.202 (1972). It may be noted that in addition to African and Arab States, representatives of some Communist States expressed disapproval of the Secretary-General's proposal. The representative of the USSR, for example, stated that it could be used as a pretext for "imperialists, colonialists, neo-colonialists and racists" to suppress all national liberation groups. *Id.* at para. 39. China also signalled disapproval. *Id.* at para. 33. The proposal was supported, *inter alia*, by Western and Latin American States. See the comments of the representatives of Belgium, Paraguay, the UK, the US and Colombia, *id.* at paras. 12, 16, 19, 43 & 45, respectively.

[105] UN Doc A/C.6/L.850, *reprinted in* 11 ILM 1382-87 (1972).

[106] *Id.* at Arts. 1-4.

international organization."[107] The draft was ambitious in the sense that it allowed for no exceptions; its prohibitions applied to all such offences, regardless of the cause of the offenders, other than those committed by or against members of armed forces of a State during military hostilities.[108] If the draft convention had been adopted, the international terrorist crimes covered by conventions at that point would have included hijacking and sabotage of aircraft (pursuant to the ICAO instruments), murder, serious bodily injury, kidnapping (pursuant to the US draft) and attacks on diplomats (pursuant to the New York Convention which was being drafted at that time).

However, during the Sixth Committee's subsequent consideration of the issue of terrorism in general, and of the US draft convention in particular, the debate continued along the same lines as it had in the General Committee,[109] and neither the draft convention nor attempts to compromise (for example, by calling for an international conference to draft a convention on terrorism) were acceptable to developing States.[110] Some commentators have noted that the timing of the US draft — as with the Secretary-General's initiative — was wrong: coming on the heels of the Munich incident, many Arab States saw it as a hostile US-Israeli swipe at the cause of liberation (when the perpetrators were considered to be martyrs in some States) and, moreover, at a time when US credibility in developing States was at a low point.[111] In this connexion, it may

---

[107] *Id.* at Art. 1(a) & (b) & (d).

[108] *Id.* at Art. 1(c).

[109] The representative of the US, for example, argued that regardless of the cause for which they are committed certain acts of violence threaten the "fabric of international order". See UN GAOR, 27th Sess., C.6 (1357th mtg.), para. 26, UN Doc A/C.6/SR.1357 (1972). The representative of Libya, by way of contrast, stated that there could be "no link" between terrorism "and the lawful acts committed by liberation movements and freedom fighters to regain their invaluable rights by all means at their disposal". UN GAOR, 27th Sess., C.6 (1369th mtg.), para. 6, UN Doc A/C.6/SR.1369 (1972). He also argued that some States were using the term terrorism as a means of vitiating the principles of freedom and self-determination enshrined in the Charter. *Id.* at para. 1. The representative of Uganda stated that the US draft could not cover actions by African liberation groups. UN GAOR, 27th Sess., C.6 (1360th mtg.), para. 3, UN Doc A/C.6/SR.1360 (1972).

[110] The various counter-proposals and compromise positions are contained in Report of the Sixth Committee, UN GAOR, Annexes (Agenda item 92), pp. 2-9, UN Doc A/8969 (1972).

[111] See Gal-Or, note 2, *supra*, at p. 84; Murphy, "The United Nations Proposals on the Control and Repression of Terrorism", in Bassiouni (ed.), *International Terrorism and Political Crimes* 502 (1975). Another commentator states that the lack of concern shown by the US with African liberation problems in the 1960s and 1970s encouraged African refusal to co-operate with the US efforts. See Yoder, "United Nations Resolutions on Terrorism", 6 Terr. J. 503, 505 (1982-3). Papers read to the American Society of International Law by J.N. Moore and John Dugard, on the one hand, and Ibrahim Abu-Lughad, on the other, reflect the contrasting points of view of many States at that time. Compare Moore, "Toward Legal Restraints on International Terrorism", 67 Proc. ASIL, No. 5, p. 88 (1973) and Dugard, "Towards the Definition of International Terrorism", *id.* at p. 94, with Abu-Lughod, "Unconventional Violence and International Politics", *id.* at p. 100.

be assumed that many developing States which did not actually support the violence conducted by various groups nevertheless, for domestic political reasons as well as relations with other developing States, were reluctant to enter into an agreement with the US and other Western States which would require them to punish certain types of offenders. Whether or not the US draft convention would have been accepted at another time is an open question, but certainly debate in the General Assembly expressed concern with the timing of the Secretary-General's initiative.[112]

The Ad Hoc *Committee on International Terrorism*

Thus, the 1972 session's treatment of the issue resulted not in the adoption of a draft convention to suppress terrorism, but in Resolution 3034, proposed by Algeria, Kenya, Yugoslavia and other States,[113] entitled (as would be subsequent General Assembly resolutions on the subject):

> Measures to prevent international terrorism which endangers or takes innocent human lives or jeopardizes fundamental freedoms, and study of the underlying causes of those forms of violence which lie in misery, frustration, grievance and despair and which cause some people to sacrifice human lives, including their own, in an attempt to effect radical change.[114]

Developing States, while seemingly willing to address the issue of terrorism, successfully shifted the focus of the debate (or at least divided it) from the immediate suppression and punishment of terrorist offences to a study of the "underlying causes" of terrorism, an activity which could only stand in the way of the immediate imposition of preventative measures. The resolution reaffirmed the legitimacy of self-determination and the national liberation struggle and condemned "repressive and terrorist" acts by colonial, racist and alien regimes in denial of self-determination. It further requested the President of the General Assembly to establish an *ad hoc* Committee charged with recommending measures for possible co-operation in

---

[112] The representative of Tanzania, for example, stated that the Munich affair was too recent to allow the issue to be considered in a "serene and calm" manner. UN GAOR, 27th Sess., C.6 (1362nd mtg.), para. 7, UN Doc A/C.6/SR.1362 (1972). See also the comments of the representatives of Saudi Arabia, pp. 33-34 (note 103 and accompanying text), and Sudan, UN GAOR, 27th Sess., C.Gen. (202nd mtg.), para. 47, UN Doc A/BUR/SR.202 (1972).

[113] See Report of the Sixth Committee, note 110, *supra*, at p. 5.

[114] GA Res 3034 (XXVIII) of 18 December 1972, UN GAOR, 27th Sess., Supp. 30, UN Doc A/8730 (1973). The vote was 76 in favour and 35 against, with 17 abstentions. See UN GAOR, 27th Sess., Annexes (Agenda item 92), p. 10 (1972).

the "speedy elimination" of the problem of terrorism. Although the first part of the title of Resolution 3034 appears at first glance to be promising, referring to "[m]easures to prevent international terrorism which endangers or takes innocent human lives", the closest the resolution came to criticizing acts of individual terrorism was to invite States to become party to existing multilateral conventions on the subject (i.e., the ICAO instruments).

The proceedings of the "*Ad Hoc* Committee on International Terrorism" served simply to demonstrate just how far apart States were on all the issues relating to international terrorism. The Terrorism Committee met from 16 July to 11 August 1973.[115] After some general debate, it was divided into three subcommittees, one to deal with each of the following issues: the definition of terrorism; the study of the underlying causes of terrorism; and measures to prevent terrorism.[116] Deadlock was reached in all three groups. With respect to the first subcommittee, States were divided both as to the necessity of formulating a definition of terrorism and as to what the content of such a definition should be.[117] Some States argued that before any work could proceed it was necessary to define precisely the term terrorism; others, however, argued that it was not necessary (and probably not possible) to formulate an abstract definition since it was more expedient simply to list, in a non-exhaustive fashion, acts which constitute terrorism and which must be eliminated.[118] Some States expressed fear that an attempt to define terrorism would widen, rather than narrow, the controversy.[119] But the crux of the problem, as earlier noted, was that many developing States felt that acts of national liberation movements should be left out of the definition of terrorism.[120] Western States, however, could not accept such a principle, arguing that the legitimacy of the cause could not legitimize the use of certain forms of violence.[121] They pointed out that certain acts are so brutal that States are prohibited from engaging in them

---

[115] See Report of the *Ad Hoc* Committee on International Terrorism, UN GAOR, 28th Sess., Supp. 28, para. 3, UN Doc A/9028 (1973).

[116] *Id.* at para. 8.

[117] The debate on the definition of terrorism is summarized, *id.* at paras. 14-25 & 35-38.

[118] *Id.* at paras. 14-16 & 35-38.

[119] *Id.* at para. 35.

[120] *Id.* at paras. 22, 37 & 45. In a proposal submitted to the Terrorism Committee by the non-aligned group, it was stated that "[w]hen a people engage in violent action against colonialist, racist and alien regimes as part of a struggle to regain its legitimate rights or to redress an injustice of which it is the victim, the international community, when it has recognized the validity of these objectives, cannot take repressive measure against any action which it ought, on the contrary, to encourage, support and defend". *Id.* at Annex, p. 26.

[121] *Id.* at para. 23. This view had earlier been put forward by the Secretariat. See Study of Secretariat, note 73, *supra*, at para. 66.

even during wartime; so too, these States asserted, there should be limits to the violence engaged in by groups and individuals.[122] Further, some developing States insisted that the question of State terrorism must be addressed by the Committee, defining State terrorism as various types of force used by one State to dominate, interfere with or attack another State.[123] Western States, however, wanted to avoid dealing with State action since numerous other documents, including the UN Charter and the Declaration on Principles of International Law, cover uses of State violence and there are other rules regarding violence by armed forces.[124]

Similar differences of opinion arose with respect to the interrelated issues of the study of the underlying causes of terrorism and of the preventative measures to be taken.[125] Many developing States argued that a study of the causes of international terrorism — e.g., the pursuit by certain countries of colonialism, occupation, racism, *apartheid*, domination and exploitation, as well as poverty and a lack of political participation — was the starting point for any UN treatment of the problem.[126] They maintained that until there was an agreed upon definition of terrorism and a study of its underlying causes, punitive measures should not proceed.[127] Many of these States opined, moreover, that any steps which are ultimately taken should be directed against State terrorism, not only because it is the worst type of terrorism but also because it led to the other types. In this view, when colonialism, etc., ended, other forms of terrorism would disappear automatically.[128] Western States, however, argued that a study of underlying causes would be long and complex and that, in the meantime, the increase in terrorist acts must be dealt with immediately through the imposition of effective punitive measures. Moreover, some States pointed out that even if the underlying causes were studied, it was unrealistic to assume that they could be so eradicated as to result in the elimination of terrorism. These States noted that in the domestic sphere, all States impose criminal sanctions for such crimes as murder even though the causes of those crimes have not yet been singled out and eradicated. Some States argued, therefore, that if a study on underlying causes must proceed, it should do so parallel to the imposition of suppressive measures, and not before.[129] Thus, while Western and some other States wanted

[122] Report of Terrorism Committee, note 115, *supra*, at para. 45.
[123] *Id.* at paras. 24-25, 28 & 38. See p. 16 (note 17 and accompanying text).
[124] Report of the Terrorism Committee, note 115, *supra*, at paras. 24-25, 38, 64 & 68.
[125] The debate on these issues is summarized, *id.* at paras. 26-34 & 40-68.
[126] *Id.* at paras. 26, 41 & 49-50.
[127] *Id.* at para. 53.
[128] *Id.* at paras. 49, 54 & 62-63.
[129] *Id.* at paras. 17, 43-44 & 53-54. They also argued that other organs of the UN, such as the Security Council, the Economic and Social Council and the Committee on

measures to be taken against terrorist acts, many developing States wanted any measures taken to be directed at the underlying causes, as they perceived them to be, feeling that it was illogical and dangerous to draw up legal formulations before having resolved the political problems.[130] Even amongst States which wanted to elaborate preventative and punitive measures, moreover, there were differences of opinion as to what these should be and how they should be enacted.[131]

In light of the differences of opinion expressed in the Terrorism Committee, it is not surprising that there was a great variation in the nature of the proposals submitted by States with respect to the issue.[132] In the end, the Terrorism Committee could do no more than to submit a report on its proceedings to the General Assembly and to state that there had been a "frank and extensive exchange of ideas" which brought out the "diversity of existing views".[133] It made no recommendations on measures to deal with the problem.

(ii) *1976-1987*

After the failure of the *Ad Hoc* Committee on Terrorism to reach any sort of consensus regarding appropriate action to be taken against terrorism, the issue was deferred for a number of years by the General Assembly.[134] Despite the unpromising performance of the Terrorism

---

Human Rights, are charged with such issues as oppression, violations of human rights, etc. and that the Terrorism Committee should not attempt to duplicate the work of those groups. *Id.* at para. 46.

[130] *Id.* at paras. 54, 57 & 68.

[131] Various approaches to the prevention and punishment of terrorism were suggested, including a single convention based on the principle *aut dedere aut judicare*, a series of conventions, each relating to a particular type of act, a General Assembly resolution condemning terrorism and a recommendation that States implement national measures as well as bilateral and regional co-operation. *Id.* at paras. 27, 29-30 & 55-61.

[132] The representatives of the non-aligned group, for example, proposed that acts of terrorism should include violent and repressive acts of colonial, racist and alien regimes as well as "[a]cts of violence committed by individuals or groups of individuals which endanger or take human lives or jeopardize fundamental freedoms"; however, this latter aspect "should not affect" groups fighting for self-determination and independence. By way of contrast, the United States submitted its draft convention which focused upon individual or group terrorism by listing certain offences which were always to be considered unlawful. A middle approach was seemingly taken by Venezuela whose proposal stated that terrorism consists of repressive measures by colonial or racist regimes as well as certain acts of individual violence, without exception. See *id.* at Annex, pp. 21-34.

[133] *Id.* at para. 69.

[134] The 2197th plenary meeting of the General Assembly deferred the issue to the 29th session, the 2319th plenary meeting deferred it to the 30th session and the 2441st meeting deferred it to the 31st meeting. See UN GAOR, 28th Sess., Plen. (2197th mtg.), UN Doc A/PV.2197 (1973); UN GAOR, 29th Sess., Plen. (2319th mtg.), UN Doc A/PV.2319 (1974); UN GAOR, 30th Sess., Plen. (2441st mtg.), UN Doc A/PV.2441 (1975). The representative of Uruguay charged that these delays were procedural manoeuvres designed to block effective action against terrorism. UN GAOR, 31st Sess., C.6 (62nd mtg.), para. 21, UN Doc A/C.6/31/SR.62 (1976).

Committee, in 1976 the General Assembly considered a proposal to resurrect that body. A number of Western States, which nevertheless wanted to deal with the issue of terrorism, were against the proposal, believing that since the Committee was to return to work with the same agenda as in 1973, i.e., the study of the underlying causes of terrorism, it was not likely to be any more successful than before.[135] However, the General Assembly passed a resolution inviting the Terrorism Committee to resume its work according to the same mandate. The resolution reaffirmed the right to self-determination and the legitimacy of the struggle for national liberation and urged States to find solutions to the underlying causes of terrorism. While it also condemned the continuation of "repressive and terrorist" acts by regimes which deny peoples the right to self-determination, the closest it came to condemning other forms of terrorism was to express "concern" over the increase in such acts. The resolution also urged States both to become parties to existing international conventions on the subject and to take measures under their domestic laws to prevent terrorism.[136] The Terrorism Committee met in early 1977; however, debate proceeded along the same lines as earlier and it was unable to make any recommendations.[137]

In 1977, the General Assembly again adopted a resolution inviting the Terrorism Committee to continue its work. The resolution was essentially identical to the 1976 resolution, although it stressed that the Committee should *first* study the underlying causes of terrorism and *then* recommend practical measures to deal with it.[138]

In 1979, the Terrorism Committee issued a report which indicates that, although the differences of opinion still existed and the various groups were still talking at cross purposes, some slightly more

---

[135] See the comments of the representatives of Canada, the Netherlands, the UK, Austria and Australia, respectively, in UN GAOR, 31st Sess., C.6 (70th mtg.), paras. 42-43, 44, 45, 49 & 52-53, UN Doc A/C.6/31/SR.70 (1976). Western and Latin American States largely abstained or voted against the proposal. *Id.* at para. 39. It might be noted that the debate in the Sixth Committee on the proposal to resurrect the Terrorism Committee followed the same lines as it had three and four years earlier. Compare the comments of the representatives of Yemen and the US, respectively, in UN GAOR, 31st Sess., C.6 (63rd mtg.), para. 1 & paras. 14, 17-20, UN Doc A/C.6/31/SR.63 (1976). The debate was marked, moreover, by accusations between delegations. The PLO representative, for example, stated that "zionism" is international terrorism. *Id.* at para. 51. The representative of Israel called Libya the "guiding force behind international terrorism". UN GAOR, 31st Sess., C.6 (65th mtg.), para. 9, UN Doc A/C.6/31/SR.65 (1976).

[136] See GA Res 31/102 of 15 December 1976, UN GAOR, 31st Sess., Supp. 39, p. 185, UN Doc A/31/39 (1977).

[137] See Report of the *Ad Hoc* Committee on International Terrorism, UN GAOR, 32nd Sess., Supp. 37, UN Doc A/32/37 (1977). Compare the comments of the representatives of Canada and Tanzania, respectively, in *id.* at p. 21, para. 11 & p. 35, para. 35.

[138] GA Res 32/147 of 16 December 1977, UN GAOR, 32nd Sess., Supp. 45, p. 212, UN Doc A/32/45 (1978).

meaningful discussions were conducted in the Committee's third attempt than in its earlier efforts.[139] The Committee was able actually to recommend to the General Assembly a number of measures for co-operation in the elimination of terrorism, including that the General Assembly should: condemn all acts of international terrorism; take note of the study of underlying causes contained in the Committee's report and urge all States to contribute to the elimination of those causes; call upon States to fulfil their obligations under international law to refrain from organizing, instigating, assisting or participating in terrorist acts in other States and allowing their territory to be used for such acts; appeal to States to join the existing conventions on international terrorism; invite all States to take measures at the national level to eliminate terrorism; recommend to appropriate specialized and regional organizations that they consider measures to prevent and combat international terrorism; urge all States to co-operate with each other to prevent terrorism, especially through the exchange of information and the adoption of extradition treaties; consider the need for additional international conventions to combat acts of terrorism not yet covered by other such conventions; and pay attention, along with the Security Council, to all situations, including colonialism, racism and alien occupation, which give rise to terrorism.[140]

In resolution 34/145 of 17 December 1979, the General Assembly adopted the recommendations of the Terrorism Committee.[141] The resolution represented a breakthrough of sorts. The fact that member States made any recommendations at all indicates that they had come to some sort of an agreement that acts of international terrorism represent a danger to world order. More importantly, although the resolution went through the usual formula of reaffirming the right to self-determination and national liberation and condemning terrorist acts by those States denying the right to self-determination, it also

---

[139] See Report of the *Ad Hoc* Committee on International Terrorism, UN GAOR, 34th Sess., Supp. 37, UN Doc A/34/37 (1979).

[140] *Id.* at para. 118. The Committee also considered a "working paper on underlying causes of terrorism", which mentioned as causes, *inter alia*, colonialism, racism, aggression, interference, expansionism, an unjust economic order, violations of human rights, poverty, and foreign exploitation. *Id.* at paras. 69-83. However, many States objected to this approach, noting that other underlying causes of terrorism exist, including the granting of safe havens to terrorists and State-sponsorship of terrorism. *Id.* at para. 76.

[141] UN GAOR, 34th Sess., Supp. 46, p. 244, UN Doc A/34/46 (1980). The Resolution was adopted by a vote of 118 in favour and none against, with 22 abstentions. Western States abstained, apparently because of the language referring to the "underlying causes" of terrorism and to the "terrorism" of colonialism, etc., and also because of their belief that agreement on a stronger resolution had been broken in bad faith. See generally Yoder, note 111, *supra*, at p. 507. It might be noted that this resolution was adopted immediately before the Hostages Convention was adopted.

"unequivocally condemn[ed] all acts of international terrorism which endanger or take human lives or jeopardize fundamental freedoms" — the first such condemnation of political acts of terrorism by the General Assembly. While it is not entirely clear why this progress was possible, it may well be that it reflected the climate of détente and the lessened tensions after the Vietnam war. Moreover, such events as the OPEC hostage-taking[142] made it clear that it is not just Western States which are vulnerable to terrorist attacks and may have given some developing States new interest in controlling the phenomenon. In 1981, a resolution on terrorism was adopted which, for the first time, condemned terrorism without also condemning terrorism by colonial regimes, etc.[143]

The next breakthrough came in 1985 when, in the immediate aftermath of the *Achille Lauro* hijacking, the General Assembly adopted without a vote a resolution which reiterated much of the 1979 resolution and (again reaffirming the right to self-determination and the legitimacy of the struggle for national liberation) addressed the issue in even stronger terms, stating that it: "[u]nequivocally condemns, as criminal, all acts, methods and practices of terrorism wherever and by whomever committed, including those which jeopardize friendly relations among States and their security"; "[d]eeply deplores the loss of innocent human lives which results from such acts of terrorism"; and "deplores the pernicious impact of acts of international terrorism on relations of co-operation among States".[144] The resolution further urges States to take measures for the "speedy and final elimination of the problem of international terrorism", such as: the harmonization of domestic legislation with existing anti-terrorism conventions; the prevention of preparations in their territories for terrorist attacks; the apprehension and prosecution or extradition of terrorists; and the avoidance of any circumstances which would "obstruct the application of appropriate law enforcement measures provided for in the relevant conventions". This language is very far indeed from the inability of the General Assembly in 1972 to issue even a mild condemnation of individual acts of terrorism.

---

[142] See p. 2 (note 10 and accompanying text in the Introduction).

[143] See GA Res 36/109 of 10 December 1981, UN GAOR, 36th Sess., Supp. 51, p. 241, UN Doc A/36/51 (1982). See also GA Res 38/130 of 19 December 1983, UN GAOR, 38th Sess., Supp. 47, p. 266, UN Doc A/38/47 (1984).

[144] GA Res 40/61 of 9 December 1985, UN GAOR, 40th Sess., Supp. 53, p. 301, UN Doc A/40/53 (1986). In this resolution, the GA encouraged ICAO to continue its work regarding aviation security and requested IMO to study the problem of maritime terrorism. Also as a result of the *Achille Lauro* incident, the Security Council passed a resolution condemning the taking of hostages and other forms of terrorism. See SC Res of 18 December 1985, UN SCOR, 40th Sess., Resolutions & Decisions, p. 42, UN Doc S/INF/41 (1985).

In December 1987, the General Assembly adopted a resolution on terrorism which reiterates and strengthens the strong condemnations of terrorism and the recommendations contained in the 1979 and 1985 resolutions.[145] The resolution is extensive in both preambular and textual paragraphs; however, it is as significant for what it does not say as for what it does say. In the Sixth Committee, Syria introduced a draft resolution which called for the convening of an international conference for the purpose of defining the difference between terrorism and the legitimate right of oppressed peoples to fight for freedom. Significantly, however, Western States, developing States and Eastern bloc States joined together to defeat the proposal.[146] As regards the issue of such a conference, the resolution ultimately adopted by the General Assembly simply requests the Secretary-General to seek the views of member States on international terrorism in all its aspects and on ways to combat it, including the calling of such a conference. Moreover, this resolution, similar to the 1985 resolution, contains unequivocal condemnation of terrorism without referring to "terrorism" by colonial, alien and racist regimes. Of course, this in no way indicates that States have lost their interest in opposing such regimes, and both resolutions reaffirm the right to self-determination and national liberation. However, these resolutions are able at last to focus on the issue of terrorism without obscuring it by reference to other, unquestionably very serious, problems. With respect to the underlying causes of terrorism, the 1985 and 1987 resolutions both urge the eradication of such problems as colonialism, racial discrimination and violations of human rights. As indicated above, the greatest objection to earlier references to underlying causes is that they were framed in such a way as both to indicate justification for acts of terrorism and to delay co-operation on the implementation of preventative measures until the causes were eliminated. By way of contrast, these resolutions address the underlying causes in only a few of many paragraphs; paragraphs which predominantly concern preventative measures and do not in any way indicate that the

---

[145] GA Res 42/159 of 7 December 1987. The resolution was adopted by a vote of 153 in favour and two against, with one abstention. The United States and Israel voted against the resolution, while Honduras abstained. The reasons for the US vote are unclear; it abstained in the Sixth Committee, its representative stating that the draft resolution was insufficiently "focused upon the problem of terrorism as such". See *International Herald Tribune*, Dec. 3, 1987, p. 3. The US may have objected to the references to the underlying causes of terrorism and to the somewhat ambiguous language regarding national liberation movements. See p. 44 (note 147 and accompanying text).

This resolution also approved of ICAO and IMO efforts with regard to terrorism and requested other organizations, such as the Universal Postal Union, the World Tourism Organization and the International Atomic Energy Agency, to consider measures to combat terrorism.

[146] *International Herald Tribune*, Dec. 3, 1987, p. 3.

eradication of underlying causes is a condition precedent to the implementation of preventative measures. Couched in this way, there can be no objection to this reference to the need to deal with underlying causes.

The change in language in the most recent General Assembly resolutions must be seen as some progress towards a universal consensus that acts of terrorism are not to be tolerated regardless of the cause. It must also be recognized, however, that the General Assembly continues to send out somewhat mixed signals regarding the issue of national liberation movements. While the 1987 resolution did not call for the convening of an international conference to define the difference between terrorism and the struggle for national liberation, it kept alive the possibility of such a conference. Moreover, the resolution also states in its penultimate paragraph that the provisions of the resolution could not "in any way prejudice the right to self-determination . . . particularly peoples under colonial and racist regimes and foreign occupation or other forms of colonial domination, nor . . . the right of these peoples to struggle to this end and to seek and receive support".[147] As indicated earlier, the efforts to condemn and prevent terrorism are not intended to prejudice the right to self-determination and national liberation; nor do they seek even to prohibit the use of force for such a cause. They are concerned rather with the prevention of certain types of violence regardless of why or by whom committed. Given the unequivocal condemnation of terrorism in the resolution ("wherever and by whomever committed"), it does not seem that this language could seriously be interpreted as excluding national liberation groups from the terms thereof. However, some States may hope that this language leaves open the door to the argument that activities of national liberation groups cannot be considered as terrorism and that such groups can use every possible means to achieve their ends. After all, despite the strong condemnation of terrorism, none of the GA resolutions defines the concept of terrorism.

Moreover, strong differences of opinion were still expressed in the debates on the more recent resolutions, and the comments of some States indicate that the international community is still far from fashioning a consensus on terrorism. In the 1985 debate, for example, the representative of Algeria, in comments which could have been taken from the 1972 and 1973 debates, stated that any attempts to equate national liberation struggles with terrorism must be rejected and urged that the Assembly focus its attention instead on acts of State

---

[147] This language is similar to that contained in the resolution to which the New York Convention is annexed. See note 162, *infra*.

terrorism.[148] The representative of Kuwait stated that attention must be paid to the underlying causes of terrorism and to the development of a definition of terrorism before any other steps are taken.[149] Additionally, diplomats explaining Syria's defeat in the 1987 resolution did not indicate that all States had fundamentally changed their attitudes regarding the need to take immediate effective measures to combat all acts of terrorism, regardless of the cause of the perpetrators. Rather, they referred to the moderate tone which characterized the 1987 session and to the desire to avoid confrontation due to concern over the poor image of the UN in Western States, the financial crisis at the UN and the improving relationship between East and West.[150]

And, of course, condemning terrorism and actually taking steps to prevent it are two different matters. The prevalence of international terrorism and the reluctance of some States to take any measures to check or condemn it go beyond the fact that they are sympathetic to the goals of revolutionary violence. As discussed above, a small number of States, in violation of existing UN principles, actively encourage terrorism against other States and engage in such activity themselves as regular components of their foreign policy.[151]

One final point may briefly be made in the context of this discussion regarding the obstacles to co-operation between States to combat terrorism: such co-operation is not only hard to achieve as between States with different ideological perspectives. It is elusive also even as between Western States. Difficulties in co-operation may partly be attributed to such factors as cumbersome bureaucracies and nationalistic jealousies; however, they are also caused by a lack of political will on the part of many Western governments, which may be afraid of provoking increased terrorist attacks on their own population or of losing valuable economic contacts with States which support or sympathize with groups which use terrorist tactics.[152]

---

[148] UN GAOR, 40th Sess., C.6 (21st mtg.), para. 19, UN Doc A/C.6/40/SR.21 (1985).
[149] *Id.* at paras. 5-9. See also the comments of the representatives of China, Iran and Angola, respectively, in UN GAOR, 40th Sess., C.6 (22nd mtg.), paras. 15, 7, 9 & 62, UN Doc A/C.6/40/SR.22 (1985).
[150] *International Herald Tribune*, Dec. 3, 1987, p. 3.
[151] See generally pp. 19-21 (notes 33-43 and accompanying text).
[152] The *Achille Lauro* incident is a good example of this problem. See note 65, *supra*. See generally Wilkinson, note 33, *supra*, at pp. 286-89. However, in recent years there has been increasing co-operation between such States. See generally pp. 129-131(notes 36-49 and accompanying text in the commentary on Article 4); 88 Dep't St. Bull., No. 2130, pp. 44-50 (1988).

4. ACHIEVEMENTS OF THE UNITED NATIONS AND THE SPECIALIZED AGENCIES WITH RESPECT TO TERRORISM: THE FIVE CONVENTIONS AND TWO PROTOCOLS IMPOSING THE OBLIGATION *AUT DEDERE AUT JUDICARE*

(A) *Segmentation of the problem of terrorism*

Given the fundamental divisions in the world community on the issue, it is not surprising that progress towards effective international co-operation to prevent and punish acts of terrorism has been halting. Despite the recent positive change in tone of GA resolutions on the subject, it seems unlikely that a universally acceptable definition of terrorism will be formulated in the near future, if ever. Similarly, the possibility that States will soon adopt a single multilateral convention which lists in a comprehensive fashion all those acts which may be considered to be terrorism appears remote. It remains difficult to identify offences which the bulk of States consider to be of sufficient gravity that they are willing to undertake to suppress them regardless of the cause for which they are committed.[153]

However, some notable progress has been made in codifying

---

[153] See generally Fourth Interim Report of the Committee on International Terrorism, in ILA *Report of the Sixtieth Conference* 349-350 (1982). It is not only in the highly political atmosphere of the UN that agreement on a comprehensive convention has been elusive. In 1982, the ILA's Committee on International Terrorism decided to postpone its efforts at drafting a terrorism convention, not because it felt that such an instrument was undesirable but because so "many problems of both a practical and theoretical nature" existed with respect to that exercise, particularly the problem of identifying offences which all States would agree to suppress. *Id.* Without abandoning the idea altogether, the Committee decided that a more modest approach was appropriate at that time, and recommended instead that States should not refuse to extradite or try persons whose acts, if committed in wartime, would subject them to trial or extradition. *Id.* at pp. 349 & 354. This proposal would essentially make all the grave breaches of warfare applicable to peacetime. See generally Rubin, "Current Legal Approaches to International Terrorism", 7 Terr. J. 147-161 (1984-85). But see the dissenting statement of ILA members L.C. Green and J. Lador-Lederer who argued that the analogy to the laws of war is conceptually and legally misleading. They argued that if States want to avoid their obligations to extradite or prosecute terrorists, they will do so regardless of whether the acts come under the laws of war or the laws of peace. See Fourth Interim Report, *supra*, at pp. 354-356. On other objections to assimilating the law of armed conflict to the law of peace as it relates to terrorist offences, see generally pp. 265 & 266 (notes 7 & 10 and accompanying text in the commentary on Article 12). It might be noted that the ILA's Terrorism Committee seemed to return to the drafting of a comprehensive convention shortly after its Fourth Interim Report, and went so far as to adopt a set of principles which would be suitable for inclusion in a subsequent convention. These principles include, *inter alia, aut dedere aut judicare*, the liability of individuals under international law, non-exculpation based on political motive and the prohibition of State-sponsored terrorism. See Report of the Committee on International Terrorism, in ILA, *Report of the Sixty-First Conference* 313-319 (1984). These principles were endorsed by the ILA in a resolution. *Id.* at p. 6. However, no such convention has as yet been adopted.

ACHIEVEMENTS: THE CONVENTIONS AND PROTOCOLS 47

international rules regarding the prevention and punishment of terrorism. The UN and the specialized agencies ICAO and IMO have been able (to a certain extent *forced* by the inability to develop a comprehensive approach to the problem) to deal in a piecemeal fashion with a number of international offences favoured by terrorist groups. Conventions and protocols have been adopted with respect to the hijacking of civil aircraft, sabotage of civil aircraft and air navigation facilities, attacks in international airports, attacks on diplomats, attacks on maritime targets and on platforms on the continental shelf and the taking of hostages. Despite the rhetoric on the part of some States to the effect that national liberation groups should be allowed to achieve their goals by whatever means possible, most States obviously consider the offences covered by the anti-terrorism conventions to be sufficiently grave or sufficiently contrary to their interests to justify their accepting obligations to repress and punish them (or at least to justify their not blocking the consensus by which the instruments were adopted). In these limited areas, ideology has yielded to some practical concerns.[154] With respect to hijacking and sabotage of civil aircraft, all States have a manifest interest in curbing such activity since experience has shown that it is not simply the aircraft of Western States which have been so victimized.[155] Moreover, from a commercial standpoint developing States have much to lose if air traffic from developed States avoids their airports because of fears of hijacking and sabotage. Similarly, diplomats and other internationally protected persons from all parts of the world have been subjected to attacks.[156] All States have a strong interest in the

[154] The ILA's Terrorism Committee noted that these conventions are able to provide for a certain level of co-operation because the offences proscribed therein are detrimental to "basic international value[s]" such as civil aviation, etc. It further stated that it "appears that the quest for justice as defined by the actors and those governments that agree with them are generally considered to be lower on the scale of values protected by the law than at least some practical interest." See Fourth Interim Report, note 153, *supra*, at pp. 350-51. Another commentator agrees, stating that when drafting its conventions, ICAO "skirted the basic ideological question of the ends to which the rash of international hijackings of aircraft were being directed in the 1960s and 1970s, and sought to invoke, in addition to humanitarian legal principles, other postulated imperative principles of international law such as freedom of the air and freedom of international communication" in which all three blocs in the UN had a common interest. McWhinney, "International Terrorism: United Nations Projects for Legal Controls", 7 Terr. J. 175, 179 (1984-85).

[155] For example, in a 1986 ICAO survey of 27 incidents which occurred between February 1984 and December 1985 and which constituted offences against the Hague Convention, only seven were committed against aircraft registered to Western States. Three offences were committed against aircraft from Latin American States, two against aircraft from Eastern European States, and 15 against aircraft from Asian and African countries, mostly those in the Middle East. See ICAO Doc A26-WP/29 EX3, Appendix F (1986).

[156] For example, in March 1973, months before adoption of the New York Convention, members of the "Black September" group burst into the Saudi Arabian

(*continued on p. 48*)

smooth exchange of diplomatic relations which can only exist if the safety of such persons is ensured.

This is not to say that all States have, at least as yet, seen it to be in their best interests to commit themselves to suppress equally all the offences covered by the conventions. While the Hague and Montreal Conventions are approaching universal acceptance — as of early 1989 the Hague Convention had 141 States Parties and the Montreal Convention had 140[157] — the New York Convention, as of the same period, had only 78 States Parties[158] and the Hostages Convention only 56.[159] It may be noted that agreement was not easily reached on either the Hostages or the New York Conventions. During the drafting of the New York Convention a number of States proposed that the draft convention should be inapplicable to national liberation movements,[160] and similar demands threatened the successful drafting of the Hostages Convention.[161] However, in the end the Conventions were drafted in such a way as to ensure that all the offences covered thereunder are subject to the rule *aut dedere aut judicare*[162] and were

([156] *continued*)
embassy in Sudan, fired machine guns and revolvers, and took as hostages the American ambassador and chargé d'affaires, the Belgian chargé d'affaires, the Saudi Arabian ambassador, the Jordanian chargé d'affaires and the Japanese chargé d'affaires. The hostage-takers threatened to kill all six diplomats if demands made upon Jordan, the US, West Germany and Israel were not met. On the second day of the incident, the hostage-takers killed the three Western diplomats. The remaining diplomats were held for two more days before the terrorists surrendered. See XIX *Keesing's Contemporary Archives* 25805 (1973).

[157] Bowman & Harris, *Multilateral Treaties Index and Current Status* 344 & 353 (1984) & 5th Supp. (1988); 89 Dep't St. Bull, No. 2146, p. 86 & No. 2147, p. 68 (1989); 88 Dep't St. Bull., Nos. 2135, p. 68, 2136, p. 76 & 2139, p. 83 (1988).

[158] Bowman & Harris, note 157, *supra*, at p. 386; 89 Dep't St. Bull., Nos. 2148, p. 76, 2147, p.69, 2145, p. 62 & 2144, p. 92; 88 Dep't St. Bull., Nos. 2139, p. 84, 2136, p. 76 & 2134, p. 83 (1988).

[159] See note 19, *supra*, in the Introduction.

[160] See Report of the Sixth Committee, UN GAOR, 28th Sess., Annexes (Agenda item 90), p. 19, UN Doc A/9407 (1973).

[161] See pp. 62-63 (notes 222 & 223 and accompanying text); pp. 264 & 268 (notes 3, 4 & 17 and accompanying text in the commentary on Article 12).

[162] With respect to the New York Convention, as a result of a compromise between those States which wanted to exclude acts of national liberation movements from the scope of the instrument and those which insisted that the draft convention should allow for no exceptions, the resolution to which that instrument is annexed provides that "the provisions of the annexed Convention could not in any way prejudice the exercise of the legitimate right to self-determination and independence . . . by peoples struggling against colonialism, alien domination, foreign occupation, racial discrimination and *apartheid*". It also states that "the present resolution, whose provisions are related to the annexed Convention, shall always be published together with it". GA Res 3166 (XXVIII), UN GAOR, 28th Sess., Supp. 10, p. 146, UN Doc A/9030 (1973). While the terms of the Convention remain unequivocal, this language at least leaves open the argument that the prohibitions therein do not pertain to national liberation movements. No such provision is in the resolution to which the Hostages Convention is attached. While Article 12 envisages the possibility that acts of hostage-taking by national liberation groups may fall outside the scope of the Convention, this will be so only when those acts must result in the obligation *aut dedere aut judicare* pursuant to the laws of armed conflict.

adopted by consensus in the General Assembly. Despite the relatively low number of parties, moreover, the pace of ratifications of, and accessions to, both instruments remains steady.[163] It is, as of this writing, too early to determine how readily the instruments adopted in 1988, i.e., the Rome Convention and Protocol and the Montreal Protocol, will be accepted by States.[164]

Thus, as things stand, the UN and the specialized agencies have managed to adopt instruments dealing with many common terrorist crimes. Instead of dealing with the issue of "terrorism" as a whole, with all its political baggage and resulting definitional polemics, the approach has been to draft a number of treaties, each listing in an objective fashion discrete offences which are to be suppressed and punished without regard to the cause or motive of the offender. None of the instruments even mentions the word "terrorism" in any of its substantive provisions. One commentator has termed this the "object-oriented" or "segmented" approach.[165] Given the objective listing of prohibited offences in each convention, another term, borrowed from extradition law,[166] which could be employed is the "enumerative" approach. Whatever it is called, the break-up of the larger problem of terrorism into smaller and more manageable units of individual and clearly defined offences has proved to be the only way of obtaining any sort of international agreement on the suppression of terrorist offences. Thus, although some commentators, without specifically taking issue with this approach, continue to argue that a definition of terrorism is necessary,[167] there is widespread agreement that this is the most expedient way of dealing with terrorism on a universal basis.[168]

Not all commentators, however, agree that an objective listing of offences which must be suppressed is an appropriate way to deal with

---

[163] Between the years 1984 and 1988, the New York Convention gained 12 States Parties and the Hostages Convention gained 25. See Bowman & Harris, note 157, *supra*, at pp. 386 & 448 & 5th Supp.

[164] However, it may be noted that 23 States signed the Rome Convention on the date of its adoption, 10 March 1988 (see Halberstam, "Terrorism on the High Seas: The *Achille Lauro*, Piracy and the IMO Convention on Maritime Safety", 82 AJIL 269 (1988)), and 47 States signed the Montreal Protocol on the closing day of the ICAO Diplomatic Conference, 24 February 1988. See Milde, "International Conference on Air Law", 13 Air Law, No. 2, 95, 96 (1988).

[165] Gal-Or, note 2, *supra*, at p. 87.

[166] See p. 229 (note 6 and accompanying text in the commentary on Article 10).

[167] One commentator, for example, has argued that the failure to reach a generally acceptable definition of terrorism has resulted in vacillations in anti-terrorism policies and in "the complete failure of the international community to launch any effective multi-lateral initiatives to combat the problem". Wardlaw, note 3, *supra*, at p. 4.

[168] See e.g., McWhinney, note 154, *supra*, at p. 179; see also Palmer, "Codification of Terrorism as an International Crime", in Bassiouni (ed.), note 2, *supra*, at pp. 507-08. Murphy notes that "paradoxically, success in combatting international terrorism may depend in part on avoiding the definitional problem." Murphy, "Comments on the Fourth Interim Report of the ILA Committee on International Terrorism", 7 Terr. J. 193, 195 (1984-85).

terrorism. Schmid has criticized the enumerative method as employed in Article 1 of the European Convention on the Suppression of Terrorism (which lists those acts which are not to be the subject of the political offence exception to extradition) on grounds that are equally applicable to the universal anti-terrorism conventions. He argues that "[t]he nature of terrorism is not inherent in the violent act itself". In his view, a particular act can be terroristic or not, depending upon "intention and circumstance".[169] Part of his criticism is that not all hijackings, for example, are terroristic: some may fall outside of his definition of "terrorism", discussed earlier,[170] in that there is no "target of terror". For example, the hijacker may simply be looking to get to a destination other than the intended one of the aircraft.[171] The other — related — part of his criticism is that it can "place a hijacker [or, presumably, a hostage-taker] who is attempting to escape from a terror regime in the same category as a 'real' ... terrorist".[172]

However, simply because a hijacker is not really a "terrorist" in the sense that he is trying to instil "terror" on the part of some segment of the population does not mean that his act is not reprehensible and should not be suppressed and punished by all States. Hijacking and hostage-taking are very serious crimes regardless of the element of "terror" (and, in any event, it may be wondered whether it is possible to commit the offence of hostage-taking, with its requirement that demands be made, without causing "terror"). With respect to the hijacker or hostage-taker who is trying to escape a repressive or terroristic regime, as a moral and legal matter it may be queried whether even an oppressed person should be given the right to take hostages or hijack a civil aircraft in order to gain his freedom. As a practical matter, an explicit exception on that basis would be so subjective as to be unworkable: who would decide what States are "terror" regimes? Western States would be free to refuse to prosecute or extradite any offender who hijacked an aircraft from any Eastern-bloc or hostile Arab State and *vice versa*. Any international co-operation on the subject of terrorism would break down immediately. The decision to make all such acts illegal, regardless of the underlying motivation, was the only way to achieve and keep any sort of international consensus in this area.

Moreover, even such a worthy definition as Schmid's, while undoubtedly helpful to a political scientist or a sociologist who is examining the phenomenon of terrorism, is not much help from a law enforcement perspective (even assuming that it would be acceptable

---

[169] Schmid, note 3, *supra*, at p. 101.
[170] See pp. 17-18 (note 26 and accompanying text).
[171] Schmid, note 3, *supra*, at p. 102.
[172] *Id.* at p. 103.

to most States). It would require fact-finders to engage in such activities as deciding whether there was truly a "target of terror" or "targets of attention". Particularly from a lawyer's point of view, therefore, the listing of certain offences which are always prohibited, regardless of motivation, is preferable to a definition of terrorism.[173]

At this point it will be helpful to examine briefly the specifics of the instruments which have been adopted to suppress terrorism.

(B) *Offences covered by the anti-terrorism conventions and protocols*

(i) *ICAO instruments*

The first multilateral convention concerning terrorism to enter into force was the 1963 Tokyo Convention, promulgated under the auspices of ICAO. The provisions of that instrument are very modest, dealing primarily with gaps in jurisdiction which exist, or which did exist,[174] with respect to crimes committed on board civil (i.e., not military, customs or police) aircraft. In particular, the Convention requires States Parties to take such measures as are necessary to establish their jurisdiction over crimes committed on board aircraft registered by them.[175] It also provides that offences committed on board aircraft shall be treated, for the purposes of extradition, as if they were committed not only in the place where they occurred but also in the territory of the registering State.[176] Other provisions concern such matters as taking offenders into custody, restoring control of the aircraft to the commander and continuation of the aircraft's journey.[177]

Although the Tokyo Convention was designed to deal with the growing problem of hijacking, it can readily be seen that its provisions are inadequate to do so in any meaningful way. The Convention neither defines nor lists any offences which States Parties are required to suppress, and it imposes no obligations regarding the extradition or

---

[173] See generally Rubin, note 153, *supra*, at p. 148, who notes that definitions of terrorism "seem irrelevant to lawyers and legislators, who are concerned with making and enforcing rules to limit all political (or any other) violence, whether the victim is a primary target or merely a means of attacking a different protected interest". However, even within groups of lawyers attempts to define terrorism continue. A recent version of the ILC's draft code of offences against the peace and security of mankind, for example, contains a definition of terrorism which is essentially identical to that contained in the Terrorism Convention adopted by the League of Nations. See 1986 YBILC, Vol. II, Part 2, p. 43 n. 105. On the League's definition, see p. 29 (notes 76-77 and accompanying text).

[174] On this issue, see p. 138 (notes 18 & 19 and accompanying text in the commentary on Article 5).

[175] Art. 3.
[176] Art. 16.
[177] Arts. 6-15.

prosecution of offenders. However, the Convention was the start of the international effort to deal with terrorism.

In 1970, a Diplomatic Conference held by ICAO adopted the Hague Convention which, by way of defining the offence of hijacking, provides that any person "who on board an aircraft in flight . . . unlawfully, by force or threat thereof, or by any other form of intimidation, seizes, or exercises control of, that aircraft . . . commits an offence".[178] Attempt and participation are also offences under the Hague Convention, as they are under all the other anti-terrorism instruments.

In 1971, in order to deal with other types of violence against civil aviation, another Diplomatic Conference adopted the Montreal Convention which provides that a person commits an offence if he "unlawfully and intentionally" does any of a number of listed things, namely, "performs an act of violence against a person on board an aircraft in flight if that act is likely to endanger the safety of that aircraft", "destroys an aircraft in service or causes damage to such an aircraft which renders it incapable of flight or which is likely to endanger its safety", "places or causes to be placed on an aircraft in service . . . a device or substance which is likely to destroy that aircraft, or to cause damage to it which renders it incapable of flight" or endangers its safety, "destroys or damages air navigation facilities or interferes with their operation, if any such act is likely to endanger the safety of aircraft in flight", or "communicates information which he knows to be false, thereby endangering the safety of aircraft in flight".[179]

In 1988, a Diplomatic Conference held under the auspices of ICAO adopted the Montreal Protocol, which adds to the list of offences in the Montreal Convention the use of "any device, substance or weapon" to perform "an act of violence against a person at an airport serving international civil aviation which causes or is likely to cause serious injury or death" and the use of any such "device, substance or weapon" which "destroys or seriously damages the facilities of an airport serving international civil aviation or aircraft not in service located thereon or disrupts the services of the airport, if such an act endangers or is likely to endanger safety at that airport".[180]

(ii) *IMO instruments*

In 1988, an International Conference held in Rome under the auspices of IMO adopted the Rome Convention which provides that a

[178] Art. 1.
[179] Art. 1.
[180] Art. II.

ACHIEVEMENTS: THE CONVENTIONS AND PROTOCOLS 53

person commits an offence if he "unlawfully and intentionally" does any of a number of listed things, namely, "seizes or exercises control over a ship by force or threat thereof or any other form of intimidation", "performs an act of violence against a person on board a ship if that act is likely to endanger the safe navigation of that ship", "destroys a ship or causes damage to a ship or to its cargo which is likely to endanger the safe navigation of that ship", "places or causes to be placed on a ship . . . a device or substance which is likely to destroy that ship, or cause damage to that ship or its cargo which endangers or is likely to endanger the safe navigation of that ship", "destroys or seriously damages maritime navigation facilities or seriously interferes with their operation, if any such act is likely to endanger the safe navigation of a ship", knowingly communicates false information, thereby endangering the safe navigation of a ship, or injures or kills any person in connexion with the foregoing offences.[181] The Conference also adopted the Rome Protocol which addresses acts committed against fixed platforms located on the continental shelf. The offences under the Protocol are almost identical to those under the Rome Convention, differing only in so far as is necessary to take into account the differences between ships and such platforms.[182]

(iii) *UN Conventions*

In 1973, in an effort to deal with the problem of terrorist attacks against diplomats, the General Assembly adopted by consensus a resolution attached to which was the New York Convention. That Convention seeks to protect certain categories of persons from the offences of murder, kidnapping or other attacks upon their person or liberty, as well as violent attacks upon their official premises, private accommodation and means of transport.[183] The class of persons protected includes heads of States, including members of a collegial body performing the functions of a head of State, heads of governments and ministers for foreign affairs, whenever such persons are in a foreign State, as well as their family members who accompany them. It also includes "any representative or official of a State or any official or other agent of an international organization of an intergovernmental character who, at the time when and in the place where a crime against him, his official premises, his private accommodation or his means of transport is committed, is entitled pursuant to international law to special protection from any attack on

[181] Art. 3.
[182] Art. 2.
[183] Art. 2.

his person, freedom or dignity, as well as members of his family forming part of his household".[184]

In 1979, the General Assembly adopted by consensus a resolution attached to which is the Hostages Convention which provides that a person commits the offence of hostage-taking if he "seizes or detains and threatens to kill, to injure or to continue to detain another person (hereinafter referred to as the "hostage") in order to compel a third party, namely, a State, an international intergovernmental organization, a natural or juridical person, or a group of persons, to do or abstain from doing any act as an explicit or implicit condition for the release of the hostage".[185]

(C) *Characteristics of the anti-terrorism instruments*

(i) *Common provisions*

While the Hague, Montreal, New York, Rome and Hostages Conventions are not identical, they are remarkably similar and the confluence of obligations imposed by all of them (and the two protocols) is great. The central obligation contained in all of the instruments is that of *aut dedere aut judicare*, i.e., that all offenders who are not extradited by the State Party in whose territory they are found must, "without exception whatsoever", be submitted to the appropriate authorities for the purpose of prosecution.[186] Moreover, all the instruments require States Parties, *inter alia*, to make the listed offences punishable under their domestic laws,[187] to establish their jurisdiction over the offences in certain circumstances, including when an offender is subsequently found in their territories and they do not extradite him to another State,[188] to take steps to prevent the offences,[189] to render assistance to each other in connexion with criminal proceedings brought in respect of the listed offences[190]

---

[184] Art. 1.
[185] Art. 1.
[186] Art. 7, Hague Convention; Art. 7, Montreal Convention; Art. I, Montreal Protocol; Art. 7, New York Convention; Art. 8(1), Hostages Convention; Art. 10(1), Rome Convention; Art. 1, Rome Protocol.
[187] Art. 2, Hague Convention; Art. 3, Montreal Convention; Art. I, Montreal Protocol; Art. 2(2), New York Convention; Art. 2, Hostages Convention; Art. 5, Rome Convention; Art. 1, Rome Protocol.
[188] Art. 4, Hague Convention; Art. 5, Montreal Convention; Arts. I & III, Montreal Protocol; Art. 3, New York Convention; Art. 5, Hostages Convention; Art. 6, Rome Convention; Art. 3, Rome Protocol.
[189] Art. 10(1), Montreal Convention; Art. I, Montreal Protocol; Art. 4, New York Convention; Art. 4, Hostages Convention; Art. 13(1), Rome Convention; Art. 1, Rome Protocol. No such provision is contained in the Hague Convention.
[190] Art. 10, Hague Convention; Art. 11, Montreal Convention; Art. I, Montreal Protocol; Art. 10, New York Convention; Art. 11, Hostages Convention; Art. 12, Rome Convention; Art. 1, Rome Protocol.

ACHIEVEMENTS: THE CONVENTIONS AND PROTOCOLS 55

and to consider the offences as extraditable ones in certain circumstances.[191]

(ii) *Reliance on municipal law*

All of these instruments are concerned only with offences which have an international dimension.[192] However, as can readily be seen from the immediately preceding discussion, and as discussed in greater detail in the commentary on Article 2,[193] these instruments rely solely on the municipal law of each State for the prevention and punishment of the target crimes. States are required to prohibit the listed offences and to exercise their jurisdiction over alleged offenders who appear in their territories. Although it is possible that individuals can be directly liable under international law for criminal offences, no international police force or judicial system exists which could enforce an international criminal law. These instruments, therefore, do not attempt directly to create individual liability under international law for the specified offences.

It is worth noting that these instruments do not describe offences which are novel (with the exception, perhaps, of the ICAO Conventions which describe offences which were essentially products of the 1960s). All States can be assumed to have pre-existing laws which prohibit such activity as hostage-taking (e.g., kidnapping), assaults on diplomats and crimes on board ships registered therein. But it is not adequate for the suppression of international terrorism that States have pre-existing legislation against the described conduct. The real value of these instruments is that they require States Parties actually to deal with offenders and they establish generally an international framework for co-operation in the suppression of such acts.[194] Despite the reliance on municipal law, the enforcement of rules regarding the described offences is no longer a domestic matter:

---

[191] Art. 8, Hague Convention; Art. 8, Montreal Convention; Art. I, Montreal Protocol; Art. 8, New York Convention; Art. 10, Hostages Convention; Art. 11, Rome Convention; Art. 1, Rome Protocol. Despite the many similarities, however, as earlier noted, the instruments are not identical. For example, Article 9 of the Hostages Convention imposes an obligation upon States not to extradite alleged offenders in circumstances wherein political persecution would result. This obligation is not contained, at least explicitly, in any of the other conventions. Some of the differences in obligations relate simply to the nature of the crime concerned. For example, Article 9 of the Hague Convention requires the State in which the hijacked aircraft is present to return the aircraft to the person lawfully entitled to possession thereto.

[192] See pp. 299-300 (notes 1-5 and accompanying text in the commentary on Article 13).

[193] See generally pp. 93-100 (notes 1-35 and accompanying text in the commentary on Article 2).

[194] Cf. US Senate, Committee on Foreign Relations, *Report on the International Convention Against the Taking of Hostages*, S. Exec. Rep. 17, 97th Cong., 1st Sess., p. 1 (1981).

States Parties have incurred international obligations with respect thereto.

(iii) *Shortcomings of the instruments*

The anti-terrorism conventions have a number of weaknesses. Because they are the result of many political compromises, many important provisions are obscure or ambiguous. Moreover, the conventions leave many vital matters — such as the decision as to whether or not an alleged offender who is not extradited will, in the end, be compelled to stand trial — to the discretion of individual States Parties. The fragile agreements on some provisions may lead to differing interpretations and a tendency by some States Parties to search for loopholes in the instruments. The weaknesses of the Hostages Convention, and to a certain extent the other instruments, are discussed in depth in the appropriate sections of the commentary. Worth particular mention at this point, however, is the fact that, other than dispute resolution procedures, the instruments lack enforcement machinery to secure compliance by States Parties which fail to live up to their obligations incurred thereunder. Various proposals for sanctions in connexion with the ICAO Conventions were advanced, but not accepted,[195] and it does not appear that the issue of sanctions

---

[195] At the time of the drafting of those instruments, a number of States maintained that a mechanism for sanctions should be developed for use against States which fail to comply with the obligation *aut dedere aut judicare*. The United States, at first by itself and then in conjunction with Canada, proposed a system whereby States could decide to impose legally binding sanctions against other States which harbour hijackers; the possible sanctions included a halt in air traffic to and from the defaulting States. See ICAO Docs 8910-LC/163, Part III, Annex 2 (1970) & LC/SC-Report-24/4/71, pp. 29-37 (1971). However, many States had strong legal and political objections to these proposals, arguing, *inter alia*, that only the Security Council could impose such sanctions, that the proposals would clash with other aviation agreements, that they would violate Article 34 of the Vienna Convention on the Law of Treaties by imposing obligations on third States and that they would be incompatible with the dispute resolution provision in the Hague Convention. On the proposals and objections see Fitzgerald, "Concerted Action Against States Found in Default of their International Obligations in Respect of Unlawful Interference with International Civil Aviation", 10 Can. YBIL 261 (1972); Chamberlain, "Suspension of Air Services with States which Harbour Hijackers", 32 ICLQ 616 (1983). See also the proposals made during the drafting of the Hague Convention by the International Federation of Airline Pilots Associations and Costa Rica, respectively, in ICAO Doc 8979-LC/165-2, p. 110 & p. 134 (1972). Calls for the adoption of mechanisms for imposing sanctions continue to be made. See, e.g, Sofaer, "Fighting Terrorism through Law", 85 Dep't St. Bull., No. 2103, p. 41 (1985). See also Wilkinson, note 33, *supra*, at p. 299. The refusal of several nations to extradite or prosecute hijackers led in 1978 to the "Bonn Declaration" by the governments of the "Economic 7" (Canada, France, the FRG, Italy, Japan, the UK and the US), in which it was declared that when a State refused to comply with its obligations, the declaring governments would halt air traffic to and from that country. To date, the Bonn Declaration seems only to have been invoked against Afghanistan (and was used to bring pressure to bear on South Africa). Determined use of such declarations might be effective substitutes for binding sanctions contained in a

was raised during the drafting of the Hostages Convention. Taken as a whole, these defects make the conventions less sturdy instruments than they could otherwise be.

5. THE EMERGENCE OF THE HOSTAGES CONVENTION

(A) *Establishment of the* Ad Hoc *Committee on the Drafting of an International Convention Against the Taking of Hostages*

In September 1976, in the wake of the Israeli operation to rescue its nationals held hostage at Entebbe, and following the successful conclusion of the other international conventions dealing with particular types of terrorist offences, the Federal Republic of Germany proposed that the topic of the drafting of an international convention against the taking of hostages be included on the agenda of the thirty-first session of the General Assembly.[196]

convention. See Chamberlain, *supra*, at pp. 624-32; Busuttil, "The Bonn Declaration on International Terrorism: A Non-Binding International Agreement on Aircraft Hijacking", 31 ICLQ 474 (1982). In June 1987, the Economic 7 countries decided to strengthen the Bonn Declaration by extending it to offences against the Montreal Convention. See 87 Dep't St. Bull., No. 2125, pp. 3-4 (1987). For its part, ICAO relies on a reporting system, established in Article 11 of the Hague Convention and Article 13 of the Montreal Convention, whereby States are required to inform the ICAO Council of the circumstances of all offences, the measures they have taken to restore the *status quo* and the measures they take with respect to alleged offenders, "in particular, the results of any extradition proceedings or other legal proceedings." The rationale for such a system is that disclosure of the relevant facts will prompt governments to take their obligations seriously, for fear of world opinion. However, ICAO does not scrutinize the reports or assess the action taken. Moreover, in many cases reports are never received. See Sochor, "Terrorism in the Sky: The Rhetoric and Realities of Sanctions", 10 Terr. J. 311, 319 (1987). No such reporting system is envisaged by the Hostages Convention; States are only required, pursuant to Article 7, to notify the Secretary-General of the results of any actual prosecution.

[196] UN GAOR, 31st Sess., Annexes (Agenda item 123), p. 1, UN Doc A/31/242 (1976). A memorandum attached to the letter of request stated that the taking of hostages, in addition to endangering the lives of its immediate victims, affects the "security of many other persons as well and frequently also endangers international peace and transnational relations". Rosenstock states that in the aftermath of the successful conclusion of the Hague, Montreal and New York Conventions, many governments began to look for "another area capable of identification as a specific and demarcated area which would not be so broad in its sweep as to suffer the fate of the League of Nations and United Nations efforts to deal with all forms of terrorism in one fell swoop". Although it was considered briefly that the practice of sending letter bombs should be the subject of the next instrument, that practice abated and was not, therefore, deemed a priority. The FRG then fixed on the idea of a convention against the taking of hostages. See Rosenstock, pp. 172-73. Although the FRG's proposal came just two months after the Entebbe raid, the FRG apparently began to build informal support for the idea of such a convention in January 1976, following the April 1975 siege of its embassy in Stockholm by members of the Holger Meins Kommando. See McDonald, p. 546. Those commentators who were involved in the drafting of the Hostages Convention note the leadership of the FRG, and particularly of Dr. Karl Fleischauer, throughout the drafting process. See *id.* at p. 173, n.15; Rosenne, p. 146; McDonald, p. 559.

The matter was referred to the Sixth Committee, where the FRG proposed the establishment of an *ad hoc* committee charged with drafting a convention on the subject which would contain, as its central provision, the obligation *aut dedere aut judicare*.[197] After some debate, the FRG proposal, slightly revised so as to remove the reference to the principle *aut dedere aut judicare*, was adopted and the Sixth Committee recommended to the General Assembly the establishment of such a committee.[198] On 15 December 1976, the General Assembly adopted by consensus Resolution 31/103 which, noting that the "taking of hostages is an act which endangers innocent human lives and violates human dignity" and recognizing "the urgent need for further effective measures to put an end to the taking of hostages", established the *Ad Hoc* Committee on the Drafting of an International Convention Against the Taking of Hostages. The resolution instructed the Hostages Committee to draft the convention at the earliest possible date, to be submitted for consideration during the Assembly's thirty-second session.[199] The resolution also requested the President of the General Assembly to appoint the members of the Committee after consultation with the various regional groups. Members were appointed from Algeria, Barbados, Bulgaria (appointed in 1979), Byelorussian Soviet Socialist Republic, Canada, Chile, Democratic Yemen, Denmark, Egypt, France, FRG, Guinea, Iran, Italy, Japan, Jordan, Kenya, Lesotho, Libya, Mexico, Netherlands, Nicaragua, Nigeria, Philippines, Poland, Somalia, Surinam, Sweden, Syria, USSR, United Kingdom, Tanzania, USA, Venezuela, and Yugoslavia.[200]

---

[197] UN GAOR, 31st Sess., Annexes (Agenda item 123), pp. 2-3, UN Doc A/31/430 (1976).

[198] *Id.* at pp. 3-4. The debate contained familiar themes from the earlier debates on the issue of terrorism, such as the desire of some States to focus on the underlying causes of such acts and the fear that such a convention would be used to thwart national liberation movements. See, e.g., the comments of the representatives of Kenya and China, respectively, in UN GAOR, 31st Sess., C.6 (57th mtg.), para. 34, UN Doc A/C.6/31/SR.57 (1976) & UN GAOR, 31st Sess., C.6 (58th mtg.), paras. 26 & 27, UN Doc A/C.6/31/SR.58 (1976). But the debate also concerned a Libyan proposal to insert the word "innocent" before the word "hostages" (see UN Doc A/C.6/31/L.11, in UN GAOR, 31st Sess., Annexes (Agenda item 123), p. 3, UN Doc A/31/430 (1976)) and the FRG's draft resolution which stated that the newly-formed committee should include the principle *aut dedere aut judicare* in the draft convention. Many developing States felt that the reference to this principle would prejudice the committee's work. See, e.g., the comments of the representative of Somalia, UN GAOR, 31st Sess., C.6 (mtg. 58), para. 55, UN Doc A/C.6/31/SR.58 (1976). In a compromise, Libya dropped its proposal and the FRG agreed to delete the reference to *aut dedere aut judicare*. UN GAOR, 31st Sess., C.6 (mtg. 59), paras. 1-8, UN Doc A/C.6/31/SR.59 (1976).

[199] UN GAOR, 31st Sess., Supp. 39, p. 186, UN Doc A/31/39 (1977).

[200] See Report of the *Ad Hoc* Committee on the Drafting of an International Convention Against the Taking of Hostages, UN GAOR, 32nd Sess., Supp. 39, p. 2, para. 2, UN Doc A/32/39 (1977); Report of the *Ad Hoc* Committee on the Drafting of an International Convention Against the Taking of Hostages, UN GAOR, 34th Sess., Supp. 39, p. 2, para. 2 & n.4, UN Doc A/34/39 (1979).

(B) *The bypassing of the ILC and the Terrorism Committee*

By thus establishing an *ad hoc* committee to draft the Hostages Convention, the General Assembly bypassed at least two already existing bodies which might conceivably have dealt with the matter — the International Law Commission and the *Ad Hoc* Committee on International Terrorism. The extensive codification of international law is one of the greatest achievements of the United Nations,[201] and the ILC is the UN organ charged with the codification and progressive development of international law. It has thus been responsible for the development of many important multilateral conventions, including the 1958 Geneva Conventions on the Law of the Sea,[202] the 1961 Vienna Convention on Diplomatic Relations,[203] the 1963 Vienna Convention on Consular Relations[204] and the 1969 Vienna Convention on the Law of Treaties.[205] It was, moreover, responsible for the initial drafting of the New York Convention and it completed that task with dispatch.[206] It may seem, therefore, that the ILC would have been the natural body to deal with the Hostages Convention, an instrument which was, and was intended to be, drafted along the same lines as the New York Convention.

The General Assembly's decision not to assign the task of the

---

The Hostages Committee submitted a total of three reports to the General Assembly. In addition to the two just cited, there is a report in UN GAOR, 33rd Sess., Supp. 39, UN Doc A/33/39 (1978). These reports, from the 32nd, 33rd and 34th sessions of the General Assembly, will subsequently be cited as "First Report of the Hostages Committee", "Second Report of the Hostages Committee", and "Third Report of the Hostages Committee", respectively, followed by a page reference and, where applicable, a paragraph reference.

[201] See generally, Hambro, "Codification of International Law under the League and under the United Nations", in *Mélanges Fernand Dehousse* 57 (1979).

[202] Convention on the Territorial Sea and the Contiguous Zone, 516 UNTS 205; Convention on the High Seas, 450 UNTS 82; Convention on Fishing and Conservation of the Living Resources of the High Seas, 559 UNTS 285; Convention on the Continental Shelf, 499 UNTS 311.

[203] 500 UNTS 95.

[204] 596 UNTS 261.

[205] See El Baradei & Franck, "The Codification and Progressive Development of International Law: A UNITAR Study of the Role and Use of the International Law Commission", 76 AJIL 630, 631 (1982). On the ILC's work on these and other conventions, see generally Sinclair, *The International Law Commission* (1987).

[206] In Resolution 2780 (XXVI) of 3 December 1971, the General Assembly requested the ILC, *inter alia*, to study the issue of the protection of diplomats with a view to preparing a set of draft articles dealing with offences against diplomats and other persons protected under international law. UN GAOR, 26th Sess., Supp. 29, p. 136, UN Doc A/8429 (1972). In 1972, the Commission began and finished its work on the subject and submitted its draft articles to the General Assembly. See 1972 YBILC, Vol. II, pp. 309-323. On the drafting of the articles, see generally Kearney, "The Twenty-Fourth Session of the International Law Commission", 67 AJIL 84, 86-94 (1973); Sinclair, note 205, *supra*, at pp. 92-93. The General Assembly adopted the New York Convention in December 1973. Thus, the entire procedure took only two years from start to finish.

drafting of the Hostages Convention to the ILC is not, however, altogether surprising. A 1981 UNITAR study examined a number of reasons why the General Assembly has been increasingly reluctant to assign topics to the ILC. These include: the generally slow pace of the ILC's work (an average of 7-10 years between the ILC's initial investigation of a topic and the production of a draft instrument) and the need for greater speed; the fact that the Commission is made up of independent lawyers and the desire in some quarters to have State representatives draft negotiating texts; the expansion of international law in both economic and technical fields, which requires the attention of bodies with more specialized knowledge; and the view of many developing States that the ILC takes an approach to international law which is too static and traditional.[207] The result has been the assignment of a number of topics, which might otherwise have gone to the ILC, to a "proliferating gaggle of *ad hoc* bodies",[208] and an attendant loss of the ILC's central role in multilateral treaty-making.[209] It might be noted, however, that the precise reasons why the drafting of a convention against hostage-taking was not assigned to the ILC are unclear from the record.[210]

As regards the decision not to assign the task to the Terrorism

---

[207] See El Baradei, Franck & Trachtenberg, *The International Law Commission: The Need for a New Direction* 6-16 (UNITAR, 1981). See also El Baradei & Franck, note 205, *supra*.

[208] *Id.* at p. 632.

[209] See El Baradei, Franck & Trachtenberg, note 207, *supra*, at p. 7, who note that the ILC has not been involved in some of the "most important areas in the development of international law", such as the law of the sea (since 1958), the law of economic relations, the law of outer space and human rights. See also El Baradei & Franck, note 205, *supra*, at p. 634, who note that some feel that the ILC's agenda is "trivia" and a "parody of the world's urgent agenda", consisting of such issues as treaty-making by international organizations and the status of the diplomatic bag. The result of this tendency to avoid the ILC is a "growing incoherence" in the UN legislative system as a whole. *Id.* at p. 639. Others have also called for a greater centralization of UN treaty-making. See, e.g., Szasz, "Improving the International Legislative Process", 9 Georgia J. Int'l L. 519-533 (1979). The UNITAR study gives mixed marks to the results of *ad hoc* bodies established to draft conventions. See El Baradei, Franck & Trachtenberg, note 207, *supra*, at p. 7. However, the Hostages Committee must be seen as one of the successes, given that it drafted a sound convention on an extremely controversial subject in just three years (and only nine actual weeks of meetings).

[210] In addition to the general reasons just cited, it may simply have been that the GA believed that a committee established with a specific mandate could work faster than a committee which already had an extensive agenda. The representative of the Netherlands to the Sixth Committee, for example, stated that he believed that the Hostages Committee could complete its task in one year since its mandate was limited in scope. See UN GAOR, 31st Sess., C.6 (56th mtg.), para. 17, UN Doc A/C.6/31/SR.56 (1976). Since the principle of the inviolability of diplomats was already established under customary international law and the Vienna Conventions, it may have been perceived that the New York Convention would not be difficult to draft. In contrast, the issue of hostage-taking promised to be more controversial, requiring a group that could devote its full attention to the subject. Moreover, it may have seemed more appropriate to have the political question regarding the scope of the Convention decided by draftsmen who were the representatives of States, rather than by the ILC.

Committee, as earlier noted,²¹¹ that body, reflecting the deep divisions within the world community on the issue of terrorism, had essentially broken down in 1973 in deadlock over such issues as the definition of international terrorism (and the inclusion of acts of national liberation movements therein), the problem of State terrorism and the relative importance of studying and addressing the causes of international terrorism *vis-à-vis* taking actions to prevent it. On the same day that the General Assembly resolved to establish the Hostages Committee, it voted to resurrect the Terrorism Committee with the same agenda as earlier.²¹² Although some members of the Sixth Committee seemed to suggest that the Terrorism Committee should be charged with drafting the Hostages Convention,²¹³ most States obviously felt that it was better to assign the task to a new, more promising, *ad hoc* committee, established with a specific and limited mandate. The drafting of a convention against hostage-taking was thus separated from the larger, and more divisive, issue of terrorism.²¹⁴

(C) *Procedural and substantive drafting progress of the Convention*

The first session of the Hostages Committee was held in New York between 1 and 19 August 1977.²¹⁵ This session was taken up by organizational matters, a general debate and consideration of various working papers submitted by member States.²¹⁶ A draft convention was submitted by the FRG;²¹⁷ this draft (although undergoing many changes ranging from the refinement of language to the addition of

---

²¹¹ See pp. 37-39 (notes 115-133 and accompanying text).

²¹² See p. 40 (note 136 and accompanying text).

²¹³ See, e.g., the comments of the representatives of the USSR and German Democratic Republic, respectively, in UN GAOR, 31st Sess., C.6 (58th mtg.), paras. 31-34, UN Doc A/C.6/31/SR.58 (1976) & UN GAOR, 31st Sess., C.6 (59th mtg.), para. 6, UN Doc A/C.6/31/SR.59 (1976). Rosenne reports that throughout the drafting of the Hostages Convention there was "some interaction" between the two agenda items (i.e., the drafting of the Convention and the work of the Terrorism Committee) and that some groups hoped that this would "blunt" the Hostages Convention. However, the General Assembly decided to keep the two items separate and deliberately delayed consideration of the Terrorism Committee's report until 1979 in the hope that the Hostages Convention would be completed by then. Rosenne, pp. 111-112. A subsequent attempt to link the two items for Sixth Committee consideration was also unsuccessful. *Id.* at pp. 123-24.

²¹⁴ One commentator notes that Entebbe "created the international political climate conducive to the adoption of a 'piecemeal' approach to international terrorism by isolation of hostage-taking from its other elements ... [h]ostage-taking had to and could be removed from the agenda of the Terrorism Committee". Boyle, *World Politics and International Law* 139 (1985).

²¹⁵ First Report of the Hostages Committee, p. 3, para. 3.

²¹⁶ *Id.* at pp. 3-4, paras. 4-11. The general debate and consideration of working papers can be found at pp. 14-95 of this report.

²¹⁷ UN Doc A/AC.188/L.3, in *id.*, at pp. 106-110. Subsequent references to this draft are cited only as "FRG draft", followed by an article number. The FRG draft is included in this study as Appendix II.

new provisions) served as the focus of the drafting process and remained the core of the final product.[218]

In the Hostages Committee, it quickly became clear that the differences of opinion which had earlier plagued the Terrorism Committee and the General Assembly had not abated. States were very far apart on many issues relevant to the proposed convention, particularly regarding the interrelated issues of the definition of hostage-taking and the scope of the instrument. In its original draft, the FRG proposed a definition of hostage-taking which was very similar to the final version, providing without exception that "[a]ny person" who seizes or detains and threatens another person with death, injury or continued detention in order to compel a third party to do or abstain from doing anything commits the offence of hostage-taking.[219] However, numerous attempts were made to alter this simple definition. First, it was proposed by Libya that the definition of hostage-taking should be drafted as follows:

> the term 'taking of hostages' is the seizure or detention, not only of a person or persons, but also of masses under colonial, racist or foreign domination, in a way that threatens him or them with death, or severe injury or deprives them of fundamental freedoms.[220]

Second, many delegations mooted the idea that the definition of hostage-taking should be drafted in such a way as to prohibit only the taking of "innocent" hostages, suggesting that "guilty" individuals, i.e., those connected with colonialism or foreign domination, could be taken hostage.[221] Third, a number of developing States proposed the insertion into the draft convention of language providing that the term "taking of hostages" does not include any acts "carried out in the process of national liberation against colonial rule, racist and foreign régimes, by liberation movements recognized by the United Nations or regional organizations".[222] The Libyan proposal did not seem to receive much attention when the drafting efforts began in earnest,

---

[218] Changes from and additions to the FRG draft are noted in the appropriate place in the commentary.
[219] FRG draft, Art. 1.
[220] UN Doc A/AC.188/L.9, in First Report of the Hostages Committee, p. 112.
[221] See, e.g., the comments of the representative of Libya, *id.* at p. 39, para. 10. The representative of Tanzania stated that oppressed and colonized peoples "could not be stopped from taking oppressors hostage if that became inevitable". *Id.* at pp. 35-36, para. 28. The proposal regarding "innocent" hostages was first mooted by Libya when the General Assembly was considering the FRG's proposal to establish an *ad hoc* committee to draft the Hostages Convention. See note 198, *supra*.
[222] UN Doc A/AC.188/L.5, in First Report of the Hostages Committee, p. 11. This proposal was sponsored by Lesotho, Tanzania, Algeria, Egypt, Guinea, Libya, and Nigeria.

and the proposal regarding "innocent" hostages seemed to fade away rather quickly. However, the underlying idea of this latter proposal was subsumed into the third position, which turned out to be the most vexing problem faced by the draftsmen. This issue is developed further in the commentary on Article 12.[223] It is enough for now to note that the problem stayed with the Committee during its entire existence and threatened to turn its work into a stalemate. In the end, however, no exceptions based on the motive of the offender or the identity of the victim were drafted into the Hostages Convention.

Given the magnitude of the task and the fundamental disagreements which appeared, the Hostages Committee was not able to submit a draft convention to the General Assembly by the end of its first session. The Committee thus adopted a resolution recommending that the General Assembly invite it to continue its work in 1978.[224] In resolution 32/148, the General Assembly did so, inviting governments to submit or update suggestions and proposals and requesting the Hostages Committee to make every effort to submit a draft convention to the General Assembly at the latter's thirty-third session.[225]

The second session of the Hostages Committee was held in Geneva from 6 to 24 February 1978.[226] On 9 February, the Committee decided that it would be best to proceed with its work by establishing two working groups.[227] Working Group I was assigned the "thornier questions" connected with the drafting, in particular: "(a) The scope of the Convention and the question of national liberation movements; (b) The question of the definition of taking of hostages; (c) The questions concerning extradition and right of asylum;" and "(d) The respect for the principles of sovereignty and territorial integrity of States with regard to the release of hostages."[228] Working Group II was assigned those draft articles which were not generally controversial and those which had been agreed upon by Working Group I.[229] At the end of the second session, both groups submitted reports which were approved by the entire Committee.[230] Although considerable progress

---

[223] See pp. 266-272 (notes 12-38 and accompanying text in the commentary on Article 12).
[224] First Report of the Hostages Committee, p. 5, para. 14.
[225] UN GAOR, 32nd Sess., Supp. 45, p. 213, UN Doc A/32/45 (1978).
[226] Second Report of the Hostages Committee, p. 2, para. 3.
[227] Id. at p. 3, para. 10.
[228] Id. at p. 5, paras. 14-15.
[229] Id. at p. 7, para. 23.
[230] Id. at pp. 3-4, paras. 11-12. The report of Working Group I is contained in pp. 5-6, paras. 14-22, and the report of Working Group II is contained in pp. 7-15, paras. 23-56, of the Second Report of the Hostages Committee.

64   TERRORISM AND THE INTERNATIONAL RESPONSE

had been made on the controversial issues,[231] the Hostages Committee was unable to complete a draft convention during its second session. Again, it adopted a resolution recommending that the General Assembly invite it to continue its work in the following year.[232] In resolution 33/19 of 29 November 1978, the General Assembly did so, and requested the Hostages Committee to make every effort to submit a draft convention to the General Assembly at its thirty-fourth session. The item "Drafting of an international convention against the taking of hostages" was included in the provisional agenda of the thirty-fourth session of the General Assembly.[233]

The third session of the Hostages Committee took place in Geneva from 29 January to 16 February 1979.[234] Work on the draft convention resumed where it left off in the second session and the working groups were again assigned their respective tasks.[235] The two groups again submitted reports to the entire Hostages Committee.[236] By the end of the session, the Committee was able to submit a draft convention to the General Assembly.[237] The draft had an incomplete preamble and two bracketed, i.e., not agreed upon, articles (those which ultimately became Articles 9 and 15); however, agreement had been reached on most vital issues and the draft was largely complete.

On 21 September 1979, at the 4th plenary meeting of its thirty-fourth session, the General Assembly referred the draft convention to the Sixth Committee which referred it to a working group made up of representatives of those States which had been members of the Hostages Committee.[238] After examining the draft convention article by article, making certain changes and preparing text for the preamble, the working group submitted a report and a revised draft convention to the Sixth Committee.[239] The draft was considered between 27 November and 7 December 1979.[240] On 7 December, the Sixth Committee adopted without a vote a draft resolution submitted by the FRG to which was annexed the final draft of the convention; a

[231] See Second Report of the Hostages Committee, pp. 5-6, paras. 14-22.
[232] Id. at p. 16, para. 57.
[233] UN GAOR, 33rd Sess., Supp. 45, p. 215, UN Doc A/33/45 (1979).
[234] Third Report of the Hostages Committee, p. 2, para. 3.
[235] Id. at pp. 3-4, para. 10.
[236] Id. at p. 4, para. 11. The report of Working Group I is contained in pp. 5-8, paras. 12-26, and the report of Working Group II is contained in pp. 9-21, paras. 27-88, of the Third Report of the Hostages Committee.
[237] Id. at pp. 22-29.
[238] See Report of the Sixth Committee, UN GAOR, 34th Sess., Annexes (Agenda item 113), p. 1, paras. 5-7, UN Doc A/34/819 (1979).
[239] Id. at pp. 2-5, paras. 3-16.
[240] Id. at p. 2, paras. 9-12.

separate vote on Article 9, however, was taken at the behest of the Soviet Union. Article 9 was adopted by a recorded vote of 103 in favour and 10 against, with 4 abstentions and 2 States not participating.[241] The draft was thus recommended to the General Assembly.[242] On 17 December 1979, the General Assembly adopted without a vote Resolution 34/146 to which the Convention was annexed.[243] Again, however, a separate vote was taken on Article 9. The Article was adopted by a vote of 125 in favour and 10 against, with 3 abstentions.[244] The Convention came into force on 4 June 1983, 30 days after deposit of the 22nd ratification.[245]

It should be noted that the period surrounding the drafting of the Hostages Convention was marked by a number of dramatic and well-publicized incidents of hostage-taking and subsequent rescue operations by non-territorial States. As earlier noted, the proposal to draft the Convention came soon after the Entebbe incident.[246] During the life span of the Hostages Committee, two other hostage-takings and rescue operations took place: the 1977 hijacking of a Lufthansa aircraft and holding of hostages at Mogadishu, Somalia, which precipitated a rescue operation by commandos from the FRG; and the 1978 hijacking of an Egyptian aircraft and holding of hostages at Larnaca, Cyprus, which resulted in a raid by Egyptian commandos.[247] Moreover, the US hostages in Iran were seized only one month before the General Assembly's consensus adoption of the Convention.[248] It would appear that the revulsion of the world community at these acts of hostage-taking, coupled with the realization by small and developing States that they are vulnerable to rescue operations, helped lead to the success of the drafting process.[249]

(D) *The drafting records of the Hostages Convention*

As earlier noted,[250] the Hostages Committee submitted three reports to the General Assembly on the progress of its work, one for each of

---

[241] *Id.* at para. 14 & n. 6. See pp. 214-215 (notes 24-26 and accompanying text in the commentary on Article 9).

[242] See Report of the Sixth Committee, note 238, *infra*, at p. 2, para. 16.

[243] See p. 1 (note 7 and accompanying text in the Introduction).

[244] See p. 215 (note 27 and accompanying text in the commentary on Article 9).

[245] See generally Bowman & Harris, note 157, *supra*, at p. 448; Art. 18, Hostages Convention.

[246] See p. 57 (note 196 and accompanying text).

[247] For the facts of these incidents, see pp. 317 & 319-320 (notes 21 & 38 in the commentary on Article 14).

[248] For the facts of this incident, see p. 3 (note 12 and accompanying text in the Introduction).

[249] For an examination of these incidents and how they affected the drafting of the Hostages Convention, see Boyle, note 214, *supra*, at pp. 136-154.

[250] See pp. 58-59 (note 200 and accompanying text).

the years that it convened. The first and second reports, moreover, contain fairly extensive summary records of the Committee's proceedings; less detailed summary records exist from the third session of the Hostages Committee.[251] These materials, coupled with a report by the Sixth Committee[252] and some summary records of the Sixth Committee's consideration of the draft convention,[253] constitute the principal *travaux préparatoires* of the Hostages Convention.

This commentary makes use in general of all the relevant rules of treaty interpretation contained in the Vienna Convention on the Law of Treaties.[254] Wherever possible, the ordinary meaning is given to the terms employed in the instrument; however, many provisions are ambiguous, perhaps deliberately so, and, therefore, recourse is often had to the *travaux préparatoires* in order to ascertain their

---

[251] For the summary records of the first session, see First Report of the Hostages Committee, pp. 10-105. In the subsequent two sessions of the Hostages Committee, most of the work was carried out in an informal manner, and, consequently, fewer summary records were kept, although the records from the second session are fairly detailed. For the summary records of the second session, see Second Report of the Hostages Committee, pp. 19-83. Since the summary records of the first two sessions of the Hostages Committee are contained in the relevant reports, when reference is made in this study to the Committee's proceedings, the reports, rather than the summary records, are cited. The summary records of the third session are very sparse and were released separately from the Committee's report. See UN Docs A/AC.188/SR. 30-35 & Corr. (1979).

Working in informal sessions where no records were kept led to a reduction in posturing by delegations and was, therefore, conducive to meaningful negotiations. See McDonald, p. 549. However, the lack of summary records from the later stages of the Hostages Committee's work makes it more difficult to discern what the various positions of the delegations were on certain issues and how consensus developed. Some light is shed on this process, particularly with regard to the issue of national liberation movements, by those authors who were present during the drafting process. See, e.g., Rosenne; Rosenstock; McDonald; Verwey. The insights of these writers are utilized where helpful.

[252] See note 238, *supra*.

[253] The Hostages Convention was considered in a number of meetings of the Sixth Committee in 1979. See UN GAOR, 34th Sess., C.6 (3rd, 4th, 10th-15th, 53rd, 56th, 58th-62nd mtgs.), UN Docs A/C.6/34/SR.3, SR.4, SR.10-15, SR.53, SR.56 & SR.58-62 (1979). The bulk of the Sixth Committee's work on the Convention was also conducted informally, without summary records; however, the summary records include a statement by the Chairman-Rapporteur of the Committee's working group as to how and why agreement was reached on various articles, as well as the reactions of various States to the draft convention. It should be noted that whenever a draftsman is quoted in this commentary the quote has been taken verbatim from the relevant summary record. Quotes, therefore, may thus not be the actual words of the speaker.

[254] Article 31(1) of the Vienna Convention provides that: "A treaty shall be interpreted in good faith in accordance with the ordinary meaning to be given to the terms of the treaty in their context and in the light of its object and purpose." Article 32 provides:

> Recourse may be had to supplementary means of interpretation, including the preparatory work of the treaty and the circumstances of its conclusion, in order to confirm the meaning resulting from the application of article 31, or to determine the meaning when the interpretation according to article 31:
> (a) leaves the meaning ambiguous or obscure; or
> (b) leads to a result which is manifestly absurd or unreasonable.

meaning.[255] Moreover, since the instrument was drafted along the same lines as the earlier anti-terrorism instruments, recourse is often had to the *travaux préparatoires* of those instruments in cases where it was thought helpful.

---

[255] Even in the absence of ambiguity, the *travaux préparatoires* are sometimes referred to for the purpose of confirming the plain or ordinary meaning of the text. This is in conformity with Article 32 of the Vienna Convention on the Law of Treaties. Although some dicta of the International Court indicate that reference should not be had to the preparatory works when the meaning of the text is clear (see, e.g., *Conditions of Admission of a State to Membership in the United Nations (Article 4 of the Charter), Advisory Opinion*, ICJ Rep. 1947-48, p. 57, 63), other dicta indicate otherwise (see, e.g., *Interpretation of the Convention of 1919 concerning Employment of Women during the Night, Advisory Opinion*, PCIJ (1932), Series A/B, No. 50, p. 365, 380) and it appears that even before the adoption of the Vienna Convention it was the practice of international tribunals to examine the *travaux préparatoires* to confirm the ordinary meaning of the text. See 1966 YBILC, Vol. II, pp. 222-23. That the International Court has generally, explicitly or implicitly, relied on the *travaux préparatoires* of treaties in order to confirm the "clear" meaning of the text is convincingly argued in Lauterpacht, *The Development of International Law by the International Court* 116-141 (1958).

PART II

THE HOSTAGES CONVENTION: COMMENTARY

Preamble

The States Parties to this Convention,
Having in mind the purposes and principles of the Charter of the United Nations concerning the maintenance of international peace and security and the promotion of friendly relations and co-operation among States,
Recognizing in particular that everyone has the right to life, liberty and security of person, as set out in the Universal Declaration of Human Rights and the International Covenant on Civil and Political Rights,
Reaffirming the principle of equal rights and self-determination of peoples as enshrined in the Charter of the United Nations and the Declaration on Principles of International Law concerning Friendly Relations and Co-operation among States in accordance with the Charter of the United Nations, as well as in other relevant resolutions of the General Assembly,
Considering that the taking of hostages is an offence of grave concern to the international community and that, in accordance with the provisions of this Convention, any person committing an act of hostage taking shall either be prosecuted or extradited,
Being convinced that it is urgently necessary to develop international co-operation between States in devising and adopting effective measures for the prevention, prosecution and punishment of all acts of taking of hostages as manifestations of international terrorism,
Have agreed as follows:

1. INTRODUCTION

The primary rule of treaty interpretation as contained in Article 31, paragraph 1, of the Vienna Convention on the Law of Treaties is that the text must be interpreted in accordance with the ordinary meaning to be given its terms in their context and in light of the object and purpose of the treaty. The context of the terms, according to paragraph 2 of that Article, includes the preamble of the treaty. The preamble of a treaty can thus be an important aid to the interpretation of a treaty.

In this Convention, the Preamble appears to be carefully worded compromise language crafted to reflect the various concerns expressed during the drafting process. Some of the paragraphs were easily agreed upon, while others required significant negotiation before compromise could be reached. As a result, the provisions are fairly innocuous and will be of somewhat limited assistance in the interpretation of this Convention. Despite the foregoing, however, it may be noted that the Preamble is significant in that it quite clearly states that the taking of hostages is an offence of grave international concern and that all acts of hostage-taking should result in extradition or prosecution.

It should be noted that there exists very little recorded discussion concerning the drafting of the Preamble. The Hostages Committee devoted little attention to the issue, and the draft convention submitted by that body to the Sixth Committee contained only one preambular paragraph, upon which tentative agreement had been reached[1] (and which appears in the final version as the fifth paragraph). Some light on the drafting of the Preamble, however, is shed by those commentators who participated in the drafting process, and their comments are taken into account below.

2. INTERPRETATION

The first two preambular paragraphs correspond to concerns expressed by the FRG when it first proposed that the General Assembly undertake the drafting of an international convention against hostage-taking, namely, that acts of hostage-taking not only endanger individual rights but also endanger international peace and transnational relations.[2] Similar language was contained in the preamble of the FRG draft, and the Sixth Committee Working Group easily approved of these paragraphs.[3]

The first preambular paragraph recognizes, in a negative sense, that international incidents of hostage-taking can compromise the purposes and principles of the United Nations to maintain peace and security and to promote friendly relations and co-operation between States. The incidents themselves can create tension between States, particularly when the State in which hostages are held (or the State which exercises effective control either over the territory in which hostages are held or over the groups which hold them) is suspected of being sympathetic to the hostage-takers or of taking insufficient steps to secure the release of hostages. Moreover, incidents of hostage-taking can result in the unilateral use of force by States to rescue hostages held in the territory of other States.[4] Even if such rescue operations are not directly contrary to the Charter, they are conducive neither to peace and security nor to the promotion of friendly relations and co-operation. In a positive sense, the first preambular paragraph recognizes that the adoption of a convention against

---

[1] See Third Report of the Hostages Committee, p. 23 & n.41.
[2] See p. 57 (note 196 and accompanying text in Part I).
[3] See UN GAOR, 34th Sess., C.6 (53rd mtg.), p. 7, para. 17, UN Doc A/C.6/34/SR.53 (1979).
[4] On such uses of force, see the commentary on Article 14 (pp. 313-325).

hostage-taking is consistent with the purposes and principles of the United Nations.

The second preambular paragraph recognizes that the taking of hostages is inconsistent with the individual rights to life, liberty and security of person as provided for in the Universal Declaration of Human Rights[5] and the International Covenant on Civil and Political Rights.[6] Although this might be considered an obvious point, in light of discussions conducted early on in the drafting process regarding the rights of certain groups to take certain categories of persons hostage,[7] its inclusion in the Preamble has some significance.

The third preambular paragraph simply reaffirms the principle of equal rights and self-determination as enshrined in the Charter and in numerous resolutions of the General Assembly.[8] According to Rosenstock, it was included for four reasons: 1) since some governments, such as that of South Africa, cloak their repressive laws under the rubric of "antiterrorism" it was thought "reasonable to ensure that actions of the international community are drafted in such a manner as not to permit them to be used, or more accurately, abused, as an instrument of repression rather than a tool for protecting such basic rights as life, liberty, and security of person"; 2) the desire of many developing countries to reiterate the principle of self-determination whenever possible; 3) the perception by developing States that the legitimacy of the use of force to achieve self-determination would be strengthened by the inclusion of such language and would, conversely, be weakened by its exclusion; and 4) the view of some of the draftsmen that the operative portions of a text should be foreshadowed in the preamble. With regard to this final reason, since Article 12 refers to self-determination it was considered by some that the Preamble should also include such a reference.[9] According to Verwey, inclusion of this reaffirmation of the right to self-determination was part of the compromise by which agreement was ultimately reached on the issue of the applicability of the Convention to acts of hostage-taking committed in the name of

---

[5] Art. 3, GA Res 217 A (III), UN Doc A/810, p. 71 (1949).

[6] Arts. 6(1) & 9(1), 999 UNTS 171, *reprinted in* 6 ILM 368 (1967).

[7] See generally pp. 62-63 (notes 221-223 and accompanying text in Part I); pp. 267-268 (notes 15-17 and accompanying text in the commentary on Article 12).

[8] See, e.g., Declaration on the Granting of Independence to Colonial Territories and Peoples, GA Res 1514 (XV), UN GAOR, 15th Sess., Supp. 16, p. 66, UN Doc A/4684 (1961); Declaration on Principles of International Law concerning Friendly Relations and Cooperation among States in accordance with the Charter of the United Nations, GA Res 2625 (XXV) of 24 October 1970, UN GAOR, 25th Sess., Supp. 28, p. 121, UN Doc A/8028 (1971).

[9] Rosenstock, pp. 175-76. Another commentator also notes the desire of some draftsmen to foreshadow some of the substantive provisions of the Convention in the Preamble. See Rosenne, p. 125.

national liberation,[10] an issue which is discussed in detail in the commentary on Article 12.

The important point to be made about this paragraph is that it does not even vaguely suggest that the principle of equal rights and self-determination is a legitimate justification for the taking of hostages. This conclusion is clear enough from the language of the paragraph itself, but, as will be seen below, is more than adequately supported by the language of Article 1, Article 8 and Article 12 of the Convention, and by the drafting history of those provisions. It is also supported by the language of the following preambular paragraph.

The fourth preambular paragraph establishes that the taking of hostages is a grave offence of concern to the international community and that, "in accordance with the provisions of the Convention", all hostage-takers shall either be extradited or prosecuted. The latter part of the paragraph thus foreshadows Article 8, which imposes the obligation *aut dedere aut judicare*. Moreover, this paragraph, as part of the compromise referred to by Verwey, balances the preceding paragraph by making it clear that the right to self-determination is not a justification for the taking of hostages and that "all" hostage-takers should be extradited or prosecuted. As envisaged by Article 12, this universal bringing to justice of hostage-takers should come about pursuant either to this Convention or to the relevant instruments on the laws of armed conflict. It may be noted that the third and fourth preambular paragraphs reflect the repeatedly manifested concerns of the various groups during the drafting process: the fear on the part of many developing States that the Convention would be used to the detriment of national liberation struggles and the insistence of Western and other States that the Convention should allow for no exceptions based on the motives of the offenders.[11] Given the attempt to create this balance, drafting the third and fourth preambular paragraphs proved to be more difficult than drafting the first two paragraphs.[12]

Finally, the fifth preambular paragraph refers to the necessity of developing international co-operation to prevent, prosecute and punish all acts of taking of hostages "as manifestations of international terrorism". The fourth preambular paragraph of the FRG draft contained similar language, but made no reference to "manifestations of international terrorism". This language was added upon the proposal of the Soviet Union during the final session of the Hostages

---

[10] Verwey, p. 76.

[11] See generally pp. 266-268 (notes 12-21 and accompanying text in the commentary on Article 12).

[12] See UN GAOR, 34th Sess., C.6 (53rd mtg.), p. 7, para. 17, UN Doc A/C.6/34/SR.53 (1979).

Committee.[13] On its face, this paragraph seems simply to reflect the fact that the Hostages Convention is, and was designed to be, part of the effort to deal with the larger problem of terrorism. However, given the lack of a generally accepted notion of what exactly constitutes "terrorism", the reference is somewhat obscure. In fact, it seems that the proposal was designed by the USSR partially to indicate that the Convention should only apply in times of peace and should not cover acts of hostage-taking committed during armed conflicts, including those conflicts involving national liberation movements, since such acts were not, in that State's view, "manifestations of international terrorism". According to the representative of the USSR to the Hostages Committee, acts committed in such situations should be covered solely by the laws of armed conflict.[14]

However, many delegations to the Hostages Committee objected to this proposal, mainly, it appears (at least from the record), on the ground that they did not want to commit themselves to one preambular paragraph before the remaining paragraphs were drafted.[15] According to Verwey, when the issue was considered by the Sixth Committee Working Group, this language was included as part of the larger compromise.[16] Despite the reference to international terrorism, however, as noted below, the terms and drafting history of Article 1 and Article 12 make it abundantly clear that this Convention applies in times of peace or war, whether the act is political in nature or motivated by greed, unless an equal obligation to extradite or prosecute is imposed by the laws of armed conflict.[17] Nevertheless, this language properly ties this Convention into the larger struggle against international terrorism, which is, manifestly, the primary purpose of this Convention.

---

[13] See UN Doc A/AC.188/WG.II/ CRP.13, in Third Report of the Hostages Committee, p. 21, para. 87.

[14] See UN Doc A/AC.188/SR.33, p. 3, paras. 7-9; UN Doc A/AC.188/SR.35, p. 2, para. 2. The USSR also seemed to want to emphasize that the Convention should apply only to international acts of hostage-taking, and not to internal offences.

[15] See, e.g., the comments of the representatives of Canada and Japan, respectively, in *id.* at p. 3, para. 10, p. 4, para. 16 & p. 3, para. 12.

[16] Verwey, p. 77. Two delegations, however, continued to object to this paragraph, particularly to the reference to "manifestations of international terrorism". See UN GAOR, 34th Sess., C.6 (53rd mtg.), p. 7, para. 17, UN Doc A/C.6/34/SR.53 (1979).

[17] See generally p. 78 (note 3 and accompanying text in the commentary on Article 1); pp. 266-272 (notes 12-37 and accompanying text in the commentary on Article 12). In light of these Articles, the door is no longer open to any argument that the reference in this paragraph to international terrorism indicates that the Convention cannot be applicable to struggles for national liberation on the ground that the activities of such groups cannot be considered to be terrorism.

Article 1

THE OFFENCES OF HOSTAGE-TAKING, ATTEMPT AND PARTICIPATION*

1. Any person who seizes or detains and threatens to kill, to injure or to continue to detain another person (hereinafter referred to as the "hostage") in order to compel a third party, namely, a State, an international intergovernmental organization, a natural or juridical person, or a group of persons, to do or abstain from doing any act as an explicit or implicit condition for the release of the hostage commits the offence of taking of hostages ("hostage-taking") within the meaning of this Convention.

2. Any person who:
 (a) attempts to commit an act of hostage-taking, or
 (b) participates as an accomplice of anyone who commits or attempts to commit an act of hostage-taking
likewise commits an offence for the purposes of this Convention.

1. INTRODUCTION

This Article sets forth the elements of the offence of hostage-taking and establishes that both an attempt to commit an act of hostage-taking and participation in an act, or attempted act, of hostage-taking are also offences under the Convention. Pursuant to Article 2, Parties must make these offences punishable under their domestic laws. Although all States may be presumed to have offences under their domestic laws which would cover the offence of hostage-taking as here defined, e.g., kidnapping, false imprisonment and unlawful detention,[1] this Article provides a uniform definition of a discrete offence, the essential elements of which must be covered by the domestic laws of all Parties. It should be noted that this Convention is not concerned with all acts of abduction or kidnapping which have an

---

* Captions identifying the subject matter of each article are supplied by the author and are not part of the official text of the Hostages Convention.

[1] See, e.g., Swedish Penal Code, Chap. 4, §1, which provides that a person is guilty of the offence of kidnapping if he "seizes and carries away or confines . . . [a] person with the intent of injuring him in body or health or forcing him into service, or to practise extortion". (English translation by the National Council for Crime Prevention, Stockholm, 1984.) Under English law there exists the offence of false imprisonment, which consists of the restraint of a victim's freedom of movement from a particular place; an aggravated form of the offence is kidnapping, which consists of the stealing and carrying away or secreting of the person. See Smith & Hogan, *Criminal Law* 381-82, 388 (5th ed., 1983). The offence of hostage-taking seemingly fits under these provisions.

international dimension; this Article is drafted in such a way as to include only those offences which are directed towards compelling some act or forbearance from a third party.² It should also be noted that although the Convention is clearly aimed at the taking of hostages in political acts of terrorism, the definition contained in this Article is not restricted to such activity. Rather, the Convention may also cover the taking of hostages for private gain with no political element.³

Except for various drafting changes, noted where relevant, this Article is very similar to the corresponding provision in the FRG draft.⁴ The interrelated questions of the definition of hostage-taking and the scope of this Convention, however, were the most hotly debated and time consuming issues faced by the draftsmen. While most of the debate centred around the scope of the Convention, particularly whether or not it should cover acts of hostage-taking committed by national liberation movements (and acts committed

---

² This also appears to be the position under the 1949 Geneva Conventions on the laws of armed conflict and 1977 Additional Protocols thereto. See citations at p. 263 (note 1 in the commentary on Article 12). As noted in detail in the commentary on Article 12, the Geneva instruments contain various prohibitions against the taking of hostages. While "hostage-taking" is not defined anywhere in those instruments, the official commentaries thereto shed some light on the meaning of the term. The commentary to Article 147 of the Civilians Convention states that: "Hostages might be considered as persons illegally deprived of their liberty . . . there is an additional feature, i.e., the threat either to prolong the hostage's detention or to put him to death." See Pictet (ed.), *Commentary to the Geneva Convention Relative to the Protection of Civilian Persons in Time of War* 600 (1958). The commentary to Article 34 notes that the word "hostage" has been given various meanings, is not easy to define, and should, in the spirit of the Convention, be understood in the widest possible sense; however, it states, "[g]enerally speaking, hostages are nationals of a belligerent State who of their own free will or through compulsion are in the hands of the enemy and are answerable with their freedom or their life for the execution of his orders and the security of his armed forces." In its modern form, the commentary continues, hostage-taking is a means of preventing breaches of the law and sabotage. Examples given are, *inter alia*, the taking of hostages by an Occupying Power from amongst prominent persons in a city to prevent disorder or attacks on occupation troops and the taking of hostages by such a power in order to obtain the delivery of foodstuffs and supplies. *Id.* at pp. 229-230. These examples all contain an element of compulsion directed towards a third party. A similar definition is contained in the commentary to the 1977 Additional Protocols. See Sandoz, Swinarski & Zimmermann (eds.), *Commentary on the Additional Protocols of 8 June 1977 to the Geneva Conventions of 12 August 1949* 874 & 1375 (1987). See also *In re List*, 15 Annual Digest and Reports of Public International Law Cases 632, 642 (US Military Tribunal at Nuremberg, 1948), wherein the court stated that "[f]or the purposes of this opinion the term 'hostage' will be considered as [meaning] those persons of the civilian population who are taken into custody for the purpose of guaranteeing with their lives the good conduct of the population of the community from which they are taken".

³ This is also the case with respect to the implementing legislation of various States. See the UK Taking of Hostages Act 1982, §1; 18 USC §1203(a). See also the comments of the UK Under-Secretary of State, Foreign and Commonwealth Office, in the House of Commons debate on the UK implementing legislation, H.C. Debs., Vol. 25, 11 June 1982, col. 57; comments of the representative of the Justice Department, in US Senate, Committee on the Judiciary, *Hearings before the Subcommittee on Security and Terrorism on*, inter alia, *S. 2624, Act for the Prevention and Punishment of the Crime of Hostage-taking*, 98th Cong., 2d Sess., p. 48 (1984).

⁴ FRG draft, Art. 1.

during armed conflicts generally), there was also considerable debate over the definition itself, resulting from the efforts of many developing States to create exceptions based on the motives of the hostage-takers and to focus attention on other problems such as colonialism, foreign occupation, etc.[5] In the end, however, no exceptions were provided for in this Article, and it maintained its original focus.

This Article corresponds to Article 1 of the Hague Convention, Article 2 of the Montreal Convention, Article 2 of the Montreal Protocol, Article 2 of the New York Convention, Article 3 of the Rome Convention and Article 2 of the Rome Protocol.[6] All of the other instruments similarly provide that attempt and participation are offences thereunder.

2. INTERPRETATION

PARAGRAPH 1: THE DEFINITION OF THE OFFENCE OF HOSTAGE-TAKING

Paragraph 1 lists the acts necessary for the commission of the offence of hostage-taking. These are 1) the seizure or detention of a hostage; and 2) a threat to kill, injure or continue the detention. These acts must be committed in order to compel a third party to behave in a certain way.[7]

"Any person who . . ."

The words "Any person" make it clear that this Convention applies regardless of the identity of, or cause espoused by, the offender. They also make it clear that the Convention is directed towards individual liability, rather than State action. This is not to say, however, that the Convention does not apply to acts committed by a person acting at the

---

[5] See pp. 62-63 (notes 220-223 in Part I); pp. 266-268 (notes 12-17 in the commentary on Article 12).

[6] The corresponding provisions of the Hague, Montreal and Rome Conventions and Protocols similarly describe in some detail the proscribed conduct, while Article 2 of the New York Convention differs slightly in that it simply lists certain offences by name, e.g., murder and kidnapping.

[7] It may be noted that the corresponding provisions of the Montreal Convention and Protocol, the New York Convention and the Rome Convention and Protocol provide that an offence is committed only if the acts are committed intentionally. However, as with the offence of hijacking as defined in the Hague Convention, no such specific requirement was necessary in this instrument since the proscribed acts could hardly be committed in anything but an intentional manner. Moreover, all the other anti-terrorism instruments provide that an offence is committed only if the actions are done "unlawfully". In this case, it may be assumed that the Convention is concerned with unlawful conduct. See generally Shubber, pp. 211-212.

behest of a State. No exception for State agents can be implied from this wording. Indeed, the draftsmen made it clear that this definition includes acts by such persons. During the first session of the Hostages Committee, the representative of the FRG stated that in his opinion the Convention covers "the case of a person who, acting on behalf of a public institution or State, committed an offence within the terms of the convention".[8] Similarly, during the second session of the Hostages Committee, the Chairman noted that individual responsibility would arise if a government official of any State committed an act of hostage-taking.[9] This was not the subject of further debate on record and it may be assumed that the words "Any person", unconditional as they stand, cover acts committed by State agents as well as those committed by private persons.

". . . seizes or detains . . ."

The seizure or detention of another person constitutes the first act necessary to commit the offence of hostage-taking. The variety of ways in which this seizure and/or detention may be carried out seems almost limitless and would include, for example, detention inside the victim's home, abduction in the street with subsequent detention elsewhere, and, overlapping with the Hague Convention, seizure and detention in an aircraft hijacking.[10]

The words "detain" and, particularly, "seize" imply the use of force, although the Article does not specifically provide that the seizure or detention must be effected by force. In fact, the Article makes no reference to the manner of seizure or detention. By way of contrast, Article 1 of the Hague Convention prohibits seizure of an aircraft "by

---

[8] First Report of the Hostages Committee, p. 64, para. 21. This was in response to a comment by the Mexican representative that "responsibility for hostage-taking in many cases rested with an authority for which the individual was merely acting as agent". He further stated that although it was implicit that agents of an authority were also prohibited from taking hostages, it might be useful to make a specific reference to such a case. *Id.* at p. 63, para. 18.

The coverage of acts of hostage-taking by individuals acting pursuant to the authority of a State is consistent with the rules under the Geneva instruments. In fact, although those instruments clearly provide for individual liability, the problem faced in armed conflicts is with "hostages taken by an authority — and not by individuals". See *Commentary to the Protocols*, note 2, *supra*, at p. 874.

[9] Second Report of the Hostages Committee, p. 58, para. 5. This statement arose in the context of the report of the Chairman that, while many States wanted the Convention to cover acts committed by States, others maintained that hostage-taking was a matter of individual responsibility, "a concept established and enhanced by international law since the Second World War". *Id.*

[10] The French delegation to the Hostages Committee submitted a proposal that would have required the detention to be in a "secret place". UN Doc A/AC.188/L.13, in First Report of the Hostages Committee, p. 113. However, as the UK representative pointed out, there are cases of hostage-taking where the place of detention is not secret. Second Report of the Hostages Committee, p. 55, para. 57.

force or threat thereof, or by any other form of intimidation". During the Sixth Committee deliberations on the present Convention, the representative of Austria stated that he would have preferred Article 1 to include a reference to the means by which the act was committed, e.g., use of force, threat of force, etc., although he did not insist on the inclusion of such a reference.[11] It would seem that the vast majority of cases of seizure and detention of hostages will result from the use of force;[12] however, the absence of such a requirement suggests that, similar to the Hague Convention, the threat of force or other means of intimidation, e.g., blackmail, or indeed any other method used to effect the seizure or detention, would suffice to bring the conduct within the scope of this Convention.[13] As the UK Under-Secretary of State for Foreign and Commonwealth Affairs stated in the House of Commons debate concerning the UK implementing legislation, the relevant consideration is not how the detention came about, but whether it in fact happened.[14]

It is worth noting that the use of both the word "seizes" and the word "detains" is essentially tautologous. It is difficult to discern how a seizure, coupled with a threat, could be seen as anything other than a detention, no matter how short the duration. This fact is recognized in the UK implementing legislation which uses only the word "detains", and contains no mention of a seizure.[15] The Under-Secretary of State for Foreign and Commonwealth Affairs explained in the House of Commons debate on the UK legislation that use of the word "seizes" would have added nothing to the word "detains" within the context and purpose of the bill. He stated that if there is no detention, there is no offence of hostage-taking and that, therefore, the seizure must amount to a detention for an offence to be committed under the Act. He explained away the use of both "seizes" and "detains" in the

---

[11] UN GAOR, 34th Sess., C.6 (14th mtg.), p. 5, para. 19, UN Doc A/C.6/34/SR.14 (1979).

[12] See, e.g., the OPEC hostage-taking in 1975 and the Entebbe incident in 1976, pp. 2-3 (notes 10-11 and accompanying text in the Introduction).

[13] See Shubber, p. 213, who reaches the same conclusion.

[14] In the Commons, a proposal had been mooted to add the words "or makes a threat with the purpose of detaining" to the Taking of Hostages Act, thus covering "constructive detention". H.C. Debs., note 3, *supra*, at cols. 565-566. The Under-Secretary of State responded that such an addition was not necessary since a court could determine whether the facts and circumstances amount to a detention; if they do, it "should not matter one whit whether the detention has come about through physical restraint or because of threats or other action which ... have led to [the hostage] remaining in a place in which he would not have chosen to remain but for the action of the accused". *Id.* at cols. 567-568.

[15] Taking of Hostages Act 1982, §(1)(a). Some other jurisdictions, however, have chosen to use both words. See, e.g., the US legislation at 18 USC §1203(a), and the New Zealand legislation, the Crimes (Internationally Protected Persons and Hostages) Act 1980 (No. 44), §8.

Convention as required by the need to be more flexible in a document drafted in many languages.[16]

"... and threatens to kill, to injure or to continue to detain ..."

The threat to kill, to injure or to continue the detention in order to compel a third party is the second of two acts necessary to complete the offence of hostage-taking. A detention or seizure of an individual is not enough, therefore, to commit the offence. If there is no threat, or if the acts of the offenders are not directed towards the compulsion of a third party, no offence within the meaning of this Convention is committed.

The FRG draft provided that the threat must be to kill, to continue the detention or to cause "severe" injury to the hostage.[17] In the first session of the Hostages Committee, the representative of Canada argued that since the threat of continued detention was considered sufficient to incur criminal liability, it was not necessary to qualify the word "injury" with the word "severe".[18] The FRG representative replied that his delegation might have trouble deleting the word "severe" since in his country's legal system the notion of "injury" without any qualifying adjective would include minor forms of physical harm.[19] The Sixth Committee Working Group deleted the word "severe" from the draft instrument, although it is not clear from the record why.[20] Deletion of the word "severe" may have resulted from a lack of consensus as to a proper definition of the word[21] or from agreement with the Canadian point of view. In any event, it may be assumed that the injury threatened does not have to be severe for the Convention to apply (although it is unlikely that a hostage-taker would ever threaten injury which is less than "severe").[22]

In a case where the threat is of continued detention, it would seem that the threat of any continued detention, regardless of how short the duration, would be sufficient for the act to fall within the Convention.

The scope of liability for "threats"

The threat to kill, injure or continue the detention is an

---

[16] H.C. Debs., note 3, *supra*, at cols. 565-567.
[17] FRG draft, Art. 1.
[18] First Report of the Hostages Committee, p. 74, para. 2.
[19] *Id*. at p. 92, para. 2.
[20] UN GAOR, 34th Sess., C.6 (53rd mtg.), p. 7, para. 18, UN Doc A/C.6/34/SR.53 (1979).
[21] Cf. pp. 106-107 (note 59 and accompanying text in the commentary on Article 2).
[22] In any event, a threat to injure unless another person does or forbears from doing an act is really also a threat to continue the detention.

indispensable element of the offence of hostage-taking which will normally occur either at the time of or subsequent to the seizure of the hostage. It is worth noting that similar to the Hague Convention, Montreal Convention and Protocol and Rome Convention and Protocol, but unlike the New York Convention, this Convention does not cover the case of a threat to commit the proscribed offence.[23] The delegate of Mexico to the Hostages Committee suggested that the Convention should cover threats, arguing that they "had become a major international problem: potential kidnappers travelled from country to country, extracting ransoms merely by threatening to take hostages".[24] Other delegations disagreed for various reasons, arguing, *inter alia*, that the concept of threat is too "subjective", that it would be difficult to apply the Convention in a case that involved only a threat, and that no such reference was included in the Hague and Montreal Conventions.[25] The proposal does not appear to have been pressed.

The decision to omit coverage of threats to take hostages was probably a wise one. Extending the Convention in that way would have meant that it could be invoked in every case of threatened hostage-taking containing an international element, even where there is no real probability that a hostage-taking will actually take place. Although threats are covered by the New York Convention, the threat of injury to a diplomat or other internationally protected person for the purposes of extortion can be appreciated as a more likely occurrence than a threat to take other persons hostage and one which, moreover, seemingly has more international significance.[26] Even so,

---

[23] Article 2(1)(c) of the New York Convention requires Parties to make punishable threats to commit any of the attacks covered by that instrument. Article 3(2)(c) of the Rome Convention and Article 2(2)(c) of the Rome Protocol also cover certain threats to commit proscribed acts. Article 1 of the Hague Convention does not cover threats to commit the act of hijacking but, as noted above, prohibits the use of the threat of force actually to effect the hijacking.

[24] First Report of the Hostages Committee, p. 77, para. 24. The representative of Denmark agreed that the Convention should cover threats. *Id.* at p. 85, para. 12.

[25] See, e.g., the comments of the Chairman of the Hostages Committee and the representatives of the Netherlands, the US and Italy, *id.* at p. 64, para. 19, p. 65, para. 28, p. 66, para. 36, & p. 78, para. 27, respectively. The FRG representative appeared ambivalent, noting that if other delegations wanted the Convention to cover threats, it would not be outside the Committee's mandate. *Id.* at p. 64, para. 20. One commentator states that the Hostages Convention covers the offence of threats to take hostages. Rosenstock, p. 177. However, this is clearly not the case.

[26] Many members of the ILC expressed the opinion that threats to commit violence against internationally protected persons in an attempt at blackmail, e.g., to extort money or to obtain the release of prisoners, are a very serious form of terrorism which should be covered by the New York Convention. See, e.g., the comments of Commission members Bilge, Thiam, Sette Camara, Ushakov & Reuter, 1972 YBILC, Vol. I, p. 238. In the Sixth Committee debate on the New York Convention, the delegate of Mexico argued that "[t]elephone calls made to threaten the life of a diplomat or his family were not negligible matters and interfered with the normal work of an embassy or mission, thus hampering normal communications between States". UN GAOR, 28th Sess., C.6 (1434th mtg.), para. 30, UN Doc A/C.6/SR.1434 (1973).

inclusion of threat liability in the New York Convention was the cause of much debate during the drafting of that Convention, with many draftsmen opposed on various grounds, including the prospective problems of proof, the possibility of frivolous threats, the difficulty of deciding what constitutes a threat when no steps towards commission are made, and the "danger of abuse".[27] It would appear that it was best to establish the threshold of liability under the Hostages Convention at the point where steps are actually taken to perpetrate the crime, i.e., attempt. Threats to commit the offence are best left to internal law.

". . . another person . . ."

As regards the identity of the hostage, this Article simply states that it must be "another person". Early in the drafting process, some delegations from developing countries indicated their belief that the Convention should only protect "innocent" hostages, suggesting that leaders or citizens of States considered to be "colonialist" or "racist", etc., may legitimately be taken hostage.[28] These proposals were not adopted, however, and it is clear that the Convention will apply without regard to the identity of the hostage.

". . . in order to compel . . ."

The acts of taking the hostage and uttering the threat must be done for the purpose of compelling a third party to do or abstain from doing a certain act. Although the United Kingdom representative to the Hostages Committee suggested that the definition in Article 1 was somewhat restrictive in so far as it did not take into account situations in which the offender had no desire to compel any person to do or abstain from doing anything, or in which the element of compulsion

---

[27] See, e.g., the comments of ILC members Ramangasoavina and Quentin-Baxter, 1972 YBILC, Vol. I, p. 238. This division of opinion was noted by the ILC in its commentary to that instrument, although it also stated that the concept of threat is "well-defined . . . under most systems of criminal law" and, therefore, needed no detailed explanation. 1972 YBILC, Vol. II, p. 315. Earlier, the Chairman of the ILC noted that the Convention should not apply to every form of threat, e.g., those of an unbalanced individual who had no intention of carrying out the threat, and spoke of limiting coverage of threats to those which were serious enough to bring in the relevant State's machinery for the protection of diplomats. See YBILC, Vol. I, p. 239. The ILC, however, seemed unable to reach agreement on how the concept should be limited. *Id.* at p. 250. In the Sixth Committee, not all draftsmen were in favour of including threats in the New York Convention. See, e.g., the comments of the representative of Cuba. UN GAOR, 28th Sess., C.6 (1412th mtg.), para. 12, UN Doc A/C.6/SR.1412 (1973). However, a Tunisian proposal to delete the reference to threats was defeated. UN GAOR, 28th Sess., C.6 (1435th mtg.), para. 4, UN Doc A/C.6/SR.1435 (1973).

[28] See p. 62 (note 221 and accompanying text in Part I).

was not clearly identified,[29] no concrete action was suggested or taken in this regard and it must be concluded that the motivation to compel a third party is an indispensable element of the offence. Thus, for example, an abduction, coupled with a threat to kill, is not enough to trigger the mechanisms of the Convention if there is no element of compulsion involved. However, the words "in order to compel" seem to relate to the motivation of the hostage-taker, rather than to any physical acts which he might take. Thus, while the seizure and threat will usually be accompanied or followed by a demand that a third party act in a certain way, there is no actual requirement that a demand be uttered. Thus, if there is a detention and threat, yet no demands, there will still be a hostage-taking if the offender is seeking to compel a third party.[30]

"... a third party, namely, a State, an international intergovernmental organization, a natural or juridical person, or a group of persons ..."

The compulsion must be directed towards a "third party", and the Convention specifically lists these as a "State, an international intergovernmental organization, a natural or juridical person, or a group of persons". Most political acts of hostage-taking are committed in order to obtain concessions from a State; however, this Article makes it clear that the offence of hostage-taking is committed regardless of the identity of the third party. That this listing covers all possible third parties is confirmed by the comments of the Chairman-Rapporteur of the Sixth Committee Working Group who explained that, according to an agreed interpretation, the listing of third parties was intended to be "exhaustive". He also stated that the category of "a group of persons" was added to the original FRG draft article "for the sake of completeness".[31]

It would appear that States also consider that the offence of hostage-taking is committed regardless of the identity of the third party. The US implementing legislation as originally sent to Congress simply prohibited compulsion against a "third party", omitting the

---

[29] Second Report of the Hostages Committee, p. 54, para. 56.

[30] In this connexion it might be noted that many kidnappings and hostage-takings do not involve any demands. One author notes that 54 out of 146 kidnappings and seizures in Western Europe between 1970 and 1982 did not result in demands upon a third party. See Aston, "Political Hostage-Taking in Western Europe", in Gutteridge, *The New Terrorism* 61 & 71 (1986). Incidents wherein demands are not made will not necessarily fall outside the scope of this Convention; however, in such cases the intent to compel will be difficult to discern.

[31] UN GAOR, 34th Sess., C.6 (53rd mtg.), p. 7, para. 18, UN Doc A/C.6/34/SR. 53 (1979).

listing of possible third parties contained in the Convention.[32] A section-by-section analysis of the bill contained in the Presidential message to Congress explained that the omission was intended

> to make it clear that attempts to influence third parties not expressly listed in the definition, such as US state governments and unincorporated local governments, would violate the statute. There is no need to define 'third parties' in the legislation since the phrase speaks for itself and is intended to have the broadest possible meaning.[33]

The Department of Justice added that the wide construction of "third party" is intended to "avoid possible loopholes".[34] Although the statute as finally adopted refers to "third person or a governmental organization",[35] this appears to be a clarification of, rather than a restriction on, the meaning of "third party". The United Kingdom legislation refers to "a State, intergovernmental organisation or person", similarly exhaustive language.[36]

Another issue related to the category of third persons is the scope of the word "international" as used in "international intergovernmental organization". In the Sixth Committee deliberations on the Convention, the representative of the Philippines stated that he favoured the deletion of the word "international", positing that it would exclude intergovernmental organizations at the regional level.[37] After the Sixth Committee Working Group had completed its work on the draft, however, the Chairman-Rapporteur stated that, according to an agreed interpretation, the phrase "international intergovernmental organization" covers "universal, regional and subregional organizations of an intergovernmental character".[38]

---

[32] See *Message from the President Transmitting Four Drafts of Proposed Legislation to Attack the Pressing and Urgent Problem of International Terrorism*, H.R. Doc 98-211, 98th Cong., 2nd Sess., p. 7 (1984).

[33] *Id.* at pp. 7-8.

[34] See *Hearings before the Subcommittee on Security and Terrorism*, note 3, *supra*, at p. 122.

[35] See 18 USC §1203(a).

[36] See Taking of Hostages Act 1982, §1(1)(b). In the UK, the word "person" in an Act "includes a body of persons corporate or unincorporate". Interpretation Act 1978, Schedule 1.

[37] UN GAOR, 34th Sess., C.6 (13th mtg.), p. 20, para. 98, UN Doc A/C.6/34/SR.13 (1979).

[38] UN GAOR, 34th Sess., C.6 (53rd mtg.), p. 7, para. 18, UN Doc A/C.6/34/SR.53 (1979). It may be noted that Article 1 of the FRG draft listed as third parties "international organizations" and "international conferences". However, these did not need to be listed separately inasmuch as they fall under other categories. International organizations of a non-governmental type would fit under the descriptions "juridical person" or "group of persons", while international conferences, if made up of the representatives of States, could fall under the category of "State", and, if made up of private persons, could fall under the category "group of persons".

ARTICLE 1

"... to do or abstain from doing any act ..."

The goal of a hostage-taker may be to compel a third party to take some positive action, e.g., release prisoners as in the Entebbe incident,[39] or, alternatively, to refrain from some activity, e.g., extraditing an accused criminal.[40] This Convention applies to both situations. The words "any act" indicate that this Convention will apply regardless of the nature of the act which must be done or abstained from.

"... as an explicit or implicit condition for the release of the hostage ..."

This phrase was not included in the FRG draft; it was added to paragraph 1 during the third session of the Hostages Committee without any explanation appearing on the record.[41] Most likely, it was added simply to cover situations wherein an offender takes a hostage, utters a threat to kill, injure or continue the detention and demands that an act be done or abstained from, yet never states that the hostage will be released upon compliance with the demand. In such a case, it may normally be assumed that the release of the hostage will be the *quid pro quo* for the third party's action or forbearance (indeed, otherwise there would be little reason for the third party to submit to

---

[39] See pp. 2-3 (note 11 and accompanying text in the Introduction).

[40] Such a situation was recently faced by the FRG. In early 1987, German authorities in Frankfurt arrested Mohammed Ali Hamadeh, a member of Hezbollah, in connexion with the 1985 hijacking of a TWA airliner that resulted in the murder of an American passenger. A few days later, two German businessmen were taken hostage in Beirut, allegedly by a group with ties to the pro-Iranian group Hezbollah, in an attempt to force the release of Hamadeh. Subsequently, Bonn refused a US extradition request made in accordance with the bilateral treaty between those two States, later acknowledging that it did so as a result of threats by the hostage-takers that they would kill the two German hostages. However, in January 1988, the FRG placed on trial Abbas Ali Hamadeh, the brother of Mohammed Hamadeh, on charges relating to the hostage-takings committed in order to secure his brother's release, despite the fact that another German hostage was seized in January 1988, apparently on the orders of a third Hamadeh brother. *International Herald Tribune*, Jan. 27, 1988, p. 5 & Jan. 28, 1988, p. 1. Two of the German hostages have been released and, in April 1988, Abbas Hamadeh was convicted and sentenced to 13 years' imprisonment. Although one of the Germans remained held hostage, in July 1988 the trial of Mohammed Hamadeh on charges of hijacking and murder began. *International Herald Tribune*, July 5, 1988, p. 2 & July 6, 1988, p. 2. The FRG assured the US that Mohammed Hamadeh would be prosecuted to the full extent of the law. 87 Dept St. Bull., No. 2125, p. 85 (1987). In May 1989, Mohammed Hamadeh was convicted of murder, air piracy and other crimes committed in connexion with the hijacking and was sentenced to life imprisonment. The cycle continued, however, in as much as shortly before the Hamadeh verdict three West German relief workers in southern Lebanon were seized, in an apparent effort to pressure the FRG to release Hamadeh. See *The Washington Post*, May 18, 1989, p. A1 & p. A41.

[41] See Third Report of the Hostages Committee, p. 10, para. 33.

the compulsion). This provision makes it clear that the Convention will apply even when the offender makes no express promise to release the hostage upon compliance with the demand.

The words "as an explicit or implicit condition for the release of the hostage" do not seem particularly necessary or helpful in this context.[42] While they do serve to make it clear that the release of the hostage does not have to be explicitly promised in order for the Convention to apply, as just noted where a hostage is seized and a threat and demand are made, it may normally be assumed that submission to the demand is a condition for the release of the hostage. The words "in order to compel" seem to make it clear that the hostage-taker is bargaining for the health, safety and release of the hostage in exchange for the act or forbearance. Because of the qualifying words "as an explicit or implicit condition for the release of the hostage", it appears that the Convention would not apply in a case where the hostage-taker makes it clear that he will never release the hostage, that he fully intends to kill him, but bases the compulsion upon a threat, for example, to brutally torture the hostage before the ultimate killing. However unlikely such a scenario may appear, the phrase "explicit or implicit condition for the release of the hostage" seems an unnecessary limitation of the scope of the definition of hostage-taking.

Indeed, while the legislation adopted by the United States to implement the Convention employs the "explicit or implicit condition" language,[43] the United Kingdom apparently felt it unnecessary or undesirable and did not include the phrase in its legislation. The statute states simply that "A person . . . who . . . (a) detains any person ("the hostage"), and (b) in order to compel a State, international governmental organisation or person to do or abstain from doing any act, threatens to kill, injure or continue to detain the hostage, commits an offence".[44] This appears to be a more flexible approach, and, if employed in this Convention, would have required its application when release of the hostage is neither implicitly or explicitly the *quid pro quo* for the submission of the third party to the compulsion.

". . . commits the offence of taking of hostages (hostage-taking) within the meaning of this Convention."

While this language suggests that all acts of hostage-taking as

---

[42] One commentator approves of the language, stating that it more clearly defines the aims of the hostage-takers, "an important re-emphasis of the element of duress". Rosenne, p. 127.
[43] See 18 USC §1203(a).
[44] Taking of Hostages Act 1982, §(1)(b).

defined by this Article will be offences under this Convention, subsequent provisions place a limitation on this wording. Specifically, pursuant to Article 12, if Parties to this instrument are obliged to extradite or prosecute an alleged offender in a given hostage-taking situation under the 1949 Geneva Conventions on the laws of armed conflict or additional protocols thereto, then this Convention will not apply to that act. Further, pursuant to Article 13, the Convention will not apply to acts of hostage-taking which are essentially of domestic concern.

PARAGRAPH 2: ATTEMPT AND PARTICIPATION AS OFFENCES UNDER THE CONVENTION

Paragraph 2 provides that anyone who attempts to commit hostage-taking or participates in such acts "likewise commits an offence for the purpose of this Convention".

"Any person who: (a) attempts to commit an act of hostage-taking . . ."

In its commentary to the New York Convention, the International Law Commission stated that attempt is a "well-defined" concept under most systems of criminal law and does "not require, therefore, any detailed explanation in the context of the present draft".[45] Because there will be different definitions of attempt in various States, however, the precise nature of liability under this paragraph could differ from State to State. It could in theory transpire that the elements of attempt in a particular case will be satisfied in one jurisdiction but not in another. Since one State will not normally employ the criminal law of another,[46] the possibility exists, for example, that an alleged offender could be tried for attempted hostage-taking in a State other than that in which his conduct took place, and ultimately acquitted, even though his conduct may have constituted attempt under the criminal law of the territorial State and/or of other States Parties. However, it seems that definitions of attempt are essentially similar in most jurisdictions,[47] and it is unlikely

---

[45] 1972 YBILC, Vol. II, p. 315.
[46] See Akehurst, "Jurisdiction in International Law", 46 BYIL 145, 165-66 (1972).
[47] For example, in the UK, Section 1 of the Criminal Attempts Act 1981 provides that a person who, with intent to commit an offence to which the act applies (all offences which, if completed, would be triable in England or Wales with some exceptions not relevant here), "does an act which is more than merely preparatory to the commission of the offence, [is] guilty of attempting to commit the offence". In the US, although there is no comprehensive statutory definition of attempt in federal law (see *US* v. *Heng*
(*continued on p. 90*)

that any steps which come dangerously close to the commission of the offence of hostage-taking will fall outside the scope of any State's definition of the offence of attempt.

The inclusion of attempt liability in this instrument recognizes that those who attempt to commit terrorist acts such as hostage-taking, but who are, for whatever reason, unsuccessful, pose as great a threat to the stability of the international order as those who are successful. It can be appreciated that many terrorist acts are unsuccessful and the thwarted perpetrators may simply keep looking for the right opportunity. Success may be more elusive if the Parties are required to extradite or prosecute those who attempt to take hostages.

". . . or (b) participates as an accomplice of anyone who commits or attempts to commit an act of hostage-taking . . ."

Participation in a hostage-taking or an attempted hostage-taking is also an offence under this Convention.

As with attempt, the ILC stated in its commentary to the New York Convention that participation is a well-known concept in most criminal law systems.[48] During the drafting of this Convention, some light on this subparagraph was shed by the Chairman-Rapporteur of the Sixth Committee Working Group who stated that "according to an agreed interpretation, the concept of participating as an accomplice was intended to cover aiding and abetting, conspiring or otherwise being an accessory".[49] Thus, it is clear that the scope of the phrase "participates as an accomplice" is very wide indeed.

([47] *continued*)
Awkak Roman, 356 F. Supp. 434, 437 (SDNY, 1973), *aff'd* 484 F. 2d 1271 (2d Cir. 1973), *cert. den.* 415 US 978 (1974)), many federal courts have applied the "substantial step" test, i.e., whether the defendant, acting with the kind of culpability required for the commission of the crime which he is charged of attempting, actually engaged in conduct which constitutes a substantial step towards commission of the crime. See *US v. Mandujano*, 499 F. 2d 370, 376 (5th Cir. 1974), *cert. den.* 419 US 1114 (1975); *US v. Jackson*, 560 F. 2d 112, 120, 121 (2d Cir. 1977), *cert. den.* 434 US 941 (1978), *cert. den.* 434 US 1017 (1978). In Sweden, liability for attempt occurs when a person "has begun to commit a crime without bringing it to completion . . . if there had been a danger that the act would lead to the completion of the crime or such danger had been precluded only because of accidental circumstances". See Swedish Penal Code, note 1, *supra*, at Chap. 23, §1. Thus, the UK and US definitions of attempt, at least, are very similar in so far as they both require an intent to commit the underlying crime plus an act in furtherance of the crime which is more than simply preparatory. In Sweden, the definition of attempt is somewhat less refined; however, it is not substantially different from the UK and US models.

[48] 1972 YBILC, Vol. II, p. 315.

[49] UN GAOR, 34th Sess., C.6 (53rd mtg.), p. 7, para. 19, UN Doc A/C.6/34/SR.53 (1979). The only recorded objection to this interpretation came from the representative of Pakistan who stated that he did not think that participation should include conspiracy. UN GAOR, 34th Sess., C.6 (62nd mtg.), p. 2, para. 2, UN Doc A/C.6/34/SR.62 (1979).

As regards the Chairman-Rapporteur's reference to "conspiring", the question arises as to whether his comments can be interpreted as meaning that conspiracy to take hostages is a distinct offence under this Convention, i.e., an offence regardless of whether or not an act of hostage-taking, or attempted hostage-taking, has been committed.[50] It would seem that such an interpretation is strained. Conspiracy is not specifically listed as an offence under this Convention (or under the other anti-terrorism instruments). Moreover, while many or most States generally consider conspiracy to be a distinct offence under their laws,[51] this does not appear to be universally so: in its commentary to the New York Convention, the ILC stated that it did not include as an offence "conspiracy to commit any of the violent acts referred to . . . because of the great differences in its definition under the various systems . . . some systems do not even recognize it as a separate crime".[52] It would seem that if the draftsmen of the Hostages Convention had intended conspiracy to be a distinct offence under the instrument, they would have provided so expressly, as has been done in some other conventions dealing with international offences.[53]

Given the context in which the reference to "conspiring" was made, i.e., in a clarification of the concept of "participating as an accomplice", the better interpretation of the Chairman-Rapporteur's statement is that when an offence of hostage-taking, or attempted hostage-taking, has occurred, those who have acted as conspirators must be considered as accomplices.[54] If a Party's laws on participation are not broad enough to include conspirators as accomplices, those laws must be altered accordingly.

---

[50] One commentator has apparently interpreted the Chairman-Rapporteur's comments in this way. See Rosenne, p. 128.

[51] In the UK, for example, the Criminal Law Act 1977, §1(1) (as amended by the Criminal Attempts Act 1981) provides that "[i]f a person agrees with any other person or persons that a course of conduct shall be pursued which, if the agreement is carried out in accordance with their intentions . . . will necessarily amount to or involve the commission of any offence or offences by one or more of the parties to the agreement . . . he is guilty of conspiracy".

[52] 1972 YBILC, Vol. II, p. 316. Moreover, in the Sixth Committee deliberations on the New York Convention, it was proposed that conspiracy be included in that instrument as an ancillary offence. See the proposal of the Spanish delegation in UN Doc A/C.6/L.913 (1973). While there appeared to be considerable support for the proposal, it was not adopted. See, e.g., the comments of the representatives of Yugoslavia, Uganda, Oman and Pakistan in UN GAOR, 28th Sess., C.6 (1413th mtg.), paras. 8, 25, 45 & 58, respectively, UN Doc A/C.6/SR.1413 (1973).

[53] See, e.g., Art. III(b), 1948 Convention on the Prevention and Punishment of the Crime of Genocide, 78 UNTS 277; Art III(a), 1973 International Convention on the Suppression of the Crime of Apartheid, 1015 UNTS 244.

[54] In the UK, for example, the Accessories and Abettors Act 1861, §8 (as amended by the Criminal Law Act 1977), provides that "[w]hosoever shall aid, abet, counsel or procure the commission of any indictable offence . . . shall be liable to be tried, indicted and punished as a principal offender". Conspiracy to commit an offence constitutes counselling if the offence is actually committed. See Smith & Hogan, *Criminal Law* 121 (1983).

The importance of the Convention's coverage of accomplice liability can hardly be overstated. International acts of terrorism such as hostage-taking very often rely on the assistance, and indeed direction, of sympathetic groups and individuals who do not appear at the scene of the crime but whose criminal culpability is at least as great as that of the perpetrators themselves. Moreover, these accomplices may be residents of and/or present in different States from each other and from the actual perpetrators. The provisions of this Convention can assist States in bringing such participants to justice.

Article 2

ESTABLISHMENT OF PENALTIES FOR CONVENTION OFFENCES

Each State Party shall make the offences set forth in article 1 punishable by appropriate penalties which take into account the grave nature of those offences.

1. INTRODUCTION

While Article 1 sets forth the essential elements of the offence of hostage-taking, it imposes no obligations upon States with respect to that offence. This Article, by way of contrast, imposes a fundamental obligation upon Parties: they must ensure that the offence of hostage-taking, as well as the offences of attempt and participation, are punishable by "appropriate" penalties under their domestic laws. It may be noted, however, that no obligations regarding the *imposition* of penalties are imposed upon States Parties.

This Article corresponds to Article 2 of the Hague Convention, Article 3 of the Montreal Convention, Article 2, paragraph 2, of the New York Convention and Article 5 of the Rome Convention.

The role of municipal law in the suppression and punishment of hostage-taking and other "international crimes"

This is the first of many articles in this Convention which impose obligations upon Parties regarding the suppression and punishment of the offences of hostage-taking, attempted hostage-taking and participation. Other such provisions include Article 5, which requires Parties to establish their jurisdiction over the offences in various circumstances, and Article 8, which requires them to either extradite or submit for prosecution all alleged offenders who appear in their territory. It can thus be seen that the enforcement of the prohibition against hostage-taking, and of the offences listed in the other anti-terrorism conventions, relies entirely upon municipal legal systems. This is the case generally with what may loosely be called "international crimes", i.e., both those offences which by customary international law are considered to be crimes against the law of nations[1] and those

---

[1] Piracy may be the only definite example of such an offence; however, certain war crimes can also probably be included in this category. See generally United Nations
(*continued on p. 94*)

offences which are considered to be so harmful to international order that some or most States have become party to conventions designed to combat them.[2] Although directed against acts committed by individuals, most conventions designed to suppress international crimes impose obligations only upon States; with a few exceptions,[3] as far as these conventions are concerned individuals remain responsible only under domestic law.[4]

There are two, closely related, reasons for this approach to the suppression of international crimes. The first is that the extent of individual liability under international law for criminal offences is unclear. The second is that no judicial (or enforcement) mechanism separate and apart from those in municipal legal systems exists to deal with international offences. Because of this second reason, even if it could be said as a theoretical matter that individuals may be criminally liable under international law, and even if agreement existed as to the offences which could occasion such liability, jurisdiction over

---

([1] *continued*)
Secretariat, *Historical Survey of the Question of International Criminal Jurisdiction* 1, UN Doc A/CN.4/7/Rev. 1 (1949); p. 135 (note 6 and accompanying text in the commentary on Article 5).

[2] In addition to the anti-terrorism instruments, conventions exist, *inter alia*, concerning drug trafficking, counterfeiting, slavery, obscene publications, war crimes, genocide, *apartheid* and torture. See pp. 136-139 (notes 10-21 and accompanying text in the commentary on Article 5). Although various drafts have been advanced (see, e.g., ILA, *Report of the Sixty-First Conference* 257 (1984)), there exists no international criminal code. As suggested in the text, therefore, the term "international crime" is imprecise. One commentator states that it refers to those offences "which endanger the fundamental values of the international community as a whole". Feller, "Jurisdiction over Offences with a Foreign Element", in Bassiouni & Nanda (eds.), *A Treatise on International Criminal Law*, Vol. II, 41 (1973). Bassiouni states that a common crime becomes an international crime when it is committed in more than one State or where no State has exclusive national jurisdiction or if it affects citizens of more than one State or an internationally protected person or object. See Bassiouni, "Methodological Options for International Legal Control of Terrorism", in Bassiouni (ed.), *International Terrorism and Political Crimes* 487 (1975). Another source states simply that a "modern use" of the term international crime refers to an offence over which there is multistate jurisdiction. Parry & Grant, *et al.*, *Encyclopaedic Dictionary of International Law* 79-80 (1986). Finally, one writer maintains that the term should be given a narrow construction, *inter alia*, limited to those offences which give rise to direct individual liability under international law without the intermediate provisions of municipal law. See Jescheck, "International Crimes", in Bernhard (ed.), *Encyclopedia of Public International Law*, Vol. 8, 332, 333 (1985). As employed in this discussion, the term international crime refers both to those offences which are considered to be against the law of nations under customary international law and to those offences the prevention and punishment of which have been the subject of multilateral conventions.

[3] See pp. 96-97 (notes 16 & 17 and accompanying text).

[4] The process by which the suppression and punishment of international crimes rely upon municipal law has been called "adjective international criminal law". This concept is in contrast to "substantive international criminal law", which would involve an international criminal code with supporting structures for implementation and enforcement. See Bassiouni, note 2, *supra*, at p. 490.

international crimes would still remain with individual States. To fully appreciate the fact that the suppression of terrorism does and will continue, at least in the foreseeable future, to rely on municipal law, some attention should be paid to these issues.

Turning first to the issue of individual liability under international law, one aspect of what one author terms the "[d]octrinal debates of almost bitter intensity" over whether the individual is a subject of international law[5] is the question of whether an individual can be held directly responsible under international law for criminal offences, or whether, alternatively, individuals can only be liable under municipal law which has incorporated international law.[6] The classic example of an international offence is piracy, and many commentators have argued that customary international law does not merely allow, or require, States to exercise universal jurisdiction over pirates, but that customary law also imposes direct responsibility upon individuals who commit that offence.[7] Whatever the position may be with respect to piracy, developments since World War II have made it difficult to sustain the argument that individuals can never be directly criminally responsible under international law. The Charter of the International Military Tribunal at Nuremberg (and of its counterpart in the far east, the Tokyo Tribunal) made it clear that individuals would be liable for the offences of crimes against the peace, war crimes and crimes

---

[5] Briggs, "The Position of Individuals in International Law", 62 US Naval War College International Law Studies 415, 417 (1980).

[6] Sir Hersch Lauterpacht, for example, believed that individuals were liable under international law for international criminal offences, and "not only in exceptional situations as . . . pirates or war criminals . . ." Oppenheim, *International Law*, Vol. I, 357 n.1 (8th ed., H. Lauterpacht, ed., 1955). Schwarzenberger, however, has doubted whether it could be said that there are rules of customary international law which prescribe offences in which direct individual liability under international law could be imputed to individuals. Schwarzenberger, "The Problem of an International Criminal Law", 13 Current Legal Problems 263 (1960). Generally, one with a "dualist" conception of international law would argue that an individual can only be liable for an international offence once that offence has been incorporated into municipal law, while a "monist" would believe that an individual can be directly liable under international law for an international offence, regardless of the content of municipal law. For summaries of these positions, see Stone & Woetzel (eds.), *Toward a Feasible International Criminal Court* 87-95 (1970); Sinha, "The Position of the Individual in an International Criminal Law", in Bassiouni & Nanda, note 2, *supra*, Vol. I, pp. 126-132.

[7] See, e.g., Kelsen, *Peace Through Law* 76 (1944), wherein it is stated that the rule that States are allowed to seize and punish pirates regardless of the venue of the offence is a rule "imposing a legal duty directly upon individuals and establishing individual responsibility." Moreover, "[t]he fact that the specification of the punishment is left to national law, and the trial of the pirate to national courts, does not deprive the delict and the sanction of their international character." On the other hand, Briggs argued that in cases of piracy and "other so-called 'offences against the law of nations', the situation is usually one in which national courts try individuals for offences against national legislation which may be labelled 'offences against the law of nations'". Briggs, *The Law of Nations* 96 (2nd ed., 1953).

against humanity.[8] In its Judgment, the Nuremberg Tribunal stated that "crimes against international law are committed by men, not by abstract entities, and only by punishing individuals who commit such crimes can the provisions of international law be enforced".[9] Accordingly, the Tribunal held the defendants individually liable for their criminal offences, and did so employing, for the first time, international law as the controlling substantive law.[10]

While the decision of a tribunal established by a Charter which had only 23 Parties[11] may not, by itself, be considered overwhelming evidence that a principle of international law exists that individuals can be liable under that system for criminal acts, subsequent developments indicate that the international community of States is ready to accept such a principle. In 1946, the entire General Assembly of the UN affirmed the Nuremberg Charter and Judgment, and instructed the newly formed Committee for the Progressive Development of International Law and its Codification to "treat as a matter of primary importance plans for the formulation, in the context of a general codification of offences against the peace and security of mankind, or of an International Criminal Code, of the principles" recognized in that Charter and Judgment.[12] That committee's successor, the ILC, did so in 1950, the first principle being that "any person who commits an act which constitutes a crime under international law is responsible therefor and liable to punishment".[13] Also in 1946, the General Assembly adopted Resolution 96(I) which states that genocide is a crime "under international law".[14] In 1948, it adopted Resolution 260(III),[15] annexed to which is the Convention on the

---

[8] See Art. 6, 1945 London Agreement for the Prosecution and Punishment of the Major War Criminals of the European Axis Powers and Charter of the International Military Tribunal, 82 UNTS 279, *reprinted in* 39 AJIL Supp. 258 (1945); Article 5, Special Proclamation of the Supreme Commander for the Allied Powers of 19 January 1946, *reprinted in* 14 Dep't St. Bull. 361 (1946).

[9] 41 AJIL 172, 220-221 (1947). The tribunal also stated: "That international law imposes duties and liabilities upon individuals as well as upon States has long been recognized."

[10] See generally Baxter, "The Municipal and International Law Basis of Jurisdiction over War Crimes", 28 BYIL 385-386 (1951). One commentator states that the Nuremberg judgment "discarded any pretense" that international law applies only to States. See Janis, "Individuals as Subjects of International Law" 17 Cor. Int'l L. J. 61, 65 (1984).

[11] See Bowman & Harris, *Multilateral Treaties Index and Current Status* 115 (1984).

[12] GA Res. 95 (I) of 11 December 1946, UN Doc A/64/Add. 1, p. 188 (1947).

[13] 1950 YBILC, Vol. II, pp. 374-78. Under the second principle, the fact that municipal law does not impose a penalty for such a crime does not relieve an individual from liability under international law. *Id.* The ILC decided that its task was only to formulate the principles and not to decide their status under international law, and it submitted the text of the principles without recommendation. See 1949 YBILC, Vol. I, p. 282; 1950 YBILC, Vol. II, p. 374.

[14] UN Doc A/64/Add. 1, pp. 188-89 (1947).

[15] UN Doc A/810, pp. 174-77 (1949).

Prevention and Punishment of the Crime of Genocide which "confirm[s]" that genocide is a crime under international law and imposes obligations upon States regarding its prevention and punishment.[16] Similarly, the 1973 Convention on the Suppression and Punishment of the Crime of Apartheid declares that offence to be a "crime against humanity", resulting in "[i]nternational criminal responsibility".[17]

Further evidence that the international community is ready to accept the principle of individual criminal liability under international law is the fact that since 1949 the ILC has been preparing a "Draft Code of Offences Against the Peace and Security of Mankind", an instrument which is intended to codify the Nuremberg principles.[18] Progress on the code of offences has been held up for a number of reasons,[19] and, although the ILC has returned to work on the code after a long absence,[20] it appears that it will be some time before it is completed and adopted.[21] However, it is significant that the various

[16] Arts. I & V-VII, 78 UNTS 277.

[17] Arts. I & III, 1015 UNTS 244. It may be noted that while the conventions on genocide and *apartheid* purport to give rise to individual liability under international law, enforcement of the prohibitions contained therein still relies on municipal law. Both instruments provide that an international penal tribunal could have jurisdiction over the offences (Articles VI & V respectively); however, no such tribunal currently exists. See pp. 99-100 (notes 29-35 and accompanying text).

[18] In Resolution 177 (II) of 21 November 1947, UN Doc A/519, pp. 111-12 (1948), the General Assembly requested the ILC to prepare a draft code of offences against the peace and security of mankind, "indicating clearly the place to be accorded to the principles" recognized in the Charter and Judgment of the Nuremberg Tribunal. The first draft of the code was submitted to the General Assembly in 1951, and included the following offences: aggression, the incursion of armed bands into the territory of a State with a political purpose, the undertaking or encouragement of organized activities calculated to foment civil strife or terrorist activities in another State, violations of treaties designed to ensure international peace and security, forcible annexation of territory, acts with intent to destroy a national, ethnic or religious group, inhuman acts against any civilian population, and acts against the laws or customs of war. 1951 YBILC, Vol. II, pp. 134-137.

[19] The biggest obstacle was the difficulty in the General Assembly of formulating a generally acceptable definition of aggression, one of the primary offences to be included in the draft code. In light of this problem, the General Assembly decided to defer consideration of the code by the ILC pending the formulation of such a definition. See GA Res 897 (IX) of 4 December 1954, UN GAOR, 9th Sess., Supp. 21, p. 50, UN Doc A/2890 (1955); GA Res 1186 (XXI) of 11 December 1957, UN GAOR, 12th Sess., Supp. 18, pp. 51-52, UN Doc A/3805 (1958). See generally, Ferencz, "Draft Code of Offences Against the Peace and Security of Mankind", 75 AJIL 674 (1981).

[20] The General Assembly agreed upon a definition of aggression in 1974. See GA Res 3314 (XXIX) of 14 December 1974, UN GAOR, 29th Sess., Supp. 31, p. 142, UN Doc A/9631 (1975). Consideration of the draft code was reinstated to the ILC's agenda pursuant to GA Res 36/106 of 10 December 1981, UN GAOR, 36th Sess., Supp. 51, p. 239, UN Doc A/36/51 (1982).

[21] See Sinclair, *The International Law Commission* 104 (1987), who notes that, at the time of publication of his book, the ILC was still at a "very early stage" of its work regarding the draft code, that the topic is "highly political" and that certain basic issues were not yet decided. There was as yet no agreement, *inter alia*, on the precise offences to be included, on the meaning of "crimes against humanity", on the scope of "war crimes" and of complicity under the code, and on the means of implementing the instrument.

(*continued on p. 98*)

drafts of the code have always provided for direct individual criminal liability under international law.[22]

It can thus probably be said that there is at least an emerging consensus on the principle of individual criminal liability under international law.[23] However, while the strongest cases can probably be made with respect to piracy, the offences covered by the Nuremberg Charter, genocide and *apartheid*, it is uncertain as to which offences can give rise to such liability. One of the continuing obstacles to completion of the Code of Offences Against the Peace and Security of Mankind seems to be the absence of agreement regarding the precise offences which should be included therein.[24] But even if that code is ultimately completed and adopted, the question of which crimes can occasion individual liability under international law will not be settled. That code will not purport to include all such crimes; it will simply list those offences which are considered to be against the "peace and security of mankind". Reports of the ILC since it resumed work on the subject indicate that there is general agreement that only the most serious international crimes should be covered by the code,[25] and that the offence of piracy, for example, will not be included.[26] The

---

([21] *continued*)
Id. at pp. 166-167. See also 1986 YBILC, Vol. II, Part 2, at pp. 43 *et seq*. As at the end of 1987, the ILC had provisionally adopted four draft articles. See "Report of the International Law Commission on the Work of its Thirty-ninth Session", UN GAOR, 42nd Sess., Supp. 10, p. 11, UN Doc A/42/10 (1987). Moreover, it seems that some States, including Western States, are less than enthusiastic about the adoption of such a code. See Ferencz, note 19, *supra*, at pp. 675-77; Jescheck, note 2, *supra*, at p. 334.

[22] Article 1 of the 1951 draft states that the listed offences "are crimes under international law, for which the responsible individuals shall be punishable". See 1951 YBILC, Vol. II, pp. 134-35. See also, Art. 1, 1954 YBILC, Vol. II, p. 150; Arts. 1-3, 1986 YBILC, Vol. II, Part 2, p. 41, n. 105. A review of the ILC's reports indicates no controversy over the issue of individual liability under international law; the only controversy *ratione personae* appears to relate to whether the draft code should apply to States and other entities as well as to individuals. See 1950 YBILC, Vol. II, p. 260. However, in 1984, the ILC decided to limit the code to criminal liability of individuals, without prejudice to subsequent consideration of extending it to States. See 1984 YBILC, Vol. II, Part 2, p. 17.

[23] It is difficult to be more definite than this since there is very little "hard" law on the subject other than the Nuremberg Judgment. As Briggs noted, the Nuremberg principles have not been formally adopted by the General Assembly, the draft code of offences is far from complete, and there is no international tribunal with jurisdiction over criminal offenders. See Briggs, note 5, *supra*, at p. 424.

[24] See Sinclair, note 21, *supra*, at p. 166; 1986 YBILC, Vol. II, Part 2, p. 46.

[25] See 1983 YBILC, Vol. II, Part 2, p. 16; 1986 YBILC, Vol. II, Part 2, p. 40. In 1984 the ILC decided to include in its revised draft the offences contained in the first drafts, with modifications of form and substance taking into account developments in international law. Moreover, there is a "trend" in favour of including such offences as colonialism, *apartheid* and, perhaps, damage to the environment and economic aggression if appropriate formulations can be found. Other possibilities include the use of nuclear weapons and mercenarism. See 1984 YBILC, Vol. II, Part 2, p. 17.

[26] *Id.* Although recognizing that piracy is an international crime under customary international law, the ILC states that it is doubtful whether in present times the offence constitutes a threat to the peace and security of mankind. For similar reasons, sentiment appears to be against the inclusion of the offence of drug trafficking. *Id.*

exclusion of certain crimes of international concern will not necessarily indicate that their commission cannot occasion individual liability under international law, but it would leave that question unsettled.

It is worth noting in the context of this study that the various drafts of the code have always included terrorism as an offence, and the most recent drafts specifically include as aspects of terrorism such offences as hostage-taking and hijacking.[27] It is also worth noting that the International Law Association has similarly taken the position that acts of international terrorism, including acts of hostage-taking, hijacking, etc., "no less than crimes against humanity", are violations of international law by individuals.[28]

But even if it can be said that terrorist or other offences may result in direct individual responsibility under international law, of more practical importance is the fact that there exists no international judicial body which can take jurisdiction over international crimes. The Nuremberg and Tokyo tribunals were able to impose international liability only because they were, in a sense, international courts, made up of judges from the victorious powers. There exists no permanent international criminal tribunal which could perform a similar function. It is thus really a theoretical question whether individuals who commit certain offences are liable under international law since States have the exclusive right to try and punish offenders.

The case for an international criminal court has been argued in many quarters,[29] and efforts have been made by intergovernmental organizations to draft a statute for such a court. In 1937, the League of Nations promulgated a Convention on the Establishment of an International Criminal Court which would have had jurisdiction in some cases over the offences set forth in the League's Terrorism Convention.[30] However, neither Convention ever came into force.[31] The UN drafted statutes for an international criminal court in the

---

[27] See Art. 2(6), 1951 YBILC, Vol. II, pp. 135-36; Art. 4(D), 1985 YBILC, Vol. II, Part 2, p. 17 & n.50; Art. 11(4), 1986 YBILC, Vol. II, Part 2, p. 43 n.105.
[28] ILA Report, note 2, *supra*, at p. 7.
[29] See e.g., Stone & Woetzel, note 6, *supra*; Ferencz, *An International Criminal Court: A Step Towards World Peace*, 2 Vols. (1980).
[30] See LN Doc C.547(I).M.384(I).1937.V (1937), *reprinted in* Hudson (ed.), *International Legislation*, Vol. VII, 878 (1941). On the terms of the League's Terrorism Convention, see pp. 28-29 (notes 76-78 and accompanying text in Part I). Article 2 of the Convention on the Establishment of an International Criminal Court provided that each State Party was entitled, but not required, to commit to the court a person accused of one of the crimes contained in the Terrorism Convention instead of prosecuting that person itself or instead of extraditing him to another State. Other provisions dealt in detail with the composition and operation of the court.
[31] See p. 29 (note 79 and accompanying text in Part I).

1950s,[32] but these were not adopted and the issue seems now to be dormant.[33] The ILC is awaiting guidance from the General Assembly regarding whether its mandate concerning the drafting of the Code of Offences Against the Peace and Security of Mankind extends to the drafting of a statute establishing a competent jurisdiction.[34] However, it appears to be leaning towards including in the draft code a provision creating universal jurisdiction over the offences, based on the principle *aut dedere aut judicare*.[35]

---

[32] See Report of the Committee on International Criminal Jurisdiction, UN GAOR, 7th Sess., Supp. 11, UN Doc A/2136 (1952); Report of the 1953 Committee on International Criminal Jurisdiction, UN GAOR, 9th Sess., Supp. 12, UN Doc A/2645 (1954). The UN efforts in this regard began in 1948 when the General Assembly requested the ILC to study the "desirability and possibility of establishing an international judicial organ for the trial of persons charged with genocide or other crimes over which jurisdiction will be conferred upon that organ by international conventions". See GA Res 260B (III), UN Doc A/810, pp. 177-78 (1949). See also Finch, "Draft Statute for an International Criminal Court", 46 AJIL 89 (1952); Liang, "The Establishment of an International Criminal Jurisdiction", 47 AJIL 638 (1953). For historical studies of UN and earlier efforts to draft a statute for such a court, see Stone & Woetzel, note 6, *supra*, at pp. 160-207; Ferencz, note 29, *supra*; "Historical Survey", note 1, *supra*; UN GAOR, 12th Sess., Annexes (Agenda Item 56), UN Doc A/3649 (1959). It might be noted that various non-intergovernmental organizations have also promulgated statutes for such a court. See, e.g., First International Criminal Law Conference, *The Establishment of an International Criminal Court* (1971); ILA Report, note 2, *supra*, at pp. 257-267.

[33] There was a good deal of disagreement in the ILC and the Sixth Committee regarding both the desirability and the feasibility of an international criminal court. See Ferencz, note 29, *supra*, at pp. 23-39. It was decided in 1954, and again in 1957, to defer consideration of the question until such time as the General Assembly again took up the issue of a draft code of offences against the peace and security of mankind. See GA Res 898 (IX) of 14 December 1954, UN GAOR, 9th Sess., Supp. 21, p. 50, UN Doc A/2890 (1955); GA Res 1187 (XII) of 11 December 1957, UN GAOR, 12th Sess., Supp. 18, p. 51, UN Doc A/3805 (1958). The ILC has not yet returned to this matter. The obstacles to the formation of such a court remain formidable. Powerful States, in particular, will be reluctant to cede the sovereignty necessary to allow such a court to function (and expose their leaders to the jurisdiction of the court), and, in any event, doubts exist as to the efficacy of such a court in the absence of an international executive power which could enforce the court's jurisdiction. See generally Stone & Woetzel, note 6, *supra*, at pp. 142 & 149; Dautricourt, "The International Criminal Court: The Concept of International Criminal Jurisdiction — Definition and Limitation of the Subject", in Bassiouni & Nanda, note 2, *supra*, Vol. I, 652.

Of particular relevance to international terrorism, it may be noted that in June 1988 the International Air Transport Association proposed to ICAO both the establishment of an international court with jurisdiction to try captured aircraft hijackers and the establishment of an international detention centre for convicted hijackers. See "Internationalizing the Response" (Paper Submitted to ICAO Aviation Security Panel, June 1988). However, there is no reason to expect that such proposals will soon be embraced by States.

[34] See 1983 YBILC, Vol. II, Part 2, p. 16; *Report on the Thirty-Ninth Session*, note 21, *supra*, at p. 32.

[35] One recent draft states that an offence against the peace and security of mankind is a "universal offence" with respect to which every State has the duty *aut dedere aut judicare*. It also states, however, that this provision does "not prejudice the question of the existence of an international criminal jurisdiction". See Art. 4, 1986 YBILC, Vol. II, p. 41 n.105. The 1987 report of the ILC indicates that the Commission is still far from consensus on this issue. See *Report on the Thirty-Ninth Session*, note 21, *supra*, at pp. 11-13.

Given the above state of affairs, the Hostages Convention and its predecessors do not address the issue of individual liability under international law for the specified offences. Whatever may be the status of individuals under international law, it is not affected by these instruments. Moreover, whatever the merit of creating an international criminal court, enforcement of international criminal law will for some time continue to rely on municipal law.

2. Interpretation

"Each State Party shall make the offences set forth in article 1 punishable..."

The essential obligation imposed by this Article is that Parties must ensure that the offences set forth in Article 1 — hostage-taking, attempted hostage-taking, and participation — are punishable under their domestic laws. Although the wording "shall make the offences ... punishable" indicates that Parties must take some affirmative steps in this regard, i.e., by enacting legislation specifically establishing such penalties, it appears in fact that no steps must be taken if a State's laws already provide penalties for the conduct described in Article 1. States are not generally required to execute their obligations under international law in a particular fashion; international law "imposes an obligation not of way, but of result".[36] Accordingly, as can be seen more clearly from the survey below, there can be and have been two distinct responses by Parties to the obligation imposed by this Article. Some Parties have enacted legislation specifying penalties for the offence of hostage-taking; these laws generally also contain definitions of the offence which follow the definition in Article 1 in a more or less verbatim fashion. Other States do not appear to have enacted any specific legislation making the offence of hostage-taking punishable, relying instead on their existing laws dealing with such offences as kidnapping. As noted in the commentary on Article 1,[37] the definition of the offence of hostage-taking is more narrowly drafted than such crimes as kidnapping and false imprisonment; however, hostage-taking may well fit within a State's laws regarding those crimes. It would seem to be of little consequence whether States enact legislation specifically in response to this Convention or whether they rely on their existing legislation. It is enough if the end result is that the offences are punishable by "appropriate" penalties.

---

[36] Wildhaber, *Treaty-Making Power and Constitution: An International and Comparative Study* 183 (1971).
[37] See p. 77 (note 1 and accompanying text in the commentary on Article 1).

There would appear to be a number of reasons, by no means mutually exclusive, why a State would chose to enact specific legislation establishing penalties for the offence of hostage-taking. The first and most obvious is that its existing laws might not adequately cover the conduct described in Article 1 or provide "appropriate" penalties therefor. The second is that its laws might cover the specified conduct, but do not have the jurisdictional reach required by Article 5 of this Convention. The third is that its constitution or other laws require the enactment of legislation in order to incorporate treaties into domestic law, and the implementing legislation has been drafted in such a way as to include penalties for the offences.[38] It might be noted that it is generally States with common law systems, e.g., the US, the UK and New Zealand, which have found it necessary to enact legislation providing penalties for the offences contained in this Convention.

"... by appropriate penalties which take into account the grave nature of those offences."

The penalties established by Parties for offences under this Convention must be "appropriate", taking into account their "grave nature". There is a certain element of intended obscurity in this language (i.e., what penalties are "appropriate"?), reflecting the fact that systems of punishment vary from State to State and that, therefore, it would be difficult and undesirable (from the point of view of many States) for the Convention to set down any specific penalties, or range of penalties, for the offences. It could certainly be argued that a convention dealing with a crime of international concern, under which an offender may be prosecuted by a State simply on the basis of custody, should set forth a uniform range of penalties, both for the sake of consistency and to ensure that some punishment is ultimately imposed. However, it seems unlikely that States are ready to accept any such obligation.[39] It is clear that States Parties have a good deal of

---

[38] It seems that the United States, for example, has enacted legislation for all three reasons. That country has a federal statute against kidnapping which pre-dates the legislation enacted to implement the Hostages Convention. However, the kidnapping law has a somewhat different definition than that contained in the Hostages Convention and does not have a sufficiently broad jurisdictional reach. See 18 USC §1201. But even if the offence of kidnapping as defined in that statute covered all the elements of hostage-taking, and even if that statute had a sufficiently broad jurisdictional reach to satisfy Article 5 of this Convention, the United States would have had to enact legislation to implement the Hostages Convention since, as noted below, such a treaty would not be self-executing in that country. See note 43, *infra*.

[39] During the drafting of the Hague Convention, for example, the chairman of the ICAO Legal Committee Sub-Committee on the Subject of Unlawful Seizure of Aircraft explained to the Committee that delegates generally felt that the draft convention should not contain any specific penalties since systems of punishment vary from one

ARTICLE 2 103

discretion as to the specific penalties they may establish for the offences set forth in Article 1; however, the use of the word "grave" emphasizes that the penalties established should be akin to those normally established by Parties for serious, rather than minor, crimes.

The response of certain States Parties to the obligation set forth in this Article

Set forth below are the penalties which may be imposed by a sampling of States Parties to this Convention for the offence of hostage-taking. This survey may be useful from two points of view. First, it reveals the range of penalties that Parties consider to be "appropriate" for the offence of hostage-taking and, second, it demonstrates the ways in which Parties have complied with the obligation contained in this Article.

1) The United Kingdom — In the UK, the Taking of Hostages Act 1982 has been enacted to implement the Hostages Convention. The Act defines hostage-taking in a similar fashion to the Convention and provides that a convicted hostage-taker is liable to imprisonment for life.[40] Pursuant to the Criminal Attempts Act 1981 one who attempts to commit an act of hostage-taking is also liable to life imprisonment,[41] and pursuant to the Accessories and Abettors Act 1861 a participant can be tried and punished in the same manner as a principal.[42]

2) The United States — In the US, legislation has been enacted which contains a definition of hostage-taking which is very similar to that in the Hostages Convention and which provides that offenders, including those who attempt to commit an act of hostage-taking, shall

country to another. See ICAO Doc 8877-LC/161, p. 42 (1970). Subsequently, in the diplomatic conference, proposals were mooted to more clearly delineate the types of penalties which should be imposed for hijacking. The representatives of Austria and Italy, for example, proposed that the draft convention should provide that the penalty for hijacking "shall be no less than the penalties provided for attempted voluntary offences against the life of a person under the law of that State". ICAO Doc 8979-LC/165-2, p. 116 (1972). However, many States objected to this proposal. The representative of the United Arab Republic, for example, stated that it was "unnecessarily expansive at the cost of encroaching on national legislation". ICAO Doc 8979-LC/165-1, p. 62 (1972). See also the comments of the representatives of India, Costa Rica, Kuwait and France, *id.* at pp. 64-65.

[40] §1. In the UK, treaties are not self-executing and thus require Parliamentary action before they become part of domestic law. An unincorporated treaty has no formal standing in British law. See McNair, *The Law of Treaties* 81 (2nd ed. 1961). However, very few treaties are actually incorporated into the domestic law of the UK; Parliament generally incorporates only those treaties which, *inter alia*, would change domestic law. See Higgins, in Jacobs & Roberts (eds.), *The Effect of Treaties in Domestic Law* 125-27 (1987).
[41] §4.
[42] §8.

be subject to a term of imprisonment "for any years or for life".[43] Pursuant to another federal statute, participants may be punishable as a principal.[44]

3) The Philippines — The Republic of the Philippines has not enacted legislation specifically establishing penalties for the offence of hostage-taking. However, its penal code provides for the offence of "kidnapping and serious illegal detention", which states that a "private individual" who kidnaps, detains or otherwise deprives another of his liberty, shall suffer the penalty of *reclusion perpetua* to death if any of the following circumstances obtain: 1) the detention lasts more than five days; 2) it has "been committed simulating public authority"; 3) serious physical injuries are inflicted upon the detainee, or threats to kill him are made; or 4) the detainee is a minor, woman or public officer. Moreover, the penalty will be death "where the kidnapping or detention was committed for the purpose of extorting ransom from the victim or any other person, even if none of the circumstances above-mentioned were present in the commission of the offense".[45] The penal code provides for another offence, "slight illegal detention", wherein if none of the circumstances mentioned above obtains, the penalty of *reclusion temporal* shall be imposed.[46] It may be noted that these laws may not satisfy that State's obligations under the Convention: the reference to "private individual[s]" seems to indicate that it does not apply to those acting on behalf of a State whereas, as mentioned in the commentary on Article 1, this Convention applies to the acts of State agents.[47]

4) Sweden — In Sweden, no legislation has been enacted specifically to provide for penalties for the offences contained in this Convention. When a defendant is accused in that country of an act of hostage-taking he will be charged with an analogous offence under Swedish law.[48] The Swedish Penal Code provides for the offence of kidnapping which covers the essential elements of hostage-taking, prohibiting the seizure and carrying away or confinement of a person

---

[43] 18 USC §1203(a). In the United States many types of treaties are not self-executing, including those which define crimes. See Jackson, in Jacobs & Roberts, note 40, *supra*, at p. 150. See also the *Over the Top* case, 5 F. 2d 838, 845 (D. Conn. 1925); Evans, "Self-Executing Treaties in the United States of America", 30 BYIL 178-205 (1953).
[44] 18 USC §2.
[45] Revised Penal Code of the Philippines, Title Nine, Chap. 1, §1, Art. 267.
[46] *Id.* at Art. 268.
[47] See pp. 79-80 (notes 8-9 and accompanying text in the commentary on Article 1).
[48] Information received from Swedish Ministry for Foreign Affairs via letter dated 12 November 1986 from the First Secretary of the Swedish Embassy to the United Kingdom.

with the intent, *inter alia*, of injuring him or of practising extortion. The penalty for the offence is "imprisonment for a fixed period of at least four and at most ten years, or for life". For less serious crimes, the penalty is imprisonment for at most six years.[49]

5) Spain — Spain has enacted legislation dealing with terrorism which prohibits the offence of hostage-taking and makes it punishable by imprisonment for a term of up to 12 years. If the victim is an officer or authority performing his duties the penalty is a term of imprisonment of from 20 years and one day to 30 years.[50] If terrorism is not involved, the crime will be treated as a normal case of kidnapping which, pursuant to that country's penal code, is punishable by a term of imprisonment of up to 12 years unless a ransom is demanded, in which case the penalty is increased to imprisonment for up to 17 years and 4 months.[51]

6) New Zealand — Pursuant to legislation which contains a definition of hostage-taking substantially similar to the Hostages Convention, those who commit the offence are liable to imprisonment for a term not exceeding 14 years.[52]

7) The Federal Republic of Germany — The law of the Federal Republic of Germany has contained a provision against hostage-taking, which defines the offence in a similar way to the Convention, since before the Convention was promulgated. Pursuant to that legislation, hostage-taking is punishable by at least three years' imprisonment.[53]

It can be seen from the above survey that States Parties differ significantly with respect to the range of penalties that they consider to be "appropriate" for the offence of hostage-taking. The most severe penalty — death — can be imposed by the Philippines, while the least severe maximum penalty — 14 years — is provided for under the law of New Zealand. Other States commonly provide for a term of imprisonment for a number of years or for life. Regardless of the differences, it is clear that all of the States have enacted a range of penalties which recognizes that the offence of hostage-taking is a serious one.

---

[49] Swedish Penal Code, Chap. 4, §1 (English translation by the National Council for Crime Prevention, Stockholm, 1984).
[50] Organic Law of 26 December 1984, Arts. 1(c) & 8.
[51] Spanish Penal Code (Codigo Penal), Art. 480.
[52] Crimes (Internationally Protected Persons and Hostages) Act 1980 (No. 44), §8.
[53] StGB, §239b.

"Appropriate" penalties under this Convention compared to "severe" penalties under the ICAO Conventions

The wording of this Article received a significant amount of attention during the drafting of this Convention. Article 4 of the FRG draft was identical to Article 2 of the Hague Convention and Article 3 of the Montreal Convention, which differ from this Article in that they provide that Parties must make the offences therein "punishable by severe penalties". The drafting history of the Hague Convention indicates that the "severe" formulation was chosen by the draftsmen because they believed that it adequately conveyed two important but distinct messages: 1) that seizures of aircraft should be dealt with "severely"; but that 2) each State should determine the specific penalties it might impose.[54]

The language employed in the Hostages Convention was first used in the New York Convention. The Sixth Committee draftsmen of the New York Convention rejected the "severe" language and adopted the "appropriate" formulation at least partly it seems on the rationale that some of the many offences under that instrument might not call for "severe" penalties (since that instrument may cover minor attacks on internationally protected persons).[55] When the issue was addressed by the draftsmen of this Convention, the "severe" language was rejected by the Hostages Committee and replaced with the language employed in the New York Convention.[56] While the rationale put forth by the draftsmen of the New York Convention did not as easily apply to this Convention, numerous arguments — of varying degrees of clarity — were advanced against use of the "severe" formulation. Amongst these arguments were: use of the word "severe" would inappropriately place an obligation upon national courts regarding the severity of the penalty to be imposed;[57] use of the term "severe" could lead to a misuse of the Convention to infringe upon human rights;[58] there is a lack of a uniform definition or agreement as to what

---

[54] The original proposal submitted by the sub-committee initially charged with drafting the Convention provided that States Parties undertake "to make the offense punishable in a manner commensurate with the gravity of such offense." ICAO Doc 8838-LC/157, p. 14 (1970). The "severe" language was added by the Legal Committee at the behest of the representative of the United States who stated that it would place very clearly on record that the seizure of aircraft would not be tolerated and that severe penalties were necessary to deter such actions. ICAO Doc 8877-LC/161, pp. 42 & 88 (1970).

[55] See the comments of the US representative in First Report of the Hostages Committee, p. 81, para. 48. See also the comments of ILC member Ramangasoavina during the drafting of the New York Convention in 1972 YBILC, Vol. I, p. 201.

[56] See Second Report of the Hostages Committee, p. 11, paras. 41-43.

[57] See the comments of the representative of Denmark in First Report of the Hostages Committee, p. 85, para. 12.

[58] See, e.g., the comments of the representatives of Iran and Nicaragua, *id.* at p. 72, para. 17 & p. 83, para. 1, respectively.

constitutes "severe" penalties;[59] and, similar to the argument advanced during the drafting of the New York Convention, the formula does not distinguish, with respect to possible penalties, between the gravity of the various offences set out in Article 1, i.e., actual taking of hostages, attempt and complicity.[60]

Arguments advanced in favour of retaining the language contained in the FRG draft were to the following effect: the word "severe" would provide a more adequate safeguard against the imposition of insufficient penalties such as short prison terms or fines;[61] use of the word "severe" was preferable since it was used in the instruments most closely related to the Hostages Convention, i.e., the Hague and Montreal Conventions;[62] the word "severe" is unambiguous and there are precedents in international law for its use;[63] and inclusion of the "severe" formulation would constitute a greater psychological deterrent to would-be hostage-takers.[64] However, the delegations favouring retention of the word "severe" were apparently in the minority and, in any event, many of them seemed to feel less strongly about the issue than did those which opposed the use of the word. The representative of the UK, for example, although preferring use of the word "severe", stated that he would have no objection to the use of the word "appropriate" provided that it was accompanied, as it was in the New York Convention, by a requirement that States Parties should take into account the "grave" nature of the offences when establishing penalties.[65]

Indeed, while a specific requirement that Parties must establish "severe" penalties for offences under this Convention might arguably have been a somewhat greater safeguard against inadequate penalties, as can be seen from the above survey, none of the surveyed States Parties to this Convention have established what might be regarded as minor penalties for the offence. Moreover, there does not really seem to be much difference between the two formulations. Both emphasize that the possible penalties must be more than minor while making it clear that it is up to each State Party to determine the specific type of penalties to be imposed. And it does not appear that States Parties

---

[59] See the comments of the representative of the Netherlands, *id.* at p. 80, para. 39.
[60] See the comments of the representative of Mexico, *id.* at p. 78, para. 25.
[61] See the comments of the representative of the Federal Republic of Germany, *id.* at p. 92, para. 6.
[62] See the comments of the representative of the United States, *id.* at p. 81, para. 48.
[63] See the comments of the representative of Poland in Second Report of the Hostages Committee, p. 31, para. 35.
[64] See the comments of the representative of Japan, *id.* at p. 32, para. 43.
[65] *Id.* at p. 30, para. 28. The representative of the United States said that both formulations were sufficiently clear and "would roughly have the same effect within the context of the various legal systems". First Report of the Hostages Committee, p. 81, para. 48.

have considered that the types of penalties which should be imposed under this Convention are to be any less severe than those imposed under the ICAO Conventions.

For example, in the UK, the statutes enacted to implement the Hague and the Montreal Conventions both provide, as does the Taking of Hostages Act, that offenders are liable for imprisonment for life.[66] In the US, the legislation enacted to implement the Hague Convention provides that convicted offenders shall be liable for imprisonment for not less than twenty years, or death if death to another person results from the prohibited acts,[67] while its legislation which deals with those acts prohibited by the Montreal Convention provides that offenders shall be subject to not more than a $100,000 fine or not more than twenty years' imprisonment or both.[68] As noted, the legislation enacted by the US regarding the taking of hostages provides that offenders shall be subject to a term of imprisonment for any years or for life. In New Zealand, the hijacker of an airplane can be imprisoned for life,[69] while one who commits an act against the Montreal Convention can be imprisoned for up to 14 years,[70] the same penalty that can be imposed upon hostage-takers. Finally, in the Philippines a hijacker, depending upon whether injury is inflicted, can receive a punishment ranging from imprisonment for at least 12 years to death, with a fine of between twenty thousand and fifty thousand pesos.[71] This may be compared to the penalty for hostage-taking in the Philippines which, as noted, ranges from imprisonment to death.

Thus, while there are variations within some States with respect to the range of penalties which might be imposed for the crimes of hijacking, other interference with civil aviation and hostage-taking, these differences do not appear to have anything to do with the different language contained in the penalty provisions of the various conventions (and it may be noted that in the United States, the maximum penalty for a violation of the Montreal Convention, which uses the "severe" formulation, is lower than that for a violation of the Hostages Convention which does not). More likely, they reflect the assessment of the lawmakers of each country as to the seriousness of the various offences. In any case, the possible penalties for all the offences in all of the countries surveyed may be said to be "severe".

---

[66] See Hijacking Act 1971, §1; Protection of Aircraft Act 1973, Part I, §4.
[67] See 49 USC §1472.
[68] See 18 USC §32.
[69] See Aviation Crimes Act 1972 (No. 137), §3.
[70] Id., at §5.
[71] See Philippine Hijacking Law 1971 [Rep. Act No. 6253] §2. A comprehensive listing of the penalties established by States for violations of the ICAO Conventions may be found in ICAO Doc A26-WP/29 EX/3, Appendix G (1986).

Article 3

EASING THE SITUATION OF THE HOSTAGES

1. The State Party in the territory of which the hostage is held by the offender shall take all measures it considers appropriate to ease the situation of the hostage, in particular, to secure his release and, after his release, to facilitate, when relevant, his departure.

2. If any object which the offender has obtained as a result of the taking of hostages comes into the custody of a State Party, that State Party shall return it as soon as possible to the hostage or the third party referred to in article 1, as the case may be, or to the appropriate authorities thereof.

1. INTRODUCTION

This Article imposes various obligations upon Parties which are designed to mitigate the effects of a hostage-taking and, to the extent possible, return the situation to the *status quo ante*. Specifically, a Party in whose territory a hostage is held must work towards securing his release and must facilitate his subsequent departure as well as take such other steps as it considers appropriate to ease his situation. Moreover, all Parties are required to return to the hostage or third party any object in their custody that was obtained by the offender as a result of the offence. Some of the draftsmen stressed the humanitarian considerations which make this Article, particularly paragraph 1, one of the most important in the Convention.[1]

As discussed in greater detail below, however, the Article has great significance beyond its humanitarian purpose: by authorizing a State to take "all measures it considers necessary" to ease the situation of the hostage, the Article seemingly creates a potential exception to the extradite or prosecute requirement in that it would appear to allow a State to grant immunity to the hostage-taker in return for the release of the hostage.

The Article is identical in substance to the FRG draft, although some drafting changes were made.[2] Paragraph 1 is somewhat similar to Article 9 of the Hague Convention, which provides, in paragraph 1, that:

---

[1] See, e.g., the comments of the representatives of Yugoslavia and the Soviet Union in Second Report of the Hostages Committee, p. 35, para. 67 & p. 36, para. 73, respectively.
[2] FRG draft, Art. 3.

> [w]hen any of the acts mentioned in Article 1(a) has occurred or is about to occur, Contracting States shall take all appropriate measures to restore control of the aircraft to its lawful commander or to preserve his control of the aircraft.

and, in paragraph 2, that:

> any Contracting State in which the aircraft or its passengers or crew are present shall facilitate the continuation of the journey of the passengers and crew as soon as possible, and shall without delay return the aircraft and its cargo to the persons lawfully entitled to possession.

Article 10(2) of the Montreal Convention is similar to this latter provision, while Article 13(2) of the Rome Convention places a State Party under the obligation to exercise all possible efforts to avoid the undue delay of a ship or a ship's passengers, crew or cargo present in its territory when an offence under that Convention has been committed.[3]

2. INTERPRETATION

PARAGRAPH 1: THE OBLIGATION TO EASE THE SITUATION OF THE HOSTAGE

"The State Party in the territory of which the hostage is held by the offender . . ."

The obligation contained in paragraph 1 appears to be imposed only upon the Party in whose territory the hostage is held. Parties do not, therefore, seem to be under an obligation to take any steps whatsoever to ease the situation of a hostage who is held in the territory of another State Party (and the principle of territorial sovereignty, would, in any event, place limitations on the actions the non-territorial States could take in this regard). By way of contrast, Article 9(1) of the Hague Convention imposes an obligation upon "Contracting States" (and, by implication, all of them which are in a position to do so) to preserve or restore control of the aircraft to its lawful commander.

---

[3] See also Article 11 of the Tokyo Convention which is very similar to Article 9 of the Hague Convention. The absence of a corresponding provision in the New York Convention can probably be attributed to existing duties under international law regarding the protection of diplomats. See, e.g., Art. 29, 1961 Vienna Convention on Diplomatic Relations, 500 UNTS 95; *Case Concerning US Diplomatic and Consular Staff in Tehran*, ICJ Rep. 1980, paras. 61-62, 67-69. See generally Rosenstock, p. 179.

ARTICLE 3

". . . shall take all measures it considers appropriate to ease the situation of the hostage, in particular, to secure his release . . ."

The general obligation imposed upon the territorial State by this paragraph is to take measures to "ease the situation of the hostage". Presumably the territorial State may seek to ease the hostage's situation in any number of ways (including, for example, attempting to provide food and other material comforts to him and opening the lines of communication between him and his family). However, it is specifically obliged by this paragraph to attempt to secure his release. There are a number of ways in which a State may secure the release of hostages, including, *inter alia*, negotiation, acquiescence in the hostage-takers' demands,[4] and the use of force. This latter approach has been employed many times, an example being the actions of the government of Pakistan in September 1986 when its commandos stormed a Pan American jet which, along with its passengers and crew, was held by four gunmen at the Karachi airport.[5]

This provision requires the territorial State only to take such steps as "it" thinks appropriate. During the drafting of the Convention, the representatives of some States expressed concern that this provision is too imprecise and gives too much latitude to the territorial State, particularly in cases where it is another State against whom the compulsion is directed.[6] Other representatives, however, including those of the United Kingdom and Nigeria, agreed that the State in which the hostage is held would be the best judge of the proper measures to take.[7] Both the language of this provision and the *travaux préparatoires* thus indicate that the determination of what measures are appropriate to secure the hostage's release is left exclusively to the discretion of the territorial State. Absent a showing of bad faith, there

---

[4] The representative of the Federal Republic of Germany noted that such acquiescence is authorized, but of course not required, by this Article. See First Report of the Hostages Committee, p. 47, para. 6.

[5] During the incident, fifteen passengers were killed and scores injured by the terrorists who began shooting and detonating grenades. After the Pakistani action, the other passengers escaped and the gunmen were captured. See *New York Times*, Sept. 6, 1986, pp. A1 & A4, and Sept. 7, 1986, p. A1. The territorial State's authority to use force, however, may be limited when the hostage-taking occurs in diplomatic premises such as an embassy or consulate. Because such premises are inviolable (see Art. 22, 1961 Vienna Convention on Diplomatic Relations, 500 UNTS 95; Art. 31, Vienna Convention on Consular Relations, 596 UNTS 261), consent of the government whose mission is involved will be necessary before force may be used. See generally Aston, "Political Hostage-Taking in Western Europe", in Gutteridge, *The New Terrorism* (1986).

[6] See, e.g., the comments of the representatives of Poland, Iran and Libya in Second Report of the Hostages Committee, p. 34, para. 58, p. 35, para. 64 & p. 35, para. 65, respectively.

[7] See the comments of the representative of the United Kingdom in First Report of the Hostages Committee, p. 71, para. 15, and those of the representative of Nigeria in Second Report of the Hostages Committee, p. 35, para. 60.

does not appear to be any basis upon which another party may claim that a State's decisions under this Article constituted a breach of the Convention or upon which an arbitral body or the International Court of Justice, exercising its jurisdiction in a dispute regarding the "interpretation or application" of this Convention pursuant to Article 16, could substitute its judgment as to what steps should have been taken.[8]

Despite the wide measure of discretion given to the territorial State, however, the absence of such qualifying words as "if any" connected to the obligation to take "all measures it considers appropriate" indicates that the State must actually take measures designed to secure the hostage's release. It cannot sit idly by while the hostage is being held, and a territorial State which makes no attempt to secure the release of the hostage is in breach of this Convention. At a minimum, it would seem that the territorial State should attempt to ascertain the hostage's whereabouts, request his release, and examine all viable alternatives which could lead to that end. Moreover, its efforts should continue for the entire duration of the incident. It might be noted that if the hostage is a foreigner, the obligation to attempt to secure his release may fall within a State's general obligation to protect aliens.[9]

The potential conflict between Article 3 and Article 8: A grant of immunity in return for the release of hostages

One possible method by which a State may secure the release of hostages is to agree to grant the hostage-takers immunity from prosecution or extradition in exchange for the release of the victims. The question thus arises as to whether this is an acceptable course of action by a State Party to this Convention. On the one hand, this

---

[8] The discretion granted by this Article may be contrasted with that granted by Article 15 of the 1950 European Convention for the Protection of Human Rights and Fundamental Freedoms, ETS 5, which states that Parties, under certain circumstances, "may take measures" derogating from their obligations under the instrument. On the face of it, Article 15 does not grant as much discretion as does the provision under consideration. Decisions of the European Commission and Court of Human Rights, moreover, confirm that while States have a "domestic margin of appreciation", the Commission and Court are competent to substitute their judgment both as to whether or not circumstances justified derogation from the Convention and as to whether the measures taken in derogation were strictly required by the situation. See *Greece* v. *United Kingdom*, 2 Yearbook of the European Convention on Human Rights 174, 176 (1958-59); the *Lawless* case, Judgment of 1 July 1961 (Merits), Series A, no. 3, p. 55, para. 22 & pp. 57-59, paras. 36-38; *Ireland* v. *United Kingdom*, Judgment of 18 January 1978 (Merits), Series A, Vol. 25, pp. 78-79, para. 207. See also Higgins, "Derogations under Human Rights Treaties", 48 BYIL 281, 296-301 (1975-76). That a State has acted in good faith would not prevent such a substitution of judgment. See Robertson, "Lawless v. The Government of Ireland (Second Phase)", 37 BYIL 536, 542-546 (1961).

[9] See generally Freeman, *International Responsibility of States for Denial of Justice* 27 & 367 (1938).

Article clearly allows, indeed requires, a State to take whatever measures it considers appropriate to secure the release of the hostages. The range of possible measures is not expressly limited by this Article, and a State could well decide that a grant of immunity is the most appropriate step to take. On the other hand, Article 8 — probably the most important obligation imposed by this Convention — requires States in whose territory an alleged offender is present to comply with the obligation *aut dedere aut judicare* "without exception whatsoever". Thus, it appears that a conflict between the two provisions could arise.

Keeping in mind that the interpretation of a treaty must begin with the plain meaning of the text,[10] it might be argued that the wording of Article 8 — "without exception whatsoever" — is so unqualified as to place a limitation on the discretion granted in Article 3. However, this argument is not entirely persuasive. The words "all measures it considers necessary" found in Article 3 are very broad indeed, and do not easily lend themselves to a restrictive interpretation. From a teleological standpoint, moreover, there is no compelling basis to conclude that the wording of Article 8 must take precedence over Article 3. One purpose of this Convention, as seen in the Preamble and throughout the text, is to ensure that all those who commit acts of hostage-taking are either prosecuted or extradited. However, it is also the purpose of the instrument to protect victims, or potential victims, of such acts.

Given this uncertainty, reference to the *travaux préparatoires* of this Convention is particularly justified, and seems, moreover, to provide an answer to the problem. In the Hostages Committee, the representative of the Netherlands pointed out the potential conflict between the two Articles and, asserting that the territorial State should have broad latitude in obtaining the release of the hostages, argued that Article 3 should take precedence over the extradite or prosecute obligation.[11] The representative of Canada disagreed, arguing that the obligation to prosecute or extradite should not be affected by any conditions which the offender tries to impose upon a third party.[12] However, other representatives agreed with that of the Netherlands, including the representative of Italy who argued that a Party should be allowed in extremely serious circumstances to negotiate immunity in exchange for the release of the hostages. He pointed out, moreover, that if the State had an absolute obligation to punish the

---

[10] See Art. 31(1), 1969 Vienna Convention on the Law of Treaties; 1966 YBILC, Vol. II, pp. 220-221.
[11] See Second Report of the Hostages Committee, p. 72, para. 18.
[12] *Id.* at p. 74, para. 4.

offender any negotiation based upon a promise of immunity would be pointless.[13]

With respect to this debate, the representative of the FRG ultimately explained that while Articles 3 and 8 are in principle of equal rank, Article 3 gives the territorial State *carte blanche* to take the measures it deems appropriate. Therefore, if a State decides not to extradite or prosecute in order to obtain the release of the hostage, it is authorized under the Convention to act accordingly. He also noted, however, that this determination would not be binding upon the other Parties: if the hostage-taker was subsequently apprehended in the territory of a State other than the State which made the deal, he must be prosecuted or extradited by that State.[14] The interpretation of the FRG representative appears to have been accepted by the Hostages Committee and no further discussion regarding this issue appears on the record.

It appears, therefore, that a Party has the authority under this Article to negotiate immunity for the hostage-takers in return for the release of the hostages. If this interpretation is correct this paragraph allows a State unilaterally to decide that it will not comply with one of its fundamental obligations under the Convention — to extradite or prosecute all offenders found in its territory. It can thus be appreciated that this provision significantly weakens the Convention from a law enforcement perspective. It may be that this exception is a necessary evil since for political and humanitarian reasons it seems unlikely that States would so bind themselves that they could never legitimately grant immunity in exchange for the safe release of hostages.[15] However, because of the enormous potential this provision has for weakening the law enforcement value of the Convention, the exception should be viewed as narrowly as possible. States should only grant immunity as a last resort, after a good faith determination that such is the only way to secure the safe release of the hostages. While the representative of the Netherlands may have been overstating the case when he called paragraph 1 of Article 3 the most important provision in the Convention,[16] the possible exception it creates to the extradite or prosecute rule certainly makes it one of the most significant.

---

[13] Second Report of the Hostages Committee, p. 78, para. 29.
[14] *Id.* at p. 92, para. 4.
[15] It might be noted that, with respect to the Hague Convention, at least one source argues that a grant of immunity is not consistent with a Party's obligations under that instrument. See Sofaer, "Fighting Terrorism Through Law", 85 Dept St. Bull., No. 2103, p. 39 (1985).
[16] Second Report of the Hostages Committee, p. 34, para. 53.

The Achille Lauro *incident*

An example of a grant of immunity made in exchange for the release of hostages can be found in the *Achille Lauro* incident, during which terrorists connected with the Palestine Liberation Front hijacked an Italian cruise ship in international waters off the coast of Egypt and held its occupants hostage.[17] Although the facts regarding the negotiations are somewhat unclear, it seems that the governments of Egypt and Italy, in conjunction with the Palestine Liberation Movement, came to an agreement with the terrorists whereby they would surrender to the PLO and be granted safe passage to an undisclosed location outside of Egypt in return for the safe release of all the hostages and the ship.[18] From what has already been said, it would appear that such a deal is within the legitimate discretion of a State acting under this Article.[19]

It is worth noting, however, that in this case the hostage-takers did not live up to their end of the bargain and had in fact murdered one of the passengers, an elderly American Jewish man.[20] There are

---

[17] *New York Times*, Oct. 8, 1985, p. A1. For additional facts concerning this incident, see p. 4 (note 13 and accompanying text in the Introduction).

[18] *New York Times*, Oct. 10, 1985, pp. A1, A10, & A11. Subsequently, Egyptian officials, under criticism for letting the offenders leave the country, stated that they were not party to the deal but rather were acting as intermediary between Italy and the PLO. *New York Times*, Oct. 10, 1985, p. A14.

[19] One commentator asserts that Egypt failed to live up to its obligations under the Hostages Convention by granting the terrorists safe passage. However, it does not appear that this commentator took account of this Article in making that assessment. See Murphy, "The Future of Multilateralism and Efforts to Combat International Terrorism", 25 Colum. J. Trans. L. 35, 82 (1986). It might be noted that this incident is referred to merely as an example of such a deal. It is not considered that this incident provides evidence of subsequent practice which could assist in interpreting this provision pursuant to Article 31(3)(b) of the Vienna Convention on the Law of Treaties. This single incident, vigorously objected to by the only other State Party to the Convention involved, the United States, can hardly be seen as indicating the understanding of the "parties as a whole". See 1966 YBILC, Vol. II, p. 222. It might be noted in this context, moreover, that it does not seem that Egypt expressly justified its action pursuant to this Article.

Another example of a bargain for immunity in return for the release of hostages occurred in April 1988. An armed gang, apparently connected with the pro-Iranian groups Hezbollah and Islamic Jihad in Lebanon, hijacked a Kuwait Airways Boeing 747 en route from Bangkok to Kuwait with 97 passengers and 15 crew. During the incident, which lasted for 15 days, the aircraft flew to Iran, Cyprus and, finally, Algeria. The hijackers demanded the release of 17 prisoners held in Kuwait. Early in the incident, 57 hostages — women, non-Arabs and a Jordanian— were released; however, the other passengers, some of whom were members of the Kuwaiti ruling family, remained as hostages and two were killed. After intensive negotiations, first in Cyprus with Cypriot and PLO officials, and then in Algeria with Algerian officials, the hijackers and Algeria reached an agreement whereby the remaining hostages were released in return for safe conduct for the hijackers to either Iran or Lebanon. See XXXIV *Keesing's Record of World Events* 35916-17 (1988). Although Algeria is not party to the Hostages Convention, such a deal would, apparently, be permissible under this instrument. However, it may not be permissible under the Hague Convention. See note 15, *supra*.

[20] *New York Times*, Oct. 10, 1985, p. A1.

conflicting reports as to whether or not this fact was known by Egyptian officials before they allowed the offenders to leave the country;[21] but the conduct of those officials in letting the terrorists leave was severely criticized by the governments of the United States and Israel.[22] Indeed, when the Egyptian aircraft carrying the hijackers to Tunis was over international waters, it was intercepted by US F-14s and diverted to Italy where the hijackers were taken into custody and ultimately tried.[23] Officials of the Italian government asserted that the interception was the result of an accord between the United States, Italy, Egypt and the Palestine Liberation Movement, a charge which was denied by both Egyptian and American authorities.[24]

As noted, in the *Achille Lauro* affair one of the conditions of the bargain was that the hostages would all be released unharmed. But this Article does not require that a deal made with hostage-takers must contain such a condition. Even if a State Party knows that one or more hostages have been killed by the offenders, it seemingly could still negotiate immunity from prosecution in return for the release of the remaining hostages. However, such a deal can create political problems. As can clearly be seen from the reaction of Israel and the United States in the *Achille Lauro* incident, if the bargaining State actually lives up to that deal it may well meet the opposition of other interested States.

". . . and, after his release, to facilitate, when relevant, his departure."

The final phrase of paragraph 1 requires the territorial State to facilitate, if relevant, the departure of the hostage from that State after he has been released. The inclusion of this provision was not controversial and only minor changes were made from the FRG draft, most notably the addition of the words "when relevant" to cover the case of a hostage who had been held in his own State or who otherwise did not wish to depart.[25] The representative of the FRG explained that under this provision, the action taken would depend upon the will of the hostage himself,[26] and the representative of Italy added that the obligation to facilitate departure must be viewed strictly in terms of the hostage's desire to leave the country.[27]

---

[21] *New York Times*, Oct. 11, 1985, p. A11 & Oct. 14, 1985, p. A1.
[22] *New York Times*, Oct. 10, 1985, p. A1.
[23] *New York Times*, Oct. 11, 1985, p. A1 & July 11, 1986, p. A1.
[24] *New York Times*, Oct. 11, 1985, p. A11 & Oct. 12, 1985, p. A5.
[25] See UN GAOR, 34th Sess., C.6 (53rd mtg.), p. 8, para. 22, UN Doc A/C.6/34/SR.53 (1979).
[26] First Report of the Hostages Committee, p. 64, para. 22.
[27] *Id.* at p. 78, para. 31.

The primary way in which a State may facilitate a hostage's departure is to provide him with the means of travel. The representative of the FRG explained that:

> The article had been drafted with the possibility in mind that the hostage could not afford the travel expenses involved in returning to the place to which he wished to go. In such circumstances, it was intended that the State he had been taken to would provide him with assistance in returning home.[28]

PARAGRAPH 2: THE OBLIGATION TO RETURN OBJECTS TO THE HOSTAGES OR THIRD PARTY

"If any object which the offender has obtained as a result of the taking of hostages comes into the custody of a State Party, that State Party shall return it as soon as possible to the hostage or the third party referred to in article 1, as the case may be, or to the appropriate authorities thereof."

Any object obtained by the hostage-taker as a result of the offence which subsequently comes into the hands of a Party must be returned to the hostage or to the third party (or authorities thereof) referred to in Article 1, i.e., "a State, an international intergovernmental organization, a natural or juridical person, or a group of persons". These objects would include items taken from the hostage during the incident and any ransom paid by the third party. As noted by the US representative to the Hostages Committee, this provision simply seeks restoration of the *status quo ante* once the hostage-taking has ended.[29] Obviously, the hostage-taker cannot retain the spoils of his crime,[30] and the obligation imposed upon States in this paragraph is similar to the rule under customary international law that States which come into the possession of goods taken by pirates must return them to the true owners.[31] It is worth noting that the obligation imposed by this paragraph is imposed upon all Parties, and not just the territorial State as is the case under paragraph 1.

The FRG draft required the State to "promptly" return to the "person entitled to possession" any object in its custody "illegally acquired" as a result of the hostage-taking.[32] However, various objections to this wording were voiced during the drafting process.

---

[28] *Id.* at p. 64, para. 22.
[29] Second Report of the Hostages Committee, p. 34, para. 57.
[30] Cf. 18 USC §1963 which provides for the forfeiture of proceeds and interests resulting from "racketeering activity".
[31] See Wortley, "*Pirata non mutat Dominium*", 25 BYIL 258 (1947).
[32] FRG draft, Art. 3.

Objections to the phrase "person entitled to possession" centred around the difficulty a State may have in establishing who was actually "entitled" to possession of an object obtained during a hostage-taking. Such an inquiry could involve that State in a private law dispute as to the identity of the title holder.[33] The revised wording is designed to avoid arguments regarding title by requiring simply a return to the *status quo ante*. In most cases, the object will presumably just be returned to the person or State from whom it was taken or extorted without any inquiry into title.[34]

The words "illegally acquired" were deleted by the Sixth Committee, explaining that it was difficult to see how an object could legally be obtained during a hostage-taking situation.[35]

Finally, the requirement that the object be returned "promptly" was replaced by "as soon as possible". This change was suggested by the representative of the UK to the Hostages Committee, who pointed out that custodial States may require a certain amount of time before returning an object so that they may use it "in their inquiries into the case or as evidence before their courts".[36]

---

[33] See, e.g., the comments of the representative of Canada in First Report of the Hostages Committee, p. 74, para. 5, and in Second Report of the Committee, p. 34, para. 52.

[34] See generally, Rosenstock, p. 179.

[35] See UN GAOR, 34th Sess., C.6 (53rd mtg.), p. 8, para. 22, UN Doc A/C.6/34/SR.53 (1979).

[36] Second Report of the Hostages Committee, p. 34, para. 50.

Article 4

CO-OPERATION TO PREVENT ACTS OF HOSTAGE-TAKING

States Parties shall co-operate in the prevention of the offences set forth in article 1, particularly by:
(a) taking all practicable measures to prevent preparations in their respective territories for the commission of those offences within or outside their territories, including measures to prohibit in their territories illegal activities of persons, groups and organizations that encourage, instigate, organize or engage in the perpetration of acts of taking of hostages;
(b) exchanging information and co-ordinating the taking of administrative and other measures as appropriate to prevent the commission of those offences.

1. INTRODUCTION

Most of the obligations imposed by this Convention — including the central obligation of *aut dedere aut judicare* — are concerned with the action to be taken by Parties once an act of hostage-taking has been committed. It is, of course, better if these acts can be prevented from happening in the first place, and this Article imposes upon Parties the obligation to work together to this end. Two types of co-operation are called for: first, Parties must take measures to prevent preparations in their territories for the commission of the crimes set forth in Article 1 and, second, they must exchange information and co-ordinate other preventative measures. As stated by the Yugoslav representative to the Sixth Committee, the Article reflects the principle that anti-terrorism treaties such as this one should not be restricted to actions *post factum* but, rather, should also impose obligations upon Parties to take appropriate action to prevent and suppress terrorist activities.[1] Moreover, the Article indicates that becoming a Party to this Convention is not in itself a sufficient measure of international co-operation as regards the offence of hostage-taking. As stated by the United States representative to the Hostages Committee, it is necessary after the conclusion of such treaties to seek "further agreement[s] between States . . . to ensure their co-operation not only in defining but also in preventing the offenses in question so that the need for extradition could be avoided".[2]

---

[1] See UN GAOR, 34th Sess., C.6 (62nd mtg.), p. 7, para. 30, UN Doc A/C.6/34/SR.62 (1979).
[2] First Report of the Hostages Committee, p. 68, para. 4.

There was no controversy over the inclusion of this Article in the Convention. It is virtually identical to Article 4 of the New York Convention, Article 13(1) of the Rome Convention and to the draft submitted by the FRG,[3] except that the final phrase of subparagraph (a) ("including measures . . .") is unique to this Convention. No corresponding provision is contained in the Hague Convention. The Montreal Convention, however, provides in Article 10(1) that "Contracting States shall, in accordance with international and national law, endeavour to take all practicable measures for the purpose of preventing the offences mentioned in Article 1".

The need for, and obstacles to, international co-operation to prevent acts of hostage-taking

It will be appreciated that significant co-operation between States will be more effective than unilateral action in preventing acts of hostage-taking.[4] Terrorism is a collective problem, not only because of the general interdependence of the international community, but also because of the transnational nature of the phenomenon: terrorists often travel from State to State; plans are often hatched in one or more countries for execution in another; members of a terrorist group may be nationals of and/or live in various States, and victims often come from different States from both their captors and each other; a terrorist act can take place in more than one country, e.g., by the movement of hostages from the territory of one State to the territory of another, and they often take place in international airspace and waters. And, of course, terrorist groups receive support from various States for acts to be committed in or against other States.[5] Given all of this, it is easy to see the necessity for international co-operation to prevent acts of hostage-taking, whether this co-operation is on an *ad hoc* basis or, preferably, through predetermined concerted action. And, as discussed below, co-operation can take many forms, be it the exchange of police and intelligence information, the exchange of tactical experience and training methods for anti-terrorism forces and the exchange of technology relevant to anti-terrorism operations.[6]

However, significant obstacles exist to effective co-operation between States to prevent acts of hostage-taking and other acts of

---

[3] FRG draft, Art. 2.
[4] While this point is self-evident, it is supported by claims of the government of the US that, due in part to increased co-operation with other States, it deterred or preempted more than 180 international terrorist incidents in the 18-month period prior to June 1986. See 86 Dep't St. Bull., No. 2113, p. 3 (1986).
[5] See pp. 19-20 (notes 33-38 and accompanying text in Part I).
[6] See pp. 128-131 (notes 33-49 and accompanying text).

terrorism. Prevention in general can be difficult in democratic States since such States place significant restraints on interference with individual rights, such as freedom of expression, movement and privacy. These restraints may lead to a conflict between individual rights and public security,[7] and each State must, therefore, seek a level of preventative activity which does not encroach to an unacceptable degree upon individual liberty.[8] With specific regard to inter-State co-operation to prevent terrorism, these constitutional and other legal restraints vary from State to State, resulting in the need to find a common denominator of acceptable co-operative preventative activity.[9] Other obstacles include: the clashing ideologies of various States which makes them unlikely to trust each other to the degree necessary for effective co-operation, or even to agree on the need to prevent acts of terrorism in general and hostage-taking in particular[10] (although this latter problem seems unlikely to arise as between States which have become party to this instrument); inflexible State bureaucracies; reluctance on the part of States to make the concessions regarding sovereignty that certain types of co-operation may require;[11] the expense of preventative efforts;[12] the lack of the strong political will which is sometimes necessary to institute preventative measures, particularly when States have significant economic links with other States which are suspected of supporting terrorist groups;[13] and, according to the US Department of State, the reluctance of some States which have not specifically been victimized by terrorist acts to get involved for fear of occasioning terrorist acts in their territory.[14]

---

[7] See Gal-Or, *International Cooperation to Suppress Terrorism* 52-53 n.25, 63-65 (1985). See also note 27, *infra*.

[8] See Wilkinson, *Terrorism and the Liberal State* 126-127, 142 (2nd ed., 1986), who states that it is a "dangerous illusion" to believe that one can protect liberal democracy by suspending liberal rights. At the same time, he continues, it is the job of the government to uphold constitutional authority and the rule of law.

[9] See Gal-Or, note 7, *supra*, at p. 43. An example of where co-operation between States has raised constitutional questions can be found in the FRG. Although the central police in that State exchange information regarding terrorists with the authorities of other States, it has been argued that this is a violation of the right to data protection and is not strictly permissible under the Basic Law. See Kubica & Leineweber, "*Grundfragen zu den Zentralstellenaufgaben des Bundeskriminalamtes*", 37 Neue Juristische Wochenschrift 2068-72 (1984).

[10] See pp. 28-45 (Part I, §3).

[11] See Gal-Or, note 7, *supra*, at pp. 61-63, 69, 73 & 78-79.

[12] See 86 Dep't St. Bull., No. 2113, p. 10 (1986).

[13] *Id.* See also Gal-Or, note 7, *supra*, at pp. 66-68, who notes, *inter alia*, that the oil dependence of many States makes them reluctant to take preventative measures which would adversely affect those States which support terrorism.

[14] Dep't St. Bull., note 12, *supra*. The US government also states that certain States are reluctant to co-operate with the US since they "erroneously believe that because the U.S. Government is a principal target of terrorists, working with [it] could bring more trouble; or they have nationalistic reasons for keeping a distance".

Despite these obstacles, Parties are obliged to co-operate in good faith in the generally envisaged ways to prevent acts of hostage-taking, and they should, therefore, to the extent possible, overcome these difficulties. But it seems best that this Article is rather general as to the obligations imposed upon Parties, leaving it to each one to decide the steps it will take to fulfil its responsibilities under subparagraph (a) and the precise extent of the co-operation it will undertake with each other Party pursuant to subparagraph (b). With regard to this latter point, it is clear that the degree of co-operation between individual Parties to this Convention will vary, depending particularly upon their ideological compatibility (with, of course, like-minded States attaining a degree of co-operation which is greater than that possible as between States with different political and social systems).

2. INTERPRETATION

"States Parties shall co-operate in the prevention of the offences set forth in article 1, particularly by:"

This Article is divided into two subparagraphs, both of which deal with a particular type of co-operation designed to prevent the offences listed in Article 1. The categories are not mutually exclusive; however, in general, subparagraph (a) envisages measures that a State may take (whether on its own initiative or pursuant to a more specific agreement with one or more other States) in the exercise of its law enforcement powers to keep its territory free of activities preparatory to acts of hostage-taking. While these will normally be measures that a State will take on its own, they are co-operative in the sense that they are taken towards the common goal of preventing international acts of hostage-taking. By way of contrast, subparagraph (b) requires a more active and genuine co-operation between Parties to prevent such acts.

SUBPARAGRAPH (A)

". . . taking all practicable measures to prevent preparations in their respective territories for the commission of those offences within or outside their territories . . ."

This subparagraph requires Parties to take measures to keep their territories free of activities preparatory to acts of hostage-taking. In its commentary to the New York Convention, the ILC stated that the identical language in that instrument "embodies the well established principle of international law that every State must ensure that its territory is not used for the preparation of crimes to be committed in other States".[15] In this connexion it might be noted that this subparagraph is a stronger version of the rule, adopted by the League of Nations and the General Assembly of the UN in numerous resolutions, that a State must not support, assist or acquiesce in activities within its territory directed towards the commission of terrorist acts in other States.[16] Moreover, the words "within or outside their territories" make it clear that a State's responsibility under this subparagraph is not limited to preventing preparations for acts which are to be committed in the territory of other States: it must also prevent preparations for acts which are to occur in its own territory.[17]

In general, this provision envisages such measures as the surveillance of, and intelligence gathering regarding, persons or groups who may either currently or prospectively be involved in the preparation of acts of hostage-taking,[18] and the taking of the police and judicial measures necessary to curtail such activities. However, the words "all practicable measures" are deliberately vague, leaving it to

---

[15] 1972 YBILC, Vol. II, p. 317. The ILC cited the case of *United States v. Arjona*, 120 US 479, 484 (1886). In *Arjona*, the US Supreme Court held that "[t]he law of nations requires every national government to use 'due diligence' to prevent a wrong being done within its own dominion to another nation with which it is at peace, or to the people thereof". See also *The Corfu Channel Case*, ICJ Rep. 1949, p. 22, wherein the Court noted the obligation of every State "not to allow knowingly its territory to be used for acts contrary to the rights of other States". See Brownlie, *System of the Law of Nations — State Responsibility (Part I)* 165 (1983), who notes that "a state is under a duty to control the activities of private persons within its state territory and the duty is no less applicable where the harm is caused to persons or other legal interests wihin the territory of another state". He also notes that the duty to prevent the activities of armed bands is based on a State's physical control of its territory. *Id.* at pp. 181-82. On tort liability of a State for failing to prevent injury to aliens in terrorist attacks see Lillich & Paxman, "Responsibility for Injury to Aliens in Terrorist Activities", 26 Am. U.L.R. 219 (1977).

[16] E.g., Declaration on Principles of International Law concerning Friendly Relations and Cooperation among States in accordance with the Charter of the United Nations, GA Res 2625 (XXV) of 24 October 1970, UN GAOR, 25th Sess., Supp. 28, p. 121, UN Doc A/8028 (1971). GA Res 40/61 of 9 December 1985, UN GAOR, 40th Sess., Supp. 53, p. 301, UN Doc A/40/53 (1986); see pp. 29-30 (notes 82-86 and accompanying text in Part I).

[17] Similarly, a 1987 GA resolution on terrorism provides that States should "prevent the preparation and organization in their respective territories for the commission within or outside their territory of terrorist acts and subversive acts directed against other States and their citizens". See GA Res 42/159 of 7 December 1987. The ILA has stated that "[a] state is legally obliged to exercise due diligence to prevent the commission of acts of international terrorism within its jurisdiction". See ILA, *Report of the Sixty-First Conference* 7 (1984).

[18] As one commentator notes, the terrorist thrives on surprise and picks the time, locale and circumstances of his attack. Effective intelligence gathering regarding the identity of terrorists and terrorist groups, and such matters as their whereabouts, aims, motivations, structures, supporters, finances and resouces is, therefore, an essential element of any concerted effort to prevent preparations for terrorist attacks. See Kerstetter, "Terrorism and Intelligence", 3 Terr. J. 109, 109 (1979). See also Wilkinson, note 8, *supra*, at p. 137.

each individual Party to determine the steps to be taken to prevent preparations in its territory. During the drafting of this Convention, the representative of Yugoslavia to the Hostages Committee, in order "to avoid difficulties" in determining what was "practicable", proposed that this Article be changed to require Parties to take "all measures" to prevent such preparations.[19] However, as will be seen immediately below, the representatives of other States preferred the language as it stands and the proposed change was not made.

A requirement that Parties must take "all" measures to prevent preparations for acts of hostage-taking would have been undesirable. It seems impossible that a State could ever, in fact, take "all" measures to prevent such preparations. If this were the requirement and it happened that preparations for an act of hostage-taking nevertheless took place in the territory of a Party, then that Party could find itself in breach of this Convention for not taking measures which were simply unforeseeable. Of more importance, however, the measures taken will properly vary from State to State. As noted by the representative of the United States to the Hostages Committee, use of the words "all practicable measures" reflects the differences between various legal systems and, at the same time, stresses the need for co-operation between Parties.[20] The representative of Canada agreed that the existing language properly gives Parties latitude regarding the preventative measures they could adopt.[21] This was the approach, moreover, taken by the ILC which stated with respect to the corresponding provision of the New York Convention that the manner of implementation of the obligations imposed by that Article is not specifically set forth because the nature and extent of the measures, under both (a) and (b), should be determined by the Parties on the "basis of their particular experience and requirements" (although the ILC did allow that such measures would, "of course, include both police and judicial action as the varying circumstances might demand").[22]

[19] Second Report of the Hostages Committee, p. 33, para. 47.
[20] First Report of the Hostages Committee, pp. 68-69, para. 4.
[21] Id. at p. 74, para. 3. During the drafting of the New York Convention, the representative of the UK similarly stated with respect to the corresponding provision in that instrument that it is "implicit in the text . . . that the obligations assumed in this respect must be subject to the limitations imposed by national law and by the practicalities of the situation in each case". UN GAOR, 28th Sess., Plenary (2202nd mtg.), para. 242, UN Doc A/PV.2202 (1973).
[22] 1972 YBILC, Vol. II, p. 317. Similarly, the Terrorism Committee of the ILA has stated that although "coordination of the efforts of many States is necessary and desirable if the international community is prepared to act through legal means" to prevent terrorism, "the deep and necessary rules of the international legal order reserve to individual States a wide discretion . . . as to precisely what behaviour by individuals and groups is to be forbidden by each State's municipal law". See "Fourth Interim Report of the Committee on International Terrorism", ILA, *Report of the Sixtieth Conference* 350 (1982).

The precise implementation of this provision by a Party, therefore, will be in accordance with such factors as its constitutional and other legal safeguards and limitations (i.e., the extent to which it can take measures which may infringe upon individual liberty), its national resources (e.g., finances and manpower) and the extent to which such measures are necessary. The measures which are thus "practicable" will hinge upon a Party's legal, economic and political climate, as well as the level of prohibited activity currently or prospectively taking place in its territory. It must be recognized that the discretion that Parties have under this Article is very great; nevertheless, a State must in fact take those measures which are "practicable", and its failure to do so will be a breach of this Convention.

The obligations of States under this subparagraph will presumably be fulfilled either through the exercise of their normal police powers or through the specific legislation which many States have enacted in recent years to deal with terrorism in general. In this connexion, it might be noted that the FRG, for example, has implemented a number of legislative measures which are designed to counter terrorist acts. To mention a few of these provisions, it is illegal in that State to form, participate in or aid a terrorist association, i.e., one which is directed towards the commission of certain crimes, including murder and the taking of hostages.[23] To prevent such crimes, the police may, *inter alia*, search entire premises, monitor telephone conversations and establish roadblocks for identity checks.[24] Moreover, a defence counsel may be excluded from a case, *inter alia*, if there is reason to believe that he has misused his right of contact with his client in order to commit an offence.[25]

In the UK, in addition to the normal crime preventative devices available to the authorities, legislation has been enacted which confers extraordinary powers upon the government to deal with the problem of terrorism, including international terrorism.[26] This legislation, *inter alia*: makes it illegal to support or to belong to certain proscribed organizations; authorizes the Secretary of State to issue orders excluding from Great Britain, Northern Ireland or the entire United Kingdom any person who is, or has been, involved in the "commission, preparation or instigation" of acts of terrorism, or who is attempting, or may attempt, to enter Great Britain, Northern Ireland, or the entire United Kingdom with a view to committing, preparing or instigating an act of terrorism; makes it illegal to solicit,

---

[23] *StGB*, §§129 & 129a.
[24] *StPO*, §§110a, 103, 111, 153e & d & 163b & c.
[25] *Id.*, §§138a & 148. These provisions and other anti-terrorism measures in the FRG are discussed in Wardlaw, *Political Terrorism* 121-126 (1982).
[26] Prevention of Terrorism (Temporary Provisions) Act 1984.

accept, give, lend, etc., money or property to be used in connexion with the commission, preparation or instigation of an act of terrorism; makes it an offence for a person to fail to disclose, without reasonable excuse, information which he knows or believes might be of material assistance in preventing a terrorist act or which would be helpful in bringing to justice a person who has committed, prepared or instigated a terrorist act; allows a police constable to arrest without a warrant any person whom he has reasonable grounds for suspecting has been concerned in the commission, preparation or instigation of an act of terrorism; and authorizes the Secretary of State to order the examination of persons leaving or arriving in the country who may have been involved in the commission, preparation or instigation of an act of terrorism.[27]

"... including measures to prohibit in their territories illegal activities of persons, groups and organizations that encourage, instigate, organize or engage in the perpetration of acts of taking of hostages;"

This language was proposed by the representative of Yugoslavia to the Hostages Committee, who stated that since many acts of hostage-taking are committed by individuals, groups or organizations which are already known for their terrorist activities, "one of the best ways of preventing hostage-takings would be to eliminate terrorism by asking States to ban terrorist organizations and groups and to take the necessary steps to prevent them from engaging in their activities".[28] There exists no recorded debate regarding its inclusion, but Rosenstock asserts that it is:

> the tautological result of the desire of some states to ban activity not to their liking and the impossibility or at least unwillingness for Western and some other states to limit freedom of expression and assembly. No one raised any substantive problem with prohibiting illegal activity since the denomination as illegal establishes the prohibited nature of the activity and

---

[27] *Id.* at §§1, 3, 4, 5, 6, 8, 10, 11, 12 & 13. On the development and implementation of the various Prevention of Terrorism Acts, see Walker, *The Prevention of Terrorism in British Law* (1986).

It might be noted that while such provisions will be helpful in preventing terrorist acts, they have been criticized as unwarranted infringements on civil liberties. The FRG measures noted above, together with other anti-terrorism measures in that State, have been called the "most repressive ... in existence in a liberal democracy". See Wardlaw, note 25, *supra*, at p. 121. The UK act has been similarly criticized. See Scorer, *The New Prevention of Terrorism Act: The Case for Repeal* (3rd ed., 1985). These criticisms are noted to highlight the problem liberal democracies meet in seeking a proper balance between preventative measures and civil liberties.

[28] Second Report of the Hostages Committee, p. 38, para. 1.

the text cannot be read as even suggesting the utility of making licit acts illicit.[29]

While the phrase seems to add little to the content of this Article, to the extent that it seeks to prevent illegal activity of persons or groups who would encourage, etc., the taking of hostages, it may be a helpful addition to the text. And it may be noted that some of the provisions of UK and FRG law, discussed immediately above, seem to fall within this language.

SUBPARAGRAPH (B)

"... exchanging information and co-ordinating the taking of administrative and other measures as appropriate to prevent the commission of those offences."

While the first subparagraph is concerned with the actions which each State must take to prevent preparations for acts of hostage-taking, this subparagraph envisages close and regular co-operation between Parties to prevent the commission of such acts. It may be noted that this provision is slightly more detailed than the previous one regarding the obligations imposed upon Parties. While subparagraph (a) simply requires Parties to take "all practicable measures", this provision specifically requires them to "exchange information" and to "take administrative and other measures as appropriate" for such prevention. There is, of course, room for divergence as to what administrative and other measures are "appropriate" and as to the specific nature and content of the information exchanged,[30] but Parties which do not exchange information or co-ordinate administrative and other measures to the end of preventing acts of terrorism will be in breach of their obligations.

This subparagraph is an exact duplication of the language employed in the New York Convention and was not the subject of

---

[29] Rosenstock, p. 179. See also Rosenne, p. 129. It may be noted that although the original draft of the Rome Convention contained a phrase identical to the one currently under consideration, some opposition was expressed (see Halberstam, "Terrorism on the High Seas: The *Achille Lauro*, Piracy and the IMO Convention on Maritime Safety", 82 AJIL 307 (1988)), and no such phrase was included in the final draft.

[30] It may be noted that the language of this provision, requiring Parties to take the measures "as appropriate" to prevent the offences, on its face, seems to confer less discretion than the language in Article 3, requiring the territorial State to take the measures "it considers appropriate" to ease the hostage's situation. There is no indication as to whether this was a deliberate drafting decision; however, the wording of this subparagraph leaves open the possibility that one Party could allege that another has not, in fact, taken those co-operative measures which are appropriate to prevent such acts.

significant discussion during the drafting of this instrument. In the Hostages Committee, the US representative asserted that the provision is a clear requirement of any such international convention.[31] Only one State, Libya, is on record as arguing against its inclusion, asserting that the issue of co-operation is a matter for bilateral agreements.[32] To this latter position it may be responded that the precise extent of co-operation undertaken by States in fulfilment of this subparagraph will indeed be the subject of further agreements, whether formal or informal, bilateral (which will often be best given the wide variation in the levels of co-operation which States will wish to reach with each other) or multilateral (usually regional), but there is no good reason why the general obligation to undertake such co-operation should not be imposed herein.

The exchange of information is a *sine qua non* of any co-operative effort to prevent international acts of hostage-taking. Often local police and intelligence agencies have information on such matters as planned terrorist attacks, the connexions between terrorist groups and the whereabouts and activities of persons and groups which may be involved, currently or prospectively, in the preparation of an act of hostage-taking. This information should be communicated to other interested States, since it may place them in a position to prevent or help prevent such acts.[33] The more items of information available to law enforcement officials, the greater the chance that they will be able to obtain an accurate picture of current or prospective terrorist activity.[34]

In this regard, it might be noted that this provision suffers from a certain lack of specificity regarding the types of information which should be exchanged between Parties. The sharing of intelligence information is a sensitive issue and it should be realized that the specific form, content and detail of information which is communicated as between Parties will depend upon such factors as the terms of any agreement reached between them, the degree to which one State trusts another State with intelligence information gathered by the former, and the limitations imposed by the constitution and laws of the communicating State. This reality

---

[31] First Report of the Hostages Committee, p. 69, para. 4.
[32] Second Report of the Hostages Committee, p. 29, para. 25.
[33] See generally Wilkinson, note 8, *supra*, at p. 142. For example, in 1984, information uncovered by Swiss authorities and transmitted to US and Italian officials allowed them to prevent terrorist attacks on the US embassy in Rome. See Simon, "Misunderstanding Terrorism", 67 Foreign Policy 104, 117 (1987). The importance of information exchanges, moreover, has not been overlooked by the GA. Many of its resolutions on the subject of terrorism call upon States to take such action. See, e.g., GA Res 34/145 of 17 December 1979, UN GAOR, 34th Sess., Supp. 46, p. 244, UN Doc A/34/46 (1980); GA Res 42/159, note 17, *supra*.
[34] See Kerstetter, note 18, *supra*, at p. 110.

notwithstanding, this provision would have been improved if it had listed in at least a general way the types of information which should be exchanged.[35] But this is not a very serious deficiency since the clear requirement of this Article is that one Party must provide to another Party information in its possession — albeit edited or condensed as it feels its interests require — that is necessary for the latter to prevent an act of hostage-taking.[36]

Although the requirement of exchanging information is relatively straight-forward, it is less clear as to what is meant by "administrative and other measures" in the context of co-operative efforts to prevent acts of hostage-taking. The wording properly gives a great deal of latitude to each individual Party to determine the extent of the co-operation it will undertake with each other Party, and such co-operation could include, for example, such measures as joint surveillance operations and the development of common preventative strategies. However, since no specific measures are cited, the obligation envisaged by these words is somewhat amorphous. In an attempt to understand the types of co-operation which States could undertake pursuant to this provision, it might be helpful to examine some of the types of co-operation which States have developed to prevent acts of terrorism in general.

Co-operative measures implemented by States to prevent terrorism

It does not appear that States have implemented any special co-operative measures specifically in response to this Convention. However, there has been an increasing degree of co-operation amongst many States — Parties to this Convention as well as non-

---

[35] For example, Article 14 of the 1929 International Convention for the Suppression of Counterfeiting Currency, 112 LNTS 371, states that Parties thereto should "so far as [they] think expedient", notify each other of investigations regarding counterfeiters, as well as their movements and other details which may be of use, such as their descriptions, fingerprints and photographs.

[36] In any event, information relevant to acts of hostage-taking can be exchanged through Interpol. The Constitution of that organization prohibits it from involving itself with political offences (Art. 3, *Constitution and General Regulations of the International Criminal Police Organization (Interpol), as amended*) and that organization was reluctant for many years to assist in the prevention of terrorist acts. However, it has gradually increased its involvement in this regard. In 1972, the General Assembly of Interpol decided that the services of the organization can be utilized in respect of certain types of modern criminality "such as the holding of hostages with the intention of perpetrating blackmail or other forms of extortion". See Lador-Lederer, "A Legal Approach to International Terrorism", 9 Israel L.R. 194, 204 n.31 (1974). In 1984, Interpol reinterpreted Article 3 of its constitution, allowing it to take a greater role in preventative activity, and, since 1985, it has coordinated the flow of information relevant to anti-terrorism. See Murphy, "The Future of Multilateralism and Efforts to Combat International Terrorism", 25 Colum. J. Trans. L. 35, 54 (1986); 88 Dep't St. Bull., No. 2130, p. 49 (1988).

Parties — designed to prevent acts of terrorism in general. Although it is difficult to identify the precise measure of co-operation which currently exists between States in this regard (partially because much of it is conducted in secrecy), and while it appears that even closer co-operation is certainly possible and desirable, recent years have seen the institution of such activities (particularly on the regional level) as intelligence pools, police co-ordination in the apprehension of suspected terrorists and in frontier and airport surveillance, common training programmes, exchange of experience and common operations.[37] This has particularly been evident as between European and other Western States, on both the bilateral and multilateral levels.

For example, in Western Europe there are regular meetings on the ministerial and lower levels concerning the exchange of information, discussion of tactics, common training, etc.[38] The EEC has established the TREVI group, made up of the Ministers of each country who are responsible for counter-terrorism. In 1986, this group agreed to meet more frequently and to extend counter-terrorism co-operation to States outside the EEC, including the United States. Within the TREVI group, there are a number of working groups as well as a well-established machinery for exchange of information and intelligence regarding terrorism between the police and security services of member States. Moreover, that group approved a meeting of chief police officers from European airports, who exchange information and co-ordinate methods of dealing with high-risk flights. Also within the EEC, a working group on terrorism has been established within the framework of European political co-operation.[39] Other examples of co-operation in Europe include the "Wiener Club", consisting of high-level officials of the FRG, Italy, Austria, Switzerland, and France, which discusses issues of terrorism and mutual security, and the "Berner Club", which is a forum for representatives of various security agencies to deal, *inter alia*, with terrorism.[40]

In addition, the following examples of co-operation are worthy of note:

— the United States sponsors an "Anti-Terrorism Assistance Program" which provides counter-terrorism training and equipment

---

[37] See Gal-Or, note 7, *supra*, at pp. 73-74.
[38] *Id*.
[39] See the written answer to a Parliamentary Question on European co-operation in the fight against terrorism. H.C. Debs., Vol. 96, cols. 422-23 (1985-86).
[40] See Boge, "*Komplizierte Verfahrens-vorschriften und schwerfällige Geschäftswege*", 1985 *Kriminalistik* 38, 38.

to various participating States. As of March 1989 some 7,000 people from over 60 States participated in that programme.[41]

— the governments of France and the United States announced in February 1987 that they had reached an agreement to increase co-operation in the fight against terrorism by improving intelligence exchanges and law enforcement contacts between Paris and Washington.[42] The United States has also developed close co-operative relationships with many other States, including Canada, Britain and Israel, and is negotiating others.[43] These relationships involve communications, counter-terrorism technology, and military co-operation.[44]

— some co-operative measures have recently been taken against those States which are suspected of supporting terrorists in an effort to convince them to end such support. For example, the EEC announced in April 1986, in the light of the evidence of Libya's involvement in terrorism, that it had reached agreement amongst member States to reduce the size of Libyan People's Bureaus and to impose controls upon the entry and movement of Libyans — including diplomats and governmental officials — in their territories.[45] EEC governments have also agreed not to export arms or other military equipment to States which support terrorism.[46] In November 1986, the Council of Europe passed a resolution urging States to prevent abuse by terrorists of diplomatic and consular immunities, *inter alia*, by closer scrutiny of diplomats and exchanges of information.[47] And in late 1986, the EEC announced a series of economic, political, diplomatic and security-related measures against Syria.[48]

— through NATO there is an exchange of intelligence regarding weapons, personnel and techniques of terrorists.[49]

The implementation of measures such as these would be within the scope of this subparagraph.

---

[41] US Department of State, *Patterns of Global Terrorism: 1988*, p. iv (1989)
[42] *International Herald Tribune*, Oct. 18-19, 1986, p. 3.
[43] Dep't St. Bull., note 4, *supra*, at p. 3.
[44] *Id*. at p. 8.
[45] *Id*. at p. 4.
[46] *Id*. at p. 7.
[47] Dep't St. Bull., note 41, *supra*, at p. 79.
[48] *Id*. at p. 4. See also XXXII *Keesing's Contemporary Archives* 34784 (1986). These measures were in response to evidence of Syrian involvement in terrorist activity in Britain and West Berlin. See p. 20 (note 36 and accompanying text in Part I).
[49] See Gal-Or, note 7, *supra*, at p. 75.

Article 5

ESTABLISHMENT OF JURISDICTION OVER THE OFFENCES

1. Each State Party shall take such measures as may be necessary to establish its jurisdiction over any of the offences set forth in article 1 which are committed:
    (a) in its territory or on board a ship or aircraft registered in that State;
    (b) by any of its nationals or, if that State considers it appropriate, by those stateless persons who have their habitual residence in its territory;
    (c) in order to compel that State to do or abstain from doing any act; or
    (d) with respect to a hostage who is a national of that State, if that State considers it appropriate.

2. Each State Party shall likewise take such measures as may be necessary to establish its jurisdiction over the offences set forth in article 1 in cases where the alleged offender is present in its territory and it does not extradite him to any of the States mentioned in paragraph 1 of this article.

3. This Convention does not exclude any criminal jurisdiction exercised in accordance with internal law.

1. Introduction

While Article 2 requires States Parties to make the offences set forth in Article 1 punishable under their domestic laws, this Article requires Parties to establish their prescriptive jurisdiction over those offences on various bases, and thereby seeks to ensure that those laws can be applied to acts of hostage-taking in the specified circumstances. In particular, the Article requires, in paragraph 1, the establishment of what may be called "primary" jurisdiction by the States most directly affected by a particular act of hostage-taking and, in paragraph 2, the establishment of "subsidiary" jurisdiction, based on the principle of universality, by States which may be less directly concerned, but in whose territory an offender is subsequently present.[1] Moreover, the Article, in paragraph 3, makes it clear that the Convention does not impair the right of a State to exercise jurisdiction over an offence on grounds not specifically provided for in the Convention. The wide jurisdictional net thus envisaged by this Article is designed to ensure that no "safe-havens" exist for hostage-takers.

---

[1] The terms "primary" and "subsidiary" or "secondary" jurisdiction were used by many of the draftsmen of this Convention. See, e.g., Second Report of the Hostages Committee, p. 42, para. 20.

Paragraph 1 of this Article corresponds to Article 4(1) of the Hague Convention, Article 5(1) of the Montreal Convention, Article 3(1) of the New York Convention and Article 6(1) and (2) of the Rome Convention. Many of the bases upon which this Convention requires States to establish primary jurisdiction, however, differ from those provided for in the earlier-adopted instruments, and from those provided for in the FRG draft.[2] Paragraphs 2 and 3 are identical in substance to the corresponding paragraphs in the other Conventions (except in the Rome Convention the corresponding provisions are in paragraphs 4 and 5) and remain essentially unchanged from the original draft.

During the drafting of this Article, much of the discussion centred around the following issues: the precise bases of jurisdiction which should be included in paragraph 1; whether the Convention should also require Parties to establish jurisdiction over serious acts of violence which are committed during an act of hostage-taking; and whether a system of priority of jurisdiction amongst those States listed in Article 1 should be established. All of these issues are treated in some depth below.

The expansion of jurisdictional bases by multilateral conventions dealing with international offences

The legal literature on the subject of jurisdiction is virtually unanimous in listing five principles upon which States base their jurisdiction over criminal offences: the territorial principle, the nationality principle, the passive personality principle, the protective, or security, principle and the universality principle.[3] The territorial principle, i.e., jurisdiction based on the location of the offence, is "everywhere regarded as of primary importance and of fundamental character",[4] but beyond that the extent to which States utilize these principles varies greatly. At the risk of over-simplification (and these points will be developed more completely below), it may be stated that the common law States view the exercise of jurisdiction on a basis other than territorial as somewhat unusual, while the civil law States commonly employ the nationality principle, i.e., jurisdiction based on the nationality of the offender, in addition to the territorial principle.

---

[2] FRG draft, Art. 5(1).

[3] See, e.g., "Introductory Comment", 1935 Harvard Research Draft Convention on Jurisdiction with Respect to Crime, 29 AJIL Supp. 443, 445 (1935); Bowett, "Jurisdiction: Changing Patterns of Authority over Activities and Resources", 53 BYIL 1, 4-12 (1982); Akehurst, "Jurisdiction in International Law", 46 BYIL 145, 152-169 (1972-73); Schachter, "International Law in Theory and Practice", 178 RC (1982-V) 239-265.

[4] Harvard Research, note 3, *supra*, at 445.

ARTICLE 5

The passive personality principle, i.e., jurisdiction based on the nationality of the victim, is somewhat controversial, generally opposed by many States but employed by others, and the protective principle, i.e., jurisdiction based on the harm done to the State concerned, is used to some degree by most States with respect to specific types of offences. Finally, the universality principle, which is based solely on custody of the offender and does not require any other link between the State exercising jurisdiction and the offence, is employed by some States in certain circumstances,[5] and has recently been sanctioned in many multilateral treaties dealing with specific crimes of international significance. However, the only offence which is indisputably "universal" in nature — i.e., amenable under customary international law to the jurisdiction of all States regardless of where and by whom committed — is piracy.[6]

It is, in general, desirable that as many States as possible establish their jurisdiction over international offences, i.e., those crimes which are considered to be of concern to the entire community of States. Perpetrators of such crimes will often be found outside of the State in whose territory the crime was committed, and often extradition to the territorial State will be impractical or impossible due to such factors as the lack of an extradition treaty, other restrictions in the requested State's laws and the lack of a request from the territorial State.[7] Because such crimes present a threat to the entire international order, it is imperative that offenders are prosecuted, and the greater the number of States which have jurisdiction over the offences, the greater the possibility that this will happen. Thus, most of the existing multilateral conventions dealing with crimes of international concern have at least authorized, if not required, some departure from the principle of territoriality.[8] Provisions which expand the bases upon which many States would otherwise establish jurisdiction over

---

[5] See, e.g., *StGB*, §7(2)(ii), which provides that the German criminal code will apply to an offence committed abroad if the offence is punishable in the place where it was committed and the offender is subsequently present in German territory and cannot be extradited because there is no request, or the request is refused or the request cannot be complied with. See also Sørensen (ed.), *Manual of Public International Law* 366 (1968).

[6] See Bowett, note 3, *supra*, at pp. 10-12; *In re Piracy Jure Gentium*, [1934] AC 586, 589; United Nations Secretariat, *Historical Survey of the Question of International Criminal Jurisdiction* 1, UN Doc A/CN.4/7/Rev. 1 (1949). Other crimes often mentioned as being universal in nature as a matter of customary international law are slavery and war crimes. See, e.g., Sørensen, note 5, *supra*, at pp. 365-67; UK War Office, *British Manual of Military Law*, Part III, para. 637 (1958).

[7] See generally the commentary on Article 10 (pp. 227-244).

[8] However, not all such Conventions contain provisions regarding jurisdiction. The 1926 Convention with the Object of Securing the Abolition of Slavery and Slave Trade, 60 LNTS 253, and the 1956 Supplementary Convention on the Abolition of Slavery, 266 UNTS 3, require Parties to punish those involved in slavery, but make no mention of jurisdiction.

criminal offences not only ensure the jurisdictional competence of a larger number of municipal courts, and provide in theory a better chance of bringing offenders to justice, they foster a degree of tolerance — if not actually harmonizing State practice in this area — between States with respect to the exercise of jurisdiction, and thus reduce the possibility that one State will assert that another has exceeded the limits of jurisdiction acceptable under international law. The extent to which such Conventions actually depart from the territorial principle, however, varies greatly from instrument to instrument, with, in general, the more recent instruments containing bolder provisions in this regard than earlier ones.[9]

Some Conventions are quite restrictive and do not go beyond the most traditional notions of jurisdiction. For example, Article 1 of the 1923 Convention on the Suppression of the Circulation of and Traffic in Obscene Publications requires States Parties to take "all measures to discover, prosecute and punish any person engaged" in the listed offences. Article 2, however, provides that persons committing such offences shall "be amenable to the Courts of the Contracting Parties in whose territories the offence, or any of the constitutive elements of the offence, was committed". That Article further provides that offenders shall be amenable also to the "Courts of the Contracting Party whose nationals they are", but only if "the laws of such country shall permit it".[10] Thus, that instrument requires application of the territorial principle and authorizes, but does not require, application of the nationality principle. Article VI of the 1948 Convention on the Prevention and Punishment of the Crime of Genocide provides that offenders shall be tried by the State in whose territory the offence was committed. Drafted at a time when there was movement towards the establishment of an international criminal court,[11] that Article also provides that offenders may be tried by an international penal tribunal which may have jurisdiction over the offence by agreement of the Parties.[12] Because no such tribunal exists, however, and because the Convention in any event imposes no obligations upon Parties

---

[9] Some authors cite generally the existing multilateral conventions on international crimes and state that they provide for the principle of universality. Mann, for example, states that "[t]raffic in women and children, trade in narcotics, falsification of currency, piracy and trade in indecent publications are crimes covered by such treaties and therefore by the principle of universality". Mann, *Studies in International Law* 81 (1973). See also Feller, "Jurisdiction over Offences with a Foreign Element", in Bassiouni & Nanda, *A Treatise on International Criminal Law*, Vol. II, 32-33 n.38 (1973). However, as the following discussion indicates, some of these conventions manifestly do not provide for universal jurisdiction.
[10] 27 LNTS 217.
[11] See generally pp. 97 & 100 (notes 17 & 32 in the commentary on Article 2).
[12] 78 UNTS 277.

regarding the acceptance of the jurisdiction of such a tribunal, that instrument effectively provides only for territorial jurisdiction.[13]

Some Conventions take a somewhat bolder approach, envisaging, but not requiring, jurisdiction based upon universality. Article 9 of the 1929 Convention for the Suppression of Counterfeiting Currency requires application of the universality principle in some cases, but only when the accused is in a State whose internal law generally recognizes that principle.[14] Article 36(2)(iv) of the 1961 Single Convention on Narcotic Drugs is drafted in stronger terms, stating that an offender should be tried by the State in whose territory the offence was committed, or by the State in whose territory he is found if extradition is not possible. While this latter provision would seem to require application of the universality principle, the Article goes on to provide, in paragraph 3, that it is subject to a State's internal laws regarding jurisdiction.[15] Thus, that Convention encourages application of the universality principle, but it does not require States to amend their laws to make this possible.

However, many conventions on international offences actually

---

[13] Of course, if genocide is a crime under customary international law, and there is a strong case that it is, then, notwithstanding the obligations regarding jurisdiction which Parties undertake pursuant to the Genocide Convention, jurisdiction over the offence may be universal by customary law. See *Attorney-General of the Government of Israel v. Eichmann*, 36 ILR 5, 34-35 (1968).

[14] 112 LNTS 371. Specifically, the Article provides that foreigners who have committed abroad any of the offences proscribed in the Convention, "and who are in the territory of a country whose internal legislation recognises as a general rule the principle of the prosecution of offences committed abroad, should be punishable in the same way as if the offence had been committed in the territory of that country". However, this obligation is subject to the condition that "extradition has been requested and that the country to which application is made cannot hand over the person accused for some reason which has no connection with the offence". Article 8 of the Counterfeiting Convention provides for application of the nationality principle in some cases, specifically in "countries where the principle of the extradition of nationals is not recognised" and the national has returned to his State after committing the offence abroad. However, the scope of this provision is limited by the condition that it will not apply "if, in a similar case, the extradition of a foreigner could not be granted".

[15] 520 UNTS 204. Earlier in paragraph 2, moreover, the Article states that the obligations imposed therein are subject to the constitutional limitations of a State Party as well as its "legal system and domestic law". Similar qualifications can be found in Article 22 of the 1971 Convention on Psychotropic Substances, UN Doc E/CONF 58/6, *reprinted in* 10 ILM 261 (1971).

The position with respect to the 1973 Convention on the Prevention and Punishment of Apartheid, 1015 UNTS 244, is somewhat unclear. Article IV of that instrument provides that Parties should "adopt legislative, judicial and administrative measures to prosecute, bring to trial and punish [offenders] in accordance with their jurisdiction". Article V states that persons charged with the specified acts "may be tried by a competent tribunal of any State Party to the Convention which may acquire jurisdiction" over them (or by an international penal tribunal which has jurisdiction pursuant to an agreement of the Parties). These provisions indicate that States may adopt a very wide jurisdiction, including universal, to deal with the crime of *apartheid*, but that they are not actually required to adopt a wider jurisdiction to deal with that offence than they normally use for criminal offences.

require States to establish their jurisdiction on specified bases, some of which go beyond the limits of which many or most States would normally respect. One far-reaching and early example of such a provision can be found in the four 1949 Geneva Conventions on the laws of armed conflict, which require each State Party to enact legislation providing penal sanctions for those committing "grave breaches" of the instruments and to "bring such persons, regardless of their nationality, before its own courts", if it does not hand them over to another Party.[16] These instruments are widely (although not unanimously) interpreted as creating, and requiring, "universal" jurisdiction over those offences which constitute grave breaches.[17]

Less demanding provisions may be found in many other instruments. Article 3 of the Tokyo Convention, for example, requires each State Party to establish its jurisdiction over offences committed on board aircraft registered in that State, without regard to the location of the aircraft at the time of the offence or to the nationality of the victim or offender.[18] While the establishment of jurisdiction by the State of registration of an aircraft seems to have been fully acceptable under customary international law and is now commonplace, State practice in this regard was not entirely consistent prior to the Tokyo Convention.[19] The 1977 European Convention on the Suppression of Terrorism takes a somewhat modest approach to the issue of jurisdiction, providing that each State Party must establish

---

[16] Convention I, Art. 49; Convention II, Art. 50; Convention III, Art. 129; Convention IV, Art. 146. See full citations on p. 263 (note 1 in the commentary on Article 12). It may be noted that the Geneva Conventions do not specifically require States to *establish* universal jurisdiction over the offences concerned. However, the obligation *aut dedere aut judicare* implies such a requirement. In this connexion, it might be noted that paragraph 2 of this Article may not strictly be necessary because establishment of jurisdiction over the offences would in any event be necessary in order to comply with the alternative obligation *aut judicare* in Article 8 of this Convention. However, paragraph 2 is a helpful clarification of States' obligations in this regard.

[17] See, e.g., Akehurst, note 3, *supra*, at p. 160; Draper, *The Red Cross Conventions* 105 (1958). Not all commentators agree, however. Bowett, for example, maintains that the right to exercise jurisdiction over war crimes belongs only to a victorious belligerent. Bowett, note 3, *supra*, at p. 12.

[18] Article 4 of that instrument, moreover, authorizes certain States to interfere with an aircraft in flight in order to exercise criminal jurisdiction. These include a State in whose territory an offence has effects, a State whose national or permanent resident has been the victim of an offence, a State against whose security an offence has been committed and the State of registration.

[19] Even prior to World War II, some sources maintained that offences committed on board aircraft were subject to the jurisdiction of the State of registration in much the same way as are ships. See, e.g., Harvard Research, note 3, *supra*, at pp. 508-09. However, in the past not all States so extended their jurisdiction. See Shubber, *Jurisdiction over Crimes on Board Aircraft* 48-56 (1973). The Tokyo Convention now has over 120 States Parties (see Bowman & Harris, *Multilateral Treaties Index and Current Status* 280 (1984) & 4th Supp. 68 (1987)) and such jurisdiction is widespread. See, e.g., the Tokyo Convention Act 1967, §1(1) of which extends the criminal jurisdiction of the United Kingdom to acts committed on board aircraft registered in that State.

its jurisdiction over offences wherein the alleged offender is present in its territory and it does not extradite him after receiving a request for extradition from another State Party whose "jurisdiction is based on a rule of jurisdiction existing equally in the law of the requested State".[20] In other words, a Party must only establish its jurisdiction over offences wherein: 1) an alleged offender is present in its territory; 2) it turns down a request for extradition from another State Party; and 3) that other Party requested extradition relying on a basis of jurisdiction that is employed also by the requested State with respect to the crime concerned.[21] If, for example, a person accused of one of the acts prohibited in that instrument is present in State A and State B requests his extradition based on the fact that the alleged offender is a national of State B, then State A must only have established its jurisdiction over that offence if it normally employs the nationality principle with respect to that particular offence.

The most comprehensive provisions regarding the establishment of jurisdiction by States Parties may be found in the anti-terrorism Conventions. The pattern established in the Hague Convention and followed in the Montreal, New York, Rome and Hostages Conventions, is to create a two-tiered system for the establishment of jurisdiction. The first tier ("primary" jurisdiction) requires each Party to establish its jurisdiction over offences in a number of specified situations, e.g., territorial offences or offences committed by its nationals. The second tier ("secondary" or "subsidiary" jurisdiction) is based on the principle of universality, requiring each Party to establish its jurisdiction over any offences wherein the offender is subsequently present in its territory and it does not extradite him to any of the States with primary jurisdiction.[22] There is little difference in effect between the first and second category, although States in the second

---

[20] Art. 6.
[21] As the Council of Europe pointed out, for example:
the United Kingdom extradition arrangements are generally based on the territorial principle. Similarly the jurisdiction of the domestic courts is generally based on the territorial principle. In general there is no jurisdiction over offences committed by nationals abroad but there are certain exceptions, notably murder. Because of this jurisdictional limitation the United Kingdom in most cases cannot claim extradition of a national for an offence committed abroad. In the reverse situation there would be no obligation for the United Kingdom under Article 6 arising from a request for extradition from a State able to exercise such a jurisdiction. If, however, the request was for extradition of a national for a murder falling under Article 1 and committed abroad, the obligation under Article 6 would apply because the United Kingdom has a similar jurisdiction in respect of this offence.
See Council of Europe, *Explanatory Report on the European Convention on the Suppression of Terrorism* 16-17 (1977).
[22] Similar provisions are contained in Article 4 of the 1984 Convention Against Torture and Other Cruel and Inhuman or Degrading Treatment or Punishment, UN Doc A/RES/39/46, *reprinted in* 23 ILM 1027 (1984) & 24 ILM 535 (1985), and in Article 8 of the 1980 Convention on the Physical Protection of Nuclear Material, Misc. 27 (1980), Cmnd. 8112, *reprinted in* 18 ILM 1419 (1979).

group would not normally request extradition of an alleged offender, while those in the first have at least a moral responsibility to do so and, given their close connexion to the offence, will often want to. Moreover, extradition to the States listed in paragraph 1 will be facilitated by Article 10, paragraph 4.

2. Interpretation

Paragraph 1: Establishment of Primary Jurisdiction over the Offences

This paragraph lists six bases upon which States Parties must — or, in the case of two of the bases, may — establish their primary jurisdiction over acts of hostage-taking and over attempts to take hostages and participation in those offences. As earlier noted, some of the bases are similar to those set forth in the other anti-terrorism treaties. However, these instruments diverge significantly with respect to the precise bases upon which they require States to establish their jurisdiction. Article 4 of the Hague Convention requires each State Party to establish primary jurisdiction on three grounds: when the offence is committed on board aircraft registered therein; when a hijacked aircraft lands in its territory with the alleged offender still on board; and when the offence is committed on board an aircraft leased without crew and the lessee has his principal place of business in that State or, if he has no principal place of business, his residence in that State. Article 5 of the Montreal Convention requires establishment of jurisdiction on the same three bases and adds the State in whose territory the offence is committed. Article 3 of the New York Convention requires the establishment of jurisdiction by the territorial State or the State of registration of a ship or aircraft on which the offence takes place, the national State of the alleged offender and the State on whose behalf the internationally protected person enjoys his status (a basis which overlaps with both the passive personality principle and the protective principle). Article 6 of the Rome Convention provides for the same bases of jurisdiction as the Hostages Convention, although establishment of jurisdiction by the State which is the target of compulsion is optional (and that Article does not, of course, refer to the State of registration of an aircraft). Article 3 of the Rome Protocol is also similar to the Hostages Convention in this regard.

To some extent, these variations reflect the fact that the different conventions are all directed towards different crimes. For example, the New York Convention deals with crimes against diplomats, and this explains the obligation to establish jurisdiction by States on whose behalf a victimized internationally protected person enjoys his status. By way of contrast, this Convention requires the establishment of jurisdiction by a State when the offence is committed "in order to compel that State to do or abstain from doing any act", a basis which, although very often relevant as well to other terrorist offences such as hijacking, is tailored particularly to the nature of the offence of hostage-taking. However, not all the variations can be attributed to the different interests protected by the Conventions. This Convention (and the Rome Convention) envisages the establishment of jurisdiction on more bases than do the earlier ones, and most of these bases could just as easily find a rationale for use in the earlier instruments. Indeed, paragraph 1 of this Article contains a textbook-like listing of the bases of jurisdiction extant under customary international law (except the universality principle which is provided for in paragraph 2). The increase in the number of bases of jurisdiction can probably be attributed partially to an insistence upon such an expansion by States which favour certain types of extraterritorial jurisdiction, such as the passive personality principle, and partially also to a recognition on the part of most of the draftsmen that it is desirable to have as many States as possible establish jurisdiction over the offences.

However, it appears that most States wanted some restrictions on the number of States which would be required to establish primary jurisdiction over the offences. The draft submitted by the FRG would have required the establishment of jurisdiction by the territorial State, including the State of registration of a ship or aircraft, the national State of the offender and the State which is the object of compulsion. Moreover, the FRG draft would have required the establishment of jurisdiction by a State when an international organization of which it is a member was the target of compulsion.[23] This last basis would have meant that if the United Nations, for example, was the target of compulsion, all member States of that organization would have primary jurisdiction over the crime. The French delegation to the Hostages Committee proposed that the draft be amended to require also that each State Party establish jurisdiction over offences wherein the hostage is a national of that State.[24] However, the representative of the Netherlands proposed the deletion of the provision regarding international organizations[25] and urged rejection of the French proposal, asserting that primary jurisdiction under the Convention should be limited to the territorial State, the national State of the

---

[23] FRG draft, Art. 5.
[24] UN Doc A/AC.188/L.13 (1977), in First Report of the Hostages Committee, p. 113.
[25] UN Doc A/AC.188/L.14 (1977), in First Report of the Hostages Committee, p. 114.

offender and the State which was the target of the compulsion. He argued that extending primary jurisdiction to a greater number of States might weaken the system of enforcement established by the Convention since it would be very difficult to determine which State should properly exercise jurisdiction when there were competing claims from so many different Parties.[26] The FRG representative replied that he was not in favour of reducing the number of States which would be required to establish primary jurisdiction since it would not be desirable to have to resort too often to the subsidiary jurisdiction provided for in paragraph 2.[27] In the end, the provision regarding international organizations was deleted and the French proposal was amended to make jurisdiction on that basis optional.[28]

In one sense, therefore, the argument of the representative of the Netherlands can be seen to have prevailed since the only States which are actually required to establish primary jurisdiction under the Convention are the territorial State, the national State of the offender and the State which is the target of the compulsion. However, given the potentially larger number of States with primary jurisdiction, i.e., those which establish jurisdiction on a permissive basis, States should not often have to resort to the secondary jurisdictional basis provided in paragraph 2. In most cases, at least one of the States with primary jurisdiction will request the extradition of an alleged offender when he has fled to a State with no such jurisdiction, thus ensuring that the State ultimately exercising jurisdiction will have a significant connexion with the offence and, therefore, a genuine interest in seeing that the offender is brought to justice.

"Each State Party shall take such measures as may be necessary to establish its jurisdiction . . ."

This provision requires each State Party to take whatever measures are necessary under its internal law to establish its jurisdiction over acts of hostage-taking in specified circumstances. Of course, if a State's jurisdiction is already wide enough to cover such situations, no steps must in fact be taken in this regard.

Some question might arise as to the scope of the obligation envisaged by these words. In particular, some writers have suggested, somewhat obscurely, with respect to both this Article and the identical provisions in the earlier anti-terrorism treaties, that these words require States not only to *establish* jurisdiction, i.e., by enacting prescriptive legislation which would ensure that their domestic laws

---

[26] Second Report of the Hostages Committee, p. 39, para. 6.
[27] *Id.* at p. 42, para. 20.
[28] See *id.* at p. 10, para. 39; Third Report of the Hostages Committee, p. 12, para. 47.

regarding criminal jurisdiction authorize their courts to deal with offences in the envisaged circumstances, but also actually to *exercise* it with respect to such offences.[29] But this interpretation cannot stand. The exercise of jurisdiction is dealt with in Article 8 of this Convention, which requires the State in whose territory the offender is present, if it does not extradite him, to submit the case to its authorities for the purpose of prosecution. It is a fundamental principle of international law that one State cannot, without permission, exercise enforcement jurisdiction in the territory of another State,[30] and the writers just referred to do not suggest how, for example, the national State of an offender can exercise jurisdiction over him when he is in another State. Other commentators thus take the better view that this provision is concerned only with the establishment of jurisdiction and not with its exercise.[31]

When an alleged offender is not present in its territory, the best that a Party can do is attempt to exercise its jurisdiction by requesting extradition from the State in which the alleged offender is present, and the requirement that States Parties must establish primary jurisdiction over the offences in certain circumstances is designed to increase the probability that they will do so. However, there is no specific requirement under this Convention that a State with primary jurisdiction must actually request extradition. The conclusion that States other than the one in whose territory the alleged offender is found are not obliged to exercise, or attempt to exercise, their jurisdiction over him is implicit in the statement of the representative of the Netherlands to the Sixth Committee that the States with primary jurisdiction have "at least a moral obligation to request extradition when the alleged offender was found in a State which, under normal jurisdictional rules [the reference was to States with subsidiary jurisdiction under paragraph 2], would have no involvement with the crime at all".[32]

"... over any of the offences set forth in article 1 which are committed:"

"... in its territory ..."

The first part of subparagraph (a) requires each Party to establish its

---

[29] See Shubber, pp. 219-20; Shubber, "Aircraft Hijacking under the Hague Convention 1970 — A New Regime?", 22 ICLQ 687, 706-707 (1973); Wadegaonkar, "Hijacking and International Law", 22 Indian J. Int'l L. 360, 365 (1982).

[30] See generally, Jennings, "Extraterritorial Jurisdiction and the United States Antitrust Laws", 33 BYIL 146, 149 (1957); the *Lotus* case, PCIJ (1927), Series A, No. 10, p. 18.

[31] See White, pp. 41-42; Wood, p. 807.

[32] UN GAOR, 34th Sess., C.6 (13th mtg.), p. 9, para. 40, UN Doc A/C.6/SR.13 (1979).

jurisdiction over offences which are committed in its territory. As earlier noted, the territorial principle of jurisdiction is the fundamental basis upon which States establish jurisdiction over criminal offences. Although this Convention does not establish any priority of jurisdiction for the territorial State, most acts of hostage-taking should be dealt with in the State in which the crime is committed.[33]

The inclusion of this basis of jurisdiction in the Convention was non-controversial. The only recorded discussion which appears is a suggestion by the representative of the Netherlands to the Hostages Committee that the words "wholly or partly" be added to this provision.[34] The representative of the United States replied that while he had no objection to such an addition, it was unnecessary since that principle was implicit in the existing wording.[35] No more recorded discussion was held regarding this issue and it would seem that this provision requires Parties to establish their jurisdiction over situations wherein one or more of the constitutive elements of the offences takes place in their territories. This is in accord with common State practice.[36]

The question could arise whether a State Party is obliged pursuant to this subparagraph to establish its jurisdiction over offences which are committed in dependent or non-self-governing territories under its control. The answer would appear to be no. This subparagraph provides that a State must only establish jurisdiction over offences committed in "its" territory. While States commonly establish and exercise jurisdiction which is essentially "territorial" in nature over criminal offences committed in dependent territories to which they have title or which are otherwise under their control,[37] such areas are not, strictly speaking, the territory of those States.[38] In contrast to this

---

[33] This fact was noted by a representative of the US Department of Justice during hearings on that country's implementing legislation for this Convention. See US Senate, Committee on the Judiciary, *Hearings before the Subcommittee on Security and Terrorism*, 98th Cong., 2d Sess., pp. 48-49.

[34] Second Report of the Hostages Committee, p. 39, para. 8.

[35] *Id.* at p. 42, para. 23.

[36] See generally, Harvard Research, note 3, *supra*, at p. 495; Akehurst, note 3, *supra*, at pp. 152-53 (and sources cited). Bowett notes that when States determine whether a crime has been committed in their territory, the "general tendency, which accords with common sense, is to ascertain whether one of the constituent elements has been committed within their territory". Bowett, note 3, *supra*, at pp. 6-7.

[37] See, e.g., 18 USC §5, which provides that "[t]he term 'United States', as used in this title [dealing with criminal offences] in a territorial sense, includes all places and waters, continental or insular, subject to the jurisdiction of the United States, except the Canal Zone".

[38] The Declaration on Principles of International Law concerning Friendly Relations and Co-operation among States in accordance with the Charter of the United Nations, GA Res 2625 (XXV) of 24 October 1970, UN GAOR, 25th Sess., Supp. 28, p. 121, UN Doc A/8028 (1971) states that "the territory of a colony or other non-self-governing

language certain other conventions dealing with international criminal offences contain language which makes it clear that States Parties thereto must establish jurisdiction in dependent territories.[39] Had the draftsmen of this Convention intended that States Parties must establish such jurisdiction they presumably would similarly have so provided. The absence of such a requirement in this Convention seems unfortunate, in so far as it may result in a gap in jurisdiction.[40]

Another issue which arises is the extent to which States should establish jurisdiction over offences committed in certain off-shore areas outside their territorial sea. This provision presumably requires Parties to establish their jurisdiction over offences committed in their territorial waters (and in their airspace) since these areas are generally considered to be part of a State's territory.[41] Somewhat less clear is the position with respect to offences which might be committed on an artificial island or installation (such as an oil rig) located on the continental shelf or in the exclusive economic zone (EEZ) of a particular State Party. States have long claimed and been granted certain sovereign rights with regard to exploration and exploitation of natural resources on their continental shelves[42] and, to a lesser extent, the EEZ.[43] Moreover, Article 5 of the 1958 Geneva Convention on the Continental Shelf provides that the coastal State is entitled to construct and maintain "installations and other devices" necessary for the exploration and exploitation of the continental shelf "and to

territory has, under the Charter of the United Nations, a status separate and distinct from the territory of the State administering it ...". Further to this issue, see Shaw, "Territory in International Law", 13 Netherlands J. Int'l L. 61, 88-91 (1982). Similarly, see Oppenheim, *International Law*, Vol. I, p. 460 (H. Lauterpacht, ed., 8th ed., 1958), in which it is noted that a mandated or trust territory is not the territory of a State, notwithstanding the many aspects of sovereignty that State may exercise therein.

[39] See, e.g., Article 5(a) of the Torture Convention, note 22, *supra*, which provides that each State Party must establish jurisdiction over offences "committed in any territory under its jurisdiction ...".

[40] The language of this subparagraph is essentially identical to that contained in Article 5(a) of the FRG draft, and it is unclear from the record whether the draftsmen considered any alternative language. To the extent, if any, that the issue may have been considered during the drafting of this Convention, the somewhat restrictive language of this subparagraph may have been preferred by some of the draftsmen due to their reluctance to concede the establishment and exercise of "territorial" jurisdiction by certain States in territories to which they claim title.

[41] See generally, Arts. 1 & 2, 1958 Geneva Convention on the Territorial Sea and Contiguous Zone, 516 UNTS 205; Arts. 1 & 2, 1944 Chicago Convention on International Civil Aviation, 15 UNTS 295. It might be noted that Article 6(1)(b) of the Rome Convention specifically requires the establishment of jurisdiction by each State Party over offences committed in its territorial sea.

[42] See, e.g., Art. 2, 1958 Geneva Convention on the Continental Shelf, 499 UNTS 311; Art. 77, 1982 Convention on the Law of the Sea, 21 ILM 1261, 1285 (1982); 1945 Truman Proclamation on the Continental Shelf, *reprinted in* Whiteman, *Digest of International Law*, Vol. 4, 756 (1965).

[43] See, e.g., Art. 56, 1982 Convention on the Law of the Sea, Misc. 11 (1983), Cmnd 8941, *reprinted in* 21 ILM 1261, 1280 (1982); Phillips, "The Exclusive Economic Zone as a Concept in International Law", 26 ICLQ 585 (1977).

establish safety zones around such installations and devices and to take in those zones measures necessary for their protection". The Article also provides that such installations are under the jurisdiction of the coastal State.[44] Articles 60 and 80 of the 1982 Convention on the Law of the Sea similarly grant the coastal State exclusive rights to construct, operate and use artificial islands and installations in the EEZ and on the continental shelf, respectively, and provide that such are under the exclusive jurisdiction of the coastal State for the purposes of "customs, fiscal, health, safety and immigration laws and regulations".[45]

While a coastal State's rights in the EEZ and on the continental shelf are less than territorial sovereignty, the jurisdiction that they are granted under those instruments and the jurisdiction which many have in fact assumed (particularly with respect to the continental shelf, but increasingly with regard to the EEZ) is similar to territorial jurisdiction, albeit only to the extent that such is consistent with their rights in those areas.[46] This would include criminal jurisdiction. In the United Kingdom, for example, the Continental Shelf Act 1964 provides that any act or omission which "takes place on, under, or above an installation in a designated area or any waters within 500 metres of such an installation" which would be an offence in any part of the United Kingdom will be treated as an offence under the law of that part.[47] Thus, while the matter may not be entirely free from doubt given the uncertain status of these rules under customary international law, it would seem to be the better interpretation of this Convention that a State's "territory" for the purposes of establishing territorial jurisdiction over acts of hostage-taking would include any artificial islands and installations which it may have constructed on its continental shelf or in its EEZ.[48] It may be noted that the Rome Protocol, of course, specifically requires States to establish jurisdiction over terrorist offences committed against fixed platforms located on their continental shelves.

[44] 499 UNTS 311.
[45] 21 ILM 1261, 1280-81 & 1286.
[46] See Bowett, note 3, *supra*, at pp. 5-6 (and sources cited).
[47] §3. See also 43 USC §1331, *et seq.*, which extends US laws to artificial islands and substructures engaged in exploration and exploitation of the resources of the seabed and subsoil on the continental shelf.
[48] See generally Nyhart & Kessler, "Ocean Vessels and Offshore Structures", in Evans & Murphy, *Legal Aspects of International Terrorism* 198-203 (1978). Cf. *In re Schtraks*, [1962] 2 All ER 176, 180-81, in which the court noted that the concept of "territory" as used in extradition treaties includes areas in which a State exercises *de jure* and *de facto* control. While this willingness to extend the "territory" of a State for the purpose of establishing jurisdiction under this Convention may, at first glance, appear inconsistent with the conclusion reached above with respect to dependent territories, it might be noted that in considering areas such as the continental shelf and EEZ, the problems of the rights of self-determination, etc., as held by inhabitants of dependent territories do not arise.

"... or on board a ship or aircraft registered in that State ..."

Acts of hostage-taking, overlapping with the offence of hijacking, are commonly committed on board aircraft. Moreover, as the *Achille Lauro* incident demonstrated, ships are also possible locations for such offences. The second part of subparagraph (a) requires States to establish their jurisdiction over offences which are committed on board ships and aircraft registered therein. It is generally accepted under international law that ships and aircraft are, for the purposes of jurisdiction, assimilated to the territory of the State in which they are registered,[49] and this provision did not cause any debate during the drafting process.

"... by any of its nationals ..."

The first part of subparagraph (b) requires each Party to establish jurisdiction over offences which are committed by its nationals. No other connexion with the offence need exist. The nationality principle, which is justified by the allegiance which the person charged owes to the State of which he is a national, is fully accepted under customary international law,[50] and inclusion of this provision in the Convention appears to have been generally non-controversial.[51] It may be noted, however, that this basis of jurisdiction is more commonly employed by civil law jurisdictions than by common law jurisdictions. For example, the criminal code of the FRG specifically provides that the criminal laws of that State apply to a crime committed by a German national abroad if the offence is punishable in the place where it was committed or if there is no power to impose punishment in the place where it was committed.[52] By way of contrast, nations such as the US and the UK, although often extending their jurisdiction to nationals abroad, follow a rule of interpretation that their criminal legislation will not be applied extra-territorially, even with respect to their nationals, unless the legislature provides

---

[49] See Harvard Research, note 3, *supra*, at p. 509; *US v. Flores*, 289 US 137 (1933); note 19, *supra*. The exercise of jurisdiction over ships and aircraft by the State of registration has been called "quasi-territorial". See Cheng, "Crimes on Board Aircraft", 12 Current Legal Problems 177, 182 (1959). With respect to British jurisdiction over offences committed on board ships and aircraft, see generally Merchant Shipping Act 1894, §686(1); Tokyo Convention Act 1967, §1(1).

[50] Harvard Research, note 3, *supra*, at p. 519; Sørensen, note 5, *supra*, at pp. 356-57.

[51] Some objections were raised, however. The representative of Chile, for example, argued that there was no real justification for any State other than the territorial and compelled States to have primary jurisdiction. First Report of the Hostages Committee, p. 86, para. 15.

[52] *StGB*, §7(2)(i).

otherwise.[53] With respect to this Convention, the US implementing legislation for the Hostages Convention specifically states that it will apply, regardless of where the offence takes place, when the offence is committed by a US national.[54] The UK legislation appears to establish jurisdiction over any act of hostage-taking, regardless of where or by whom it was committed, thus, of course, subsuming the nationality principle.[55]

". . . or, if that State considers it appropriate, by those stateless persons who have their habitual residence in its territory . . ."

The second part of subparagraph (b) provides for permissive primary jurisdiction, authorizing States to establish jurisdiction over offences with which their only connexion is that they are committed by stateless persons who are habitually resident in their territory. Establishment of jurisdiction on this basis is required only if "that State considers it appropriate". The decision as to whether or not it will establish its jurisdiction on this basis, as with the passive personality principle below, is, therefore, left wholly to the discretion of that Party and its failure to do so will not be a breach of this Convention.

It is not unknown for a State to claim the right to assert jurisdiction over an offence on the sole basis that it was committed by a resident thereof, thus assimilating residents to nationals for the purposes of criminal jurisdiction. Such assertions of jurisdiction may relate only to specific offences or they may be more general in nature. For example, the UK Exchange Control Act 1947 provides for jurisdiction over permanent residents of the UK with respect only to matters covered therein,[56] while the penal code of Sweden states that aliens domiciled in Sweden who commit crimes outside Sweden will be tried according to Swedish law and in a Swedish court.[57] Article 4, paragraph (a), of the Tokyo Convention, moreover, allows a State to interrupt an aircraft in flight for the purpose of exercising its jurisdiction over a

---

[53] See Jennings, note 30, *supra*, at p. 149; Sørensen, note 5, *supra*, at p. 357; Hirst, "The Criminal Law Abroad", 1982 Crim. L. R. 496. See also *United States v. Bowman*, 260 US 94, 97-98 (1922); *R. v. Martin*, [1956] 2 WLR 975. Notable exceptions under British law exist with respect to the crimes, *inter alia*, of murder, manslaughter, bigamy and treason. See Offences Against the Person Act 1861, §§9 & 57; *R. v. Casement*, [1917] 1 KB 98. Exceptions also exist under United States law. See, e.g., *Bowman, supra*.
[54] See 18 USC §1203 (b)(1)(A).
[55] See Taking of Hostages Act 1982, §1.
[56] §1 & Fifth Schedule, Part II.
[57] See Swedish Penal Code, Chap. 2, §2(1) (English translation by the National Council for Crime Prevention, Stockholm, 1984). This section, however, is not applicable to certain circumstances, including "if the act is not punishable under the law at the place where it was committed".

crime on board that aircraft when the offence has been committed by "a permanent resident of such State". With respect to the exercise of jurisdiction over stateless persons under customary international law, since normally an objection to a State's exercise of jurisdiction over an individual will be lodged by that person's national State, it would appear that an exercise of jurisdiction over a stateless person may be done with impunity.[58]

This provision was added by the Sixth Committee Working Group without explanation on record.[59] Some light on the addition is shed by Verwey, a participant in the drafting process, who indicates that it was added at the behest of Arab States,[60] which presumably would prefer that they exercise jurisdiction over certain offenders than to have such jurisdiction exercised by other States which may be less sympathetic to the cause of the alleged offenders. In any event, as one commentator states, the inclusion of this provision seems reasonable "in light of the role such persons from certain areas may play".[61] Not all States have established their jurisdiction over such offences. The United States legislation, for example, would not cover such situations, although the legislation of the United Kingdom and New Zealand would.[62]

Two interpretive points should be addressed: the meaning of the terms "stateless persons" and "habitual residence", neither of which is defined in this Convention. With respect to the definition of "stateless person", it is generally accepted under international law that that term relates simply to a person who is not considered to be a national by any State under its laws.[63] There seems to be no reason why this definition should not apply to the term as used in this Convention.[64] With regard to "habitual residence", that term has been interpreted by various international tribunals. In its Advisory Opinion in the *Acquisition of Polish Nationality* case, the PCIJ stated that "habitual residence" is the establishment of residence "in a permanent manner with the intention

---

[58] Akehurst, note 3, *supra*, at p. 169.
[59] UN GAOR, 34th Sess., C.6 (53rd mtg.), p. 8, para. 23, UN Doc A/C.6/34/SR.53 (1979).
[60] Verwey, p. 90.
[61] Rosenstock, p. 180.
[62] Compare 18 USC §1203 with Taking of Hostages Act 1982, §1 and Crimes (Internationally Protected Persons and Hostages) Act 1980 (No. 44), §8 (New Zealand).
[63] See Art. 1, 1954 Convention Relating to the Status of Stateless Persons, 360 UNTS 117; Weis, *Nationality and Statelessness in International Law* 161 (2nd ed., 1979); Mutharika, *The Regulation of Statelessness in International and National Law* 1 (1976).
[64] It could be argued that the term "stateless persons" as used in this Article should apply not only to such "*de jure*" stateless persons, but also to "*de facto*" stateless persons, i.e., those who have a nationality but no longer enjoy the protection and assistance of their State, e.g., refugees. But for reasons discussed in greater detail below (see pp. 179-180 (notes 42-47 and accompanying text in the commentary on Article 6)), it is submitted that this is an unduly wide interpretation of this provision. It is, however, possible that a State's establishment of jurisdiction over refugees and other aliens resident in its territory would be permissible under paragraph 3 of this Article.

of remaining" in the State.⁶⁵ In the *Interpretation of Minorities Treaty* (Germany v. Poland), the arbitrator examined this definition further, stating that the "establishment" aspect of the definition implies a certain concentration of personal and economic relations in that place (the degree of which depending upon the facts and circumstances of each case) and that the "intention of remaining" aspect means the intention of making the establishment one for life or for an indefinite period.⁶⁶ Again, there seems to be no reason why this definition should not apply to this Convention, although it is also possible that if a stateless person fits within a State Party's own definition of "habitual residence" which differs from the one set forth herein, then that State may also establish the envisaged jurisdiction.

". . . in order to compel that State to do or abstain from doing any act . . ."

Subparagraph (c) requires each State to establish jurisdiction over offences in which it is the third party, referred to in Article 1, which the offender seeks to compel to do or abstain from an act. This is a somewhat unusual basis of jurisdiction. The Hostages Convention was the first anti-terrorism convention to include such a basis, and it was subsequently included in the Rome Convention in non-mandatory terms. Justification for this basis can easily be found in the nature of the offence of hostage-taking: it is very often a State which is the target of compulsion in such acts and that State will have a strong interest in seeing that the offender is brought to justice.

In most cases, the State which is the target of compulsion will also have some other link to the crime, e.g., the offence will have taken place in its territory and/or the offender and/or victim will be a national of that State. However, jurisdiction under this provision does not require any such connexion between the compelled party and the offence. While it would seemingly be the unusual case where an offender, who has no national or residential connexion with a State, would attempt to compel that State to do or abstain from doing something by taking hostage, outside of its territory, a person who similarly has no connexion with that State, such an occurrence is not strictly hypothetical. In fact, this was precisely the situation in the *Achille Lauro* affair, in which Palestinian terrorists hijacked an Italian cruise ship on the high seas and held as hostage nationals of various

---

⁶⁵ PCIJ (1923), Series B, Advisory Opn. 7, p. 20.
⁶⁶ 2 Annual Digest and Reports of Public International Law Cases 230, 234 (1923-24). It might be noted that the arbitrator also held that the concept of "establishment" does not imply exclusiveness, leaving open the possibility that a person can have more than one habitual residence. If this is correct, then the possibility exists that two States could establish jurisdiction on this basis with respect to the same offender.

States, none of whom, apparently, were Israeli, and demanded the release of Palestinian prisoners from Israeli jails in return for the release of the hostages.[67] Certainly a State in the position of Israel can justify an assertion of jurisdiction over such an act.[68]

Jurisdiction based on the status of the State as the compelled party is similar to jurisdiction based on the "protective principle", which, according to one source, determines jurisdiction "by reference to the national interest injured by the offence".[69] Although the extent to which the protective principle is employed by States varies, it is used to some extent by most States and is accepted under customary international law.[70] Generally, this basis of jurisdiction is used in relation to crimes which affect the "integrity", "security", "safety" and economic interests of a State.[71] As one commentator states, one rationale for application of the principle is that the "consequences [of the offence] may be of utmost gravity and concern to the State against which [it is] directed".[72] The case of a hostage-taker seeking to compel a sovereign State to do or abstain from an act can fit into this rationale for jurisdiction. If, for example, a hostage-taker seeks to compel a State to release prisoners duly convicted of serious crimes under that State's laws, it can certainly be seen as an offence against that State's "integrity" or "security".

It may briefly be mentioned that this basis of jurisdiction is also somewhat similar to the "effects" principle of territorial jurisdiction, a

---

[67] For a somewhat more detailed exposition of the facts of the *Achille Lauro* affair, see p. 4 (note 13 and accompanying text in the Introduction).

[68] It may be noted that this basis of jurisdiction will be particularly helpful to a State which has not adopted the passive personality principle in situations wherein its nationals are taken hostage outside its territory by non-nationals in order to compel that State into action or forbearance.

[69] Harvard Research, note 3, *supra*, at p. 445. The comparison of this basis of jurisdiction with the protective principle may be somewhat flawed, however, since, as one writer points out, the latter principle is partially justified by the fact that "the State against which the crime is committed is generally the only State which has an interest in its repression". Schachter, note 3, *supra*, at p. 245. Such a situation would not generally exist with respect to international acts of hostage-taking such as those contemplated by this Convention.

[70] Harvard Research, note 3, *supra*, at p. 445. Swedish law, for example, takes a very wide approach to this basis of jurisdiction, providing that a person who commits a crime outside of Sweden "shall be tried according to Swedish law and in a Swedish court", *inter alia*, if "the crime was committed against Sweden". Swedish Penal Code, Chap. 2, §3(3) (English translation, note 57, *supra*). Anglo-American jurisdictions generally take a more restrictive view of this basis of jurisdiction. See Harvard Research, note 3, *supra*, at p. 552. But for an example of the application of the principle in the United Kingdom, see *Joyce v. Director of Public Prosecutions*, [1946] AC 347, 372.

[71] See Harvard Research, note 3, *supra*, at p. 552; Feller, note 9, *supra*, at p. 26. A 1931 resolution of the *Institut de Droit International* states in Article 4 that any State has the right to punish acts committed outside its territory, even by aliens, when the acts constitute an attack against its security or a falsification of its money, its stamps, seal or official marks. *Cited in* Sørensen, note 5, *supra*, at p. 363.

[72] Starke, *Introduction to International Law* 226 (9th ed., 1984).

principle which has been the subject of some controversy.[73] Under the "effects" doctrine, a State exercises "territorial" jurisdiction not because one of the constitutive elements have occurred in its territory, but because the act has "effects" therein.[74] Its similarity to the basis of jurisdiction provided for in this subparagraph would be particularly evident in a case wherein the State submits to the compulsion, e.g., by releasing prisoners, thereby creating adverse effects in its territory.

Very little debate regarding this basis of jurisdiction appears on the record, and it appears that most States favoured its inclusion. However, some States did voice opposition to the proposal[75] and, according to Verwey, it was generally opposed by Arab States which, he continues, "had in mind a particular State which happens to be a traditional and potential object of compulsion by Palestinian hostage-takers".[76]

". . . or . . . with respect to a hostage who is a national of that State, if that State considers it appropriate."

The passive personality principle, i.e., jurisdiction over an offence by a State on the sole basis that its national was the victim thereof, has generally been employed by some States. However, many States traditionally do not accept the principle, and it has been "vigorously opposed" by common law jurisdictions.[77] One commentator states that this basis of jurisdiction has been more widely attacked than any other.[78] The main objections to the principle appear to be that 1) an injury to a national abroad is of generally insufficient concern to a State to justify its assertion of jurisdiction and is, rather, best left to the jurisdiction of the territorial State, and 2) the principle theoretically leaves an individual subject to the laws of every State at all times and in all places.[79] As will be seen below, however, the opposition which some States have had to this principle appears to be eroding, at least with respect to certain offences.

The inclusion of the passive personality principle in this Con-

---

[73] See generally, Akehurst, note 3, *supra*, at pp. 153-154.

[74] See generally, Bowett, note 3, *supra*, at p. 7.

[75] See e.g., the comments of the representative of the Byelorussian SSR to the Sixth Committee, UN GAOR, 34th Sess., C.6 (13th mtg.), p. 19, para. 90, UN Doc A/C.6/34/SR.13 (1979).

[76] Verwey, p. 89 & n.55.

[77] See Harvard Research, note 3, *supra*, at p. 579. See also Akehurst, note 3, *supra*, at p. 163.

[78] Sørensen, note 5, *supra*, at p. 369. Mann suggests that the principle should be treated as an excess of jurisdiction, except where it coincides with the protective principle. See Mann, note 9, *supra*, at pp. 79 & 81.

[79] See generally Bowett, note 3, *supra*, at p. 10; dissenting opinion of Judge Moore in the *Lotus* case. PCIJ (1927), Series A, No. 10, p. 92.

vention was most obviously the result of a compromise between those States which accept the principle as a common basis for jurisdiction and those which have traditionally avoided its use. Those States which supported its inclusion argued that it would fill a gap in jurisdiction and that, in any event, a State whose national is held hostage has a strong enough interest in the offence to justify its assertion of jurisdiction.[80] Opposing States asserted that inclusion of this principle would only lead to problems of conflicting claims of jurisdiction, and for extradition, if there were a number of hostages and they were from different States.[81] One commentator who was present during the drafting of the Convention states that, while a number of jurisdictions such as the US and the UK were willing to accept the passive personality principle in the case of the protection of diplomats (the New York Convention), "a comparable rationale did not exist with regard to nationals generally." However, civil law States "insisted on retaining the ability under their law of applying the principle, and subparagraph 1(d) was the resultant compromise."[82]

Since the Convention does not actually require States to establish jurisdiction on this basis, or on the stateless person basis, it might be wondered why the draftsmen felt it necessary or desirable to mention them specifically in the Convention.[83] This is particularly so given paragraph 3 of this Article, which states that the Convention does not "exclude any criminal jurisdiction exercised in accordance with internal law", a provision which would seemingly allow States to establish jurisdiction on those two grounds if they so desired.[84] Two possible reasons can be identified. The first is that specifically authorizing those bases in the text may encourage States to establish their jurisdiction thereon (thus increasing the number of States with

---

[80] See, e.g., the comments of the representative of France, Second Report of the Hostages Committee, p. 41, para. 15.

[81] See, e.g., the comments of the representatives of the Netherlands and the United Kingdom, *id.* at p. 39, para. 6 & p. 40, para. 9, respectively. Another objection was voiced during the Sixth Committee deliberations by the representative of Jordan, who argued that the passive personality principle would "expose [an alleged offender] to a number of jurisdictions". UN GAOR, 34th Sess., C.6 (62nd mtg.), p. 3, para. 8, UN Doc A/C.6/34/SR.62 (1979).

[82] Rosenstock, p. 180.

[83] It might be noted that the specific inclusion of these permissive bases in this paragraph will not necessarily facilitate extradition. Article 10(4) provides that the offences shall only be treated, for the purpose of extradition, as having been committed in the territories of the States which are *required* to establish jurisdiction pursuant to Article 5(1).

[84] Some States argued that the passive personality principle should not be specifically included in the Convention on the ground that States which wished to exercise such jurisdiction could properly do so under paragraph 3. See the comments of the representatives of the US and Sweden, Second Report of the Hostages Committee, p. 43, para. 24 and para. 27, respectively.

primary jurisdiction), without, however, requiring reluctant States to do so. The second is that some States may have wanted to clarify beyond the somewhat ambiguous language of paragraph 3 that the exercise of jurisdiction on these bases is permissible, and thus obviate in advance any objections which might be raised thereto.

In any event, the main objections to the passive personality principle generally seem less compelling when dealing with terrorist offences since the victims thereof are often attacked precisely because of their nationality. Moreover, since terrorists can be seen as *hostes humani generis*, all States have a strong interest in seeing that there are no gaps in jurisdiction. Indeed, States seem increasingly willing to accept the principle in connexion with terrorist offences. The US and the UK, for example, although they opposed the inclusion of the principle in this Convention, have both enacted implementing legislation which covers offences with which their only connexion is the nationality of the hostage.[85] Moreover, versions of the principle appear in the Tokyo, New York and Rome Conventions.[86] And, in the aftermath of the *Achille Lauro* affair, during which an American citizen was murdered by terrorists on board an Italian cruise ship in the Mediterranean, the US enacted a law dealing with "[t]errorist acts abroad against US nationals". This law makes it illegal to: 1) kill a US national when he is outside the US; 2) conspire or attempt outside the US to kill a US national; and 3) engage in physical violence outside the US which has either the intent or the result of causing serious bodily injury to a US national. No prosecution will be brought with respect to these offences, however, unless the Attorney General of the US or his subordinate certifies in writing that "in the judgment of the certifying official, such offence was intended to coerce, intimidate, or retaliate against a government or civilian population".[87] Notwithstanding the fact that this legislation applies only to terrorist offences, it is a significant expansion of the normal US criminal jurisdiction.

---

[85] 18 USC §1203(b)(1)(A); Taking of Hostages Act 1982, §1.

[86] See Art. 4, Tokyo Convention; note 18, *supra*. Article 3(1)(c) of the New York Convention requires each State Party to establish its jurisdiction over the offence "when the crime is committed against an internationally protected person . . . who enjoys his status as such by virtue of functions which he exercises on behalf of that State". Moreover, the requirement in Article 4 of the Hague Convention and Article 5 of the Montreal Convention regarding the establishment of jurisdiction by a State over offences committed on board aircraft leased without crew when the lessee has his principal place of business or residence in that State is not unlike the passive personality principle. Article 6(2)(b) of the Rome Convention and Article 3(2)(b) of the Rome Protocol authorize the establishment of jurisdiction by States over offences wherein their nationals are "seized, threatened, injured or killed".

[87] See 1986 Omnibus Diplomatic Security and Antiterrorism Act, §1202, Public Law No. 99-399, 100 Stat. 895, 896 (1986), *codified in* 18 USC §2331.

ARTICLE 5

PARAGRAPH 2: ESTABLISHMENT OF SUBSIDIARY JURISDICTION OVER THE OFFENCES

Pursuant to Article 8, paragraph 1, the State Party in whose territory an alleged offender is present must, if it does not extradite him, submit the case to its appropriate authorities for the purpose of prosecution. This paragraph seeks to ensure that a State which has no connexion with the offence other than the offender's subsequent presence in its territory has the authority, under its domestic law, to prosecute him. This provision is mandatory in nature and is identical in substance to corresponding provisions in the other anti-terrorism instruments.

"Each State Party shall likewise take such measures as may be necessary to establish its jurisdiction over the offences set forth in article 1 in cases where the alleged offender is present in its territory..."

Under this subparagraph, each State Party must establish its jurisdiction over offences on the mere basis of the offender's subsequent presence in its territory. As stated by the representative of the Netherlands to the Sixth Committee, this provision is based on the principle of "universality".[88] This type of jurisdiction, as earlier noted, is for most (but not all)[89] States an extraordinary extension of criminal jurisdiction,[90] and is justified by the need of the entire community of States to ensure that those who commit such crimes do not escape punishment. The legislation enacted by the US to implement the Hostages Convention provides that the offence of hostage-taking applies to acts committed outside the US if the offender is found in the US.[91] In the UK, the Taking of Hostages Act 1982 prohibits hostage-taking by "[a] person, whatever his nationality ... in the United Kingdom or elsewhere",[92] a very wide provision indeed. During the House of Commons debate on the legislation, one MP, noting the proposed statute's shift from the traditional policy that the courts of the United Kingdom cannot prosecute an offender if the

---

[88] UN GAOR, 34th Sess., C.6 (13th mtg.), p. 9, para. 40, UN Doc A/C.6/34/SR.13 (1979).
[89] See pp. 134-135 (notes 3-6 and accompanying text).
[90] *Id.* For example, during the Congressional hearings on the United States implementing legislation for the Hostages Convention, a representative of the Department of Justice noted that the provision was unusual since there is generally "no basis to prosecute an offender whose crime had no nexus to the United States simply because of his subsequent presence in this country ..." See *Hearings before the Subcommittee on Security and Terrorism*, note 33, *supra*, at p. 123.
[91] 18 USC §1203(b)(1)(B).
[92] §1.

crime has no ties with the State, explained that modern technology and travel, coupled with the nature of terrorism, necessitated the expanded jurisdiction.[93] As can be seen, the UK legislation covers all acts of hostage-taking no matter where or by whom committed. It is unclear as to whether the UK will ever actively seek to prosecute an offender, i.e., by seeking extradition, whose crime has no connexion with the UK and who does not otherwise subsequently appear in that State.

". . . and it does not extradite him to any of the States mentioned in paragraph 1 of this article."

There are two reasons why an alleged offender who is found in the territory of a Party which has no other connexion with him or with the offence would not be extradited: 1) although one or more of the States listed in paragraph 1 have requested extradition, the State in which the offender is present has denied the request(s), for whatever reason; and 2) none of the States listed in paragraph 1 have requested extradition.

With respect to the first reason — a State's refusal to grant extradition — it may be noted briefly (since this point is discussed in more detail in the commentaries on Articles 8 and 10) that this Convention does not actually require Parties to extradite an alleged offender. It simply requires Parties which do not extradite to submit the case to its authorities "for the purpose of prosecution". Decisions regarding extradition are left to the domestic legislation and treaties of each Party.

With respect to the second reason for non-extradition — the lack of a request — the representative of the Netherlands to the Hostages Committee proposed the addition of the words "after receiving a request for extradition from one of those states", i.e., those required to establish primary jurisdiction, to the end of this paragraph.[94] This addition would have meant that a State must only establish jurisdiction pursuant to this paragraph over offences with respect to which a request for extradition from a State with primary jurisdiction has been made and refused. A corresponding proposal was made with respect to the exercise of jurisdiction pursuant to Article 8.[95] The representative of the Netherlands argued that it was unreasonable to

---

[93] See H.C. Debs, Vol. 25, 11 June 1982, cols. 568, 572. The same MP noted that the legislation was mainly directed at crimes which took place outside of the UK. If the crime took place in the UK, he explained, the authorities would probably prosecute under existing legislation which would cover the situation, such as kidnapping, murder, firearms offences, etc. *Id.* at col. 573.
[94] UN Doc A/AC.188/L.14 (1977), in First Report of the Hostages Committee, p. 114.
[95] *Id.* See pp. 196-197 (notes 33-38 in the commentary on Article 8).

require a State which has no connexion with the offence other than the offender's subsequent presence in its territory to prosecute him when the States with primary jurisdiction did not have enough interest in the case to request extradition, or were, for whatever reason, unwilling to prosecute the offender.[96] However, the representatives of other States disagreed, expressing the belief that such a provision would leave gaps in jurisdiction, and the proposal was not adopted.[97] Jurisdiction under this paragraph must, therefore, be established regardless of the reason for the failure to extradite.

The legal effect of the establishment of universal jurisdiction

As earlier noted, there are very few offences, perhaps only one, piracy, which, by customary international law, are subject to the jurisdiction of all States, based solely on custody of the offender. White reports that during the drafting of the Hague Convention it was thought important that if an offender fled to a State other than one with primary jurisdiction that State should have jurisdiction to prosecute him. The proposal was, therefore, mooted that the Convention should declare that hijacking, like piracy, was an international offence so that any State in which an offender was found had jurisdiction. However, it was recognized that piracy became an international offence under customary international law only after general acceptance by all States over many centuries. It was doubted that the same result could be brought about simply by declaring it so in a convention. The result was the requirement that States Parties must establish their jurisdiction over all offenders who are subsequently found in their territory, a requirement which achieves a "similar result".[98]

It is possible that a State which establishes universal jurisdiction over acts of hostage-taking will actually exercise such with respect to an offender who is a national of a non-party to this Convention. If the non-party complains, the question would thus arise as to the effect this provision might have upon the rights of States which are not parties to this Convention. Of course, in general, treaties can impose no obligations upon non-parties thereto without their consent.[99] However, it may be argued that the fact that the Hostages Convention was adopted by consensus in a resolution of the General Assembly of the UN elevates the rules set forth therein to the level of customary

---

[96] First Report of the Hostages Committee, p. 89, para. 9.
[97] See, e.g., the comments of the representatives of the US, Mexico, and the FRG, *id.* at p. 89, para. 10, p. 90, para. 11 & p. 93, para. 8, respectively.
[98] See White, p. 41.
[99] Art. 34, Vienna Convention on the Law of Treaties.

international law. As Schachter states, there are two possible interpretations of the legal nature of provisions such as this paragraph.[100] The first is that, because the provisions have been adopted in the framework of multilateral treaties through the processes of international organizations, the community of States has recognized that universal jurisdiction exists for the offences and that, therefore, any State may exercise such.[101] Under this interpretation, all States have the right, but not the obligation (unless they are States Parties to the relevant instrument), to exercise jurisdiction on this basis. The second theory is that the conventions are simply agreements among States Parties not to object to the exercise of jurisdiction on this basis by any other State Party, and that the rights of non-parties are not affected.

It is not proposed to review here the lively debate on the legal effects of General Assembly resolutions (or of lawmaking treaties in general). It is enough to say that certainly the fact that the Hostages Convention was adopted by consensus in the General Assembly makes the rules therein — including those regarding jurisdiction — evidence of the content of customary international law.[102] However, it would probably be too much to conclude that all those rules are definitely customary rules: they are contained, after all, in a Convention which currently has fewer than 60 States Parties. While State practice may ultimately justify the conclusion that universal jurisdiction over offences of hostage-taking is permissible under customary international law, it is unclear if this is currently the case.[103]

---

[100] Schachter, note 3, *supra*, at pp. 262-64.

[101] See also Wood, p. 809, where he suggests that the adoption of the New York Convention by consensus in the General Assembly amounts to a sufficient degree of State acceptance to establish that such jurisdiction is permissible under international law with respect to the crimes contained therein.

[102] See, e.g., Schwebel, "The Effect of Resolutions of the UN General Assembly on Customary International Law", 73 Proc. ASIL 301-310 (1979); Brownlie, *Principles of International Law* 12-13, 14-15 (3rd ed., 1979).

[103] See, e.g., Paust, "Extradition of the *Achille Lauro* Hostage-Takers: Navigating the Hazards", 20 Vand. J. Trans. L. 235, 254 (1987), who states that the exercise of universal jurisdiction over nationals of non-parties or non-signatories would be "highly suspect". Schachter, on the other hand, suggests that a State which is not party to the relevant convention could only object to an assertion of universal jurisdiction over its national if it opposed the jurisdiction clause at the time of the adoption of the convention. However, he states that the ultimate resolution of this question will depend upon State practice. See Schachter, note 3, *supra*, at 263-64. In this connexion, it might be noted that the criteria set down by the ICJ in the *North Sea Continental Shelf Cases* regarding whether a conventional rule can be considered to have become a general rule of international law do not seem to have been satisfied in the case of Article 5(2) of this Convention. While Article 5(2) may be considered to be of a "fundamentally norm creating character", the Convention does not yet seem to have reached the necessary "widespread and representative participation". Although the fact that only six years have passed since the Convention came into force cannot be regarded as a bar to considering Article 5(2) as a new rule of customary law, State practice, so far seemingly non-existent, cannot be said to be "extensive and virtually uniform". See ICJ Rep. 1969, at pp. 41-43.

ARTICLE 5

PARAGRAPH 3: JURISDICTION EXERCISED IN ACCORDANCE WITH INTERNAL LAW

"This Convention does not exclude any criminal jurisdiction exercised in accordance with internal law."

This paragraph is meant solely to convey the simple message that it is acceptable for States to exercise jurisdiction over an offence of hostage-taking on a basis which is not expressly included in this Convention. Almost identical wording exists in the Hague, Montreal, New York and Rome Conventions and there is no recorded debate about its inclusion in this Convention.

This provision seems less helpful in this Convention than it might be in the earlier anti-terrorism instruments. As already noted, many of the bases of jurisdiction extant under customary international law are not expressly provided for in those earlier instruments, and wording such as this serves as a helpful clarification in those instruments. This Convention, by way of contrast, specifically includes almost all of the bases of jurisdiction known to customary international law.

3. Problems Relevant to the Establishment of Jurisdiction under the Convention

A. JURISDICTION OVER CRIMES ATTENDANT TO ACTS OF HOSTAGE-TAKING

Many acts of hostage-taking are accompanied by serious acts of violence against the hostages. This Article, however, requires Parties only to establish their jurisdiction over the offences set forth in Article 1, i.e., hostage-taking, attempt and participation. It does not require Parties to establish their jurisdiction over other crimes committed during the course of the offences.

During the second session of the Hostages Committee, the representative of the Netherlands proposed that Parties should be required to extend their jurisdiction under the Convention to "any serious act of violence against a hostage committed by the alleged offender in connexion with one of the offences mentioned in article 1". Thus, he explained, if a hostage was murdered the offender could be extradited and prosecuted for that murder as well as the hostage-taking. Since both offences are part of the same act, he argued, that "complex act" should be judged under this Convention.[104] Precedent for such a provision is found in Article 4(1) of the Hague Convention

---

[104] Second Report of the Hostages Committee, p. 39, para. 7.

which requires Parties with primary jurisdiction to take the measures necessary to establish jurisdiction not only over the offences referred to in Article 1 of that Convention (hijacking, attempt and participation) but also over "any other act of violence against passengers or crew committed by the alleged offender in connexion with the offence".

The little recorded debate which exists regarding this issue indicates that many delegations looked favourably upon the proposal submitted by the Netherlands,[105] and, according to the final report of the Hostages Committee, agreement was tentatively reached to adopt the proposal. However, that same report stated that it was finally agreed to exclude the amendment, explaining only that "[s]everal delegations expressed reservations" regarding its inclusion.[106] The Chairman of the Hostages Committee explained to the Sixth Committee only that after a "thorough debate" agreement could not be reached on the issue.[107] Since most of the debate (and the actual decision) regarding this issue appears to have been held informally, it is not entirely clear why the proposal was rejected. It would seem, however, that many of the draftsmen felt that the additional language would undesirably have expanded the scope of the Convention beyond originally intended and required amendments to other provisions as well. For example, acceptance of the Dutch proposal would have made little sense unless Article 10 were amended so as to require States Parties also to consider attendant acts of violence as extraditable offences.[108] An additional question which could have been raised is whether a

---

[105] See, e.g., the comments of the representatives of the UK, FRG and the US, *id.* at p. 40, para. 12, p. 42, para. 21 & p. 42, para. 23, respectively. The Report of Working Group II stated, moreover, that there was a "strong trend" towards accepting compromise language which would have required establishment of jurisdiction over such serious acts of violence if they caused "death or bodily injury" to a hostage. See *id.* at p. 9.

[106] Third Report of the Hostages Committee, p. 12, paras. 45-46.

[107] UN GAOR, 34th Sess., C.6 (4th mtg.), p. 5, para. 20, UN Doc A/C.6/34/SR.4 (1979).

[108] This is because the rule of speciality, contained in most extradition laws and treaties (see, e.g., 1982 FRG Law on Mutual Assistance in Criminal Matters, §11, *translated in* 24 ILM 945 (1985); Art. XVI(1)(a), Treaty on Extradition, 13 October 1983, United States-Italy, TIAS 10, 837), prohibits a State to which an alleged offender has been extradited from prosecuting him (without the consent of the requested State) for any offence other than the one for which extradition was granted. If a State which established its jurisdiction over accompanying acts of violence wanted to exercise such by requesting extradition, it would have to formulate that request in terms of both hostage-taking and the accompanying act of violence. The chances that such a request would be granted would be greatly increased if States Parties were required to consider such acts of violence as extraditable offences. On the meaning of "extraditable offences", see generally pp. 229-232 (notes 6-21 in the commentary on Article 10). It may be noted, however, that Article 8 of the Hague Convention does not require States Parties to consider attendant acts of violence as extraditable offences, notwithstanding the requirement in that Convention that States Parties must establish jurisdiction over such offences.

State would be required to *exercise* jurisdiction over such acts of violence pursuant to Article 8(1) with respect to alleged offenders found in their territory and not extradited. Presumably for reasons such as these, the representative of France, although expressing his interest in the proposal, suggested that the language would introduce to Article 5 a provision which was "too comprehensive for the scope of the Convention."[109]

Problems connected with obtaining the extradition of alleged offenders for attendant acts of violence aside,[110] the difficulty presented by the lack of a provision such as that proposed by the Netherlands is the possibility that a Party will exercise jurisdiction, or will want to exercise jurisdiction, over a particular act of hostage-taking when its internal law does not allow it to assert jurisdiction over another act of violence which occurred during that offence. The type of dilemma just described can occur whenever a State asserts jurisdiction over the hostage-taking on a basis not generally permissible under its laws, but which was established with respect to hostage-taking because of that State's obligations under this Convention. States in such a position could thus prosecute and punish the offender for the act of hostage-taking, but not for the attendant act of violence.

The very real nature of this problem was illustrated in the aftermath of the *Achille Lauro* affair. As earlier noted,[111] during that hostage-taking a Jewish American tourist, Leon Klinghoffer, was shot by the terrorists and his body was thrown overboard. Once the offenders were in Italian custody, the US government indicated that it would seek their extradition under the Italian-American extradition treaty; however, it was subsequently agreed by the two governments that Italy would prosecute them.[112] The four men, plus eleven others, mostly *in absentia*, were subsequently tried and convicted in Italy for various offences, including one of them for the murder of Mr. Klinghoffer.[113] Despite the fact that the American government's real interest in the case was the murder of Mr. Klinghoffer, the offenders could not have been tried for murder in an American court — whether custody was obtained by extradition or otherwise — because the criminal jurisdiction of the United States does not generally extend to crimes committed abroad against its nationals.[114] By way of

[109] Second Report of the Hostages Committee, p. 41, para. 16.
[110] In this regard, see generally p. 160 (note 108 and accompanying text); note 117, *infra*.
[111] For the facts of the *Achille Lauro* incident, see p. 4 (note 13 in the Introduction).
[112] *New York Times*, Oct. 12, 1985, p. A4.
[113] *New York Times*, July 11, 1986, p. A1.
[114] See generally pp. 152-153 (notes 77-82 and accompanying text); "Briefing of National Security Advisor Robert McFarlane on the Apprehension of the *Achille Lauro* Hijackers", 24 ILM 1516, 1521-22 (1985).

contrast, as noted above, the US law implementing the Hostages Convention covers situations wherein the only connexion between the crime and the US is that the hostage is a national of that country.[115] Thus, the US arrest warrant for the hostage-takers mentioned the offences of hostage-taking, piracy and conspiracy, but not murder.[116] While the US will not again find itself in that precise type of situation, since it has, as earlier noted, amended its laws to cover terrorist attacks upon its nationals abroad,[117] any State could find itself in similar difficulties whenever it exercises, or wants to exercise, jurisdiction over an act of hostage-taking in a situation wherein it does not have jurisdiction over accompanying crimes.

The problems connected with the exercise of jurisdiction by a State over an act of hostage-taking when it does not have jurisdiction over accompanying acts of violence were addressed during the House of Commons debate on the UK implementing legislation. One MP suggested that the proposed legislation could lead to a situation in which a judge sitting on a case wherein a hostage was murdered but where, due to jurisdictional limitations, the only charged offence is hostage-taking, might impose a sentence which takes the murder into account. Since evidence would not have been offered on a murder charge, and since the defendant would not have had the opportunity to defend himself therefrom, taking the death of the hostage into account when imposing sentence would be unfair.[118] The Under-Secretary of State for Foreign and Commonwealth Affairs replied that imposing a life sentence in a case where a hostage was killed would be

---

[115] See p. 154 (note 85 and accompanying text).

[116] See 24 ILM 1554 (1985).

[117] See p. 154 (note 87 and accompanying text). It might be noted, however, that just because a State has established jurisdiction over accompanying acts of violence does not mean that the exercise of that jurisdiction will always be an easy matter. As earlier indicated, States are not required by this Convention to consider such acts of violence as extraditable offences (see p. 159 (note 104 and accompanying text); see also Article 10 of this Convention). Even if a State grants extradition for hostage-taking, if it does not also grant extradition for the accompanying act of violence the requesting State may not exercise its jurisdiction over that latter act. Moreover, difficulties in this regard might exist even with respect to States which have a bilateral extradition treaty in force as between themselves. While serious acts of violence will generally be considered as extraditable offences, many treaties provide that if the offence for which extradition has been requested has not been committed in the territory of the requesting State, then extradition must only be granted if the requested State would have jurisdiction over that offence in similar circumstances. See, e.g., Art. III, United States-Italy treaty, note 104, *supra*. See also pp. 243-244 (note 65 in the commentary on Article 10). Thus, under such a treaty it is not enough that the United States, for example, has established jurisdiction over the murder of its national abroad. Unless the requested State has similar jurisdiction it is not required, and may not be authorized, to grant extradition for that act. This problem would not arise had the draftsmen adopted the Dutch proposal requiring States to establish their jurisdiction over acts of violence accompanying acts of hostage-taking.

[118] H.C. Debs., Vol. 25, 11 June 1982, cols. 573 & 575.

reasonable; the sentence would not be for murder but for a serious act of hostage-taking.[119]

In a case where a State which has jurisdiction over the hostage-taking finds itself without jurisdiction over an attendant act of violence, it could prosecute the offender for the hostage-taking and then extradite (or return) him to a State with jurisdiction over the attendant act of violence for prosecution thereof. This assumes, of course, that the second State makes such a request. If no such request is made, the offender must stand charged only with the hostage-taking offence. Alternatively, it could honour or defer to an extradition request from a State which has jurisdiction over both offences (similar to the United States action in the *Achille Lauro* incident, although the Italian government did not actually need to seek extradition of the offenders since they were already present in its territory). A State exercising jurisdiction pursuant to paragraph 2, and which has no jurisdiction over the attendant act of violence, presumably has reasons for refusing to extradite the offender and in such a case the attendant act of violence will probably not be prosecuted. It might be noted in this connexion that such problems will not arise under the Rome Convention since Article 3(1)(g) thereof specifically includes as distinct offences, subject to all the obligations contained in that instrument, the injuring or killing of persons in connexion with the commission or attempted commission of any of the other offences under that instrument.

B. PRIORITY OF JURISDICTION

Under customary international law, no system of priority exists amongst those States which have a legitimate claim to jurisdiction over a particular crime. Even a State which has territorial jurisdiction over an offence has no claim superior in law to that of another State which also has jurisdiction and which would like to prosecute the offender. Priority would seem to depend solely on custody.[120] Although

---

[119] *Id.* at cols. 574-575.

[120] See generally Harris, *Cases and Materials on International Law* 211 (3rd ed., 1983). Similarly, many extradition treaties do not provide for any priority in requests for extradition. The 1978 extradition treaty between the United States and Mexico, for example, provides, in Article 16, that where there is more than one request for extradition of the same person, whether for the same or different offences, the requested State has the right to decide which request it will grant. Treaty on Extradition, 4 May 1978, United States-Mexico, TIAS 9656, *reprinted in* 17 ILM 1058, 1067 (1978). However, some treaties do provide for priority. Article 15 of the 1981 Inter-American Convention on Extradition, for example, requires the requested State to give priority to the territorial State where there are two or more requests for the extradition of a person for the same offence. If there are two or more requests for extradition, but for different offences, extradition must be granted to the State which
(*continued on p. 164*)

paragraph 1 of Article 5 requires various States to establish primary jurisdiction over the offences set forth in Article 1, this Convention, following the model of the earlier anti-terrorism Conventions, does not provide for any system of priority of jurisdiction amongst the States listed therein.[121] Nor can one be implied from the language of Article 5, from any other provision of the Convention or from the *travaux préparatoires* of this or the Hague, Montreal or New York Conventions.

Priority of jurisdiction was discussed during the drafting of this Convention. Although most of the debate appears to have been held informally, the record of the Sixth Committee deliberations indicates that at least a few States would have preferred that the Convention establish such a system. The representative of Jordan, for example, asserted that, while it could accept the final draft of Article 5, it would have been a "greater contribution to the codification and progressive development of international law had [the Article] embodied provisions for a system of priority of jurisdiction" and a system of priority in the case of a State receiving more than one request for extradition.[122] Moreover, Verwey reports that the Arab States wanted a system which provided for absolute priority for the territorial State.[123]

([120] *continued*)
seeks the offender for the crime which is punishable by the most severe penalty. If the offences are of equal gravity, priority shall be determined by the order in which the requests were received. PAUTS 60, *reprinted in* 20 ILM 723 (1981). Still other treaties and laws contain general guidelines for determining priority. See, e.g., Article 15 of the 1972 extradition treaty between the United States and Argentina which states that where there are two or more requests for extradition, the requested State shall determine which request it will grant, taking into account all the circumstances, including the possibility of later extradition between the requesting States, the seriousness of each offence, the place where the crime was committed, the nationality of the person sought and the dates of the requests. Treaty on Extradition, 21 January 1972, United States-Argentina, TIAS 7510. Similar criteria are contained in Article 13 of the 1957 Swedish Extradition Act.

[121] For an apparently different view, see Bassiouni, *International Criminal Law*, Vol. I, 480 (1986).

[122] UN GAOR, 34th Sess., C.6 (62nd mtg.), p. 3, para. 7, UN Doc A/C.6/34/SR.62 (1979).

[123] Verwey, p. 89. As earlier noted, moreover, Verwey reports that Arab nations opposed the provision requiring the establishment of jurisdiction by the State which was the object of compulsion. A compromise was reached whereby the Arab proposals to establish a system of priority with respect to Article 5 were withdrawn in return for a final draft of paragraph 1 which 1) placed the provision requiring the establishment of jurisdiction by the compelled State after that based on nationality and 2) expanded the nationality provision to include stateless persons. *Id.* This compromise, however, does not imply any sort of priority system. It might be noted that the USSR representative also urged a system of priority favouring the territorial State. See UN GAOR, 34th Sess., C.6 (13th mtg.), p. 14, para. 67, UN Doc A/C.6/34/SR.13 (1979). Moreover, the ILC draft of the New York Convention established a priority in favour of the territorial State, but this was apparently omitted by the Sixth Committee. See 1972 YBILC, Vol. II, p. 319. Article 11(5) of the Rome Convention, without actually establishing a priority, requires a State which has received more than one extradition request to "pay due regard to the interests and responsibilities" of the flag State.

ARTICLE 5

The arguments against a system of priority advanced during the drafting of this Convention do not appear in the record. According to White, proposals which would have established a system of priority for the Hague Convention were rejected on the grounds that it would be too difficult to agree on what the priority should be and a belief, moreover, that the decision as to which State should in fact prosecute a hijacker should in each case depend upon the circumstances.[124] It may be presumed that similar arguments prevailed during the drafting of this Convention.

The lack of a system of priority raises the possibility of a conflict of jurisdiction between two or more Parties which wish to exercise jurisdiction over the same act of hostage-taking. For example, consider the case of a national of State A who takes control over a ship registered in State B and holds hostage nationals from States B, C & D in an attempt to compel State C to release from its jails prisoners who have been tried and convicted of grievous crimes against State C. After State C complies with the demand, the offender flees to State E where he is subsequently taken into custody. Under paragraph 1 of Article 5, States A, B, C & D have all been required to establish primary jurisdiction over the offences. Although one might argue that States B & C have been most harmed by the particular act, there is no objective rationale in the Convention from which to favour the jurisdictional claim of any one of the four States. Assuming that State E has no interest in exercising its subsidiary jurisdiction under paragraph 2, and that all of the other four States request extradition under the Convention, State E must then decide which request to honour. The decision rests solely within the discretion of State E, subject to any conditions imposed by its extradition treaties and laws.

---

[124] White, p. 12.

Article 6

MATTERS PRIOR TO TRIAL OR EXTRADITION

1. Upon being satisfied that the circumstances so warrant, any State Party in the territory of which the alleged offender is present shall, in accordance with its laws, take him into custody or take other measures to ensure his presence for such time as is necessary to enable any criminal or extradition proceedings to be instituted. That State Party shall immediately make a preliminary inquiry into the facts.

2. The custody or other measures referred to in paragraph 1 of this article shall be notified without delay directly or through the Secretary-General of the United Nations to:
   (a) the State where the offence was committed;
   (b) the State against which compulsion has been directed or attempted;
   (c) the State of which the natural or juridical person against whom compulsion has been directed or attempted is a national;
   (d) the State of which the hostage is a national or in the territory of which he has his habitual residence;
   (e) the State of which the alleged offender is a national or, if he is a stateless person, in the territory of which he has his habitual residence;
   (f) the international intergovernmental organization against which compulsion has been directed or attempted;
   (g) all other States concerned.

3. Any person regarding whom the measures referred to in paragraph 1 of this article are being taken shall be entitled:
   (a) to communicate without delay with the nearest appropriate representative of the State of which he is a national or which is otherwise entitled to establish such communication or, if he is a stateless person, the State in the territory of which he has his habitual residence;
   (b) to be visited by a representative of that State.

4. The rights referred to in paragraph 3 of this article shall be exercised in conformity with the laws and regulations of the State in the territory of which the alleged offender is present subject to the proviso, however, that the said laws and regulations must enable full effect to be given to the purposes for which the rights accorded under paragraph 3 of this article are intended.

5. The provisions of paragraphs 3 and 4 of this article shall be without prejudice to the right of any State Party having a claim to jurisdiction in accordance with paragraph 1(b) of article 5 to invite the International Committee of the Red Cross to communicate with and visit the alleged offender.

6. The State which makes the preliminary inquiry contemplated in

paragraph 1 of this article shall promptly report its findings to the States or organization referred to in paragraph 2 of this article and indicate whether it intends to exercise jurisdiction.

1. INTRODUCTION

Seeking both to ensure compliance with the obligation *aut dedere aut judicare* which is set forth in Article 8 and to protect the human rights of alleged offenders, this Article imposes a number of obligations upon the State Party in whose territory an alleged offender is found. These obligations include taking measures to ensure an alleged offender's presence for any extradition or prosecution proceedings, holding a preliminary inquiry into the facts, notifying certain other States of the measures taken and of the findings of the preliminary inquiry, and allowing the alleged offender to communicate with and be visited by a representative of the protecting State.

This Article corresponds to Article 6 of the Hague, Montreal and New York Conventions and Article 7 of the Rome Convention, but is somewhat more complex than those provisions. In particular, paragraphs 4 and 5 of this Article have no counterpart in the first three of those instruments and paragraph 5 has no counterpart in the Rome Convention. There is little recorded debate regarding the drafting of this Article and its inclusion herein seems to have been generally non-controversial.

2. INTERPRETATION

PARAGRAPH 1: TAKING MEASURES TO ENSURE THE PRESENCE OF THE ACCUSED

This paragraph requires a State Party in whose territory an alleged offender is present to take him into custody or take other measures to ensure his presence at criminal or extradition proceedings.

"Upon being satisfied that the circumstances so warrant . . ."

The obligation to take custodial or other measures to ensure the presence of the alleged offender is applicable only if the Party in whose territory he is present is "satisfied that the circumstances so warrant". The decision as to whether or not any such steps will be taken in a given case is thus left to the discretion of the relevant State Party. While this Article provides no guidance as to what "circumstances" may, or should, be taken into account by a Party when making its decision, clearly this phrase recognizes that most States will not (and should not) take any measures against an alleged offender when there are no grounds to believe that he has committed an offence. However, the "circumstances" which can be taken into account do not appear to be limited to evidentiary considerations. This phrase was adapted from a similar provision in the Tokyo Convention,[1] and essentially identical language can be found in all the other anti-terrorism instruments. It was part of the original FRG draft[2] and there is no recorded debate regarding its inclusion in this Convention. However, the *travaux préparatoires* of some of the earlier conventions support the conclusions just mentioned, i.e., that: 1) it is left to the discretion of the relevant Party to decide whether or not it will take measures to ensure the presence of an alleged offender; and 2) the "circumstances" which may be taken into account are primarily, but not exclusively, evidentiary ones.

During the drafting of the Tokyo Convention, the French representative stated that this phrase was designed to give "freedom of judgment" to the relevant State.[3] Seven years later, during the drafting of the Hague Convention, the delegations of Argentina and Brazil proposed that the words "upon being satisfied that the circumstances so warrant" be deleted from the corresponding provision of that instrument.[4] Asserting that the phrase was ambiguous and would weaken the text, the representatives of those States maintained that unless the Convention contained an unequivocal obligation to arrest or otherwise ensure an alleged offender's presence, States could arbitrarily invoke any "circumstances" they liked to justify a claim that they had no duty to undertake the measures envisaged. A loophole would, therefore, be present in the Convention. Moreover, they argued, deletion of the words would not change the meaning of the text because, in any case, the action taken by States would depend "upon the circumstances".[5]

Other delegations, however, favoured inclusion of the words. The representative of the UK, supported by that of the US, asserted that deletion of the phrase would result in obliging Parties to arrest any person against whom the allegation of hijacking was made, even if that allegation was not supported by evidence. This was an obligation, he maintained, that no State could accept.[6] The delegate of Mexico

---

[1] Art. 13(2).
[2] FRG draft, Art. 6.
[3] ICAO Doc 8565-LC/152-1, pp. 332-333 (1963).
[4] ICAO Doc 8979-LC/165-2, p. 96 (1972).
[5] ICAO Doc 8979-LC/165-1, pp. 100-101 & 173-174 (1972).
[6] *Id.* at p. 174.

agreed, stating that it was inconceivable that a person could be taken into custody if the circumstances did not warrant such action,[7] and the delegate of Costa Rica added that an obligation to take action regardless of the circumstances might be too much of an encroachment upon the sovereignty of the State concerned.[8]

In response to the British argument, the representative of Barbados pointed out that the provision does not impose an unequivocal obligation to place an alleged offender in custody; rather, it merely requires the State to ensure his presence, whether this be achieved by arrest or by other measures.[9] The Greek delegate added that the obligation to ensure only that the alleged offender did not leave the State concerned was not an unacceptable one, particularly when compared with the dangerous implication of the words "upon being satisfied that the circumstances so warrant", i.e., that a State Party could on the basis of its subjective judgment ignore the requirement contained in this paragraph.[10]

Despite the arguments advanced to delete the phrase, a significant majority of State delegations favoured its retention.[11] They clearly did not want to appear to bind themselves unequivocally to take measures against all alleged offenders, without being able to have regard to the surrounding circumstances. It may be noted, however, that deleting the phrase would probably not have had the effect of absolutely requiring States to take offenders into custody, or to take other measures, when such action was not warranted by the circumstances. Most States have fundamental principles of law which do not allow deprivations of liberty without some supporting evidence. For example, in the United States a person cannot be arrested without probable cause to believe that he has committed a crime.[12] Indeed, while the ILC did not include this phrase in its draft of the corresponding Article of the New York Convention, in its commentary thereto it nevertheless stated that action taken by a State in this regard "must be considered in light of the requirement . . . that there be grounds to believe that the alleged offender has committed one or more of the crimes set forth".[13] The insistence of States that the phrase not be deleted from these Conventions, however, obviates in advance any argument which could otherwise be made that they must take such measures without having regard to the surrounding circumstances.

[7] ICAO Doc 8979-LC/165-1, p. 174 (1972).
[8] *Id.* at p. 101.
[9] *Id.* at p. 175.
[10] *Id.*
[11] The vote in the Legal Committee was 49 in favour and 11 against. *Id.* at p. 176.
[12] See generally, Amnd. 4, *Constitution of the United States; Gerstein v. Pugh*, 95 S.Ct. 854 (1975).
[13] 1972 YBILC, Vol. II, p. 317.

It should be emphasized, however, that a State must, of course, act in good faith in exercising its discretion, and a decision not to take such measures that is based, for example, on sympathy with the hostage-taker's political motives or a disinclination to get involved in a political situation cannot be justified by reference to the words of this Convention. Normally, when there exists that degree of evidence which a State generally requires before it takes measures against a suspect under its domestic criminal law, then that State should take such measures against a person who is suspected of committing one of the offences set forth in this Convention. Its failure to do so, in the absence of other justifying "circumstances", may be evidence of bad faith. In this connexion it might be noted that the failure of Yugoslavia to hold Abu Abbas, the alleged mastermind of the *Achille Lauro* hijacking, pending an extradition request by the United States, despite having been shown evidence of his involvement in the offence, would appear to have been a breach of its obligation under this Article.[14]

Although the foregoing discussion demonstrates that the draftsmen of these conventions were concerned primarily with ensuring that States Parties would have the freedom to determine whether or not the evidence justified taking preliminary action against alleged offenders, this paragraph does not expressly or impliedly limit to evidentiary considerations the circumstances which may be taken into account. The draftsmen seemed more generally to want to avoid tying the hands of States Parties.[15] What other circumstances, then, could a State Party legitimately take into account when deciding whether or not to take such measures? While it is not possible to draw up a definitive list, two such circumstances are worth particular mention.

One is the possible danger that the offender still presents to his victims. As noted, the ILC deleted the phrase "[u]pon being satisfied that the circumstances so warrant" from its draft of the New York

---

[14] See p. 26 (note 65 in Part I). As one commentator points out, Yugoslavia's explanation that it refused to hold Abbas on the grounds that he had diplomatic immunity as an official of the PLO is inadequate. The PLO is not a State, and, in any event, Abbas was neither accredited to Yugoslavia nor in transit between diplomatic posts at the time of the incident, the circumstances under which a diplomat is generally accorded immunity from local criminal jurisdiction. See Murphy, "The Future of Multilateralism and Efforts to Combat International Terrorism", 25 Colum. J. Trans. L. 35, 49 (1986). See also Arts. 31 & 40, 1961 Vienna Convention on Diplomatic Relations, 500 UNTS 95.

[15] For example, the sub-committee initially charged with drafting the Tokyo Convention reported that the similar formula employed in that Convention was "a more general and less precise condition which would enable the State to decide as a matter of policy whether the circumstances called for this action, instead of being obliged to act if there is a *prima facie* case of a serious offense under its laws." ICAO Doc 8565-LC/152-2, p. 233 (1963).

Convention. It was restored by the Sixth Committee, however, the Chairman of the drafting group explaining only that:

> [m]ost members of the Drafting Committee believed that without that specification, the obligation imposed on the State party concerned would be too absolute and would not permit that State to take into consideration certain factors of the utmost importance, such as the threat posed by the alleged offender to the lives of his victims.[16]

While this explanation is not entirely clear, it seems to reflect the fairly obvious proposition that one circumstance which would justify a Party's decision not to take custodial or other measures would be if the victims (in the case of this Convention, the hostages) were still in the hands of the offender and a State's attempt to take measures pursuant to the provision would present a danger to them.

Another example of a circumstance wherein a State would be justified in not taking such measures is if it had promised immunity to the offender in exchange for the release of the hostages pursuant to its discretion under Article 3.[17] This, however, would not affect the obligation of another State Party in whose territory an alleged offender might subsequently be present to take such action.

". . . any State Party in the territory of which the alleged offender is present . . ."

The obligation imposed by this paragraph applies to any State Party in whose territory the offender is present. This would include the State in whose territory the crime was committed, if the offender is still present therein, as well as any other Party to which the offender fled subsequent to the offence. If the offence has occurred in the territory of another State, it would seem that a State's action in this regard will often be taken at the request of that other State, for example, pursuant to a request for provisional arrest pending a formal request for extradition.[18] However, even if no such request comes from another State, these measures must be taken. Each State may be presumed to have procedures which allow it to take measures with respect to a person suspected of violating its criminal laws, and, pursuant to Article 5 and Article 2 of this Convention, an offence

---

[16] UN GAOR, 28th Sess., C.6 (1436th mtg.), para. 61, UN Doc A/C.6/SR.1436 (1973).
[17] See pp. 113-115 (notes 10-19 and accompanying text in the commentary on Article 3).
[18] On requests for provisional arrests, see generally Bassiouni, *International Extradition United States Law & Practice* 524-30 (2d ed., 1987); Stanbrook, *The Law and Practice of Extradition* 18-20 (1980); Art. XII, Treaty on Extradition, 13 October 1983, United States-Italy, TIAS 10, 837, *reprinted in* 24 ILM 1527, 1529 (1985).

which is committed outside of a State must be an offence under that State's laws if the offender subsequently appears in its territory.

"... shall, in accordance with its laws, take him into custody or take other measures to ensure his presence for such time as is necessary to enable any criminal or extradition proceedings to be instituted."

The essential obligation imposed upon Parties by this paragraph is to ensure the presence of the offender for the time necessary to enable extradition or criminal proceedings to commence. Such preliminary measures are necessary if the obligation *aut dedere aut judicare* is to be satisfied adequately. The precise way in which this obligation is implemented is left to the internal law of the relevant State. The measures may include taking the alleged offender into custody, but there is no absolute requirement that the State must do so (indeed, the ILC deleted the express reference to "custody" and "other measures" from the New York Convention, explaining that it was "unnecessarily confusing").[19] Other methods could include, for example, the requiring of bond or the revocation of the alleged offender's passport.[20] However, it is unclear whether these latter measures would truly "ensure" the alleged offender's presence, and it seems that, given the serious nature of the offences, custodial measures would most often be best.

The custodial or other measures are to last only for such time "as is necessary" to enable the proceedings to be instituted. An early draft of the Hague Convention contained the words "reasonably necessary";[21] however, the word "reasonably" was deleted upon the proposal of the French delegation.[22] Although it is unclear from the record as to why most delegations favoured deletion of the word "reasonably", some of them emphasized that the question of reasonableness is implied in the words "for such time as is necessary".[23] And it would indeed seem that

---

[19] 1972 YBILC, Vol. I, p. 206. During the Sixth Committee deliberations on the New York Convention, the delegate of Brazil noted that the Article quite rightly made no mention of any specific measures which should be taken since these "would differ according to the specific legal system". UN GAOR, 28th Sess., C.6 (1418th mtg.), para. 18, UN Doc A/C.6/SR.1418 (1973).

[20] See generally the comments of Prof. Ago in the ILC (1972 YBILC, Vol. I, p. 207) and of the representative of the Netherlands to the ICAO Tokyo Diplomatic Conference. ICAO Doc 8565-LC/152-1, p. 394 (1963).

[21] ICAO Doc 8979-LC/165-1, p. 173 (1972). This is the wording contained in Article 13(2) of the Tokyo Convention.

[22] ICAO Doc 8979-LC/165-1, p. 175 (1972).

[23] See, e.g., the comments of the representatives of Brazil and the United Kingdom, *id.* at p. 174. On the other hand, the representative of Mexico, arguing for the retention of the word "reasonably", stated that even if it lacks precision "it gives some sort of norm to guide national authorities in determining the period of custody necessary to permit the preparation of criminal or extradition proceedings". *Id.*

while the time necessary to institute the procedures is a matter of internal law, it should not be unreasonably long.[24]

Finally, although this phrase would seem to indicate that the measures should last only so long as is necessary to allow the proceedings to be "instituted", a reasonable interpretation of this obligation would be that the measures must ensure his presence not only for the institution of the proceedings but also for their duration.

"That State Party shall immediately make a preliminary inquiry into the facts."

This paragraph requires a Party taking measures pursuant to paragraph 1 to make a preliminary inquiry into the facts. The Article imposes no obligations regarding the form of the inquiry, i.e., whether it should be formal or informal or whether it should be conducted by a judge or by police or prosecutorial officials. It would seem, therefore, that the question of the form of the inquiry is strictly a matter for internal law (and Article 7(2) of the Rome Convention specifically so provides). Although it may be assumed that most or all States already have some sort of provision for such a hearing,[25] this requirement serves a useful human rights function as well as a law enforcement one — it seeks to ensure that accused persons do not have their liberty infringed unnecessarily. A similar obligation is imposed by the Hague, Montreal and Rome Conventions, but was omitted from the New York Convention for reasons which are unclear from the record.

PARAGRAPH 2: NOTIFICATION TO OTHER STATES OF THE MEASURES TAKEN

"The custody or other measures referred to in paragraph 1 of this article shall be notified without delay . . ."

Paragraph 2 requires a Party which is taking measures pursuant to paragraph 1 to notify various other States (and, if relevant, the international organization which has been the target of compulsion) of any measures it has taken pursuant to paragraph 1. According to the ILC, the purpose of this provision is two-fold:

> In the first place, it is desirable to notify States that are carrying on a search for the alleged offender that he has been found. In the second place it will

---

[24] An unreasonable delay pending extradition or prosecution may constitute a breach of international law. See generally Art. 9(3), 1966 International Covenant on Civil and Political Rights, 999 UNTS 171.

[25] See, e.g., Rule 5, *Federal Rules of Criminal Procedure* (United States).

permit any State with a special interest in the particular crime committed to determine if it wishes to request extradition and to commence the preparation of necessary documents and the collection of the required evidence.[26]

Another purpose served by this provision is that it ensures that the State entitled to protect the alleged offender pursuant to paragraph 3 of this Article will receive notice of the custodial or other measures independently of any request by the alleged offender to communicate with the representative of that State.

Notification under this paragraph must be effected "without delay". The original FRG draft provided, as do the corresponding provisions of the Hague, Montreal and Rome Conventions, that notification must be made "immediately". However, during the drafting of the New York Convention, it was suggested by the Soviet representative to the Sixth Committee that it might be difficult in practice to effect notification "immediately".[27] Subsequently, the Sixth Committee changed the phrase to read "without delay",[28] and these words were adopted by the draftsmen of this Convention as well. It is somewhat difficult to calibrate what the difference in practice will be between notice which must be given "immediately" and notice which must be given "without delay". In any event, it is clear that notification under this provision must be effected as soon as is practicable after the measures have been taken.

". . . directly or through the Secretary-General of the United Nations . . ."

A Party may make the necessary notification either directly to the relevant States or through the Secretary-General of the United Nations. The Hague, Montreal and Rome Conventions provide only for direct notification, as did the ILC draft of the New York Convention.[29] In the Sixth Committee deliberations regarding the New York Convention, however, it was proposed by the delegation of Singapore that notification under this paragraph should be conducted through the Secretary-General.[30] Two reasons were advanced for this proposal: 1) the notifying State might not have diplomatic relations with one or more of the States entitled to notice and, therefore, might not in fact communicate the information to those States; and 2) notification through the Secretary-General would ease the burden on

---

[26] 1972 YBILC, Vol. II, p. 318.
[27] UN GAOR, 28th Sess., C.6 (1418th mtg.), para. 16, UN Doc A/C.6/SR.1418 (1973).
[28] UN GAOR, 28th Sess., C.6 (1436th mtg.), para. 63, UN Doc A/C.6/SR.1436 (1973).
[29] See 1972 YBILC, Vol. II, p. 317.
[30] UN GAOR, 28th Sess., C.6 (1436th mtg.), para. 31, UN Doc A/C.6/SR.1436 (1973).

small States which might not have the material means to effect communication to many States.[31] Some of the draftsmen, however, expressed the view that direct communication would be preferable given the bureaucratic nature of notification through the Secretary-General.[32] In the end, a compromise was reached whereby States may choose between the two systems of notification.

"... to: ... the State where the offence was committed ... the State against which compulsion has been directed or attempted ... the State of which the natural or juridical person against whom compulsion has been directed or attempted is a national ... the State of which the hostage is a national or in the territory of which he has his habitual residence ... the State of which the alleged offender is a national or, if he is a stateless person, in the territory of which he has his habitual residence ... the international intergovernmental organization against which compulsion has been directed or attempted ... all other States concerned."

The States which must be notified of the measures taken are all those which would normally have some interest in the particular act of hostage-taking. Indeed, the list of States entitled to such notification includes, *inter alia*, all those States which, if they are Parties to the Convention, are required, or entitled, to establish primary jurisdiction over that offence pursuant to Article 5, paragraph 1. It should be emphasized, however, that States are obliged to give notice even to those listed States which are not party to the Convention.

One minor problem which could arise in connexion with this provision is that, although it requires that notification be given to "all other States concerned", it provides no guidance as to what other States might be "concerned" with a particular act of hostage-taking. It could be argued that the class of "concerned" States includes all other States Parties to this Convention. However, such an interpretation is weakened by the fact that during the drafting of the New York Convention the ILC omitted a provision of an early draft of that instrument which would have required that notice be given to all States Parties thereto. The ILC replaced that provision with a requirement that notice be given to all "interested States", explaining that, in view of the urgency of the requirement, the substituted language would "ease delays".[33]

The search for a precise meaning of "other concerned States" is made more difficult because it seems that all of the States most

---

[31] UN GAOR, 28th Sess., C.6 (1436th mtg.), para. 31, UN Doc A/C.6/SR.1436 (1973).
[32] *Id.* at para. 50.
[33] 1972 YBILC, Vol. I, p. 240.

concerned with a particular act of hostage-taking are already specifically included in the list of those entitled to notice. Since there is really no basis upon which to determine a fixed content of the term "concerned" States, it is probably enough to say that States Parties which know of another State which has some particular interest in the case should notify that State of the measures taken.[34]

PARAGRAPH 3: RIGHT OF THE ACCUSED TO VISITATION AND COMMUNICATION

Pursuant to this paragraph, the State Party taking measures in accordance with paragraph 1 of this Article must allow the alleged offender: 1) to communicate with the appropriate representative of a protecting State; and 2) to be visited by a representative of that State. As the ILC noted in its commentary to the draft New York Convention, this paragraph "is designed to safeguard the rights of the alleged offenders, thereby strengthening in this specific instance the general obligation established under [Article 8, paragraph 2]"[35] (which requires the fair treatment of alleged offenders). The rights to communicate and to be visited are basic to the enjoyment by the individual of effective protection, allowing as they do a determination of whether a prisoner is receiving humane treatment and enjoying other procedural rights guaranteed by international law, such as the assistance of counsel.[36] These rights are codified in Article 36, paragraph 1, of the 1963 Vienna Convention on Consular Relations,[37] and are provided for in many other consular agreements, bilateral[38] and multilateral.[39] To the extent that the similar provisions in the Vienna Convention and other agreements are more comprehensive than this paragraph, they will, of course, apply as between States Parties thereto.

[34] It may be noted that the language of the corresponding paragraphs in the Hague, Montreal and Rome Conventions seems preferable to that employed here, providing that a State Party which takes custodial measures should, "if it considers it advisable, [notify] any other interested States ..." Although this formula similarly does not provide any guidance as to what other States are "interested", the obligation is less absolute than that contained herein.

[35] 1972 YBILC, Vol. II, p. 318.

[36] See generally Lee, *Consular Law and Practice* 120 (1961).

[37] 596 UNTS 261. That Article provides that consular officers and nationals of the sending State shall be free to communicate with and have access to each other, that consular officers shall be informed when a national of the sending State is placed in custody pending trial or is otherwise detained and that "consular officers shall have the right to visit a national of the sending state who is in prison, custody or detention, to converse and correspond with him and to arrange for his legal representation."

[38] See, e.g., Art. 5, Consular Convention, 8 January 1963, United States-Republic of Korea, 493 UNTS 103. See also Lee, *The Vienna Convention on Consular Relations* 107 (1966).

[39] See Art. 6, 1967 European Convention on Consular Functions, 61 ETS (not yet in force).

The corresponding provisions of the Hague and Montreal Conventions are more limited in that they provide only that a person in custody "shall be assisted in communicating immediately with the nearest appropriate representative of the State of which he is a national". The corresponding provisions of the New York and Rome Conventions are, however, almost identical to this one.

"Any person regarding whom the measures referred to in paragraph 1 of this article are being taken shall be entitled ... to communicate without delay ..."

The protections under this paragraph are extended to "[a]ny person"; however, they are in fact relevant only when the accused is held in a State other than that of which he is a national. The alleged offender must be allowed to exercise his right to communicate with the protecting State's representative "without delay". The Hague and Montreal Conventions, by way of contrast, require that the alleged offender be allowed to establish such communication "immediately". The current language was adopted by the Sixth Committee during the drafting of the New York Convention, explaining that it was consistent with the terminology of the Vienna Convention on Consular Relations.[40] In any event, the communication must be allowed as soon as is practicable, and any delay can be seen as a breach of this Convention.

"... with the nearest appropriate representative of the State of which he is a national or which is otherwise entitled to establish such communication ..."

The alleged offender must be allowed to communicate with an appropriate representative, i.e., a diplomatic or consular official, of either his national State or of some other State which is entitled to exercise some measure of protection with respect to him. This provision recognizes that situations exist wherein a national of one State falls within the international protection of another State, for example, because of a lack of diplomatic relations between the custodial State and the offender's national State.[41] This provision, which appears in essentially identical form in the New York and Rome Conventions, is an improvement over the corresponding provisions in the Hague and Montreal Conventions which refer only to the "national" State of the alleged offender.

---

[40] UN GAOR, 28th Sess., C.6 (1436th mtg.), para. 63, UN Doc A/C.6/SR.1436 (1973).
[41] See generally Oppenheim, *International Law*, Vol. I, 646-647 (8th ed., H. Lauterpacht, ed., 1955).

ARTICLE 6

"... or, if he is a stateless person, the State in the territory of which he has his habitual residence;"

The State taking measures pursuant to paragraph 1 must allow a stateless person to communicate with and be visited by a representative of the State in whose territory he has his habitual residence. This provision thus follows the pattern, established in Article 5, paragraph 1(b), and continued in the second paragraph of this Article, to assimilate stateless persons, for many of the purposes of this Convention, to nationals of the State in which they are habitually resident. It recognizes that persons accused of such crimes may well be stateless persons and that such persons also need the assistance which can only be provided by a protecting State.

As noted earlier, the definition of a stateless person is a person who is not considered to be a national under the laws of any State.[42] In the absence of any contrary indication, it should be assumed that it is this definition of stateless person which should be ascribed to the term as employed in this Convention. However, it is worth noting that there has been a certain tendency in legal literature and in studies to assimilate to such "*de jure*" stateless persons "*de facto*" stateless persons, i.e., those persons who "without having been deprived of their nationality no longer enjoy the protection and assistance of their national authorities", particularly refugees.[43] A broad interpretation of this provision would, therefore, include refugees in the category of "stateless" persons who are entitled to communicate with, and to be visited by, the appropriate representatives of the State in which they are habitually resident. Such an interpretation would have the admirable humanitarian effect of enlarging the class of potential offenders who could enjoy the protection of the representatives of a State.[44] But in the absence of a specific reference to refugees it is probably too much to say that this provision includes refugees who are not, strictly speaking, stateless persons. However similar the plight of refugees and stateless persons, and regardless of the fact that the

---

[42] See p. 149 (note 63 and accompanying text in the commentary on Article 5); Art. 1, 1954 Convention Relating to the Status of Stateless Persons, 360 UNTS 117.

[43] See UN Secretariat, *A Study of Statelessness*, UN Doc E/1112 & E/1112/Add.1 (1949); Weis, *Nationality and Statelessness in International Law* 44, 164, 202 (2nd ed., 1979); von Mangoldt, "Stateless Persons", in Bernhardt (ed.), *Encyclopedia of Public International Law*, Vol. 8, 490-494 (1985).

[44] It may be noted in this connexion that Article 2 of the Protocol Concerning the Protection of Refugees to the European Convention on Consular Functions, ETS 61, specifically provides that the consular official of the State in whose territory a refugee has his habitual residence is entitled to protect him in conformity with the Convention, in consultation, whenever possible, with the United Nations High Commission for Refugees or with any other agency of the UN which might succeed it.

categories may in some cases overlap,[45] the two terms have distinct meanings in international law.[46] Thus, it must be concluded that refugees who are not stateless persons fall outside the scope of this provision; such persons must rely on whatever protection is afforded by the appropriate UN agencies, such as the High Commission for Refugees.[47]

The corresponding paragraph of the New York Convention differs somewhat, providing that a stateless person may communicate with and be visited by a representative of any State which he requests and which is willing to protect his rights. The draftsmen of this Convention rejected this wording, the Chairman of the Sixth Committee stating that it put stateless persons in a "more favourable position" than nationals.[48] Although this is not explained further, the statement reflects the fact that nationals of a State cannot request and receive protection from any other State just because the latter is willing to do so. The result of this change, however, is that, in contrast to the situation under the New York Convention, if a stateless person is not habitually resident in any State,[49] he is not entitled to the protection contained in this paragraph.

". . . to be visited by a representative of that State."

The alleged offender has the right not only to communicate with a representative of the protecting State but also to be visited by that

---

[45] In particular, a stateless person can be a refugee. See Art. 6(A)(ii) of the Statute of the Office of the United Nations High Commissioner for Refugees, annexed to GA Res 428 (V) of 14 December 1950, UN GAOR, 5th Sess., Supp. 20, p. 46, UN Doc A/1775 (1951), which provides that persons protected include not only those who, because of a fear of persecution, are outside their State of nationality and are unable or unwilling to avail themselves of the protection of that State, but also persons "who, not having a nationality and being outside the country of [their] habitual residence", are in a similar position. See also Art. 1(A)(2), 1951 Convention Relating to the Status of Refugees, 189 UNTS 150.

[46] For definitions of a refugee, see Art. 6, Statute of the Office of the United Nations High Commissioner for Refugees, note 44, *supra*; Art. 1, 1951 Convention Relating to the Status of Refugees, 189 UNTS 150; Goodwin-Gill, *The Refugee in International Law* 17-20 (1983). Therefore, despite the similarities of the two groups and the tendency to address their problems in a similar manner, they are distinct entities and their statuses are treated in separate international instruments. The Convention Relating to the Status of Stateless Persons, 360 UNTS 117, thus deals only with *de jure* and not *de facto* stateless persons.

[47] On the international protection afforded refugees by UN agencies, see generally Goodwin-Gill, note 46, *supra*, at pp. 56, 129-140. It might be noted that during the drafting of the Vienna Convention on Consular Relations the UNHCR indicated that it would undertake, with respect to refugees, to provide protections such as those contemplated in that instrument. See Lee, note 36, *supra*, at pp. 69-70.

[48] UN GAOR, 34th Sess., C.6 (53rd mtg.), p. 8, para. 25, UN Doc A/C.6/34/SR.53 (1979).

[49] On the meaning of "habitual residence", see p. 150 (notes 65-66 and accompanying text in the commentary on Article 5).

representative. No similar provision exists in the Hague or Montreal Conventions, but the same right is accorded by the New York and Rome Conventions. As earlier noted, this right is expressly provided for in the Vienna Convention on Consular Relations, and in many other consular agreements.

PARAGRAPH 4: EFFECTIVE EXERCISE OF THE RIGHTS IN PARAGRAPH 3 GUARANTEED

"The rights referred to in paragraph 3 of this article shall be exercised in conformity with the laws and regulations of the State in the territory of which the alleged offender is present subject to the proviso, however, that the said laws and regulations must enable full effect to be given to the purposes for which the rights accorded under paragraph 3 of this article are intended."

A State may impose its own procedural rules, e.g., regarding the time and place, upon the alleged offender's communication and visits with the representative of the protecting State. However, local law cannot impede the exercise of these rights so as to destroy the benefit of the protective functions. Thus, for example, if a State's procedural laws somehow interfere with the accused's right to arrange for legal assistance through the representative of the protecting State, that State is in breach of this Convention. The language is taken directly from Article 36(2) of the Vienna Convention on Consular Relations. No comparable provisions are contained in the earlier anti-terrorism conventions, although identical wording is contained in Article 7(4) of the Rome Convention.

PARAGRAPH 5: PROTECTION BY THE INTERNATIONAL COMMITTEE OF THE RED CROSS

"The provisions of paragraphs 3 and 4 of this article shall be without prejudice to the right of any State Party having a claim to jurisdiction in accordance with paragraph 1(b) of article 5 to invite the International Committee of the Red Cross to communicate with and visit the alleged offender."

This paragraph provides that the provisions of paragraphs 3 and 4 are "without prejudice" to the "right" of a Party which has a claim to jurisdiction under Article 5, paragraph 1(b), i.e., when the offence is committed "by any of its nationals or, if that State considers it appropriate, by those stateless persons who have their habitual residence in its territory", to invite the ICRC to communicate with and visit the accused. This paragraph has no counterpart in the Hague, Montreal, New York or Rome Conventions; it was added to this Convention by the Sixth Committee.[50]

This provision is somewhat curious. On the one hand, it "reflects commendable concern with the right to communicate with accused persons and a creative approach to facilitating communication in precisely the circumstances in which it may be most necessary, that is, when relations between the states involved are such that no diplomatic or consular communication exists".[51] Moreover, it "diminishes the potential scope of article 9, paragraph 1, subparagraph (a)(ii) [which requires a State Party to refuse extradition when the alleged offender's position would be prejudiced by reason of the fact that he cannot communicate with the protecting State], by broadening the possible means of communication".[52] On the other hand, the reference to the "right" of the State to invite the ICRC to communicate with the alleged offender is somewhat obscure. The wording of this provision seems, at first glance, to be referring to a right which exists independently of this Convention. However, it is unclear as to what right to this effect such a State would already have. Although it could have been phrased better (e.g., "A State Party having a claim to jurisdiction in accordance with paragraph 1(b) of article 5 shall have the right to invite the International Committee of the Red Cross to communicate with and visit the alleged offender. The provisions of paragraphs 3 and 4 of this article shall be without prejudice to that right"), the better interpretation of this paragraph is that it gives the State with a claim to jurisdiction based on Article 5(1)(b) the right to make such an invitation to the ICRC, and imposes a corresponding duty upon the custodial State to allow the visit.

The Chairman of the Sixth Committee Working Group received and read into the record a letter from the Delegate to International Organizations of the ICRC regarding this provision.[53] In that letter, the ICRC indicated that the role it may be called upon to play under Article 6(5) is consistent with its own statutes and those of the International Red Cross to study any matter and take any humanitarian initiative falling within its function as a neutral and independent institution and intermediary. However, the letter placed the following conditions upon the involvement of the ICRC:

---

[50] UN GAOR, 34th Sess., C.6 (53rd mtg.), p. 8, para. 26, UN Doc A/C.6/34/SR.53 (1979).
[51] Rosenstock, p. 181.
[52] *Id.*
[53] UN GAOR, 34th Sess., C.6 (53rd mtg.), p. 11, paras. 42-44, UN Doc A/C.6/34/SR.53 (1979).

ARTICLE 6

1) the ICRC must remain free to accept or refuse, in light of the circumstances, any invitation of the kind envisaged;

2) the ICRC would not act without the agreement of the States in which the offender is held and of which he is a national;

3) the ICRC would prefer to act only if the visit of a State representative, as provided for in the draft, proved impossible;

4) it must be clear that the ICRC does not represent the requesting State but, rather, that it acts independently and only on the basis of humanitarian criteria;

5) the custodial State must agree that the ICRC may visit the detained person without witnesses and repeatedly; and

6) the ICRC only communicates with a detainee by visiting him but may agree to transmit family messages to the detained person and vice versa if no other means of doing so exist; and finally

7) any report prepared will be sent to both the requesting and custodial States.[54]

PARAGRAPH 6: NOTIFICATION OF THE FINDINGS OF THE PRELIMINARY INQUIRY

"The State which makes the preliminary inquiry contemplated in paragraph 1 of this article shall promptly report its findings to the States or organization referred to in paragraph 2 of this article and indicate whether it intends to exercise jurisdiction."

This paragraph requires the State in whose territory the alleged offender is found to communicate promptly the results of its preliminary inquiry to those States and organizations which are entitled, pursuant to paragraph 2, to notice of the measures earlier taken against him. Moreover, it requires the State to indicate whether or not it intends to exercise jurisdiction over the offence. Similar provisions are to be found in the Hague, Montreal and Rome Conventions but not in the New York Convention (since that instrument does not require that such an inquiry be held).

Notification both of the results of the preliminary investigation and of whether or not the State in whose territory the alleged offender is present intends to exercise its jurisdiction will be of assistance to those States which have primary jurisdiction in deciding whether or not they will request extradition of the offender. Such notification also has the desirable result of keeping those States and the international organization most concerned with the offence, including the protecting power, up to date regarding developments. It is unclear

[54] *Id.*

from the language or the *travaux préparatoires* as to whether this notification must be direct or whether it may instead be through the Secretary-General of the United Nations. There is no apparent reason, however, as to why this provision would differ in that respect from paragraph 2.

Article 7

NOTIFICATION OF THE RESULTS OF PROSECUTION

The State Party where the alleged offender is prosecuted shall in accordance with its laws communicate the final outcome of the proceedings to the Secretary-General of the United Nations, who shall transmit the information to the other States concerned and the international intergovernmental organizations concerned.

1. INTRODUCTION

This Article requires States which have prosecuted an alleged offender to communicate the results of the prosecution to the Secretary-General, who shall then transmit the information to other interested parties. No such provision was included in the FRG draft; it was proposed by the representative of Nigeria during the final session of the Hostages Committee.[1] No problems were raised regarding this language, and an essentially identical provision may be found in Article 11 of the New York Convention. However, the ICAO conventions impose more stringent notification requirements upon States Parties. Pursuant to Article 11 of the Hague Convention and Article 13 of the Montreal Convention, States Parties must report to the ICAO Council all relevant information in their possession concerning: the circumstances of offences under those instruments; the action they have taken to restore the *status quo* (i.e., in the case of the Hague Convention to restore control of the aircraft to the commander and in the case of both instruments to facilitate the continuation of the journey of the passengers and crew and to return the aircraft to the person entitled to possession); and the results of "the measures taken in relation to the offender or the alleged offender, and, in particular, the results of any extradition or other legal proceedings." Article 15 of the Rome Convention imposes substantially similar obligations to the ICAO instruments.[2]

---

[1] See Third Report of the Hostages Committee, p. 14, para. 55.
[2] Article 5 of the New York Convention, moreover, requires a State Party in whose territory an offence has been committed, if it has reason to believe the alleged offender has fled from its territory, to notify other States concerned of the pertinent facts of the crime and information regarding the identity of the alleged offender. Moreover, whenever an offence under that Convention has been committed, any State which has information regarding the victim or the circumstances of the crime shall report such to the State Party on whose behalf he was exercising his functions.

2. INTERPRETATION

The interpretation of this Article presents no particular problems. If a State prosecutes an alleged offender, it must communicate the results of that prosecution to the Secretary-General, who will then transmit the information to other "States concerned and the international intergovernmental organizations concerned." There being no specific listing of the States or international organizations which might be "concerned" with a particular offence, it may be assumed that notification will be made to those States and the international intergovernmental organization which are listed in Article 6(2). The option for direct notification to the concerned parties (rather than solely through the Secretary-General) which is contained in Article 6(2) has presumably been excluded due to the fact that the urgency extant in circumstances under Article 6 is not present in situations envisaged by this Article.[3]

It should be emphasized that the notification requirement under this Article would appear to obtain only when an actual prosecution has taken place. States need not notify the Secretary-General of other action, if any, taken with respect to an alleged offender (other than the preliminary measures, if any, taken pursuant to Article 6). Moreover, they need not reveal other information in their possession regarding the details of an act of hostage-taking or of any action they take with respect to that incident. This Article thus compares unfavourably with the corresponding provisions in the ICAO conventions and the Rome Convention, noted above. Because of the very limited nature of the information which must be communicated pursuant to this Article, concerned States may remain ignorant of relevant facts regarding acts of hostage-taking and of the whereabouts of alleged offenders. Moreover, as earlier noted, the stringent notification requirements of the ICAO instruments were designed partially on the rationale that disclosure of the relevant facts — regarding both the incidents themselves and the disposition of the alleged offender — will prompt governments to take their obligations under those instruments seriously, for fear of world opinion.[4] No such effect can be expected from the very limited obligation imposed by this Article.

---

[3] See generally pp. 175-176 (notes 29-32 and accompanying text in the commentary on Article 6).
[4] See pp. 56-57 (note 195 in Part I).

Article 8

AUT DEDERE AUT JUDICARE

1. The State Party in the territory of which the alleged offender is found shall, if it does not extradite him, be obliged, without exception whatsoever and whether or not the offence was committed in its territory, to submit the case to its competent authorities for the purpose of prosecution, through proceedings in accordance with the laws of that State. Those authorities shall take their decision in the same manner as in the case of any ordinary offence of a grave nature under the law of that State.

2. Any person regarding whom proceedings are being carried out in connexion with any of the offences set forth in article 1 shall be guaranteed fair treatment at all stages of the proceedings, including enjoyment of all the rights and guarantees provided by the law of the State in the territory of which he is present.

1. INTRODUCTION

Two distinct obligations are imposed by this Article, one designed to ensure that all those who are accused of committing acts of hostage-taking are brought to justice and the other to ensure that they receive fair treatment during all the relevant proceedings.

It is not enough for a convention of this type to require the Parties to make the listed offences punishable under their domestic laws, as is done in Article 2, nor is it enough to require them to establish their jurisdiction over such offences, as is done in Article 5. It must also require them actually to deal with those persons who are accused of such offences. Paragraph 1 of this Article, therefore, contains what is probably the most important obligation imposed by this Convention, requiring any Party in whose territory an alleged offender is found to submit the case to its appropriate authorities for the purpose of prosecution, unless it decides instead to extradite him. This principle, *aut dedere aut judicare*, is well-known in extradition law and may be found in many other multilateral conventions, both universal and regional in scope. This paragraph is identical in substance to Article 7 of the Hague, Montreal and New York Conventions and Article 10(1) of the Rome Convention.

Paragraph 2 of this Article is one of the provisions of this Convention (along with Articles 6 and 9) which are concerned with safeguarding the human rights of alleged offenders. It requires Parties to accord "fair treatment" to offenders during all stages of all proceedings brought in connexion with an offence of hostage-taking. Essentially identical provisions may be found in Article 9 of the New York Convention and Article 10(2) of the Rome Convention; however, no counterparts exist in the ICAO instruments. It may briefly be noted (for this point is discussed more fully below) that this provision not only serves a laudable human rights function; it may also encourage States to become parties to this Convention and to extradite alleged offenders to the State where the crime was committed. If States have some assurance that other States will provide the rights guaranteed herein, they may become less resistant to the idea of subjecting alleged offenders to the jurisdiction of other States.

The principle aut dedere aut judicare *and its use in multilateral treaties*

Many of the multilateral treaties dealing with criminal offences contain, in some form, the principle *aut dedere aut judicare*.[1] Until recent years, these instruments were drafted in such a way as to make application of the principle non-mandatory in most cases. For example, the 1929 Convention for the Suppression of Counterfeiting Currency requires States Parties to punish foreigners who have committed abroad any offence referred to in the Convention in the same way as if the offence had been committed in their territory. However, this obligation is only applicable with regard to States "whose internal legislation recognizes as a general rule the principle of the prosecution of offences committed abroad". Moreover, the obligation to prosecute is further conditioned upon that State having received a request for extradition from another State Party and rejected it "for some reason which has no connection with the offence".[2] Similarly, and of particular relevance to terrorism, the 1937 Convention on the Prevention and Punishment of Terrorism, which was drafted by the League of Nations, but which never came into force, provides, in Article 10, that "[f]oreigners who are in the territory of a High Contracting Party and who have committed abroad any of the offences set out . . . shall be prosecuted and punished as

---

[1] See Bassiouni, *International Extradition United States Law and Practice* 13-22 (2nd ed., 1987), for an extensive list of conventions dealing with "international crimes" which may recognize the principle *aut dedere aut judicare* in one form or another, i.e., they either require prosecution of the target crimes or require extradition or specifically provide for the alternative *aut dedere aut judicare*. It might be noted that the current discussion is directly related to, and overlaps with, the discussion of the obligation to establish jurisdiction over the offences in various circumstances. See pp. 135-139 (notes 7-22 and accompanying text in the commentary on Article 5).

[2] 112 LNTS 371. See p. 137 (note 14 and accompanying text in the commentary on Article 5).

though the offence had been committed in the territory of the High Contracting Party". However, this obligation would only have been applicable if the following conditions had been satisfied: 1) extradition had been requested and denied for a reason not connected with the offence; 2) the law of the State where the alleged offender was present recognized the jurisdiction of its courts regarding offences committed abroad by foreigners; and 3) the foreigner was a national of a State which recognized the jurisdiction of its courts regarding offences committed abroad by foreigners.[3] Particularly since most States do not generally recognize the principle of prosecution of foreigners for offences committed abroad,[4] it can be appreciated that these conditions left the mandatory scope of the principle *aut dedere aut judicare* very narrow indeed.

However, since World War II, many conventions dealing with international offences have made application of the principle mandatory.[5] For example, the four 1949 Geneva Conventions on the laws of armed conflict require each High Contracting Party to "bring before its own courts" those persons who have allegedly committed grave breaches of those instruments, or "if it prefers . . . hand such persons over for trial to another High Contracting Party concerned".[6] It may be noted, moreover, that the principle is also imposed in some form by the regional instruments dealing with terrorism, i.e., the OAS Convention[7] and the European Convention.[8] The most absolute statement of the rule, however, is that formulated in the Hostages Convention and in the other anti-terrorism conventions promulgated under the auspices of the UN, ICAO and IMO.[9]

---

[3] LN Doc C.546(1).M.383(1).1937.V. For details of this instrument, see p. 29 (notes 76-78 and accompanying text in Part I).

[4] See p. 190 (note 14 and accompanying text).

[5] But not all such conventions adopted in recent years have required application of the principle. The instruments concerning narcotic drugs, for example, leave the issue up to the relevant State's laws and do not require any changes in those laws in order to comply with the obligation *aut dedere aut judicare*. See p. 137 (note 15 and accompanying text in the commentary on Article 5).

[6] See p. 138 (note 16 and accompanying text in the commentary on Article 5). For full citations to these instruments, see p. 263 (note 1 in the commentary on Article 12).

[7] Art. 5. That Article provides that where extradition is not in order the requested State "is obliged to submit the case to its competent authorities for prosecution, as if the act had been committed in its territory." It would seem that the obligation to prosecute is contingent upon a prior request for extradition and denial of that request.

[8] Art. 7. The rule as formulated in the European Convention is slightly different from that in the universal anti-terrorism conventions. Similar to the OAS instrument, it requires the State where the alleged offender is found to prosecute him only if it has earlier received and refused a request for extradition from another State Party. For a further discussion of this condition, see pp. 196-197 (notes 32-38 and accompanying text).

[9] See generally Costello, "International Terrorism and the Development of the Principle *aut dedere aut judicare*", 10 J. Int'l L. & Econ. 483-501 (1973). Similar statements of the rule are contained in Article 7(1) of the 1984 Convention Against

(continued on p. 190)

The obligation *aut dedere aut judicare* is essential to the effectiveness of the universal anti-terrorism instruments in combatting the offences, in the sense of punishing the offenders, since none of them contains an obligation to extradite alleged offenders to a State which may have a closer connexion with the offence than the offender's subsequent presence in its territory (although Article 10 of this instrument may facilitate extradition in some cases). And the non-extradition of an offender would otherwise generally result in impunity. Some writers have claimed that there is an obligation imposed by the law of nations to prosecute or punish those persons whom a State refuses to extradite. Grotius asserted that States have the somewhat differently worded obligation *aut dedere aut punire* with respect to those in their territory who have committed crimes in another State,[10] while a more contemporary writer, Bassiouni, asserts that the principle *aut dedere aut judicare* is a *"civitas maxima* which rises to the level of a *jus cogens* principle of international law".[11] However, this is not a widely accepted view.[12] Indeed, although some States, such as the FRG, have legislation which envisages application of the principle *aut dedere aut judicare* in some cases,[13] as one commentator notes, "[m]ost domestic criminal legislation does not provide for the duty nor the possibility to prosecute a person whose extradition has been denied".[14] Nor do extradition treaties generally provide such a duty. The anti-terrorism conventions, therefore, by requiring

---

([9] *continued*)
Torture and Other Cruel and Inhuman or Degrading Treatment or Punishment, UN Doc A/RES/39/46, *reprinted in* 23 ILM 1027 (1984) & 24 ILM 535 (1985) and in Article 10 of the 1980 Convention on the Physical Protection of Nuclear Material, Misc. 27 (1980), Cmnd 8112, *reprinted in* 18 ILM 1419 (1979).

[10] *De Jure Belli ac Pacis*, Book 2, Ch. 21, §§III & IV (English translation, Carnegie Endowment for International Peace, pp. 526-529 (1925)).

[11] Bassiouni, note 1, *supra*, at xvi & 13. The adoption of such a general rule, moreover, has been advocated in other quarters. See Van den Wijngaert, *The Political Offence Exception to Extradition* 218-229 and sources cited at p. 207 n.1080 & p. 219 n.1130 (1980).

[12] See, e.g., Schultz, "The General Framework of Extradition and Asylum", in Bassiouni & Nanda (eds.), *A Treatise on International Criminal Law*, Vol. II, 310 (1973); Stein, "Extradition", in Bernhardt (ed.), *Encyclopedia of Public International Law*, Vol. 8, 223 (1985). Even Bassiouni acknowledges that contemporary practice would not support the view that there is a general obligation *aut dedere aut judicare* with respect to international crimes. However, he states that the "widespread use of the formula 'prosecute or extradite' either specifically stated, explicitly stated in a duty to extradite, or implicit in the duty to prosecute or criminalize, and the number of signatories to these numerous conventions attests to the existing general *jus cogens* principle . . . its acceptance by a significant number of states raises it to the level of a general duty under customary international law". See Bassiouni, note 1, *supra*, at 22-23. However, given the relatively small number of treaties which actually impose the duty *aut dedere aut judicare* (as opposed to authorizing it) in all situations, it seems doubtful that Bassiouni's argument is currently tenable.

[13] *StGB*, §7(2)(ii).

[14] Van den Wijngaert, note 11, *supra*, at p. 219.

application of the principle *aut dedere aut judicare*, seek to ensure that all offenders are brought to justice; if, as intended, they are universally adhered to, they could eliminate safe havens for terrorists.

Despite the improvement that the principle represents over existing non-conventional practice, however, it is not without its faults. In most cases, there will be difficulties in bringing an alleged offender to trial in a State other than the one in which the offence was committed, not the least of which is the fact that the evidence and witnesses will generally be located in the territorial State (although this problem should be alleviated somewhat by the requirements of Article 11). And it is generally true that the territorial State is more injured by a crime than any other State. Why, then, do these conventions not as a general rule require a State which has no connexion with an offence, other than the fact that the offender has subsequently appeared in its territory, to extradite him to the territorial State or, at least, to another State which has some significant link to the offence? The answer, quite clearly, is that States will not accept such an obligation. They have, in fact, specifically rejected proposals by the USSR and other States, made with respect to the Hague Convention, which would have required States to extradite offenders to the State of registration of the aircraft.[15] When States bind themselves to extradite criminals, they generally do so on either a bilateral[16] or a regional basis.[17] The other States with whom they are dealing are, therefore, not only known in advance but carefully selected. But even in such bilateral and regional treaties many limitations are often placed on extradition, such as the rules of non-extradition of nationals of the requested State

---

[15] See, e.g., the proposal of the USSR and Poland during the drafting of the Hague Convention which would have required "[e]ach Contracting State [to] make the offenders subject to extradition to the State of registration regardless of any specific agreement between the States concerned." ICAO Doc 8979-LC/165-2, p. 82 (1972). See also the Soviet proposal for a protocol to the Hague Convention which contained a similar requirement. ICAO Doc 9050-LC/169-2, p. 60 (1973). Moreover, during the drafting of the Hostages Convention, some States expressed a preference for a requirement that alleged offenders be extradited to the territorial State. See, e.g., the comments of the representative of Poland, UN GAOR, 34th Sess., C.6 (14th mtg.), p. 8, para. 40, UN Doc A/C.6/34/SR.14 (1979). It might be noted that during the drafting of the Hague Convention the US submitted a proposal which expressed a preference for extradition to the State of registration but which did not require such. ICAO Doc 8979-LC/165-2, p. 74.

[16] One source estimates the number of existing bilateral extradition treaties at 1,500. See Stein, "Extradition Treaties", in Bernhardt, note 12, *supra*, at p. 230.

[17] See, e.g., 1957 European Convention on Extradition, 359 UNTS 276; 1933 Montevideo Convention on Extradition and Optional Clause, 162 LNTS 45; 1981 Inter-American Convention on Extradition, PAUTS 60. For further details on the various regional arrangements, see Bassiouni, note 1, *supra*, at pp. 25-30; Shearer, "The Current Framework of International Extradition: A Brief Study of Regional Arrangements and Multilateral Treaties", in Bassiouni & Nanda, note 12, *supra*, at pp. 326-335 (1973); Shearer, *Extradition in International Law* 51-67 (1971).

and non-extradition of political offenders.[18] Thus, States do not generally bind themselves "automatically" to extradite alleged offenders, but rather leave themselves with a measure of control over whether or not a particular request will be granted.

With specific regard to multilateral treaties designed for universal adherence, for both political and humanitarian reasons States are less willing to bind themselves to extradite alleged offenders. Thus, while many States are willing to accept that certain types of international crimes should be punished without regard to the location of the offence, the motives of the offender or the identity of the victim, they do not want to find themselves bound to extradite alleged offenders to other States with which they would not otherwise choose to deal on that basis or which they may fundamentally distrust.[19] Humanitarian considerations preclude States from extraditing alleged offenders to other States which they perceive as not guaranteeing such rights as a fair trial.[20] Although provisions such as paragraph 2 of this Article are designed to assuage the apprehensions of States, encouraging them to extradite by obliging all States to protect certain fundamental human rights, the reluctance of States in this regard is aptly demonstrated by Article 9 of this Convention which requires States *not* to extradite under certain circumstances. While in a more perfect world multilateral treaties dealing with substantive criminal offences might require that the alleged offender be extradited to the State in whose territory the crime was committed, or at least to another State which has a more substantial connexion with the offence than simply the fact that the offender has subsequently appeared there, it has not as yet been possible to conclude a treaty which contains such a requirement. Nor in the current international climate, wherein many States routinely disregard fundamental human rights, is such a requirement desirable.

[18] See pp. 231-232 (notes 18-22 and accompanying text in the commentary on Article 10). It may briefly be noted, however, that there is a trend, at least amongst certain Western States, to narrow these restrictions. *Id.*

[19] For example, during the debate in the ICAO Diplomatic Conference on the drafting of the Hague Convention, various representatives expressed their disapproval not only of the proposals just mentioned (note 15, *supra*) which would have required extradition to the State of registration, but also to proposed language which would have made the Hague Convention the legal basis for extradition for those States which require an extradition treaty between themselves and other States as a condition for extradition. These States were concerned that the proposed language would force them into unwanted extradition relationships with certain other States with which they did not want to deal, particularly South Africa. See ICAO Doc 8979-LC/165-1, pp. 129, 182 (1972). For a more thorough discussion of this debate, see pp. 238-240 (notes 42-50 and accompanying text in the commentary on Article 10).

[20] See generally, Van den Wijngaert, note 11, *supra*, at p. 159; Costello, note 9, *supra*, at pp. 491-494; Rosenstock, p. 182. As one commentator states, the inclusion of the principle *aut dedere aut judicare* is "acknowledgement that even the serious criminal may deserve protection against persecution or prejudice, while not escaping trial or punishment". Goodwin-Gill, *The Refugee in International Law* 80 (1983).

Although this issue is discussed in further detail in the commentary on Article 10, mention should be made in this context of the political offence exception to extradition. This principle, although stated and applied in various ways, holds that extradition may not be had for political offences or for offences "connected" with political offences. This exception is commonly contained in extradition laws and treaties and "can be considered as a generally accepted principle, at least insofar as 'western nations' are concerned".[21] Terrorist offences are commonly committed in a political context, and the reluctance of States to derogate from the political offence exception must be seen as at least partially responsible for the failure of this instrument and the other universal anti-terrorism conventions to contain a more substantial duty to extradite. While the political offence exception remains intact under this Convention, and States may thus refuse to extradite on the ground that the act of hostage-taking was political in nature (assuming that they could otherwise do so under their domestic laws and other treaties), the case must still be submitted to the requested State's appropriate authorities for the purpose of prosecution. Thus, no political offence exception to *prosecution* exists under this or the other anti-terrorism conventions.

2. INTERPRETATION

PARAGRAPH 1: SUBMISSION OF THE CASE FOR THE PURPOSE OF PROSECUTION WHEN EXTRADITION DOES NOT OCCUR

With respect to the obligation *aut dedere aut judicare* as formulated in this and the other anti-terrorism conventions, the ILC stated in its commentary to its draft of the New York Convention:

> In other words, the State party in whose territory the alleged offender is present is required to carry out one of the two alternatives specified in the article, it being left to that State to decide which that alternative will be. It is, of course, possible that no request for extradition will be received, in which case the State where the alleged offender is found would be effectively deprived of one of its options and have no recourse save to submit the case to its competent authorities for prosecution. On the other hand, even though it has been requested to extradite, it may submit the

---

[21] Van den Wijngaert, note 11, *supra*, at p. 1. It does not seem to be a feature in extradition treaties between Communist countries. *Id.* at n. 3. The literature on the political offence exception to extradition is vast, but Van den Wijngaert's book provides the most thorough and excellent treatment of the issue. See also Shearer, *Extradition in International Law* 166-193 (1971); Bassiouni, *International Extradition and World Public Order* 370-487 (1974).

case to its competent authorities for the purpose of prosecution, for whatever reasons it may see fit to act upon.[22]

Although this paragraph leaves it to the Party in whose territory the offender is present to decide whether it will comply with a request for extradition or instead submit the case for prosecution, as will be discussed in more detail in the commentary on Article 10, a State may well be required under some other instrument to extradite an alleged offender in a particular case. Moreover, when legal and humanitarian circumstances permit, it will usually be desirable to extradite the alleged offender to the territorial State.[23]

"The State Party in the territory of which the alleged offender is found . . ."

The obligation to extradite or prosecute an alleged offender is imposed upon the State Party in whose territory he is found. This may be the State to which the offender has fled subsequent to the offence or any other Party in whose territory he is present for whatever reason. It should be emphasized that this includes the State Party in whose territory the offence is committed. Unless the circumstances envisaged in Article 13 are satisfied, the territorial State cannot consider the offence to be an internal matter falling outside the obligation *aut dedere aut judicare*.

". . . shall, if it does not extradite him . . ."

It is worth emphasizing that this paragraph does not impose any binding obligation upon States to extradite an alleged offender. Rather, it is formulated in such a way as to make the controlling obligation one of submitting the case for the purpose of prosecution in the event that a State does not, for whatever reason, extradite.

" . . . be obliged, without exception whatsoever . . ."

This phrase establishes that, subject to what has earlier been said in the commentary on Article 3,[24] a Party has no discretion with respect

---

[22] 1972 YBILC, Vol. II, p. 318.

[23] The desirability of extraditing to the territorial State in most cases was noted during the drafting of both the US and the UK implementing legislation for the Hostages Convention. See the comments of Lord Trefgarne during the debate in the House of Lords. H.L. Debs., Vol. 427, 1 March 1982, col. 1116. See also the comments of the representative of the US Department of Justice in *Hearings before the Subcommittee on Security and Terrorism*, 98th Cong., 2d Sess., p. 49 (1984).

[24] See pp. 112-114 (notes 10-16 and accompanying text in the commentary on Article 3).

to application of the principle *aut dedere aut judicare*. The State *must* either extradite the offender or submit the case for the purpose of prosecution, without regard to such factors as the motive for the crime or the identity of the offender.

The words "without exception whatsoever" were added to the Hague Convention by the ICAO Diplomatic Conference after a proposal to use the words "whatever the motive for the offence" was objected to by some developing States on the somewhat obscure ground that such language would remove the matter of motivation from the competence of judicial authorities and prejudice the course of justice.[25] After some debate, the delegate of the United Arab Republic stated that if the intent was to punish all acts of hijacking, he would prefer wording such as "without any exception".[26] The representative of the USSR proposed the current language, noting that it was identical to the language contained in General Assembly Resolution 2645 (XXV) which condemns, "without exception whatsoever, all acts of aerial hijacking . . ."[27]

Rejection of the express reference to motive, however, in no way indicates that politically motivated offences fall outside the ambit of the obligation *aut dedere aut judicare*. The language "without exception whatsoever" unambiguously requires all offences to result in extradition or submission for prosecution. As the United Kingdom delegate to the Hague Conference stated, the wording is as comprehensive as that which it was designed to replace and would "exclude not only all considerations of motive, but also any considerations of nationality or ethnic origin".[28] It may be recalled in this context that attempts made by some State delegations during the drafting of the Hostages Convention to remove certain politically motivated offences from the obligation *aut dedere aut judicare* were unsuccessful. These attempts are discussed more fully in Part I[29] and in the commentaries on Article 1[30] and Article 12.[31] As it stands, the only acts of hostage-taking with respect to which States Parties are not obliged to either extradite the offender or submit the case for the purpose of prosecution pursuant to this Convention are: 1) those

---

[25] See, e.g., the comments of the representatives of Kenya, the United Arab Republic, Tanzania, and Congo, ICAO Doc 8979-LC/165-1, pp. 130-131 (1972). For the text of the proposal to use the words "whatever the motive for the offence", see ICAO Doc 8979-LC/165-2, p. 131 (1972).

[26] ICAO Doc 8979-LC/165-1, p. 131.

[27] *Id.* at p. 178. The text of that resolution is at UN GAOR, 25th Sess., Supp. 28, p. 126, UN Doc A/8028 (1971), *reprinted in* 9 ILM 1288 (1970).

[28] ICAO Doc 8979-LC/165-1, p. 178.

[29] See pp. 62-63 (notes 220-223 in Part I).

[30] See p. 79 (note 5 and accompanying text in the commentary on Article 1).

[31] See pp. 266-268 (notes 12-17 and accompanying text in the commentary on Article 12).

which are subject to the same obligation pursuant to the Geneva Conventions on armed conflicts and Protocols thereto (Article 12); 2) those which are strictly internal in nature within the contemplation of Article 13; and 3) those with respect to which the offenders have been granted immunity in return for the release of the hostages pursuant to Article 3 (although this would only apply to the bargaining State).

The obligation to prosecute when no request for extradition is made

Under this Article the obligation *aut judicare* is applicable whenever, and for whatever reason, the State in whose territory the offender is present does not extradite him. This Article may thus be contrasted with Article 7 of the European Convention on the Suppression of Terrorism which makes the obligation *aut judicare* contingent upon that State having received and denied a request for extradition from another State Party "whose jurisdiction is based on a rule of jurisdiction existing equally in the law of the requested State".[32] In other words, under that instrument if the State Party in whose territory the alleged offender is found (even if it is the territorial State or another State which has a close connexion with the offence) does not receive a request for extradition from another State Party, then it has no obligation to submit the case for the purpose of prosecution. But not only must that State receive and refuse a request for extradition before its obligation to prosecute is activated, that request must be from a Party which is relying on a basis of jurisdiction which the requested State also employs for that type of offence. If, for example, the requesting State is relying on the nationality principle for a crime committed outside of its territory and the requested State would not have jurisdiction over that offence if its own national had committed the particular crime abroad, then the requested State's refusal to extradite would not result in the obligation *aut judicare*.

During the drafting of the Hostages Convention, the delegations of the Netherlands and France submitted proposals which would similarly have conditioned a State's obligation *aut judicare* upon its having received and denied a request for extradition from a State which is required by this Convention to establish primary jurisdiction over the offence.[33] In advocating that delegation's proposal, which complemented a proposal made with respect to Article 5, paragraph

---

[32] With respect to this provision, see also pp. 138-139 (notes 20 & 21 and accompanying text in the commentary on Article 5).
[33] See UN Docs A/AC.188/L.13 & A/AC.188/L.14, in First Report of the Hostages Committee, pp. 113 & 114 respectively. A similar proposal was made by the Netherlands, and rejected, during the drafting of the New York Convention. See Wood, p. 811.

2,[34] the representative of the Netherlands argued that it was unreasonable to oblige a State which has no connexion with the offence, other than the offender's subsequent presence therein, to prosecute the offender when none of the States with primary jurisdiction had enough interest to request extradition. As drafted, he argued, the language gives a State in which an offence was committed an excuse not to mount a prosecution which it might find undesirable for a number of reasons. In effect, the "no safe havens" principle would permit them to foist the responsibility for prosecution on an otherwise uninvolved State in which the offender happened to be.[35] Moreover, the representative of the Netherlands expressed his belief that the primary responsibility to prosecute the alleged offender lay with the State which was most directly concerned, i.e., the territorial State.[36]

Other delegations, however, such as those of the US, the UK, the FRG and Japan, disagreed. The FRG representative warned that the Dutch and French proposals would create a loophole in a system which was designed to ensure that hostage-takers would face prosecution everywhere. Although recognizing that it might not be fair to impose the obligation to prosecute upon a State that had nothing to do with a given case apart from the fact that the hostage-taker subsequently happened to be found in its territory, while other States with a closer relationship to the case refrained from requesting extradition, he argued that it was better to increase rather than reduce the number of States having jurisdiction.[37]

In the end, the delegations of the Netherlands and France did not insist on their proposals, and it is clear that a State's duty to prosecute an alleged offender present in its territory is in no way contingent upon a request for extradition from another State.[38] Any risk of a State which has no real connexion with the crime having to bear the burden of prosecuting an offender simply because he happened to make his way to its territory is outweighed by the need to ensure that no safe havens exist for hostage-takers. And in the absence of a requirement upon States with primary jurisdiction to request extradition, this approach is the only effective way of eliminating all safe havens.

[34] See pp. 156-157 (notes 94-97 and accompanying text in the commentary on Article 5).
[35] See First Report of the Hostages Committee, pp. 90-91, para. 18.
[36] Second Report of the Hostages Committee, p. 47, para. 46.
[37] *Id.* at p. 49, para. 5. See also the comments of the representatives of the US, UK and Japan, *id.* at p. 47, para. 48, pp. 47 & 48, paras. 50 & 51, & p. 51, para. 18, respectively.
[38] One commentator states, without further analysis, that this provision and the corresponding provisions in the Hague, Montreal and New York Conventions require a request for extradition before the obligation to prosecute is activated. See Murphy, "The Future of Multilateralism and Efforts to Combat International Terrorism", 25 Colum. J. Trans. L. 35 (1986) at p. 45 & n. 48. However, both the text of this paragraph and the *travaux préparatoires* demonstrate that this is not the case.

"... and whether or not the offence was committed in its territory ..."

The obligation to submit the case for the purpose of prosecution in the absence of extradition exists regardless of where the offence was committed. It may reasonably be queried whether the phrase "whether or not the offence was committed in its territory" is strictly necessary, given the first phrase of this paragraph, and it was in fact left out of the New York Convention. However, to the extent that it emphasizes the duty of all States Parties to extradite or prosecute all alleged offenders subsequently found in their territories, regardless of where the offence occurred, its inclusion in this paragraph does no harm.

"... to submit the case to its competent authorities for the purpose of prosecution ..."

A Party which does not extradite an alleged offender must turn the case over to its relevant authorities for the "purpose of prosecution". While at first this language could appear to require States Parties actually to prosecute all such offenders, the language of this paragraph as a whole, particularly the second sentence, and the *travaux préparatoires* of the earlier anti-terrorism conventions establish clearly that this is not the case.

During the drafting of the Hague Convention, many States, including the US and the USSR, expressed the opinion that all cases of hijacking should result either in the extradition or the prosecution, i.e., the bringing to trial, of alleged offenders.[39] However, other States argued that such an absolute obligation would be an impermissible trespass upon the discretion of their prosecuting authorities.[40] As White notes, many States maintained that there could be:

> exceptional cases where, perhaps for lack of evidence or for humanitarian reasons, the circumstances would not justify bringing a prosecution. Those States considered that, although cases where proceedings were not brought would be rare, they could not accept a fetter on the discretion enjoyed by their prosecuting authorities to decide whether or not to prosecute in the light of all the facts of a case.[41]

---

[39] See the comments of the US representative in ICAO Doc 8838-LC/157, p. 145 (1970); the proposal of the delegation of New Zealand in ICAO Doc 8979-LC/165-2, p. 133 (1972). See also White, p. 42.

[40] *Id.*

[41] *Id.* The Chairman of the ICAO Subcommittee charged with the initial drafting stated that it was decided not to include an absolute requirement to prosecute when the alleged offender was not extradited since it "was not considered possible to trespass upon the jurisdiction of the [public prosecutor] in this regard." ICAO Doc 8877-LC/161, p. 69 (1970).

ARTICLE 8

As a result, the Legal Committee of ICAO submitted to the Diplomatic Conference a draft article which would have obliged a Party which did not extradite an alleged offender to "submit the case to its competent authorities for their decision whether to prosecute him".[42] This provision, explained the Chairman of the ICAO Legal Committee's Subcommittee on the Subject of the Unlawful Seizure of Aircraft, was taken from the European Convention on Extradition which provides that States which choose not to extradite an alleged offender must at least submit the question to their authorities for their decision as to whether prosecution should be undertaken.[43]

However, in the Diplomatic Conference a large number of States co-sponsored an amended draft article which contained the words "purpose of prosecution".[44] Although the delegates of some States, such as Malaysia and Tanzania, expressed concern that these words were ambiguous as to whether prosecution under the Convention was mandatory or discretionary,[45] the UK representative explained that the words were understood to mean that the case must simply be submitted to a State's competent authorities who would then employ their discretion to decide whether or not to prosecute.[46] Thus, under this provision a Party is under no obligation to punish an alleged offender or even to conduct a trial. As the ILC stated in its commentary to its draft of the New York Convention, the obligation of a Party is:

> fulfilled once it has submitted the case to its competent authorities, which will, in most States, be judicial in character, for the purpose of prosecution. It will be up to those authorities to decide whether to prosecute or not, subject to the normal requirement of treaty law that the decision be taken in good faith in the light of all the circumstances involved. The obligation of the State party in such case will be fulfilled under the article even if the decision which those authorities may take is not to commence criminal trial proceedings.[47]

---

[42] ICAO Doc 8865-LC/159, p. 33 (1970).

[43] ICAO Doc 8877-LC/161, p. 69 (1970). Article 6(2) of the European Convention on Extradition, 359 UNTS 276, recognizes the principle *aut dedere aut judicare* in some cases, providing that if the requested State does not "extradite its national, it shall at the request of the requesting Party, submit the case to its competent authorities in order that proceedings may be taken if they are considered appropriate".

[44] ICAO Doc 8979-LC/165-2, p. 131 (1972). The proposal was adopted by a vote of 60 in favour, 2 against, with 13 abstentions. ICAO Doc 8979-LC/165-1, p. 182 (1972).

[45] *Id.* at pp. 180-181.

[46] *Id.* at p. 181.

[47] 1972 YBILC, Vol. II, p. 318. See also DeSchutter, "Problems of Jurisdiction in the International Control and Repression of Terrorism", in Bassiouni (ed.), *International Terrorism and Political Crimes* 386 (1975), who notes with respect to this type of provision that the appropriate authorities must in good faith decide whether to prosecute and that this "formulation clearly respects the rule of separation of powers, giving the

(continued on p. 200)

It is worth emphasizing that any discretion reserved by this paragraph belongs only to those authorities of a State which normally make decisions on prosecutions, i.e., its judicial or prosecutorial officials. This paragraph limits the freedom of action of a State's political authorities in so far as they are obliged to submit every case wherein extradition is not granted to the competent authorities.[48]

". . . through proceedings in accordance with the laws of that State."

The proceedings conducted in connexion with the submission of the case to a State's appropriate authorities are to be in accordance with the criminal procedure law of that State. Inclusion of this phrase does not appear to have been strictly necessary, both because it may be assumed that such would be the case in any event and because the second sentence of this paragraph — "Those authorities shall take their decision in the same manner as in the case of any ordinary offence of a grave nature under the law of that State" — makes a similar point. This phrase first appeared in the corresponding paragraph of the New York Convention, the draftsmen of that instrument employing it as a substitute for the language contained in the second sentence of this paragraph, which earlier appeared as the second sentence of the corresponding paragraphs of the ICAO conventions. The ILC explained that it replaced that sentence both because it appeared redundant given the requirement that the offences must be made punishable under internal law and, somewhat more cryptically, because:

> [a]s the obligation imposed on a State party is that of submitting the case to its competent authorities for the purpose of prosecution, the Commission considered it beyond the scope of the present draft to provide specific requirements as to the manner in which those authorities should exercise their functions under internal law.[49]

During the drafting of this Convention the representatives of some States indicated that they would prefer that this paragraph follow the

---

([47] *continued*)
judiciary a free hand, a fundamental principle in any democratic system". Another commentator warns, however, that if the prosecuting State's criminal justice system lacks integrity, there is a risk of political intervention in the prosecution which may prevent the trial or conviction of the alleged offender. Murphy, note 38, *supra*, at p. 43.

[48] See the comments of the representative of Israel to the Sixth Committee during the drafting of the New York Convention. UN GAOR, 28th Sess., C.6 (1419th mtg.), para. 11, UN Doc A/C.6/SR.1419 (1973). See also Sundberg, "Piracy: Air and Sea", in Bassiouni & Nanda, note 12, *supra*, at pp. 481-482 & n.121, who states, *inter alia*, that this formulation moves "the possible decision *not* to prosecute to the level of the grand jury in the United States and to the level of the Attorney General in England".

[49] 1972 YBILC, Vol. II, pp. 318-19.

model of the New York Convention, by including this phrase rather than the ICAO language. The representative of Poland stated that the New York language was "short, simple, and clear and did not lend itself to misinterpretation",[50] a sentiment basically echoed by the delegate of the Byelorussian SSR.[51] The FRG representative stated that he could accept either formulation.[52] In the end, the appearance of both formulations in this Convention appears to have been a compromise between those States which preferred this phrase and those which preferred the ICAO language.

"Those authorities shall take their decision in the same manner as in the case of any ordinary offence of a grave nature under the law of that State."

When the appropriate authorities of a non-extraditing State are taking their decision as to whether or not an actual prosecution will take place, they must (and may) do so in the same way as they would with respect to other serious crimes under their laws. This sentence thus both serves as a restraint on the prosecuting authorities in so far as they must treat the offences as they would any ordinary — as opposed to political — crime and ensures them a measure of latitude by leaving intact the discretion that they may normally exercise when making decisions regarding other ordinary crimes. Similar provisions may be found in the corresponding paragraphs of the Hague, Montreal and Rome Conventions and in Article 7 of the European Convention on the Suppression of Terrorism. As the ILC noted in its commentary to the New York Convention, this sentence was included in the ICAO conventions "in order to provide a necessary degree of tolerance to the officials charged with making the decision to prosecute or not to prosecute".[53]

According to White, this sentence was included in the Hague Convention because:

> some South American States apparently take different factors into consideration in deciding whether to prosecute for a 'political' offence from those taken into account in deciding whether to prosecute for an ordinary offence with the result that a political offender may be treated more leniently than an ordinary offender. The Convention, therefore, requires that for the purpose of deciding whether to prosecute or not (though not for the purpose of deciding whether to extradite or not) hijacking must always be treated as an 'ordinary' (though serious) offence.[54]

[50] Second Report of the Hostages Committee, p. 49, para. 2.
[51] *Id.* at p. 50, para. 14.
[52] *Id.* at p. 49, para. 4.
[53] 1972 YBILC, Vol. II, p. 318.
[54] White, p. 42.

The drafting records of the Hague Convention, moreover, confirm that this sentence was included to clarify that no account should be taken of the political context of the crime when the decision is being made as to whether or not the alleged offender will be prosecuted (although as suggested by White, and as noted earlier,[55] the political context may be taken into account in deciding whether or not to extradite). The representative of Yugoslavia to the Hague Conference, for example, noted, as did other delegates, that the purpose of this wording is to ensure that prosecution is not inhibited by any political aspects of the offence. He asserted, moreover, that the language of the Article removes all possibility of ambiguity by ensuring that those who commit acts of hijacking are uniformly treated as criminals.[56] The representative of Canada similarly noted that under the Article the prosecution of hijackers would be governed by the same considerations as are ordinary criminal offences.[57]

In deciding whether or not to prosecute an individual suspected of committing a particular criminal offence, the authorities of a State may exercise discretion in any number of ways. The most obvious, of course, is a decision based on the opinion that the evidence is not strong enough to justify prosecution. Clearly, no breach of the Convention exists where officials decide in good faith that no *prima facie* case of hostage-taking can be made. Moreover, as mentioned above, States may decide not to prosecute a given offender on humanitarian grounds. Some States may also allow their officials to decide not to prosecute an alleged offender in return for his agreement to testify against his co-defendants. Such considerations would appear to be permissible under this Article, but, again, only if they are normally available to the authorities of that State when making decisions regarding the prosecution of ordinary crimes.[58]

The extent to which this sentence provides leeway to the State in deciding whether or not to prosecute was the subject of debate in the ILC during the drafting of the New York Convention. Mr. Reuter argued that the sentence constituted a necessary "loophole" by virtue of which States Parties could observe faithfully their obligations under

---

[55] See p. 193 (text accompanying note 21).
[56] ICAO Doc 8979-LC/165-1, p. 134 (1972).
[57] *Id.* at p. 135.
[58] In the UK, for example, prosecutors have a great deal of discretion in deciding whether to bring a case to trial. The primary consideration, of course, concerns whether there is admissible, substantial and reliable evidence of the accused offender's guilt. Prosecutors must also consider whether the public interest justifies the bringing of proceedings, taking into account such factors as the severity of the likely penalty, the staleness of the case and the youth, old age or mental illness of the accused. See *Code for Crown Prosecutors* (HMSO, undated).

the relevant convention and also "deal with embarrassing situations without having recourse to extradition or prosecution" by submitting a case to the proper authorities who could then decide not to prosecute; the State could then take "shelter behind the judicial authority".[59] While Mr. Reuter mentioned only two situations wherein the appropriate authorities could properly decide not to prosecute — "either because it could see at once that there was not sufficient evidence, or because the circumstances were such that the guilty person — who was none the less a criminal — had the support of public opinion, so that to prosecute would be to run the risk of an improper trial"[60] — his references to a "loophole" and "embarrassing situations" indicate a belief that the State Party could hide behind any decision taken by the prosecutorial authorities without regard to the reason behind that decision.

Other members of the Commission, however, took a somewhat more restrictive view of this sentence. One member argued that the discretion of the prosecuting authorities was subject to certain limits and that the State Party's obligation will not be discharged if its judicial authority, for example, "gave an improper dismissal".[61] Similarly, the Chairman of the Commission argued that this sentence could not be interpreted as an "escape clause that might enable a government to take a decision on the question of prosecution without due regard to the legal considerations".[62] That a State Party cannot hide behind an improper decision made by its appropriate authorities seems clear, and is confirmed by the ILC commentary, as quoted above, wherein it states that decisions made in this regard are "subject to the normal requirement of treaty law that the decision be taken in good faith in the light of all the circumstances involved".[63] While the discretion in this regard is broad, therefore, it must, of course, be exercised in good faith.

In the end, this provision may well be a serious weakness of this Convention. Much latitude is left to each State Party's officials to determine whether or not prosecution will be had, and it would be difficult in most cases to prove that a decision not to prosecute was taken in bad faith. However, it is unlikely that a better provision could have been drafted since States are loath to give up their discretion in this regard. In any event, a State's decision not to prosecute in the face of overwhelming evidence of guilt and no compelling humanitarian reasons could be seen as *prima facie* evidence of bad faith.

---

[59] 1972 YBILC, Vol. I, pp. 208, 219 & 222-223.
[60] *Id.* at p. 223.
[61] See the comments of Prof. Ago, *id.*
[62] *Id.* at p. 241.
[63] 1972 YBILC, Vol. II, p. 318.

PARAGRAPH 2: FAIR TREATMENT OF THE OFFENDER

"Any person regarding whom proceedings are being carried out in connexion with any of the offences set forth in article 1 shall be guaranteed fair treatment . . ."

All persons, nationals and non-nationals of the relevant State alike, are entitled to "fair treatment" during the course of proceedings taken in connexion with the offences. The crucial words "fair treatment" contain a significant degree of ambiguity since they are not precisely defined by this paragraph or by international law generally. A question may thus arise as to the specific obligation imposed by this paragraph. In its commentary to its draft of the New York Convention, the ILC stated:

> The expression 'fair treatment' was preferred, because of its generality, to more usual expressions such as 'due process', 'fair hearing' or 'fair trial' which might be interpreted in a narrow technical sense. The expression 'fair treatment' is intended to incorporate all the guarantees generally recognized to a detained or accused person. An example of such guarantees is found in article 14 of the International Covenant on Civil and Political Rights.[64]

It may thus be helpful to examine the guarantees contained in Article 14 of the 1966 International Covenant on Civil and Political Rights.[65] Paragraph 1 of that Article provides, *inter alia*, that:

> All persons shall be equal before the courts and tribunals. In the determination of any criminal charge against him, or of his rights and obligations in a suit at law, everyone shall be entitled to a fair and public hearing by a competent, independent and impartial tribunal established by law.

Additionally, paragraphs 1 to 7 of Article 14 provide a number of other guarantees to an accused person. In particular, during the determination of a criminal charge, each person is guaranteed, at a minimum and "in full equality": to be informed promptly and in detail in a language which he understands of the charges against him; to have adequate time and facilities for the preparation of his defence and to communicate with counsel of his choosing; to be tried without undue delay; to be tried in his presence and to defend himself in

---

[64] 1972 YBILC, Vol. II, p. 320. It may be noted that Article 4 of the OAS Convention provides that persons deprived of "freedom through the application of this convention shall enjoy the legal guarantees of due process."
[65] 999 UNTS 171.

person or through legal counsel of his own choosing; to have legal counsel assigned to him where the interests of justice so require, and without payment by him in any such case if he does not have the means; to examine witnesses against him and to obtain the attendance and examination of witnesses on his behalf under the same conditions as witnesses against him; to have the free assistance of an interpreter if he cannot understand or speak the language used in court; and to be free from compulsion to testify against himself or to admit guilt. Moreover, each person shall be presumed innocent until proved guilty and will have the rights to have his conviction and sentence reviewed by a higher tribunal "according to law" and to be free from trial or punishment for an offence for which he has already been finally convicted or acquitted "in accordance with the law and penal procedure of each country".

The ILC's reference to the International Covenant on Civil and Political Rights is instructive. That instrument was adopted unanimously by the General Assembly with 106 votes,[66] has more than 80 parties and, as Brownlie states, "the nature of the subject-matter is such that even for non-parties [its content] represents authoritative evidence of the content of the concept of human rights as it appears in the Charter of the United Nations".[67] Moreover, while the Covenant is more extensive than most other instruments on the subject, many of the rights mentioned in Article 14 are included in other conventions and documents such as the 1950 European Convention for the Protection of Human Rights,[68] the 1969 American Convention on Human Rights,[69] and, to a lesser extent, the 1981 African Charter on Human and People's Rights.[70] They are also provided for in such

---

[66] See GA Res 2200 (XXI), UN GAOR, 21st Sess., Supp. 16, p. 49, UN Doc A/6316 (1967). See also UN GAOR, 21st Sess., 2 Annexes (Agenda item 62), p. 67 (1966).

[67] Brownlie, *Basic Documents in International Law* 257 (3rd ed., 1983).

[68] Art. 6, 213 UNTS 221. The European Convention does not, however, specifically provide for equality before the law, for the presence of the accused at his trial (although this may be implicit), for the right to an appeal, for the right against self-incrimination (although in European continental civil law systems, the accused may not testify) or for the principle *non bis in idem*. For a more thorough examination of the differences between the various human rights instruments as they relate to accused persons, see Sieghart, *The Lawful Rights of Mankind* 133-137 (1985); Sieghart, *The International Law of Human Rights* 259-307 (1983); Harris, "The Right to a Fair Trial in Criminal Proceedings as a Human Right", 16 ICLQ 352 (1972). See also Robertson, *Human Rights in the World* (2nd ed., 1982).

[69] Arts. 8 & 24, PAUTS 36, *reprinted in* 9 ILM 673 (1970). The American Convention does not specifically provide for a public trial or for the presence of the accused at his trial but, as with the European Convention, this latter right may be implicit.

[70] Arts. 3 & 7, OAU Doc CAB/LEG/67/3/Rev. 5, *reprinted in* 21 ILM 59 (1982). The African Charter is less comprehensive than the other regional instruments. It does not provide for the rights to a public trial, assigned or free counsel, an interpreter, prompt information of the charges in a language which the accused understands, to examine witnesses, against self-incrimination, *non bis in idem*, appeal, and to be tried in person.

non-binding instruments as the 1948 Universal Declaration of Human Rights.[71]

In light of the ILC's comments, one authority, writing with respect to the New York Convention, has stated that a violation of any of the rights referred to in Article 14 of the International Covenant would leave it open to a State Party to allege that there has been a breach of the New York Convention. Resort could then be had to the dispute resolution provision of the latter instrument.[72] However, this conclusion is somewhat difficult to reach with certainty. While the ILC's reference to Article 14 of the International Covenant may provide a general sense as to what the term "fair treatment" may require (with respect to this Convention as well as the New York Convention), it is doubtful that this subparagraph incorporates all of the protections contained in Article 14. As earlier noted, international law does not provide a definite content to the term "fair treatment". Despite the widespread acceptance of the International Covenant, moreover, most States are not party to the instrument. Further, regional human rights instruments generally guarantee fewer rights than does the International Covenant. In the end, the term "fair treatment" remains ambiguous.

Finally, it should be noted that the obligation imposed upon States Parties under this paragraph may be difficult to fulfil when the proceedings are being conducted in a State which is not the territorial State. Evidence and witnesses which are essential to a fair trial may be located in the territorial State. If the territorial State or any other State which has such evidence does not comply with the obligation to render judicial assistance contained in Article 11, or if such States are not parties to this instrument and do not render the evidence voluntarily or pursuant to another obligation, it will be difficult for the State in which the proceedings are being held to ensure that the alleged offender receives fair treatment.

". . . at all stages of the proceedings . . ."

The "proceedings" during which fair treatment must be guaranteed would presumably include all measures which may be taken with respect to the alleged offender, including preliminary custody, extradition hearings, trial, and sentencing. As stated by the ILC, this provision is intended to "safeguard the rights of the alleged offender from the moment he is found and measures are taken to ensure his presence until a final decision is taken on the case".[73]

---

[71] Arts. 7, 10 & 11, GA Res 217A (III), UN Doc A/810, p. 71 (1949).
[72] Costello, note 9, *supra*, at pp. 491-494.
[73] 1972 YBILC, Vol. II, p. 320.

"... including enjoyment of all the rights and guarantees provided by the law of the State in the territory of which he is present."

This phrase was added to this paragraph at the suggestion of the representative of the USSR to the Hostages Committee who argued that the expression "fair treatment" had connotations which were more ethical than legal and that, therefore, it would be better to say that the accused "shall enjoy the rights and guarantees provided for by the legislation of the country in whose territory he is present".[74] This language was agreed to by the Hostages Committee, although it maintained the original language as well.[75] There is no recorded debate or explanation regarding this provision, and it is somewhat difficult to discern its meaning. It could be interpreted as an attempt to establish the "national treatment" or "equality" principle, i.e., requiring only that the accused be given the same rights as are accorded nationals of the State in which the proceedings are taking place,[76] as the rule of this Convention, but the retention of the first phrase of this paragraph by the draftsmen would effectively vitiate any such conclusion. Alternatively, it could simply be a restatement of the principle that all persons are equal before the law. In any event, it does not seem that this provision adds anything to this paragraph since the "enjoyment of all the rights and guarantees provided by the law of the State in the territory of which he is present" would appear to be a necessary element of "fair treatment".

The inclusion of human rights provisions in anti-terrorism conventions

While there did not appear to be much controversy concerning inclusion of this paragraph in the Hostages Convention, at least one draftsman, the representative of Sweden to the Hostages Committee, expressed doubts about this paragraph. This representative pointed out that there are other international instruments that set standards for the treatment of suspected persons and asserted that it was, therefore, "invidious" to single out one aspect of those standards in the draft convention.[77] However, it does not appear that this objection was pressed and most delegations obviously agreed that it is desirable to include in this type of Convention some provisions regarding human rights.

The inclusion of such provisions is to be applauded. While the

---

[74] Second Report of the Hostages Committee, p. 47, para. 49.
[75] *Id.* at p. 12, para. 47.
[76] See generally Freeman, *International Responsibility of States for Denial of Justice* 532-537 (1938).
[77] Second Report of the Hostages Committee, p. 50, para. 13.

reinforcement of States' obligations in this regard may be important generally, it takes on an added importance in instruments which seek to deal with terrorists. The phenomenon of international terrorism has resulted in a backlash of anger and disgust in many States. There is a danger that official and public opinion in a State which has been victimized by terrorist activities may be so intolerant and so aroused with passion that it might lead to practices, *de facto* or *de jure*, which deny certain fundamental rights to accused persons. However reprehensible the nature of the offence, a civilized society must provide all criminals with certain fundamental guarantees, and this provision may help to secure those guarantees.[78] From a more practical point of view, this provision might encourage States to become parties to the Convention: many States may well be concerned about the ability or desire of other States to accord "fair treatment" to alleged offenders in their custody and will, therefore, be reluctant to agree to measures which might subject their nationals to the criminal jurisdiction of those other States. And even if they do become party to this instrument, they might be reluctant to extradite offenders in particular cases. Provisions such as this one may ease such apprehensions.

---

[78] See generally Rozakis, "Terrorism and the Internationally Protected Persons in the Light of the ILC's Draft Articles", 23 ICLQ 32, 61 (1974).

Article 9

DISCRIMINATION CLAUSE

1. A request for the extradition of an alleged offender, pursuant to this Convention, shall not be granted if the requested State Party has substantial grounds for believing:
   (a) that the request for extradition for an offence set forth in article 1 has been made for the purpose of prosecuting or punishing a person on account of his race, religion, nationality, ethnic origin or political opinion; or
   (b) that the person's position may be prejudiced:
      (i) for any of the reasons mentioned in subparagraph (a) of this paragraph, or
      (ii) for the reason that communication with him by the appropriate authorities of the State entitled to exercise rights of protection cannot be effected.

2. With respect to the offences as defined in this Convention, the provisions of all extradition treaties and arrangements applicable between States Parties are modified as between States Parties to the extent that they are incompatible with this Convention.

1. INTRODUCTION

This Article, one of a number of provisions of this Convention concerned with protecting the human rights of alleged offenders, prohibits States from extraditing individuals under certain circumstances. In particular, States must deny an extradition request made pursuant to this Convention when the request is in reality made for the purpose of prosecuting or punishing an alleged offender, not for his offence, but because of his race, religion, nationality, ethnic origin or political opinion. Extradition must also be denied when, although the request is not actually made in order to prosecute or punish the alleged offender for his race, political opinion, etc., his position would be prejudiced by reason of one of those circumstances or by reason of the fact that he could not, in the requesting State, communicate with the State entitled to exercise diplomatic protection. In one sense, this Article contemplates the granting of asylum to persecuted individuals; however, a State which denies an extradition request pursuant to this provision must still submit the case to its appropriate authorities for the purpose of prosecution.[1]

---

[1] See the comments of the Jordanian representative to the Sixth Committee. UN GAOR, 34th Sess., C.6 (12th mtg.), pp. 5-6, paras. 20-23, UN Doc A/C.6/34/SR.12

(continued on p. 210)

This Article was included upon the proposal of the representative of Jordan made during the final session of the Hostages Committee[2] and, as discussed below, was the subject of much controversy during the drafting process. In fact, this Article was the subject of the only votes taken during the drafting of the Convention. There are no counterparts to this Article in the other anti-terrorism conventions, although Article 11(6) of the Rome Convention provides that when considering a request for the extradition of an alleged offender, a requested State "shall pay due regard" to whether the rights of visitation and communication (as set forth in Article 6(3) of this Convention) "can be effected in the requesting State".

The role of "discrimination clauses" in the law of extradition

Although inclusion of this Article caused a good deal of debate amongst the draftsmen, this type of provision, which may be referred to as a "discrimination clause",[3] is not unknown to the law of extradition. Similar provisions exist in the 1957 European Convention on Extradition,[4] the 1981 Inter-American Convention on Extradition[5] and the 1977 European Convention on the Suppression of Terrorism.[6] Moreover, discrimination clauses, while not as widespread as the political offence exception, can be found in various forms in the

---

([1] *continued*)
(1979). See also Council of Europe, *Explanatory Report on the European Convention on the Suppression of Terrorism* 15 (1977), which states that one purpose of the similar clause contained in that Convention is to "safeguard the traditional right to asylum". However, the report also states that if extradition is refused, "the requested State must submit the case to its competent authorities for the purpose of prosecution".

[2] See Third Report of the Hostages Committee, p. 16, paras. 64-66. The original Jordanian proposal read as follows:
   No Contracting State shall extradite an alleged offender if that State has substantial grounds for believing:
   (a) that the request for extradition for an offence set forth in article 1 has been made for the purpose of prosecuting or punishing a person on account of his race, religion, nationality or political opinion;
   (b) that that person's position may be prejudiced for any of these reasons;
   (c) that the appropriate authorities of the State of which he is a national or, if he is a Stateless person, the appropriate authorities of the State which he requests and which is willing to protect his rights, cannot communicate with him to protect his rights in the requesting State.

[3] See Van den Wijngaert, *The Political Offence Exception to Extradition* 2 (1980); Stein, "Extradition", in Bernhardt (ed.), *Encyclopedia of Public International Law*, Vol. 8, 222 (1985). Van den Wijngaert, particularly at pages 64-93, provides a detailed examination of the discrimination clause, as well as a study of its relationship to such concepts as the political offence exception to extradition, humanitarian asylum and *non-refoulement* of refugees. Van den Wijngaert states that "the right of *humanitarian asylum*, the principle of *non-refoulement*, and the *discrimination clause* are three different legal embodiments of the same basic principle, although each having a different legal construction". Van den Wijngaert, *supra*, at p. 65.

[4] Art. 3(2), 359 UNTS 276.
[5] Art. 4(5), PAUTS 60.
[6] Art. 5.

domestic laws of some States[7] and in some other extradition treaties and arrangements.[8] In its early forms, the discrimination clause seems to have been concerned only with "disguised" requests for extradition, i.e., those requests which were formulated in terms of a common crime but which were, in fact, designed to obtain custody of the alleged offender and prosecute him for a political crime or purpose.[9] As drafted in this and other more recent instruments, however, such clauses seek also to protect those persons whose positions would be prejudiced because of political reasons. Moreover, many recent clauses extend protection to those who may be persecuted also on account of race, religion, nationality and, in this Convention, ethnic origin. The first of this modern type of clause appears in the European Convention on Extradition.

While the discrimination clause is similar to the political offence exception, the two principles are somewhat different. The political offence exception focuses upon the crime itself, examining its political context and providing that extradition may be refused when the crime is a political one.[10] The discrimination clause focuses more upon the nature of the extradition request,[11] i.e., the motives of the requesting State in seeking extradition, rather than on the nature of the crime, and also upon the treatment that the alleged offender is likely to receive in the requesting State.

The principle underlying the discrimination clause — that an individual should not be extradited to a State in which he might be persecuted or prejudiced for reasons extraneous to his guilt of the charged offence — is based in humanitarian law. It is similar to the principle of *non-refoulement* of refugees which, as set forth in Article 33 of the 1951 Convention Relating to the Status of Refugees, provides that States Parties may not "expel or return ('refouler') a refugee in

---

[7] See, e.g., §6(2), 1982 FRG Law on International Assistance in Criminal Matters, *translated in* 24 ILM 945 (1985); Art. 10(1), 1967 Netherlands Extradition Act; Art. 7, 1957 Swedish Extradition Act.

[8] See, e.g., §9, Scheme Relating to the Rendition of Fugitive Offenders within the Commonwealth, Cmnd 3008; Art. 7(1)(b) & (c), Treaty on Extradition, 12 May 1976, United Kingdom-Finland, UKTS 23 (1977), Cmnd 6741; Art. V(1), Treaty on Extradition, 13 October 1983, United States-Italy, TIAS 10,837, *reprinted in* 24 ILM 1527 (1985).

[9] See, e.g., §3(1), UK Extradition Act 1870; Stein, note 3, *supra*; Van den Wijngaert, note 3, *supra*, at pp. 80-82. It may be noted that even some recent discrimination clauses are concerned only with extradition requests which ostensibly concern ordinary offences but which are in reality for political offences. See, e.g., US-Italy treaty, note 8, *supra*; Art. V(c)(ii), Treaty on Extradition, 8 June 1972, United States-United Kingdom, TIAS 8468. In the United States, the Secretary of State has the discretion to determine whether the extradition request is a subterfuge, i.e., a request for a political offence disguised as a request for an ordinary crime. See *In re Lincoln*, 228 F. 70, 74 (E.D.N.Y. 1951), *aff'd* 241 US 651 (1916).

[10] See generally *In re Castioni*, [1891] 1 QB 149; *Eain v. Wilkes*, 641 F. 2d 504, 518 (7th Cir. 1981), *cert. den.*, 454 US 894 (1981).

[11] See Van den Wijngaert, note 3, *supra*, at p. 2.

any manner whatsoever to the frontiers of territories where his life or freedom would be threatened on account of his race, religion, nationality, membership of a particular social group or political opinion".[12] Indeed, although the issue is not all that clear (and is, moreover, beyond the scope of this discussion) some writers argue that the principle of *non-refoulement* should or does apply generally to the extradition as well as to the expulsion of refugees.[13] In fact, although no discrimination clause can be found in the ICAO, New York or Rome Conventions, the following statement by the ILC in its commentary to its draft of the extradite or prosecute provision of the New York Convention indicates that an implied discrimination clause may be read into those instruments (and that, moreover, at least in the view of the ILC, the principle of *non-refoulement* is generally of relevance to extradition):

> Some members of the Commission had been concerned to ensure that there is no impairment of the principle of *non-refoulement*. The article as drafted makes this point clear. Thus, if the State where the alleged offender is found considers that he would not receive a fair trial or would be subjected to any type of abusive treatment in a State which has requested extradition, that request for extradition could, and should, be rejected.[14]

---

[12] 189 UNTS 150. It may be noted that the discrimination clauses contained in the Hostages Convention and in the other instruments noted (see p. 210 (notes 4-6 and accompanying text)) are formulated in stronger terms than is often the case with the rule of *non-refoulement*. For example, Article 33(2) of the Refugees Convention states that the rule of *non-refoulement* will not apply when there are reasonable grounds to regard the particular refugee as a danger to the security of the State in which he is present or when the refugee has been convicted of a particularly serious crime and represents a danger to the community of that State. See *Deportation to U. Case* (Federal Republic of Germany, Superior Administrative Court of Rhineland-Palatinate, 1972), 73 ILR 614 (1987). No such exceptions obtain with respect to this Article. Moreover, the rule of *non-refoulement* as stated in the Refugees Convention protects only against threats to a refugee's life and freedom, whereas the rule as stated in this instrument protects persons whose position would be prejudiced.

[13] See Van den Wijngaert, note 3, *supra*, at p. 75 (and sources cited); Goodwin-Gill, *The Refugee in International Law* 78-83 (1983). Goodwin-Gill states that there is "every indication" that the Committee of Experts of the Council of Europe intended the discrimination clause contained in the European Convention on Extradition to "close the gap between the political offender and the refugee". *Id.* at pp. 78-79. He also stated that there is a clear tendency to extend the principle of *non-refoulement* to include non-extradition. *Id.* at p. 80. See also *Folkerts v. State-Secretary of Justice* (Netherlands, Council of State, Judicial Division, 1978) 74 ILR 472, 474-75 (1987), wherein the court noted the close relationship between Article 33 of the Refugees Convention and Article 3(2) of the European Convention. In deciding whether Article 3(2) would be a bar to extradition in that case, the court took into consideration information from a UNHCR representative as to whether the evidence furnished in support of that claim would be sufficient to grant a request for recognition as a refugee.

[14] 1972 YBILC, Vol. II, p. 318. See also the comments of various members of the ILC during the drafting of the New York Convention. *Id.*, Vol. I, pp. 207-208, paras. 26, 28 & 31. During the drafting of the Hague Convention, moreover, the delegation of the US recognized the existence of discrimination clauses. In advocating that the political

ARTICLE 9

The inclusion of a discrimination clause in this Convention

As earlier noted, this provision was added to the Convention upon the proposal of the Jordanian delegation. In advocating its inclusion, the representative of Jordan to the Sixth Committee argued that, although the Convention would not be an extradition treaty as such:

> to the extent that the extradition option was concerned and to the extent that the future Convention could under article 10 be invoked as the basis of extradition, it was a multilateral extradition treaty limited, however, to the offence of the taking of hostages and a few other offences. In a bilateral extradition treaty between neighbouring friendly States, there would normally be provisions to safeguard the rights of persons claimed. A convention that might have the effect of exposing persons to different legal systems should have similar if not more safeguards.[15]

He indicated, moreover, that his delegation could accept the principle *aut dedere aut judicare* only if the draftsmen incorporated this safeguard into the Convention. The provision was necessary, he maintained, in order to prevent potential abuse, particularly in such circumstances where State practice might depend upon "extra-legal factors".[16]

Other States took various positions regarding the inclusion of this Article, some of which are discussed more fully below. At one end of the spectrum were the Arab countries, along with some other developing States, which strongly supported the Jordanian proposal. The Syrian representative, for example, argued that it was "essential to ensure a humanitarian spirit",[17] while the Algerian delegate asserted that the Convention must contain a provision which allows for the denial of extradition where there is a danger of an offender being prosecuted or punished as a result of religious or racial discrimination.[18] The delegations of Iraq and Pakistan indicated that they viewed Article 9 as a necessary balance to Article 8.[19] At the other end of the spectrum were States, most notably the Soviet Union and

---

offence exception be prohibited with respect to the offence of hijacking, the US representative stated that its proposal "would not affect, however, an extradition law which permitted refusal of extradition if the requested State determined that the alleged offender was in fact sought, not for that offence, but on account of his religious or political beliefs". ICAO Doc 8979-LC/165-2, p. 75 (1972).

[15] UN GAOR, 34th Sess., C.6 (12th mtg.), p. 6, para. 22, UN Doc A/C.6/34/SR.12 (1979).
[16] *Id.* at p. 5, para. 19.
[17] UN GAOR, 34th Sess., C.6 (14th mtg.), p. 2, para. 6, UN Doc A/C.6/34/SR.14 (1979).
[18] *Id.* at pp. 13-14, para. 74.
[19] UN GAOR, 34th Sess., C.6 (61st mtg.), p. 12, para. 49, UN Doc A/C.6/34/SR.61 (1979) (Iraq) & UN GAOR, 34th Sess., C.6 (62nd mtg.), p. 2, para. 3, UN Doc A/C.6/34/SR.62 (1979) (Pakistan).

its allies, which were vehemently opposed to inclusion of this type of provision. These States asserted that such a provision would allow Parties to avoid their obligations under the Convention and would undermine the "principle of inevitability of punishment".[20] Somewhere in the middle were the Western States, which, though they expressed some reservations about the provision, seemed flexible in their approach,[21] and some Latin American States which appeared ambivalent, noting that the Article would not affect the obligation to submit each case for the purpose of prosecution.[22]

Verwey, who was part of the Netherlands delegation during the drafting of the Convention, gives an interesting account of the history of Article 9. He states that the original proposal for the Article was submitted by Jordan after the failure of Algeria and Libya, amongst others, to introduce the element of "political motive" into Article 8, i.e., exceptions to the principle *aut dedere aut judicare* based on the motive of the hostage-takers. In response to the proposal, the Western and Eastern European delegations pointed to the novelty of introducing such prohibitive language ("*shall* not be granted") to the law of extradition. However, it became clear that the Arab delegations considered the proposal a *sine qua non* for acceptance of the entire Convention. The Western delegations, therefore, approached the proposal in a constructive spirit and made a number of efforts to "soften" the wording, e.g., by replacing the word "shall" with the word "may". As the main elements of a compromise reached after lengthy informal negotiations it was agreed that: the prohibitive word "shall" would remain in the first paragraph; the second paragraph would remain in its entirety; and both paragraphs would be reworded so as to make it clear that Article 9 is restricted only to the scope of the Convention, i.e., it is applicable only with respect to treaty relations as between States Parties to the Hostages Convention and does not introduce an innovation to the general law of extradition. The Eastern bloc nations and their allies, however, "could not accept such an alleged restriction of their sovereignty" and, moreover, objected to the use of the term "political opinion" in the first paragraph.[23]

Indeed, the Eastern-bloc countries were never reconciled to inclusion of this provision and one delegation, that of the USSR, requested a roll-call vote on the Article in the Sixth Committee. The Article was approved by a vote of 103 in favour and 10 against, with 4

---

[20] See p. 220 (note 50 and accompanying text).
[21] See pp. 216-217 (notes 33-37 and accompanying text).
[22] See, e.g, the comments of the representatives of Peru and Uruguay, respectively, in UN GAOR, 34th Sess., C.6 (13th mtg.), p. 5, para. 19, UN Doc A/C.6/34/SR.13 & UN GAOR, 34th Sess., C.6 (14th mtg.), p. 12, para. 67, UN Doc A/C.6/34/SR.14 (1979).
[23] Verwey, pp. 90-92.

abstentions.[24] States voting against were Bulgaria, Byelorussian SSR, Cuba, Czechoslovakia, GDR, Hungary, Mongolia, Poland, Ukrainian SSR, and the USSR.[25] The representative of the USSR, moreover, stated that because of the inclusion of this Article, his delegation would have abstained if the Convention as a whole had been put to a vote.[26] Another vote regarding this Article was held in the General Assembly with a similar result.[27]

Acquiescence to the inclusion of this Article seems a small price to have paid for a more widespread acceptance of the Convention — and, therefore, of the principle that there should be no safe-havens for those who commit acts of hostage-taking — by Arab and other States. Despite the compromise, however, as of August 1989 only four Arab States, Egypt, Jordan, Kuwait and Oman had become party to the Convention and only one other, Iraq, had signed it.[28] But it may be noted that their opposition to this Article did not prevent Eastern bloc States from becoming party to this instrument. In 1987, a number of them deposited instruments of accession with the UN.[29]

2. INTERPRETATION

PARAGRAPH 1: OBLIGATION NOT TO EXTRADITE WHEN PERSECUTION OR PREJUDICE WOULD RESULT

"A request for the extradition of an alleged offender, pursuant to this Convention, shall not be granted . . ."

The terms of this provision are mandatory: States "shall not" grant extradition, as between themselves and other States Parties to this Convention, for the acts set forth in Article 1 when substantial grounds exist to believe that any of the circumstances envisaged by this Article exist. A State which grants extradition despite such circumstances will be in breach of this Convention. The original

---

[24] UN GAOR, 34th Sess., C.6 (62nd mtg.), p. 9, paras. 47 & 48, UN Doc A/C.6/3/34/SR.62 (1979).

[25] *Id.* at para. 47. The States that abstained were Botswana, Congo, Romania, and Vietnam. Although some other States expressed their disapproval of the provision in the drafting stages, these objections were apparently dropped. See, e.g., the comments of the representative of Uganda. UN GAOR, 34th Sess., C.6 (13th mtg.), p. 3, para. 10, UN Doc A/C.6/34/SR.13 (1979).

[26] UN GAOR, 34th Sess., C.6 (62nd mtg.), pp. 10-11, para. 55, UN Doc A/C.6/34/SR.62 (1979).

[27] The Article passed by a vote of 125 in favour and 10 against, with three abstentions (Botswana, Cuba & Romania). UN GAOR, 34th Sess., Plenary (105th mtg.), para. 34, UN Doc A/34/PV.105 (1979).

[28] See generally p. 5 (note 19 in the Introduction).

[29] *Id.*

Jordanian draft article stated that: "No Contracting State shall extradite an alleged offender ..."[30] The words "pursuant to this Convention" were added by the Sixth Committee, although its explanation for the change is obscure.[31] As noted, Verwey reports that the addition was intended to make it clear that the prohibition on extradition applies only with respect to treaty relations as between States Parties to the Convention, and is not a general innovation in the law of extradition.[32]

As noted above, it was the mandatory nature of this provision which caused some concern amongst many Western and other delegations during the drafting of this Convention. The representative of Canada, for example, stated that his delegation had "reservations about a provision which called in question the traditional discretion of States regarding extradition and which, by permitting States to take all the circumstances of each case into account, went beyond the scope of the Convention and introduced a new element into extradition law".[33] Moreover, the Belgian delegate asserted[34] that that provision might cause a conflict with the principle of "freedom of action" regarding extradition as expressed in Article 5 of the European Convention on the Suppression of Terrorism (which contains a discrimination clause

---

[30] See note 2, *supra*.

[31] See UN GAOR, 34th Sess., C.6 (53rd mtg.), p. 9, para. 29, UN Doc A/C.6/34/SR.53 (1979).

[32] See p. 214 (note 23 and accompanying text). A narrow interpretation of the wording "pursuant to this Convention" would indicate that the prohibition contained in this paragraph would not apply when the request for extradition for one of the offences set forth in Article 1 is formulated strictly in terms of a bilateral extradition treaty existing between States Parties to this Convention, without any reference being made to this Convention. Although it is not entirely clear, such an interpretation seems to have been made by the US Senate Committee on Foreign Relations in stating that: "As a result of the qualifying phrases 'pursuant to this Convention' in paragraph 1 and 'with respect to the offenses as defined in this Convention' in paragraph 2, Article 9 will not affect normal US extradition practice which is carried out pursuant to bilateral extradition treaties." See US Senate, Committee on Foreign Relations, *Report on the International Convention Against the Taking of Hostages*, 97th Cong., 1st Sess., S. Exec. Rep. 17 (1981). However, in light of paragraph 2 of this Article, such an interpretation seems somewhat strained. See generally pp. 223-225.

[33] UN GAOR, 34th Sess., C.6 (13th mtg.), pp. 2-3, para. 6, UN Doc A/C.6/34/SR.13 (1979). The Canadian representative's reference to "permitting States to take all the circumstances of each case into account" is somewhat unclear. However, he may have been referring to the "rule of non-inquiry" which is followed by some States, i.e., that principle by which courts deciding upon an extradition request will refuse to inquire into the prospective treatment of an accused in the requesting State. This is the general rule in the United States. See, e.g., *In re Burt*, 737 F. 2d 1477, 1485-87 (7th Cir. 1984); *Gallina v. Fraser*, 278 F. 2d 77, 78 (2nd Cir. 1960), *cert. den.* 364 US 851 (1960). But it may be noted that in the US, at least, this is a rule followed by the judiciary. The Executive would, apparently, generally have the discretion to deny an extradition request where persecution would occur in the requesting State. See *Peroff v. Hylton*, 563 F. 2d 1099 (4th Cir. 1977). See also Bassiouni, *International Extradition United States Law and Practice* 374 & 603 (2d ed. 1987).

[34] UN GAOR, 34th Sess., C.6 (14th mtg.), p. 13, para. 69, UN Doc A/C.6/34/SR.14 (1979).

couched in non-mandatory terms)[35] and the representative of the Philippines stated that the mandatory language of the provision weakened the entire instrument.[36] Despite these objections, however, many of these delegations indicated a willingness to reach agreement on the provision.[37]

In one sense, it does appear that because of this language States Parties lose a certain measure of discretion that they might otherwise have had in deciding whether or not to extradite an alleged offender. However, the mandatory terms of this provision will be softened somewhat in practice because it is the requested State which will determine whether substantial grounds exist to believe that the circumstances envisaged by this Article are satisfied.[38] Moreover, the mandatory nature of the provision would appear to provide better protection for the individual accused. The Jordanian representative made a fair point in noting that a person alleged to have committed an offence under this Convention may need extra protection due to the fact that he might be exposed to many different legal systems.[39]

---

[35] Article 5 of that instrument states that "*[n]o obligation is imposed by this Convention to extradite* if the requested State has substantial grounds for believing that the request for extradition for an offence mentioned in article 1 or 2 has been made for the purpose of prosecuting or punishing a person on account of his race, religion, nationality or political opinion, or that that person's position may be prejudiced for any of those reasons" (emphasis added). The explanatory report to that Convention states that if the requisite conditions exist, the requested State *may* refuse extradition. See Council of Europe, *Explanatory Report to the European Convention Against the Suppression of Terrorism* 15 (1977). By way of contrast, the language in the European Convention on Extradition is mandatory in nature, i.e., it prohibits extradition if the envisaged circumstances obtain. Article 3 of that instrument states that extradition "shall not be granted . . . if the requested party has substantial grounds for believing that a request for extradition for an ordinary criminal offence has been made for the purpose of prosecuting or punishing a person on account of his race, religion, nationality or political opinion, or that that person's position may be prejudiced for any of these reasons." 359 UNTS 276.

[36] UN GAOR, 34th Sess., C.6 (13th mtg.), p. 21, para. 100, UN Doc A/C.6/34/SR.13 (1979).

[37] See, e.g., the comments of the representatives of Canada and the Philippines.

[38] One writer, referring to the fact that it is the requested State which will determine whether or not such substantial grounds exist, concludes that "there is a strong element of optical illusion" in the absolute nature of this prohibition. Rosenne, p. 133.

[39] See generally *Explanatory Report*, note 35, *supra*, at p. 15, which states that the discrimination clause was included despite the fact that "in the member States of the Council of Europe, all but one of which has signed the European Convention on Human Rights, prosecution, punishment or discrimination of a person on account of his race, religion, nationality or political opinion is unlikely to occur". In a document which is intended to have universal scope, such as the Hostages Convention, the argument for inclusion of such a clause is even more compelling. It may be noted in this regard that the Committee of Ministers of the Council of Europe has recommended that extradition should not be granted to States which are not parties to the European Convention on Human Rights, 213 UNTS 221, when there are "substantial grounds for believing that the request has been made for the purpose of prosecuting or punishing the person concerned on account of his race, religion, nationality or political opinion, or that his position may be prejudiced for any of these reasons". See Recommendation No. R (80) 9, in Council of Europe, Committee of Ministers, *Recommendations to Member States 1980* (1982).

Finally, it should be noted that, despite the suggestions of some States to the contrary, the mandatory aspect of this clause is not entirely novel: Article 3, paragraph 2, of the European Convention on Extradition contains similar mandatory language,[40] as does the Inter-American Convention on Extradition,[41] which was, however, drafted after the Hostages Convention.

"... if the requested State Party has substantial grounds for believing:"

Absent "substantial grounds" to believe that the envisaged circumstances obtain, the prohibition on extradition will not be in effect. The words "substantial grounds" were adopted from the corresponding provisions of the European Convention on Extradition and the European Convention on the Suppression of Terrorism, and there was no recorded discussion at the time of the drafting of the present Convention which concerns their precise meaning. However, the words are clear enough in themselves and, for example, a mere allegation by an alleged offender that the envisaged circumstances obtain would not be enough to trigger a State's obligation not to extradite.[42] The factors which could lead a State to conclude that such "substantial grounds" exist will, of course, vary from case to case. However, they could include the prior persecution of the alleged offender by the requesting State or a history in the requesting State of persecution of others similarly situated because of their political opinion, ethnic origin, etc.[43] Moreover, a history in that State of persons being unable to obtain a fair trial because of their political opinion, etc. would be an example of substantial grounds to believe that an alleged offender's position would be prejudiced upon extradition.

During the drafting of this provision, some States expressed concern about the fact that the determination of whether such grounds exist was left solely to the subjective judgment of the requested State.[44] It is unlikely, however, that any other practical

---

[40] See note 35, *supra*.

[41] See note 5, *supra*.

[42] Cf. *T. v. Swiss Federal Prosecutor's Office* (Swiss Federal Tribunal, 1966), 72 ILR 632, 635-36 (1987), wherein the court rejected an applicant's claim that Article 33 of the Refugees Convention would bar his extradition (even assuming that the Convention was relevant to extradition), noting that he had made no attempt to prove that his freedom would be threatened in the requesting State and that such a possibility was not otherwise apparent.

[43] See generally *Folkerts*, note 13, *supra*, at p. 475.

[44] See, e.g., the comments of the representatives of the Philippines and Poland, respectively, in UN GAOR, 34th Sess., C.6 (13th mtg.), p. 20, para. 100, UN Doc A/C.6/34/SR.13 & UN GAOR, 34th Sess., C.6 (62nd mtg.), p. 10, para. 52, UN Doc A/C.6/34/SR.62 (1979).

alternative could have been found and the determination of whether such grounds exist remains, at least in the first instance, a matter for the discretion of the requested State. It would be within the scope of the dispute resolution procedure set forth in Article 16 to inquire as to whether such a determination was made in good faith.

". . . that the request for extradition for an offence set forth in article 1 has been made for the purpose of prosecuting or punishing a person on account of his race, religion, nationality, ethnic origin or political opinion . . ."

This Article does not prohibit extradition of offenders whose acts are motivated by politics, religion, nationality, etc. Rather, it prohibits extradition when the request is made for the purpose of prosecuting or punishing an alleged offender because of his "race, religion, nationality, ethnic origin or political opinion". In other words, extradition is not prohibited, for example, just because it was an alleged offender's religious or political viewpoints which motivated him to take hostages in State A; rather, it is prohibited when State A's extradition request is in reality made so that it may prosecute the alleged offender because of those viewpoints, rather than for the act of hostage-taking.

The statuses mentioned in this Article are identical to those listed in the two European Conventions, although that of "ethnic origin", added by the Sixth Committee,[45] is new to this instrument.

As earlier noted, the most serious and sustained objections to the inclusion of this Article came from the Eastern bloc States. The delegate of the USSR set the tone by asserting that the Article "in actual fact meant that a State Party to the Convention would have the right not to discharge an international obligation it had assumed on the basis of its own appraisal of the administration of justice in the other State Party concerned".[46] Article 9, he argued, undermines

> the principle of inevitability of punishment for a crime by making it possible for a criminal to escape punishment in many cases, especially those involving the question of extradition between states with different political views. Therefore, the basic principle that hostage-taking is a criminally punishable act without exception whatsoever was violated, since hostage-taking was encouraged in cases where a criminal disagreed with the policies of a certain Government.

---

[45] UN GAOR, 34th Sess., C.6 (53rd mtg.), p. 9, para. 29, UN Doc A/C.6/34/SR.53 (1979).
[46] UN GAOR, 34th Sess., C.6 (13th mtg.), p. 14, para. 68, UN Doc A/C.6/34/SR.13 (1979).

The provision, he concluded, would make it more difficult to combat the phenomenon of hostage-taking.[47] The delegate of Poland asserted that the Article was inconsistent with the general scope of the Convention in that it virtually eliminated the principle of extradition. Moreover, he asserted that it was imprecise and would be subjectively interpreted, thus militating against interpretation of the Convention in accordance with the principles of justice.[48] Similar comments were made by the representatives of Romania and Bulgaria.[49]

The arguments put forth by these States indicate a failure to give due weight to the true nature of the obligations undertaken by Parties to this Convention. States are not obliged by this instrument to grant extradition; rather, they are required only to submit for the purpose of prosecution those alleged offenders who are not extradited. When extradition does not take place, for whatever reason, submission for the purpose of prosecution must follow. That obligation is not affected by this provision. Therefore, this provision is clearly not a licence to "refuse to discharge an international obligation". It is thus somewhat difficult to discern the true nature of the objections voiced by the Eastern bloc delegations. Their recalcitrance regarding the inclusion of this Article may have stemmed generally from their belief that these anti-terrorism conventions should always result in extradition to the territorial State (or the State of registration of an aircraft).[50] Alternatively, they may have been concerned, as has at least one writer, that such clauses are in reality designed as political weapons, disguised as humanitarian protections, to be used against socialist countries.[51] And it is certainly true that generally speaking this type of provision would most often be invoked as between States which are on generally unfriendly terms or which have fundamentally different political and legal systems, rather than as between friendly States with similar systems.[52] It is in the nature of things that a

---

[47] UN GAOR, 34th Sess., C.6 (62nd mtg.), pp. 10-11, para. 55, UN Doc A/C.6/34/SR.62 (1979).

[48] *Id.* at p. 10, para. 52.

[49] *Id.* at p. 10, para. 54 (Romania) & p. 11, para. 58 (Bulgaria).

[50] See generally p. 191 (note 15 and accompanying text in the commentary on Article 8).

[51] See, e.g., Zlataric, *"Les problèmes actuels de l'extradition"*, 39 *Rev. int'l d. pén* 773, 781 (1968). It may be noted, moreover, that Eastern bloc States have objected to the inclusion of such provisions in documents other than the Hostages Convention. The USSR and GDR resisted proposals during the 1977 UN Conference on Territorial Asylum which would have protected refugees from extradition to a State where they might be persecuted. See Goodwin-Gill, note 13, *supra*, at pp. 80-81.

[52] See generally Van den Wijngaert, note 3, *supra*, at pp. 85-89 where she makes the point that the discrimination clause "is likely to be relatively seldom and always hesitantly applied between friendly nations . . . it is indeed a very delicate and politically disagreeable task to determine that extradition cannot be granted because the extradition request is politically motivated or because the requested person is liable to be persecuted in the requesting state."

requested State's perception of whether or not substantial grounds exist to believe that the circumstances envisaged by this Article obtain will be coloured by its general view of the fairness of the requesting State's judicial system.

However, the argument presented by the Eastern bloc States would have had more force if this Convention imposed a general obligation to extradite, with this Article constituting permissible grounds for derogation from that obligation. As it stands (and as discussed in detail throughout the commentary on Article 10), extradition under this Convention is governed by the relevant treaties and domestic laws of each State Party. If no extradition treaty exists between two relevant States, when the envisaged circumstances obtain the requested State would probably not, and perhaps could not, depending upon the terms of its laws, grant extradition even if this Article was not included in the Convention. Thus, while such a State might well use this Article as part of its reason for refusing to extradite, it need not do so to justify its decision since it is not otherwise obliged to extradite to the requesting State. Even if an extradition treaty exists between the two relevant States (and it would seem that such a treaty is less likely to exist as between States with such fundamental differences),[53] many of the situations envisaged by this Article could probably fit within a broad interpretation of the political offence exception,[54] and the requested State could deny extradition on that basis. Therefore, this Article does not substantially alter the existing state of affairs.[55] If anything, its practical effect will be to serve more as a bar to States which wish to extradite, since they are prohibited from doing so under the envisaged circumstances, than as a "loophole" for States which do not.[56] But even though this provision might prevent extradition in some cases wherein it would otherwise be required, given its compelling humanitarian basis, and the fact that it should not result in impunity for the offender, it is to be applauded.

It is worth noting that there appear to be two ways in which this Article could be the centre of a dispute as between two Parties, and thus the subject of the dispute settlement procedure set forth in Article 16. The first is if a requested State decides that there are substantial grounds to believe that one or more of the circumstances envisaged by this Article obtain and refuses extradition. It would be

---

[53] But such treaties do exist. The US, for example, has over 100 extradition treaties (a list is contained in Bassiouni, note 33, *supra*, at pp. 933-948), including with such partners as Romania. See Treaty on Extradition 23 July 1924, United States-Romania, TS 713.
[54] See generally Van den Wijngaert, note 3, *supra*, at p. 82.
[55] See generally Rosenstock, p. 182.
[56] See the comments of the Jordanian representative to this effect. UN GAOR, 34th Sess., C.6 (62nd mtg.), p. 3, para. 9, UN Doc A/C.6/34/SR.62 (1979).

open to the requesting State to challenge that determination if — and only if — the requested State is generally under a treaty obligation to extradite alleged offenders thereto. The second is if a State decides that no such substantial grounds exist and grants extradition. It would be open to another concerned Party, i.e., the national State of the offender, to challenge that determination.

". . . or . . . that the person's position may be prejudiced: . . . for any of the reasons mentioned in subparagraph (a) of this paragraph . . ."

The first part of this Article requires that extradition must be denied when the request is in reality made for the purpose of prosecuting or punishing the alleged offender because of his race, religion, nationality, ethnic origin or political opinion. The above language, however, by way of contrast, makes it clear that extradition must also be denied when the requested person's position will be prejudiced because of one of those circumstances, even if the request is not actually made for the purpose of persecuting him and is *bona fide*. This language is quite broad, for it seems that a person's position could be prejudiced in any number of ways. However, some examples of how an alleged offender's position could be prejudiced within the meaning of this Article are if, by reason of one of the listed conditions, he would be unable to prepare his defence adequately or to receive a fair trial, or where his sentence or treatment would be unduly harsh.[57]

". . . or . . . for the reason that communication with him by the appropriate authorities of the State entitled to exercise rights of protection cannot be effected."

This Article, containing a safeguard not found in other discrimination clauses, provides that extradition must also be denied when the defendant's position would be *prejudiced* because he is not permitted to communicate with a protecting State. The original proposal by Jordan would automatically have prohibited extradition when substantial grounds existed to believe that an alleged offender would not be able to communicate with the protecting State.[58] The representative of Jordan recognized that such language might cause some difficulties, but, asserting that the provision was similar to

---

[57] As indicated, the ways in which a person's position could be "prejudiced" due to the listed factors seem numerous. An example cited by the Council of Europe with respect to the discrimination clause contained in the European Convention on the Suppression of Terrorism is "if the person to be extradited would, in the requesting State, be deprived of the rights of defence as they are guaranteed in the European Convention on Human Rights." See Explanatory Report, note 35, *supra*, at p. 15.

[58] See note 2, *supra*.

Article 6, paragraph 3, he argued that it was proper to impose the same obligation with respect to communication rights upon the State to which an alleged offender is extradited as is imposed upon the State which apprehended him.[59] However, some States expressed reservations concerning that language,[60] and the provision was redrafted in such a way as to condition the prohibition upon the existence of substantial grounds to believe that the alleged offender's position will actually be prejudiced by the lack of such communication.

Thus, one writer notes that where "the legal system of the requesting state is such as to give every reason to believe due process and a fair trial are assured, there would seem to be no reason for any bar to extradition",[61] presumably since no prejudice would actually result from the failure to allow communication. This observation seems sound, although it is arguable that if such communication cannot take place the alleged offender is prejudiced *per se*. The same commentator also states that the subparagraph requires not only that there be no consular or diplomatic relations but that the State entitled to exercise protection *cannot* do so, as opposed to being unwilling to do so. Therefore, he concludes, an offer by the requesting State to allow such communication seems to remove any bar to extradition. The scope of the subparagraph as a bar to extradition is narrowed even further by the practice of appointment of protecting powers and by the provision in Article 6, paragraph 5, regarding visits by a representative of the ICRC.[62]

PARAGRAPH 2: MODIFICATION OF INCONSISTENT TREATIES

"With respect to the offences as defined in this Convention, the provisions of all extradition treaties and arrangements applicable between States Parties are modified as between States Parties to the extent that they are incompatible with this Convention."

If States Parties to this Convention have extradition treaties with

---

[59] UN GAOR, 34th Sess., C.6 (12th mtg.), p. 6, para. 21, UN Doc A/C.6/34/SR.12 (1979).

[60] See, e.g., the comments of the representatives of Belgium and the Netherlands, respectively UN GAOR, 34th Sess., C.6 (14th mtg.), p. 13, para. 70, UN Doc A/C.6/34/SR.14 & UN GAOR, 34th Sess., C.6 (13th mtg.), p. 9, para. 39, UN Doc A/C.6/34/SR.13 (1979).

[61] Rosenstock, p. 182. See also *Folkerts*, note 13, *supra*, at p. 475, where the court stated that a claim under Article 3(2) of the European Convention must be examined in light of the fact that the requesting State (the FRG) is a constitutional State and a Party to the European Convention on Human Rights, and is governed by a legal regime in which human rights and fundamental freedoms are generally protected and respected.

[62] *Id.* at pp. 182-83.

each other which do not contain discrimination clauses, or which are otherwise inconsistent with the terms of paragraph 1 of this Article or other provisions of this Convention, those treaties are modified by this paragraph, with respect only to the offences of hostage-taking, attempted hostage-taking and participation therein. This provision thus seeks to ensure that such other instruments are compatible with this Convention.

During the drafting of this Convention, some States expressed concern that the prohibitory language in paragraph 1 of this Article would affect the obligations of Parties under their extradition treaties, i.e., it would prohibit extradition in some circumstances where it may previously have been allowed or even required. The representative of Canada, for example, stated that the Article might create interpretive problems for national courts and cause conflicts between contradictory treaty obligations.[63] In response to these concerns, the representative of Jordan stated:

> As to the possible conflict with existing treaty relations, if it existed at all, such conflict was minimal and perhaps inevitable because of the very nature of contracts at the international level ... if [a State] wished to participate in regulating a new phenomenon, [it] should [be ready] to accept some conflict of obligation.[64]

This paragraph was subsequently added by the Sixth Committee Working Group, the Chairman-Rapporteur explaining that it was intended "to take care of possible incompatibilities between the provisions of article 9 and existing extradition treaties and arrangements".[65] The provisions of this Article thus supersede any other obligation as between two States Parties to extradite in the circumstances envisaged by this Article.

The Eastern bloc States and their allies objected to this provision also. The representative of Bulgaria asserted that it would be better to allow States Parties themselves to resolve the question of existing treaties and arrangements.[66] Similarly, the Cuban representative stated that he could not accept the idea that the sovereign will of States, as expressed in bilateral treaties, was subject to modification by multilateral norms. This objection was also applicable to Article 10.[67]

---

[63] UN GAOR, 34th Sess., C.6 (13th mtg.), p. 3, para. 6, UN Doc A/C.6/34/SR.13 (1979).

[64] UN GAOR, 34th Sess., C.6 (12th mtg.), p. 6, para. 23, UN Doc A/C.6/34/SR.12 (1979).

[65] UN GAOR, 34th Sess., C.6 (53rd mtg.), p. 9, para. 29, UN Doc A/C.6/34/SR.53 (1979).

[66] UN GAOR, 34th Sess., C.6 (62nd mtg.), p. 11, para. 58, UN Doc A/C.6/34/SR.62 (1979).

[67] *Id.* at p. 12, para. 59.

In any event, paragraph 2 appears to be nothing more than a statement of the rules regarding successive treaties codified in Article 30 of the Vienna Convention on the Law of Treaties.

Article 10

FACILITATION OF THE EXTRADITION OPTION

1. The offences set forth in article 1 shall be deemed to be included as extraditable offences in any extradition treaty existing between States Parties. States Parties undertake to include such offences as extraditable offences in every extradition treaty to be concluded between them.

2. If a State Party which makes extradition conditional on the existence of a treaty receives a request for extradition from another State Party with which it has no extradition treaty, the requested State may at its option consider this Convention as the legal basis for extradition in respect of the offences set forth in article 1. Extradition shall be subject to the other conditions provided by the law of the requested State.

3. States Parties which do not make extradition conditional on the existence of a treaty shall recognize the offences set forth in article 1 as extraditable offences between themselves subject to the conditions provided by the law of the requested State.

4. The offences set forth in article 1 shall be treated, for the purpose of extradition between States Parties, as if they had been committed not only in the place in which they occurred but also in the territories of the States required to establish their jurisdiction in accordance with paragraph 1 of article 5.

1. INTRODUCTION

Article 8, paragraph 1, requires a State Party in whose territory an alleged offender is present either to extradite him or to submit the case to its appropriate authorities for the purpose of prosecution. The present Article deals in more detail with the option of extradition. In general, it is preferable that an alleged offender is tried in a State which has a close connexion with the offence, whether that State is the territorial State or one of the other States which are required under Article 5, paragraph 1, to establish primary jurisdiction over the offences. However, no general duty exists under customary international law to extradite alleged offenders; indeed, in the absence of a treaty many States may not grant extradition.[1] This

---

[1] See Shearer, *Extradition in International Law* 24-27 (1972). Extradition may be defined as "the formal surrender, based upon reciprocating arrangements, by one nation to another of an individual accused or convicted of an offence outside its own territory and within the jurisdiction of the other which, being competent to try and punish him, demands the surrender". *Id.* at p. 21.

Article seeks to provide the legal bases for extradition in some situations, thus facilitating the extradition option in many cases and resulting in some cases in an obligation to extradite.

Apart from some drafting differences, this Article is virtually identical to Article 8 of the Hague, Montreal and New York Conventions, and similar provisions are also contained in Article 11 of the Rome Convention. Adoption of this Article caused little debate in either the Hostages Committee or the Sixth Committee. In its commentary to its draft of the New York Convention, the ILC explained the purpose of this Article as follows:

> If the option recognized in article 6 [article 8 of the Hostages Convention] is to be effective, either alternative envisaged therein should be capable of implementation when an alleged offender is found in the territory of a State Party. It is desirable, therefore, to provide in the present draft the legal basis for extradition of alleged offenders in a variety of situations so that the State in which the alleged offender is present will be afforded a real rather than an illusory choice ... *Paragraph 1* will apply when the States concerned have an extradition treaty in effect between them which does not include the offence for which extradition is sought. *Paragraph 2* covers the situation of States party which make extradition conditional on the existence of an extradition treaty and no such treaty exists at the time when extradition is to be requested. *Paragraph 3* covers the situation between those States which do not make extradition conditional on the existence of a treaty.[2]

The ILC emphasized that these provisions are intended to facilitate the decision whether to extradite, rather than to make the option of extradition controlling.[3] Indeed, as discussed in greater detail below, it is clear from the language of each of the paragraphs in this Article and from the *travaux préparatoires* of the Hague and New York Conventions that none of the provisions herein create, by themselves, an obligation to extradite; rather, the most stringent requirement imposed is that Parties must recognize hostage-taking, attempt and participation as extraditable offences. Extradition under this Convention remains an essentially bilateral matter, subject to the terms of existing extradition treaties and laws. Moreover, it is important to note that this Article does not require any changes in the extradition laws of Parties which would, for example, require that different criteria be used in a decision whether or not to extradite an alleged hostage-taker from those which are used with respect to other extraditable crimes (although Article 9 might represent a different criterion).

---

[2] 1972 YBILC, Vol. II, p. 319.
[3] *Id.*

While the provisions contained in this Article serve a useful purpose in that they go some way towards providing legal bases for extradition in some cases where perhaps they would otherwise not exist, the Article is complicated and gives rise both to various interpretive difficulties and to discrepancies between the obligations of various States Parties.

2. INTERPRETATION

PARAGRAPH 1: THE OFFENCES INCLUDED AS EXTRADITABLE OFFENCES IN EXTRADITION TREATIES BETWEEN STATES PARTIES

"The offences set forth in article 1 shall be deemed to be included as extraditable offences in any extradition treaty . . ."

Through the use of a legal fiction ("shall be deemed"), this paragraph modifies, where necessary, all extradition treaties existing between Parties such that all the offences set forth in Article 1 — hostage-taking, attempted hostage-taking and participation therein — are considered to be extraditable offences within the meaning of those instruments.[4] A similar fiction is contained not only in the other anti-terrorism treaties but also in many other conventions dealing with international criminal offences.[5]

In general, extradition treaties deal with "extraditable offences" in one of two ways. The first approach, which may be referred to as the "enumerative" method,[6] is to list specifically in the treaty those offences for which extradition may be granted as between the Parties thereto. This method became the standard international form in the late 19th century, and is still employed in many existing treaties.[7] Thus, for example, the 1972 extradition treaty between the United States and Argentina lists approximately 30 substantive offences (and attempt and participation with respect to those crimes) which are "extraditable" within the meaning of that instrument as long as they

---

[4] Some States have made express provision for this fiction in their legislation implementing the Hostages Convention. See, e.g., UK Taking of Hostages Act 1982, §3 of which provides that hostage-taking shall be included in the lists of extraditable crimes contained in the Extradition Act 1870 and the Fugitive Offenders Act 1967. See also New Zealand Crimes (Internationally Protected Persons and Hostages) Act 1980 (No. 44), §10.

[5] See, e.g., Art. 10, 1929 Convention for the Suppression of Counterfeiting Currency, 112 LNTS 371; Art. 8(1), 1984 Convention Against Torture and Other Cruel and Inhuman or Degrading Treatment or Punishment, UN Doc A/RES/39/46, *reprinted in* 23 ILM 1027 (1984) & 24 ILM 535 (1985).

[6] See Shearer, note 1, *supra*, at p. 133.

[7] *Id.*

are punishable by the laws of each party by imprisonment for at least one year.[8] With respect to such treaties, this provision has the effect of adding the offence of hostage-taking (as well as attempt and participation if the particular treaty does not include those ancillary offences) to the specifically listed offences. It is with respect to this type of treaty that this provision is of most relevance.

The second (and more modern)[9] approach, which may be referred to as the "eliminative" or "no-list" method,[10] is for the treaty to define extraditable offences as all offences which are punishable by both Parties by a certain penalty, e.g. (and most commonly) imprisonment for a period of one year or more. Thus, this type of treaty dispenses with the need for a specific list of offences.[11] For example, Article II of the 1982 extradition treaty between the United States and Italy states that any "offense, however denominated, shall be an extraditable offense only if it is punishable under the laws of both Contracting Parties by deprivation of liberty for a period of more than one year or by a more severe penalty".[12] Similarly, the European Convention on

---

[8] Art. 2, Treaty on Extradition, 21 January 1972, United States-Argentina, TIAS 7510. The enumerative method was the predominant US practice. See Whiteman, *Digest of International Law*, Vol. 6, 772-73 (1968). However, this appears to be changing. See generally pp. 230-231 (notes 11-12 & 15 and accompanying text). In the UK, extradition may not be had unless the offence is listed in the first schedules, supplemented by subsequent legislation, to both the Extradition Act 1870 (relevant to extradition to foreign States) and the Fugitive Offenders Act 1967 (relevant to extradition within the Commonwealth). See Stanbrook, *The Law and Practice of Extradition* 8-9 & 40-42 (1980). Proposed legislation in the UK, however, would define an "extraditable" offence as any offence which would constitute an offence punishable under the laws of the United Kingdom with imprisonment for a term of 12 months, or any greater punishment. See H.L. Bill 20 (1987).

Shearer notes that the enumerative method has been criticized on numerous grounds, including: 1) the fact that many such treaties are old and are not amended or replaced to keep abreast of the increasing range of offences; 2) the possibility of chance omissions of serious crimes; and 3) the tendency of some municipal courts to restrictively interpret the listed crimes. Shearer, note 1, *supra*, at p. 133.

[9] See US Senate, Committee on Foreign Relations, *Report on the Extradition Treaty with Italy*, 98th Cong., 2d Sess., Exec. Rep. 98-33, p. 3 (1984), *reprinted in* 24 ILM 1531, 1532 (1985); Schultz, "The General Framework of Extradition and Asylum", in Bassiouni & Nanda (eds.), *A Treatise on International Criminal Law*, Vol. II, 312 (1973).

[10] Shearer, note 1, *supra*, at 134-35.

[11] For the advantages of this method, see *id*. See also *Report on the Extradition Treaty*, note 9, *supra*, where it is stated that "[o]mitting the list of offenses obviates the need to renegotiate the treaty or to supplement it should both countries pass criminal laws dealing with new types of criminal activity ... and assures that no offenses are inadvertently excluded." It may be noted that some extradition treaties adopt a mixed approach to the treatment of extraditable offences, i.e., they contain lists, but also provide that extradition will be granted as well for other offences which carry a certain minimum penalty in both States. See, e.g., Art. 2, Treaty on Extradition, 20 June 1978, United States-Federal Republic of Germany, TIAS 9785 (although this particular treaty was amended in 1986 to provide simply for the eliminative method. See Supplementary Treaty on Extradition, 21 October 1986, Treaty Doc 100-6, 100th Cong., 1st Sess. (1987)).

[12] Treaty on Extradition, 13 October 1983, United States-Italy, TIAS 10,837, *reprinted in* 24 ILM 1527 (1985).

Extradition provides in Article 2 that extraditable offences are those which are punishable under the laws of the requested and the requesting Parties by deprivation of liberty for a maximum period of at least one year or a more severe penalty.[13]

This paragraph will be of less relevance to this second type of treaty. When such a treaty is in effect as between two States Parties, hostage-taking would normally fall within its scope even without this paragraph. This is because Article 2 of this Convention requires each Party to make hostage-taking punishable by "appropriate penalties", which will, presumably, always be greater than the penalty provided in such an extradition treaty as the threshold to be considered as an extraditable offence.[14] For example, Article II of the 1983 supplementary extradition convention between the United States and Sweden provides that extradition may be had for offences which are punishable by both Parties by deprivation of liberty for a period of 2 years or more.[15] Under US law, hostage-taking is punishable by up to life imprisonment,[16] while under Swedish law, kidnapping, the crime for which a hostage-taker would be charged in that country, is punishable by at least four years' imprisonment.[17] By the express terms of the extradition treaty between those two countries, therefore, hostage-taking is an "extraditable offence". However, in the (seemingly unlikely) event that a Party to this Convention establishes a penalty for hostage-taking which is less severe than the threshold penalty provided for in an extradition treaty with another Party, then that extradition treaty is modified to include hostage-taking, notwithstanding the fact that the penalty for that offence is less than the treaty threshold (and it may be noted that such a penalty would probably not be "appropriate" within the meaning of Article 2 of this Convention and could, therefore, constitute a breach of this Convention).

The meaning of "extraditable offence"

As earlier indicated, the inclusion of hostage-taking as an

---

[13] 359 UNTS 276. See also Art. 1, 1933 Montevideo Convention on Extradition, 162 LNTS 45. Shearer reports that the majority of eliminative treaties specify imprisonment for one year, or a more severe penalty, as the standard of severity to be considered as extraditable. Shearer, note 1, *supra*, at p. 135. Article 2 of the 1981 Inter-American Treaty on Extradition provides that imprisonment for two years or more is the threshold penalty for the offence to be considered as extraditable. PAUTS 60, *reprinted in* 20 ILM 723 (1981).

[14] See generally the comments of the ILC in this regard in 1972 YBILC, Vol. II, p. 319.

[15] TIAS 10,812, *reprinted in* 22 ILM 736 (1983).

[16] 18 USC §1203(a).

[17] Swedish Penal Code, Ch. 4, §1 (English translation by the National Council for Crime Prevention, Stockholm, 1984).

extraditable offence in extradition treaties existing between States Parties, by itself, does not automatically oblige States Parties to those instruments actually to extradite an alleged offender. It simply means that hostage-taking is one of the crimes for which extradition *may* be granted. The offence of hostage-taking is subject, as are other extraditable offences, to all the terms and conditions of each particular treaty in which it is "deemed to be included". Extradition treaties (and domestic laws) include some or all of a number of conditions, exceptions and exclusions, including, *inter alia*, the political offence exception,[18] the rule of non-extradition of nationals of the requested State,[19] non-extradition where the alleged offender could be subject to the death penalty in the requesting State,[20] the non-extradition for offences under military law[21] and the rule of *ne bis in idem*.[22] As

---

[18] See, e.g., Art. 7(1)(e), US-Argentina treaty, note 8, *supra*; Art. 3, European Convention, note 13, *supra*. See generally Shearer, note 1, *supra*, at pp. 166-193; Bassiouni, *International Extradition United States Law and Practice* 383-450 (2nd ed., 1987).

[19] See, e.g., Art. 4, US-Argentina treaty, note 8, *supra*; 1957 Swedish Extradition Act, §2; Art. 6, European Convention, note 13, *supra*. See generally Shearer, note 1, *supra*, at pp. 94-125. This exception is favoured more by the civil law States than by common law States. See Bassiouni, note 18, *supra*, at p. 457. Some treaties, such as the US-Argentina instrument, require the requested State to prosecute its national itself if it denies extradition on this basis, a requirement which would, in any event, obtain pursuant to Article 8 of the Hostages Convention regardless of the reason for denial of extradition.

It may briefly be noted in this context that some modern extradition treaties have eliminated or narrowed the exceptions based on the political nature of the offence and the nationality of the accused. See, e.g, the US-Italy treaty, note 12, *supra*, which, in Article IV, prohibits the denial of an extradition request on the ground that the requested person is a national of the requested State, and, in Article V, restricts the scope of the political offence exception by, *inter alia*, prohibiting its invocation with respect to crimes for which both Parties have the obligation *aut dedere aut judicare* pursuant to a multilateral instrument. On restrictions of the political offence exception, see pp. 234-235 (notes 32-35 and accompanying text).

[20] See, e.g., Art. VIII, Convention on Extradition, 24 October 1961, United States-Sweden, TIAS 5496, 494 UNTS 141; Art. 3(4), Extradition Treaty, 12 May 1976, United Kingdom-Finland, UKTS 23 (1977), Cmnd 6741; Art. 11, European Convention, note 13, *supra*; 1982 FRG Law on International Assistance in Criminal Matters, §8, *translated in* 24 ILM 945 (1985). Such provisions commonly require extradition, however, where assurances are made by the requesting State that the death penalty will not be carried out with respect to that offence.

[21] See, e.g., Art. V(4), US-Sweden treaty, note 20, *supra*; Art. 4, European Convention, note 13, *supra*; FRG law, note 20, *supra*, §7.

[22] See, e.g., Art V(1)(a), Treaty on Extradition, 8 June 1972, United States-United Kingdom, TIAS 8468; Art. V(1), US-Sweden treaty, note 20, *supra*; Art. 9, European Convention, note 13, *supra*. On the whole range of exceptions, exclusions and conditions regarding extradition, see Bassiouni, note 18, *supra*, at pp. 381-496. One important limitation on extradition not yet mentioned is the fact that common law States generally require, before extradition may be granted, that such evidence be presented as would justify holding the accused for trial in the requested State. Unless such a *prima facie* case is made out, extradition will not be granted. In civil law States, however, extradition is generally more administrative than judicial in nature; such States do not examine the strength of the case against the accused. It is generally enough that the warrant has been regularly issued, the identification of the accused is established and the requirements of the relevant treaty are fulfilled. See Shearer, note 1, *supra*, at p. 150; Bassiouni, note 18, *supra*, at pp. 552-554.

White states with respect to the corresponding Article in the Hague Convention, the "Convention does not require such rules to be waived: it merely provides that hijacking is an extraditable offence and leaves it to national law to determine whether in any given case the hijacker should be extradited".[23] However, unless a specific exception to extradition preserved in the relevant treaty obtains in a particular situation, extradition for the offence of hostage-taking will in fact be mandatory as between the two Parties to that treaty. It may thus be noted that the precise nature of the obligation assumed by Parties under this paragraph with respect to the extradition of hostage-takers will vary in accordance with the terms of both their bilateral treaties and their domestic legislation.

The effect of this Article on the political offence exception to extradition

It follows from the above comments that if the political offence exception is included in a relevant treaty (or domestic law), this Article has no effect on the right of a State to invoke that exception. Two writers, however, have asserted that this provision limits the ability of a State to invoke the political offence exception. Shubber, referring to the corresponding paragraph of the Hague Convention, suggests that it "means that, if previously some States could claim that hijacking was a political offence and as such was not covered by extradition treaties, this plea is no longer available".[24] Similarly, Rosenne, writing with respect to this Convention, states that "[w]henever the Convention is applicable, it removes, as between the States Parties, the excuse of political crime or political motivation from the defences available to a detained person whose extradition is requested, and to that extent may enlarge the obligation of the requested State to effect the extradition in accordance with the Convention".[25]

However, neither of these commentators explains precisely how they reach this conclusion, and such an interpretation of this Article is not readily justifiable either from the language of this provision or from the *travaux préparatoires* of the anti-terrorism conventions. Unlike Article VII of the Genocide Convention, which states that the

---

[23] White, p. 43.

[24] Shubber, "Aircraft Hijacking under The Hague Convention 1970", 22 ICLQ 718 (1973).

[25] Rosenne, p. 144. See also the comments of Mr. Ago during the ILC deliberations concerning the New York Convention where he states that the corresponding provision in that instrument was "intended to ensure that extradition is not rendered impossible by the existence of a treaty or of internal laws excluding political crimes from the list of extraditable offences". 1972 YBILC, Vol. I, p. 219. It is unclear whether he believed that the crimes under that instrument could not be subject to the political offence exception or whether he was simply making the point that the crimes enumerated therein are not necessarily political in nature.

offences contained in that instrument "shall not be considered as political crimes for the purpose of extradition",[26] and Article XI(1) of the Apartheid Convention, which contains similar language,[27] this Article is conspicuously silent as regards the political offence exception. During the drafting of the Hague Convention the draftsmen made it clear that they did not intend this provision to affect a State's existing laws regarding the decision to extradite an alleged offender.[28] Moreover, the proposals of some States, including the USSR and the US, to prohibit invocation of the political offence exception with respect to hijacking were not adopted.[29] White, it would seem, is therefore quite correct, and by no means alone, in her belief that this provision has no effect on the political offence exception to extradition.[30] Rosenne himself goes on to assert that this Article does not affect "fundamental aspects of a country's extradition law and practices, such as limitations on the extradition of nationals, the conditions of reciprocity, the application of the speciality rule and so forth".[31] It is difficult to discern how he singles out the political offence exception as the one aspect of domestic law which is affected by this Article. It should be emphasized, however, that even if a State refuses extradition because of the political nature of the offence (or indeed for any other reason), it must still submit the case to its authorities for the purpose of prosecution, and those authorities must, at that point, treat the offence as they would other ordinary offences.

Significantly, although none of the anti-terrorism conventions actually precludes States from invoking the political offence exception, some States have undertaken, as between themselves and certain other States only, not to invoke that exception with respect to the offences covered in these conventions. For example, Article 4(3)(b) of the 1978 extradition treaty between the US and the FRG provides that offences "which the Contracting Parties or the Requesting State have the obligation to prosecute by reason of a multilateral international agreement" shall not fall within the scope of

---

[26] 1948 Convention on the Prevention and Punishment of the Crime of Genocide, 78 UNTS 277.

[27] 1973 Convention on the Suppression and Punishment of the Crime of Apartheid, 1015 UNTS 243.

[28] See, e.g., the comments of the representatives of France, Sweden, and the UK in ICAO Doc. 8877-LC/161, pp. 57-58 (1970).

[29] See the proposals of Ghana, the US, the USSR and Poland, New Zealand and Paraguay in ICAO Doc 8979-LC/165-2, pp. 34, 69 & 74-75, 80, 133 & 135, respectively. See also White, p. 43; Abramovsky, "Multilateral Conventions for the Suppression of Unlawful Seizure and Interference with Aircraft Part I: The Hague Convention", 13 Colum. J. Trans. L. 401-03 (1974).

[30] See, e.g., Van den Wijngaert, *The Political Offence Exception to Extradition* 149 (1980); Wood, p. 812.

[31] Rosenne, p. 144.

the political offence exception.[32] A similar provision, worded somewhat differently, is contained in Article 1 of the supplementary extradition treaty between the US and the UK, which provides that the political offence exception shall not be invoked with regard to, *inter alia*, offences under the Hague, Montreal, New York and Hostages Conventions.[33] Article 1 of the European Convention on the Suppression of Terrorism similarly provides that certain offences are not subject to the political offence exception; these include offences within the scope of the Hague, Montreal and New York Conventions and offences "involving kidnapping, the taking of a hostage or serious unlawful detention". These instruments thus provide for an "exception to the exception".[34] This is an encouraging trend; however, it can be appreciated that it is one thing to depoliticize certain crimes as between two States which enter into a bilateral extradition treaty with each other, or even as between States within a common grouping such as the Council of Europe, but quite another thing to be able to achieve such a result in an instrument designed for universal adherence. Moreover, it must be acknowledged that attempts to depoliticize certain offences may not be as successful as might be hoped. Article 13 of the European Convention on the Suppression of Terrorism allows States to enter reservations to Article 1 and numerous States have done so, preserving their right to deny extradition on political grounds.[35]

---

[32] See note 11, *supra*.

[33] Supplementary Extradition Treaty, 25 June 1985, United States-United Kingdom, 24 ILM 1104 (1985). The US plans to continue negotiating instruments which so limit the political offence exception. See Note, "Elimination of the Political Offense Exception for Violent Crimes: The Proposed United States-United Kingdom Supplementary Treaty", 26 Va. J. Int'l L. 755, 756-57 (1986).

[34] For an argument that "international" offences, i.e., those which are the subject of international conventions, should be excluded from the political offence exception (and should thus be an "exception to the exception"), see Bassiouni, note 18, *supra*, at pp. 438-450. See also Johnson, "The Draft Code of Offences Against the Peace and Security of Mankind", 4 ICLQ 445, 456 (1955).

[35] See Van den Wijngaert, note 30, *supra*, at p. 160 n.866. The depoliticizing approach may not, in any event, ensure extradition in cases concerning terrorism, even with respect to bilateral treaties. For example, in 1987, because of pressure put on it by terrorist groups victimizing its nationals, the FRG denied a US request for the extradition of a hijacker (although the FRG did undertake to prosecute him itself). See p. 87 (note 40 in the commentary on Article 1). With particular respect to the European Convention on the Suppression of Terrorism, it might be noted that the effects of Article 13 allowing reservations will be reduced by the fact that the member States of the European Community have adopted a convention which provides for the application of the former instrument without reservations as between themselves. See 1979 Agreement Concerning the Application of the 1977 European Convention on the Suppression of Terrorism Among the Member States of the European Communities, Misc. 5 (1980), Cmnd 7823.

It may be noted that at least one example exists wherein the political offence exception was narrowed even as between two States which are generally distrustful of each other. An agreement between the United States and Cuba called for the

(*continued on p. 236*)

". . . existing between States Parties."

According to this provision, hostage-taking is deemed to be an extraditable offence in those treaties "existing" between States Parties. Some confusion could attach to the meaning of the word "existing". Rosenne has criticized the use of this word on the ground that it "cannot in good faith be interpreted as referring to any fixed point of time, such as the date of the adoption of the Convention or the date upon which a given State expressed on the international plane its consent to be bound by the treaty". He further argues that this and other objections he voices with respect to this Article "are not a matter of pedantry or formalism" since treaties dealing with extradition "are vulnerable to conflicting national laws and tendencies, and this often opens the way to astute lawyers bent (as is their duty) on obtaining an acquittal for their clients".[36] Although his point is not entirely clear, Rosenne seems to be arguing that certain interpretations of the word "existing" may facilitate an alleged offender's attempt to avoid extradition.

For example, suppose "existing" is interpreted as referring to the date the Convention came into force. It is possible that two States which were not parties to the Hostages Convention at that time will, after entry into force, and before they become parties to the instrument, enter into an extradition treaty with each other which does not specifically include hostage-taking as an extraditable offence. Since that treaty was not "existing" at the relevant point in time, hostage-taking will not be deemed to be included in that treaty. Moreover, since those States were not party to this Convention when they entered into the bilateral treaty, they were under no obligation specifically to include hostage-taking in that treaty pursuant to the second sentence of this paragraph. Thus, hostage-taking will not be an extraditable offence within the meaning of that instrument and an alleged offender may thereby avoid extradition (but not prosecution).

([35] *continued*)
extradition or prosecution of aircraft hijackers; the political aspect of the case only affected the agreement in so far as States could take into account, as extenuating or mitigating circumstances, whether the alleged offender was sought for strictly political reasons and was in danger of death without a viable alternative for leaving the country. Memorandum of Understanding on Hijacking of Aircraft and Vessels and Other Offenses, 15 February 1973, United States-Cuba, TIAS 7579.

[36] Rosenne, pp. 134-35. Rosenne made similar objections to this phrase during the drafting of the New York Convention, stating that the word "existing" is not adequate "inasmuch as, in some States, a duly ratified international treaty did not *ipso facto* become part of the law of the land. The meaning of 'existing' was not sufficiently clear, and it might well be asked whether it was really necessary to link Article 7 to a specific point in time". UN GAOR, 28th Sess., C.6 (1419 mtg.), para. 25, UN Doc A/C.6/SR.1419 (1973).

However, it is submitted that the only reasonable interpretation of this paragraph would appear to be that the word "existing" must refer to that point in time at which both the requesting and the requested State became bound by this Convention on the international plane. Only under this interpretation will no gaps exist in extradition treaties between Parties with respect to the inclusion of hostage-taking: all treaties between two Parties which were entered into before they were both bound by this instrument will include hostage-taking through the means of the legal fiction "shall be deemed" and those entered into as between two Parties after that point must specifically include the offence pursuant to the obligation imposed in the second sentence of this paragraph.

"States Parties undertake to include such offences as extraditable offences in every extradition treaty to be concluded between them."

Under this paragraph, Parties are obliged to include hostage-taking as an extraditable offence in future extradition treaties concluded between them (however, there is no obligation imposed upon States Parties to enter into such extradition treaties). In effect, this provision is relevant only to treaties which specifically list those offences which are subject to extradition since, as noted above, hostage-taking will normally fall within those treaties which do not contain lists but which rather include as extraditable offences those crimes punishable under the laws of both Parties by a certain penalty.

The original draft of the corresponding paragraph of the Hague Convention, submitted by the ICAO Legal Committee's Sub-committee on the Subject of the Unlawful Seizure of Aircraft, provided that "[t]he offense shall be deemed to be an extraditable offense in any extradition treaty existing or to be concluded between Contracting States".[37] However, the delegate of Spain to the Legal Committee argued that *rather* than deeming the offence to be included in future treaties, the Convention should impose an obligation upon Contracting States to include it expressly in such future treaties.[38] The proposal was adopted without much debate. It follows from this history and from the language of this provision that if Parties to this Convention negotiate an extradition treaty that contains a list of extraditable offences which does not include the offence of hostage-taking (or which otherwise excludes hostage-taking), they are in breach of this Convention; however, it does not

---

[37] ICAO Doc 8838-LC/157, p. 15 (1970). This is the approach taken in some other multilateral conventions concerning criminal offences. See, e.g., the Counterfeiting Convention, note 5, *supra*.

[38] ICAO Doc 8838-LC/161, p. 55 (1970).

appear that the offence of hostage-taking would be deemed to be included in that treaty.[39]

PARAGRAPH 2: THE HOSTAGES CONVENTION AS THE LEGAL BASIS FOR EXTRADITION

"If a State Party which makes extradition conditional on the existence of a treaty receives a request for extradition from another State Party with which it has no extradition treaty . . ."

Some States, such as the UK, the US and the Netherlands, have domestic laws which make the existence of a treaty with a requesting State a prerequisite to extradition.[40] Whereas paragraph 1 seeks to provide the legal basis upon which two Parties which have an extradition treaty as between themselves will consider hostage-taking an extraditable offence, this paragraph seeks to do the same as between two Parties which have no such treaty but where the requested State's domestic law requires a treaty before extradition can be granted. In accordance with this provision, section 3, paragraph 3 of the UK Taking of Hostages Act 1982 provides that where no extradition "arrangement" exists with a foreign State the Act may be treated as such an arrangement, limited to the offences under the Act.[41]

". . . the requested State may at its option consider this Convention as the legal basis for extradition in respect of the offences set forth in article 1."

When no extradition treaty exists between a requesting State and a requested State whose law requires the existence of such a treaty, this Convention may, in effect, serve as that treaty. However, this is at the option of the requested State. It is under no obligation to consider this Convention as an extradition treaty and its failure to do so in no way gives rise to a claim that it has breached this Convention.

The optional nature of this provision was the cause of considerable debate during the drafting of the Hague Convention and, to a lesser extent, the New York Convention. During the Diplomatic Conference at The Hague, the representative of the Netherlands, supported by a

---

[39] For a different point of view, see Shubber, p. 719.

[40] See UK Extradition Act 1870, §2; 18 USC §§3181 & 3184; 1967 Netherlands Extradition Act.

[41] The United States, however, has apparently declined to consider the anti-terrorism conventions to be "treaties on extradition" as required by 18 USC §3181. See Murphy, "The Future of Multilateralism and Efforts to Combat International Terrorism", 25 Colum. J. Trans. L. 35 (1986) at p. 45 n. 48.

number of other States, notably the US, the UK, Italy and Spain, proposed that this paragraph be amended to *require* a State which makes extradition conditional on the existence of a treaty to "recognize the present Convention as the legal basis for extradition" when extradition is requested by another State Party with which it has no such treaty.[42] In support of his proposal, the representative of the Netherlands argued that the amendment would not actually make extradition mandatory since the law of each nation regarding extradition "might involve all kinds of restrictions". Rather, he continued, the proposed language would simply remove the possibility of a State asserting that it was unable to grant extradition on the ground that it had no extradition treaty with the requesting State, since the Hague Convention would in effect constitute such a treaty, the conditions of which were to be found in the law of the requested State.[43] In support of the proposal, the Canadian representative noted that while some States would have to amend their laws under the proposed paragraph, it would help close existing gaps regarding extradition between Parties.[44] In line with this proposal, the drafting committee tentatively changed this paragraph to state that the Convention should be considered "as constituting an extradition treaty" in respect of the offences therein.[45]

However, a large number of States, particularly developing nations, asserted, for various reasons, that the proposal was unacceptable. The representative of the Congo, for example, stated that the proposal treated in an off-hand manner the requirement of some States that they must have an extradition treaty in order to extradite, supplying the necessary treaty in one sentence.[46] The representatives of some other States, such as Tanzania, asserted, somewhat obscurely, that the proposal would make extradition mandatory.[47] For all the various objections voiced, the crux of the problem was framed by the representative of India when he stated that the paragraph would force countries into treaty relationships with other nations with which they would not normally want to deal.[48] The representative of Uganda stated that it would not sign a convention that was also signed by South Africa if the effect of such was that it would be signing an extradition treaty with that nation.[49] Agreement could not be reached

---

[42] See ICAO Doc 8979-LC/165-2, p. 66 (1972); ICAO Doc 8979-LC/165-1, p. 125 (1972).
[43] *Id.* at pp. 125-26.
[44] *Id.* at pp. 126-27.
[45] *Id.* at p. 160.
[46] *Id.* at p. 182.
[47] *Id.* at p. 183. See also the various objections of the representatives of Uganda, Kenya and Tunisia, *id.* at pp. 126, 127 & 183, respectively.
[48] *Id.* at p. 183.
[49] *Id.* at p. 129.

on the Netherlands amendment and, in the end, the current compromise formula was proposed by Zambia and accepted by the Conference.[50]

During the drafting of the New York Convention, attempts were again made to couch this paragraph in such a way as to require States which make extradition conditional on the existence of a treaty to consider the Convention as the relevant treaty. The ILC's first draft of that Convention contained such wording but was amended upon the objections of some members.[51] Similarly, in the Sixth Committee, a French proposal[52] to adopt such language was rejected.[53] The position of the UK, in an apparent reversal since the time of the drafting of the Hague Convention, was that it would be "wrong and unfair to impose on a State which made extradition conditional on the existence of a treaty an obligation to extradite to a State with which it did not have an extradition treaty; that might raise difficulties in practice".[54] Somewhat surprisingly, given that State's previous attempts to require extradition of hijackers to the State of registration of the aircraft,[55] the representative of the USSR also supported the non-mandatory language, stating that such an option as contained in paragraph 2, was "part of the sovereign rights of each State". Moreover, he added that "there was little point in changing the wording at the present juncture, since it had now become part and parcel of the international legal machinery accepted by a large number of States".[56]

"Extradition shall be subject to the other conditions provided by the law of the requested State."

As already noted, extradition of hostage-takers will always be governed by the laws of the relevant Parties. In a case which falls within paragraph 1, the conditions governing extradition will already be provided for in the relevant extradition treaty between the two Parties. In a case which falls within this paragraph, however, the Parties will not have an existing set of agreed-upon conditions for extradition. This sentence, therefore, makes it clear that extradition in such a case will be governed by the law of the requested State. If, for example, the law of that State does not allow the extradition of

---

[50] ICAO Doc 8979-LC/165-1, pp. 188 & 191 (1972).
[51] See 1972 YBILC, Vol. I, p. 218.
[52] UN Doc A/C.6/L.945 (1973).
[53] See UN GAOR, 28th Sess., C.6 (1437th mtg.), para. 41, UN Doc A/C.6/SR.1437 (1973).
[54] *Id.* at para. 37.
[55] See p. 191 (note 15 and accompanying text in the commentary on Article 8).
[56] See UN GAOR, 28th Sess., C.6 (1437th mtg.), para. 40, UN Doc A/C.6/SR.1437 (1973).

nationals or extradition to a State where the death penalty could be imposed, then those conditions may be applied to a request pursuant to this Convention.

PARAGRAPH 3: THE OFFENCES AS EXTRADITABLE WHERE THE STATES PARTIES DO NOT REQUIRE AN EXTRADITION TREATY

"States Parties which do not make extradition conditional on the existence of a treaty shall recognize the offences set forth in article 1 as extraditable offences between themselves subject to the conditions provided by the law of the requested State."

Many States, including Sweden, France, the FRG and some Latin American States,[57] do not make the existence of a treaty a prerequisite to extradition. Rather, extradition from those States is governed by domestic laws which set down in detail the terms and conditions thereof, including the types of offences for which extradition may be had (usually offences punishable by the law of the requested State by deprivation of liberty for more than a certain period of time, such as one year). This paragraph requires such States to recognize the offences set forth in paragraph 1 as extraditable as between themselves. Before extradition will be granted, States which do not require a treaty often require assurances of reciprocity, i.e., that if the roles of the States were reversed, a similar request would be granted by the requesting State.[58] This provision would seem to guarantee that reciprocity. As with the previous paragraph, extradition pursuant to this paragraph is subject to the laws of the requested State.

It may be noted that this paragraph refers only to situations wherein neither the requested State nor the requesting State requires a treaty in order to extradite. None of the provisions in this Article covers a case wherein a State which does not require a treaty receives a request from a State which does. It would appear that in such a case the requested State is not under any obligation to consider hostage-taking as an extraditable offence as between those two States. Such a requirement would result in an unequal obligation as between the two relevant States since no such obligation would be imposed upon the requesting State if the roles of the States were reversed. It might be noted that while the requested State in such a situation is under no obligation to do so, it is, of course, free to consider hostage-taking as an extraditable offence as between those two States.

---

[57] See 1957 Swedish Extradition Act; FRG law, note 20, *supra*; 1927 French Extradition Act; Shearer, note 1, *supra*, at p. 26.
[58] *Id.*, at pp. 31-33. See, e.g., FRG law, note 20, *supra*, §5.

The inequality of obligations created by this Article

During the drafting of this Convention the representative of France to the Hostages Committee stated that this paragraph establishes a sharp distinction between the obligations of those States which make extradition conditional on the existence of a treaty and the obligations of those States which have no such requirement.[59] Similar objections were voiced during the drafting of the earlier conventions, both by the representative of France and by other draftsmen. The essence of these objections was that the three-tiered regime provided for in this Article creates an inequality of obligation amongst States Parties to this instrument.[60] States which fall within paragraph 1, i.e., those which have extradition treaties with each other, and those which fall into paragraph 3, i.e., those which do not require such treaties, *must* treat the offences set forth in Article 1 as extraditable as between themselves. By way of contrast, States which fall into paragraph 2, i.e., those which do not have an extradition treaty with the requesting State but whose law requires the existence of such as a prerequisite to extradition, are under no such obligation. Rather, they have the option to treat this Convention as the legal basis for extradition.

As earlier noted, to rectify this situation, proposals were made during the drafting of the earlier conventions to require States falling within paragraph 2 to consider the relevant convention as the legal basis for extradition.[61] Moreover, Rosenne, who played a role in the drafting of both the Hostages Convention and the New York Convention, states that "it was once suggested that the whole matter could have been simply covered by a short and uncomplicated clause stating that the offences recognised in Article 1 would be recognised by the contracting parties as extraditable offences, notwithstanding any other treaties binding them." While suggestions such as this at one time attracted some support, he continues, "the dead hand of precedent unfortunately prevailed and these (to us) imperfect texts have appeared in a whole series of treaties".[62] It would certainly seem that language such as that suggested by Rosenne or, at least, language requiring States which fall within paragraph 2 to recognize this Convention as the legal basis for extradition, would be a simpler and more consistent approach to creating a legal basis for extradition.

---

[59] See UN GAOR, 34th Sess., C.6 (62nd mtg.), p. 8, para. 37, UN Doc A/C.6/34/SR.62 (1979).

[60] See, e.g., the comments of the Dutch representative during the drafting of the Hague Convention, ICAO Doc 8979-LC/165-1, p. 125 (1972); the comments of the French representative during the drafting of the New York Convention, UN GAOR, 28th Sess., C.6 (1437th mtg.), paras. 29 & 30, UN Doc A/C.6/SR.1437 (1973).

[61] See pp. 238-240 (notes 42-56 and accompanying text).

[62] Rosenne, p. 135.

However, it appears that the wording of this Article is the best that could have been done by way of a compromise between the differing views of the various States involved in the drafting of the Hague Convention. It is unclear as to whether, as Rosenne asserts, these paragraphs were maintained in the Hostages Convention simply because of the "dead hand of precedent" (an analysis which is given some support by the statement of the USSR representative to the Sixth Committee during the drafting of the New York Convention)[63] or whether the unwillingness of some States to bend on this issue simply was undiminished during the years between the drafting of the Hague Convention and the drafting of the Hostages Convention. Whichever, and it may be a combination of both, it does not appear that any serious attempt was ever made during the drafting of the Hostages Convention to adopt alternative language.

Despite the drawbacks of this Article, in the final analysis its effect is to provide a legal basis for extradition in many cases wherein one may not have existed before. It will thus facilitate extradition in some cases and is, therefore, a welcome provision.

PARAGRAPH 4: THE OFFENCES TREATED AS HAVING TAKEN PLACE IN THE TERRITORIES OF THE STATES WITH PRIMARY JURISDICTION

"The offences set forth in article 1 shall be treated, for the purpose of extradition between States Parties, as if they had been committed not only in the place in which they occurred but also in the territories of the States required to establish their jurisdiction in accordance with paragraph 1 of article 5."

As noted in the commentary on Article 5,[64] those States which are required to establish primary jurisdiction over the offences have at least a moral responsibility to request extradition of alleged offenders. This provision seeks to facilitate the grant of extradition to one of those States by creating a legal fiction whereby the offences shall be treated, for the purpose of extradition, as having occurred in the territory of those States. This provision was added to the Hague Convention and each of the subsequent anti-terrorism conventions to cover the case of any requirement which may exist in treaties or domestic laws wherein extradition may only be had when the offence was committed in the territory of the requesting State.[65] It may be

---

[63] See p. 240 (note 56 and accompanying text).
[64] See p. 143 (note 32 and accompanying text in the commentary on Article 5).
[65] See White, p. 43; Shubber, note 24, *supra*, at p. 722. Section 3(3) of the UK Taking of Hostages Act 1982 accordingly provides for this fiction. Although the fiction created in this Article will be helpful in many cases, it may be noted that it will not strictly be
(continued on p. 244)

noted that this fiction relates only to those States which are *required* to establish primary jurisdiction pursuant to Article 5(1). It would not appear to relate to those States which have established their jurisdiction pursuant to that provision on a permissive basis, i.e., the passive personality principle, and over stateless persons resident in their territory.

(65 *continued*)
necessary as regards all treaties which provide as a general rule that extradition may only be had for offences committed in the territory of the requesting State. This is because many of those treaties provide exceptions to that rule which would require extradition as between parties thereto, assuming that they are both parties to this Convention as well, when a request for extradition is based on one of the grounds of jurisdiction set forth in Article 5, paragraph 1. For example, Article I of the extradition treaty between the US and Australia provides that extradition may be had for offences committed in the territory of the requesting State. However, Article IV of that instrument provides that when the offence for which extradition has been requested has been committed outside the territory of the requesting State, extradition shall be granted if the requested State would have jurisdiction over the offence in similar circumstances. See Treaty on Extradition, 14 May 1974, United States-Australia, TIAS 8234. If both Australia and the US are parties to the Hostages Convention they will both have been required to establish their jurisdiction on the bases listed in Article 5, paragraph 1. Thus, when one of those States requests extradition pursuant to that bilateral treaty for an offence of hostage-taking which has been committed extra-territorially on one of the bases provided for in Article 5, paragraph 1, of the Hostages Convention, then that bilateral treaty would require extradition even if this paragraph 4 of this Article did not exist. See also proposed legislation in the UK which would include as an "extraditable" offence any extra-territorial offence against the law of a foreign State which is punishable under that law with imprisonment for a term of 12 months, or any greater punishment, if *inter alia*, equivalent conduct outside the UK would constitute an extra-territorial offence similarly punishable in the UK. See H.L. Bill 20 (1987).

Article 11

MUTUAL ASSISTANCE IN CRIMINAL PROCEEDINGS

1. States Parties shall afford one another the greatest measure of assistance in connexion with criminal proceedings brought in respect of the offences set forth in article 1, including the supply of all evidence at their disposal necessary for the proceedings.

2. The provisions of paragraph 1 of this article shall not affect obligations concerning mutual judicial assistance embodied in any other treaty.

1. Introduction

This Article seeks to facilitate criminal proceedings brought in respect of offences under this Convention by requiring States Parties to provide each other with "the greatest measure" of assistance in connexion therewith. The course of criminal proceedings will normally involve a number of different State entities and officials, such as police, prosecutors and courts. Some or all of these will be involved at one stage or another in such activities as gathering evidence, locating witnesses and serving documents. Because of the often transnational nature of the offence of hostage-taking, and also because this Convention contemplates that offenders may sometimes be tried (or will be found) in a State other than that in which an offence occurred, when proceedings are brought for an offence under this Convention these activities must sometimes take place in the territory of a State other than the one conducting the proceedings.

However, it is a basic principle of international law that the officials of one State may not, without permission, perform sovereign acts — which may include such activities as the gathering of evidence and serving of documents — in the territory of another State.[1] Therefore, co-operation between States in these activities is essential. While it is possible that one State will allow the officials of another State to conduct in its territory certain activities relevant to a criminal proceeding to be held in the latter State,[2] more usually the officials of

---

[1] See generally Grützner, "International Judicial Assistance and Cooperation in Criminal Matters" in Bassiouni & Nanda (eds.), *A Treatise on International Criminal Law*, Vol. II, 189 (1973); Paikin, "Problems of Obtaining Evidence in Foreign States for Use in Federal Criminal Prosecutions", 22 Colum. J. Trans. L. 233, 234-35 (1984).

[2] An example of this would be allowing the consul of a requesting State to take evidence, in the form of the interrogation of his co-national, in the State in which he is based. See Geiger, "Legal Assistance Between States in Criminal Matters", in Bernhardt (ed.), *Encyclopedia of Public International Law*, Vol. 9, 249 (1986).

the requested State will conduct these activities in their territory on behalf of the requesting State. The process by which one State thus assists another in a criminal proceeding has variously been called such terms as "judicial assistance in criminal matters"[3] and "mutual assistance in criminal matters".[4]

This Article completes a two-tiered system of co-operative obligations begun in Article 4 (which requires States to co-operate in the prevention of offences of hostage-taking). As stated by the representative of the US to the Hostages Committee, this Article is "an essential element in a legal scheme intended to allow for the hostage-taker to be tried in a State other than that in which the criminal act had been committed ... [and is] consistent with the goal of eliminating safe havens for hostage-takers".[5] Indeed, the obligation to prosecute those alleged offenders who are not extradited cannot adequately be complied with if a State which decides to prosecute cannot obtain the necessary evidence. In addition to its obvious law enforcement value, moreover, mutual assistance also has an important human rights function: if one State refuses to supply evidence — which may be exculpatory — to another State which is conducting a proceeding, it may thus affect an accused offender's right to a fair trial.[6]

This Article corresponds to Article 10 of the Hague Convention, Article 11 of the Montreal Convention, Article 10 of the New York Convention and Article 12 of the Rome Convention. It is virtually unchanged from Article 9 of the original FRG draft and was not the subject of contention during the drafting of this Convention. However, as discussed below, this Article gives rise to some problems of interpretation, in particular with respect to the precise meaning of the words "greatest measure of assistance".

The existing state of mutual assistance in criminal matters under international law

The most basic form of mutual assistance in criminal matters is the transmission of evidence by a State for use in a foreign proceeding,

---

[3] See, e.g., Harvard Research Draft Convention on Judicial Assistance, 33 AJIL (Supp. 1939).
[4] This appears to be the modern and more favoured term. See, e.g., 1959 European Convention on Mutual Assistance in Criminal Matters, 472 UNTS 185; Treaty on Mutual Assistance in Criminal Matters, 9 November 1982, United States-Italy, *reprinted in* 24 ILM 1539 (1985). The terms are, however, interchangeable. See generally Mueller, "International Judicial Assistance in Criminal Matters", 7 Villanova L. R. 193, *reprinted in* Mueller & Wise, *International Criminal Law* 412-13 (1965).
[5] First Report of the Hostages Committee, pp. 93-94, para. 13.
[6] See Grützner, note 1, *supra*, at pp. 190-191.

traditionally upon the receipt of a letter rogatory.[7] However, the term "mutual assistance in criminal matters" is not inherently limited to any particular activities and may refer to any assistance given by the authorities of one State to further the criminal processes of another State, ranging from formal and informal police co-operation to co-operation between courts.[8]

Although some sources have indicated otherwise, States have no obligation under customary international law to render assistance to each other with respect to criminal proceedings.[9] Any obligation which exists to render mutual assistance is imposed by treaty, either multilateral or bilateral. While many States have laws which allow them to render various types of assistance even in the absence of a treaty, a grant of assistance rendered thereunder is generally a matter of comity, subject to the discretion of judges and other officials.[10]

---

[7] Letter rogatory is the term given to a request by a judicial authority to a foreign judicial authority. See generally *The Signe Tiedmann v. The Signe, et al.*, 37 F. Supp. 819, 920 (E.D. La., 1941). Generally letters rogatory must be transmitted through diplomatic channels and the procedures involved can be obscure, cumbersome and time-consuming. See US Senate, Committee on Foreign Relations, *Report on Mutual Legal Assistance Treaty with Italy*, 98th Cong., 2nd Sess., Exec. Rep. 98-36, p. 2 (1984), *reprinted in* 24 ILM 1542 (1985). One commentator argues that the use of letters rogatory is no longer defensible and that police and prosecutors should be able to handle requests directly, avoiding diplomatic channels. Paikin, note 1, *supra*, at p. 256. A modern trend in mutual assistance arrangements seeks to avoid this process by designating central authorities in each State to process requests. See, e.g., Art. 2, US-Italy treaty, note 4, *supra*, §4, Scheme Relating to Mutual Assistance in Criminal Matters within the Commonwealth, *reprinted in* UK Home Office, *International Mutual Assistance in Criminal Matters A Discussion Paper*, Annex B (February 1988). In some cases, direct communication between the authorities concerned is authorized. See, e.g., Art. 15(2), European Convention, note 4, *supra*. In this connexion, it might be noted that with respect to terrorist offences the Council of Europe has recommended that direct communication between the relevant authorities takes place, where permissible. This is so that such offences can be dealt with speedily. See Recommendation No. R (82) 1, in Council of Europe, Committee of Ministers, *Recommendations to Member States 1982* (1984).

[8] A discussion paper by the UK Home Office states simply that mutual assistance "is the means whereby one State provides assistance to another in the investigation and prosecution of criminal offences". See Home Office Discussion Paper, note 7, *supra*, at p. 1. Similarly, another source states that mutual assistance is "any assistance with a view to the tracing, arrest and trial of suspects". See Sandoz, Swinarski & Zimmermann (eds.), *Commentary on the Additional Protocols of 8 June 1977 to the Geneva Conventions of 12 August 1949* 1028 (1987). See also Jones, "International Judicial Assistance: Procedural Chaos and a Program for Reform", 62 Yale L.J. 515 (1953); Grützner, note 1, *supra*, at p. 193.

[9] See *id.*, at p. 234; Mueller, note 4, *supra*, at p. 415.

[10] Paikin, note 1, *supra*, at pp. 234, 254-55. A Canadian court, for example, has noted that: "The enforcement of letters rogatory is always a matter within the discretionary power of the Court . . . [and is] based upon international comity or courtesy proceeding from the law of nations." *Re Westinghouse Electric Corp. and Duquesne Light Co., et al.*, (1977) 78 DLR (3d) 3, 20. The degree of discretion, of course, varies from State to State. One US court has indicated that the district courts' discretion regarding such requests is not terribly wide, holding that a court abused its discretion in denying a request on the grounds of lack of reciprocity and admissibility. The court stated that the liberal intent
(continued on p. 248)

Moreover, to the extent that States have adopted such, domestic laws (and treaties) on the matter vary considerably, both with respect to the types of assistance which may be rendered and with respect to the nature of the officials who may grant assistance.[11]

The differences in laws on the subject of mutual assistance in criminal matters may be attributed partly to the fact that the concept of one State assisting another in criminal proceedings is still a relatively new one and the rules regarding practice in this regard are still evolving. Historically, States considered criminal matters to be strictly within the domestic domain and would not involve themselves in other States' criminal proceedings. However, modern developments in communications and transportation and the increased movement of persons from country to country, which have both coincided with and contributed to the advent of such transnational criminal activity as drug smuggling and other organized crime, corporate offences and terrorism, have led to an increased need for co-operation between States in criminal matters.[12] Generally speaking, European civil law States took the lead in this regard, adopting over the years many treaties on the subject as between themselves,[13] most notably the 1959 European Convention on Mutual Assistance in Criminal Matters.[14] Until recently, the practice in common law and other States regarding mutual assistance arrangements has been much less developed. However, this situation is changing. The countries of the British Commonwealth have developed a Scheme Relating to Mutual Assistance in Criminal Matters, which is similar to the European Convention.[15] Moreover, since 1973 the United States has entered into a series of comprehensive bilateral treaties with other States — of both the common law and civil law systems — on the subject of mutual assistance in criminal matters.[16] And, in 1984, the Asian-African Legal

---

([10] *continued*)
of the drafters of the US legislation means that "[a]s long as the discovered information is intended for use in a foreign proceeding which comports with notions of due process, the requirements of [US law] have been met". *John Deere Ltd. v. Sperry Corp.*, 754 F. 2d 132, 138 (3rd Cir., 1985).

[11] See generally pp. 251-253 (notes 36-50 and accompanying text).
[12] See generally Grützner, note 1, *supra*, at p. 190.
[13] *Id.* at pp. 196-201.
[14] 472 UNTS 185. This Convention, as of 1 January 1987, was in force as between 18 European States and Israel. See Bowman & Harris, *Multilateral Treaties Index and Current Status* 238 (1984) & 4th Supp., p. 61 (1987). On the forms of assistance provided for under the European Convention, see generally pp. 250-251 (notes 25-34 and accompanying text).
[15] See note 7, *supra*.
[16] See, e.g., Treaty on Mutual Legal Assistance in Criminal Matters, 25 May 1973, United States-Switzerland, TIAS 8302, *reprinted in* 12 ILM 916 (1973); Treaty on Mutual Assistance in Criminal Matters, 7 June 1979, United States-Turkey, TIAS 9891; Treaty on Mutual Assistance in Criminal Matters, 12 June 1981, United States-

Consultative Committee promulgated a "Draft of Model Bilateral Arrangements on Mutual Assistance on Letters Rogatory in Criminal Matters" for use by member States.[17] Thus, many States have changed their attitudes with respect to such co-operation and the law in this area is rapidly developing.[18] However, the international system has not yet been able to develop a uniform practice with respect to assistance in criminal matters and no general multilateral convention on the subject has as yet been adopted.[19]

It might be noted that some difficulties in co-operation in criminal matters stem from the differences in the various legal systems with respect to the conduct of criminal proceedings, particularly in the manner of taking evidence[20] and in the applicable privileges of witnesses and other holders of evidence.[21] Recent treaties between the US and civil law countries, however, have demonstrated that the gap between the legal systems can be bridged successfully and are encouraging signs in the search for more extensive co-operation between States.[22] It may be noted that even amongst States with similar legal systems, however, there may be discrepancies in the

---

Netherlands, TIAS 10, 734; United States-Italy treaty, note 4, *supra*; Treaty on Mutual Assistance in Criminal Matters, 18 March 1985, United States-Canada, *reprinted in* 24 ILM 1092 (1985); Treaty Concerning the Cayman Islands and Mutual Assistance in Criminal Matters, 3 July 1986, United States-United Kingdom, *reprinted in* 26 ILM 536 (1987). The US treaties take as their point of departure the European Convention, but are somewhat more sophisticated as regards the types of assistance required. See generally pp. 250-251 & 256 (notes 25-34 & 63-64 and accompanying text); Ellis & Pisani, "The US Treaties on Mutual Assistance in Criminal Matters: A Comparative Analysis", 19 International Lawyer 189 (1985).

[17] Doc AALCC/XXIII/4, *reprinted in* 23 ILM 103 (1984).

[18] In addition to the developments just cited, moreover, the UK is currently reassessing its rather restrictive legislation in this area. See Home Office Discussion Paper, note 7, *supra*. See generally Havers, "Legal Cooperation: A Matter of Necessity", 21 International Lawyer 185, 191 (1987). On current UK law, see pp. 252-253 (notes 43-50 and accompanying text). The UK has, moreover, recently entered into its first significant treaty on the subject (other than an exchange of notes with the FRG concerning police co-operation, 414 UNTS 3), albeit limited in scope to the Cayman Islands. See note 16, *supra*.

[19] At least one commentator has urged the convening of an international conference devoted to the drafting of such a convention. See Bassiouni, "An International Control Scheme for the Prosecution of International Terrorists: An Introduction", in Evans & Murphy (eds.), *Legal Aspects of International Terrorism* 490 (1978).

[20] In particular, this relates to the differences between the adversarial and inquisitorial systems. In civil law States, evidence can only be taken in front of a judge while in common law countries evidence gathering is primarily the task of the parties. See generally Markees, "The Difference in Concept between Civil and Common Law Countries as to Judicial Assistance and Cooperation in Criminal Matters", in Bassiouni & Nanda, note 1, *supra*, at pp. 171-175; Jones, note 8, *supra*, at pp. 520 & 526-27.

[21] On conflicting privileges, see Markees, note 20, *supra*, at pp. 179-84.

[22] With respect to the taking of evidence, for example, under the US-Italy treaty, note 4, *supra*, when evidence is taken in Italy at the behest of the US, it will be done in the presence of a judge. See *Report on Mutual Assistance Treaty*, note 7, *supra*, at p. 9. With respect to privileges, generally treaties and laws on the subject provide that when evidence is taken in the requested State, the privileges of that State will obtain. See, e.g., 18 USC §1782; Art. 14(1), US-Italy treaty, note 4, *supra*.

applicable laws. For example, as will be seen below, the legislation of the UK and the US in this field differ from each other.[23]

2. Interpretation

PARAGRAPH 1: RENDERING ASSISTANCE IN CRIMINAL PROCEEDINGS

"States Parties shall afford one another . . ."

The obligation to render assistance under this Article applies in each given case to *all* States Parties to this Convention. This is because, as noted by the ILC, "part of the required evidence may be located in third States"[24] (a reference, apparently, to those States other than the State in which the proceedings are being held and the State where the crime was committed). Thus, a State which has even a minimal connexion with a particular offence may be requested to supply evidence or provide some other form of assistance to a State which is conducting proceedings against an alleged hostage-taker.

". . . the greatest measure of assistance . . ."

At first glance the obligation imposed upon States Parties by this Article appears to be substantial: they must render to each other the "greatest measure" of assistance in connexion with criminal proceedings. Extrapolating from various laws, as well as treaties (which tend to be more detailed than States' domestic laws on the subject), on mutual assistance, the types of assistance rendered under this Article could include such acts as serving documents,[25] taking testimony,[26] providing documents and records and other articles of evidence,[27] locating persons,[28] transferring persons in custody for

---

[23] See pp. 252-253 (notes 41-47 and accompanying text).
[24] 1972 YBILC, Vol. II, p. 321.
[25] See, e.g., Art. 7, European Convention, note 4, *supra*; Art. 2(2)(a), Asian-African Bilateral Model, note 17, *supra*; Arts. II(2)(d) & XI, US-Canada treaty, note 16, *supra*; Arts. 1(2)(b) & 11, US-Italy treaty, note 4, *supra*; 18 USC §1696.
[26] See, e.g., Art. 3, European Convention, note 4, *supra*; Art. 2(2)(b), Asian-African Bilateral Model, note 17, *supra*; Arts. II(2)(e) & XII, US-Canada treaty, note 16, *supra*; Arts. 1(2)(e) & 14, US-Italy treaty, note 4, *supra*; 18 USC §1782; UK Evidence (Proceedings in Other Jurisdictions) Act 1975, §5.
[27] See, e.g., Art. 3, European Convention, note 4, *supra*; Art. 2(2)(b), Asian-African Bilateral Model, note 17, *supra*; Arts. II(2)(b) & (f) & XII-XIII, US-Canada treaty, note 16, *supra*; Arts. 1(2)(e) & 12-13, US-Italy treaty, note 4, *supra*; 1982 FRG Law on Mutual Assistance in Criminal Matters, §66, *translated in* 24 ILM 945 (1985); 18 USC §1782.
[28] Arts. II(2)(c) & X, US-Canada treaty, note 16, *supra*; Arts. 1(2)(a) & 10, US-Italy treaty, note 4, *supra*.

testimonial purposes,[29] executing requests for searches and seizures,[30] local examination of objects and sites,[31] exchanging information (including from judicial records),[32] immobilizing and forfeiting assets[33] and requesting or compelling non-custodial persons to testify in the requesting State.[34] It is not difficult to see how each of these services can render more effective the prosecution of hostage-takers, particularly when the proceeding is conducted in a State in which the crime did not occur and/or when the accused is part of an international band with members located in more than one State.

However, while all these types of assistance *could* be rendered pursuant to this Article, it is unclear as to which of them, if any, *must* be afforded by one State Party to another. Upon closer scrutiny the exact nature of the obligation imposed by this Article becomes difficult to discern. This Article creates the treaty link necessary to impose an obligation to render assistance in criminal matters, but, unlike those treaties which are specifically devoted to the subject, it does not delimit the parameters of that obligation by setting forth the measures which must be rendered. The Article does specifically require States to supply all evidence at their disposal to a requesting State, and the transmission of evidence is certainly the most important type of assistance which can be rendered. Indeed, most of the types of assistance listed above are related to the supply of evidence. However, as discussed below, since the types of evidence which must be transmitted are similarly not listed in this Article, questions may arise as to when evidence is at a State's "disposal". Further, the supply of evidence is not, in any event, the "greatest measure" of assistance conceivable. As earlier indicated, there is no definite content to the words "assistance in criminal matters"; the term may apply to any act designed to assist the criminal processes of another State.[35] But domestic laws (and treaties) on the subject, although containing many similarities, vary considerably as to the types of assistance they authorize.

For example, in the Federal Republic of Germany legislation specifically authorizes certain types of assistance to be rendered to

---

[29] See, e.g., Art. 11, European Convention, note 4, *supra*; Arts. II(2)(g) & XV, US-Canada treaty, note 16, *supra*; Arts. 1(2)(f) & 16, US-Italy treaty, note 4, *supra*; FRG law, note 27, *supra*, §62.

[30] See, e.g., Art. 5, European Convention, note 4, *supra*; Arts. II(2)(h) & XVI, US-Canada treaty, note 16, *supra*; FRG law, note 27, *supra*, §67.

[31] See, e.g., Art. II(2)(a), US-Canada treaty, note 16, *supra*.

[32] See, e.g., Arts. 13 & 21-22, European Convention, note 4, *supra*; Arts. II(2)(b) & XIII, US-Canada treaty, note 16, *supra*.

[33] See, e.g., Arts. 1(2)(g) & 16, US-Italy treaty, note 4, *supra*; Arts. 1(2)(g) & 16, US-UK treaty, note 16, *supra*.

[34] See, e.g., Arts. 10 & 11, European Convention, note 4, *supra*; Arts. 1(2)(f) & 15, US-Italy treaty, note 4, *supra*.

[35] See p. 247 (note 8 and accompanying text).

other States, including the surrender of objects "which may serve as evidence in foreign proceedings",[36] the search for and seizure of objects which may be subject to surrender[37] and the temporary transfer of a person held in custody for the purposes of testimony, confrontation or inspection by a foreign court (if, *inter alia*, that person consents).[38] In addition, the statute has a general clause which allows for all other forms of assistance that are not mentioned specifically.[39] This would apparently include the service of documents and the examination of non-custodial witnesses in the FRG and the sending of a record of that examination to the foreign court.[40] In the United States, legislation exists which authorizes district courts to order a person to give his testimony or statement or to "produce a document or other thing" for use in a foreign court.[41] District courts may also order that a person be served with any document issued in connexion with a proceeding in a foreign tribunal.[42] In the United Kingdom, a Secretary of State may require a police magistrate or justice of the peace to take evidence for the purposes of any criminal matter pending in any court or tribunal in any foreign State. The evidence must be taken from a witness in the same manner as if he had appeared on a charge against a defendant for an indictable offence in the UK. A witness may be compelled to attend and give evidence and answer questions.[43] Moreover, the High Court, Court of Session or High Court of Justice in Northern Ireland may, for the benefit of a criminal proceeding in a foreign court, order the examination of a witness and the production of documents.[44] It should be noted that UK law does not authorize the transmission to a foreign State of types of evidence other than documents, i.e., physical evidence such as the *instrumenta sceleris*.

From this brief comparison, it can be seen that there are many differences between the laws of these three countries. The legislation of the FRG is quite detailed, specifically authorizing certain types of assistance and impliedly authorizing many others. Under that law,

[36] FRG law, note 27, *supra*, §66.
[37] *Id.* at §67.
[38] *Id.* at §62.
[39] *Id.* at §59.
[40] These forms of assistance are provided for in Articles 3 and 7 of the European Convention, note 4, *supra*. See Council of Europe, *Explanatory Report on the European Convention on Mutual Assistance in Criminal Matters* 14 (1969). Insofar as the FRG is party to the European Convention, it may be assumed that these types of assistance are permissible under the FRG law. The FRG law limits assistance which may be granted only to those forms which would violate basic principles of the German legal system. FRG law, note 27, *supra*, §72.
[41] 18 USC §1782.
[42] 18 USC §1696.
[43] Extradition Act 1873, §5.
[44] Evidence (Proceedings in Other Jurisdictions) Act 1975, §5.

moreover, assistance may be granted and requested both by courts and by other governmental authorities.[45] The legislation of the US, by way of contrast, authorizes fewer types of assistance than does the FRG statute and, while any court or authority or other interested person may request the assistance, it may be granted only by a court.[46] The UK legislation is even more restrictive as to the types of assistance which may be granted — limited only to certain types of evidence — and, moreover, provides that the request must be made both by and to a court.[47] Both the UK and US require that the assistance must be needed for use by a court or tribunal,[48] while the FRG statute states that assistance may be granted regardless of whether the foreign proceedings are conducted by a court or by a governmental authority.[49] It might be noted, moreover, that some States' laws on the subject also provide exceptions and limitations even as regards those types of assistance which are generally authorized. For example, the UK legislation mandates refusal of assistance with respect to political offences.[50]

What, then, is the nature of a Party's obligation under this Article? Two possibilities exist. The first is that States must only render in good faith those types of assistance which are provided for under their domestic laws. Alternatively, there may be an objective content to this obligation, i.e., there may be certain types of assistance which States Parties must render to each other pursuant to this Article such that if their laws do not authorize such assistance, they must be changed accordingly. This is not an abstract inquiry. The possibility exists that one State Party may, in connexion with the prosecution of a hostage-taker, request that another Party (with which it has no mutual assistance treaty) render to it a form of assistance for which there is no provision in the requested Party's laws. While it would seem that this would not often be the case with the more common forms of mutual assistance, such as the taking of testimony, the problem could arise with more sophisticated forms of assistance, such as the transfer of persons in custody or the execution of requests for searches and

---

[45] FRG law, note 27, *supra*, §59.
[46] 18 USC §§1696 & 1782.
[47] See Extradition Act 1873, §5; Evidence (Proceedings in Other Jurisdictions) Act 1975, §5.
[48] *Id.*; 18 USC §§1696 & 1782.
[49] FRG law, note 27, *supra*, §59.
[50] See Extradition Act 1873, §5; Evidence (Proceedings in Other Jurisdictions) Act 1975, §5(3). Moreover, assistance will not be granted if it would prejudice British security. *Id.* at §3(2). Some States, moreover, will only grant assistance upon receiving assurances of reciprocity, i.e., that the requesting State would provide similar forms of assistance to the requested State if their roles were reversed. See Home Office Discussion Paper, note 7, *supra*, at p. 3. On exceptions contained in mutual assistance treaties, see note 84, *infra*.

seizures. The question thus arises as to whether a refusal by the requested Party constitutes a breach of this Convention.

On balance, it appears that the first interpretation mentioned above must obtain and that States must only provide such assistance as is generally permissible under their laws. In this connexion, it might be noted that the corresponding Articles of the Hague and Montreal Conventions provide with respect to a request for assistance that: "The law of the State requested shall apply in all cases." Similar provisions are contained in other conventions dealing with international crimes.[51] Moreover, the Rome Convention, drafted after the Hostages Convention, provides that assistance between States Parties shall be rendered "in conformity with any treaties on mutual assistance that may exist between them" or, in "the absence of such treaties ... in accordance with their national law."[52] Under those instruments, therefore, no objective content to the obligation to render assistance exists. In the absence of a relevant treaty, States must only render such assistance as is generally possible under their laws and, moreover, those laws need not necessarily be changed in order to comply with the conventions. For reasons which do not appear in the record, that qualification was omitted from the New York Convention,[53] and the draftsmen of this Convention did not restore it. While it could be argued that this omission indicates that the draftsmen wanted to establish a broader and more uniform obligation that would not hinge strictly upon the laws of each individual State Party, there is no indication from the *travaux préparatoires* that this was the case. Although there is little recorded discussion concerning this Article from the drafting of this Convention, there is reason to believe that the draftsmen of the New York Convention, at least, viewed the obligation contained in the corresponding provision of that instrument as identical to that contained in the ICAO instruments, notwithstanding their deletion of the reference to the requested State's laws.[54] Moreover, as noted below, the Chairman of the Sixth Committee Drafting Group, when referring specifically to the

---

[51] See, e.g., Art. 88(3), 1977 Protocol Additional to the Geneva Conventions of 12 August 1949, and Relating to the Protection of Victims of International Armed Conflicts, Misc. 19 (1977), Cmnd 6927, *reprinted in* 16 ILM 1391 (1977).

[52] See also Art. 9, Convention Against Torture and Other Cruel, Inhuman or Degrading Treatment or Punishment, UN Doc A/RES/39/46 (1984), *reprinted in* 23 ILM 1027 (1984) & 24 ILM 535 (1985), which provides, with respect to paragraph 1 of that Article which is identical to the provision currently under consideration, that: "States Parties shall carry out their obligations under paragraph 1 of this Article in conformity with any treaties on mutual judicial assistance that may exist between them."

[53] One source states that it was omitted "presumably on the ground that [it] is redundant". See Bloomfield & FitzGerald, *Crimes Against Internationally Protected Persons: Prevention and Punishment* 116 (1975).

[54] The ILC noted that its draft of the Article "substantially reproduces" the provisions of the earlier conventions. 1972 YBILC, Vol. II, p. 321.

obligation to supply evidence as contained in the New York Convention, indicated that the requested State's laws will guide whether or not a particular request should be granted,[55] thus evincing a generally deferential posture regarding existing State laws on the subject.

The compelling nature of this conclusion becomes evident upon an attempt to construct an objective content for this Article. What criteria could possibly be used that would justify concluding that certain types of assistance must be rendered by States Parties? Suppose, for example, it is argued that the fact that the draftsmen chose wording for this Article which is very similar to that contained in Article 1 of the European Convention on Mutual Assistance in Criminal Matters (which requires States Parties to afford one another the "widest measure of assistance")[56] indicates that they intended that States Parties to this Convention must render to each other those types of assistance which are specifically listed in the European Convention. One problem with this argument is that the European Convention does not really represent the "greatest measure" of assistance possible. Recent bilateral treaties entered into between the United States and other States, for example, call for greater measures of assistance than the European Convention.[57] We are then led to the argument that the US treaties should represent the objective content of the obligation to render assistance under this Article since they are, perhaps, the "greatest measure of assistance".

Of course, neither of these arguments is particularly convincing in and of itself. The discrepancies between States' laws in this regard are too great to assume that some objective content can be given to this obligation without that content being set forth specifically. In addition to the differences noted above, a few examples from State laws and treaties suffice to establish this point. In its introduction to its draft model bilateral treaty on mutual assistance, the Asian-African Legal Consultative Committee stated that no provision had been made in the draft for "compelling persons to appear before the courts or tribunals of the requesting States in response to the process issued, or for the obligation of the requested State to transfer persons to the requesting State for that purpose". Although "[s]uch provisions do exist in the European Convention", the introduction continues, it was "felt that in the context of the present needs of the Asian-African region, it would be far too ambitious to attempt mutual co-operation at the level existing between a group of Western European nations".[58]

---

[55] See p. 259 (note 75 and accompanying text).
[56] See note 4, *supra*.
[57] See generally notes 16 & 25-34, *supra*.
[58] Doc AALCC/XXIII/4, *reprinted in* 23 ILM 78, 81 (1984).

Differences in laws do not only exist as between developed and developing States, however. The law of the FRG, for example, specifically authorizes searches and seizures at the request of another State.[59] In the UK, however, there is no authority for the execution of searches and seizures at the request of a foreign authority for the benefit of foreign proceedings.[60] Even as regards some types of assistance which are generally authorized, moreover, differences may exist. Under the law of the FRG a person in custody has the right to refuse to be transported to another State for the purposes of testimony or confrontation.[61] Under the treaty between the US and Italy, however, no such right of refusal exists.[62] Similarly, under the European Convention a non-custodial witness cannot be penalized for failing to respond to a summons to give testimony in a foreign proceeding.[63] Under the US-Italy treaty, however, penalties can be imposed.[64]

If this Article were intended to require specific forms of assistance which would perhaps require changes in the laws of some Parties it would presumably have contained language similar to that contained in Article 2 and Article 5, stating, for example, that: "States Parties shall take such measures as are necessary under their laws to ensure that they may comply with a request from another State: (a) to transport to that State a person in custody for testimonial purposes; (b) to serve documents in their territory . . ." It must be concluded that, as with the ICAO instruments and the Rome Convention, a requested State's laws will govern all requests, both as to the types of assistance generally permissible and as to exceptions and limitations.[65] At the same time, however, it must be kept in mind that this Article imposes an obligation upon Parties to provide each other with assistance in criminal proceedings. That obligation is illusory if a State's laws are so restrictive as to require it to deny assistance in most

---

[59] FRG law, note 27, *supra*, §67.

[60] It may be noted, however, that as of February 1988 this situation was under review. See Home Office Discussion Paper, note 7, *supra*, at p. 3.

[61] FRG law, note 27, *supra*, §62(1)(1).

[62] Art. 16, US-Italy treaty, note 4, *supra*.

[63] Art. 12, European Convention, note 4, *supra*.

[64] Art. 15, US-Italy treaty, note 4, *supra*. This Article provides that the "Requested State . . . shall compel that person to appear and testify in the Requesting State by means of the procedures for compelling the appearance and testimony of witnesses in the Requested State". A person who fails to appear "shall be subject to sanctions under the law of the Requested State as if that person had failed to appear in similar circumstances in that State". Such sanctions, however, shall not include removal of that person to the Requesting State.

[65] On limitations, see generally p. 253 (note 50 and accompanying text). With respect to the political offence exception, it might be noted that while invocation of that exception might not be against the letter of this Convention, it is certainly against its spirit. Similarly, a requirement of reciprocity would seem to have little place with respect to the offences under this Convention.

circumstances. States are under an obligation to comply with their treaty obligations in good faith and they should, therefore, endeavour to ensure that their laws are broad enough to allow them to render such assistance as is compatible with their fundamental principles of law.

". . . in connexion with criminal proceedings brought in respect of the offences set forth in article 1 . . ."

The obligation to render assistance is applicable whenever "criminal proceedings" are brought with respect to an act of hostage-taking or attempted hostage-taking. It is apparent from this language that the obligation to render assistance is not only applicable to actual trials of alleged offenders. But what precisely is meant by "criminal proceedings"? According to the Harvard Research in International Law, the definition is very wide indeed: a "criminal proceeding" is "any proceeding before a tribunal of a State, directed to the investigation of a crime or to conviction or punishment for a crime".[66] During the drafting of the New York Convention, the Chairman of the Sixth Committee drafting group stated with respect to the identical provision in that Convention that "'assistance in criminal proceedings' in paragraph 1 should be understood as covering assistance not only in connection with the trial of a case but also in connection with the proceedings leading up to trial".[67] While most relevant to an actual prosecution, the obligation to render assistance would thus seem to apply to any pre-trial proceeding held in connexion with an offence under this Convention, including preliminary hearings and extradition hearings. Given the non-limitative nature of the language of this Article, moreover, it would appear that the obligation also obtains to post-trial proceedings such as sentencing.

It should also be noted that the obligation to render assistance is applicable only with respect to proceedings "brought" in connexion with an offence of hostage-taking. This language indicates that a proceeding must actually have been instituted before the obligation to render assistance is applicable, i.e., the obligation does not pertain to a purely preliminary investigation. It should be noted that there is no inherent limitation of mutual assistance under international law to proceedings which have already been instituted. For example, the treaty between the US and Canada on the subject states that the

---

[66] Art. 1(g), Harvard Research Draft Convention, note 3, *supra*, at p. 41. This would include investigations by a Grand Jury or a *juge d'instruction*, but not by police or prosecutors. *Id.*

[67] UN GAOR, 28th Sess., C.6 (1437th mtg.), para. 49, UN Doc A/C.6/SR.1437 (1973).

assistance contemplated therein should be rendered in respect of "all matters relating to the investigation, prosecution, and suppression of offences".[68] And the US generally allows assistance in preliminary stages even before indictment.[69] On the other hand, the UK statutes on the matter are only applicable to proceedings which have already been instituted.[70]

". . . including the supply of all evidence at their disposal necessary for the proceedings."

This phrase provides some degree of specificity to the obligation to render assistance. The ICAO instruments do not contain a phrase such as this; it was added by the ILC in identical terms to the corresponding provision of the New York Convention. After noting the addition, the Chairman of the ILC Working Group stated to the Commission simply that the phrase was intended to "overcome the difficulties which the State concerned would have in proving the case against the offender if it did not receive the evidence which other States had at their disposal".[71] Although there is little material concerning this addition in the drafting records, it can be assumed that the draftsmen of that instrument felt that the obligation to render the "greatest measure" of assistance was too vague and should be given some content. However, the obligation to supply evidence seems as far as they were willing or able to go in this regard.[72] In any event, it can readily be seen that the single most important type of assistance that one State can render to another is the supply of evidence, whether in the form of testimony taken in the requested State, documents, records or some other form of physical evidence such as the *instrumenta sceleris*.

---

[68] Art. II(1), US-Canada treaty, note 16, *supra*.

[69] Paikin, note 1, *supra*, at p. 255.

[70] See Extradition Act 1873, §5; Evidence (Proceedings in Other Jurisdictions) Act 1975, §5.

[71] 1972 YBILC, Vol. I, p. 228.

[72] It does not appear from the drafting records of this Convention that any specific attempts were made to define more clearly the obligation to render assistance. It might be noted, however, that the addition by the draftsmen of the New York Convention of the specific obligation to supply evidence was an achievement that the draftsmen of the Hague Convention were not able to obtain. The chairman of the ICAO subcommittee charged with preparing the initial draft of the Hague Convention stated that, despite lengthy discussions on the matter, it had not been possible to set out in more detail the obligations of States under the corresponding provision in that Convention, and that the draft was limited to the idea that States should give each other the "greatest possible measure of assistance". ICAO Doc 8877-LC/161, p. 79 (1970). During the Diplomatic Conference, various proposals were submitted to develop that provision further. See ICAO Doc 8979-LC/165-2, p. 44 (1972); ICAO Doc 8979-LC/165-1, p. 166 (1972). However, these proposals were opposed by some States on the ground, *inter alia*, that they might be interpreted as restrictive. See, e.g., the comments of the representatives of Spain and the United States, *id*. at p. 97.

What, then, is the precise nature of a State's obligations with regard to the supply of evidence to a requesting State? The words "all evidence" indicate that a State is not entitled to withhold any evidence which might be found in its territory. However, questions may arise as to when evidence is at a State's "disposal" and as to which State may determine what evidence is "necessary". During the drafting of this Convention, this latter issue was taken up by the representative of the Philippines who "requested clarification regarding who was to determine what evidence was necessary".[73] In response, the representative of the FRG stated that in his opinion only the requesting State could judge what evidence was required.[74] However, during the drafting of the New York Convention the Chairman of the Sixth Committee Drafting Group stated with reference to this phrase that, as a point of "clarification [which] should be made to avoid any possible future error in interpretation ... [the provision] would require States Parties to supply only such evidence as was at their disposal in accordance with their national legislation".[75] Obviously, the initial determination as to what evidence is "necessary" will be made by the appropriate authorities of the State in which the proceedings are taking place who will then make their request in accordance with that determination. However, the decision as to what evidence will actually be forwarded will be made by the requested State in accordance with its laws.

Thus, as with the rendering of other assistance, the nature of the obligation to supply evidence depends upon the content of the requested State's laws. While it could be argued that the above statement by the Chairman of the Sixth Committee drafting group should be interpreted as meaning that a particular item of evidence is at a requested State's "disposal" for the purpose of transmission for use in a foreign State proceeding whenever that evidence could normally be gathered for use in the requested State's own courts, such an interpretation seems somewhat strained. It would appear rather that evidence is at a State's "disposal" for use in a foreign State proceeding only when its national legislation authorizes the gathering and use of such evidence for that purpose. If, for example, as is the case in the UK, a State's laws do not allow searches and seizures at the request of a foreign State, then a State's refusal to supply such evidence would not appear to be a breach of this Convention.

With respect to the form of the evidence rendered, the ILC stated that "[c]learly if the alleged offender is to be tried in a State other than that in which the crime was committed it will be necessary to make

---

[73] Second Report of the Hostages Committee, p. 53, para. 43.
[74] *Id.* at para. 44.
[75] UN GAOR, 28th Sess., C.6 (1438th mtg.), para. 49, UN Doc A/C.6/SR.1438 (1973).

testimony available to the court hearing the case and in such form as the law of that State requires".[76] This indicates that the requested State must transmit the evidence, in so far as its own legislation allows, in the form needed by the requesting State, even if such form is different from that usually employed by the requested State. This requirement, while perhaps somewhat burdensome to the requested State, will help ensure that the evidence rendered will actually assist the foreign proceedings. It may be noted, moreover, that similar requirements are commonly contained in treaties and domestic laws on mutual assistance.[77] An example of this would be the swearing in of a witness under oath in a State where this is not usually done, but which has no fundamental obstacle to such in its laws.[78]

One final issue which arises with respect to the obligation to supply evidence is whether evidence should be transmitted (or some other service performed) even if no request is submitted therefor. One commentator has written that judicial assistance should be rendered only if it is requested and only to the extent specified in the request. Assistance in addition to that requested, he asserts, could "interfere with the course of the criminal proceeding and possibly disturb the *modus procendi* intended by the requesting authority".[79] Indeed, laws and treaties on the subject commonly provide that evidence will be transmitted, or some other form of assistance rendered, only upon the request of a court or other appropriate official of a foreign State.[80] It would seem, however, that a State Party which is aware of evidence in its territory relevant to a foreign criminal proceeding concerning an act of hostage-taking should notify the appropriate State of its existence, thus giving that State an opportunity to formulate a request.

PARAGRAPH 2: PRESERVATION OF OTHER OBLIGATIONS REGARDING MUTUAL ASSISTANCE

"The provisions of paragraph 1 of this article shall not affect obligations concerning mutual judicial assistance embodied in any other treaty."

This paragraph makes it clear that the provisions of paragraph 1

---

[76] 1972 YBILC, Vol. II, p. 321.

[77] See, e.g., 18 USC §1782, which provides that a district court order requiring the gathering of evidence for use in a foreign proceeding "may prescribe the practice and procedure which may be in whole or in part the practice and procedure of the foreign country ... for the taking of testimony or statement or producing the document or other thing".

[78] See, e.g., Art. 3, European Convention, note 4, *supra*.

[79] Grützner, note 1, *supra*, at pp. 228-29.

[80] See, e.g., 28 USC §1782; FRG law, note 27, *supra*, §59; Art. 1, US-Italy treaty, note 4, *supra*.

shall not affect any other treaty obligations that a State may have with respect to mutual assistance. Similar provisions are contained in the earlier anti-terrorism conventions, and this paragraph was included in the original FRG draft. The representative of the Netherlands to the Hostages Committee asserted that this paragraph serves no purpose.[81] Other delegations, however, replied that since existing treaties on mutual assistance may be more complete, the terms thereof should take precedence over this paragraph and that this should be made clear.[82] It does not appear that much more attention was directed to this paragraph and it was included in this Convention unchanged. It may be noted that some treaties on the subject of mutual assistance contain similar provisions.[83] However, it does not appear that this Article is strictly necessary, since it is difficult to discern how an obligation so general in its terms could affect any existing treaty on the subject.[84]

---

[81] Second Report of the Hostages Committee, p. 52, para. 36. A similar comment was made by the Israeli delegate to the Sixth Committee during the drafting of the New York Convention. UN GAOR, 28th Sess., C.6 (1420th mtg.), para. 64, UN Doc A/C.6/SR.1420 (1973).

[82] See, e.g., the comments of the representatives of the Philippines, FRG & France in Second Report of the Hostages Committee, p. 52, para. 37, pp. 52-53, para. 38 & p. 53, para. 39, respectively.

[83] See, e.g., Art. 26, European Convention, note 4, *supra*; Art. 19, US-Italy treaty, note 4, *supra*.

[84] It may be noted, however, that one effect of this provision is to obviate in advance any argument that might be made that the conditions and limitations under existing treaties on mutual assistance are somehow nullified by this Article. Treaties on mutual assistance generally contain exceptions to the obligations imposed therein. For example, many such treaties contain provisions which allow a refusal to execute a request for judicial assistance when that assistance would be detrimental to the essential interests of a State Party. Article 2(b) of the European Convention (note 4, *supra*), for example, allows a refusal when "the requested Party considers that execution of the request is likely to prejudice the sovereignty, security, *ordre public* or other essential interests of its country". See also Art. 3(1)(a), US-Switzerland treaty, note 16, *supra*; Art. 5(1)(a), US-Italy treaty, note 4, *supra*. Some treaties also authorize refusal when there is a danger of double jeopardy. See Art. 3(1)(b), US-Switzerland treaty, note 16, *supra*. Treaties on the subject, moreover, often provide that assistance may or shall be refused in connexion with military or political offences. See Art. 2(a), European Convention, note 4, *supra*; Art. 2(1)(c)(1) & (2) & (3), US-Switzerland treaty, note 16, *supra*; Art. 5(1)(b), US-Italy treaty, note 4, *supra*. All these exceptions would seem to be preserved under this Article. However, as earlier noted (note 65, *supra*), there would seem to be little room for invocation of the political offence exception with respect to offences under this Convention. In this connexion, it might be noted that the European Convention on the Suppression of Terrorism specifically prohibits a refusal to grant a request for mutual assistance on the ground that it concerns a political offence.

Article 12

RELATIONSHIP BETWEEN THE CONVENTION AND THE LAWS OF ARMED CONFLICT

In so far as the Geneva Conventions of 1949 for the protection of war victims or the Additional Protocols to those Conventions are applicable to a particular act of hostage-taking, and in so far as States Parties to this Convention are bound under those conventions to prosecute or hand over the hostage-taker, the present Convention shall not apply to an act of hostage-taking committed in the course of armed conflicts as defined in the Geneva Conventions of 1949 and the Protocols thereto, including armed conflicts mentioned in article 1, paragraph 4, of Additional Protocol I of 1977, in which peoples are fighting against colonial domination and alien occupation and against racist régimes in the exercise of their right of self-determination, as enshrined in the Charter of the United Nations and the Declaration of Principles of International Law concerning Friendly Relations and Co-operation among States in accordance with the Charter of the United Nations.

1. INTRODUCTION

This Article provides that the Hostages Convention will not apply to an act of hostage-taking committed during an armed conflict if (and only if) that act is covered by the four 1949 Geneva Conventions or the two 1977 Additional Protocols thereto[1] such that the offender must be prosecuted or extradited pursuant to those instruments.

The tortuous development of this Article presents an interesting study of the dynamics of multilateral treaty making, particularly when the proposed convention is to deal with issues which are of a highly controversial and political nature and is meant to be universally accepted. As discussed in greater detail below, the Article evolved from proposals, submitted by some developing States, designed

---

[1] Convention for the Amelioration of the Condition of the Wounded and Sick in Armed Forces in the Field, 75 UNTS 31 (Convention I); Convention for the Amelioration of the Condition of Wounded, Sick, and Shipwrecked Members of Armed Forces at Sea, 75 UNTS 85 (Convention II); Convention Relative to the Treatment of Prisoners of War, 75 UNTS 135 (Convention III); Convention Relative to the Protection of Civilian Persons in Time of War, 75 UNTS 287 (Convention IV or Civilians Convention); Protocol Additional to the Geneva Conventions of 12 August 1949, and Relating to the Protection of Victims of International Armed Conflicts, Misc. 19 (1977), Cmnd 6927, *reprinted in* 16 ILM 1391 (1977) (Protocol I); Protocol Additional to the Geneva Conventions of 12 August 1949, and Relating to the Protection of Victims of Non-International Armed Conflicts, Misc. 19 (1977), Cmnd 6927, *reprinted in* 16 ILM 1442 (1977) (Protocol II).

specifically to exclude from the scope of the instrument acts of hostage-taking which are committed by national liberation movements.[2] The representatives of some States even suggested initially that such acts were in fact permissible under international law. These somewhat extreme positions were totally unacceptable to Western and some other States which wanted nothing less than for the Convention to apply to all acts of hostage-taking, wherever and by whomever committed. Given the wide difference between these two starting points, this issue became the most difficult and time consuming problem faced by the draftsmen.[3] Indeed, it would not be too much to say that this issue threatened the prospect of ever reaching agreement on a draft convention.[4]

As discussed below, by a series of compromises agreement was finally reached on acceptable wording for this Article. As a result of these many compromises, however, the language employed herein is less clear than it could have been and leads to some difficulties in interpretation. Ambiguities in this language will be discussed in the interpretation section.

It is, perhaps, because of its less than precise language that this Article has been misinterpreted by some commentators. One writer states that this Article provides that the Hostages Convention "is not applicable for an act of hostage-taking committed during armed conflicts in the sense of the Geneva Conventions of 1949 and their additional protocols, including struggles for national liberation and self-determination." This commentator thus concludes that "the convention becomes actually void of any suppressive significance since most hostage-taking terrorists define themselves and are widely accepted as freedom fighters."[5] Two other writers go even further and

---

[2] See pp. 267-268 (notes 13-17 and accompanying text). The Article had its actual genesis in Article 10(1) of the original FRG draft, which stated that the Hostages Conventions would not "affect" the Geneva Conventions, the Hague Conventions, the Montreal Convention or the New York Convention. This "collision clause" was not contained in the final draft.

[3] This fact is noted by commentators who were involved in the drafting of the Convention. See Rosenstock, p. 183; Verwey, p. 69; McDonald, p. 550. It is also reflected in the amount of debate devoted to the issue and in the various reports of the Hostages Committee. See, e.g., Second Report of the Hostages Committee, pp. 5-6, paras. 15-22. For behind-the-scenes examinations of the development of this Article, see Verwey and McDonald.

[4] See generally the comments of the representative of Democratic Yemen, p. 268 (note 17 and accompanying text). As far as Western States were concerned, McDonald reports that in 1978, the year of the Hostages Committee's second session, some delegations thought that further progress on the Convention would be impossible because of deadlock on this issue and felt that it would be best to abandon the drafting process. It was finally agreed, however, to give the effort one more chance in the third session. At the beginning of the third session, a US representative estimated the chances of success at 10%. McDonald, pp. 550-51.

[5] See Gal-Or, *International Cooperation to Suppress Terrorism* 96 (1985).

state that this Article recognizes that the taking of hostages by national liberation movements is a legitimate means of their struggle.[6]

Despite the ambiguous language of this Article, neither of these interpretations can stand. The latter interpretation is manifestly incorrect and cannot be justified by any reasonable reading of this Article. The clear intent of this Article is that all acts of hostage-taking shall be punished, either pursuant to this Convention or pursuant to the Geneva instruments as "grave breaches" thereof. It is thus difficult to discern how acts of hostage-taking by national liberation movements, even if covered by the Geneva instruments rather than by this Convention, are "legitimized". The former interpretation is also incorrect. As drafted, the Article does not exclude from the scope of this Convention all acts of hostage-taking committed during armed conflicts. It excludes such acts only when States Parties have the obligation pursuant to the Geneva instruments to prosecute or extradite the alleged offender.[7] As will be seen below, there will be many cases wherein acts of hostage-taking committed during armed conflicts will not result in such an obligation pursuant to the Geneva instruments and will, therefore, be covered by this Convention. This Convention thus applies not only in peacetime, but it fills in gaps which may exist in the prohibition against the taking of hostages during armed conflicts. With particular respect to acts of hostage-taking committed during struggles for national liberation, i.e., those "in which peoples are fighting against colonial domination and alien occupation and against racist régimes", it is possible, at least in theory, that such acts may fall within the scope of Protocol I in such a way as to result in the obligation *aut dedere aut judicare*. However, as discussed below, it will, in fact, be the rare case which is so covered, and most acts of hostage-taking committed during such struggles will, therefore, fall within the scope of this Convention. In any event, it

---

[6] See Wardlaw, *Political Terrorism* 113 (1982); Aston, "The United Nations Convention Against the Taking of Hostages: Realistic or Rhetoric?", 5 Terr. J. 139, 156 (1981-82). These commentators thus conclude that there is a conflict between this Article and Article 75(2) of Protocol I which prohibits the taking of hostages, including by national liberation movements. However, no such conflict exists since, as the following discussion indicates, this Article does not in any way legitimize hostage-taking by national liberation groups.

[7] Other commentators take this view. See Rosenstock, p. 184; Verwey, p. 92; Rosenne, p. 137; Murphy, *The United Nations and the Control of International Violence* 195 (1983). One commentator, while regretting what he calls the "rhetorical and symbolic" reinforcement in Article 12 of the idea that wars of national liberation are international conflicts, similarly notes that Article 12 allows for no gaps in the rule that acts of hostage-taking are subject to the obligation *aut dedere aut judicare*. See Sofaer, "Terrorism and the Law", 64 Foreign Affairs 901, 915-16 (1986). This is the view of the US government. See *Message from the President on the International Convention Against the Taking of Hostages*, S. Exec. Doc N., 96th Cong., 2d Sess., p. 2 (1980). See also Nash, "Contemporary Practice of the United States Relating to International Law", 74 AJIL 418, 420-21 (1980).

might be noted that, contrary to the suggestion of the first commentator mentioned above, it would make little difference how a group defines itself. While there is an element of uncertainty in the words "colonial domination", etc., they clearly exclude most armed struggles not involving the forces of two States.[8] Acts of hostage-taking by other insurgent groups (regardless of their self-designation as "freedom fighters") have not even a theoretical possibility of falling within the scope of Protocol I, and must, therefore, fall within the scope of the Hostages Convention.

Another criticism of this Article is that it goes some way towards blurring the lines between acts of terrorism and wartime delicts by combatants. This Article is, in fact, the only provision in any of the anti-terrorism conventions which deals with the interrelationship between international criminal law and the laws of armed conflict as they relate to national liberation movements.[9] One commentator has criticized the Article on the grounds that it leaves the door open to an argument that "the structure and language of Article 12 represent some measure of acceptance that members of national liberation movements are combatants, not terrorists".[10] Indeed, if an act of hostage-taking by a national liberation movement is covered by the laws of armed conflict in such a way as to impose an obligation to extradite or prosecute, the offenders will be entitled, as combatants, to prisoner of war status and all the attendant benefits granted by Convention III and Protocol I.[11] However, this situation is created not by the Hostages Convention but by Protocol I. This Article simply recognizes the developments in the laws of war — whether they are desirable ones or not — which could lead to a situation in which such acts fall under Protocol I.

Development of the Article

During the course of the first session of the Hostages Committee, it became clear that States were very far apart on the issue of the applicability of the draft convention to acts of hostage-taking committed by national liberation groups. The debate in this regard developed along similar lines as had the General Assembly debates on

---

[8] See p. 295 (note 102 and accompanying text).

[9] On this interrelationship generally, see Hailbronner, "International Terrorism and the Laws of War", 25 Ger. YBIL 169 (1982).

[10] See Sofaer, note 7, *supra*, at p. 916. See also Friedlander, "Unmuzzling the Dogs of War", 7 Terr. J. 169, 171 (1984-5).

[11] Pursuant to Article 44(4) of Protocol I, moreover, even a combatant who forfeits his right to POW status by failing to carry his arms openly during each military engagement and "during such time as he is visible to the adversary" in a deployment preceding an attack, shall be entitled to "protections equivalent in all respects to those accorded to prisoners of war by the Third Convention and by this Protocol."

terrorism in general.[12] The representative of Syria, voicing the concerns of many other developing countries, supported to some extent by Eastern-bloc States, asserted that "acts perpetrated by criminals under ordinary law could not be placed on equal footing with the struggle of national liberation movements which, by their very nature and their objectives, were entirely different."[13] Other comments along these lines were followed by concrete proposals to exclude from the Convention acts of hostage-taking committed by national liberation groups. The delegations of Lesotho and Tanzania, later joined by those of Algeria, Egypt, Guinea, Libya and Nigeria, proposed that the following provision be included in the Convention:

> For the purposes of this Convention, the term "taking of hostages" shall not include any act or acts carried out in the process of national liberation against colonial rule, racist and foreign regimes, by liberation movements recognized by the United Nations or regional organizations.[14]

In support of this proposal, the representative of Tanzania not only argued that the Convention should be inapplicable to acts of hostage-taking committed by national liberation groups, but suggested (as did the representatives of some other States) that such acts were permissible under international law. He argued that "under no circumstances [should the Convention] be capable of being invoked against national liberation movements which took their oppressors hostage in the course of a struggle against a colonial Government or a racist foreign régime."[15] The representative of Lesotho suggested that

---

[12] See generally §3, *supra*, in Part I (pp. 28-45).

[13] First Report of the Hostages Committee, p. 36, para. 31. Other representatives seemed concerned that the Convention would impair the right of self-determination of those persons fighting against "colonialism, alien domination, racial discrimination and *apartheid*". See, e.g, the comments of the representatives of Iran, Algeria, Poland, Libya and Yugoslavia, *id.* at p. 41, para. 20, p. 30, para. 4, p. 69, para. 6, p. 76, para. 12, and p. 28, para. 12, respectively.

[14] UN Doc A/AC.188/L.5, in First Report of the Hostages Committee, p. 111. See also the similar proposal of Syria. UN Doc A/AC.188/L.10, in *id.* at p. 112. As noted earlier, similar attempts were made to remove the actions of national liberation groups from the scope of the New York Convention. Although no such exception was drafted into that instrument, paragraph 4 of the resolution to which that instrument is annexed could be interpreted as allowing such an exception. See p. 48 (note 162 in Part I). No such provision is contained in the Hostages Convention or accompanying resolution.

[15] First Report of the Hostages Committee, p. 58, para. 42 & p. 35, para. 28. See also the proposal of Algeria and Libya which stated:
   when a population engages in violent acts against colonialist, neo-colonialist, racist and foreign régimes within the framework of a struggle to restore its legitimate rights or to redress an injustice of which it is the victim, the international community, once it has recognized the validity of those goals, cannot take repressive measures against acts which it must on the contrary encourage, support and defend.
UN Doc A/AC.188/L.4, in *id.* at pp. 110-11. The representative of Guinea argued that "[t]he nationalists of Zimbabwe or the revolutionary peoples of Mozambique, who were
(*continued on p. 268*)

the "state of mind and motives of the perpetrator" must be taken into account,[16] and the representative of Democratic Yemen seemingly summed up the position of many developing countries when he said "either there would be an internationally accepted convention against the taking of hostages which did not apply to acts carried out by recognized national liberation movements in the course of their struggle, or there would be no convention at all."[17]

A sharply different opinion was held by the representatives of Western States, who argued that there should be no exceptions to the Convention based on the cause of the hostage-takers. The representative of the US, for example, argued that the "question of whether there were circumstances in which oppressed peoples could resort to force to obtain their fundamental rights, including the right to self-determination, was not at issue."[18] Rather, it is "impossible even in the name of the noblest causes, in the name of the struggle for the most sacred rights, to admit certain acts such as the hijacking of aircraft, the commission of crimes against diplomatic agents or the use of poison gas or explosive bullets, and one must consider precisely the question whether the taking of hostages was not an equally repugnant act."[19] He stated that "a definition of the act of taking of hostages that would take account of the motives or causes prompting the commission of the act would set the international community back several decades . . . to the barbarous age when there still had been talk of just and unjust wars".[20] Similarly, the delegate of the Netherlands stated that the prosecution of persons who resorted to such actions was not an attack on their aims but "a rejection of their choice of methods."[21]

It was Protocol I Additional to the Geneva Conventions which most contributed to the erosion of the most extreme positions taken by developing States in this regard. The Protocol, which had just been completed at the time of the first session of the Hostages Committee,[22] specifically applies to armed conflicts involving national liberation

([15] *continued*)
the victims of constant aggression, could not be blamed if one day they took someone like Ian Smith or Vorster hostage." *Id.* at p. 40, para. 13. See also the comments of the representative of Nigeria, *id.* at pp. 76-77, para. 18.

[16] *Id.* at p. 57, para. 39. Similarly, the representative of Algeria stated that politically motivated offences committed by national liberation movements must be removed from the scope of the Convention. Second Report of the Hostages Committee, p. 50, para. 8.

[17] First Report of the Hostages Committee, pp. 83-84, para. 5.

[18] *Id.* at p. 55, para. 26.

[19] *Id.* at pp. 52-53, para. 9.

[20] *Id.* at p. 52, para. 9.

[21] *Id.* at p. 50, para. 21. See also the comments of the representative of Sweden, *id.* at p. 71, para. 12.

[22] The Protocols were completed in June 1977 (Bowman & Harris, *Multilateral Treaties Index and Current Status* 419 (1984)) and the first session of the Hostages Committee was held in August 1977 (First Report of the Hostages Committee, p. 3, para. 3).

movements, i.e., conflicts "in which peoples are fighting against colonial domination and alien occupation and against racist régimes in the exercise of their right of self-determination . . ."[23] The Geneva Conventions and Protocol I prohibit absolutely acts of hostage-taking committed against civilians during armed conflicts.[24] The growing realization that Protocol I prohibits acts of hostage-taking committed by national liberation movements[25] made it impossible to maintain arguments that such acts were actually permissible, and they were soon abandoned. Indeed, the Hostages Committee Working Group entrusted with this issue reported at the end of the 1978 session that:

> negotiations revolved around the generally agreed principle that the taking of hostages was an act prohibited under international law. In this respect, there was general agreement that no one should be granted an open license for taking hostages.[26]

This statement reflected a significant reversal on the part of some developing nations.

The movement towards a compromise position was started in the 1977 session of the Hostages Committee by the representative of Mexico, who proposed language that would have removed from the scope of the Convention any act of hostage-taking:

> covered by the rules of international law applicable to armed conflicts, including conflicts in which people are fighting against colonial domination and foreign occupation and against racist regimes.[27]

The Mexican representative stated that "[t]here were adequate

---

[23] Art. 1(4).
[24] See Art. 34, Civilians Convention; Art. 74(2), Protocol I; pp. 283 & 294 (notes 58-59 & 98 and accompanying text).
[25] Given that the first session of the Hostages Committee took place so soon after the Additional Protocols were completed, there seemed to be some confusion on the part of some delegations as to just how the Protocols treated acts of hostage-taking by liberation groups. The representative of Lesotho, for example, suggested that the Secretariat provide copies of the revisions introduced by the Protocols. First Report of the Hostages Committee, p. 49, para. 17. The representative of Tanzania "wondered just what 'the rules of international law applicable to armed conflicts' were in the context of liberation struggles". *Id.* at p. 58, para. 42. See also the comments of the representatives of Algeria and Nigeria, *id.* at p. 60, para. 1 & p. 61, para. 9, respectively. The representative of the US stated that "[w]hile recognizing the strong support that existed for those movements, he had to point out that those same Governments, when negotiating the additional Protocol in Geneva, had accepted precisely the idea that the liberation movements should not take hostages." He suggested that "[s]ince the views which had been expressed by some representatives appear to be at variance with what their Governments had decided at Geneva . . . [delegations should] . . . check on that matter." *Id.* at p. 62, para. 11.
[26] Second Report of the Hostages Committee, p. 5, para. 16.
[27] UN Doc A/AC.188/L.6, in First Report of the Hostages Committee, p. 111.

instruments setting forth the rules of war, and the convention should not try to regulate what was already regulated."[28]

During the 1978 session of the Hostages Committee, the question of national liberation movements was entrusted to Working Group I, where it became the central issue of the drafting process.[29] Language such as that proposed by the Mexican delegation gradually won the support of many developing countries, which apparently felt that, while it would not legitimize acts of hostage-taking by national liberation groups, it would prevent such acts from coming within the scope of the Convention, and thus from being lumped together with terrorist acts.[30] Essentially, these States would have liked to develop two mutually exclusive legal regimes regarding the taking of hostages, one in force during armed conflicts, including "national liberation" struggles, and the other applicable to peacetime.[31]

For their part, Western States did not feel that the language proposed by Mexico, and similar proposals made during the 1978 session, went far enough towards ensuring that all acts of hostage-taking were subject to the obligation *aut dedere aut judicare*.[32] As just noted, those proposals would have removed from the scope of the Convention acts of hostage-taking which are "covered" by the laws of armed conflict. However, as will be seen below, there are many conceivable situations in which the rules of armed conflict, specifically the Geneva instruments, may "cover" a particular act of hostage-taking in the sense that they *prohibit* that act but do not impose an obligation upon States Parties thereto to prosecute or extradite the offenders. Further, the Mexican language could be interpreted as removing all acts of hostage-taking committed during armed conflicts from the scope of the Convention.[33] If such were the case, even if the relevant States Parties to this Convention were not parties to one or

---

[28] First Report of the Hostages Committee, p. 49, para. 16.

[29] Second Report of the Hostages Committee, p. 5, para. 15.

[30] See *id.* at pp. 5-6, para. 19. The Chairman *ad interim* of the Hostages Committee stated:

> even the proponents of safeguards for the rights of national liberation movements had maintained that they were in no way suggesting that those movements should be granted an open licence to take hostages. However, it had been pointed out that a clear distinction should be drawn in the convention between genuine activities of national liberation movements and acts of terrorist groups which had nothing in common with them.

Id. at p. 58, para. 3.

[31] See, e.g., the comments of the representative of Mexico. First Report of the Hostages Committee, p. 81, para. 43. See also Second Report of the Hostages Committee, pp. 5-6, para. 19.

[32] See Rosenstock, p. 184.

[33] This seemed to be the interpretation of the representative of Mexico. He stated that his State's proposed language, in contrast to the proposal of Tanzania which referred only to struggles for national liberation, would remove from the scope of the Convention all acts of hostage-taking occurring during armed conflicts. See First Report of the Hostages Committee, p. 57, para. 33 & pp. 80-81, para. 43.

more of the instruments dealing with armed conflicts, and thus not bound by a relevant provision contained therein to extradite or prosecute in a given case (which, as discussed below, will often be the case in respect of Protocol I), this Convention would not apply to that act. Western States thus wanted a more "comprehensive" approach such that the Hostages Convention would "encompass all cases of hostage-taking", supplementing, where necessary, the law of Geneva.[34]

According to the 1979 report of Working Group I:

> a number of representatives maintained that agreement on the question of national liberation movements was a key to the solution of other outstanding issues, in particular those of the scope of the Convention and the definition of hostage-taking. Thus the deliberations within the Group first and foremost focused on this question.[35]

A number of compromise proposals were submitted informally until the present language was submitted and accepted by consensus "as establishing an equitable balance between the desired objectives".[36] Unfortunately, most of the work of the 1979 session of the Hostages Committee was conducted off the record, and the precise nature of the positions taken and the movements towards compromise are, therefore, unclear. With respect to the final compromise, however, Verwey reports that:

> As it turned out, [i]t involved nine basic elements: (1) the legitimacy of the struggle of peoples for self-determination against colonial, racist, or foreign regimes would be reaffirmed in the Convention; (2) this would be done not in any operative paragraph, but in the Preamble; (3) in order to indicate that this reaffirmation was not intended to establish a basis for an exception to the prohibition of hostage taking, a "balancing" paragraph would be added emphasizing this point; (4) some reference to the prohibition of hostage taking as "acts of terrorism" would be made; (5) this reference would also find a place in the Preamble; (6) Article [12], on the scope of the Convention, would make clear that the Hostages Convention would only supplement, not replace, preexisting conventions dealing with the problem, conventions both on the law of peace and, in particular, on

---

[34] See Second Report of the Hostages Committee, p. 6, para. 20. The representative of France, for example, urged that the Convention should be drafted in such a way as to supplement, if necessary, the Geneva Conventions such that all acts of hostage-taking are subject to the obligation *aut dedere aut judicare. Id.* at pp. 63-64, paras. 1-6. McDonald reports that the position of the US going into the final session was that: 1) there could be no provision acknowledging the right of national liberation movements to take hostages; 2) the motives of the hostage-takers were irrelevant; 3) the words "national liberation movement" could not appear in the text; and 4) the text could leave no gaps in the prohibition against hostage-taking. McDonald, p. 551.
[35] Third Report of the Hostages Committee, p. 5, para. 16.
[36] *Id.* at pp. 5-7, paras. 16-19.

the law of war, notably the Geneva Conventions of 1949 and Additional Protocol I thereto of 1977; (7) the definition of the offense incorporated in Article 1 could thus remain comprehensive and unconditional; (8) certain provisions would be inserted to guarantee to all alleged offenders a fair trial, including those who were members of national liberation movements and others who might fear being subjected to prejudiced judgment; and (9) on this basis, the principle *aut dedere aut judicare* could remain unconditional, without any exception.[37]

Although most delegations to the Sixth Committee obviously agreed that the language adopted by the Hostages Committee was a satisfactory compromise formula (inasmuch as it was retained in the final draft), the representatives of some States continued to express dismay that this Article does not expressly exclude from the Convention acts of hostage-taking committed by national liberation movements.[38]

It is not entirely clear from the record as to why many developing States were willing to compromise so far from their original position. Certain factors, however, can be identified as most probably contributing to the eventual consensus:

1) The prohibition against hostage-taking during armed conflicts involving national liberation movements contained in Protocol I made it impossible to argue that hostage-takings by such groups are permissible under international law. Once such activity was recognized as illegitimate, the argument for specifically excluding such acts from this Convention lost much of its force;

2) This Convention will apply to all acts of hostage-taking committed during armed conflicts which are not covered by the Geneva instruments in such a way as to give rise to the obligation *aut dedere aut judicare*. Thus, the Convention could not be seen as directed against national liberation movements, or as necessarily equating members of such groups with terrorists;

3) Since it might have been expected that all States would eventually become parties to Protocol I (a situation which, as discussed below, now appears unlikely, at least for the foreseeable future) it might also have been expected that all or most acts of hostage-taking by national liberation movements would fall under the Geneva regime rather than under this Convention;

4) The concessions, mentioned above, which reaffirmed the

---

[37] Verwey, p. 76.

[38] See, e.g., the comments of the representatives of Pakistan, Tanzania and Mali during the Sixth Committee deliberations, in UN GAOR, 34th Sess., C.6 (14th mtg.), p. 16, para. 94, UN Doc A/C.6/34/SR.14 (1979), UN GAOR, 34th Sess., C.6 (53rd mtg.), p. 14, para. 55, UN Doc A/C.6/34/SR.53 (1979) & UN GAOR, 34th Sess., C.6 (62nd mtg.), p. 8, para. 41, UN Doc A/C.6/34/SR.62 (1979), respectively.

legitimacy of national liberation movements represented an acceptable level of compromise by Western States;

5) Deadlock on this issue jeopardized the prospects for eventual agreement on a draft convention, and there was little to be gained politically by developing States by being seen as standing in the way of such a positive development in international criminal law.[39]

Whatever their reasons for ultimately coming to terms on this issue, most developing States have not yet become party to this Convention.[40] As just indicated, and as will be discussed below, it will in practice be the rare case that an act of hostage-taking committed by a national liberation movement will be covered by the Geneva instruments rather than by this Convention. Although it is by no means clear, this may have something to do with the fact that so few developing States have so far bound themselves to this instrument.

2. INTERPRETATION

"In so far as the Geneva Conventions of 1949 for the protection of war victims or the Additional Protocols to those Conventions are applicable to a particular act of hostage-taking, and in so far as States Parties to this Convention are bound under those conventions to prosecute or hand over the hostage-taker, the present Convention shall not apply to an act of hostage-taking . . ."

It is only "in so far as" States Parties to this Convention are bound under the Geneva "conventions" — either the four original instruments or the two Additional Protocols thereto[41] — to extradite

---

[39] McDonald attributes over-all success in the drafting process to the following factors: 1) the timing of the initiative and the fact that no State wanted to be seen to be responsible for failure; 2) the high quality and serious approach of the delegations sent to the third, and final, session of the Hostages Committee; 3) the flexible working structure which allowed much of the negotiations to be conducted off the record; 4) the strong professional rapport and spirit of the Western delegations; and 5) the strong leadership of the FRG. McDonald, pp. 558-59.

[40] A list of States Parties is given on p. 5 (note 19 in the Introduction).

[41] This Article refers to the Geneva Conventions and Additional Protocols and states that the Hostages Convention will not apply when "those conventions" require States Parties to prosecute or hand over the offender. The reference to "conventions" could lead to the conclusion that the Hostages Convention is only rendered inapplicable when the Geneva Conventions require *aut dedere aut judicare*, and not in those additional circumstances where Protocol I imposes that obligation. However, the drafting history of this Convention argues forcefully against such a conclusion, and Rosenne states that the use of the word "conventions" — with the lower case "c" — was intended to make it clear that the reference was both to the Conventions proper and to the Protocols. Rosenne, p. 137. See also Nash, note 7, *supra*, at p. 421. It must thus be concluded that this Convention is displaced whenever any of the Geneva instruments impose the obligation *aut dedere aut judicare*.

or prosecute the offender in a particular incident of hostage-taking that this Convention will not apply to that act. Where no such obligation is imposed by those instruments, then this Convention is fully operative. This Convention and the Geneva instruments, therefore, are designed to complement each other in such a way as to ensure that all acts of hostage-taking, whether committed in peacetime or during an armed conflict, result in the obligation *aut dedere aut judicare*.

At first glance, the above language indicates that two distinct conditions must be fulfilled before the Hostages Convention is rendered inapplicable to a particular act of hostage-taking: the Geneva instruments must be "applicable" to that act *and* those instruments must impose upon States Parties to this Convention an obligation to extradite or prosecute the offender. However, the reference to the instruments being "applicable" to the particular act is in fact superfluous since they could hardly require the Parties to extradite or prosecute that offender if they were not "applicable" to that act. Thus, upon closer scrutiny it may be discerned that only one condition must exist in order to make this Convention inapplicable to a particular act of hostage-taking: the Geneva instruments must impose the obligation *aut dedere aut judicare* with respect to that act. Therefore, this wording is unduly long and unnecessarily complex. All that really needs to be said is that: "In so far as the Geneva Conventions of 1949 for the protection of war victims or the Additional Protocols to those Conventions bind States Parties to this Convention to prosecute or hand over the offender in a particular act of hostage-taking . . ."

It may briefly be noted in this connexion (and this issue is discussed in detail below) that while it is not possible for the Geneva instruments to impose the obligation *aut dedere aut judicare* with respect to a particular act of hostage-taking without being "applicable" to that act, the reverse situation could exist. There can be circumstances wherein the Geneva instruments are "applicable" to a particular act of hostage-taking in the sense that they prohibit that act, but where they do not impose the obligation to extradite or prosecute the offender. In such cases the Hostages Convention will still apply to that act (assuming it is otherwise applicable), notwithstanding the concurrent "applicability" of the Geneva instruments.[42]

Two problems of interpretation may arise with respect to the above quoted language. The first relates to the identification of the "States Parties" which must be bound under the Geneva instruments to extradite or prosecute an alleged offender in order for the Hostages

---

[42] See pp. 280-281 (text accompanying notes 54-55).

Convention not to apply to a particular act of hostage-taking. This Article provides that the Hostages Convention will not apply only "in so far as States Parties" thereto are obliged to extradite or prosecute a given offender under the Geneva regime. Confusion could well arise as to which "States Parties" this language refers to. Two possible interpretations can be made of this language. First, it can be interpreted as requiring that *all* States Parties to the Hostages Convention must be bound by the relevant Geneva instruments in a particular case in order for this Convention not to apply to that act of hostage-taking. Under this interpretation, if any State Party to this Convention is not a party to the Geneva instrument which covers the situation, then it cannot be said that the "States Parties" to this instrument are bound under those instruments. Therefore, the Hostages Convention will still apply to that act. Alternatively, this language can be interpreted as requiring only that the State in whose territory the alleged offender is found must be obliged to extradite or prosecute him pursuant to the Geneva instruments before this Convention will not apply to that act. Although the proper interpretation of this language is far from clear, it seems, on balance, that this latter possibility is the better interpretation.

The problem presented by this language is perhaps best understood by way of illustration: Suppose that during an armed conflict between State A and State B, soldiers of State B take as hostage certain civilian nationals of State A who are present in State B. That act of hostage-taking is prohibited by the Civilians Convention in such a way as to give rise to an obligation under that instrument to prosecute or extradite the hostage-takers.[43] Subsequently, those soldiers are found in the territory of State D. State A, State B and State D are parties to the Geneva Conventions and to the Hostages Convention. Another State, State C, is a party to the Hostages Convention but not to the Geneva Conventions.

Under the first of the above interpretations, the Hostages Convention will still apply to that act of hostage-taking because not all "States Parties" to this instrument are bound to prosecute or extradite the alleged offender under the Geneva instruments. However, this interpretation does not seem right. The simple fact that one State Party to this Convention, which may have absolutely no connexion with the offence, is not bound under the Civilians Convention should not be enough to keep that act within the scope of the Hostages Convention. Indeed, even if State C had some connexion with the offence, e.g., one of the offenders was its national working as a mercenary for State B, this should not be enough to keep the offence

---

[43] See pp. 282-283 (notes 57-60 and accompanying text).

within the scope of the Hostages Convention. The draftsmen clearly intended that whenever possible the laws of armed conflict should apply to offences, and that in such cases this Convention would not apply. This intention should not be defeated by an interpretation of this instrument which would require every State Party to this Convention to be bound by the relevant rule of armed conflict in order for this Convention not to apply to an act of hostage-taking.

It should be noted that this is a problem which was probably not considered by the draftsmen of this Convention. Virtually every State is party to the four Geneva Conventions: those instruments had 165 States Parties as of 1 January 1988.[44] It is, therefore, almost certain that every State Party to the Hostages Convention will also be a State Party to the Geneva Conventions. Thus, the type of dilemma just described will never occur when the hostage-taking situation is one which falls under the four Conventions. However, the same cannot be said of Protocol I, which, as discussed below, may impose the obligation *aut dedere aut judicare* with respect to some acts of hostage-taking not similarly covered by the original four instruments.[45] At the time of the drafting of the Hostages Convention it might have been expected that Protocol I would obtain the same universal acceptance as the Geneva Conventions. If such were the case, then the type of dilemma above described would similarly never occur when that Protocol imposed the obligation *aut dedere aut judicare*. However, only 72 States had become parties to that instrument as of 18 January 1988[46] and, as discussed below, many States are unlikely to ratify or accede to that instrument in the near future, if ever.[47] If the first interpretation of this language is accepted as correct, then Protocol I will, therefore, rarely apply to an act of hostage-taking in such a way as to preclude the applicability of the Hostages Convention in situations wherein the four original Conventions do not impose the obligation *aut dedere aut judicare*.

The second interpretation of this language, i.e., that this Convention will not apply to a particular act when the State where the alleged offender is found is obliged pursuant to the Geneva instruments to extradite or prosecute him, seems the better interpretation. In fact, in a given case only *one* State Party to this Convention or the Geneva instruments will be bound to prosecute or extradite an alleged offender, i.e., the State in whose territory he is found. Thus, this interpretation seems both more workable in practice and more consistent with the terms of this Convention and this Article

---

[44] See Bowman & Harris, note 22, *supra*, at pp. 154-55 & 5th Supp. (1988).
[45] See generally pp. 294-298 (text accompanying notes 97-108).
[46] See International Review of the Red Cross (Jan.-Feb 1988) p. 95.
[47] See pp. 291-292 & 296-297 (notes 86-90 & 105 and accompanying text).

("... in so far as States Parties to this Convention are bound under those conventions to prosecute or hand over ..."). However, if the alleged offender flees from the State where he is found before justice can be done, or if that State refuses to comply with its obligation to extradite him or submit the case for the purpose of prosecution, and he is subsequently found in the territory of a State Party to this Convention which is not bound under the Geneva instruments, then that act will then fall within the scope of the Hostages Convention.[48]

The second, much less difficult, problem of interpretation arises with respect to the requirement that States Parties must be "bound under those conventions" to extradite or prosecute the alleged offender in order for the Hostages Convention not to apply to a particular act of hostage-taking. The widespread acceptance of the four Geneva Conventions raises the possibility that all or most of the rules contained therein are now binding upon all States by customary international law.[49] If this is the case, then it is possible that even those few States which are not parties to those instruments will be obliged to extradite or prosecute offenders in cases where such an obligation is envisaged by the Geneva Conventions. However, the language of this Article — "in so far as States Parties to this Convention are *bound under those conventions*" — indicates that the Hostages Convention will not be rendered inapplicable simply because customary international law imposes an obligation to extradite or prosecute the offender. Rather, in order for this Convention to be inoperative, that obligation must flow directly from the Geneva instruments. Besides being more faithful to the language of this Article, this interpretation obviates the need to determine whether or not the extradite or prosecute

---

[48] It should be emphasized in this connexion that if for *any* reason a State Party to this Convention is not obliged pursuant to the Geneva regime to extradite or prosecute a hostage-taker then this Convention will apply to that act. For example, while the better view is that all States Parties to the Geneva Conventions are obliged to extradite or prosecute a person who appears in their territory who has committed a grave breach of the Conventions (see p. 138 (note 17 and accompanying text in the commentary on Article 5)), some writers have argued that neutral States have no such obligation. See, e.g., Röling, "Aspects of Criminal Responsibility for Violations of the Laws of War", in Cassese (ed.), *The New Humanitarian Law of Armed Conflict* 202 (1979). See also p. 138 (note 17 in the commentary on Article 5). If such an interpretation is correct, then that neutral State would be obliged pursuant to the Hostages Convention to extradite or prosecute the offender.

[49] The question of whether the rules laid down in these instruments now represent customary international law has been the subject of much commentary, and it is difficult to reach any definite conclusions in this regard. See, e.g., Meron, "The Geneva Conventions as Customary Law", 81 AJIL 348 (1987); Baxter, "Treaties and Custom", 129 RC (1970-I) 25, 96. Baxter noted that there exists a paradox in this area: simply because so many States have become parties to the instruments, it is virtually impossible to determine whether they have indeed passed into customary international law.

obligation is in fact binding even as to States which are not parties to the Civilians Convention.[50]

"... committed in the course of armed conflicts as defined in the Geneva Conventions of 1949 and the Protocols thereto..."

The Geneva Conventions and Protocols thereto are only applicable during the course of armed conflicts. However, it is somewhat inaccurate to say that the instruments "define" armed conflicts: no such definition appears in any of the instruments. Rather, the Conventions merely set forth the circumstances under which they are applicable. For example, common Article 2 of the four original Conventions states that the instruments "shall apply to all cases of declared war or of any other armed conflict which may arise between two or more High Contracting Parties... [and also] to all cases of total or partial occupation of the territory of a High Contracting Party". This Article thus leaves open the question of what, precisely, constitutes an "armed conflict". The ICRC's commentaries on the conventions, however, define an armed conflict within the meaning of common Article 2, i.e., an international armed conflict, as "[a]ny difference arising between two States and leading to the intervention of members of the armed forces". Further, "[i]t makes no difference how long the conflict lasts, or how much slaughter takes place."[51] Article 1 of Protocol I provides that that instrument will apply in the same circumstances as common Article 2 and, moreover, during armed conflicts for national liberation. As noted below, the Geneva Conventions do not define non-international armed conflicts either, although some attempt to do so is contained in Article 1 of Protocol II.[52]

Despite the lack of an actual definition of "armed conflicts" expressly contained in the Geneva instruments, the present wording is sufficient to convey the intended meaning of this Article: that this Convention will not apply to a particular act or hostage-taking if that act must result in the prosecution or extradition of the offender pursuant to the Geneva regime.

"... including armed conflicts mentioned in article 1, paragraph 4,

---

[50] It might briefly be noted that even if the substantive humanitarian rules set forth in the Conventions are binding under customary international law, it is less than clear if such procedural obligations as the requirement *aut dedere aut judicare* would similarly be binding under customary law. See generally Murphy, "Sanctions and Enforcement of the Humanitarian Law of the Four Geneva Conventions of 1949 and Geneva Protocol I of 1977", 103 Military L. R. 3, 5 (1984).

[51] See Pictet (ed.), *Commentary to the Geneva Convention Relative to the Protection of Civilian Persons in Time of War* 20 (1958).

[52] See note 56, *infra*.

of Additional Protocol I of 1977, in which peoples are fighting against colonial domination and alien occupation and against racist régimes in the exercise of their right of self-determination, as enshrined in the Charter of the United Nations and the Declaration of Principles of International Law concerning Friendly Relations and Co-operation among States in accordance with the Charter of the United Nations."

As will be seen below, a State Party to Protocol I may be under an obligation pursuant to that instrument to prosecute or extradite hostage-takers for acts committed in struggles against "colonial domination", etc. However, it is unclear as to what purpose is served by specifically mentioning in this Article this particular type of armed conflict. Most likely, it was added to satisfy those States which wanted to emphasize that national liberation struggles can be seen as "armed conflicts" rather than as terrorist activity (indeed, this language is taken directly from Article 1(4) of Protocol I). However, as a result, it is just another example of the obscurity of this Article. It should be emphasized that inclusion of this language in no way means that acts of hostage-taking committed during national liberation struggles are always outside the scope of this Convention: they are so only in those limited circumstances wherein a State Party is obliged pursuant to Protocol I to extradite or prosecute alleged hostage-takers during such conflicts.

3. THE GENEVA INSTRUMENTS AND THE OBLIGATION TO PROSECUTE OR HAND OVER HOSTAGE-TAKERS

To assess the effect of this Article upon the operation of the Hostages Convention, it is necessary to examine the extent to which the Geneva Conventions and Additional Protocols thereto require States Parties to "prosecute or hand over" those who have committed acts of hostage-taking during armed conflicts. In addition to clarifying the position with respect to national liberation movements under this Convention, this exercise will identify those acts of hostage-taking committed during armed conflicts which do not result in the obligation *aut dedere aut judicare* pursuant to the Geneva instruments, and which, therefore, fall within the scope of the Hostages Convention. It will be seen that this Convention fills in gaps which exist under the Geneva regime, particularly under the four original Conventions. To approach the problem, it may be best to make a distinction — as do the Geneva instruments — between international armed conflicts and non-international armed conflicts. The discussion regarding non-international conflicts is brief, examining first the situation under the four original Geneva Conventions and then the situation under Protocol II. The discussion concerning international armed conflicts focuses first upon the four original Conventions since, for most States, these are still the only applicable law. The discussion will then turn to hostage-takings committed during the course of conflicts wherein "peoples are fighting against colonial domination and alien occupation and against racist régimes", all of which will be referred to as "national liberation movements".[53] Given the controversial status under international law of struggles for national liberation, this discussion has not been included under the rubric of either international or non-international armed conflicts. It is during this discussion that the changes to the law introduced by Protocol I will be addressed, both with respect to national liberation movements and with respect to traditional international armed conflicts.

A. NON-INTERNATIONAL ARMED CONFLICTS

Common Article 3 of the four Geneva Conventions and Protocol II

The first prohibition against hostage-taking contained in the Geneva Conventions is found in Article 3 common to all four instruments. Article 3 applies to all armed conflicts not of "an international character" and sets forth a minimum standard of conduct to which each side to the conflict must adhere with respect to "persons taking no active part in the hostilities, including members of armed forces who have laid down their arms and those placed *hors de combat* by sickness, wounds, detention or any other cause ..." Subparagraph 1 lists a number of acts "which are and shall remain prohibited at any time and in any place whatsoever with respect to the above mentioned persons". This list includes the "taking of hostages". Thus, it can be seen that during internal conflicts common Article 3 prohibits absolutely the taking as hostage any of the persons specifically mentioned therein. Further, this prohibition applies both to the State Party to the Convention and to the rebel faction.

However, it does not appear that the provisions of Article 3 may operate in such a way as to preclude the applicability of the Hostages

---

[53] Although UN and ICRC practice has generally avoided such terms as "wars of national liberation" and "national liberation movements", preferring to list more specifically the types of struggles to which resolutions and instruments refer, i.e., against colonial domination, racist regimes and alien occupation (see, e.g., p. 288 (note 73 and accompanying text)), these terms are commonly employed by writers. See, e.g., Verwey; Abi-Saab, "The Legal Nature of Wars of National Liberation", 165 RC (1979-IV) 363-445; Schindler, "The Different Types of Armed Conflicts According to the Geneva Conventions and Protocols", 163 RC (1979-II) 133-144.

Convention. While Article 3 *prohibits* the taking of hostages in an internal conflict, it does not require States Parties to prosecute or extradite alleged offenders. In fact, Article 3 does not impose any obligation upon States Parties with respect to dealing with alleged offenders; it settles merely for a prohibition. Article 3 is the only provision of the Geneva Conventions which deals with internal armed conflicts, and it is not affected by any of the other provisions of those instruments. Any obligation imposed by subsequent provisions to prosecute or extradite hostage-takers in international armed conflicts, therefore, does not apply to situations envisaged by Article 3.[54] Thus, while it might be said that common Article 3 is "applicable" to an act of hostage-taking committed during an internal conflict, it does not impose an obligation to "prosecute or hand over" offenders. The Hostages Convention will, therefore, still apply in such situations, assuming that it is otherwise applicable.

Protocol II, which is also applicable to non-international armed conflicts, repeats in Article 4 the prohibition against hostage-taking; however, it similarly imposes no obligation to extradite or prosecute hostage-takers.[55] Therefore, the above situation is not different with respect to an internal conflict occurring in the territory of a State Party to that instrument.

Of course, the foregoing discussion does not address one crucial question: when is a conflict "not of an international character" such that it is covered only by the minimal protections contained in common Article 3 of the Conventions and Article 4 of Protocol II? This question is addressed more fully below; it is sufficient to note for now that, with the possible exception of certain "wars of national liberation", all civil wars, i.e., those which take place in the

---

[54] Article 3 has thus been called a "Convention in miniature". See ICRC Commentary, note 51, *supra*, at p. 41. Some sources have indicated that an act of hostage-taking in violation of common Article 3 would result in an obligation to extradite or prosecute offenders. See the comments of the representative of the FRG in First Report of the Hostages Committee, p. 47, para. 8; Boyle, "International Law in Time of Crisis: From the Entebbe Raid to the Hostages Convention", 75 Northwestern U. L.R. 769, 834 (1980). However, a close examination of the text of the Civilians Convention indicates that this is not the case, and the author just mentioned indicates in a later work that there is not, in fact, an obligation to extradite or prosecute for violations of common Article 3. See Boyle, *World Politics and International Law* 143 (1985). It might be noted that common Article 3 encourages parties to such internal conflicts to bring all or part of the other provisions of the Geneva Conventions into force, by means of special agreements. However, it would not appear that even if such a special agreement were concluded which required the extradition or prosecution of those who commit acts of hostage-taking the Hostages Convention would necessarily be displaced. This is because the State Party to that special agreement would not be "bound under" the Geneva Conventions to prosecute or hand over the hostage-taker; rather, it would be bound pursuant to that special agreement.

[55] As with common Article 3, Article 4 of Protocol II simply lists certain acts which "are and shall remain prohibited at anytime and in any place whatsoever".

territory of a single State and which do not involve the armed forces of other States, are considered to be non-international in nature.[56]

Note on acts of hostage-taking which are strictly internal in nature

As noted, since the prohibition of acts of hostage-taking committed during internal armed conflicts does not include an obligation to "prosecute or hand over" offenders, there is nothing in common Article 3 or Protocol II which precludes application of the Hostages Convention to such situations. However, if the act is also internal within the meaning of the Hostages Convention, it will be outside of the scope of that instrument. Pursuant to Article 13, the Hostages Convention does not apply "where the offence is committed within a single State, the hostage and the alleged offender are nationals of that State and the alleged offender is found in the territory of that State." If these criteria are satisfied with respect to a particular act of hostage-taking occurring during an internal armed conflict, then there will be no internationally binding obligation to extradite or prosecute the offenders imposed by either the Geneva instruments or the Hostages Convention.

B. INTERNATIONAL ARMED CONFLICTS

The four Geneva Conventions of 1949

Each of the four Geneva Conventions contains an article which sets forth those acts which are considered to be "grave breaches" of the particular instrument.[57] Each of the instruments also contains an Article which provides that each State Party:

> shall be under the obligation to search for persons alleged to have committed, or to have ordered to be committed, such grave breaches, and shall bring such persons, regardless of their nationality, before its own courts. It may also, if it prefers, and in accordance with the provisions of its own legislation, hand such persons over for trial to another High

---

[56] See pp. 286-287 & 295-296 (notes 66-70 & 102 and accompanying text). It might be noted that Article 1 of Protocol II provides that a non-international conflict within the scope of that instrument is one which is not covered by Article 1 of Protocol I and "which take[s] place in the territory of a High Contracting Party between its armed forces and dissident armed forces or other organized armed groups which, under responsible command, exercise such control over a part of its territory as to enable them to carry out sustained and concerted military operations and to implement this Protocol."

[57] See Art. 50, Convention I; Art. 51, Convention II; Art. 130, Convention III; Art. 147, Convention IV.

Contracting Party concerned, provided such High Contracting Party has made out a *prima facie* case.[58]

In short, States Parties are required to extradite or prosecute those who commit grave breaches of the Geneva Conventions.

A review of the four Geneva Conventions reveals that only Convention IV, the Convention Relative to the Protection of Civilian Persons in Time of War, makes any reference to hostage-taking during international armed conflicts. Pursuant to Article 34, "[t]he taking of hostages is prohibited."[59] Moreover, pursuant to Article 147, hostage-taking is a "grave breach" of the Convention when it is committed against a "person . . . protected" by the Convention. Thus, in certain cases acts of hostage-taking may be covered by the Civilians Convention in such a way as to displace the Hostages Convention. It would seem that acts of hostage-taking committed against any persons other than those protected by the Civilians Convention, however, do not give rise under the other Geneva Conventions to an obligation to extradite or prosecute the offenders. In fact, such acts do not even appear to be prohibited.[60] Moreover, it must be noted that the Civilians Convention applies only when the hostages are in the hands of an "authority", i.e., agents of one of the parties to the conflict.[61] If private individuals take hostages during the armed conflict, that act will still be covered by the Hostages Convention. Further, attempts to commit grave breaches are nowhere prohibited in any of the Geneva instruments.[62] It would, therefore, appear that all attempts to take hostages will be covered by the Hostages Convention.

---

[58] See Art. 49, Convention I; Art. 50, Convention II; Art. 129, Convention III; Art. 146, Convention IV.

[59] As noted earlier, the Civilians Convention does not define the taking of hostages; however, some guidance is provided in the ICRC Commentary. See p. 78 (note 2 in the commentary on Article 1). See also note 61, *infra*.

[60] It might be noted that before the adoption of the Geneva Conventions, the taking of civilian hostages was probably permitted during war. See Draper, *The Red Cross Conventions* 35 (1958).

[61] This is apparent from the immediately following discussion regarding "persons protected" under the Convention. Moreover, the ICRC Commentary states that "hostages are nationals of a belligerent State who of their own free will or through compulsion are in the *hands of the enemy* and are answerable with their freedom or their life for the execution of his orders and the security of his armed forces." ICRC Commentary, note 51, *supra*, at p. 229 (emphasis added). The ICRC Commentary to the 1977 Protocols states that the term 'hostages' "must be understood in the same way as in Article 34 of the Fourth Convention . . . [w]e are therefore faced here with the problem of hostages taken by an authority — and not by individuals." Sandoz, Swinarski & Zimmermann (eds.), *Commentary on the Additional Protocols of 8 June 1977 to the Geneva Conventions of 12 August 1949* 874 (1987).

[62] See generally *id*. at p. 980. As regards participation, those who order such crimes are also expressly liable under the relevant provisions (Article 146 of the Civilians Convention) for grave breaches, and other participants would also seem to be covered thereby. *Id*. at p. 979. This view is consistent with Nuremberg Principle VII. See 1950 YBILC, Vol. II, pp. 374-78.

Two basic questions must be asked in order to determine whether or not a given act of hostage-taking is covered by the Civilians Convention in such a way as to require the prosecution or extradition of an alleged offender: 1) does the instrument apply to that armed conflict?; and, if so, 2) is the victim of the hostage-taking a person protected by the Civilians Convention? If these two questions are not answered affirmatively, the Hostages Convention, rather than the Civilians Convention, will apply to the act of hostage-taking.

A resolution of the first inquiry — whether or not the Civilians Convention applies to the conflict — requires reference to common Article 2 of the instruments. That Article provides that the Convention "shall apply to all cases of declared war or of any other armed conflict which may arise between two or more High Contracting Parties, even if the state of war is not recognized by one of them." It further provides that even if one of the conflicting Powers is not party to the Convention, the Powers which are party "shall remain bound by it in their mutual relations." Moreover, they shall "be bound by the Convention in relation to the said Power [i.e., the non-party], if the latter accepts and applies the provisions thereof."[63] Finally, the "Convention shall also apply to all cases of partial or total occupation of the territory of a High Contracting Party".

Once it is determined that the Convention applies to the conflict, it must be ascertained whether the particular act of hostage-taking has been committed against a person protected by the Civilians Convention. As earlier noted, a grave breach of the Civilians Convention is committed only when the act is directed against a person protected by that instrument, and in the absence of a grave breach there is no obligation pursuant to that instrument to extradite or prosecute the alleged offender. Pursuant to Article 4 of the Convention, protected persons are "those who, at a given moment and in any manner whatsoever, find themselves, in case of a conflict or occupation, in the hands of a Party to the conflict or Occupying Power of which they are not nationals."

However, certain categories of civilians are specifically excluded from the protection of the instrument, including:

1) "nationals of a State which is not bound by the Convention"; and

2) "[n]ationals of a neutral State who find themselves in the territory of a belligerent State, and nationals of a co-belligerent State

---

[63] An express declaration is not necessary. It is enough if a party to the conflict indicates by its behaviour that it has accepted the rules of the Convention. See ICRC Commentary, note 51, *supra*, at pp. 23-24; Commentary to the Protocols, note 61, *supra*, at pp. 1087-88.

... while the State of which they are nationals has normal diplomatic representation in the State in whose hands they are".

Moreover, Article 4 expressly provides that the protection of the Civilians Convention does not extend to any person protected by any of the other Geneva Conventions, i.e., those members of armed forces who are wounded, sick, shipwrecked or prisoners of war (including civilians who become members of the *levée en masse*).[64] It should be emphasized, moreover, that persons protected by common Article 3 applicable to internal armed conflicts do not fit into the definition of persons protected by the other provisions of the Civilians Convention. Given the almost universal acceptance of the Civilians Convention, virtually all cases of hostage-taking committed against civilians during an armed conflict occurring between States will be covered by that instrument in such a way as to give rise to an obligation to extradite or prosecute offenders. This is true, apparently, even if both parties to the conflict deny that a "war" exists.[65] Pursuant to Article 146,

---

[64] See Art. 4(A)(6), Convention III.

[65] As noted, Article 2 of the Civilians Convention states that that instrument will apply "even if the state of war is not recognized by one of [the High Contracting Parties]." On its face, this wording indicates that if the state of war is denied by *both* parties to the conflict, the Civilians Convention will not apply. Under such an interpretation, the Hostages Convention will apply to that act of hostage-taking since no prosecute or extradite obligation will be imposed by the Geneva Conventions. However, this interpretation probably cannot stand. As stated in the ICRC Commentary to the Civilians Convention:

> There is no need for a formal declaration of war, or for recognition of the existence of a state of war, as preliminaries to the application of the Convention. The occurrence of *de facto* hostilities is sufficient ... The Convention only provides for the case of one of the Parties denying the existence of a state of war. What would the position be, it may be wondered, if both the Parties to an armed conflict were to deny the existence of a state of war. Even in that event it would not appear that they could, by tacit agreement, prevent the Conventions from applying. It must not be forgotten that the Conventions have been drawn up first and foremost to protect individuals, and not to serve State interests.

ICRC Commentary, note 51, *supra*, at pp. 20-21. See also Commentary to the Protocols, note 61, *supra*, at p. 40.

This commentary indicates that even if both sides deny the existence of a state of war, the Civilians Convention will apply, requiring the prosecution or extradition of the hostage-takers and precluding application of the Hostages Convention. The general editor of the ICRC Commentary seems to indicate in a later publication that the denial of a state of war by both Parties would indeed render the Geneva Conventions inapplicable:

> What would happen if neither Party recognizes the state of war? This will not happen very often; in general, at least one of the parties will be quick to accuse the other of aggression. Nevertheless, it has occurred, and in that case the Convention as it now stands — *even if the state of war is not recognized by one of the Parties* — cannot be invoked, otherwise words would be meaningless.

Pictet, *Humanitarian Law and the Protection of War Victims* 50 (1975). Most commentators, however, agree that the Conventions will apply even if both Parties do not recognize the state of war, an interpretation, moreover, which appears to be borne out by State practice. See, e.g., Oppenheim, *International Law*, Vol. II, p. 369, n.6 (H. Lauterpacht, ed., 7th ed., 1952); Schindler, note 53, *supra*, at p. 131; Greenwood, "The Concept of War in Modern International Law", 36 ICLQ 283, 295 (1987); Murphy, note 50, *supra*, at pp. 20-21.

moreover, any State Party in whose territory the alleged offender is found, whether or not it was party to the conflict, must either extradite or prosecute him.

However, the exceptions to the class of persons protected by the Civilians Convention — particularly with respect to those persons protected by the other instruments — leave a number of possible situations wherein an act of hostage-taking committed during an armed conflict will not result in an obligation to extradite or prosecute pursuant to the Geneva Conventions. Moreover, as noted, if the hostage-taking is done by private individuals, the Civilians Convention will not apply. In all these cases, the Hostages Convention may apply.

C. ARMED CONFLICTS FOR "NATIONAL LIBERATION"

Assume that in the territory of State A members of an organized and popular "national liberation movement", which has been engaged in continuous low-level hostilities against the regime for many years, take as hostage two civilian nationals of State A who are supporters of the regime. As a condition for the release of the hostages, the hostage-takers demand that the government of State A release members of their group who have been tried, convicted and imprisoned on criminal charges for activity related to their movement. State A is party both to the Civilians and the Hostages Conventions. After the incident, the hostage-takers flee to the territory of State B, which is also party to both the Hostages Convention and the Geneva Conventions.

The Civilians Convention

In this case, it will be difficult to establish either that the Civilians Convention applies to the conflict or that the victims are persons protected under that instrument.

The situation under traditional international law

Under traditional international law, all civil wars, no matter how intense and regardless of the particular grievance or cause of the rebels, are considered to be within the domestic sphere, in the absence of a recognition of belligerency.[66] And it is clear that the draftsmen and States Parties to the Geneva Conventions intended that all civil

---

[66] See generally, Draper, note 60, *supra*, at p. 14; Schindler, note 53, *supra*, at pp. 133, 145; Abi-Saab, note 53, *supra*, at p. 367.

wars should fall within the scope of Article 3, i.e., subject, as internal conflicts, only to minimal safeguards. Thus, the ICRC Commentary, without precisely defining the term "armed conflict not of an international nature", states:

> Speaking generally, it must be recognized that the conflicts referred to in Article 3 are armed conflicts, with armed forces on either side engaged in hostilities — conflicts, in short, which are in many respects similar to an international war, but take place within the confines of a single country. In many cases, each of the Parties is in possession of a portion of the national territory, and there is often some sort of a front.[67]

In line with this, common Article 2 of the Geneva Conventions, as noted above, states that the instruments apply to armed conflicts between "High Contracting Parties" or in armed conflicts between a "Power" which is party to the Convention and a "Power" which is not, "if the latter accepts and applies the provisions thereof." A "High Contracting Party" was surely intended to refer only to a State. And most probably the term "Power" had the same limitation since in traditional diplomatic usage a "Power" was synonymous with a "State".[68] Thus, while some writers, such as Sir Hersch Lauterpacht, suggested that a "Power" in this context could refer to an entity other than a State (specifically a recognized belligerent),[69] others, such as Draper, argued:

> the expression "Powers" does not readily lend itself to the idea of rebels having the status of belligerents. It is suggested that in the context of Article 2, para. 3, "Powers" means States capable then and there of becoming Contracting Parties to these Conventions either by ratification or by accession. If that be so, then it is apparent that Article 2, para. 3 would not apply to a civil war of any description.[70]

Under this traditional interpretation, a national liberation movement cannot bind itself to the Civilians Convention (or to the other Geneva Conventions) either as a "High Contracting Party" or on an *ad hoc* basis as a "Power" in such a way as to make that instrument applicable to its struggle. And if this interpretation is still valid, the Hostages Convention will apply to the above situation, imposing upon State B the obligation to extradite or prosecute.

---

[67] ICRC Commentary, note 51, *supra*, at p. 36. See also Murphy, note 50, *supra*, at p. 50.

[68] See Baxter, "The Geneva Conventions of 1949 and Wars of National Liberation", in Bassiouni (ed.), *International Terrorism and Political Crimes* 123 (1925). See also Abi-Saab, note 53, *supra*, at p. 400.

[69] Oppenheim, note 65, *supra*, at pp. 370-372.

[70] Draper, note 60, *supra*, at p. 16.

Moreover, the definition of persons protected by the Civilians Convention militates against wars of national liberation coming within the scope of that instrument. As noted, pursuant to Article 4, that instrument protects only those civilians who are "in the hands of a Party to the conflict or Occupying Power of which they are not nationals." Stated in another way, the Convention does not apply when the civilians are in the hands of a Party of which they are nationals. As stated in the ICRC Commentary:

> it is intended to cover anyone who is *not* a national of the Party to the conflict or Occupying Power in whose hands he is. The Convention thus remains faithful to a recognized principle of international law: it does not interfere in a State's relations with its own national.[71]

It would thus seem that the Civilians Convention could not include as a protected person a civilian sympathizer of a national liberation group who is taken hostage by the armed forces of his State. It is difficult to conclude, therefore, that the Convention would protect the civilian if the opposite situation obtained, i.e., when the movement took as hostage a supporter of the regime.

The case reconsidered in light of modern developments in international law

Consideration must be given to developments in international law since the 1960s which raise the possibility that wars of national liberation (but not other civil wars) may come within the scope of the Geneva Conventions in such a way as to displace the Hostages Convention in some cases. Specifically, many States consider that wars of national liberation, sanctioned by the principle of self-determination, are now international in nature. Thus, in a number of resolutions during the 1960s and 1970s, the General Assembly called for the application of the Geneva Conventions to such armed conflicts,[72] and, in Resolution 3103 (XXVIII) of 12 December 1973, it stated that "armed conflicts involving the struggle of peoples against colonial and alien domination and racist régimes are to be regarded as international armed conflicts in the sense of the 1949 Geneva Conventions".[73]

However, even if armed conflicts involving national liberation are

---

[71] ICRC Commentary, note 51, *supra*, at p. 46.
[72] See, e.g., GA Res 2621 (XXV) of 12 October 1970, UN GAOR, 25th Sess., Supp. 28, p. 1, UN Doc A/8028 (1971); GA Res 2508 (XXIV) of 21 November 1969, UN GAOR, 24th Sess., Supp. 30, p. 67, UN Doc A/7630 (1970).
[73] UN GAOR, 28th Sess., Supp. 30, p. 142, UN Doc A/9030 (1974). A thorough treatment of the issue of whether such conflicts are international in nature is contained in Abi-Saab, note 53, *supra, passim*.

now considered to be international in nature pursuant to customary international law, this would not be enough to render the Hostages Convention inapplicable to an act of hostage-taking committed during the course of such a struggle. As earlier noted, the Hostages Convention is only displaced when the States Parties are "bound under" the Geneva instruments to prosecute or hand over an alleged offender.[74] States Parties will not be so bound unless the Geneva Conventions are applicable to that conflict pursuant to common Article 2. Thus, before the Hostages Convention will be displaced, the national liberation movement must become bound under the Civilians Convention in such a way as to make that instrument applicable to the conflict. Two possibilities have been suggested as to how this can be done.[75] The first is that a national liberation movement can be seen as a "Power" within the meaning of common Article 2 which can accept and apply the provisions of the Geneva Conventions in an armed conflict with a "Power" which is a State Party, thus binding itself to those instruments for the purposes of that particular conflict. Alternatively, each of the Geneva Conventions contains a provision — Article 155 in the case of the Civilians Convention — which states that any "Power" can accede to the Convention. If a national liberation movement is a "Power" it could, therefore, become a full party to the instrument pursuant to that provision. One proponent of these possibilities argues that they find their justification in the following: 1) the widespread view of wars of national liberation as international armed conflicts; 2) the fact that the term "Power" has sometimes been used to refer to entities other than States; and 3) the humanitarian purpose of the Conventions requires that they be as widely applied as possible.[76]

With respect to the issue of protected persons, as noted above the definition of that group would seemingly exclude those persons who are held hostage by the armed forces of the State of which they are nationals and, conversely, those who are held by rebels who share their nationality.[77] However, supporters of the theory that national liberation movements can become bound by the Geneva Conventions

---

[74] See pp. 277-278 (text accompanying notes 49 & 50).

[75] See, e.g., Abi-Saab, note 53, *supra*, at p. 400; Schindler, note 53, *supra*, at p. 135. See also Veuthey, "Guerilla Warfare and Humanitarian Law", International Review of the Red Cross (May-June 1983) 119, 123.

[76] Abi-Saab, note 53, *supra*, at p. 400. Similarly, one view expressed by some draftsmen of the 1977 Protocols was that since wars of national liberation are international according to the UN, then the term "Power" should refer not only to States but also to non-State entities which enjoy the right to self-determination. See Commentary to the Protocols, note 61, *supra*, at p. 47.

[77] This fact was noted by Western delegates during the drafting of the 1977 Additional Protocols. See generally Lysaght, "The Attitude of Western Countries", in Cassese (ed.), *The New Humanitarian Law of Armed Conflict* 352 (1979).

would argue that since the notion of nationality is technically inoperative in the context of wars of national liberation, protected persons within the meaning of the Civilians Convention should include, in the case of an alien or colonial regime, the local inhabitants of that territory and, in the case of a racist regime, the group which is discriminated against.[78]

If it is accepted that such conflicts are international in nature, that the Conventions can come into force during such conflicts in one or both of the ways suggested (and it appears that some liberation groups have attempted to bring the Conventions into force as between themselves and their adversaries),[79] and that the victims can be persons protected under the Civilians Convention, then the above hypothetical situation, and other hostage-takings committed during struggles for national liberation, can fall within the Civilians Convention and result in the obligation to extradite or prosecute the alleged offenders. This will only be so, however, if the national liberation movement has, in fact, taken the steps necessary to bind itself to the Civilians Convention. In that event, the Hostages Convention will not apply to that situation.

However, the conclusion that an act of hostage-taking committed during a war of national liberation can be covered by the Civilians Convention in such a way as to require the extradition or prosecution of the alleged offenders is tenuous at best. Initially, despite the widespread support for the idea, it is difficult to conclude with certainty that wars of national liberation are international armed conflicts pursuant to customary international law. Many Western and other States did not embrace the GA resolutions, mentioned above, which proclaimed the international nature of such conflicts. Resolution 3103, for example, passed by a vote of 83 in favour and 13 against, with 19 abstentions, failing to receive the support of most Western nations.[80] While it could be argued that the adoption of

---

[78] See, e.g., Abi-Saab, note 53, *supra*, at pp. 427-28.

[79] The African National Congress, for example, has submitted a declaration to the ICRC stating that it "intends to respect and be guided by the general principles of international humanitarian law applicable in armed conflicts", and that "[w]henever possible" it will "endeavour to respect the rules" of the four Geneva Conventions and Protocol I. See International Review of the Red Cross (Jan.-Feb. 1981), p. 21. Abi-Saab has argued that a "very strong case" can be made for considering this declaration and others like it as satisfying common Article 2 to the four Conventions. Abi-Saab, note 53, *supra*, at p. 434. Also, in 1960, the Provisional Government of Algeria notified the depositary of its accession to the Geneva Conventions, although it did not formally obtain its independence until 1962. See Roberts & Guelff (eds.), *Documents on the Law of War* 326 (1982). However, many States, particularly France, objected to this "accession" on the basis that the Provisional Government was not a State. See Taubenfeld, "The Applicability of the Laws of War in Civil War", in Moore (ed.), *Law and Civil War in the Modern World* 510 (1974).

[80] UN GAOR, 28th Sess., Plenary (2197th mtg.), p. 4, para. 29, UN Doc A/28/PV.2197 (1973).

Article 1(4) of Protocol I, which expressly declares wars of national liberation to be international armed conflicts, confirms or establishes a customary rule to that effect,[81] such an argument is less than compelling. Most Western States at first voted against that provision,[82] and abstained when it came up for a final vote.[83] Western States were concerned that Article 1(4) politicizes humanitarian law by making the motives behind the conflict a criterion for the applicability of that law.[84] While their subsequent abstention in the final vote may, to a certain extent, represent at least acquiescence in the idea that such conflicts are international in nature,[85] some Western States remain opposed to Protocol I precisely because of Article 1(4). The United States and France have declared that they will not ratify Protocol I.[86] The US government has objected particularly to what it considers the legitimization of liberation and "terrorist" groups by the instrument.[87]

---

[81] Abi-Saab, for example, suggests that Article 1(4) confirms the view that such conflicts are international by customary law. See Abi-Saab, note 53, *supra*, at pp. 369-72, 433. Cassese states that the adoption of Article 1(4) "testified to the formulation of a rule binding on all States participating in the conference (irrespective of whether or not they ratify the *Protocol I*), save for Israel, which consistently rejected the provision". See Cassese, "Wars of National Liberation and Humanitarian Law", in Swinarski (ed.), *Studies and Essays in Honour of Jean Pictet* 322 (1984).

[82] The vote was 70 in favour and 21 against, with 13 abstentions. See *Official Records of the Diplomatic Conference on the Reaffirmation and Development of International Humanitarian Law Applicable in Armed Conflicts*, Geneva 1974-1977 (1978), Vol. VIII, p. 102, para. 42, Doc CDDH/I/SR. 13.

[83] *Id.* at Vol. VI, pp. 40-41, para. 58, Doc CDDH/SR. 36. The vote was 87 in favour and 1 against, with 11 abstentions. Israel voted against the provision. As one commentator states, the issue of the applicability of Protocol I to national liberation movements was the subject of almost "crippling debate". See Keith, "The Present State of International Humanitarian Law", 9 Aust. YIL 13, 17 (1985). See also Commentary to the Protocols, note 61, *supra*, at p. 41.

[84] See Roberts, "The New Rules for Waging War: The Case Against Ratification of Additional Protocol I", 26 Va. J. Int'l L. 109, 126-27 (1986); Aldrich, "Progressive Development of the Laws of War: A Reply to the Criticisms of the 1977 Protocol I", 26 Va. J. Int'l L. 693, 701 (1986); Wortley, "Observations on the Revision of the 1949 Geneva 'Red Cross' Conventions", 54 BYIL 143, 151 (1983); Levie (ed.), *Protection of War Victims*, Vol. I, 68 (1979); Baxter, "Humanitarian Law or Humanitarian Politics? The 1974 Diplomatic Conference of Humanitarian Law", 16 Harv. Int'l L. J. 1, 17 (1975). The view as expressed during the drafting of the 1977 Protocols was that it was not possible to dismiss the "fundamental distinction" between international conflicts and conflicts of a non-international character — a distinction based on "objective legal criteria" — simply on the basis of the reasons underlying the armed conflict. See Commentary to the Protocols, note 61, *supra*, at p. 47. It may be noted that even the experts involved in the drafting of the Protocols concluded that wars of national liberation could not be seen as international pursuant to customary international law. *Id.* at pp. 47 & 49. However, inclusion of wars of national liberation in the category of international armed conflicts was a major goal of many developing States during the drafting of the Protocols. Baxter, *supra*, at p. 11.

[85] See Cassese, note 81, *supra*, at p. 323.

[86] See *International Herald Tribune*, Feb. 17, 1987.

[87] See *Letter of Transmittal from the President, Protocol II Additional to the 1949 Geneva Conventions and Relating to the Protection of Victims of Noninternational Armed Conflicts*, S. Treaty Doc. No. 2, 100th Cong., 1st Sess. (1987), *reprinted in* 81 AJIL 910 (1987). But

(*continued on p. 292*)

But of most importance, however, those States which would be most directly affected by a rule of customary international law to the effect that such conflicts are international in nature — South Africa and Israel — have completely rejected such a notion.[88] South Africa, moreover, did not participate in the Diplomatic Conference which drafted the Protocols after the first session, and Israel voted against Article 1(4).[89] Neither State, moreover, has become party to the Protocol.[90]

However, even if such conflicts are now considered to be international in nature, the more important question for the purpose of this study is whether a national liberation movement can bind itself to the Geneva Conventions in such a way as to bring them into force during its conflict with the colonial, alien or racist power.[91] If national liberation movements cannot so bind themselves, then the obligation *aut dedere aut judicare* cannot arise with respect to an act of hostage-taking committed in the course of such a conflict, and the Hostages Convention will not be displaced. On balance, it would appear that national liberation movements cannot be considered as "Powers" such that they may bring the Geneva Conventions into force. As Cassese states, the "whole context and wording of the various provisions of the Geneva Conventions make it clear that when they mention 'Powers' they intend to apply to States only", an interpretation, he concludes, which is "borne out by subsequent practice."[92] It might be noted, for example, that the ICRC Commentary to Article 155 of the Civilians Convention states that it is open to all "States".[93] While it appears that many States now consider that national liberation movements are "Powers" which may accept and apply or accede to the Geneva

---

([87] *continued*)
this may be a passing attitude, particular to the Reagan administration. It appears that the US delegation, despite serious misgivings regarding the wisdom of including national liberation movements within the scope of Protocol I, attempted to have Article 1(4) adopted by consensus. See Abi-Saab, note 53, *supra*, at p. 391.

[88] See Schindler, note 53, *supra*, at p. 136; Greenwood, "The Application of the Geneva Protocols of 1977 and Their Impact on General International Law in Humanitarian Matters", in Conderelli (ed.), *The Geneva Protocols of 1977 Additional to the Conventions of 1949: Ten Years On* (1988), at pp. 23-24. Schindler thus argues that the opposition of these and other States militate against the existence of a rule of customary law that such conflicts are international in nature.

[89] See note 83, *supra*; Cassese, note 81, *supra*, at p. 323.

[90] The fact that neither of these States, whose interests are so directly affected, have ratified Protocol I make it difficult to argue that Article 1(4) has become a rule of customary law. See generally *North Sea Continental Shelf Cases*, ICJ Rep. 1969, p. 43, para. 73. Even Cassese would not argue that it is a rule binding as against South Africa or Israel. See generally note 81, *supra*.

[91] To say that such conflicts are international in nature does not mean *ipso facto* that national liberation groups may bring those Conventions into force as between themselves and their adversaries. It simply means that the customary rules of international law regarding international armed conflicts must be applied to struggles for national liberation. Cf. Cassese, note 81, *supra*, at p. 324.

[92] *Id.*, at p. 316.

[93] ICRC Commentary, note 51, *supra*, at p. 621.

Conventions,[94] even some proponents of this view recognize that it is not one which is generally held.[95] It was the uncertainty in this area which, in part, led to the drafting of Article 1(4) and Article 96(3) of Protocol I.[96]

Thus, while it is certainly desirable from a humanitarian point of view to extend the protections of the Geneva Conventions as far as possible, it seems best to conclude that the Civilians Convention cannot in the current state of international law apply to the above hypothetical situation, or to other hostage-takings by national liberation movements, in such a way as to render the Hostages Convention inapplicable. It remains to be seen what effect Additional Protocol I has on the law with respect to national liberation movements.

1977 Additional Protocol I Relating to the Protection of Victims of International Armed Conflicts

It is possible, at least in theory, that certain acts of hostage-taking committed during the course of a struggle for national liberation will be covered by Protocol I in such a way as to require the prosecution or extradition of the hostage-taker. In accordance with the trend to "internationalize" armed conflicts for national liberation, Article 1, paragraph 4, of Protocol I provides that the instrument shall apply, in addition to those circumstances envisaged by common Article 2 of the Geneva Conventions, to:

> armed conflicts in which peoples are fighting against colonial domination and alien occupation and against racist régimes in the exercise of their right of self-determination, as enshrined in the Charter of the United Nations and the Declaration on Principles of International Law concerning

---

[94] See Commentary to the Protocols, note 61, *supra*, at p. 1091.

[95] See Schindler, note 53, *supra*, at p. 136. Even Abi-Saab recognizes that there was heavy resistance to the idea that national liberation movements could bind themselves to the Geneva Conventions in the ways suggested. However, he argues that the subsequent adoption of Protocol I, which establishes a mechanism by which that instrument may be brought into force in struggles for national liberation, vindicates the interpretation of the term "Powers" as including national liberation movements. See Abi-Saab, note 53, *supra*, at p. 433. In this connexion, it might be noted that an international instrument should be interpreted "within the framework of the entire legal system prevailing at the time of the interpretation." See *Legal Consequences for States of the Continued Presence of South Africa in Namibia, Advisory Opinion*, ICJ Rep. 1971, p. 31, para. 53. However, given the continued resistance both to the idea that wars of national liberation are international in nature and to the interpretation of the term "Powers" as including national liberation movements — particularly by those States which are most directly affected by such conflicts and which have not ratified Protocol I — it does not appear that this maxim would compel an interpretation of the term "Powers" as employed in the Civilians Convention as including such movements.

[96] See generally Schindler, note 53, *supra*, at p. 136.

Friendly Relations and Co-operation among States in accordance with the Charter of the United Nations.

The precise way in which the Protocol, and, therefore, the Conventions themselves, become applicable to such conflicts and binding upon the liberation movement as well as other Parties to the Protocol is set forth in Article 96, paragraph 3. It is worth setting out that paragraph in full:

> The authority representing a people engaged against a High Contracting Party in an armed conflict of the type referred to in Article 1, paragraph 4, may undertake to apply the Conventions and this Protocol in relation to that conflict by means of a unilateral declaration addressed to the depositary. Such declaration shall, upon its receipt by the depositary, have in relation to that conflict the following effects:
> (a) the Conventions and this Protocol are brought into force for the said authority as a Party to the conflict with immediate effect;
> (b) the said authority assumes the same rights and obligations as those which have been assumed by a High Contracting Party to the Conventions and this Protocol; and
> (c) the Conventions and this Protocol are equally binding upon all Parties to the conflict.

It can be seen from this provision that the Geneva Conventions, supplemented by Protocol I, will apply to a struggle for national liberation only if: 1) the State against whom the struggle is conducted is party to Protocol I; and 2) the appropriate authority of the national liberation movement makes the necessary declaration.[97] If these conditions are satisfied, all the provisions of the Civilians Convention will apply to that conflict, including the prohibition against hostage-taking[98] and the requirement that hostage-takers must be extradited or prosecuted. The Hostages Convention will not apply to an act of hostage-taking committed in such circumstances. Without such a declaration, however, the Conventions and Protocol cannot "apply" to that conflict within the meaning of common Article 2 of the four Conventions and Article 1(4) of the Protocol. If the instruments do not apply to that conflict, then the obligation *aut dedere aut judicare* cannot arise with respect to an act of hostage-taking which occurs

---

[97] If the State against which the national liberation group is fighting is not party to Protocol I, such a declaration will not bring the Protocol into effect as regards that struggle. The declaration will serve only as a "unilateral undertaking of obligations". See Commentary to the Protocols, note 61, *supra*, at p. 1092. It may be noted, moreover, that, in contrast to the situation of a "Power" under common Article 2 of the Geneva Conventions (see note 63, *supra*), an express declaration must be made.

[98] It may be noted, moreover, that in addition to the relevant provisions of the Civilians Convention, Article 75(2) of Protocol I contains an additional prohibition against the taking of hostages as a fundamental guarantee.

therein. There will thus be no bar to the operation of the Hostages Convention. It should be emphasized moreover, that in order for the Hostages Convention to be displaced in favour of the Geneva regime, the act of hostage-taking must be committed by an "authority", that is, by the movement itself.[99] Acts of hostage-taking committed by groups or individuals who are sympathetic to the movement but who are not factually linked thereto will not fall under the Geneva instruments.[100] As regards protected persons, it would seem that the reference to "peoples" in Article 1(4) (as in "peoples fighting against colonial domination", etc.) recognizes a "separate corporate existence" between the regime and the oppressed group such that for the purposes of the class of protected person, they are of different nationalities.[101]

Despite the possibilities that are opened up by Protocol I, however, there is in fact very little prospect that it will be applicable to a particular act of hostage-taking committed during a national liberation struggle in such a way as to give rise to the obligation *aut dedere aut judicare*. In the first place, it should be reiterated that the class of groups which fall within Article 1(4) — those fighting for self-determination "against colonial domination, and alien occupation and against racist régimes" — is quite restricted. The Protocol cannot, therefore, be applicable in the majority of civil wars or armed conflicts which are not conducted between the armed forces of two States, regardless of how valid the grievances of the rebels are.[102] Moreover,

---

[99] See p. 283 (note 61 and accompanying text).

[100] Cf. Hailbronner, note 9, *supra*, at p. 178.

[101] See Abi-Saab, note 53, *supra*, pp. 428-429. As earlier noted, the class of persons protected under the Civilians Convention includes only persons who are "in the hands of a Party to the conflict or Occupying Power of which they are not nationals", thus indicating that the obligation to extradite or prosecute does not obtain when a State has taken one of its own nationals as hostage. Despite the extension of the category of international armed conflicts to include those involving national liberation movements, no provision of Protocol I expressly changes this limitation in the definition of protected persons. However, such a change must be implied since, as stated in the ICRC Commentary to the Protocols, "to insist on the 'official' nationality would result in depriving these provisions of a large part of their purpose, and it is therefore necessary to resort to concepts such as 'belonging' or 'allegiance'. Note 61, *supra*, at p. 56.

[102] Commentators are in general agreement on this point. See, e.g., Cassese, "The Status of Rebels under the 1977 Geneva Protocol on Non-International Armed Conflicts", 30 ICLQ 416, 417 (1980); Schindler, note 53, *supra*, at p. 137; Abi-Saab, note 53, *supra*, at p. 396; Commentary to the Protocols, note 61, at p. 55. Thus, not every insurgent, secessionist or dissident group which calls itself a national liberation movement will be entitled to that status. The struggles which are, in fact, conducted "against colonial domination and alien occupation and against racist régimes" would appear to be quite limited. The ICRC Commentary notes that the category of "colonial domination" covers classical colonial situations, where a people have taken up arms to free itself from the domination of another people. The category of "alien occupation", by way of contrast, "covers cases of partial or total occupation of a territory which has not yet been fully formed as a State" (Abi-Saab, note 53, *supra*, at p. 394, explains further that these would include "colonies of settlement", i.e., where the settlers sever

(continued on p. 296)

the Protocol only enters into force with respect to a struggle for national liberation if the authority representing the people in the struggle makes the necessary declaration.[103] Of critical importance, such a declaration is only valid *when the government against which the movement is fighting has already become a party to the Protocol*. This provision is the greatest weakness of the attempt to bring such struggles into the ambit of the law of Geneva.[104] Those States which

([102] *continued*)
their ties with their mother countries and exercise a colonial policy *vis-à-vis* the local population), while "racist régimes" involve "cases of régimes founded on racist criteria". The first two categories, according to the ICRC, "imply the existence of distinct peoples", while the third, "if not the existence of two completely distinct peoples, at least a rift within a people which ensures hegemony of one section in accordance with racist ideas". These categories are not mutually exclusive. The ICRC commentary concludes that the listing "colonial domination, alien occupation and racist régimes" is exhaustive; no other types of struggles will fit within Article 1(4). Commentary to the Protocols, note 61, *supra*, at p. 54. Other commentators agree. Schindler, for example, adds that "[o]nce the last remains of European colonialism and of the predominance of the white race will be overcome, the provisions on wars of national liberation" will become superfluous. Schindler, note 53, *supra*, at p. 144. It is clear that the draftsmen of the Protocol had in mind the struggles in Southern Africa, Palestine and other areas where there are (or were) colonies and non-self-governing territories. *Id*. at p. 138. The legitimacy of wars of national liberation would not appear to extend to struggles in post-colonial and independent States. *Id*. at pp. 137-38. See also Aldrich, note 84, *supra*, at p. 702; Higgins, "The Attitude of Western States Towards Legal Aspects of the Use of Force", in Cassese (ed.), *The Current Regulation of the Use of Force* 435, 449 (1986); Gasser, "An Appeal for Ratification by the United States", 81 AJIL 912, 917 (1987). However, even if it is agreed that the listing in Article 1(4) is exhaustive (and Abi-Saab, note 53, *supra*, at pp. 396-398, for one, posits that it might not be and that other struggles for self-determination could exist which fall within that provision), there will be room for disagreement over whether a particular struggle is, in fact, "against colonial domination and alien occupation and against racist régimes". Because there are no definite legal standards in this regard, some commentators have noted that application of Article 1(4) would be highly subjective. See Baxter, note 84, *supra*, at p. 16; Roberts, note 84, *supra*, at p. 127.

[103] It may briefly be noted that it is not entirely clear as to what "authority" is entitled to make the necessary declaration on behalf of the "people" engaged in the struggle. No criteria in this regard are expressly set forth in the text, and a proposal that would have required recognition by the relevant regional intergovernmental organization was not adopted. See Commentary to the Protocols, note 61, *supra*, p. 1089. Abi-Saab lists four considerations which have been suggested as relevant to a determination of whether an "authority" is entitled to that status: 1) recognition by the regional intergovernmental organization (the easy case since it is the formula employed by the UN and was used by the Diplomatic Conference which drafted the Protocols); 2) territorial control by the group (a doubtful criterion); 3) that the liberation movement be "truly representative of the people"; and 4) that it attain a minimum degree of effectiveness as a belligerent. Abi-Saab, note 53, *supra*, at pp. 407-15. Schindler argues that several provisions of Protocol I indicate that an "authority" must exhibit "a minimum amount of organization and influence to secure the application of the Conventions and Protocol I." Since Article 96 requires equal application of the instruments by the parties to the conflict, this Article implies that the authority can secure their application. Moreover, Article 43 of Protocol I requires a minimal degree of organization of the armed forces of each party to the conflict, a requirement which, according to Schindler, can only be satisfied by an "authority exerting a minimal amount of governmental power". Schindler, note 53, *supra*, at p. 140. In the end, however, the law in this regard remains unclear.

[104] Writers are in general agreement on this point. See, e.g., Schindler, note 53, *supra*, at pp. 141 & 144; Veuthey, note 75, *supra*, at p. 122.

are the actual targets of such a struggle — particularly South Africa and Israel — have not become party to the Protocol and are extremely unlikely to do so in the foreseeable future.[105]

This weakness was recognized by some of the draftsmen of the Hostages Convention. During the final discussions held in the Sixth Committee on this Article, the representative of Pakistan noted that "most of the movements struggling for self-determination were not recognized by the colonial or occupying States and were usually denied the rights established under Additional Protocol I". He thus expressed dismay that Article 12 was drafted in such a way as to allow the "colonial or occupying" power to determine which instruments would apply to a particular act. He urged that the Article be re-drafted in such a way as expressly to exempt national liberation movements from this Convention.[106] Alternatively, he stated that he could accept the Article on the understanding that "in cases involving a movement for self-determination, no State, or colonial or occupying Power, could invoke the Convention if, by its own actions, it had precluded the application of the Geneva Conventions and Additional Protocols thereto".[107] However, no such interpretation can be made of this Article. In light of the above, cases of hostage-taking during wars of national liberation are likely to come within the scope of the Hostages Convention, rather than the Geneva instruments, assuming that Article 13 of the former instrument does not preclude its applicability.

The expansion of the obligation to extradite or prosecute hostage-takers under Protocol I

It would appear that the scope of the obligation to extradite or prosecute hostage-takers under Protocol I is greater than that under the four original Conventions. The Protocol states that

> [a]cts described as grave breaches in the Conventions are grave breaches of this Protocol if committed against persons in the power of an adverse Party protected by Articles 44 [expanding the class of combatants and prisoners of war], 45 [other persons who have taken part in the hostilities] and 73 [refugees and stateless persons] of this Protocol, or against the wounded, sick and shipwrecked of the adverse Party who are protected by this Protocol, or against those medical or religious personnel, medical units or

---

[105] See Greenwood, note 88, *supra*, at p. 23. Thus, no declaration has been deposited pursuant to Article 96(3). *Id*.

[106] UN GAOR, 34th Sess., C.6 (14th mtg.), p. 16, para. 94, UN Doc A/C.6/34/SR.14 (1979).

[107] UN GAOR, 34th Sess., C.6 (62nd mtg.), p. 2, para. 4, UN Doc A/C.6/34/SR.62 (1979).

medical transports which are under the control of the adverse Party and are protected by this Protocol.[108]

Although it is not entirely clear, this wording indicates that all the grave breaches described in all four Conventions are grave breaches of the Protocol — requiring extradition or prosecution of the offenders — if they are committed against any of the listed categories of persons. Thus, for example, hostage-taking, a breach of the Civilians Convention, would be a breach of the Protocol if directed against a "wounded, sick or shipwrecked" person of the adverse party or against another person who has taken part in the hostilities. Since under the original Geneva instruments hostage-taking is only a grave breach of the Civilians Convention, this Article may represent a significant expansion of the obligation to prosecute acts of hostage-taking committed during international armed conflicts.

---

[108] Art. 85(2).

Article 13

LIMITATION OF THE CONVENTION TO INTERNATIONAL ACTS OF HOSTAGE-TAKING

This Convention shall not apply where the offence is committed within a single State, the hostage and the alleged offender are nationals of that State and the alleged offender is found in the territory of that State.

1. INTRODUCTION

By the terms of this Article, the Convention will not apply to a particular offence when the following four conditions are all met:

1) the offence is committed within a single State;
2) the hostage is a national of that State;
3) the offender is a national of that State; and
4) the offender is subsequently found in the territory of that State.

The Article thus removes from the scope of the Convention all acts of hostage-taking which are internal in nature. Although each State can be presumed to have laws that cover such criminal activity in its territory,[1] if the conditions envisaged by this Article obtain there will be no internationally binding obligation upon Parties to extradite or prosecute the offender or to fulfil the other provisions of the Convention. The only problem of interpretation which arises with respect to this Article is whether it excludes from the scope of the Convention acts of hostage-taking which are otherwise internal in nature, but where the target of demands is either a foreign State or a third party located in a foreign State.

All of the other anti-terrorism conventions also have provisions which make it clear that they apply only to international offences. However, the criteria in this regard vary from instrument to instrument, reflecting the fact that they were each designed to protect different interests. The Hague Convention, for example, designed to protect international civil aviation, will only apply if the place of take-off or the place of actual landing of the aircraft on board which the offence is committed is outside the territory of the State of registration of the aircraft.[2] A similar restriction is contained in the Montreal Convention, which provides that it will apply only if the

---
[1] See generally p. 77 (note 1 in the commentary on Article 1).
[2] Art. 3(3).

actual or intended place of take-off or landing of the aircraft is outside the territory of the State of registration or if the offence is committed in the territory of a State other than the State of registration.[3] The Rome Convention, designed to protect international maritime navigation, provides that it will only apply "if the ship is navigating or is scheduled to navigate into, through or from waters beyond the outer limit of the territorial sea of a single State, or the lateral limits of its territorial sea with adjacent States."[4] Similar to the Hostages Convention, however, all of the other anti-terrorism instruments will apply in situations not otherwise covered if the alleged offender is subsequently found in the territory of another State, i.e., in the case of the ICAO Conventions, in the territory of a State other than the State of registration, and, in the case of the Rome Convention, a State other than the State in whose waters the ship was navigating.[5]

It might be noted that, to a certain extent, the threshold of applicability of this Convention is lower than that of the other instruments since, for example, the mere fact that one of the hostages is of a different nationality than all the others will be enough for this Convention to apply, even to an otherwise solely internal offence. It is, therefore, possible that an offence of hostage-taking covered by this Convention will coincide with an aerial hijacking or the seizure of a ship which is not covered by the Hague or Rome Conventions. Thus, this Convention will fill in some gaps, as regards the obligation *aut dedere aut judicare*, left by those instruments.[6]

---

[3] Art. 4(2). This provision relates to all the offences in the Montreal Convention which are directed against aircraft or passengers. With respect to offences against air navigation facilities, paragraph 5 of this Article provides that the Convention will apply only if such facilities are used in "international air navigation".

[4] Art. 4(1). Article 1, paragraph 1, of the Rome Protocol states that it will apply when offences "are committed on board or against fixed platforms located on the continental shelf". The New York Convention also places limits on its applicability. Article 1 provides that an "internationally protected person" within the scope of the Convention means, *inter alia*, "a Head of State, including any member of a collegial body performing the functions of a Head of State under the constitution of the State concerned, a Head of government or a Minister for Foreign Affairs, *whenever any such person is in a foreign State* . . ." (emphasis added).

[5] See Art. 3(5), Hague Convention (which provides that only certain provisions of the Convention, i.e., those relating to the rule *aut dedere aut judicare*, will apply in such circumstances); Art. 4(3), Montreal Convention (unless the offence is against an air navigation facility used only in non-international air navigation); Art. 4(2), Rome Convention; Art. 1(2), Rome Protocol (which provides that in cases where it does not apply pursuant to paragraph 1 of the Article, "it nevertheless applies when the offender or alleged offender is found in the territory of a State Party other than the State in whose internal waters or territorial sea the fixed platform is located").

[6] These would, however, be somewhat unusual cases. Suppose, for example, an aircraft registered in State A is hijacked in the airspace of State A whilst en route to State B from a point in State A. The hijackers demand to be taken to State C. However, before proceeding to State C the aircraft stops to refuel at another point in State A, without first landing in any other State. The authorities of State A refuse to allow the refueling; the hijackers hold the passengers hostage in return for such permission and

2. INTERPRETATION

"This Convention shall not apply . . ."

When the four conditions set forth above obtain, this Convention will not be applicable to that act of hostage-taking. Thus, for example, States have no obligation to establish penalties for, or jurisdiction over, such conduct and, once such an offence is committed, the Convention imposes no duty to extradite or prosecute the alleged offender or to comply with a request for judicial assistance. In effect, no "offence" within the meaning of this Convention will have been committed and a State Party will, therefore, be unable to sustain an allegation that the way in which another State Party dealt with such a situation constituted a breach of this Convention.

". . . where the offence is committed within a single State . . ."

The first of the four conditions necessary to keep a particular act of hostage-taking outside the scope of this Convention is that the offence must have taken place "within a single State". Stated somewhat differently, if any of the constitutive elements of the offence are committed in a second State, this Convention will apply. As noted in the commentary on Article 1,[7] the elements of the offence of hostage-taking are:

---

for the release of prisoners in State A. The incident ends, either peacefully or violently, before the aircraft takes off again. While it may be assumed that State A will wish to prosecute the offenders for the offence of hijacking, it is under no obligation in this situation to do so pursuant to the Hague Convention since the place of take-off and place of actual landing of the aircraft were in the State of registration, State A. However, if even one of the passengers or hijackers were nationals of a State other than State A, then the Hostages Convention will apply to that act, requiring State A to extradite or prosecute the perpetrators for the offence of hostage-taking. Similarly, suppose a ship which is neither navigating nor scheduled to navigate "into, through or from waters beyond the outer limit of the territorial sea of a single State, or the lateral limits of its territorial sea with adjacent States" is seized and the passengers held hostage in order to compel that State to do or abstain from some act. The Rome Convention will not apply to that incident (unless the offenders are subsequently found in the territory of another State); however, if even one of the passengers or offenders is a national of another State, then the Hostages Convention will apply. While it is possible to envisage situations wherein the Hague or Rome Conventions will apply to an offence which is also a hostage-taking, but where the Hostages Convention will not apply, these would be far more unusual even than the situations just described.

It may be noted in this connexion that, pursuant to Articles 3(2) and 4(1), respectively, the Hague and Montreal Conventions do not apply to "aircraft used in military, customs or police services". Similarly, the Rome Convention, pursuant to Article 2, does not apply to a warship or to a "ship owned or operated by a State when being used as a naval auxiliary or for customs or police purposes". Hostage-takings committed on such aircraft or vessels could be covered by this Convention.

[7] See p. 79 (note 7 and accompanying text in the commentary on Article 1).

1) the seizure or detention of another person; and

2) the threat to kill, injure or continue the detention in order to compel a third party to do or abstain from doing some act.

In most situations, the wording of this Article will present no problems: if the offenders seize and detain the hostages and threaten them in the territory of a State, and do not move them to another State, then the offence has been committed "within a single State".

Status of the Convention in an otherwise internal offence when the target of demands is a foreign State or a third party located in a foreign State

While the above-quoted language seems simple enough, certain situations can be envisaged in which it would not be as easy to determine whether or not the offence has been committed entirely within a single State. Difficulty could arise from the fact that Article 1 refers to the conduct of the hostage-takers as having an objective, namely, "in order to compel a third party" to do or abstain from doing a particular act. What is the position if, though the seizure and detention take place in one State by nationals of that State against other nationals of that State (and are, therefore, *prima facie* "internal" in the contemplation of Article 13), the third party against whom the demand is addressed is outside the territory of that State or is a foreign State? Does that factor take the case outside the contemplation of Article 13 and thus within the scope of the Convention? The answer, from a plain reading of the words of this Article, would appear to be no: the Convention will not apply when the physical acts of the offenders take place solely in the territory of the State of which they and the hostages are nationals and where the offenders are subsequently found. However, the issue should not lightly be dismissed and is worthy of further examination. It may be helpful to employ a hypothetical situation in order to illustrate the problem:

In the territory of State A, nationals of State A who are members of an urban terrorist group take other nationals of State A hostage in order to compel State A to release certain other members of the group who have been convicted of crimes against State A and imprisoned. After seizing the hostages, the group issues a statement to a newspaper, which is subsequently printed, stating that the hostages will be killed unless the prisoners are released within 48 hours. After the offence, the hostage-takers do not leave State A. In this situation, the case is clear: the hostages and hostage-takers are nationals of State A, the hostage-takers are not subsequently found in the territory of another State and the elements of the offence — the detention and the threat — have both been committed entirely within the territory of

State A. Since all four conditions have been satisfied, this Convention will not apply.

However, suppose all the facts outlined above are the same but the terrorist group is seeking to compel State B, rather than State A, to release prisoners? State B hears of the threat and demand from the police in State A and/or from the news services. While in general it seems unlikely that a terrorist group would take nationals of State A hostage in order to compel State B to do or abstain from some act, such a situation is not unforeseeable. For example, the hostages from State A could be from the same ethnic group, religion or race as the citizens of State B. Moreover, not all acts of terrorism are so well planned, so perfectly executed or so rational as to preclude such a possibility.[8] Alternatively, suppose the third party is not a foreign State, but is a citizen of, or is located in, a foreign State. What if, for example, the hostage-takers are seeking to compel a corporation in State B to take some action, e.g., pay a ransom, in return for the release of hostages who are employees of that corporation, but who are located in, and nationals of, State A? Can it then be said that the offence has taken place "within a single State"? The answer to this question is not easily to be discerned. An attempt to resolve this question requires careful analysis of the elements of the offence of hostage-taking and of the *travaux préparatoires* of this Convention. Although it is not a clear-cut issue, on balance it would appear that these offences are committed "within a single State", and are thus outside the scope of this Convention.

The elements of the offence of hostage-taking

If an offence wherein the target of demands is a foreign State, or a third party located in a foreign State, is to be seen as not having been committed "within a single State" such that this Convention will apply to that incident, then one of the constitutive elements of the offence must be seen as having been committed, in whole or in part, outside of

---

[8] It might be noted in this connexion that the *Achille Lauro* hijacking occurred, apparently, only because the terrorists were discovered on board the ship while cleaning their guns. It was reported that the original plan was for the hijackers to use the ship as transport to the Israeli port of Ashdod where they were to conduct a terrorist strike. However, once they were discovered they decided to hijack the ship and take hostages (although another report had it that the hijackers changed their minds about the attack at Ashdod because of cowardice and decided instead to hijack the ship). In any event, the result was that the terrorists took hostages in an attempt to force concessions from Israel even though none of the hostages was, apparently, an Israeli citizen (although some of them were Jews). While this incident fell within the scope of the Convention for various reasons (e.g., the hostages were of different nationalities), the incident is an example of how a terrorist attack can deviate significantly from the terrorists' original plan. See XXXI *Keesing's Contemporary Archives* 34077 (1985). See also p. 4 (note 13 and accompanying text in the Introduction).

the territory of State A. It is clear that the hostages in the above hypothetical situation have been seized and detained in State A; therefore, the success of such an interpretation will depend upon an analysis of the second element, that of threatening to kill, injure or continue the detention of the hostages in order to compel the third party to do or abstain from doing some act. It could reasonably be argued that the threat either continues to be made or is not complete until it reaches the target of the demands, i.e., the third party. Under such an interpretation, the threat is made or uttered in the place where the third party hears of it, by whatever means (e.g., the media, a phone call, a letter, etc.). On this basis the offence has not taken place "within a single State", since one of the elements has taken place in State B, and it would fall within the scope of this Convention.

In this connexion, consideration should be given to the English case of *Treacy v. Director of Public Prosecutions*[9] which dealt with the roughly analogous statutory crime of blackmail — the essential element of which is a "demand with menaces".[10] The House of Lords held by a 3-2 majority that when a man in England posted a letter containing a demand to a woman in Germany, that demand was made, and the crime completed, where the letter was posted, rather than where it was received.[11] Although it would appear to be the holding that a demand in the crime of blackmail is made only in the country where first uttered or posted, two of their Lordships dissented and held that the demand can only be seen as made where received.[12] Moreover, no member of the majority precluded the possibility that if the facts were reversed, i.e., the letter posted in Germany and received in England, the demand could also be seen as made in England. Indeed, one member of the majority, in an opinion in which another member joined, left open the possibility that a demand which is posted in England can also be seen as made in the country where received on the theory of a "continuing demand".[13]

Thus, *Treacy* indicates the possibility that a threat or demand by hostage-takers could be made, not only in the place where the

---

[9] [1971] 2 WLR 112.

[10] Theft Act 1968, §21(1).

[11] [1971] 2 WLR 112, 112. See also *R. v. Owen*, [1957] 1 QB 174, 193, wherein the court held that a forged document is "uttered" in the place where the document is posted, not where it is received.

[12] [1971] 2 WLR 112, 114 [Lord Reid] & 119 [Lord Morris of Borth-Y-Gest]. See also Williams, "Venue and the Ambit of Criminal Law (Part 3)", 81 LQR 518, 521 (1965).

[13] [1971] 2 WLR 112, 120-122 [Lord Hodson, Lord Guest concurring]. Cf. *R. v. Baxter*, [1971] 2 All ER 359, 362, in which the court held that where a defendant sent letters from Northern Ireland in order to obtain money by deception in England, there were two views upon which it could be said that an attempt was committed in England: 1) that the attempt was still in being when the letters were received; and 2) that where a person dispatches a missile or a missive and arranges for its transport and delivery, part of the crime is committed in the jurisdiction by the means which he has arranged.

offenders are present at the time of the offence, but also in the place where it is received by the third party. While this was not the holding of *Treacy*, it is certainly reasonable that a State could consider that a threat or demand is "uttered" where it is received. As one commentator states with respect to situations such as in *Treacy*, the demand can be seen as "first made where the defendant acts and the system of communication used would be treated as an agent of the offender: a means by which his demand is preserved, transported and repeated".[14] Moreover, it is certainly the case that a person may commit an offence in a State in which he is not present (although this may depend upon an interpretation of the definition of the crime as requiring a consequence in that second State).[15] A construction of the crime of hostage-taking whereby the threat or demand is seen to be made where received by the third party would broaden the scope of this Convention, rendering it applicable to a potentially greater number of cases of hostage-taking. It is, therefore, entirely consistent with the purpose of this Convention to ensure that all acts of hostage-taking result in the punishment of the offenders. Moreover, there is certainly an international aspect to such a crime which would justify its coming within the scope of this instrument. However, it is somewhat difficult to conclude with confidence that this is the proper interpretation of this Article. Initially, it may be noted that a plain reading of the words "committed within a single State" would seem to lead to the conclusion that the Convention should not be interpreted as applicable (assuming that the other conditions are satisfied) when all the physical acts of the offenders take place within one State simply because a threat initially uttered in that State makes its way to another. As Lord Diplock stated in *Treacy*, an ordinary literate person would consider that he had made a demand at posting the letter, not when the letter was received.[16] The same would hold true for a demand or threat which travelled by newspaper or some other medium. Similar to Lord Diplock's rationale, the rule of treaty interpretation that terms of an instrument should be given their ordinary meaning would lead to the conclusion that this Convention should not apply in such a situation. Moreover, the fact that some States *may*, in interpreting

---

[14] See Hirst, "Jurisdiction Over Cross-Frontier Offences", 97 LQR 80, 84 (1981).

[15] Some commentators and courts make a distinction between "conduct crimes" and "result crimes". A conduct crime is one in which the elements of the *actus reas* include only the behaviour of the offender and, perhaps, the circumstances in which they take place. It is not necessary that the conduct produces any further result. In this view, *Treacy* is a conduct crime (although the dissenters seemed to see it as a result crime, requiring receipt of the demand by the victim). A result crime, by way of contrast, requires the conduct of the offender to produce some further consequence. An example would be murder. In this type of offence, an element can occur in a place other than where the offender is present. See Hirst, note 14, *supra*, at pp. 82-83.

[16] [1971] 2 WLR 112, 128.

their criminal law, consider that a threat or demand is made in the place where it is received does not seem to be a strong enough basis upon which to conclude that the element of threat in the offence of hostage-taking must be so interpreted, as a matter of international law, for all States Parties to this instrument. Any State court decisions in this regard will necessarily deal with such complex, and often interrelated, domestic law issues as the definition of the particular crime involved, that State's prior case-law, the language of its statute, its rules of statutory construction, the intention of its legislature and its rules regarding territorial jurisdiction.[17] Comparisons between such State court decisions concerning elements of domestic criminal offences and the elements of hostage-taking will necessarily be imperfect.

Moreover, a further analysis of the elements of the offence provides another argument against such an interpretation. In particular, there is not, in fact, any requirement contained in the elements of hostage-taking that a demand be made upon a third party. While a demand will, practically speaking, usually be made in an act of hostage-taking, and will be part and parcel of the threat to the hostages, the elements of the offence are the seizure and the threat to the well-being of the hostages. The words "in order to compel" do not require more than a motivation upon the part of the offender. The threat can be seen as directed towards the hostage, rather than towards the third party and, therefore, the offence is complete when the threat is initially uttered or communicated to the hostage. Thus, for example, if hostage-takers take hostages in order to compel State B to do a certain act and they threaten the lives or safety of the hostages but never make any outside communication of their intent, the offence is still complete even if State B never hears of it. Viewed in this way, no element of the offence can be seen as occurring in the second State. Even if the threat and demand are made together, however, and both are seen as directed towards the third party, there is no solid basis upon which to conclude that the element of threat takes place in the State where it is heard of by the third party.

Finally, while there is, as noted, an international aspect to cases wherein the target of demands is a foreign State or a third party located in a foreign State, and while that State is perhaps put into an uncomfortable position by such an offence, an offence which takes place in the territory of one State by nationals of that State against other nationals of that State is still an essentially internal affair. At the same time, however, it must be recognized that a certain element of ambiguity exists in the words "committed within a single State" such

---

[17] Cf. *Treacy*. On English cases regarding jurisdiction over offences which have an international dimension, see Hirst, note 14, *supra*; Williams, note 12, *supra*.

that it is at least plausible that the Convention should apply in such situations. It will be helpful, therefore, to examine the drafting history of this Convention. As will be seen, the *travaux préparatoires* support the conclusion that this Convention should not apply simply because the third party in an otherwise internal offence is a foreign State or a third party who is located in, or a national of, a foreign State.

Development of the Article

It does not appear that the draftsmen of the Convention ever examined the issue of when an offence can be said to have been "committed within a single State". However, they did consider language which would have made the Convention applicable whenever the third party to be compelled was: 1) a State; 2) an international organization; or 3) a natural or juridical person who was not a national of the territorial State. Article 10, paragraph 2, of the FRG draft provided that:

> This Convention shall not apply where the offence is committed within a single State, where the hostage, the offender, and the person or body corporate subjected to demands are all nationals of that State and where the offender is found in the territory of that State. This Convention shall, however, apply if a State, an international organization or an international conference is subjected to demands.

Thus, the FRG draft article specifically provided that the draft convention would apply *whenever* the compulsion was directed against *any* State or international organization, without regard to where the offence took place. Moreover, the FRG draft would have removed an act of hostage-taking from the scope of this Convention only if, in addition to the four conditions listed in this Article, a fifth condition was satisfied, namely, that the persons or entities subjected to demands were all nationals of the territorial State. That language indicates that the instrument *would* apply if the third party was a national of any other State. The FRG draft article would thus largely have eliminated the need to consider the issue of the location of the threat since, by the express terms thereof, the draft convention would always have applied when a foreign State, a national thereof, or an international organization (or conference) was the third party. However, the FRG version was whittled away by the Hostages Committee.

The fact that the FRG language was not adopted could suggest that the draftsmen considered that the element of "threat" takes place in the State in which it is heard of by the third party and that, therefore, there was no need for the Convention explicitly to provide that it will apply whenever another State or a national of another State was the third party. However, there is no indication from the *travaux préparatoires* that this was the case. More plausibly, it could suggest that the draftsmen did not want the Convention to apply to an otherwise internal offence simply because the third party was in another State or was itself a foreign State, believing instead that such an offence remains essentially internal in nature and is, therefore, more properly outside of the scope of this Convention.

Much of the debate on this Article appears to have occurred off the record, particularly during the crucial period in the development of the provision — the 1979 session of the Hostages Committee. However, there is some recorded debate which gives an indication as to the intentions of the draftsmen.

(i) *where a foreign State is subjected to demands*

As noted, the FRG language would have made the Convention applicable whenever any State — whether the territorial or a foreign State — was subjected to demands. With respect to this language, the representative of Mexico stated in the first session of the Hostages Committee that:

> even if a third State was involved, an international convention could not apply to an act committed by and solely involving nationals of the State where the act was committed. If the offender took the hostage in his own country, he must be brought to trial in his own country in accordance with national legislation.[18]

Although the reference to a "third State" is somewhat obscure (he probably meant to say "second State"), the Mexican representative appeared to be arguing that the Convention should not apply to an otherwise internal offence simply because a State — foreign or otherwise — was the subject of demands.

The representative of the FRG disagreed, stating in response that whenever a State was subjected to demands it was a matter of international concern. He added, however, that since reservations had been expressed, his delegation would have no objection to redrafting the Article.[19] Later in the first session, the FRG representative stated that, after reflecting on the objections expressed by the representatives of Mexico and Nigeria to the effect that the second sentence (the one which provided that the Convention would apply whenever a State, an international organization or international conference was the

---

[18] First Report of the Hostages Committee, p. 64, para. 18.
[19] *Id.* at para. 23.

subject of demands) of the FRG draft article "was in conflict with the principle that the draft convention should be limited to cases of international relevance . . . his delegation had concluded that there might be a stronger case for deleting the provision than for retaining it."[20]

During its second session, the Hostages Committee considered a proposal submitted by the French delegation to insert the word "foreign" before the word "State" in the second sentence of the FRG draft article.[21] This proposal was somewhat less restrictive than the point of view expressed by Mexico, in so far as it would have provided that the Convention would apply whenever a foreign State was subjected to demands in an otherwise internal offence. While some States such as Canada and the US seemed to prefer the original FRG language,[22] the French proposal appeared to have the support of many delegations. The delegate of the United Kingdom, for example, expressed doubt whether the Convention should apply where demands were made on a State in cases where there is no international element[23] (although this comment could also reflect a belief that the draft convention should not apply regardless of whether it was a foreign State or the territorial State which was subjected to demands in an otherwise internal offence). Similarly, the representative of the Philippines stated that it was obvious that the Convention would not apply where the offence only involved one State,[24] while the representative of the Netherlands supported the idea behind the French amendment, asserting that if the State subjected to demands was the State in whose territory the offence had been committed, the Convention should not apply.[25]

Delegations thus appeared to be divided into three groups with respect to whether the Convention should apply when compulsion was directed towards a State in an otherwise internal case. Some thought that the Convention should apply whenever any State is subjected to demands. Others believed that the Convention should apply only when the State that was subjected to demands was other than the State wherein the offence took place. A third group thought that it should never apply when the target of demands was a State, even a foreign State, if the offence was otherwise purely internal. The report of the Hostages Committee for the 1979 session indicates that it was proposed that the second sentence of the FRG draft article be deleted and that the words "or that State itself is subjected to

---

[20] *Id.* at p. 93, para. 9.
[21] UN Doc A/AC.188/L.13, in First Report of the Hostages Committee, p. 114.
[22] See Second Report of the Hostages Committee, p. 22, para. 7 (US) & p. 23, para. 12 (Canada).
[23] *Id.* at p. 22, para. 9.
[24] *Id.* at p. 23, para. 13.
[25] *Id.* at p. 23, para. 15.

demands" be inserted into the first sentence. The resulting text would have been as follows:

> This Convention shall not apply where the offence is committed within a single State, where the hostage, the alleged offender, and the person or body corporate subjected to demands are all nationals of that State or *that State itself is subjected to demands* and where the alleged offender is found in the territory of that State.[26] (emphasis added)

This language would have served the same purpose as the French proposal, explicitly removing from the scope of the Convention situations wherein the territorial State was subjected to demands in an otherwise internal situation and, thus, by implication, leaving within the scope of the Convention situations wherein a foreign State was subjected to demands. However, one delegation — it is unclear from the record which — proposed the deletion of the words "or that State itself is subjected to demands".[27] The final report of the Hostages Committee indicates that general agreement was reached on this proposal, although one delegation "noted that the deletion of the words referred to . . . restricted the scope of the future Convention".[28] The language agreed upon by the Hostages Committee was ultimately adopted by the Sixth Committee without change.[29]

Although the failure of the draftsmen to adopt language such as that contained in the FRG draft is not, by itself, conclusive proof that the Convention should not apply when a foreign State is the target of demands in an otherwise internal offence,[30] that action, combined with the plain meaning of this Article, seems to lead to the conclusion that the Convention will not be applicable in such a case. This conclusion seems also to have been reached by the delegation which noted that the deletion of the words "or that State itself is subjected to demands" resulted in a restriction of the scope of the Convention.

   (ii) *where a third party who is not a national of the territorial State is subjected to demands*

As noted, the FRG draft would have removed an offence from the

---

[26] Third Report of the Hostages Committee, p. 19, para. 79.
[27] *Id.* at para. 80.
[28] *Id.* at para. 81.
[29] UN GAOR, 34th Sess., C.6 (53rd mtg.), p. 9, para. 31, UN Doc A/C.6/34/SR.53 (1979).
[30] Cf. *Legal Consequences for States of the Continued Presence of South Africa in Namibia (South West Africa)*, Advisory Opinion, ICJ Rep. 1971, p. 36, para. 69, in which the court noted that the fact that a proposal has not been adopted by an international organization "does not necessarily carry with it the inference that a collective pronouncement is made in a sense opposite to that proposed".

ARTICLE 13

scope of the Convention only if, in addition to the four conditions listed in this Article, "the person or body corporate subjected to demands are all nationals of the [territorial] State". By implication, therefore, the FRG draft would have left within the scope of the Convention those cases, otherwise internal in nature, wherein "the person[s] or body corporate" subjected to demands were nationals of another State, presumably even if they were located in the territorial State at the time of the offence. Thus, in the above hypothetical situation, if the demands were directed at the corporation located in State B, or at any national of State B, then this Convention would have applied.

This provision remained in the Convention until the last session of the Hostages Committee when it was deleted upon the proposal of the same delegation which urged deletion of the words "that State itself is subjected to demands".[31] No reasons for the deletion can be found in the record. As the Article stands no reference is made to the nationality or location of the third party which is the subject of demands. Thus, it appears that in an otherwise internal case if the person who is the subject of demands is a national of a State other than the territorial State, even if he is outside the territorial State at the time of the offence, this Convention will not apply.[32]

Thus, the drafting history of this Convention appears to support the conclusion that the instrument will not apply in an otherwise internal offence simply because the third party is another State or is a person who is located in, or a national of, another State.[33]

---

[31] Third Report of the Hostages Committee, p. 19, para. 80.

[32] With respect to the applicability of the Convention when the target of demands is an international organization, the representative of Mexico argued that if a hostage was taken from an international organization or international conference, the offender would have to be brought to trial by the State where the crime was committed. First Report of the Hostages Committee, p. 64, para. 18. The language of the FRG draft which provided that the Convention would apply in an otherwise internal offence when the target of demands was an international organization was omitted in the final session of the Hostages Committee (Third Report of the Hostages Committee, p. 19, paras. 79-81), but no explanation appears on the record as to why this step was taken. Thus, it appears that when the offence is otherwise internal and the compulsion is directed against an international organization, whether located within or outside the territorial State, this Convention will not apply.

[33] Some support for this conclusion, moreover, may be found in the remarks of the US Justice Department regarding the US implementing legislation for the Hostages Convention. The Department noted that the Convention does not apply when the hostage-taking is in the United States, the victim and the perpetrator are US nationals and the perpetrator is found in the US. It then stated that the nationality of the third party is "immaterial" to the applicability of the Convention. See *Hearings before the Subcommittee on Security and Terrorism*, 98th Cong., 2d Sess. (1984) at p. 123. While this somewhat begs the question of whether the offence is committed "within a single State" when the third party is another State or a person located in another State, given the ambiguity to this effect which exists in the Convention it seems unlikely that the Justice Department would have stated that the nationality of the third party is "immaterial" if the Convention were to apply in such cases.

". . . the hostage and the alleged offender are nationals of that State . . ."

Many cases of hostage-taking involve more than one hostage and/or more than one offender. For the offence to remain outside of the scope of the Convention, *all* the hostages and *all* the offenders must be nationals of the State in which the offence was committed.

". . . and the alleged offender is found in the territory of that State."

In order for a particular act of hostage-taking to remain outside of the scope of this Convention, *all* the offenders must subsequently be found in the territory of that State. If, for example, in an attempt to escape one offender leaves the territory of the State in which an otherwise internal offence takes place, this Convention will apply to that act of hostage-taking. Indeed, if any offender is not brought to justice (in the sense that the obligation *aut dedere aut judicare* is not applied with respect to him) in the territorial State and then subsequently leaves that State, that offence then comes within the scope of this Convention. It may thus be noted that it will not always be clear at first as to whether or not the Convention will apply to a particular offence.

The offences of participation and attempt

It is worth noting that since under Article 1, paragraph 2, attempt and participation are also offences under this Convention, if acts of participation in a hostage-taking, or acts constituting an attempt, take place outside of the State in which an actual seizure or detention and threat takes place, the Convention will apply.

Article 14

TERRITORIAL INTEGRITY AND POLITICAL INDEPENDENCE

> Nothing in this Convention shall be construed as justifying the violation of the territorial integrity or political independence of a State in contravention of the Charter of the United Nations.

1. Introduction

This Article developed from a proposal submitted to the Hostages Committee by a number of developing States which would specifically have prohibited States Parties from undertaking operations designed to rescue hostages held in the territory of another State. The legality of the unilateral use of force by a State to combat terrorism, particularly with respect to the rescue of hostages held in the territory of another State, has been the subject of considerable debate. The original draft of this Article was an attempt by some States to resolve that debate by establishing a rule against such operations. However, as ultimately formulated, this Article simply echoes the wording of Article 2(4) of the UN Charter, which states that: "All Members shall refrain in their international relations from the threat or use of force against the territorial integrity or political independence of any State, or in any other manner inconsistent with the Purposes of the United Nations."

Development of the Article

The original draft of this Article, proposed by Tanzania, Algeria and a number of other Arab and African States during the first session of the Hostages Committee, provided that:

> States shall not resort to the threat or use of force against the sovereignty, territorial integrity or independence of other States as a means of rescuing hostages.[1]

The Israeli rescue operation at Entebbe, strongly criticized by many developing States,[2] had taken place in the year prior to the Hostages

---

[1] UN Doc A/AC.188/L.7, in First Report of the Hostages Committee, p. 111. Other States sponsoring the proposal were Egypt, Guinea, Kenya, Lesotho, Libya, Nigeria.

[2] See, e.g., the comments of the representatives of Mauritania, Qatar and Cameroon during the Security Council debate on Entebbe, respectively, in UN SCOR, 31st Sess. (1939th mtg.), p. 5, para. 41, p. 19, para. 168 & p. 23, para. 214, UN Doc S/PV.1939 (1976).

Committee's first session.³ This proposal was clearly in reaction to that mission and was designed to declare future such operations illegal.⁴ In support of the proposal, the representative of Tanzania maintained that it was a simple reaffirmation of the principles of the Charter for which there were many precedents.⁵ Other delegations, such as those from the Philippines and Mexico, also viewed the proposal as nothing more than a restatement of the Charter.⁶

However, the representatives of many Western nations seemed disinclined to include such a provision in the Convention. They did not argue that the Convention should specifically authorize rescue missions. Indeed, they did not, except for the representative of Israel,⁷ even argue, at least on the record, that such operations are legal. Rather, they seemed to think that the Hostages Convention was not a suitable instrument for dealing with the issue of such uses of force.⁸ However, the approach of these States was, at least in the discussion which appears on the record, somewhat indirect. The representative of the US indicated that he had no real objections to including in the Convention terminology from the Charter but questioned the utility both of doing so in this context and of selecting only certain terms from the Charter for inclusion. He urged that better wording be found.⁹ The representative of the FRG added that his delegation had no major difficulty with the text since it was useful in reminding the Committee of the aim of its endeavours, "namely to prevent unlawful acts by Governments which endangered international peace". However, he questioned whether it was wise to include such a provision in a document which, in his opinion, should be "self-explanatory".¹⁰ Later in the first session, another representative of the FRG stated that the proposal was generally acceptable and that it sought to achieve the same end as Article 3, paragraph 1, which leaves it to the Party in whose territory the hostage is held to decide on the

---

³ On Entebbe, see pp. 2-3 (note 11 and accompanying text in the Introduction).
⁴ It may be noted that, although not indicated in the record, this provision became known amongst the draftsmen as the "anti-Entebbe clause". See McDonald, pp. 548-49. Entebbe seemed very much on the minds of some delegates and, although it was not specifically referred to by name, numerous allusions to the incident were made throughout the first session of the Hostages Committee. See, e.g., the comments of the representatives of Yugoslavia and Libya in First Report of the Hostages Committee, p. 28, para. 12 & p. 39, para. 11, respectively. See generally Boyle, *World Politics and International Law* 142 (1985).
⁵ First Report of the Hostages Committee, p. 62, para. 13.
⁶ *Id.* at p. 77, para. 21 & p. 85, para. 14, respectively.
⁷ UN GAOR, 34th Sess., C.6 (14th mtg.), p. 3, para. 9, UN Doc A/C.6/34/SR.14 (1979).
⁸ See, e.g., the comments of the United States representative to the Sixth Committee, UN GAOR, 34th Sess., C.6 (13th mtg.), p. 18, para. 87, UN Doc A/C.6/34/SR.13 (1979).
⁹ First Report of the Hostages Committee, p. 63, para. 14.
¹⁰ *Id.* at para. 15.

appropriate measures to be taken.[11] The representative of Sweden asserted that since the underlying principle of the proposal was already embodied in the Charter, a special provision in the draft convention was superfluous. However, he continued, since several representatives favoured including a reference to the principle of territorial integrity, he was prepared to consider the matter further.[12]

The representative of Syria, "in order to facilitate" the work of the Committee, submitted an amendment to the proposal such that the wording of this Article would have been as follows:

> Nothing in this Convention can be construed as justifying in any manner the threat or use of force or any interference whatsoever against the sovereignty, independence or territorial integrity of peoples and States, under the pretext of rescuing or freeing hostages.[13]

Despite the apparent (from the drafting record) willingness of most Western States to accept wording similar to these proposals, one commentator who was present during the drafting process reports that this issue became highly emotional and developed into a serious problem. Developing States insisted on the inclusion of such a clause, while Western States were opposed.[14] This account is seemingly verified by the fact that the question was entrusted to Working Group I of the Hostages Committee, the group dealing with the "thornier issues" of the Convention.[15] The report of the Hostages Committee for 1978 indicates that there was little discussion of this issue by the working group during that session (its efforts being concentrated on the questions of the scope of the draft convention and its applicability to national liberation groups).[16] The Chairman of that group reported to the Committee, however, that the issue of respect for the sovereignty and territorial integrity of States was a "minor problem" which could be dealt with simply by "rewording the relevant provisions ... in light of the suggestions made during the negotiations".[17]

The 1979 report of the Hostages Committee indicates that the question of sovereignty and territorial integrity was considered by the working group in that session "[p]arallel with the negotiations on the question of national liberation movements". According to the report, the Working Group was divided between those members who felt that

[11] *Id.* at p. 70, para. 11.
[12] *Id.* at p. 71, para. 12.
[13] UN Doc A/AC.188/L.11, in First Report of the Hostages Committee, p. 112. See the comments of the Syrian representative, *id.* at p. 84, para. 6.
[14] McDonald, pp. 553 & 555.
[15] See Second Report of the Hostages Committee, p. 5, para. 15.
[16] *Id.*
[17] *Id.* at p. 58, para. 6.

the Convention should have a provision dealing with sovereignty and territorial integrity (and who favoured the Syrian amendment to the Tanzanian proposal) and those members who "felt that, having regard to the purposes and principles of the United Nations as contained in Articles 1 and 2 of the Charter, such a clause was not needed". A third group of members submitted informally the following compromise text (apparently for inclusion in the preamble):

> Considering that nothing in the present Convention shall either extend or restrict the permissible use of force by States under the United Nations Charter . . .

When this text failed to receive the acceptance of the other groups, the third group proposed the compromise language which was ultimately adopted.[18]

The debate concerning the use of force to rescue hostages and other uses of force occasioned by terrorism

There has for many years been a robust debate on the legality of one State's intervention in the territory of another to protect its nationals.[19] Because a vast literature already exists on the subject,[20] and because it is beyond the scope of this commentary (particularly since, as noted below, this Article does not affect the existing law on the subject), a full exposition of the arguments on either side of the issue will not be undertaken here. Nor will any attempt be made to resolve this difficult question. However, at the risk of over-simplification, a brief outline of the issue may be in order so that this Article can be placed into context and properly understood. Two other types of

---

[18] Third Report of the Hostages Committee, pp. 7-8, paras. 21-22. Solution of this problem was part of a "package deal" with the solution to the issue of the applicability of the Convention to national liberation movements. McDonald, p. 555.

[19] For a survey of opinions on the legality of such operations, the theories upon which they are justified and the facts of various operations, see Ronzitti, *Rescuing Nationals Abroad through Military Coercion and Intervention on Grounds of Humanity* (1985).

[20] See, e.g., *id.* (and sources cited throughout); Bowett, "The Use of Force for the Protection of Nationals Abroad", in Cassese (ed.), *The Current Regulation of the Use of Force* 39-55 (1986); Bowett, "The Use of Force in the Protection of Nationals", 43 Transactions of the Grotius Society for the Year 1957 111-126 (1962); Bowett, *Self-Defence in International Law* 87-105 (1958); Brownlie, *International Law and the Use of Force by States* 289-301 (1963); Brownlie, "The United Nations Charter and the Use of Force, 1945-1985", in Cassese, *supra*, at pp. 497-98; Lillich, "Forcible Self-Help by States to Protect Human Rights", 53 Iowa L.R. 325 (1967); Jefferey, "The American Hostages in Tehran: The I.C.J. and the Legality of Rescue Missions", 30 ICLQ 717 (1981); Schweisfurth, "Operations to Rescue Nationals in Third States Involving the Use of Force in Relation to the Protection of Human Rights", 23 Ger. YBIL 159 (1980); Note, "Rescue at Entebbe — Legal Aspects", 6 Is. YBHR 312 (1976); Gordon, "Use of Force for the Protection of Nationals Abroad: The Entebbe Incident", 9 Case W.R. J. Int'l L. 117 (1977).

force employed as a reaction to terrorism may also be identified: the use of force against States which are suspected of aiding or encouraging terrorist operations and the extra-territorial use of force to bring alleged terrorists to justice. All these uses of force are discussed briefly below.

A number of operations designed to rescue hostages have been conducted in recent years; some of these have been conducted with the permission of the territorial State,[21] but many have not.[22] In the latter cases — the type which concern us here — the territorial State may have given its explicit or implicit approval to the hostage-takings, either before the seizure or during the detention, or it may have been unable or unwilling to protect the hostages. This was the situation, for example, during the holding of US nationals in Tehran between 1979 and 1981, which, in 1980, resulted in a failed rescue attempt by US commandos.[23] This was also the apparent situation preceding the 1976 Israeli raid on Entebbe.[24]

[21] One example of a rescue operation conducted with the permission of the territorial State is the 1977 West German raid at Mogadishu, Somalia. In that case, a Lufthansa aeroplane was hijacked over the French Riviera and eventually landed at Mogadishu airport. The hijackers, members of the Baader-Meinhof group, demanded the release of various prisoners held in West Germany and Turkey. With the permission of the Somali government, West German commandos stormed the aircraft, killing the hijackers and freeing most of the hostages. See *New York Times*, Oct. 18, 1977, pp. A1 & A12. Another example is the 1985 Egyptian raid at the Maltese airport of Luga in an effort to release hostages held on board an Egyptian aircraft. See XXXII *Keesing's Contemporary Archives* 34326 (1986).

[22] E.g., the 1976 Israeli raid on Entebbe (see pp. 2-3 (note 11 and accompanying text in the Introduction)), the 1980 United States rescue attempt in Iran (see p. 3 (note 12 and accompanying text in the Introduction); note 23, *infra*) and the 1978 Egyptian raid at Larnaca (see pp. 319-320 (note 38 and accompanying text)).

[23] Although the hostages were originally seized by Muslim fundamentalist students, no steps to rectify the situation were taken by Iranian authorities, and it became increasingly clear that the students had the full support and approval of the Khomeini regime. This fact was recognized by the ICJ in the *Case Concerning the United States Diplomatic and Consular Staff in Tehran*, ICJ Rep. 1980, at paras. 70-75. Some four and one half months after the hostage-taking began, the US commandos landed in Tabas, Iran, in the launch of a rescue operation. However, the mission was abandoned after the crash of some of their aircraft. See *New York Times*, April 26, 1980, p. A1; 80 Dep't St. Bull., No. 2039, p. 38 (1980).

[24] The Entebbe raid resulted in the freeing of the hostages and remains the most important example of such a unilateral use of force. It occasioned a significant debate in the Security Council, with many States expressing their opinions on the legality of such operations. See UN SCOR, 31st Sess. (1939th mtg.), UN Doc S/PV.1939 (1976); UN SCOR, 31st Sess. (1940th mtg.), UN Doc S/PV.1940 (1976); UN SCOR, 31st Sess. (1941st mtg.), UN Doc S/PV.1941 (1976); UN SCOR, 31st Sess. (1942nd mtg.), UN Doc S/PV.1942 (1976); UN SCOR, 31st Sess. (1943rd mtg.), UN Doc S/PV.1943 (1976). See also p. 313 (note 2 and accompanying text); pp. 318-319 & 320 (notes 30-32 & 45-47 and accompanying text). It appeared that Uganda did not do all that it could to secure the release of the hostages and may even have assisted the hostage-takers. See pp. 2-3 (note 11 and accompanying text in the Introduction). See also the comments of the representative of Israel in UN SCOR, 31st Sess. (1939th mtg.), pp. 10-12, paras. 93-101, UN Doc S/PV.1939 (1976). The representative of Uganda to the Security Council, however, argued that his country gave all the "help and hospitality it was capable to all the hostages". *Id.* at p. 5, para. 35.

Many writers and States have argued, on a number of theories, that unilateral military intervention by a State to protect its nationals abroad is permissible. Some have approached the issue by asserting that Article 2(4) of the UN Charter does not make the territory of a State inviolable; since the use of force to rescue nationals does not in fact violate the "territorial integrity" or the "political independence" of a State, and is not "inconsistent with the Purposes of the United Nations", it is not unlawful.[25] More commonly, the argument is couched in terms of self-defence. Bowett, for example, asserts that the right of a State to intervene to protect nationals is generally admitted and has characterized such action as a legitimate form of self-defence within the regime of Article 51 of the UN Charter.[26] Because Article 51 states that the Charter shall not impair the right of self-defence in the case of an "armed attack", there are two ways in which rescue operations can fall within that provision. First, it can be argued that the words "armed attack" are meant to be illustrative, rather than exhaustive, of the circumstances under which self-defence can be exercised.[27] Second, even if an armed attack must occur before the right of self-defence exists, an attack upon a State's nationals abroad can be seen as an attack on the State.[28] Additional theories have been advanced to justify rescue operations, including "necessity" (a theory which is particularly relevant to situations wherein the hostages are not held by the territorial State or its agents, thus militating against a justification of self-defence), self-protection or self-help and the obligation to protect human rights.[29]

States which have argued that a right exists under international law to rescue hostages held in another State have generally maintained that the right is one of self-defence (although they sometimes allude to other theories as well). During the Security Council debate on the Entebbe incident, the government of Israel stated that it had a right "to protect its nationals in mortal danger", and justified its intervention in Uganda as within its legitimate right of self-defence as preserved in the United Nations Charter. Moreover, it stated that its actions were within the limits of *The Caroline* case, i.e., "necessity of self-defence, instant, overwhelming, leaving no choice of means and

---

[25] See, e.g., Bowett, in *Current Regulation*, note 20, *supra*, at p. 40. See also Ronzitti, note 19, *supra*, at pp. 1-3.

[26] Bowett, in *Current Regulation*, note 20, *supra*, at pp. 40-44. See also Waldock, "The Regulation of the Use of Force by Individual States in International Law", 81 RC (1952-II) 451, 466-67.

[27] Bowett, in *Current Regulation*, note 20, *supra*, at p. 40.

[28] *Id.* at pp. 40-41.

[29] See Ronzitti, note 19, *supra*, at pp. 4-6 (and sources cited therein). See also Bowett, in *Current Regulation*, note 20, *supra*, at pp. 43-46. See also Fitzmaurice, "The General Principles of International Law Considered from the Standpoint of the Rule of Law", 92 RC (1957-II) 1, 172-73; Schweisfurth, note 20, *supra*, at pp. 179-180.

no moment for deliberation".[30] The representative of the United States concurred. Although he allowed that the Entebbe raid "necessarily involved a temporary breach of the territorial integrity of Uganda", he stated that:

> there is a well established right to use limited force for the protection of one's own nationals from an imminent threat of injury or death in a situation where the State in whose territory they are located is either unwilling or unable to protect them. The right, flowing from the right of self-defence, is limited to such use of force as is necessary and appropriate to protect threatened nationals from injury.[31]

Other Western States refused to criticize the Israeli action, and their comments to the Security Council implied a measure of support for it.[32]

The US justified its failed operation to rescue its nationals held hostage in Iran on various theories. In an initial statement, the President called the mission a "humanitarian" one designed to "safeguard American lives, to protect America's national interests and to reduce tensions in the world".[33] The Secretary of Defense termed the mission a "rescue operation and not a military action".[34] The mission was justified both to Congress[35] and in a report to the Security Council[36] as a measure of self-defence. The United States action was supported by various Western countries, Japan, Israel and Egypt,[37] the latter of which in 1978 had undertaken similar action with respect to hostages held in Larnaca, Cyprus (although it based its claim on the need to fight international terrorism rather than on self-defence).[38]

---

[30] UN SCOR, 31st Sess. (1939th mtg.), pp. 13-14, paras. 106 & 115, UN Doc S/PV.1939 (1976), *reprinted in* 15 ILM 1224, 1228-1231 (1976). See *The Caroline* case, in Moore, *Digest of International Law*, Vol. 2, 409, 412 (1906).

[31] UN SCOR, 31st Sess. (1941st mtg.), p. 8, para. 77, UN Doc S/PV.1941 (1976).

[32] See, e.g., the comments of the representatives of the UK and France, respectively, in UN SCOR, 31st Sess. (1939th mtg.), p. 11, para. 92 & p. 22, para. 204, UN Doc S/PV.1939 (1976).

[33] See Dep't St. Bull., note 23, *supra*.

[34] *Id.* at p. 41.

[35] See Ronzitti, note 19, *supra*, at p. 45.

[36] See letter of 25 April 1980 from the representative of the United States of America to the President of the Security Council, UN Doc S/13908 (1980). The Iranian authorities called the US action "aggression". See letter from the representative of Iran to the Secretary-General, UN Doc S/13915 (1980).

[37] See Ronzitti, *supra*, note 19, at pp. 45-47 & 57.

[38] In the Larnaca incident, terrorists burst into a meeting of the Afro-Asian Peoples Solidarity Organization (held in Nicosia), killed the Secretary (an Egyptian national) and took several hostages, some of whom were Egyptian. After a series of events, the terrorists and the hostages were on board an aircraft in the Larnaca (Cyprus) Airport. During negotiations between the Cypriot authorities and the terrorists, Egyptian commandos stormed the plane. The hostages escaped and the terrorists were arrested; however, during the incident the Cypriot national guard fired on the Egyptian

(*continued on p. 320*)

Many writers and States, however, assert that a State has no right under international law to intervene militarily in the territory of another State to rescue its nationals. Brownlie, for one, argues that "it is very doubtful if the present form of intervention has any basis in the modern law."[39] Some have refuted the argument that there can be a distinction between "territorial integrity" and "political independence" on the one hand and "territorial inviolability" on the other.[40] The concept of territorial integrity has thus been equated with territorial inviolability, and any such unilateral use of force in the territory of another State is seen as a violation of Article 2(4).[41] Moreover, the argument that use of force to protect nationals abroad is a legitimate exercise of self-defence has been criticized.[42] It has been argued, for example, that self-defence in situations where there has not been a direct attack against a State's territory is only legitimate when the attack is against a symbol of State sovereignty such as a warship or armed forces overseas.[43] The arguments of necessity and self-protection have also been challenged.[44]

During the Security Council debate on the Entebbe raid, many States objected vehemently to the Israeli action. In addition to the criticisms of the Arab and African States, the Soviet Union argued that the Israeli action was a "flagrant act of aggression",[45] while the representative of Romania argued that it was an illegal use of force.[46] Objecting States submitted a draft resolution to the Security Council condemning the Israeli action, but it was withdrawn, apparently because it had little chance of adoption.[47]

It can readily be seen from the foregoing that there exists no

---

([38] *continued*)
commandos, killing some of them. Both States acknowledged that the Cypriot authorities had given the aircraft carrying the commandos permission to land at Larnaca, but that they had prohibited military intervention. *Id.* at pp. 40-41. Inasmuch as Egypt was a sponsor of the original draft of this Article (see note 1, *supra*), its action at Larnaca contains some irony.

[39] Brownlie, *Use of Force*, note 20, *supra*, at p. 301. See also Brownlie, in *Current Regulation*, note 20, *supra*, at pp. 497-498.

[40] See, e.g., Brownlie, "Humanitarian Intervention", in Moore (ed.), *Law and Civil War in the Modern World* 222 (1974).

[41] See, e.g., the comments of the representative of Ecuador to the General Assembly, UN GAOR, 21st Sess., Plenary (1463rd mtg.), para. 14, UN Doc A/PV.1463 (1966).

[42] Ronzitti, note 19, *supra*, at pp. 11-13.

[43] *Id.* at p. 11.

[44] *Id.* at pp. 13-15.

[45] UN SCOR, 31st Sess. (1942nd mtg.), p. 22, para. 195, UN Doc S/PV.1942 (1976).

[46] *Id.* at p. 6, para. 45. See also the objections of the representative of Uganda to the Security Council who termed the Israeli raid "barbaric, unprovoked and unwarranted aggression". See UN SCOR, 31st Sess. (1939th mtg.), p. 5, para. 37, UN Doc S/PV.1939 (1976).

[47] This three-power draft by Tanzania, Libya and Benin condemned Israel's violation of Uganda's sovereignty and territorial integrity. UN Doc S/12139 (1976), *reprinted in* 15 ILM 1227-28 (1976). However, it was not pressed to a vote. *Id.* at p. 1225. See also 13 UN Chron., No. 8, p. 15 (1976).

international consensus on the legality of hostage rescue missions where the territorial State has not given its consent.

Another type of force which has been used as a reaction to terrorism, and could conceivably be used in response specifically to a hostage-taking (particularly when the danger to the hostage has passed, e.g., because of his release), is that directed against a State which is suspected of giving aid and support to terrorists. An example of this is the US bombing of Libya in April 1986[48] which was conducted partly in response to the killing of a US serviceman and the injury of over 200 other people in the bombing of a West Berlin nightclub, an act which was attributed by the US to Libyan agents.[49] The United States defended this action on the basis of self-defence, consistent with Article 51 of the Charter. A statement by the White House issued immediately after the attack provided that:

> In light of this reprehensible act of violence and clear evidence that Libya is planning future attacks, the United States has chosen to exercise its right to self-defense. It is our hope that this action will preempt and discourage Libyan attacks against innocent civilians in the future.

The statement further said that the targets were part of "Qadhafi's terrorist infrastructure".[50] In a subsequent statement, the President stated that the "mission [was] fully consistent with Article 51 of the United Nations Charter", and was undertaken only after "diplomacy, public condemnation, economic sanctions, and demonstrations of military force".[51] The Secretary of Defense stated that the "action was proportionate to the sustained, clear, continuing and widespread use of terror against Americans and others by Qadhafi's Libya".[52] Similar statements were made in the Security Council,[53] where, however, a number of participants in the debate condemned the US action as aggression and in no way sanctioned by the right of self-defence.[54]

---

[48] See *New York Times*, April 15, 1986, p. A1.
[49] See 86 Dep't St. Bull., No. 2111, p. 1 (1986).
[50] *Id.*
[51] *Id.* at p. 2.
[52] *Id.* at p. 3.
[53] See UN SCOR, 41st Sess. (2682nd mtg.), p. 31, UN Doc S/PV.2682 (1986).
[54] See, e.g., the comments of the representatives of Qatar, Poland and Saudi Arabia, respectively, in UN SCOR, 41st Sess. (2677th mtg.), pp. 4-5, 27 & 41, UN Doc S/PV.2677 (1986). A resolution condemning the US bombing (UN Doc S/18016/Rev.1 (1986)) was vetoed by France, the US and the UK. See UN SCOR, 41st Sess. (2682nd mtg.), p. 43, UN Doc S/PV.2682 (1986). It seems difficult to justify the US action in Libya under a traditional self-defence analysis. See Murphy, "The Future of Multilateralism and Efforts to Combat International Terrorism", 25 Colum. J. Trans. L. (1986) at pp. 86-88; Greenwood, "International Law and the United States' Air Operation Against Libya", 89 West Virginia L. R. 933, 937-948 (1987). Greenwood,

(continued on p. 322)

One final type of unilateral use of force which may be mentioned is that employed by a State to bring to justice an alleged offender who is outside of its territory. This type of force was employed by the US in the aftermath of the *Achille Lauro* crisis. As discussed in the commentary on Article 3,[55] pursuant to an agreement which was apparently reached between the hijackers, the PLO and the governments of Egypt and Italy, the hijackers were placed on an Egyptian aircraft bound for Tunis. The plane was intercepted by American military aircraft and diverted to a US airbase in Italy where the offenders were handed over to Italian authorities. The American action was termed "piracy" by Egypt, but the US defended its use of force.[56] Although this type of force is not a classical situation wherein the "territorial integrity" or "political independence" of a State may have been violated, there is similarly a debate over whether it is contrary to Article 2(4).[57]

2. Interpretation

"Nothing in this Convention shall be construed as justifying the violation of the territorial integrity or political independence of a State in contravention of the Charter of the United Nations."

What effect, then, does this Article have on the law regarding the use of force by a State as a reaction to a hostage-taking, and particularly with respect to the rescue of its nationals held in another State? The answer, quite simply, is that this Article has no effect on the law in this regard. Although the proposers of this Article were motivated by a desire to prohibit specifically any such future rescue operations, this Article neither prohibits nor sanctions the use of force by a State to rescue hostages or for other purposes. As finally adopted, this Article simply reaffirms the principles of the UN Charter. By simply echoing the words of Article 2(4), this Article keeps the debate on this issue in precisely the same place it was before the adoption of

---

([54] *continued*)
however, notes that the US action has added to a trend towards a wider view of self-defence, necessitated by the nature of irregular or terrorist attacks, which would justify such action as self-defence under the theory of an "accumulation of events". *Id.* at pp. 953-956.

[55] See p. 115 (note 18 and accompanying text in the commentary on Article 3).

[56] See 85 Dep't St. Bull., No. 2105, 74-81 (1985). It might be noted that the US did not seem to justify its action on any precise legal grounds.

[57] Compare Murphy, note 54, *supra*, at pp. 80-83 with Schachter, "In Defense of International Rules on the Use of Force", 53 Univ. Chi. L. R. 113, 140 (1986).

this Convention.[58] Whatever the legality of an Entebbe-like raid, it remains a matter of customary international law and the law of the Charter and it is, in essence, still unsettled.

It may be recalled that Article 3 obliges the State in whose territory the hostage is held to attempt to secure his release. No such obligation is placed on any other State, such as the national State of the hostage. But to say that this Convention does not require a State to attempt to secure the release of its nationals is not the same as saying that this Convention prohibits rescue operations if they are otherwise permissible under international law.

Thus, on the one hand, if no right exists unilaterally to use force to rescue hostages held in another State, the prohibition against the taking of hostages contained in this Convention, and attendant obligations imposed in relation thereto, cannot be used to justify such an action.[59] On the other hand, if such a right exists, it is not curtailed by this Article. Accordingly, those who previously believed that rescue operations are contrary to the Charter have expressed the view that the prohibition of such operations is upheld by this Convention. And those who have held that such operations are legal see no bar imposed by this Convention. For example, in the Sixth Committee deliberations the representative of Peru stated his belief that this Article would "prevent States from taking arbitrary action and, in particular, from resorting to the threat or use of force against other States",[60] while the representative of Israel stated that "it was in the nature of law itself to prohibit the taking of hostages and the law allowed the victimized States to take all necessary actions of self-defence, according to the circumstances."[61] The uncertain nature of

---

[58] Commentators are in agreement on this point. See, e.g., Ronzitti, note 19, *supra*, at pp. 51-52; Rosenstock, p. 186. One commentator states that the solution reached "hinted at a general prohibition against the use of transnational force, but essentially left the seminal question of the Entebbe raid unanswered". See Boyle, note 4, *supra*, p. 144 (1985).

[59] One writer, however, suggests that the obligations imposed by this Convention might serve as a justification for the use of force:
> The principle of territorial sovereignty is not the only principle of law that must be weighed in considering objections against attacks on terrorists, attempts to rescue hostages and actions against countries that sponsor terrorism. States have duties to cooperate in preventing terrorists from using their territories in perpetrating criminal acts, and many governments have explicitly undertaken to extradite or prosecute terrorists guilty of hijacking, sabotage and hostage-taking. These obligations cannot be disregarded in evaluating the propriety of anti-terrorist operations.

Sofaer, "Terrorism and the Law", 64 Foreign Affairs 901, 919 (1986).

[60] UN GAOR, 34th Sess., C.6 (13th mtg.), p. 5, para. 18, UN Doc A/C.6/34/SR.13 (1979).

[61] UN GAOR 34th Sess., C.6 (14th mtg.), p. 3, para. 9, UN Doc A/C.6/34/SR.14 (1979). This representative, Rosenne, has subsequently written that this Article "protects generally actions for the release of hostages taken in conformity with the Charter in application of relevant doctrines of self-help, self-defence . . . or even on grounds of necessity". See Rosenne, pp. 141-42.

this wording, however, is reflected in the comments of the representative of Pakistan wherein he expressed the hope that the Article would not be seen "as an obstacle to the strict application of the principle of non-intervention, for there must be no possibility of a State intervening militarily in another State to secure the release of hostages".[62]

While it may be argued that the Convention should have dealt with the issue of the legality of unilateral military operations designed to rescue hostages, it is unlikely that the draftsmen of the Convention could ever have reached agreement on the issue. And a specific attempt to either prohibit or sanction such operations would most likely have resulted in the rejection of the Convention by States which disagreed with the solution reached. Recognition of the potential divisiveness of this issue probably helped lead to what appears to have been a relatively easily arrived at compromise.[63] Smaller, militarily weaker States, on whose territory hostage-rescue operations are most likely to occur, did not secure a prohibition against them. However, their fears that the existence of the Hostages Convention could be used to justify uses of force were allayed. The compromise was also satisfactory to those States which felt that the Hostages Convention was not the proper medium for dealing with the issue of permissible uses of force.[64]

Boyle argues that it is not very significant that this Convention failed to resolve the issue of the legality of rescue operations since "Entebbe-type rescue operation[s] may be unnecessary in the future precisely because of the existence of the Hostages Convention and, more importantly, because of the profound effects that the entire sequence of events which led to its adoption over the three-and-one-half-year period after Entebbe have had upon the state members of the international system" (i.e., a series of hostage-takings and subsequent rescue operations).[65] According to this view, the existence

---

[62] UN GAOR, 34th Sess., C.6 (14th mtg.), p. 16, para. 90, UN Doc A/C.6/34/SR.14 (1979).

[63] Boyle asserts that "insistence upon a clear-cut solution to this abstract problem by either side in the Hostages Committee would have killed the hostages convention in so far as it would have been interpreted by both the opponents and the partisans of the Israeli raid at Entebbe as a *sub silentio* adjudication of the merits of that dispute". Boyle, note 4, *supra*, at p. 144.

[64] See Rosenstock, p. 186. Boyle argues that the Entebbe incident was a contributing factor to ultimate agreement on the Convention. In his view, Entebbe illustrated the vulnerability of militarily weak countries to such self-help measures. These States thus realized that a failure to control international acts of hostage-taking might prompt future military interventions, both as genuine attempts to free hostages and as pretexts for other objectives. Adoption of a convention, however, could undermine the justification for such an act, particularly where the territorial State was attempting in good faith to secure the release of the hostages. See Boyle, note 4, *supra*, at p. 139.

[65] *Id.* at pp. 152-53.

of a Convention which prohibits the taking of hostages and imposes obligations upon States with respect to the prevention and punishment of such acts, coupled with an international community that is weary both of hostage-takings and rescue operations, will result in a significant decrease of incidents of hostage-takings (and an increase in good faith attempts by territorial States to end those which do occur) and, consequently, rescue operations. However, the experience of the years since the adoption of the Convention has not entirely justified this optimism. The *Achille Lauro* incident, the situation in Lebanon and continued aerial hijackings are ample proof that the taking of hostages is still regarded as a useful tool by many terrorist groups. It may be assumed that when possible, and deemed necessary, operations to rescue hostages held in the territory of another State (and other acts of force by victimized States) will be conducted.[66] The view expressed by Boyle relies upon the assumption that all or most States will become parties to this Convention, and will genuinely attempt to fight incidents of hostage-taking. This goal is still a long way from realization.

Thus, another commentator states:

> in recent years, particularly unpleasant episodes have repeatedly occurred, such as the taking of hostages, and transnational terrorism. These events are the cause of a continuous state of danger. Unless the international community acquires suitable instruments, capable of preventing and representing such criminal events, resorting to unilateral armed force is likely to continue to increase on the part of those States whose nationals become the victims of terrorist attacks, in order to fill the vacuum created by the lack of effective control mechanisms.[67]

It is not so much that effective instruments have not been designed to deal with this problem, since this Convention, although not without its flaws, contains potentially effective devices to prevent and punish acts of hostage-taking. It is rather a continuing reluctance on the part of many States to recognize that acts of hostage-taking and other types of international terrorism are unacceptable, and should be neither supported nor tolerated. Only when all or most States become conscientious parties to this instrument will acts of hostage-taking and resultant unilateral uses of force end.

---

[66] In this vein, it might be noted that the restraint of Western States in not using force to release the hostages in Lebanon is probably attributable more to difficulties in locating them and other practical problems relating to such an operation than to a belief that such is contrary to international law.

[67] Ronzitti, note 19, *supra*, at pp. 66-67.

Article 15

PRESERVATION OF THE "TREATIES ON ASYLUM"

The provisions of this Convention shall not affect the application of the Treaties on Asylum, in force at the date of the adoption of this Convention, as between the States which are parties to those Treaties; but a State Party to this Convention may not invoke those Treaties with respect to another State Party to this Convention which is not a party to those Treaties.

1. INTRODUCTION

This Article, providing that the Hostages Convention "shall not affect the application of the Treaties on Asylum", is somewhat difficult to interpret. It appears that it creates, in certain situations, an exception to the rule set forth in Article 8, paragraph 1, that the State Party in whose territory an alleged offender is found must either extradite or prosecute him. In particular, if diplomatic asylum has been granted by a State Party to one of those treaties in its embassy, or in some other place appropriate for that purpose, located in the territory of another State Party to that treaty, the latter State is seemingly not bound, with respect to the other States Parties to that treaty, by its obligation *aut dedere aut judicare*. However, it does not appear that this provision envisages the alleged offender's impunity, since the State to which the person granted asylum is transported should then either extradite him or submit the case for prosecution. In any event, this Article will have little effect on the application of the Hostages Convention. The Article is limited to those "Treaties on Asylum" which were in force as of 17 December 1979, the date of the adoption of this Convention. Only a small number of such treaties existed at that time, and they are in force only as between certain Latin American States. Of most importance, however, those treaties may not be invoked with respect to States which are not parties thereto.

This paragraph is identical to Article 12 of the New York Convention. There are no corresponding provisions in the other anti-terrorism conventions and no mention of asylum was made in the FRG draft. The issue of the inclusion of a provision regarding asylum was raised by the representative of Mexico in the first session of the Hostages Committee and was supported by various other Latin American States. Before attempting to interpret the meaning of this Article, brief discussions on the nature of asylum and the development of this Article are in order.

The nature of asylum

Asylum has been defined as "the protection which a State grants on its territory, or in some other place under the control of certain of its organs, to a person who comes to seek it."[1] The protection is granted as against another State which is seeking to persecute the individual, either because he has committed a political offence, or an offence committed for a political purpose, or for some other political reason.[2] There are two types of asylum: territorial asylum and diplomatic asylum. Territorial asylum is that asylum which a State grants to an individual present on its territory.[3] Diplomatic asylum refers to the right of a State to grant asylum in places which are under its control, but which are in the territory of another State, for example, embassies and war vessels, and to the corresponding duty of the territorial State to allow the person granted asylum to leave the country.[4] While territorial asylum is an aspect of territorial sovereignty, dispensed at a State's discretion,[5] diplomatic asylum is a limitation upon territorial sovereignty.[6] Diplomatic asylum and territorial asylum thus have opposite bases: the right to grant territorial asylum can be restricted only by treaty, while the right to grant diplomatic asylum is largely based on treaties.[7] As will be seen below, most of the "Treaties on Asylum" deal with diplomatic asylum. It may be noted that diplomatic asylum is normally practised only by

---

[1] *Institut de Droit International*, Resolution I: "Asylum in Public International Law", 43 *Annuaire*, tome II, 388, 389 (1950). It might be noted that this discussion concerns the right *of* asylum, i.e., the right of a State to grant asylum to a person, rather than the right *to* asylum, i.e., the right of an individual to be granted asylum. Traditionally, asylum refers to the right of a State rather than to the right of an individual. Oppenheim, *International Law*, Vol. I, 676-678 (8th ed., H. Lauterpacht, ed., 1958). While some writers and documents refer to the right of an individual to asylum (see, e.g., Art. 14, Universal Declaration of Human Rights, GA Res 217A (III), UN Doc A/810, p. 71 (1949)), the "Treaties on Asylum" referred to in this Article involve only the right of States to grant asylum. See pp. 334-336 & 339 (notes 37-50 & 62-64 and accompanying text).

[2] See International Commission of Jurists, *The Application in Latin America of International Declarations and Conventions Relating to Asylum* 9 (1975); Art. 3, 1954 Caracas Convention on Territorial Asylum, PAUTS 19.

[3] See generally Grahl-Madsen, *Territorial Asylum* 1-2 (1980); Art. 1, Caracas Convention, note 2, *supra*; Art. 1(1), 1967 United Nations Declaration on Territorial Asylum, GA Res 2312 (XXII), UN GAOR, 22nd Sess., Supp. 16, p. 81, UN Doc A/6716 (1968).

[4] See generally Arts. 1 & 5, 1954 Caracas Convention on Diplomatic Asylum, PAUTS 18; de Vries & Rodriguez-Novas, *The Law of the Americas* 49 (1965). See also pp. 335-336 (notes 41-47 and accompanying text).

[5] See *Asylum Case*, ICJ Rep. 1950, p. 274; Morgenstern, "The Right of Asylum", 26 BYIL 327, 327 (1949).

[6] See *Asylum Case*, note 5, *supra*, at pp. 274-75; Ronning, *Diplomatic Asylum* 5 (1965).

[7] See *Application in Latin America of International Declarations and Conventions Relating to Asylum*, note 2, *supra*, at p. 8; Grahl-Madsen, note 3, *supra*, at p. 2.

Latin American States,[8] which have, in general, a strong tradition of asylum.[9]

One aspect of the right to grant asylum is the right not to prosecute or punish a person granted asylum or otherwise to restrict his freedom,[10] and it appears that the traditional practice for a State granting asylum is to allow the person granted asylum to go unpunished for his politically-motivated acts committed abroad.[11] However, as the International Commission of Jurists notes, "[a]sylum is intended to secure a person's safety from persecution rather than his impunity",[12] and there appears to be no rule of international law which would preclude the prosecution of a person granted asylum. That there is no doctrinal bar to such prosecutions is evident from the fact that both this Convention and the European Convention on the Suppression of Terrorism contain discrimination clauses which clearly require the granting of territorial asylum to those alleged offenders who are in danger of persecution in a requesting State, while still providing that they must be prosecuted.[13] Those provisions recognize both that persons in danger of persecution must be protected and that, nevertheless, certain types of crimes such as hijacking and hostage-taking are an unacceptable threat to the international order and must result in prosecution in all instances.

---

[8] *Id.*

[9] See generally *Application in Latin America of International Declarations and Conventions Relating to Asylum*, note 2, *supra*, at pp. 4 & 7; de Vries & Rodriguez-Novas, note 4, *supra*, at pp. 44-91.

[10] Grahl-Madsen, note 3, *supra*, at p. 12.

[11] This would appear to be due mostly to the fact that the asylum State would have little interest in punishing a politically motivated act committed abroad; most States would not, in any event, have jurisdiction over crimes committed abroad by foreigners. See generally pp. 134-135 (notes 5 & 6 and accompanying text in the commentary on Article 5); p. 190 (note 14 and accompanying text in the commentary on Article 8). That impunity generally results from a grant of asylum is implicit in works on the subject. Bassiouni, for example, states that once asylum has been granted the person granted asylum becomes inviolable. Bassiouni, *International Extradition United States Law and Practice* 109 (2nd ed., 1987). The ILA has promulgated a "Draft Convention on Diplomatic Asylum" which states in Article 3(c) that persons who have committed crimes against international order such as genocide or aerial hijacking "shall not be entitled" to asylum. However, the draft also provides that the State from which asylum is sought may prosecute the alleged offender rather than surrender him. See ILA *Report of the Fifty-Fifth Conference* 199, 200 (1972). Implicit in this wording is that prosecuting the offender after refusing to extradite him is not asylum. See also Joyner, *Aerial Hijacking as an International Crime* 285-301 (1974), who lists three "enforcement responses" — asylum, prosecution and extradition — taken by States regarding aerial hijackings prior to 1973. There did not appear to be any overlap between the categories of asylum and prosecution and Joyner concluded that the practice of asylum is the "most formidable" obstacle to the "total prosecution" of hijackers.

[12] *Application in Latin America of Declarations and Conventions Relating to Asylum*, note 2, *supra*, at p. 10. Cf. *Asylum Case*, note 5, *supra*, at p. 284.

[13] See generally the commentary on Article 9 (pp. 209-225).

Development of the Article

Early in the Hostages Committee deliberations, when the desire was still evident on the part of many delegations to exclude from the scope of the Convention acts of hostage-taking committed by national liberation movements, the representative of Mexico, asserting that importance must be attached to the question of the motivation behind an act of hostage-taking,[14] proposed that the following wording be added to the Convention:

> None of the provisions of this Convention shall be interpreted as impairing the right of asylum.[15]

The proposal presumably referred to both territorial asylum and diplomatic asylum, and was (in contrast to the language ultimately adopted for this Article) seemingly relevant to all States Parties to this Convention.

A considerable amount of debate followed on the question of whether any reference to the right of asylum should be made in the Convention. Western States argued against such a provision, asserting that it was not necessary. The representative of the US, for example, referring, it seems, particularly to territorial asylum, noted that there was no such provision in the Hague or Montreal Conventions, instruments which the "United States, like many other States, had ratified while vigorously defending the right of asylum." He added:

> in the current state of international law, no State had the obligation to extradite, but States always had the right to choose between extradition of the culprit and prosecution in their own territory. By affirming the principle of 'extradite or prosecute', the Convention upheld that choice and enabled States to continue to have the option of granting or not granting asylum.[16]

He further asserted that there was nothing inconsistent in granting asylum to offenders and then instituting prosecution proceedings.[17] The representatives of other Western States made substantially similar comments.[18]

---

[14] First Report of the Hostages Committee, pp. 49-50, para. 18.
[15] *Id.* at p. 52, para. 7. This is essentially the same language as employed in Article 6 of the OAS Convention.
[16] First Report of the Hostages Committee, p. 53, para. 10.
[17] *Id.* at p. 91, para. 22.
[18] See, e.g., the comments of the representatives of the FRG and Sweden, *id.* at p. 93, para. 10 & pp. 70-71, para. 12, respectively.

The delegations of some (but by no means all)[19] Latin American and other States disagreed. Not only did they want a provision which specifically provided for the right of asylum, they seemed to argue that once asylum is granted a State should be free to refuse to submit the case for the purpose of prosecution. The representative of Venezuela, for example, asserted that the "adoption of an international rule making it obligatory to prosecute, without any exception, an offender who had not been extradited would be contrary to a humanitarian principle, that of the right of asylum, which had always been respected by Venezuela."[20] The representative of Lesotho supported the Mexican proposal, stating that it gave sovereign States full latitude in cases where for political reasons they could not extradite or prosecute a person who had committed an act of hostage-taking.[21] The representative of Mexico was willing to concede that "[t]here was nothing in the norms relating to the right of asylum to prevent the country granting asylum to an individual and declining to extradite him from instituting proceedings against him."[22] Moreover, he stated that "under international law, the granting of asylum did not guarantee immunity from prosecution." However, he added that a decision not to prosecute would "depend upon the internal legislation of the State involved alone."[23]

The issue of asylum was so contentious that it was assigned to Working Group I of the Hostages Committee, the group concerned with the "thornier issues" of the drafting process.[24] That group was not able to agree on a draft article by the time the drafting process was turned over to the Sixth Committee, apparently both because of the difficulty of the issue and because that group was concerned primarily with the issue of the applicability of the Convention to acts of hostage-taking by national liberation movements. However, according to the Hostages Committee the following text "appeared to have widespread support" as a basis for future consideration of the issue:

> None of the provisions of this Convention shall be interpreted as impairing the right of asylum. This provision shall not however affect the obligations of Contracting States under the Convention.[25]

---

[19] The representatives of Chile and Nicaragua, for example, asserted that no provision on asylum was necessary since asylum relates to political offences and hostage-taking should not be considered to be political. *Id.* at p. 56, para. 28 & p. 91, para. 19 & p. 56, para. 30, respectively.

[20] *Id.* at p. 55, para. 24.

[21] *Id.* at p. 54, para. 17.

[22] *Id.* at p. 57, para. 35.

[23] *Id.* at p. 90, para. 16.

[24] Second Report of the Hostages Committee, p. 5, paras. 14-15.

[25] Third Report of the Hostages Committee, p. 8, paras. 24-25. It appears that only
(*continued on p. 332*)

This provision would have made it clear that a grant of asylum would not affect the obligation of the State where an alleged offender was found to submit the case to its appropriate authorities for the purpose of prosecution. As will be seen below, this language could be consistent with a grant of territorial asylum since it would allow the State where the alleged offender is present to grant asylum in the sense that it does not extradite him. However, this language is inconsistent with a grant of diplomatic asylum since in that event the State in whose territory the place of asylum is located may not exercise its jurisdiction over the person granted asylum in such a way as either to extradite or prosecute him.

Regardless of the "widespread support" for this proposal in the Hostages Committee, it was unacceptable to some of the Latin American delegations in the Sixth Committee, whose attention seemed (the drafting records are not entirely clear in this regard) to be directed mainly at the right of diplomatic asylum. The representative of Mexico asserted that it was an "absurd proposal . . . [t]he first and second sentences of article [15] were so contradictory that they cancelled each other out."[26] He stated that he could not agree with the representative of the Netherlands[27] that a decision to grant asylum could only be made after the alleged offender's case had been dealt with by the prosecuting authorities of the State in whose territory he was found. Referring, apparently, only to diplomatic asylum, he stated that in "Mexico and in the other countries that were parties to conventions on asylum, no one could be prosecuted once asylum had been granted".[28] The representative of Venezuela also objected to this proposal, stating that the second sentence rendered the first meaningless. After discussing the fundamental nature of the right of diplomatic asylum in Latin America, he seemed to shift his focus to territorial asylum by stating that Article 8 (the provision requiring *aut*

([25] *continued*)
the representatives of Mexico and Venezuela were opposed to this text. *Id.* at p. 8, n. 18. One commentator who took part in the drafting of the Convention reports that the Mexican delegation at first agreed to this proposal but subsequently changed its position. See McDonald, pp. 5 & 6.

[26] UN GAOR, 34th Sess., C.6 (13th mtg.), p. 16, para. 78, UN Doc A/C.6/34/SR.13 (1979). The representatives of other countries also argued that the proposed language was contradictory. See the comments of the representatives of Peru and Greece, *id.*, at p. 6, para. 20 & p. 19, para. 89, respectively.

[27] *Id.* at p. 9, para. 39.

[28] *Id.* at p. 17, paras. 79 & 80. Although it is not entirely clear, it seems that these comments referred only to diplomatic asylum since they were made in the context of a discussion of the nature of diplomatic asylum. Moreover, Mexico was at that time party only to treaties on diplomatic asylum. It was not party to the one existing treaty on territorial asylum. See generally Bowman & Harris, *Multilateral Treaties Index and Current Status* 191 (1984).

dedere aut judicare) would "prevent the country in which the alleged offender was found from granting him asylum."[29]

Other States continued to object to the inclusion of an express provision on asylum. Eastern European States argued that asylum relates only to political crimes, whereas acts of hostage-taking are ordinary offences, and that inclusion of such a provision would serve only to weaken the Convention.[30] Even some Latin American countries seemed opposed to including a provision regarding asylum, similarly arguing that the taking of hostages is an ordinary offence outside the scope of asylum.[31] Western opinion remained as earlier noted.[32]

Some delegations from Latin America proposed that, as a compromise, language such as that contained in the corresponding provision of the New York Convention should be included in this instrument. Some of these were delegations which did not feel strongly about the inclusion of a provision regarding asylum. The representative of Chile, for example, stated that that provision simply "reaffirmed the principle of inviolability and respect for treaties."[33] The Sixth Committee working group ultimately adopted language identical to Article 12 of the New York Convention, explaining only that "although there had been some prior discussion of certain issues with some relation to the material covered by the article, the working group regarded [the article] as self-explanatory."[34] The delegations of some States, including Latin American ones, were dissatisfied with this provision. The representative of Ecuador voiced an "express reservation" to this Article, stating that it should have been drafted in stronger terms.[35] The representative of Venezuela asserted that it fails

---

[29] *Id.* at p. 10, para. 44.

[30] See, e.g., the comments of the representatives of Romania and the Soviet Union, respectively, in *id.* at p. 21, para. 105 & UN GAOR, 34th Sess., C.6 (62nd mtg.), pp. 10-11, para. 55, UN Doc A/C.6/34/SR.62 (1979).

[31] See, e.g., the comments of the representatives of Chile and Uruguay, respectively, in UN GAOR, 34th Sess., C.6 (12th mtg.), p. 8, para. 29, UN Doc A/C.6/34/SR.12 (1979) & UN GAOR, 34th Sess., C.6 (14th mtg.), p. 12, para. 68, UN Doc A/C.6/34/SR.14 (1979).

[32] See, e.g., the comments of the representatives of Canada and the Netherlands, respectively, in UN GAOR, 34th Sess., C.6 (13th mtg.), p. 2, para. 6 & p. 9, para. 39, UN Doc A/C.6/34/SR.13 (1979).

[33] See note 31, *supra*. The representative of Colombia, who seemed to feel strongly about the inclusion of a provision on asylum, also expressed approval of language such as that found in the New York Convention, asserting that such would safeguard the right of asylum. UN GAOR, 34th Sess., C.6 (13th mtg.), p. 15, para. 69, UN Doc A/C.6/34/SR.13 (1979).

[34] UN GAOR, 34th Sess., C.6 (53rd mtg.), p. 9, para. 33, UN Doc A/C.6/34/SR.53 (1979).

[35] UN GAOR, 34th Sess., C.6 (62nd mtg.), p. 5, paras. 18-21, UN Doc A/C.6/34/SR.62 (1979).

to recognize international practice with respect to asylum in so far as it is limited to the States Parties to the "Treaties on Asylum".[36]

Thus, it can be seen that the scope of this Article developed quite some way from the original Mexican proposal. In part, this can probably be attributed to developments with respect to other provisions, particularly Article 12, which made it clear that the rule *aut dedere aut judicare* must apply to all offenders regardless of their political motives or causes. It may also be attributed to the development of Article 9 during the final stages of the Hostages Committee's work and in the Sixth Committee. That Article expressly provides that extradition should not be granted when persecution would result in the requesting State, thus safeguarding the right of territorial asylum but also providing no exception to the alternative obligation *aut judicare*.

2. Interpretation

"The provisions of this Convention shall not affect the application of the Treaties on Asylum . . ."

As is often the case with compromise language, this provision is less than clear. Does it mean that States Parties to the "Treaties on Asylum" can, as between themselves, grant asylum to an alleged hostage-taker and then refuse either to extradite or to prosecute him, thus resulting in his impunity? Or does it simply mean that they may grant asylum in the sense of providing protection from the persecuting State, without, however, permitting him to go unpunished for his offence? The starting point for the interpretation of this language must be an examination of the "Treaties on Asylum". The only "Treaties on Asylum" which are in force are four regional multilateral instruments (three of which deal with diplomatic asylum) existing as between various Latin American States. Most Latin American States are parties to one or more of those instruments, which are:

— The 1928 Havana Convention on Political Asylum[37] (diplomatic asylum);

---

[36] UN GAOR, 34th Sess., C.6 (62nd mtg.), pp. 5-6, para. 22, UN Doc A/C.6/34/SR.62 (1979). See also the comments of the representatives of Cuba, *id.* at p. 12, para. 59. The representative of Colombia, in an apparent reversal of position (see note 33, *supra*), also objected to the provision. *Id.* at para. 63.

[37] 132 LNTS 323. This Convention had 15 Latin American States Parties as of 1 January 1989. Bowman & Harris, *supra*, note 28, at p. 71 & 6th Supp. (1989).

— The 1933 Montevideo Convention on Political Asylum[38] (diplomatic asylum);
— The 1954 Caracas Convention on Diplomatic Asylum;[39] and
— The 1954 Caracas Convention on Territorial Asylum.[40]

It is the application of the treaties on diplomatic asylum which, in the absence of this Article, would be most "affected" by the provisions of this Convention, and it was with this type of asylum that Latin American States seemed most concerned during the drafting of this Convention, at least in the later stages of the development of this Article. Particular attention, therefore, will be paid in this discussion to this type of asylum. The Caracas Convention is the most detailed of the treaties on diplomatic asylum and is worth careful consideration.

The Caracas Convention provides that asylum granted in "legations, war vessels and military camps or aircraft, to persons being sought for political reasons or for political offences, shall be respected by the territorial State".[41] Asylum may not be granted to persons who are "under indictment or on trial for common offences or have been convicted by competent regular courts and have not served the respective sentence, nor to deserters from land, sea and air forces".[42] However, this limitation does not apply "when the acts giving rise to the request for asylum, whatever the case may be, are clearly of a political nature."[43] The determination of the "nature of the offence or the motives for the persecution", moreover, rests solely with the requested State.[44] Asylum is to be granted only in urgent cases and only for the time necessary for the person granted asylum to leave the

---

[38] PAULTS 37. This Convention is supplementary to the Havana Convention and also had 15 States Parties as of 1 January 1989. Bowman & Harris, note 28, *supra*, at p. 94 & 6th Supp. (1989).

[39] PAULTS 18. This Convention had 13 States Parties as of 1 January 1989. Bowman & Harris, note 28, *supra*, at p. 191 & 6th Supp. (1989).

[40] PAULTS 19. This Convention had 12 States Parties as of 1 January 1989. Bowman & Harris, note 28, *supra*, at p. 191 & 6th Supp. (1989). Another treaty on asylum, the 1939 Montevideo Treaty on Political Asylum and Refuge, Hudson (ed.), *International Legislation*, Vol. VIII, 404 (1949), deals with both diplomatic and territorial asylum but has not entered into force.

[41] Arts. 1 & 9, PAULTS 18. See also Art. 2, Havana Convention, 132 LNTS 323.

[42] Art. 3, PAULTS 18. See also Art. 1, Havana Convention, 132 LNTS 323; Art. 1, Montevideo Convention, PAULTS 37.

[43] Art. 3, PAULTS 18.

[44] Art. 4, PAULTS 18. See also Art. 2, Montevideo Convention, PAULTS 37. It might be noted that the Havana Convention does not provide that the requested State has the right unilaterally to qualify the nature of the offence as political. The ICJ has held, moreover, that such a right is not recognized by any principle of international law. *Asylum Case*, note 5, *supra*, at pp. 274 & 278. However, as noted, both the Montevideo Convention and the Caracas Convention provide for such a right, and there is no State which is party to the Havana Convention which is not party to either the Montevideo or Caracas Conventions. See Bowman & Harris, note 28, *supra*, at pp. 71, 94 & 190-91.

territorial State with the guarantees of the government thereof, "to the end that his life, liberty, or personal integrity may not be endangered, or that the asylee's safety is ensured in some other way."[45] Urgent cases are, *inter alia*, those in which the person requesting asylum is being sought by persons or mobs over which the authorities have no control, "or by the authorities themselves, and is in danger of being deprived of his life or liberty because of political persecution and cannot, without risk, ensure his safety in any other way."[46] After asylum has been granted, the territorial State must immediately comply with a request by the asylum-granting State that the person granted asylum be allowed to depart from the country with guarantees of safe conduct.[47] Once departure of the person granted asylum has been effected, the State granting asylum may not, against his wishes, return him to his country of origin,[48] but it is not obliged to settle him in its territory.[49] However, if the territorial State informs the asylum-granting State of its intention to seek extradition, the person granted asylum shall remain in the territory of the asylum State until the request for extradition is received.[50]

With these provisions in mind, it can be seen that without this Article the provisions of the Hostages Convention would certainly "affect the application of" the treaties on diplomatic asylum. Article 8, paragraph 1, of this Convention provides that the State Party in whose territory the alleged offender is found, must, if it does not extradite him, "without exception whatsoever", submit the case to its competent authorities for the purpose of prosecution. The wording of Article 8, paragraph 1, standing alone, would preclude a grant of diplomatic asylum. The territorial State would be in violation of its obligations under that provision if it acquiesced in the granting of asylum in an embassy, warship or aircraft in its territory since it could not, in that event, extradite or prosecute the accused. While, given various rules of international law regarding the inviolability of diplomatic premises,[51] a territorial State could not, in any event, forcibly remove an alleged offender from the embassy of another State in order to exercise jurisdiction over him, a grant of safe conduct out of its territory to the alleged offender would be inconsistent with the obligation *aut dedere aut judicare*. Moreover, if the State in whose

---

[45] Art. 5, PAUTS 18. See also Art. 2, Havana Convention, 132 LNTS 323.
[46] Art. 6, PAUTS 18. According to Article 7 of the Caracas Convention, moreover, it is left to the requesting State to determine whether or not urgency is involved.
[47] Arts. 5 & 12, PAUTS 18.
[48] Art. 17, PAUTS 18. See also Art. 2, Havana Convention, 132 LNTS 323.
[49] Art. 17, PAUTS 18.
[50] *Id.*
[51] See generally Art. 22, 1961 Vienna Convention on Diplomatic Relations, 500 UNTS 95.

embassy an alleged offender took refuge was a State Party to this Convention, its decision to grant asylum, thus interfering with the territorial State's obligation *aut dedere aut judicare*, would seemingly violate its duty not to frustrate the object and purpose of the Convention.[52] Since the rule of this Article is that the provisions of this Convention cannot "affect the application" of the treaties on diplomatic asylum, however, to the extent that the wording currently under consideration is not limited by the subsequent language of this Article, this Article provides an exception to Article 8, paragraph 1: the territorial State may acquiesce in the asylum and need not extradite or prosecute the alleged offender.

Does it follow from the foregoing that the alleged offender may go unpunished for any offence under this Convention that he committed prior to the grant of asylum? Some of the comments of the draftsmen of the New York Convention seemed to indicate a belief that this would be the case with respect to the identical Article in that instrument. The French representative stated that the provision "would place large geographical areas beyond" the scope of the Convention.[53] The Canadian representative stated that it "would have the effect of allowing the alleged perpetrator of an offence ... [in some cases] to escape justice".[54] The representative of Brazil, who argued against including a provision on asylum in that instrument on the ground that the offences covered therein could not be considered as political, stated that the Article was an "escape clause" which would make Latin America "a sanctuary for those who committed the very crimes whose prevention and punishment was sought".[55]

During the drafting of the Hostages Convention, it certainly appeared, at least in the early stages, that some Latin American States wanted to preserve the right not to prosecute those persons to whom they grant asylum.[56] However, this desire can hardly be seen as dispositive of the issue. Other States were totally opposed to the creation of exceptions to the obligation *aut dedere aut judicare*.[57] One commentator indicates that agreement on the issue of the "nature of the obligation to prosecute" those granted asylum was never reached

---

[52] This duty would appear to be part of the general obligation *pacta sunt servanda* as codified in Article 26 of the Vienna Convention on the Law of Treaties. See 1966 YBILC, Vol. II, p. 211.
[53] UN GAOR, 28th Sess., C.6 (1430th mtg.), para. 54, UN Doc A/C.6/SR.1430 (1973).
[54] UN GAOR, 28th Sess., C.6 (1432nd mtg.), para. 15, UN Doc A/C.6/SR.1432 (1973).
[55] UN GAOR, 28th Sess., C.6 (1439th mtg.), para. 37, UN Doc A/C.6/SR.1439 (1973).
[56] See p. 331 (notes 20 & 23 and accompanying text).
[57] The representative of Canada, for example, stated that he could accept a provision on asylum only if all acts of hostage-taking were prosecuted in accordance with the Convention. UN GAOR, 34th Sess., C.6 (13th mtg.), p. 2, para. 6, UN Doc A/C.6/34/SR.13 (1979). See also the comments of the representative of the United States, p. 330 (notes 16 & 17 and accompanying text).

by the draftsmen, and that, therefore, it was "decided to let the text speak for itself."[58] In this connexion, it may be recalled that the Chairman of the Sixth Committee working group stated that the Article was "self-explanatory".[59]

While the text may be less than "self-explanatory", it seems that the provisions of the "Treaties on Asylum" provide the answer to this problem: no provision of those treaties prohibits the subsequent prosecution of a person granted asylum. And, as earlier noted, the practice of asylum was not designed to secure the impunity of offenders. Once the immediate threat of persecution is gone, i.e., the person granted asylum has been removed from the territory of the State in which he was in danger of persecution, there is no compelling reason why the State to which he has been transported, whether it is the asylum-granting State or a third State, should not turn the case over to its authorities for their decision as to whether he will be prosecuted for his act of hostage-taking (or should not extradite him to yet another State for that offence). In effect, that State would then become the State where the "alleged offender is found", thus activating its obligations under Article 8, paragraph 1. Notwithstanding the fact that the asylum-granting State may have designated the offence as "political" for the purpose of granting asylum, the new territorial State must, when making its decision regarding prosecution, treat the offence as it would any other ordinary and grave crime under its laws.

This conclusion is quite compelling for a number of reasons. Not only is it justified by the provisions of the "Treaties on Asylum", it is consistent with the comment of the representatives of both the United States and Mexico — States on either side of the issue of whether or not a provision on asylum should have been included in this Convention — to the effect that there is no rule of international law which would preclude the prosecution of a person granted asylum.[60] Moreover, it is more compatible with the primary purpose of this

---

[58] See Rosenstock, p. 187 n. 63. It may be noted that no direct interpretive comments were made on the record by the draftsmen concerning this Article. The French representative to the Sixth Committee expressed regret at "the inclusion in the Convention of a provision which established a difference between the obligations of States Parties". UN GAOR, 34th Sess., C.6 (62nd mtg.), p. 8, para. 39, UN Doc A/C.6/34/SR.62 (1979). This statement may simply reflect the fact that the State in whose territory diplomatic asylum was granted need not itself extradite or prosecute the alleged offender. It does not support the conclusion, however, that the alleged offender may ultimately go unpunished. The representative of the USSR expressed dismay at the inclusion of this provision, stating that it would make effective punishment of such crimes more difficult. *Id.* at pp. 10-11, para. 55. This comment similarly does not indicate that this provision will result in impunity for the alleged offender. It reflects only the fact that the process leading to punishment is complicated by this provision.

[59] See p. 333 (note 34 and accompanying text).

[60] See pp. 330 & 331 (notes 17 & 22 and accompanying text).

Convention than would be a contrary interpretation. As stated in the preamble, and as indicated by the entire *travaux préparatoires*, this Convention seeks to ensure that all acts of hostage-taking result in extradition or prosecution. At the end of the drafting process moreover, the FRG representative to the Sixth Committee affirmed that the Convention upholds the principle that all hostage-takers should be prosecuted or extradited.[61]

Turning briefly to the Caracas Convention on Territorial Asylum, that instrument provides that every State has "the right, in the exercise of its sovereignty, to admit into its territory such persons as it deems advisable, without, through the exercise of this right, giving rise to complaint by any other State."[62] It further provides that no State is under an obligation to surrender or expel to any other State "persons persecuted for political reasons or offences."[63] Finally, the Convention provides that the "right of extradition is not applicable in connexion with persons who ... are sought for political offences, or for common offences committed for political ends, or when extradition is solicited for predominantly political motives."[64] That treaty thus simply reaffirms the sovereign right of States to admit whomever they choose into their territories and upholds the principle of non-refoulement as well as the political offence exception to extradition. There is nothing in that instrument that would preclude the prosecution of a person granted asylum, and it does not appear that the provisions of the Hostages Convention could, in any event, "affect the application" of that particular "Treaty on Asylum". Indeed, it may be reiterated that all States Parties to this Convention have the right to maintain their adherence to the political offence exception to extradition[65] (unless that right has been relinquished by another treaty obligation) and *must*, in fact, in accordance with Article 9, deny a request for extradition when persecution would result in the requesting State. However, this does not affect the alternative obligation *aut judicare*. For all the reasons listed in the previous paragraph, it must be concluded that a person granted territorial

---

[61] UN GAOR, 34th Sess., C.6 (62nd mtg.), p. 12, para. 61, UN Doc A/C.6/34/SR.62 (1979). As discussed in the commentary on Article 3, there are circumstances in which an act of hostage-taking may not result in the prosecution or extradition of the alleged offender, in particular when the territorial State, in an effort to secure the hostages' release, agrees to a grant of immunity. See pp. 112-114 (notes 10-16 and accompanying text in the commentary on Article 3). However, that interpretation of Article 3 is justified by both the wording of the Article and by the *travaux préparatoires*. The same cannot be said with respect to the Article currently under consideration.
[62] Art. 1, PAUTS 19.
[63] *Id.*, Art. 3.
[64] *Id.*, Art. 4.
[65] See pp. 233-234 (notes 23-30 and accompanying text in the commentary on Article 10).

asylum under the Caracas Convention must then be submitted to the appropriate authorities for the purpose of prosecution.

". . . in force at the date of the adoption of this Convention . . ."

This Article will, in any event, only be relevant to those "Treaties on Asylum" which were in force at the date of the adoption of this Convention, i.e., 17 December 1979. The only "Treaties on Asylum" which were in force on that date are those listed above.[66]

". . . as between the States which are parties to those Treaties; but a State Party to this Convention may not invoke those Treaties with respect to another State Party to this Convention which is not a party to those Treaties."

This provision is relevant only to the relations of States Parties to the "Treaties on Asylum" *inter se*.[67] A State Party to one of those treaties may not invoke it with respect to a State Party to this Convention which is not also a State Party to that instrument. Thus, assume that a national of State A, who is a member of a left-wing guerilla organization dedicated to toppling the ruling military junta in State A, takes hostages in that State in an attempt to compel that State to release members of his group from prison. The hostages are nationals of State A, State B and State D. After releasing the hostages, the offender takes refuge in the embassy of State C. All four States are parties to the Hostages Convention, and State A and State C are parties to the Caracas Convention on Diplomatic Asylum. According to that instrument, State C would have the right unilaterally to determine that the offender's crime was political in nature and grant asylum. State A would be under an obligation to respect that decision and grant safe conduct out of its territory. State D, another State Party to the Caracas Convention, could not be heard to complain that State A, the territorial State, did not comply with its obligation *aut dedere aut judicare*. However, State B, which is not party to that treaty, could insist that the obligation *aut dedere aut judicare* be complied with by territorial State C, and neither State A nor State C could invoke the

---

[66] See pp. 334-335 (notes 37-40 and accompanying text). That this provision is relevant only to a small number of treaties was not only recognized by the draftsmen of this Article, that fact was apparently what made the provision acceptable to those States which preferred not to include a provision on asylum. See, e.g., the comments of the representative of Canada to the Sixth Committee during the drafting of the New York Convention, UN GAOR, 28th Sess., C.6 (1432nd mtg.), paras. 20-21, UN Doc A/C.6/SR.1432 (1973).

[67] One commentator has likened this provision to a modification of a multilateral treaty as between certain States Parties only, pursuant to Article 41 of the Vienna Convention on the Law of Treaties. See Wood, p. 814.

Caracas Convention with respect to State B.[68] Thus, this provision will only be of relevance, if ever, to certain incidents of hostage-taking which are of concern only to those Latin American States which are States Parties to the "Treaties on Asylum".[69]

It might be noted, moreover, that even if this provision can be interpreted as allowing States Parties to the "Treaties on Asylum", as between themselves, to allow offenders to go unpunished for their acts once asylum has been granted, this provision will still have only a limited effect on this Convention. Assume, for example, that in the above hypothetical situation the offender flees to the territory of State C, rather than to State C's embassy in State A. State A, State C and State D are States Parties to the Caracas Convention on Territorial Asylum. If State C grants asylum, then as regards State A and State D it would not be obliged to extradite or prosecute the offender. However, upon the insistence of State B, it must carry out its obligations in this regard.

---

[68] See the comments of the US representative during the drafting of the New York Convention. UN GAOR, 28th Sess., Plenary (2202nd mtg.), para. 323, UN Doc A/PV.2202 (1973). See also the comments of the representatives of Canada and the United Kingdom, respectively, at UN GAOR, 28th Sess., C.6 (1432nd mtg.), para. 20 & para. 23, UN Doc A/C.6/SR.1432 (1973).

[69] It may be noted, moreover, that during the drafting of the New York Convention, the representative of Colombia to the Sixth Committee noted that none of the 11 governments sponsoring the proposal regarding asylum had ever "invoked the procedures established in the treaties on asylum to protect persons guilty" of the crimes covered in that instrument. UN GAOR, 28th Sess., C.6 (1421st mtg.), para. 4, UN Doc A/C.6/SR.1421 (1973). It may be assumed that incidents of hostage-taking will be treated in much the same way. Certainly, some Latin American States, at least, have indicated their belief that hostage-taking is a common, rather than political, offence. See p. 333 (note 31 and accompanying text).

Articles 16-20

DISPUTE SETTLEMENT AND FINAL ARTICLES

A brief word is in order regarding the dispute settlement clause in the Convention and regarding the final articles. The text of these articles may be found in Appendix I.

Article 16 establishes a third party resolution procedure, essentially identical to those contained in the other anti-terrorism conventions,[1] for disputes arising in connexion with the "interpretation or application" of the Convention. In particular, a dispute which "is not settled by negotiation" shall, at one Party's request, be submitted to arbitration. If the Parties are unable to agree on the organization of the arbitration[2] within six months of that request, any one of the Parties may refer the dispute to the ICJ. It is possible that one of the many ambiguities in the language of this Convention will give rise to a dispute between two States Parties over the proper interpretation of a particular provision. In such a case, an authoritative interpretation by an arbitral body or the ICJ will be helpful, both as regards the settlement of that particular dispute and for subsequent interpretation of that provision. This Article, moreover, may be of some value in securing compliance by States which fail to meet their obligations under the Convention. For example, if there is a prolonged hostage-taking incident in the territory of a State Party and that State takes no steps to secure the hostages' release pursuant to its obligations under Article 3 of this Convention, then it would be open to another State Party to seek a declaratory judgment that the territorial State must endeavour to secure the release of the hostages.[3]

---

[1] See Art. 12, Hague Convention; Art. 14, Montreal Convention; Art. 13, New York Convention; Art. 16, Rome Convention. The corresponding provisions of the Hague and Montreal Conventions differ in that they refer to disputes which "cannot" be settled by negotiation, while the corresponding provision in the Rome Convention refers to disputes "which cannot be settled through negotiation within a reasonable time". It may be noted that the corresponding provisions of the Hague, Montreal and Rome Conventions more clearly indicate that at least an attempt to negotiate is a condition precedent to invoking the dispute settlement procedure.

[2] The ILC noted in its draft of the New York Convention that the phrase "organization of the arbitration" may raise the question "whether 'organization' includes the appointment of members or only agreement on how members are to be appointed". 1972 YBILC Vol. II, p. 322. Article 11 of the original FRG draft would have obviated these concerns, stating that submission to the ICJ may be made "if the arrangements necessary to permit this arbitration to proceed, including the selection of the arbitrator or arbitrators, have not been completed within six months". It is unclear from the record as to why this proposed language was not accepted.

[3] Cf. *Case Concerning United States Diplomatic and Consular Staff in Tehran, Judgment*, ICJ Rep. 1980, p. 3. The applicable law in the Iranian Hostages case was not the Hostages

(*continued on p. 344*)

Similarly, if a State refuses to comply with its obligation under Article 8 to either extradite or submit for the purpose of prosecution an alleged offender present in its territory, similar relief could be sought by another State Party.

It must be noted, however, that many types of disputes which may arise under this Convention would not appear to be amenable in practice to the settlement procedure contained in Article 16. Acts of hostage-taking often take place in a crisis atmosphere and are often quickly resolved by events, for good or ill, long before a case could be brought, heard and decided. Regarding a given dispute, it may well be that there is no longer any relief that a State could obtain which would justify the time and expense involved in bringing a case before a tribunal. For example, suppose a Party in whose territory an alleged offender appears refuses either to extradite him or to submit the case for the purpose of prosecution pursuant to its obligations under Article 8. By the time the procedures established in this Article are set in motion, the alleged offender may have long departed the territory of that State and gone to a State which is not party to this Convention.[4] Further, it should be noted that many disputes which may arise under this Convention will be over matters wherein the territorial State has a good deal of discretion in its application. If, for example, a State Party submits a case to its authorities for the purpose of prosecution, unless

---

([3] *continued*)
Convention (which was not then in force) but, rather, various other treaties and customary law regarding, *inter alia*, diplomatic and consular relations. However, the case demonstrates the suitability of the dispute resolution procedure in this Convention to help resolve an on-going hostage situation, or at least to clarify the legal obligations of the territorial State. In that case, the court held (in language which could be interpreted either as a declaratory judgment or as an order: see Gray, *Judicial Remedies in International Law* 64-65, 95 (1987)), *inter alia*, that Iran was in violation of several international obligations, that it must terminate the detention of the hostages and must ensure that they have the necessary means of leaving Iranian territory. ICJ Rep. 1980, at pp. 44-45. Actual compliance with such a judgment by the territorial State is, of course, another matter.

[4] This is not to say that the arbitral tribunal or the ICJ would not have jurisdiction over such a case. Moreover, there is no reason to believe that the ICJ, for example, would refuse to exercise its jurisdiction over such a case as it did in the *Northern Cameroons* case. In that case, the court refused to exercise its judicial function both because the applicant had not sought reparations and because the Trusteeship Agreement — the interpretation or application of which was under dispute — had ended. Under those circumstances, the court said it would be impossible to render a judgment capable of effective application. See ICJ Rep. 1963, p. 37. The court also stated, however, that if the judgment were to interpret a treaty which remained in force, the judgment would have continuing applicability, relevant to future acts of interpretation or application of that treaty. *Id.* Therefore, a State Party to this Convention in a situation such as that described above which wanted to seek a declaration that the territorial State was in breach of its obligations, even if it did not seek damages, could presumably do so. The judgment of the court could, moreover, be useful in future such cases. However, it may well be wondered whether the aggrieved State Party would find it expedient to bring such a case, given that the former territorial State could not, in any event, any longer comply with the obligation *aut dedere aut judicare*.

the decision as to whether or not the offender will, in fact, be prosecuted is made in a manner other than is usually the case with respect to ordinary and grave offences under that State's laws, then there has been no breach of this Convention. Moreover, under Article 3, a State may take the measures "it" considers appropriate to secure the release of hostages in its territory. In the absence of an outright failure to comply with these obligations, i.e., by refusing to submit the case for prosecution or failing to take any steps to secure the release of the hostages, disputes concerning these matters will necessarily turn on whether or not that State has exercised good faith in complying with its obligations. While this by no means precludes resort to the dispute resolution procedure, such a case may in practice be difficult to sustain.[5]

Paragraph 2 of Article 16 provides that a State may, at the time of signature, ratification or accession, declare that it does not consider itself bound by the dispute resolution provision.[6] Other States Parties will not be bound as regards States which have made such reservations. It hardly needs to be said that this type of opt-out clause significantly erodes whatever value the dispute resolution procedure would otherwise have in securing enforcement of the Convention.[7]

---

[5] It is, of course, fundamental that States must comply with their treaty obligations in good faith. See generally, Art. 26, Vienna Convention on the Law of Treaties; *Rights of Nationals of the United States of America in Morocco, Judgment*, ICJ Rep. 1952, p. 176 at 212. While good faith is thus a justiciable issue, States are presumed to act in good faith and tribunals are loath to find that a State has acted otherwise in the exercise of discretion. Taylor, "The Content of the Rule Against Abuse of Rights in International Law", 46 BYIL 321, 333-334 (1972-73). As Fitzmaurice stated, there is a "difficulty of appreciating or estimating whether a given action or the adoption of a particular attitude was in good faith". Fitzmaurice, "Hersch Lauterpacht - The Scholar as Judge, Part I", 37 BYIL 1, 36 (1961).

[6] It may be noted that the original FRG draft article did not contain an opt-out clause. While the representatives of some States, including those of the US and Canada, appeared to approve of the FRG draft, others, such as the representative of the USSR, did not. See Second Report of the Hostages Committee, p. 25, para. 31, p. 26, para. 32, & p. 27, para. 8, respectively. The reluctance of many States to accept binding third party settlement obligations in multilateral treaties (see generally Gamble, "Reservations to Multilateral Treaties: A Macroscopic View of State Practice", 74 AJIL 372, 385-86 (1980)) was no less in evidence during the drafting of this Convention, resulting in the addition of this opt-out clause. Suggestions by some States that an alternative provision for mandatory reference of disputes to conciliation should be added to this Convention (see comments of the Observer for Switzerland, UN GAOR, 34th Sess., C.6, (15th mtg.) p. 2, para. 5, UN Doc A/C.6/34/SR.15 (1979)) were not adopted.

[7] It may be noted that as of 31 December 1986, 25 States Parties to the New York Convention (11 of which were Eastern European or other Socialist States) out of a total of 68 States Parties to that instrument had opted out of the identical dispute settlement provision in that Convention. See *Multilateral Treaties Deposited with the Secretary-General, Status as at 31 December 1986*. UN Doc ST/LEG/SER.E/5 (1987), pp. 83-86. A smaller percentage — 2 out of 36 States Parties — had, as at the same date, opted out of the dispute resolution provision in this Convention. *Id.* at p. 604. However, it may be noted that at that point no Eastern European State, save Yugoslavia, had acceded to the Hostages Convention.

Articles 17 to 20 are standard final clauses. Article 17 provides that the Convention is open for signature until 31 December 1980 at UN headquarters. Thereafter, instruments of ratification or accession may be deposited with the Secretary-General. Article 18 provides that the Convention shall enter into force on the thirtieth day following the deposit of the twenty-second instrument of ratification or accession. For States which ratify or accede to the Convention after that date, the Convention will enter into force on the thirtieth day after deposit of the appropriate instrument. Pursuant to Article 19, States Parties may denounce the Convention by written notification to the Secretary-General; denunciation shall take effect one year after receipt. It might be noted that Article 14 of the FRG draft provided that denunciation would take effect six months following the date of receipt. However, this was changed by the Sixth Committee after some States expressed concern that the shorter period would create "the risk of denouncing States being relieved of their obligations under the Convention with respect to offences committed prior to the denunciation."[8] Article 20 provides that the original of the Convention shall be deposited with the Secretary-General. The Arabic, Chinese, English, French, Russian and Spanish texts are all equally authentic.

---

[8] UN GAOR, 34th Sess., C.6 (53rd mtg.), p. 10, para. 37, UN Doc A/C.6/34/SR.53 (1979). The earlier anti-terrorism conventions provide for denunciation on six months' notice, while the Rome Convention follows the lead of this instrument, requiring one year.

Conclusion

The Hostages Convention represents an important step both in the development of a general corpus of international crimes and towards the more specific goal of suppressing international terrorism. As demonstrated in Part I, the lack of consensus on many of the issues relating to terrorism has led to a piecemeal approach to the problem, which began with the Hague and Montreal Conventions and has most recently led to the adoption in 1988 of the Montreal Protocol and the Rome Convention and Protocol. This approach, avoiding the definitional morass surrounding the concept of terrorism and seeking instead low-level agreement on the prohibition of specific acts, has proved to be the only way to obtain consensus on the suppression of international terrorism. If agreement can be reached to suppress other discrete terrorist offences which are not yet covered by international instruments, e.g., bombings of civilian targets and other violence unconnected with international aviation, maritime navigation and hostage-takings, then the formulation of a definition of terrorism will remain strictly an academic exercise, largely irrelevant to the fight against terrorism.

All of these conventions are designed to regulate the conduct of individuals; however, because of current realities of international law, this must be done through the instrumentalities of domestic law. The Hostages Convention, accordingly, imposes a number of obligations upon States Parties, all of which are essential to a scheme designed to suppress acts of terrorism. Most of these obligations relate to actions which States must take in order to bring an offender to justice once an act of hostage-taking has been completed. However, the Convention also requires activity by States prior to and during acts of hostage-taking, in order both to prevent such acts and to bring those which do occur to a speedy conclusion. It is not proposed to re-examine all of these obligations at this point. Rather, it seems best, by way of conclusion, to highlight those areas where the Convention contributes most to the development of international law, to draw attention to those areas where the Convention could have been drafted in stronger terms, and to assess briefly the efficacy of the Convention as a weapon in the fight against international terrorism.

In terms of the contribution of the Convention to international law, first and foremost, of course, it stands as an absolute prohibition on acts of hostage-taking which have an international dimension. The only international acts of hostage-taking which are excluded from the terms of the Convention are those with respect to which States Parties have an equal obligation *aut dedere aut judicare* pursuant to the Geneva

Conventions on armed conflict and Additional Protocol I thereto. The Convention thus completes a framework whereby all international acts of hostage-taking, whether motivated by political considerations or by greed, whether committed by private individuals or agents of a State, and whether committed in peacetime or during war, must result in the prosecution or extradition of the offender.

This Convention, therefore, along with Protocol I, disposes firmly of the notion, prevalent amongst many States in the 1970s, that the cause of national liberation is a licence to commit any and all acts of violence. As the first anti-terrorism convention which addresses the interrelationship between international criminal law and the laws of armed conflict, this instrument recognizes the developments in international humanitarian law which make it conceivable that some armed conflicts for national liberation could be covered by the Geneva Conventions and Additional Protocol I in such a way as to impose the obligation *aut dedere aut judicare* with respect to acts of hostage-taking committed therein. It also recognizes, however, that many such conflicts will not be covered by the Geneva instruments; in such cases, acts of hostage-taking committed by national liberation groups will remain within the scope of the Hostages Convention.

The adoption of the Convention without even a hint of an exception of coverage based on the political motivation of the offender (a goal not achieved by the draftsmen of the New York Convention just six years earlier)[1] must be seen as a major success of the United Nations. Despite the divisions within that body regarding terrorism generally, the Convention, dealing with a highly political and controversial matter, was adopted by consensus. Thus, the entire community of States has at least acquiesced in, if not firmly embraced (given both the failure of many States so far to sign or ratify the Convention and the continued involvement of some States in acts of hostage-taking), the principle that all acts of hostage-taking must result in extradition or prosecution.

The most important obligation contained in this Convention is that of *aut dedere aut judicare*. While there are many conventions requiring the suppression of international criminal offences, the anti-terrorism conventions have taken the lead in most clearly setting forth this obligation. In recent years, moreover, the formulation as contained in these instruments has been included in other conventions which do not, strictly speaking, deal with terrorism, such as those concerning torture and the protection of nuclear material. The formulation as contained in this Convention should become the model for all or most future conventions dealing with international criminal offences.

---

[1] See p. 48 (note 162 in Part I); p. 267 (note 14 in the commentary on Article 12).

Adequate compliance with the principle *aut dedere aut judicare* requires States to establish jurisdiction over offences with which their only connexion is the offender's subsequent presence in their territory. This Convention thus adds to the category of crimes with respect to which States may exercise universal jurisdiction, at least as between themselves and other States Parties thereto. This basis of jurisdiction is contained in the Convention as a subsidiary basis, i.e., one to be exercised when an offender is not extradited to a State Party which has a more significant connexion with the offence and which has primary jurisdiction over that offence.

With respect to primary jurisdiction, this Convention expands the category of States with such jurisdiction beyond that generally contained in the earlier conventions. Two bases of jurisdiction are worth particular mention, the passive personality principle and jurisdiction by the State which is the target of compulsion. Although some States, such as the United States and the United Kingdom, objected to the inclusion of the passive personality principle in this Convention, they have provided for this basis in their implementing legislation. The United States, moreover, has subsequently enacted legislation which gives its courts jurisdiction over other terrorist acts committed against its nationals abroad. It seems unlikely that these developments signify the beginning of a general acceptance of the passive personality principle by States which have traditionally opposed its use; it is probably an acceptance limited only to terrorist offences, reflecting the fact that many targets of terrorist attacks are so victimized precisely because of their nationality. Nevertheless, even this limited acceptance is a significant departure from the almost absolute rejection of the principle by those States in the past. The establishment of jurisdiction by the State which is the target of compulsion, a basis which is similar to the protective principle, is also particularly justifiable by the nature of terrorism. Terrorist acts are commonly committed in order to compel action or forbearance by a State, and such a State has a strong interest in seeing that the offender is brought to justice. The expansion in general of the category of States with primary jurisdiction should help to ensure that offenders are brought to justice in a State which has a strong interest in the offence, and the inclusion of both of these bases of jurisdiction in the subsequently adopted Rome Convention and Protocol indicates that they will remain features in future anti-terrorism conventions.

Article 3 contains a requirement that is essential in an instrument designed to protect victims of hostage-takings: it obliges the territorial State to attempt to secure the release of the hostages. While such an obligation might be part of the general obligation of a State under customary international law to protect aliens in its territory, the rule as formulated in this Article leaves no doubt as to a State's obligations in this regard. It may neither acquiesce nor remain idle when hostages are taken in its territory; rather, it must in good faith take steps to secure their release. This rule is important not only for obvious humanitarian purposes, but also for the smooth functioning of international relations. If conscientiously adhered to by the territorial State, it will reduce tensions between that State and the national State of the hostages and will, moreover, reduce the latter's need and temptation to use force to rescue its nationals.

Another important aspect of this Article, however, is that it may constitute a significant erosion of the rule that all offenders, "without exception whatsoever", must either be extradited or prosecuted, since the territorial State is, apparently, authorized under this Article to grant immunity to the offenders in return for the release of the hostages. On the one hand, this potential loophole is to be regretted since it weakens the law enforcement potential of the Convention; on the other hand, humanitarian and political considerations would seem to demand that States Parties be left with room to manoeuvre in this regard. It would appear, however, that this method of securing the release of the hostages should only be employed as a last resort and, of course, only after a good faith determination that it is an appropriate step.

With regard to extradition, this Convention follows generally the pattern established in the earlier anti-terrorism Conventions. It does not compel extradition, but it facilitates the extradition option by providing the legal bases for extradition in some cases. However, one significant innovation is the inclusion of a discrimination clause, requiring States Parties *not* to extradite an offender to a State in which he would be in danger of persecution. This follows a certain trend, established in some extradition conventions and bilateral treaties, to extend the rule of *non-refoulement* to extradition. It does not, however, affect in any other way the obligation *aut dedere aut judicare*.

Despite the international consensus represented by this Convention that all acts of hostage-taking are impermissible and must be suppressed, there are significant limits on the extent to which States are willing to restrict their freedom of action in this regard. There are numerous ways in which the Convention could have been drafted in stronger terms so as more adequately to ensure that all acts of hostage-taking result in the punishment of the offender. First, the Convention could have required the extradition of alleged offenders to States which have a significant connexion with the offence, such as the territorial State or the State which was the target of demands. Second, the Convention could have established a mechanism for the imposition of sanctions against States which fail to comply with their obligations thereunder.

However, it is highly doubtful that such obligations will soon be included in a universal anti-terrorism convention. With respect to automatic extradition, States are unlikely to give up their discretion in this regard, particularly as regards the political offence exception, in a convention designed for universal adherence. Agreement on sanctions seems equally unlikely. Even with respect to the ICAO Conventions, where the subject matter lends itself to an easily identifiable form of sanction — the suspension of air services to and from the defaulting State — legal and political disagreements thwarted attempts to design mechanisms for sanctions.[2] With respect to the taking of hostages, an offence which can occur in numerous ways, agreement on the appropriate form of sanctions would have been that much more elusive, even in the unlikely event that agreement could have been reached on the basic principle that a system of sanctions should be included in the Convention. Indeed, the issue of sanctions apparently never came up during the drafting of this Convention, and no mechanism for sanctions was included in the subsequently adopted anti-terrorism conventions — the Montreal Protocol and the Rome Convention and Protocol.

Two other important ways in which the Convention could have been strengthened can be identified. Article 6 could have been drafted so as absolutely to require the State in whose territory an alleged offender is found to take measures to ensure his presence for extradition or prosecution proceedings, rather than simply requiring it to take such measures when it is "satisfied that the circumstances so warrant". Similarly, the principle *aut dedere aut judicare*, as contained in Article 8, could have been drafted so as to require that those offenders who are not extradited must actually be prosecuted, and not just submitted for the "purpose of prosecution".

However, these particular limitations are probably unavoidable in an international criminal law enforcement scheme that relies upon municipal law processes. As deliberations during the drafting of the Hague Convention aptly demonstrated, few States would ever be willing to cede their sovereignty to such a degree as to accept absolute obligations to take alleged offenders into custody or, more particularly, to prosecute them if they are not extradited. Even the European Convention on the Suppression of Terrorism has not been drafted in such a way as to impose such obligations upon States. If such obligations are unacceptable even to States within the Council of Europe *inter se*, they are not likely to be adopted in an instrument designed for universal adherence.

---

[2] See pp. 56-57 (note 195 and accompanying text in Part I).

There are other ways in which the Convention could have been drafted in stronger terms and which, seemingly, should not have been as objectionable to States as the above-mentioned areas. For example, Article 2 could have established a certain minimum penalty for those convicted of acts of hostage-taking, thus ensuring some uniformity in domestic laws in this regard and helping to ensure that hostage-takers actually serve some punishment for their offences. Moreover, a more specific listing of the required co-operative preventative measures in Article 4 would have helped to ensure that States Parties actually take some significant steps in this regard. Article 5 should have required States Parties to establish their jurisdiction over other acts of violence which accompany acts of hostage-taking, thus obviating the possibility that the State which ultimately exercises its jurisdiction over the hostage-taking will not have jurisdiction over that attendant act of violence. Further, Article 10 could simply have provided that this Convention will serve as an extradition treaty between States Parties, subject to the laws of the requested State, and thereby contained a more uniform obligation regarding the consideration of the offences in Article 1 as "extraditable offences". The obligation in Article 11 to provide mutual assistance in connexion with criminal proceedings would have been much more effective, given the wide variation in States' laws in this regard, if it had specified in greater detail the specific forms of assistance which must be rendered and the evidence which must be supplied.

As to ambiguous provisions, Article 13 is unclear as to whether the Convention should apply when the acts of the offenders take place solely within the territory of which both they and the victims are nationals, but where the target of compulsion is a second State or a third party in a second State. Similarly, the effect of Article 15 upon the obligation of States Parties to the "Treaties on Asylum", as between themselves, to prosecute an alleged offender once asylum is granted is somewhat unclear, and that provision, in any event, creates, at least in theory, a difference in the obligations of States Parties under the Convention. All of these faults make the Convention a less effective instrument than it could otherwise have been.

However, it would appear that the terms of this Convention, as well as the other anti-terrorism conventions, are as strong as current political realities will allow. And some of the very factors which make the Convention, in one sense, weaker than it could have been, paradoxically, could make it a more effective tool in the battle against terrorism. If States are not required to give up their right to invoke the political offence exception or to otherwise refuse extradition, if they are not required in all cases actually to prosecute an alleged offender or to impose a certain penalty upon a convicted hostage-taker, then they may be less reluctant to become parties to the Convention. Manifestly, the more parties to this Convention, the greater its potential in combatting acts of hostage-taking.

It remains to assess, in the light of all that has been said above, the potential efficacy of the Convention as a tool in the battle against terrorism. Despite the foregoing litany of weaknesses, the Convention imposes significant obligations upon States Parties. Of most importance, the obligation *aut dedere aut judicare* is formulated in strong terms: those offenders who are not prosecuted must be submitted to the appropriate authorities for the purpose of prosecution. Those authorities must take their decision whether or not to prosecute in the same manner as they would with respect to other ordinary and serious offences under their laws. In other words, the political context of the crime should not be taken into account, and there should be no interference by a State's political authorities. Where there is sufficient evidence to bring an alleged offender to trial and no countervailing humanitarian considerations to prevent such, a prosecution should be instituted. There is, of course, the possibility that decisions not to prosecute will be taken in bad faith, either because of sympathy for the cause of the offender, or because of considerations of expediency, such as an unwillingness to antagonize terrorist groups and the States which sponsor them. Such decisions would be a clear breach of this Convention. Given the relatively small number of States which have so far become parties to the Convention, the practice under the instrument has been limited. There have been few instances wherein an alleged offender has come (or been brought) into the territory of a State Party to this Convention, thus activating its obligation to prosecute or extradite. Such examples as do exist show somewhat mixed results. For example, in the aftermath of the *Achille Lauro* hijacking, Yugoslavia refused to hold Abu Abbas pending a US extradition request, giving the dubious excuse that he had diplomatic immunity.[3] This action was probably a violation of that State's obligations under both Article 6(1) and Article 8(1). As a signatory to the Hostages Convention, Italy's similar conduct in allowing Abbas to go free was probably a violation of (in addition to its bilateral extradition treaty with the United States) its obligation, pursuant to the Vienna Convention on the Law of Treaties, not to take action which would defeat the object and purpose of the treaty. On the other hand, there have been some recent positive developments. In 1988 and 1989, for example, after two separate trials, Lebanese men apprehended in West German territory were convicted and sentenced to imprisonment in connexion with hostage-takings committed in

---

[3] See p. 26 (note 65 in Part I).

Beirut and on board a TWA airliner.[4] Moreover, in 1989 another Lebanese man, who was apprehended by United States officials in international waters, was convicted in the United States of hostage-taking, conspiracy and hijacking in connexion with the 1985 seizure of a Jordanian airliner.[5] Also in 1989, another Lebanese man was convicted by a Swiss court of hostage-taking, hijacking and murder, committed in connexion with the 1987 seizure of an Air Afrique airliner originating in Brazzaville, and was sentenced to life imprisonment.[6] The results of the ICAO instruments have also been mixed. In general, it seems that a large number of prosecutions have been undertaken by States Parties to those Conventions, although significant exceptions exist.[7]

In the final analysis, the most significant problem connected with the ultimate prosecution of all hostage-takers is that, notwithstanding the consensus adoption of the Convention in the General Assembly, most States have not yet become parties to this Convention (although the pace of ratifications and accessions remains steady). The result is that in many of the areas of the world in which such acts are endemic, the Convention is not in force. Lebanon, for example, is not party to the Convention. While this may be considered a matter of little practical import since it is doubtful that the government of that State

[4] See p. 87 (note 40 in the commentary on Article 1).
[5] See *New York Times*, March 15, 1989, p. A3. See also 88 Dep't St. Bull., No. 2130, p. 50 (1988). It might be noted that this was the first conviction under the US legislation enacted in furtherance of the Hostages Convention.
[6] See *International Herald Tribune*, February 25-26, 1989, p. 2.
[7] In an ICAO review of 27 aerial hijackings committed between 4 February 1984 and 19 December 1985, reports received from concerned States indicated that 14 incidents resulted, or were to result, in the prosecution of the offenders. One case resulted in the institutionalization of the offender due to his mental state, and in another the offenders were killed in a rescue attempt. In two cases, asylum was granted (by Iraq to Iranian hijackers), apparently without subsequent prosecution. In the remaining nine cases, no information regarding disposition of the case was available. In four of those cases, the incident terminated in Lebanon. See ICAO Doc A26-WP/29, pp. 24-34 (1986). There have been some recent important prosecutions in connexion with offences under the Hague Convention. For example, in July 1988, a court in Pakistan convicted and sentenced to death five Palestinians who hijacked a Pan Am aircraft, an incident which resulted in the deaths of 11 passengers. See *Time*, July 18, 1988. In 1989 West German, Swiss and US courts convicted Lebanese men on hijacking charges. See p. 87 (note 40 in the commentary on Article 1). See also notes 5 & 6, *supra*, and accompanying text.

Since the adoption of the Hague Convention, which, as earlier noted, has now reached almost universal adherence, the number of aerial hijackings has decreased significantly. For example, in the pre-Hague Convention years 1969-71, there were 245 aerial hijackings. By way of contrast, in the years 1978-80, there were only 147. See Finger, "Security of International Aviation: The Role of ICAO", 6 Terr. J. 519 (1983-84). In 1986, there were only 2 aerial hijackings, the lowest figure in at least twenty years. See 88 Dep't St. Bull., No. 2130, p. 44 (1988). While the extent to which this decrease can directly be attributed to the Hague Convention is unclear, certainly the galvanization of world opinion which led to the adoption and acceptance of that instrument has also led to the institution of such security devices as baggage and passenger screenings and sky marshalls, which have played a significant role in the prevention of such acts.

would, under present conditions, be able to fulfil its obligations under the Convention, of more importance, neither of the States — Iran and Syria — which wield effective power over the groups which are responsible for the hostage-takings in that State are parties to the Convention. It is clear, moreover, that Iran, at least, is determined to use hostages as a bargaining tool with States whose nationals are held. Humanitarian and political considerations place a tremendous pressure upon those States to deal with Iran in an attempt to secure the release of their nationals. This probably has the effect of encouraging additional hostage-takings, and results in States dealing with offences of hostage-taking in a manner which is different from that envisaged by this Convention. This fact — that many acts of hostage-taking remain beyond the pale of the Convention — is the greatest weakness of the enforcement scheme of the Convention. Without universal or near-universal adherence to the Convention, safe havens for hostage-takers will continue to exist. However, this is not a weakness of the Convention itself, but of the international system in general.

Despite the failure of many States to become parties to the Convention, the instrument could still have a significant impact on the battle against terrorism. The very fact of its adoption by consensus in the General Assembly stands as an authoritative rejection by the international community of acts of hostage-taking. The Convention makes it impossible for States to argue that such acts are permissible, and increasingly difficult for them to acquiesce in such acts in their territory. Moreover, it will have significant law enforcement value as offenders come within the jurisdiction of States which are parties to the Convention. Despite its flaws, this Convention has much to recommend it: it does not deny the right to self-determination (in fact it explicitly reaffirms that right in the Preamble) or even the right to use force to obtain national liberation. Yet it condemns and prohibits unequivocally all acts of hostage-taking. The Convention does not require extradition, and thus should not be unacceptable to States which, for domestic political or ideological considerations, cannot practically extradite an offender to a particular country. It imposes a series of obligations on States which, if fulfilled, could go a long way towards the elimination of such acts. In short, it combines an absolute prohibition on acts of hostage-taking and a sufficient law enforcement mechanism with obligations which should not be too onerous for any civilized State. It is, moreover, a multilateral instrument, designed for universal adherence. If conscientiously applied by all States it would obviate the need for divisive and tension-escalating unilateral or regional measures such as economic sanctions, extra-jurisdictional actions by States to bring alleged offenders to justice, or of more dangerous responses such as the use of force against States suspected of supporting or harbouring hostage-takers. Whether the international community is mature enough to accept it fully is a matter which remains to be seen.

Appendix I

INTERNATIONAL CONVENTION AGAINST THE TAKING OF HOSTAGES, 1979

The States Parties to this Convention,

Having in mind the purposes and principles of the Charter of the United Nations concerning the maintenance of international peace and security and the promotion of friendly relations and co-operation among States,

Recognizing in particular that everyone has the right to life, liberty and security of person, as set out in the Universal Declaration of Human Rights and the International Covenant on Civil and Political Rights,

Reaffirming the principle of equal rights and self-determination of peoples as enshrined in the Charter of the United Nations and the Declaration on Principles of International Law concerning Friendly Relations and Co-operation among States in accordance with the Charter of the United Nations, as well as in other relevant resolutions of the General Assembly,

Considering that the taking of hostages is an offence of grave concern to the international community and that, in accordance with the provisions of this Convention, any person committing an act of hostage taking shall either be prosecuted or extradited,

Being convinced that it is urgently necessary to develop international co-operation between States in devising and adopting effective measures for the prevention, prosecution and punishment of all acts of taking of hostages as manifestations of international terrorism,

Have agreed as follows:

Article 1

1. Any person who seizes or detains and threatens to kill, to injure or to continue to detain another person (hereinafter referred to as the "hostage") in order to compel a third party, namely, a State, an international inter-governmental organization, a natural or juridical person, or a group of persons, to do or abstain from doing any act as an explicit or implicit condition for the release of the hostage commits the offence of taking of hostages ("hostage-taking") within the meaning of this Convention.

2. Any person who:
(a) attempts to commit an act of hostage-taking, or
(b) participates as an accomplice of anyone who commits or attempts to commit an act of hostage-taking
likewise commits an offence for the purposes of this Convention.

Article 2

Each State Party shall make the offences set forth in article 1 punishable by appropriate penalties which take into account the grave nature of those offences.

Article 3

1. The State Party in the territory of which the hostage is held by the offender shall take all measures it considers appropriate to ease the situation of the hostage, in particular, to secure his release and, after his release, to facilitate, when relevant, his departure.

2. If any object which the offender has obtained as a result of the taking of hostages comes into the custody of a State Party, that State Party shall return it as soon as possible to the hostage or the third party referred to in article 1, as the case may be, or to the appropriate authorities thereof.

Article 4

States Parties shall co-operate in the prevention of the offences set forth in article 1, particularly by:

(a) taking all practicable measures to prevent preparations in their respective territories for the commission of those offences within or outside their territories, including measures to prohibit in their territories illegal activities of persons, groups and organizations that encourage, instigate, organize or engage in the perpetration of acts of taking of hostages;

(b) exchanging information and co-ordinating the taking of administrative and other measures as appropriate to prevent the commission of those offences.

Article 5

1. Each State Party shall take such measures as may be necessary to establish its jurisdiction over any of the offences set forth in article 1 which are committed:

(a) in its territory or on board a ship or aircraft registered in that State;

(b) by any of its nationals or, if that State considers it appropriate, by those stateless persons who have their habitual residence in its territory;

(c) in order to compel that State to do or abstain from doing any act; or

(d) with respect to a hostage who is a national of that State, if that State considers it appropriate.

2. Each State Party shall likewise take such measures as may be necessary to establish its jurisdiction over the offences set forth in article 1 in cases where the alleged offender is present in its territory and it does not extradite him to any of the States mentioned in paragraph 1 of this article.

3. This Convention does not exclude any criminal jurisdiction exercised in accordance with internal law.

Article 6

1. Upon being satisfied that the circumstances so warrant, any State Party in the territory of which the alleged offender is present shall, in accordance with its laws, take him into custody or take other measures to ensure his presence for such time as is necessary to enable any criminal or extradition proceedings to be instituted. That State Party shall immediately make a preliminary inquiry into the facts.

2. The custody or other measures referred to in paragraph 1 of this article shall be notified without delay directly or through the Secretary-General of the United Nations to:

(a) the State where the offence was committed;

(b) the State against which compulsion has been directed or attempted;

(c) the State of which the natural or juridical person against whom compulsion has been directed or attempted is a national;

(d) the State of which the hostage is a national or in the territory of which he has his habitual residence;

(e) the State of which the alleged offender is a national or, if he is a stateless person, in the territory of which he has his habitual residence;

(f) the international intergovernmental organization against which compulsion has been directed or attempted;

(g) all other States concerned.

3. Any person regarding whom the measures referred to in paragraph 1 of this article are being taken shall be entitled:

(a) to communicate without delay with the nearest appropriate representative of the State of which he is a national or which is otherwise entitled to establish such communication or, if he is a stateless person, the State in the territory of which he has his habitual residence;

(b) to be visited by a representative of that State.

4. The rights referred to in paragraph 3 of this article shall be exercised in conformity with the laws and regulations of the State in the territory of which the alleged offender is present subject to the proviso, however, that the said laws and regulations must enable full effect to be given to the purposes for which the rights accorded under paragraph 3 of this article are intended.

5. The provisions of paragraphs 3 and 4 of this article shall be without prejudice to the right of any State Party having a claim to jurisdiction in accordance with paragraph 1(b) of article 5 to invite the International Committee of the Red Cross to communicate with and visit the alleged offender.

6. The State which makes the preliminary inquiry contemplated in paragraph 1 of this article shall promptly report its findings to the States or organization referred to in paragraph 2 of this article and indicate whether it intends to exercise jurisdiction.

Article 7

The State Party where the alleged offender is prosecuted shall in accordance with its laws communicate the final outcome of the proceedings to the Secretary-General of the United Nations, who shall transmit the information to the other States concerned and the international intergovernmental organizations concerned.

Article 8

1. The State Party in the territory of which the alleged offender is found shall, if it does not extradite him, be obliged, without exception whatsoever

and whether or not the offence was committed in its territory, to submit the case to its competent authorities for the purpose of prosecution, through proceedings in accordance with the laws of that State. Those authorities shall take their decision in the same manner as in the case of any ordinary offence of a grave nature under the law of that State.

2. Any person regarding whom proceedings are being carried out in connexion with any of the offences set forth in article 1 shall be guaranteed fair treatment at all stages of the proceedings, including enjoyment of all the rights and guarantees provided by the law of the State in the territory of which he is present.

Article 9

1. A request for the extradition of an alleged offender, pursuant to this Convention, shall not be granted if the requested State Party has substantial grounds for believing:

(a) that the request for extradition for an offence set forth in article 1 has been made for the purpose of prosecuting or punishing a person on account of his race, religion, nationality, ethnic origin or political opinion; or

(b) that the person's position may be prejudiced:

(i) for any of the reasons mentioned in subparagraph (a) of this paragraph, or

(ii) for the reason that communication with him by the appropriate authorities of the State entitled to exercise rights of protection cannot be effected.

2. With respect to the offences as defined in this Convention, the provisions of all extradition treaties and arrangements applicable between States Parties are modified as between States Parties to the extent that they are incompatible with this Convention.

Article 10

1. The offences set forth in article 1 shall be deemed to be included as extraditable offences in any extradition treaty existing between States Parties. States Parties undertake to include such offences as extraditable offences in every extradition treaty to be concluded between them.

2. If a State Party which makes extradition conditional on the existence of a treaty receives a request for extradition from another State Party with which it has no extradition treaty, the requested State may at its option consider this Convention as the legal basis for extradition in respect of the offences set forth in article 1. Extradition shall be subject to the other conditions provided by the law of the requested State.

3. States Parties which do not make extradition conditional on the existence of a treaty shall recognize the offences set forth in article 1 as extraditable offences between themselves subject to the conditions provided by the law of the requested State.

4. The offences set forth in article 1 shall be treated, for the purpose of extradition between States Parties, as if they had been committed not only in

the place in which they occurred but also in the territories of the States required to establish their jurisdiction in accordance with paragraph 1 of article 5.

Article 11

1. States Parties shall afford one another the greatest measure of assistance in connexion with criminal proceedings brought in respect of the offences set forth in article 1, including the supply of all evidence at their disposal necessary for the proceedings.

2. The provisions of paragraph 1 of this article shall not affect obligations concerning mutual judicial assistance embodied in any other treaty.

Article 12

In so far as the Geneva Conventions of 1949 for the protection of war victims or the Additional Protocols to those Conventions are applicable to a particular act of hostage-taking, and in so far as States Parties to this Convention are bound under those conventions to prosecute or hand over the hostage-taker, the present Convention shall not apply to an act of hostage-taking committed in the course of armed conflicts as defined in the Geneva Conventions of 1949 and the Protocols thereto, including armed conflicts mentioned in article 1, paragraph 4, of Additional Protocol I of 1977, in which peoples are fighting against colonial domination and alien occupation and against racist régimes in the exercise of their right of self-determination, as enshrined in the Charter of the United Nations and the Declaration of Principles of International Law concerning Friendly Relations and Co-operation among States in accordance with the Charter of the United Nations.

Article 13

This Convention shall not apply where the offence is committed within a single State, the hostage and the alleged offender are nationals of that State and the alleged offender is found in the territory of that State.

Article 14

Nothing in this Convention shall be construed as justifying the violation of the territorial integrity or political independence of a State in contravention of the Charter of the United Nations.

Article 15

The provisions of this Convention shall not affect the application of the Treaties on Asylum, in force at the date of the adoption of this Convention, as between the States which are parties to those Treaties; but a State Party to this Convention may not invoke those Treaties with respect to another State Party to this Convention which is not a party to those Treaties.

Article 16

1. Any dispute between two or more States Parties concerning the

interpretation or application of this Convention which is not settled by negotiation shall, at the request of one of them, be submitted to arbitration. If within six months from the date of the request for arbitration the parties are unable to agree on the organization of the arbitration, any one of those parties may refer the dispute to the International Court of Justice by request in conformity with the Statute of the Court.

2. Each State may at the time of signature or ratification of this Convention or accession thereto declare that it does not consider itself bound by paragraph 1 of this article. The other States Parties shall not be bound by paragraph 1 of this article with respect to any State Party which has made such a reservation.

3. Any State Party which has made a reservation in accordance with paragraph 2 of this article may at any time withdraw that reservation by notification to the Secretary-General of the United Nations.

Article 17

1. This Convention is open for signature by all States until 31 December 1980 at United Nations Headquarters in New York.

2. This Convention is subject to ratification. The instruments of ratification shall be deposited with the Secretary-General of the United Nations.

3. This Convention is open for accession by any State. The instruments of accession shall be deposited with the Secretary-General of the United Nations.

Article 18

1. This Convention shall enter into force on the thirtieth day following the date of deposit of the twenty-second instrument of ratification or accession with the Secretary-General of the United Nations.

2. For each State ratifying or acceding to the Convention after the deposit of the twenty-second instrument of ratification or accession, the Convention shall enter into force on the thirtieth day after deposit by such State of its instrument of ratification or accession.

Article 19

1. Any State Party may denounce this Convention by written notification to the Secretary-General of the United Nations.

2. Denunciation shall take effect one year following the date on which notification is received by the Secretary-General of the United Nations.

Article 20

The original of this Convention, of which the Arabic, Chinese, English, French, Russian and Spanish texts are equally authentic, shall be deposited with the Secretary-General of the United Nations, who shall send certified copies thereof to all States.

IN WITNESS WHEREOF, the undersigned, being duly authorized thereto by their respective Governments, have signed this Convention, opened for signature at New York on . . .

Appendix II

INTERNATIONAL CONVENTION AGAINST THE TAKING OF HOSTAGES

FEDERAL REPUBLIC OF GERMANY, DRAFT

Preamble

The States Parties to this Convention,

Having in mind the purposes and principles of the Charter of the United Nations concerning the maintenance of international peace and the promotion of friendly relations and co-operation among States,

Recognizing that everyone has the right to life, liberty and security, as set out in the Universal Declaration of Human Rights and the International Covenant on Civil and Political Rights,

Considering that the taking of hostages is a matter of grave concern,

Convinced that there is an urgent need to adopt appropriate and effective measures for the prevention and punishment of the taking of hostages,

Have agreed as follows:

Article 1

1. Any person who seizes or detains another person (hereinafter referred to as "hostage") and threatens with death or severe injury or continued detention of that person in order to compel
   (a) A third person,
   (b) A body corporate under national law,
   (c) A State or
   (d) An international organization or international conference
to do or abstain from doing anything commits an act of taking hostages, an offence within the meaning of this Convention.

2. Any person who
   (a) Attempts to commit an act of taking hostages, or
   (b) Is an accomplice of anyone who commits or attempts to commit an act of taking hostages
also commits an offence within the meaning of this Convention.

Article 2

Contracting States shall co-operate in the prevention of the offences set forth in article 1, particularly by:

(a) Taking all practicable measures to prevent preparations in their respective territories for the commission of those offences within or outside their territories;

(b) Exchanging information and co-ordinating the taking of administrative and other measures as appropriate to prevent the commission of those offences.

Article 3

1. Each Contracting State in whose territory the offender is present with his hostage shall take such measures as it deems appropriate to ease the situation of the hostage and to secure his release.

2. After the hostage has been freed the Contracting State in whose territory he is present will facilitate his prompt departure from the country.

3. If any object which the offender has illegally acquired as a result of the taking of hostages comes into the custody of a Contracting State, that Contracting State shall return it promptly to the person entitled to possession.

Article 4

Each Contracting State shall make the offences mentioned in article 1 punishable by severe penalties.

Article 5

1. Each Contracting State shall take such measures as may be necessary to establish its jurisdiction over any of the offences set forth in article 1.
 (a) That are committed in its territory or on board a ship or aircraft registered in that State,
 (b) By which that State itself or an international organization of which the State is a member is to be compelled to do or abstain from doing anything or
 (c) That are committed by any of its nationals.

2. Each Contracting State shall likewise take such measures as may be necessary to establish its jurisdiction over the offences set forth in article 1 in the case where the alleged offender is present in its territory and it does not extradite him pursuant to article 8 to any of the States mentioned in paragraph 1 of this article.

3. This Convention does not exclude any criminal jurisdiction exercised in accordance with internal law.

Article 6

1. Upon being satisfied that the circumstances so warrant, the Contracting State in whose territory the alleged offender is present shall take the appropriate measures under its internal law so as to ensure his presence for the purpose of prosecution or extradition. Such measures shall be notified without delay directly or through the Secretary-General of the United Nations to:
 (a) The State where the offence was committed,
 (b) The State against which compulsion has been directed or attempted,
 (c) The State of which the person or the body corporate against whom compulsion has been directed or attempted is a national,
 (d) The State of which the hostage is a national,
 (e) The State of which the alleged offender is a national or, if he is a stateless person, in whose territory he permanently resides,
 (f) The international organization or conference against which compulsion has been directed or attempted.

2. Any person in custody pursuant to paragraph 1 of this article shall be assisted in communicating immediately with the nearest appropriate representative of the State of which he is a national.

Article 7

1. The Contracting State in the territory of which the alleged offender is found shall, if it does not extradite him, be obliged, without exception whatsoever and whether or not the offence was committed in its territory, to submit the case to its competent authorities for the purpose of prosecution. Those authorities shall take their decision in the same manner as in the case of any ordinary offence of a serious nature under the law of that State.

2. Any person regarding whom proceedings are being carried out in connexion with any of the offences set forth in article 1 shall be guaranteed fair treatment at all stages of the proceedings.

Article 8

1. Each of the offences set forth in article 1 shall be deemed to be included as extraditable offences in any extradition treaty existing between Contracting States. Contracting States undertake to include such offences as extraditable offences in every extradition treaty to be concluded between them.

2. If a Contracting State which makes extradition conditional on the existence of a treaty receives a request for extradition from another Contracting State with which it has no extradition treaty, it may at its option consider this Convention as the legal basis for extradition in respect of the offences set forth in article 1. Extradition shall be subject to the other conditions provided by the law of the requested State.

3. Contracting States which do not make extradition conditional on the existence of a treaty shall recognize the offences set forth in article 1 as extraditable offences between themselves subject to the conditions provided by the law of the requested State.

4. The offences set forth in article 1 shall be treated, for the purpose of extradition between Contracting States, as if they had been committed not only in the place in which they occurred but also in the territories of States required to establish their jurisdiction in accordance with article 5, paragraph 1.

Article 9

1. Contracting States shall afford one another the greatest measure of assistance in connexion with criminal proceedings brought in respect of the offences set forth in article 1, including the supply of all evidence at their disposal necessary for the proceedings.

2. The provisions of paragraph 1 of this article shall not affect obligations concerning mutual judicial assistance embodied in any other treaty.

Article 10

1. This Convention shall not affect the Geneva Conventions of 12 August

1949 for the protection of war victims, the Convention of 16 December 1970 for the Suppression of Unlawful Seizure of Aircraft, the Convention of 23 September 1971 for the Suppression of Unlawful Acts against the Safety of Civil Aviation and the Convention of 14 December 1973 on the Prevention and Punishment of Crimes against Internationally Protected Persons, including Diplomatic Agents.

2. This Convention shall not apply where the offence is committed within a single State, where the hostage, the offender, and the person or body corporate subjected to demands are all nationals of that State and where the offender is found in the territory of that State. This Convention shall, however, apply if a State, an international organization or an international conference is subjected to demands.

Article 11

Any dispute between two or more Contracting States concerning the interpretation or application of this Convention which is not settled by negotiation may be submitted to arbitration by any party to the dispute by means of a written notification to any other party to the dispute. If the arrangements necessary to permit this arbitration to proceed, including the selection of the arbitrator or arbitrators, have not been completed within six months of the date of receipt of the notification, any party to the dispute may submit the dispute to the International Court of Justice for decision in accordance with the Statute of the Court.

Article 12

1. This Convention shall be open for signature by all States until . . . . at United Nations Headquarters in New York.

2. This Convention is subject to ratification. The instruments of ratification shall be deposited with the Secretary-General of the United Nations.

3. This Convention shall remain open for accession by any State. The instruments of accession shall be deposited with the Secretary-General of the United Nations.

Article 13

1. This Convention shall enter into force on the thirtieth day following the date of deposit of the twenty-second instrument of ratification or accession with the Secretary-General of the United Nations.

2. For each State ratifying or acceding to the Convention after the deposit of the twenty-second instrument of ratification or accession, the Convention shall enter into force on the thirtieth day after deposit by such State of its instrument of ratification or accession.

Article 14

1. Any Contracting State may denounce this Convention by written notification to the Secretary-General of the United Nations.

2. Denunciation shall take effect six months following the date on which notification is received by the Secretary-General of the United Nations.

INDEX

Accomplice. *See also* Conspiracy
  conspirator as, 91
  Hostages Convention—
    —liability under, 90-2
  ILC, 90
  municipal law, under, 91
Achille Lauro, 4, 26-7, 45, 115-16, 150-1, 303
  arrest—
    —extradition, pending, 26 n. 65, 171
  deal, 4, 115-16
    —hostage-takers' failure to keep to, 115
    —Hostages Convention—
      ——compatibility with, 115 n. 19
    —parties to, 115 n. 18
    —safe passage, 115
  diplomatic immunity, and, 26 n. 65, 171 n. 14
  Egypt, and, 115-16
  extradition, and, 26-7
  General Assembly, and, 42
  Italy, and, 4, 26
  jurisdiction, 150-1, 154, 158 n. 103, 161-3
  killing of hostage, 4, 115
  Palestine Liberation Front, 26, 171
  Rome Convention, and, 9 n. 26
  US interception of aircraft, 26-7, 116
    —agreement, whether by, 116
    —legitimacy, 321
  Yugoslavia, and, 26 n. 65, 171
African National Congress—
  Geneva Conventions, respect for rules of, 290 n. 79
Afro-Asian Peoples Solidarity Organization—
  Larnaca incident, 319 n. 38
Aggression—
  definition, 97 nn. 19 *and* 20
  Draft Code of Offences against Peace and Security of Mankind, 97 n. 19
Air—
  freedom of—
    —principle of international law, 47 n. 154
Aircraft—
  interception, 4, 26-7, 116, 321
Algeria—
  asylum in, 2
  Geneva Conventions 1949—
    —accession to, 290 n. 79
  Hostages Convention, and, 115 n. 19
  Kuwaiti Airways Boeing 747, 115 n. 19
    —safe passage, 115 n. 19
    ——compatibility with Hostages Convention, 115 n. 19
  mediator, as—
    —US hostages in Tehran, 3
  OPEC incident—
    —grant of asylum, 2
  positions taken—
    —extradition, refusal, 213
    —GA Res 3034, 36
    —Hostages Convention—
      ——consistency with UN Charter, 313
    —national liberation movements, 44-5, 267, 269 n. 25
  US hostages in Tehran—
    —mediator, as, 3
Aliens—
  asylum: *q.v.*
  deportation. *See non-refoulement below*
  expulsion. *See non-refoulement below*
  extradition: *q.v.*
  non-refoulement—
    —asylum, and, 339
    —*aut dedere aut judicare*, 350
    —discrimination clauses, and, 210 n. 3, 211-12
    —extradition, 210 n. 3, 211-12
    —Refugees Convention, 212 n. 12
  protection of—
    —hostage situation, 112
    —State responsibility, 123 n. 15
    —terrorist attack, in, 123 n. 15
  treatment—
    —Hostages Convention—
      ——human rights provision, effect, 207
    —standard, 207
    ——national treatment, 207
Angola—
  position taken—
    —causes of terrorism, 45 n. 149
Apartheid—

Apartheid (cont.)
　Convention on the Suppression and Punishment of the Crime of, 1973, 91 n. 53, 94 n. 2, 97, 234
　—jurisdiction provisions, 137 n. 15
　crime against humanity, 97
Applicable law—
　treaty interpretation, and, 10
Arbitration—
　Hague Convention, 343
　Hostages Convention, 343
　Montreal Convention, 343
　New York Convention, 343
　"organization of the arbitration"—
　　—appointment of arbitrators, 343 n. 2
　　—method of appointment, 343 n. 2
　Rome Convention, 343
Arm of the Arab Revolution. See under Popular Front for the Liberation of Palestine (PFLP)
Armed conflict. See also Geneva Conventions, 1949; Hostages Convention, Article 12
　hostage-taking during, 5, 265-6, 269-70
　Hostages Convention—
　　—applicability, 75, 78-9, 89, 263-98
　individual responsibility, 80 n. 8, 95-7, 98
　law of—
　　—acts of violence, prohibition, 37-8
　　—international criminal law, and, 8
Arrest—
　Achille Lauro, 26, 171
　Hague Convention, 173
　Hostages Convention, 168-74
　　—good faith, 171
　liberty of person, and, 169-72
　New York Convention, 170
　provisional—
　　—pending formal extradition request, 26 n. 65, 171, 172
　Tokyo Convention, 169
Asian-African Legal Consultative Committee—
　Draft of Model Bilateral Arrangements on Mutual Assistance on Letters Rogatory in Criminal Matters, 1984, 248-9, 250 nn. 25-7, 255
Asylum, 327-41. See also Immunity
　asylee, obligations towards, 336

　aut dedere aut judicare, and, 330-4
　conventions. See treaties below
　definition, 328
　　—diplomatic, 328
　　—Institut de Droit International, 328
　　—territorial, 328
　diplomatic, 335-9
　　—Latin-American phenomenon, 328-9
　　—treaty-based, 328
　discrimination clauses, and, 209
　Hostages Committee, 331-2
　Hostages Convention, and, 327, 330-41
　　—immunity, and, 329
　　—preservation of treaties on asylum, 327, 334-41
　ILA—
　　—draft Convention on Diplomatic Asylum, 329 n. 11
　impunity, and, 329, 337-8
　　—European Convention on the Suppression of Terrorism, 329
　　—Hostages Convention, 329
　　—ILA draft Convention, 329 n. 11
　　—international law, and, 338
　Institut de Droit International, 328-9
　International Commission of Jurists—
　　—Application in Latin America of International Declarations and Conventions Relating to Asylum, 328 nn. 2 and 7, 329 nn. 9 and 12
　international crimes, and, 329 n. 11
　New York Convention, 333 n. 33, 337, 341 n. 69
　OAS Convention, 330 n. 45
　political offence, and, 335
　　—determination of, 335
　political reason as basis, 328
　purpose—
　　—International Commission of Jurists, 329
　　—safety from persecution, 329
　right—
　　—individual, of, 328 n. 1
　　——Universal Declaration of Human Rights, 328 n. 1
　　—State, of, 328 n. 1
　Sixth Committee, 332-4, 338
　territorial, 339-40
　　—Caracas Convention on, 328 nn. 2-4, 335, 339-40
　　—restriction of—
　　——treaty, by, 328

—UN conference on, 220 n. 52
treaties, 332 n. 28
　—Caracas Convention on Diplomatic Asylum 1954, 328 n. 4, 335-6, 340-1
　——Hostages Convention, effect of, 336
　——"urgent cases", 336
　—Caracas Convention on Territorial Asylum 1954, 328 nn. 2-3, 335, 339-40
　——Hostages Convention, effect of, 339
　——*non-refoulement*, 339
　——political offence exception, 339
　—Havana Convention on Political Asylum 1928, 334, 336 nn. 45 *and* 48
　—ILA draft Convention on Diplomatic Asylum, 329
　—Montevideo Convention on Political Asylum 1933, 335
　—Montevideo Treaty on Political Asylum and Refuge 1939, 335 n. 40
　—terrorist offences under, 341 n. 69
UN Conference on Territorial Asylum, 220 n. 51
Australia—
position taken—
　—causes of terrorism, 32 n. 94, 40
Austria—
OPEC incident, 2
　—deal with hostage-takers, 2
position taken—
　—causes of terrorism, 32 n. 94, 40
Aut dedere aut judicare—
asylum, and, 112-14, 335-8, 340-1
basic principle—
　—*Ad Hoc* Committee on International Terrorism, 39 n. 131
　—anti-terrorism conventions, 2, 48, 54, 187, 189-90
　——European Convention, 189
　——Hostages Convention. *See* Hostages Convention *below*
　——League of Nations Terrorism Convention, 29, 188-9
　——OAS Convention, 189
　——US Draft Convention for the Prevention and Punishment of International Terrorism, 34
　—Code of Offences Against the Peace and Security of Mankind, 100
　—ILA Terrorism Committee, 46 n. 153

Counterfeiting Currency Convention, 1929, 94 n. 2, 188
customary international law, 271
definition—
　—ILC commentary on New York Convention, 193
extradition, and, 187
　—request for, relevance, 196-7
extradition treaties, 190
Geneva Conventions, 1949, 189, 265, 270-98, 347-8
good faith, and, 199, 202, 203
Grotius—
　—*aut dedere aut punire*, 190
hostage-taking, 265 n. 7, 270
Hostages Convention, 48, 74, 187-208, 270-98, 347-9, 350
　—asylum under, and, 112-14, 335-8, 340-1
　—FRG draft, 58
　—GA Res 31/103, 58
liability, 193, 196-8
measures to ensure presence of alleged offender, and, 173
motivation, relevance, 195-6
municipal law, in, 190
national liberation movements, and, 270-3, 348
non-refoulement, and, 350
place of offence, relevance, 198
political offence exception, 193
prosecution—
　—obligation, nature of, 198-203, 351, 353
sanctions, and, 56 n. 195
Tokyo Convention, 51-2
universal jurisdiction, 100
US Draft Convention, 34

Barbados—
position taken—
　—"circumstances so warrant", 169
Belgium—
positions taken—
　—*Ad Hoc* Committee on Terrorism, establishment, 34 n. 104
　—extradition, refusal, 216, 223
Belligerency—
recognition of—
　—international nature of conflict, relevance to, 286-7
Benin—
position taken—
　—Entebbe, 320
Berner Club, 130
Black September group—
Munich massacre, 32

Bonn Declaration 1978, 56 n. 195
  Afghanistan, 56 n. 195
  Montreal Convention—
    —extension to, 57 n. 195
  South Africa, 56 n. 195
Botswana—
  position taken—
    —extradition, refusal, 214-15
Brazil—
  positions taken—
    —asylum treaties, 337
    —"other measures necessary for institution of proceedings", 173 nn. 19 *and* 23
British Commonwealth—
  Scheme Relating to Mutual Assistance in Criminal Matters within the Commonwealth, 247, 248
  Scheme Relating to the Rendition of Fugitive Offenders within the Commonwealth, 211
Bulgaria—
  positions taken—
    —extradition, refusal, 214-15, 220
    —modification of existing treaties, 224
Byelorussian SSR—
  positions taken—
    —extradition, refusal, 214-15
    —"in accordance with the laws", 201
    —jurisdiction, 152 n. 75

Cameroon—
  position taken—
    —Entebbe, 313 n. 2
Canada—
  judicial assistance—
    —agreements. *See under* Judicial assistance conventions
  letters rogatory—
    —*Re Westinghouse Electric Corp. and Duquesne Light Co.*, 247 n. 10
  positions taken—
    —asylum, 333 n. 32
    ——treaties, 337, 340 n. 66
    —causes of terrorism, 32 n. 94, 40
    —"entitled to possession", 118 n. 33
    —extradition—
    ——Hostages Convention as basis for, 239
    ——refusal, 216
    —jurisdiction, 309
    —modification of existing treaties, 224
    —release of hostages—
    ——*aut dedere aut judicare*, and, 113
    —"severe", need for injury to be, 82
Chile—
  position taken—
    —asylum, 331 n. 19, 333 n. 31
China—
  positions taken—
    —causes of terrorism, 45 n. 149
    —national liberation movements, 30 n. 87
Colombia—
  positions taken—
    —*Ad Hoc* Committee on Terrorism, establishment, 34 n. 104
    —asylum, 333 n. 33, 334 n. 36
    ——treaties, 341 n. 69
Colonialism. *See under* Terrorism, causes
Comity—
  judicial assistance, 247
  letters rogatory, 247 n. 10
Commonwealth. *See* British Commonwealth
Communication—
  international, freedom of—
    —international law, principle of, 47 n. 154
Compliance. *See under* International law
Congo—
  positions taken—
    —*aut dedere aut judicare*, 195 n. 25
    —extradition—
    ——Hostages Convention as basis for, 239
    ——refusal, 214-15
Conspiracy. *See also* Accomplice
  Hostages Convention—
    —whether offence under, 90-2
  ILC, 91
  International Convention on the Suppression of the Crime of Apartheid, 91 n. 53
  New York Convention, 90-2
  Prevention and Punishment of the Crime of Genocide Convention 1948, 91 n. 53
  Sixth Committee, 91 n. 52
  United Kingdom, in, 91 nn. 51 *and* 54
Consular conventions—
  European Convention on Consular Functions, 177 n. 39
    —Protocol Concerning the Protection of Refugees, 179 n. 44

Korea, Republic of-USA, 1963, 177
Consular conventions (*cont.*)
 n. 38
Consular premises—
 inviolability—
  —release of hostages by force and, 111 n. 5
Consular protection. *See also* Consular conventions; Vienna Convention on Consular Relations 1963
 communication—
  —consular right, 177 n. 37
  —nationals, of, 177
 Hague Convention, 178, 222
 Hostages Convention, 177-83
  —"prejudice" in absence of, 222-3
 ICRC, 181-3
 Montreal Convention, 178
 New York Convention, 177, 178, 180
 non-national State, by, 178-80
 refugees, 179-80
  —New York Convention, 180
  —UNHCR, 179 n. 44
 Rome Convention, 178
 stateless persons, 179-80
 visit, to—
  —consular right, 177 n. 37
  —nationals, of, 177
Continental shelf. *See* Rome Protocol 1988
Conventions—
 Abolition of Slavery and the Slave Trade Convention 1926. *See* Slavery
 Abolition of Slavery, Supplementary Convention 1956. *See* Slavery
 anti-terrorism. *See also* individual conventions
  —terrorism—
   ——definition, 22, 23
 Establishment of an International Criminal Court 1937, 99
 European Convention for the Protection of Human Rights: *q.v.*
 European Convention on the Suppression of Terrorism: *q.v.*
 European Convention on Consular Functions. *See under* Consular conventions
 Hague Convention for the Suppression of Unlawful Seizure of Aircraft, 1970. *See* Hague Convention
 Hostages Convention: *q.v.*
 International Covenant on Civil and Political Rights: *q.v.*
 League of Nations Convention on the Establishment of an International Criminal Court 1937. *See under* League of Nations
 League of Nations Convention for the Prevention and Punishment of Terrorism. *See under* League of Nations
 Montreal Convention for the Suppression of Unlawful Acts against the Safety of Civil Aviation, 1971. *See* Montreal Convention
 Montreal Protocol for the Suppression of Unlawful Acts of Violence at Airports Serving International Civil Aviation, 1988. *See* Montreal Protocol
 New York Convention on the Prevention and Punishment of Crimes against Internationally Protected Persons including Diplomatic Agents, 1973. *See* New York Convention
 Physical Protection of Nuclear Material Convention, 139 n. 22
 Prevention and Punishment of the Crime of Genocide 1948. *See under* Genocide
 Psychotropic Substances Convention, 137 n. 15
 Rome Convention for the Suppression of Unlawful Acts Against the Safety of Maritime Navigation, 1988. *See* Rome Convention, 1988
 Rome Protocol for the Suppression of Unlawful Acts Against the Safety of Fixed Platforms Located on the Continental Shelf, 1988. *See* Rome Protocol, 1988
 Single Convention on Narcotic Drugs—
  —jurisdiction provisions, 94 n. 2, 137
 Status of Refugees, 1951. *See under* Refugees
 Status of Stateless Persons, 1954. *See under* Statelessness
 Suppression of Counterfeiting Currency 1929—
  —jurisdiction, 137
  —obligation to exchange information, 129 n. 35
 Suppression of the Crime of Apartheid. *See under* Apartheid
 Terrorism Convention, 1937. *See under* League of Nations

Conventions (*cont.*)
　Status of Stateless Persons, 1954. *See under* Stateless persons
　Suppression of Counterfeiting Currency 1929, 188, 229 n. 5, 237 n. 37
　　—jurisdiction, 137
　　—obligation to exchange information, 129 n. 35
　Suppression of the Circulation of and Traffic in Obscene Publications 1923, 136
　Suppression of the Crime of Apartheid. *See under* Apartheid
　Tokyo Convention on Offences and Certain other Acts Committed on Board Aircraft 1963. *See* Tokyo Convention
　Torture and Other Cruel and Inhuman or Degrading Treatment or Punishment 1984. *See under* Torture
　Vienna Convention on Consular Relations 1963: *q.v.*
　Vienna Convention on Diplomatic Relations 1961: *q.v.*
Costa Rica—
　position taken—
　　—"circumstances so warrant", 169
Courtesy, international. *See* Comity
Cuba—
　positions taken—
　　—asylum, 334 n. 36
　　—causes of terrorism, 31 n. 91
　　—extradition, refusal, 214-15
　　—modification of existing treaties, 224
　　—national liberation movements, 31 n. 89
Customary international law. *See also* International law, codification
aut dedere aut judicare, 190, 278 n. 30
diplomatic inviolability, 60 n. 210
extradition, 227
Geneva Conventions, 1949, as, 277, 291-3
Hostages Convention, 158 n. 103
international crimes, 93-4
　—genocide, 137 n. 13
　—piracy, 93 n. 1, 135
　　——obligation of State acquiring possession to return spoils, 117
　—slavery, 135 n. 6
　—UN Secretariat, 94 n. 1
　—universal jurisdiction—
　　——genocide, 137 n. 13
　　——piracy, 135
　　——slavery, 135 n. 6
　　——war crimes, 135 n. 6
　—war crimes, 93 n. 1, 135 n. 6
judicial assistance, 247
jurisdiction—
　—aircraft—
　　——State of registration, 138
　　—continental shelf, 146
　　—EEZ, 146
　　—universal, 135 n. 6, 137 n. 13, 158
jus cogens, 190
multilateral conventions as source of, 291-3
　—persistent objection, 291, 292
national liberation, wars of—
　—international nature, 290-3
North Sea Continental Shelf Cases, 292 n. 90
rescue missions—
　—legitimacy, 323
Czechoslovakia—
position taken—
　—extradition, refusal, 214-15

Denial of justice, 112 n. 8
Denmark—
positions taken—
　—"severe" penalties, 106 n. 57
　—"threat", 83 n. 24
Dependent territories—
Hostages Convention—
　—applicability, 144-5
jurisdiction in, 144-5
territory—
　—status—
　　——Declaration on Principles of International Law Concerning Friendly Relations and Co-operation among States, 144 n. 38
Diplomatic channels—
judicial assistance, 247-8
Diplomatic premises—
inviolability—
　—release of hostages by force, and, 111 n. 5
Diplomatic privileges and immunities—
extradition, and, 171 n. 14
PLO—
　—official of, 26, 171 n. 14
Diplomatic relations—
breaking-off, 3
　—UK-Syria, 27
　—US-Iran, 3
　—US-Libya, 27
Case Concerning the United States

INDEX

Diplomatic and Consular Staff in Tehran. See under International Court of Justice
Diplomats—
 expulsion—
  —terrorist involvement, for, 20 n. 36
 protection of, duty, 110 n. 3
Discretion. *See also* Margin of appreciation
European Convention for the Protection of Human Rights—
 —derogation from, 112 n. 8
 extradition, 214, 216-23
 international obligations, 101, 123-5, 194, 198-200, 344-5
 judicial assistance, 247, 251-7
 prosecution, and, 198-203
 steps to ensure presence of accused, 168-73, 174
Discrimination clause, 209-25
 asylum, and, 209, 210
 bilateral treaties, 211
 European Convention on the Suppression of Terrorism, 210, 216-17
 Hague Convention, 212
 Hostages Convention, 213-25
 implied, 212
 Inter-American Convention on Extradition, 210
 municipal law, in, 210-11
 New York Convention, 212
 non-refoulement, distinguished, 211-12
 political offence exception, and, 210 n. 3
 Scheme Relating to the Rendition of Fugitive Offenders within the Commonwealth, 211
 treatment of aliens, and, 210 n. 3, 211-12
Dispute settlement. *See also* Arbitration; International Court of Justice; Permanent Court of International Justice; Tribunals, international
 Hague Convention, 343
 hostage-taking, during, 343-4
 Hostages Convention, 112, 219, 221, 343-5
 Montreal Convention, 343
 New York Convention, 212, 343, 345
 —opt-out clause, 343 n. 7
 opt-out clause, 343 n. 7, 345
 procedures, 56, 112, 343-5
 Rome Convention, 343
 third-party—

—reluctance to accept, 345

Ecuador—
 positions taken—
  —asylum, 333
  —rescue missions, 320
Egypt—
 Achille Lauro—
  —deal, 4
  —USA, effect on relations with, 27
 Hostages Convention—
  —accession, 215
 OPEC incident—
  —target, 2
 positions taken—
  —*Achille Lauro*, 322
  —*aut dedere aut judicare*, 195 n. 25
  —Hostages Convention—
   ——consistency with UN Charter, 313 n. 1
  —national liberation movements, 267
  —rescue missions, 319
Entebbe incident, 1976, 2-3, 317-19, 320, 324-6
 demands, 2-3
 Hostages Convention, catalyst for, 9 n. 26, 57, 65
 killing of hostage, 3
 Popular Front for the Liberation of Palestine, 2
 rescue mission, 3
  —legitimacy, 318-19, 320, 324-6
  ——customary international law, 323
 Uganda, and, 3
European Convention for the Protection of Human Rights, 205, 217 n. 39, 222 n. 57, 223 n. 61
 derogation from obligations, 112 n. 8
 —margin of appreciation—
  ——*Greece* v. *United Kingdom*, 112 n. 8
  ——*Ireland* v. *United Kingdom*, 112 n. 8
  ——*Lawless* case, 112 n. 8
European Convention on the Suppression of Terrorism, 7, 50, 351
 Agreement Concerning Application of, 1979, 235 n. 35
 aut dedere aut judicare, 189 n. 8, 196
 "discrimination clause", 210, 216-19, 329
 Explanatory Report, 139 n. 21
 jurisdiction provisions, 138-9
 offences under—
  —enumerative approach, 49-50

European Convention (*cont.*)
political persecution, and, 235
"prejudice", 222 n. 57, 223 n. 61
prosecution, obligation, 201
Evidence—
extradition, and, 26 n. 65
international law—
—General Assembly Resolution, 96-7, 158
international organization, view of—
—*Legal Consequences for States of the Continued Presence of South Africa in Namibia*, 310 n. 30
judicial assistance, and, 246-7, 249, 250-1, 252
Evidence of—
principle of international law—
—convention with limited number of signatories, 96
—GA Res, 96
threat—
—difficulty of establishing, 1, 83-84
Extradition, 160-1, 163. *See also Aut dedere aut judicare*; Extradition treaties
Achille Lauro, 26-7
agreements. *See also* Extradition treaties
—Hostages Convention—
——existing agreements, effect on, 223-5
—regional, 191
—requirement for, 191, 238
—States of different political persuasion, between, 221
anti-terrorism conventions, under, 54-5, 238-41
basis—
—multilateral convention as, 192 n. 19, 238-40, 242-3
customary international law, 227
delay—
—international law, breach, 174 n. 24
diplomatic immunity, and, 171 n. 14
discretionary, 214, 216-23
discrimination clauses, 209-25
—asylum, and, 209, 210
—bilateral treaties, 211
—European Convention on the Suppression of Terrorism, 210, 216-17
—Hague Convention, 212
—Hostages Convention, 213-25
——negotiating history, 213-15
—implied, 212

—Inter-American Convention on Extradition, 210
—municipal law, in, 210-11
—New York Convention, 212
—*non-refoulement*, and, 210 n. 3
——distinguished, 211-12
—political offence exception, and, 210 n. 3
—Scheme Relating to the Rendition of Fugitive Offenders within the Commonwealth, 211
"extraditable offences", 160 n. 108. *See also* political offence exception *below*
—"deemed to be"—
——Hostages Convention, 229-31, 241. *See also under* Hostages Convention, words and phrases
——Suppression of Counterfeiting Currency Convention, 229 n. 5
——Torture Convention, 229 n. 5
—eliminative method, 230-1
—advantages, 230 n. 11
—enumerative method, 229-30
—disadvantages, 230 n. 8
—Hostages Convention—
——Article 1 offences as, 237-8, 241
——attendant violent crimes, 160-1
——"deemed to be", 229-31
—implications, 231-2
—meaning, 233-5
—motivation, relevance, 195
—New York Convention, 242
Hague Convention, 191, 192, 201-2
—legal basis, as, 193
Hostages Convention, 153, 160-2, 163, 172, 209-44
—consular protection, absence, 222-3
—discrimination clause, 209-25
—political persecution, and, 55 n. 191
—territorial State, to, 191
jurisdiction—
—priority, 163-5
Latin America, practice in, 201-2
limitations on, 191-3, 232-3
municipal law, governed by, 240-1
non-refoulement. See under Aliens
political offence exception, 192, 193, 232
—generally accepted principle—
——Communist countries, 193 n. 21

———western countries, 193
—Hostages Convention, 193, 195, 233-7
—limitations on, 233-5
—prosecution, to, 193
political persecution, and—
—Apartheid Convention, 234
—European Convention on the Suppression of Terrorism, 235
—Genocide Convention, 233-4
—Hague Convention, 234, 235
—Hostages Convention, 55 n. 192
—Montreal Convention, 235
—New York Convention, 235
—treaty reservations, 235
priority of jurisdiction, and, 163-5
provisional arrest—
—formal request for extradition, pending, 26 n. 65, 171, 172
refusal—
—death penalty, 232
—discrimination clauses, 209, 210-23
—evidence insufficient, 26 n. 65, 233 n. 22
—fear of consequences, 26 n. 65, 87 n. 40, 235 n. 35
—military law offences, for, 232
—nationals of requested State, 191, 232
—*ne bis in idem*, 232
—political offence exception. *See above*
requesting State—
—registration of aircraft, 191, 192
—territorial State, 191, 194
Single Convention on Narcotic Drugs, 137
speciality, 160 n. 108
State sovereignty, and, 214
territorial principle, 139
Extradition treaties—
Argentina-USA, 1972, 164 n. 120, 229-30, 232 nn. 18-19
Australia-USA, 1974, 244 n. 65
European Convention on Extradition 1957, 191 n. 17, 199, 210, 211, 212 n. 13, 217 n. 35, 218, 219, 223 n. 61, 230-1, 232 nn. 18-22
Finland-UK, 211 n. 8, 232 n. 20
FRG-USA, 1978, 87 n. 40, 230 n. 11, 234
—1986 amendment, 230 n. 11
Inter-American Convention on Extradition 1981, 163-4 n. 120, 191 n. 17, 210, 218, 231 n. 13

Italy-USA, 1983, 26 n. 65, 160 n. 108, 162 n. 117, 172 n. 18, 211 nn. 8-9, 230 nn. 9 *and* 12, 232 n. 19, 353
Mexico-USA, 1978, 163 n. 120
Montevideo Convention on Extradition 1933, 191 n. 17, 231 n. 13
Romania-USA, 1924, 221 n. 53
Scheme Relating to the Rendition of Fugitive Offenders within the Commonwealth, 211 n. 8
Sweden-USA, 1961, 232 nn. 20-22
—Supplementary Treaty, 1983, 231
UK-USA, 1972, 211 n. 9, 232 n. 22
—Supplementary Treaty, 1985, 235
USA-Cuba, Memorandum of Understanding on Hijacking, 1973, 235-6 n. 35
USA-Yugoslavia, 26 n. 65

Fair treatment. *See under* Human rights
Federal Republic of Germany—
draft Convention. *See under* Hostages Convention, *individual articles*
Hostages Convention—
—obligations under—
——pre-existing legislation, 105
—role in drafting, 57-8, 61-2
judicial assistance, 251-3, 256
—agreements. *See under* Judicial assistance conventions
law of—
—Basic Law—
——exchange of information about terrorists, and, 121 n. 9
—Law on Mutual Assistance in Criminal Matters 1982, 160 n. 108, 211 n. 7, 232, 241, 250 n. 27, 251-3
—Penal Code (StGB)—
——anti-terrorism measures, 125
——*aut dedere aut judicare*, 190
——hostage-taking, 105
——penalties, 105
—Penal Code (StPO), 125
positions taken—
—*aut dedere aut judicare*, 197
—facilitation of hostage's departure, 116, 117
—Hostages Convention—
——consistency with UN Charter, 314-5
—"in accordance with the laws", 201

Federal Republic of Germany (*cont.*)
—judicial assistance agreements, 261
—jurisdiction, 157 n. 97, 160 n. 105, 308-9
—"necessary evidence", 259
—securing release of hostage—
——acquiescence in terrorists' demands, 111
—"severe", need for injury to be, 82
—"severe" penalties, 107
Syria—
—expulsion of diplomats, 20 n. 36
terrorism—
—countermeasures, 125
—West Berlin—
——German-Arab Friendship Club, bombing, 20 n. 36
Force, use of—
legitimacy—
—self-determination, and. *See* National liberation movements
protection of nationals, 318, 319, 320
rescue missions, 316-25
self-defence, 318, 321
Foreign law—
application, 89
France—
Iran, 5
—re-establishment of diplomatic relations, 5
—repayment of loan, 5
law of—
—Extradition Act 1927, 241
Lebanon, hostages in—
—deal—
——re-establishment of diplomatic relations, 5
——repayment of loan, 5
positions taken—
—asylum treaties, 337
—*aut dedere aut judicare*, 196
—"circumstances so warrant", 169
—Entebbe, 319
—extradition—
——Hostages Convention as basis for, 240
——inequality of obligations, 242
—judicial assistance agreements, 261
—jurisdiction, 153 n. 80, 161, 309
—national liberation movements, 271 n. 34
—place of detention, 80 n. 10
—release of hostages—

——*aut dedere aut judicare*, and, 113
—US bombing of Libya, 321 n. 54
terrorism—
—State agents, by—
——*Rainbow Warrior*, 21

General Assembly—
aggression—
—definition, 97 n. 19
Resolutions—
—95(I) (International Criminal Code), 96
—96(I) (Genocide), 96
—177(II) (Code of Offences against Peace of Mankind), 97 n. 18
—217A(III). *See* Universal Declaration of Human Rights
—260(III) (Genocide Convention), 96-7
—260B(III) (establishment of international criminal court), 100 n. 32
—428(V) (UNHCR Statute), 180
—897(IX) (definition of aggression), 97 n. 19
—898(IX) (establishment of international criminal court), 100 n. 33
—1186(XXI) (definition of aggression), 97 n. 19
—1187(XXI) (establishment of international criminal court), 100 n. 33
—1514(XV) (Granting of Independence to Colonial Territories and Peoples), 73
—2625(XXV) (Principles of International Law concerning Friendly Relations and Cooperation among States), 20, 30 n. 85, 73, 123 n. 16, 144 n. 38
—2645(XXV) (aerial hijacking), 195
—2780(XXVI) (protection of diplomats), 59
—3034 (XXVII) (causes of terrorism), 36-7
—3103(XXVIII), 288, 290
—3166(XXVIII) (New York Convention), 1
—3314(XXIX) (definition of aggression), 20, 30 n. 83, 97 n. 20
—31/103 (hostages), 58
—32/148 (hostages), 63
—33/19 (hostages), 64
—34/145 (Terrorism Committee

INDEX

——opposition to, 33-4
——underlying causes, 32-4, 36-7, 38-9
——consideration of, 1976-87, 39-45
——*Achille Lauro*, and, 42
——catalysts for, 42
——OPEC hostage-taking, and, 42
General Assembly Sixth Committee—
discrimination clause, 209, 213-24
establishment of Hostages Committee, 58
Hostages Convention, 58, 60 n. 209, 61, 64-5, 67, 72, 75
—applicability, 310
—asylum, 332-4, 337-9
—asylum treaties, 340-1
—denunciation, 346
—national liberation movements, 272, 297
——rescue missions, 314-15, 323-4
New York Convention—
—asylum treaties, 340
—extradition, as basis for, 240
—national liberation movements, 48
—"necessary evidence", 259
US Draft Convention, 34-6
—"international", 34
—obligations under—
——*aut dedere aut judicare*, 34
—rejection—
——reasons, 35-6
—scope—
——international terrorism, 34
——kidnapping, 34
——serious bodily injury, 34
——unlawful killing, 34
Geneva Conventions, 1949 and Additional Protocols, 1977
Additional Protocol I—
—*aut dedere aut judicare*, 276, 279, 293-8
——extent of obligation, 297-8
——customary international law, whether, 291-3
——persistent objection, 291, 292
——hostage-taking under, 295-7
——Hostages Convention, and, 268-9
—national liberation, wars of—
——applicability to, 293-8
——international conflicts, as, 290-1
—national liberation movements, 266, 268-9, 293-8
—parties to, 276

—"terrorist groups", alleged legitimation, 291
Additional Protocol II, 280-2
—*aut dedere aut judicare*, 281-2
—hostage-taking, 281-2
applicability, 274, 280, 286-9
—armed conflict, during, 278
—national liberation movements, 280, 286-9
armed conflict—
—applicability during, 278
—definition, 278
aut dedere aut judicare, 189, 265, 270-98, 347-8
—internal conflicts, in, 280-2
——supplementary agreements, necessity for, 281
——neutral States, obligation, 271 n. 48
Civilians Convention—
—applicability, 284-5
——state of war, whether necessary, 285
—Article 34, 283
—Article 146, 283 n. 62, 285-6
—Article 147, 283
—*aut dedere aut judicare*, 283, 285-6
—hostage-taking under—
——international conflicts, 283
——non-international conflicts, 286-98
—Hostages Convention, and, 283-6
—protected persons, 288, 289
customary international law, as, 277, 291-3
—*aut dedere aut judicare*, 278 n. 30
—persistent objection, 291, 292
enforcement, 278 n. 30
gaps—
—Hostages Convention, and, 265, 271-2, 273-7, 279
hostage-taking, and—
—compulsion of third party necessary element, 78 n. 2
—internal conflict, 280-2
—international conflict, 282-6
——Protection of Civilian Persons in Time of War Convention, 283
—national liberation, wars of, 286-98
—responsibility—
——"an authority", 80 n. 8, 283 n. 61
——individual, 80 n. 8, 283 n. 61

INDEX

Geneva Conventions, 1949 (*cont.*)
——Nuremberg Principle VII, 283 n. 61
——participation, 283 n. 62
hostages—
—definition—
——official commentaries, 78 n. 2, 283 n. 61
Hostages Convention, and, 263-98
—applicability of, and, 89
—Civilians Convention, 284-6
—complementary nature, 264-6, 271-2, 273-7, 279
—supplementary agreements to Geneva Conventions, and, 281 n. 54
ICRC—
—ANC submission to, 290
—Commentary, 281 n. 54, 283 nn. 59 *and* 61, 284 n. 63, 285 n. 65, 287 n. 67, 288, 293 n. 95
—"wars of national liberation", 280 n. 53
internal conflicts, 280-2
—*aut dedere aut judicare*, 280-2
—definition, 281-2
—hostage-taking, 280-2
—national liberation, wars of, 281
international conflicts—
—hostage-taking during, 282-6
—national liberation, wars of, whether, 288-93
——Additional Protocol I, 290-1
—non-international conflicts, distinction, 291 n. 84
interpretation—
—context, 292
—"Powers", 292-3
—subsequent practice, 292
jurisdiction, 138
national liberation movements, 264-6, 280, 286-9
—General Assembly resolutions, 288, 290
—hostage taking by, prohibition, 269
—parties to Conventions, whether, 286-93
non-international conflict. *See also* internal conflict *above*
—definition, 282 n. 56
parties to, 276
—Additional Protocol I, 276
—Algeria, Provisional Government of, 290 n. 79
—national liberation movements, 286-93
—"Power"—

——national liberation movements, 292-3
——recognized belligerent, 287
——States, 287, 292
protected persons—
—co-nationals, 288, 289, 295 n. 101
supplementary agreements—
—desirability, 281 n. 281
"those conventions"—
—Additional Protocols, whether included, 273 n. 41
Geneva Conventions on the Law of the Sea, 1958—
codification, as, 59
Geneva Declaration on Terrorism, 1987, 14 n. 9, 16 n. 19
Genocide—
Convention on the Prevention and Punishment of the Crime of, 91 n. 53, 96-7
customary international law, 137 n. 14
jurisdiction—
—universal, whether, 137 n. 13
German Democratic Republic—
position taken—
—extradition, refusal, 214-15
Good faith—
difficulty of establishing, 345 n. 5
grant of immunity to hostage-taker, 114
prosecution—
—discretion, 199 n. 47, 202, 203
treaties—
—compliance, 345
—violation—
——defence, as, 112 n. 8
Greece—
positions taken—
—asylum, 332 n. 27
—"circumstances so warrant", 169
Guinea—
positions taken—
—Hostages Convention—
——consistency with UN Charter, 313 n. 1
—national liberation movements, 267

Hague Convention, 1, 18 n. 27, 52. *See also under* Hostages Convention, *individual articles*
adhesion to, 48
adoption, 51
arbitration, 343
arrest, 173

Convention on the Prevention and Punishment of the Crime of, 91 n. 53, 96-7, 136, 233-4
customary international law, 137 n. 14
jurisdiction—
—universal, whether, 137 n. 13
German Democratic Republic—
position taken—
—extradition, refusal, 214-15
Good faith—
difficulty of establishing, 345 n. 5
grant of immunity to hostage-taker, 114
prosecution—
—discretion, 199 n. 47, 202, 203
treaties—
—compliance, 345
—violation—
——defence, as, 112 n. 8
Greece—
positions taken—
—asylum, 332 n. 27
—"circumstances so warrant", 169
Guinea—
positions taken—
—Hostages Convention—
——consistency with UN Charter, 313 n. 1
—national liberation movements, 267

Hague Convention, 1, 18 n. 27, 52. *See also under* Hostages Convention, *individual articles*
adhesion to, 48
adoption, 51
arbitration, 343
arrest, 173
consular protection, 178, 222
discrimination clause, 212
extradition, 191, 192, 193, 201-2
—political persecution, 234, 235
hijacking—
—definition, 18 n. 27, 52
—penalties, absence of specific, 102-3 n. 39
immunity, 114 n. 15, 115 n. 19
—drafting history, 106
—reasons for formulation, 106
implementation, 108
judicial assistance, 246, 254, 256, 258
jurisdiction, 54
—priority, 164
—territorial/nationality principles, 139

—universality principle, 139
obligations under, 54-5
offences under—
—attempt, 51
—participation, 51
penalties—
—absence of specific, 102 n. 39
prosecution, 198-9, 201-2
threat, 83
universality, 48
Hezbollah, 4, 87 n. 40, 115 n. 19
Hijacking. *See also* Hague Convention; Montreal Convention; Montreal Protocol
Achille Lauro: *q.v.*
definition—
—Hague Convention, 18 n. 27, 52
IATA proposal for international court and detention centre, 100 n. 33
incidents, 354 n. 7
International Federation of Airline Pilots Associations—
—sanctions, proposals for, 56 n. 195
motivation—
—relevance, 50
terrorism, as act of, 18
Holger Meins Kommando, 57 n. 196
Hostage—
definition—
—Geneva Conventions, 1949—
——official commentary, 78 n. 2
—Geneva Conventions, 1949, Additional Protocols, 1977—
——official commentary, 78 n. 2
—Hostages Convention, 78
——political purpose, 78
——private gain, 78
—Nuremberg Tribunal—
——*In re List*, 78 n. 2
—third party—
——compulsion of act or forbearance from, 78 n. 2
Hostage-taking. *See also* Hijacking
armed conflict, during—
—legitimacy—
——Geneva Conventions, 1949, effect of, 283 n. 60
—prohibition on, 78 n. 2
cooperation to prevent. *See also* Terrorism, cooperative measures against
—desirability, 120
—Hostages Convention, 119-31
—obstacles, 120-2
——constitutional restraints, 121
——economic interests, 121

Hostage-taking (cont.)
effects—
—international peace and relations endangered, 72
—unilateral use of force, 72
incidents. See under Terrorism
killing of hostage, 4, 47 n. 156, 115
motive. See Motivation; National liberation movements
purpose, 78 n. 2
prevention. See cooperation to prevent above
reprisals—
—legality, 321
—US bombing of Libya, 321
——self defence, 321
rescue missions, 313-26
—customary international law, 323
—Entebbe, 313-14, 317 nn. 21, 22 and 24
—Hostages Convention, and, 313-25
—Larnaca, 319
—Lebanon, hostages in, and, 326
—legitimacy, 317-21
—local authorities—
——approval of, 317
—Mogadishu, 317 n. 21
—US hostages in Tehran, 317
——justification, 319
right of. See Motivation; National liberation movements
State involvement. See Terrorism, State and State-sponsored
terrorist crime, as, 2
value, 325
Hostages Committee—
draft Convention—
—revision, 64
—Sixth Committee, referral to, 64
—submission to General Assembly, 64
establishment, 57-8
membership, 58
procedure, 61-5
—informality, 66
reasons for, 59-61
records, 65-6
—lack, 65-6
——advantages, 66 n. 254
reports—
—first, 63, 65, 80, 81, 83, 111 n. 7, 118, 119, 157, 267-8, 308, 309, 314-15, 330-1
—second, 63, 65, 80, 85, 109, 111 n. 7, 113, 114, 117, 118, 126 n. 28, 133 n. 1, 142, 144, 153, 159, 161, 201, 207, 210, 259, 261, 269-71, 309, 315 n. 15, 331
—third, 75, 87, 142, 160, 185, 271, 310, 316, 331-3
—Working Groups, by, 63
session—
—1, 61-3
—2, 63-4
—3, 64
Working Group I—
—report, 63, 64
—tasks—
——asylum questions, 63
——definition of hostage-taking, 63
——extradition questions, 63
——scope of Convention, 63
——sovereignty and territorial integrity, principles of, 63
Working Group II—
—report, 63, 64, 160
—tasks—
——issues agreed by Working Group I, 63
——non-controversial questions, 63
Hostages Convention—
adhesion to. See parties below
adoption—
—GA Res 34/146, 54
applicability—
—armed conflict, during, 75, 58-9, 89, 263-98. See also Geneva Conventions, 1949
—demands, in absence of, 85 n. 30
—dependent territories, 144-5
—international acts, 23, 89, 299-312
—international organization as target, 311 n. 32
—national liberation movements: q.v.
Article 1, 74, 75, 77-92
—Article 5, and, 133
—hostage-taking—
——causes of terrorism, 78-9
——definition for purposes of Convention, 77-9
——motive, relevance, 78-9
——national liberation movements, by, 78-9
—implementing legislation, and, 101-2
—obligations, absence of, 93
Article 1(1), 79-89
—elements of offence—
——compulsion of third party, 79

INDEX

——demands, relevance, 85
——identity of third party, relevance, 85
——seizure or detention, 79
——threat to kill or continue detention, 79
—FRG draft, 82, 87
—Geneva Conventions, 1949, and, 89
—Hague Convention, 79 n. 7, 83
—Montreal Convention, 79 n. 7, 83
—New York Convention, 79 n. 7, 83-4
—Rome Convention and Protocol, 79 n. 7, 83
—threat, 83-4
Article 1(2), 89-92
—Apartheid Convention, 91 n. 53
—attempt, 89-90
—complicity, 90-2
—conspiracy, 91
——separate offence, whether, 91
—Genocide Convention, 91 n. 53
—New York Convention, 89, 91
Article 2, 77, 93-108, 172
—establishment of penalties, 93, 101
—FRG draft, 106
—Hague Convention, 93, 106, 107, 108
—Montreal Convention, 93, 106, 107, 108
—New York Convention, 93, 106-7
—obligations under—
——establishment of penalties, 93
——imposition of penalties, 93
——legislation, need for, whether, 101-2
—penalties—
——Hague Convention, 102 n. 29, 106
——Montreal Convention, 106
——national provisions, 103-5
——New York Convention, 106
——unspecified, 102
—Rome Convention, 93
Article 3, 109-18
—Article 4(b) compared, 127 n. 30
—Article 15 compared, 339 n. 61
—FRG draft, 109
—significance, 109, 114
Article 3(1), 110-16
—Article 8, and—

——potential conflict, 112-14
—Article 14, and, 314-15
—*aut dedere aut judicare*—
——exception to, possibility, 114
—breach of—
——decisions of territorial State, whether, 111-12
—Hague Convention, 109-10, 114 n. 15
—humanitarian purpose, 109
—immunity, grant of—
——Article 6(1), effect on obligations under, 112
——permissibility, 112-14
—Montreal Convention, 110
—New York Convention, 110 n. 3
—obligations under—
——attempt to secure release, 111
——ease situation of hostage, 109, 111
——extent, 111-12
——facilitate departure, 116-17
——territorial State, 111
—Rome Convention, 110
—Tokyo Convention, 110 n. 3
Article 3(2), 117-18
—FRG draft, 117
—obligations under—
——non-territorial State, on, 117
——return of object, 117
—title—
——avoidance of issue, 118
Article 4, 119-31
—FRG draft, 120
—Hague Convention, 120
—Montreal Convention, 120
—New York Convention, 120
—obligations under—
——compared, 122
——complementary, 122
——cooperation to prevent hostage-taking, 119
——exchange of information, 119
——prevention of preparations, 119
—Rome Convention, 120
—supplementary agreements, 119
Article 4(a), 122-7
—measures under, 123-7
—New York Convention, 122, 124
—obligations under—
——implementation, 125-6
——method of meeting discretionary, 124
—principle of international law, 122-3

Hostages Convention (*cont.*)
—Rome Convention, 127 n. 29
Article 4(b), 127-31
—Article 3 compared, 127 n. 30
—exchange of information—
——lack of specificity, 128-9
—implementation, 129
—New York Convention, 127
—supplementary agreements, 128
Article 5, 133-65
—Article 1, and, 133
—attendant crimes—
——absence of provision on, 159-63
——extraditable offences, not, 159 n. 104, 162 n. 117
——extradition, relevance to, 160-2, 163
——Hague Convention, 159-60
——jurisdiction, problems of, 161-2
——reasons for exclusion unclear, 160
—avoidance of safe-havens, 133
—FRG draft, 134
—Hague Convention, 134, 139, 164
—jurisdiction—
——conflict, 165
——establishment of, 93, 133
——primary and secondary, 133, 139
——priority of, 144, 163-5
—Montreal Convention, 134, 139, 164
—New York Convention, 134, 139, 164
—obligations under—
——establishment of jurisdiction, 93, 133
——implementing legislation, need for, 102
—Rome Convention, 134, 139
Article 5(1), 140-54, 181
—FRG draft, 141, 145 n. 40
—Hague Convention, 140
—Montreal Convention, 140
—New York Convention, 140, 141, 154
—obligations under—
——establishment of jurisdiction, 142-54
——exercise of jurisdiction, 142-3
——implementation, 142, 148, 154
——national State of offender, 142

——permissive, 148, 153-4
——restriction of, 141-2
——scope, 142-3
——target State, 142
——territorial State, 142, 150-2
—primary jurisdiction—
——bases. *See* primary jurisdiction, bases of *below*
——priority of, 144
——stateless persons, over, 148-50
——States under obligation to establish, 142
——"territorial State" fiction, 243-4
—primary jurisdiction, bases of, 140-2
——effects doctrine, 151-2
——nationality, 147-8
——passive personality, 152-4
——protective principle, 151
——target State, 150-2
——territorial, 143-7. *See also* "in its territory" *under* Hostages Convention, words and phrases
—Rome Convention, 140, 141, 154
—Rome Protocol, 140
—Tokyo Convention, 154
Article 5(2), 155-9, 172
—basis. *See* universality principle *below*
—customary international law, whether, 158 n. 103
—extradition, and, 156-7
——Article 8, and, 156
—implementing legislation, 155-6
—necessary, whether, 138 n. 16
—non-signatory States, effect on, 157
—subsidiary jurisdiction, 155-9
—universality principle, 155
——legal effect, 157-8
Article 5(3), 159
—Hague Convention, 159
—Montreal Convention, 159
—New York Convention, 159
—non-exclusion of other bases of jurisdiction, 159
—Rome Convention, 159
Article 6, 167-84
—protection of alleged offender, 167-84
Article 6(1), 168-74
—extradition, relevance of request for, 172

—FRG draft, 169
—Hague Convention, 169, 174
—measures to ensure presence of offender, 168-74
——circumstances warranting, 168-72. *See also* "satisfied that the circumstances so warrant" *under* Hostages Convention, words and phrases
—Montreal Convention, 174
—New York Convention, 173 n. 19, 174
—obligations under—
——Article 3, and, 172
——detention, 169-70
——discretionary, 168-73, 174
——good faith, 171
——preliminary enquiry, 174
——States bound, 172-3
—preliminary measures, 173-4
——Article 6(6), and, 183
——discretionary nature, 173
——notification of results, 183-4
——permissible delay, 173-4
—Rome Convention, 174
—Tokyo Convention, 169, 171 n. 15, 173 nn. 20-21
Article 6(2), 174-7
——entitlement to notification, 176-7
——Article 5(1), and, 176
—FRG draft, 175
—Hague Convention, 175, 177
—Montreal Convention, 175, 177
—New York Convention, 175, 176
—obligations under—
——Article 6(6) compared, 183
——method, 175-6
——notification of measures without delay, 174
——purpose, 175
—Rome Convention, 175, 177
—UN Secretary-General, role, 175-6
Article 6(3), 177-81
—accused's rights—
——communication, 177-80
——guarantee, 181
——permissible delay, 178
——persons entitled, 178-80
——States approachable, 178-80
——visit, 180-1
—consular agreements, and, 177, 181
—diplomatic protection, and, 178-81
——UNHCR, 180 n. 46

—European Convention on Consular Functions, 177 n. 30
—Hague Convention, 178, 181
—Montreal Convention, 178, 181
—New York Convention, 177, 178, 180, 181
—refugees, 179-80
—Rome Convention, 178, 181
—stateless persons, 179-80
—Vienna Convention on Consular Relations, 177, 178, 180 n. 47, 181
Article 6(4), 181
—Hague Convention, 181
—Montreal Convention, 181
—New York Convention, 181
—Rome Convention, 181
—Vienna Convention on Consular Relations, and, 181
Article 6(5), 181-3
—Article 9, and, 182, 223
—Hague Convention, 182
—ICRC, 181
——restrictions on role, 182-3
——statutes, consistency with, 182
—New York Convention, 182
—rights under—
——invitation to Red Cross, 181-2
——States entitled to exercise, 181, 182
—Rome Convention, 182
—Sixth Committee, 182
—stateless persons, protection of, 181-3
Article 6(6), 183-4
—Article 6(2) compared, 184
—Hague Convention, 183
—Montreal Convention, 183
—New York Convention, 183
—obligations under—
——benefits, 183
——methods, 184
——notification of intention *re* exercise of jurisdiction, 183
——notification of results of preliminary enquiry, 183
—Rome Convention, 183
Article 7, 185-6
—Article 6(2), and, 186
—communication of results of prosecution, 185-6
——direct notification excluded, 186
——UN Secretary-General's role, 186
—FRG draft, 185
—Hague Convention, 185, 186

Hostages Convention (*cont.*)
—Montreal Convention, 185, 186
—New York Convention, 185
—obligation under—
——limited nature, 186
—Rome Convention, 185, 186
Article 8, 74, 187-208
—Article 3, and—
——potential conflict, 112-14
—extradition, and, 156
—jurisdiction, and, 143
——need to establish, 138 n. 16
Article 8(1), 193-203
—Article 3, and, 194
—Article 5, and, 196
—Article 10, and, 194
—Article 13, and, 194
—Article 15—
——exception to, as, 327, 334, 336-7
—attendant crimes—
——effect of inclusion, 160, 161
—breach—
——discretion, exercise in good faith, not, 202
—European Convention on Extradition, 199
—European Convention on the Suppression of Terrorism, 196, 201
—extradition—
——obligation, 194
——request for, whether necessary, 196-7
——to territorial State, desirability, 194, 220
—Hague Convention, 187, 198-9, 200-2
—importance of, 187
—*locus delicti commissi*, relevance, 198
—Montreal Convention, 187, 200-1
—New York Convention, 187, 193-4, 200-1
—obligations under—
——*aut dedere aut judicare*, 93, 187-208
——choice discretionary, 194
——discretionary, 198-200
——exceptions, 194-6
——Geneva Conventions, and, 196
——grant of immunity, and, 196
——motivation, relevance, 196
——prosecution, decision, 198-203. *See also* prosecution *below*
——territorial State equally bound, 194
—prosecution—
——discretion, 202-3
——evidence, lack of, 198, 202
——good faith, requirement of, 202, 203
——humanitarian considerations, 198, 202, 203
——obligation, whether, 198-200
——political and judicial administration authorities distinguished, 200
——political offence, treatment as, 201-2
——procedural requirements, 200-1
——prosecuting authorities, responsibility of, 198-200
—Rome Convention, 187
Article 8(2), 204-8
—African Charter on Human and People's Rights, 205
—American Convention on Human Rights, 205
—European Convention for the Protection of Human Rights, 205
—evidence—
——Article 11, and, 206
——availability, 206
—fair treatment, 187-8, 204-8
——ambiguity, 206
——"at all stages of the proceedings", 206
——equality of treatment, 207
——extradition, and, 192
——meaning, 204-6
——national treatment, 207
——value of provision, 207-8
—Hague Convention, 187
—human rights, and, 187
—International Covenant on Civil and Political Rights, 204-6
—Montreal Convention, 187
—New York Convention, 188, 189
—OAS Convention, 204 n. 64
—obligations under—
——difficulties in meeting, 206
——fair treatment, 187-8, 204-8
——non-territorial State, difficulties in meeting, 206
—political offence exception, 193
——Article 10, and, 193
——extradition and prosecution distinguished, 193
—Rome Convention, 187

INDEX

—safe-havens, avoidance of, 197
Article 9, 64-5, 209-25
—absence of equivalent in anti-terrorism conventions, 210
—Article 8—
——balance to, 213
—Article 15, and, 334
—asylum, possibility of, 209
——European Convention on the Suppression of Terrorism, 209 n. 1
—discrimination clause, as, 210-15. *See also* Discrimination clause
——bilateral extradition treaties, 211
——European Convention on Extradition, 210, 211, 218
——European Convention on the Suppression of Terrorism, 210, 216-17
——Hague Convention, 212 n. 14
——Inter-American Convention on Extradition, 210, 218
——municipal law, in, 210-11
——New York Convention, 212
——*non-refoulement*, and, 211-12
——Rendition of Fugitive Offenders within the Commonwealth Scheme, 211
—extradition, and, 192
——limitations on, 209
—motive for inclusion, 214
—negotiating history, 214
—objections to, 213-15
—Rome Convention, 210
—sovereignty, and, 214
—voting, 64-5, 210, 214-15
Article 9(1), 182, 215-23
—Article 6(5), and, 223
—desirability, 217 n. 39
—dispute—
——Article 16, 221
——unjustified extradition, 222
——unjustified refusal of extradition, 221
—European Convention on the Suppression of Terrorism—
——compatibility with, 216-17
—extradition—
——Article 10, and, 221
——general law of, effect on, 216
——governing rules, 221, 240
——obligation against, 215-23
——political offence exception, 221
——prejudice because diplomatic protection lacking, 222-3
——prejudice because of status, 222
——purpose of request, 219-22
——territorial State, to, 220
—International Committee of the Red Cross, and, 223
—objections to, 219-20
—obligations under—
——mandatory nature, 215-18
——nature of, 220
——obligation to prosecute unaffected, 220
—protecting powers, appointment of, and, 223
—requested State—
——determined by, 217
—"substantial grounds", 218-19
——dispute resolution procedures, and, 219
——European Convention on Extradition, 218
——European Convention on the Suppression of Terrorism, 218
——good faith requirement, 219
——meaning, 218
——requested State, determined by, 218-19
Article 9(2), 223-5
—existing extradition treaties—
——modification, 223-4
—reasons for, 224
—sovereignty, and, 224
—Vienna Convention on the Law of Treaties, 225
Article 10, 227-44
—Article 8(1)—
——expansion of, 227
—Article 9, 228
—attendant crimes—
——effect of inclusion, 160
—"extraditable". *See under* Hostages Convention, words and phrases
——political offence exception, 193
—extradition—
——change to extradition laws not required, 228
——controlling factor, not, 228
——criteria, 228
——facilitation of, 228
—Hague Convention, 228
—interpretation—
——difficulties of, 229
—Montreal Convention, 228
—New York Convention, 228

Hostages Convention (*cont.*)
——obligations under—
————discrepancies, 229
——purpose, 227-8
————facilitation of extradition, 228
—Article 10(1), 229-38
——Apartheid Convention, 234
——breach—
————non-inclusion of Article 1 offences in extradition treaty, 237
——European Convention on the Suppression of Terrorism, 235
——"extraditable offence". *See under* Hostages Convention, words and phrases
——extradition treaties, modification of, 229-31
——Genocide Convention, 233-4
——Hague Convention, 233, 234
——implementing legislation, 229
——legal fiction, 229
——non-inclusion of Article 1 offences in extradition treaty, effect, 237-8
——obligations under—
————inclusion of Article 1 offences in extradition treaties, 237-8
——political offence exception, effect on, 233-5. *See also* Extradition, political offence exception
—Article 10(2), 238-41
——extradition—
————governing law, 240-1
————Hostages Convention as legal basis for, 238-40
——Hague Convention, 238
——New York Convention, 238, 240
——optional nature, 238-9
————reasons for, 239-40
—Article 10(3), 241-3
——applicability, 241
——extraditable offences—
————recognition of Article 1 offences as, 241
——Hague Convention, 242
——New York Convention, 242
——obligations under—
————inequality of, 242-3
————recognition of Article 1 offences as extraditable, 241
—Article 10(4), 243-4
——Article 5(1)—
————facilitation of implementation of, 243-4
——Hague Convention, 243
——implementing legislation, 243 n. 65
——"territorial State" fiction, 243-4
————limitation to States with primary jurisdiction
————passive personality principle, 244
————stateless persons, 244
—Article 11, 245-61
——Article 8(2), and, 206
——FRG draft, 246
——Hague Convention, 246
——interpretation—
————problems of, 246
——Montreal Convention, 246
——mutual assistance in criminal proceedings, 245-61. *See also* Judicial assistance
——necessity for, 245-6
——New York Convention, 246
——Rome Convention, 246
—Article 11(1), 250-60
——Asian-African Legal Consultative Committee, 255
——breach—
————refusal of requests, 254, 259
——European Convention on Mutual Assistance in Criminal Matters, 255, 256
——evidence—
————form, 259-60
————request, need for, 260
————supply of, 258-60
——"greatest measure of assistance". *See under* Hostages Convention, words and phrases
——Hague Convention, 254, 256, 258
——Montreal Convention, 254, 256, 258
——New York Convention, 254-5, 257, 258, 259-260
——obligations under—
————criminal proceedings, in respect of, 257-8
————evidence, supply of, 258-60
————"greatest measure of assistance", 250
————limitations on, 256, 261
————municipal law, determined by, 253, 254-5, 259
————nature of, 253-7
——political offence exception, 256 n. 65, 261 n. 84
——reciprocity, 256 n. 65
——Rome Convention, 256
—Article 11(2), 260-1

Article 11(1), 250-60
—Asian-African Legal Consultative Committee, 255
—breach—
——refusal of requests, 254, 259
—European Convention on Mutual Assistance in Criminal Matters, 255, 256
—evidence—
——form, 259-60
——request, need for, 260
——supply of, 258-60
—"greatest measure of assistance". *See under* Hostages Convention, words and phrases
—Hague Convention, 254, 256, 258
—Montreal Convention, 254, 256, 258
—New York Convention, 254-5, 257, 258, 259-260
—obligations under—
——criminal proceedings, in respect of, 257-8
——evidence, supply of, 258-60
——"greatest measure of assistance", 250
——limitations on, 256, 261
——municipal law, determined by, 253, 254-5, 259
——nature of, 253-7
—political offence exception, 256 n. 65, 261 n. 84
—reciprocity, 256 n. 65
—Rome Convention, 256
Article 11(2), 260-1
—European Convention on Mutual Assistance in Criminal Matters, 261
—FRG draft, 261
—judicial assistance treaties—
——obligations unaffected, 260-1
Article 12, 73, 74, 75, 78 n. 2, 89, 263-98. *See also* Geneva Conventions, 1949
—applicability—
——Article 13, and, 297
——*aut dedere aut judicare*, alternative source of obligation, in case of, 274, 276, 277
——customary international law obligation to extradite, effect of, 277
——Geneva Conventions, applicability of, 273-7
——States bound by Geneva Conventions, 274-7
—armed conflict—

——Geneva Conventions, incomplete coverage, 270-1
——hostage-taking during, 265-6, 269-70
——international criminal law, interrelationship with laws of, 266
——meaning, 278-9
——national liberation movements, 278-9
—Article 15, and, 334
—compromise, 264
—elements of, 271-2
—interpretation, difficulty of, 264, 279
—Mexican proposal, 269-70
—reasons for, 272-3
—Geneva Conventions, and, 138 n. 16, 263-98
——application of, preference for, 276
——*aut dedere aut judicare* requirement, 265, 273-4, 279-98
——complementary nature of Article 12, 265-6, 274
——definition, 273 n. 41
——Hostages Convention, displacement of, 263, 265, 270-1, 273-5, 288-9, 293, 294, 295
——incomplete coverage, 270-1
——Protocol I, applicability, 276, 294-7
——Protocol I, relevance to negotiations, 268-9
——"States Parties to", meaning, 274-7
—hostage-taking—
——legality, possibility of, 264-6, 267
—interpretation, difficulty of, 264, 279
—motivation, relevance, 268
—national liberation movements, and, 264-73, 293, 297
—negotiating history, 263-4, 266-73
——Protocol I to the Geneva Conventions, relevance, 268-9
Article 13, 89, 299-312
—Article 1—
——converse formulation, 301
—FRG draft, 307-11
—Hague Convention, 299, 300 n. 5, 301 n. 6
—Hostages Committee, and, 307-11

Hostages Conventions (*cont.*)
    missions, 313
    —rescue mission, and, 316-22
    —UN Charter—
    ——Article 2(4), and, 313
    ——violation unjustifiable, 313
    —use of force. *See also* Force, use of
    ——effect on law regarding, 322-5
  Article 15, 64, 327-41
    —acceptability—
    ——limited applicability, on grounds of, 340 n. 66
    —applicability—
    ——limited, 340 n. 66, 341
    ——parties to asylum treaties, *inter se*, 340
    ——Treaties on Asylum in force, 340
    ——Vienna Convention on Treaties, modifications under, 340 n. 67
    —Article 3, compared, 339 n. 61
    —Article 8(1)—
    ——exception to, whether, 327, 334, 336-7
    —Article 9, and, 334
    —Article 12, 334
    —asylum—
    ——diplomatic asylum treaties, vulnerability, 336
    ——preservation of treaties on, 327, 334
    —*aut dedere aut judicare* principle, and, 327, 329, 331, 332-3, 334, 336-40
    —Caracas Convention on Territorial Asylum—
    ——effect of, 339-41
    ——effect on, 339
    —contentious issue, 331
    —FRG draft, 327
    —Mexican proposal, 330
    —negotiating history, 330-4
    —New York Convention, 327, 333, 337, 341
    —significance, 327
  Article 16, 112, 219, 221, 343-5
    —applicability—
    ——limited, 344-5
    —effectiveness, 344-5
    ——discretionary nature of obligations, and, 344-5
    —FRG draft, 343 n. 2
    —Hague Convention, 343 n. 1
    —Montreal Convention, 343 n. 1
    —New York Convention, 343 nn. 1-2
    —Rome Convention, 343 n. 1
  Article 16(2)—
    —FRG draft, 345 n. 6
    —New York Convention, 345 n. 7
    —opt-out clause, 345
  Article 17, 346
  Article 18, 346
  Article 19 (denunciation), 346
    —comparable conventions, 346 n. 8
    —FRG draft, 346
  Article 20, 346
  aut dedere aut judicare: *q.v.*
  bilateral agreements, and, 128
  catalyst for, 9 n. 26, 57, 65
  deals—
    —compatibility, 109-16
  dispute settlement procedures, 112, 343-5
    —hostage-taking, during, 343-4
    —opt-out clause, 345
  drafting, 7, 57-67
    —contentious areas, 61-3, 78-9
    —Hostages Committee: *q.v.*
    —Sixth Committee, 58, 60 n. 209, 61, 64-5, 67, 72, 75
    ——records, 66 n. 253
    —Terrorism Committee, 60-1
  enforcement—
    —dispute settlement, 343-5
    —municipal law sole instrument, 93-4
  entry into force, 65
  FRG draft. *See under individual articles*
  hostage-taking, offence of. *See* Article 1(1) *above*
  implementation—
    —legislation. *See under individual countries*
    —supplementary agreements, 128
  international acts, limitation to, 299-312
  international criminal law—
    —armed conflict, law of, interaction, 8
  international law—
    —codification, as, 7
  interpretation—
    —disputed. *See* dispute settlement procedures *above*
    —teleological, 113
    —*travaux préparatoires*: *q.v.*
  judicial assistance, 246, 250-61
  jurisdiction. *See* Article 5 *above*
  liability—

—accomplice, 90-2
—individual, 79-80
—State agent, 79-80
—threat, 82
model, as, 6
object and purposes—
—*aut dedere aut judicare*, 113
—protection of victims, 113
obligations under, 5, 8
—*aut dedere aut judicare*: q.v.
—conflict between, 112-14
—cooperation to prevent hostage taking, 119-31
—easing situation of hostage, 109, 110-17
—exchange of information, 127-9
—facilitating departure of hostage, 109
—imposition of penalties, 101-8
—making offences punishable, 93-4, 101-2
—method discretionary, 101
—nature of, 6-7, 10
—non-territorial State, of, 114, 117
—return of object obtained by offender, 109
—securing release of hostage, 109, 111-12
offences under, 54
—place of, 303-5
parties, 5 n. 19, 48
—Algeria, 115 n. 19
—Egypt, 215
—Italy, 26 n. 5
—Yugoslavia, 26 n. 65
phrases. *See* Hostages Convention, words and phrases
Preamble, 64, 71-5
—armed conflict, 75
—*aut dedere aut judicare*, 74
——Article 8, 74
—compromise language, 71
—drafting, 71-2
—FRG draft, 72, 74
—human rights, and, 73
—International Convention on Civil and Political Rights, 73
—national liberation movements, 73-4, 75
—purposes and principles of UN Charter, and, 72-3
—self-determination, and, 73
——Article 12, 73
—significance, 71
—terrorism—
——hostage-taking as element of, 74-5

—Universal Declaration of Human Rights, and, 73
signatories, 5 n. 19
supplementary agreements, 128
terrorism—
—element in fight against, as, 61 n. 213, 75
third parties, and, 157
United Nations—
—Charter—
——consistency with, 313-26
—purposes and principles of, and, 72-3
violation—
—territorial State's decisions as, 111-12
Hostages Convention, words and phrases—
"all measures ... it considers appropriate", 111-14
—acquiescence in demands, 111
—"as appropriate" distinguished, 127 n. 30
—force, 111
—immunity, grant of—
——*aut dedere aut judicare*, compatibility, 112-14
——permissibility, 112-14
—negotiation, 111
—territorial State sole judge, 111-14
——binding on third State, whether, 114
"all practicable measures to prevent", 122-6
—discretionary nature, 123-5
—examples, 123-4
—"prohibit ... illegal activities ... that encourage ... ", 126-7
—"within or outside their territories", 123
"another person"—
—identity irrelevant, 84
"any act", 87
"any person", 79-80
—individual liability, 79
—State agent, 79-80
"application of the Treaties on Asylum", 334-40
—"as between", 340-1
—"in force", 340
"appropriate penalties", 102-8
—"grave nature" determining factor, 103
—implementing legislation—
——unaffected by choice of formula, 108
—"severe penalties" formula,

Hostages Convention (*cont.*)
106-8
—— cons, 106-7
—— pros, 107
—unspecified, 102
"armed conflict", 278-9
"assistance in connexion with criminal matters", 245-57
—"mutual assistance in criminal matters", 246-9
"attempts", 89-90
"considers it appropriate", 148
"criminal proceedings", 257
"ease situation of hostage", 110-16
—measures, 111
—territorial limitation, 110
"establish its jurisdiction", 142-3
"exchanging information ... and co-ordinating ... measures as appropriate", 127-31
—"it considers appropriate" distinguished, 127 n. 30
"existing", 236-7
"explicit or implicit condition", 87-8
—implementing legislation, 88
"extraditable offence", 160 n. 108, 231-3, 237, 241-3
"facilitate, when relevant, his departure", 116-17
—hostage's wish, relevance, 116
—method, 117
"fair treatment", 204-6
"Geneva Conventions ... are applicable", 274
—"bound under those conventions", 271
—"States Parties to this Convention are bound", 274-7
"grave"—
—appropriate penalties, 103
"greatest measure of assistance", 250-7
—European Convention on Mutual Assistance in Criminal Matters, 255
—preliminary investigations, in, 257-8
—supply of evidence, 258
"habitual residence", 149-50
—*Acquisition of Polish Nationality* case, 149-50
—establishment of residence, 149-50
—intention to remain, 149-50
—*Interpretation of Minorities Treaty* case, 150
—municipal law definition, 150
"hostage". See Hostages Convention, Article 1
"hostage-taking". See Hostages Convention, Article 1
"in its territory", 143-6
—continental shelf, 145-2
—dependent territories, 144-5
—EEZ, 144-5
—territorial airspace, 145
—territorial waters, 144
"in order to compel", 84-5
"instituted"—
—duration, 174
"international intergovernmental organization", 86
"justifying ... contravention of the UN Charter", 322-4
"law[s] of the/that State", 200-3, 207, 240-1
"make offences ... punishable", 101-2
—specific legislation, necessity for—
—— common law systems, 102
—— constitutional requirements, 102
—— inadequacy of existing legislation, 102
—— jurisdictional reach insufficient, 102
—— US legislation, 102 n. 38
"manifestations of international terrorism", 74-5
—absence from FRG draft, 74
—armed conflict, hostage-taking during, and, 75
—objections to, 75
—Soviet proposal, 74
"may be prejudiced", 222-3
"ordinary offence", 201-2
"organization of the arbitration", 343
"participates as accomplice", 90-2
—accessory, 90
—aiding and abetting, 90
—conspiring, 90
"proceedings", 206, 207
"race, religion, nationality, ethnic origin or political opinion", 219
"reasonably necessary", 173-4
"return [object] as soon as possible to the hostage or third party", 117-18
—"illegally acquired", 117-8
—"person entitled to possession", 117-8
—"promptly", 117-8
"right to invite ... ICRC", 181-2
"satisfied that the circumstances so

warrant", 168-72
"secure his release", 111-16
—methods. *See* "all measures ... it considers appropriate" *above*
"seizes or detains", 80-2
—force, whether necessary, 80-1
—implementing legislation, 81
—methods—
——blackmail, 81
——intimidation, 81
——relevance, 81
—other conventions compared, 81
—tautology, 81-2
——multilingual nature of Convention, 81-2
"shall not be granted", 215-18
"stateless persons", 149, 179-80
—refugees, 79-80
"States concerned", 176-7, 186
"submit the case to its competent authorities", 198-200
"substantial grounds for believing", 218-19
"supply of all evidence", 258-60
"take all measures ... necessary"—
—exception to *aut dedere aut judicare* principle, as, 109
"third party", 85-6
—comprehensive, 85
—implementing legislation, 85-6
—relevance, 85-6
"threatens to kill, injure or continue to detain", 82-4
—length of threatened detention, relevance, 82
—"severe injury", 82
"to do or abstain from doing any act"
—nature of act irrelevant, 87
"treated as if ... committed", 243-4
"within a single State", 301-12
"without delay", 174-5, 178
"without exception whatsoever", 113, 195
—"whatsoever the motive", 195
Human rights—
anti-terrorism conventions, 207-8
conventions—
—African Charter on Human and People's Rights, 205
—American Convention on Human Rights, 205
—European Convention for the Protection of Human Rights, 205
—International Covenant on Civil and Political Rights: *q.v.*
—OAS Convention, 204 n. 64

discrimination clauses, 209-25
fair treatment—
—Hostages Convention, 187-8, 204-8
—International Covenant on Civil and Political Rights, 204-6
—New York Convention, 188, 204
—OAS Convention, 204
—Rome Convention, 188
Hostages Convention, and—
—discrimination clauses, 209-25
—fair treatment, 187-8
—liberty of person, 169-72
liberty of person—
—Hostages Convention, 169-72
—New York Convention, 170
—Tokyo Convention, 169
Universal Declaration of: *q.v.*
Humanitarian law—
politization—
—Geneva Conventions, 1949, Additional Protocol I, 1977, 291
Humanity, crimes against—
apartheid, 97
individual responsibility for—
—apartheid, 97
—Nuremberg Tribunal, 95-6
Hungary—
position taken—
—extradition, refusal, 214-15

Immunity. *See also* Asylum
Achille Lauro, 115-16
Kuwaiti Airlines Boeing 747, 115 n. 19
permissibility—
—Hague Convention, 114 n. 15, 115 n. 19
—Hostages Convention, 112-16
India—
position taken—
—extradition—
——Hostages Convention as basis for, 239
Institut de Droit International—
asylum, 328
jurisdiction—
—protective principle, 151 n. 71
Internal hostage-taking—
Hostages Convention, 299-312
International Air Transport Association—
hijackers—
—proposal for international court and detention centre, 100 n. 35

396 INDEX

International Atomic Energy Agency, 9 n. 26, 43 n. 145
International Civil Aviation Organization—
Conventions, 1, 47, 51-2. *See also* Tokyo Convention, 1963; Hague Convention, 1970; Montreal Convention, 1971; Montreal Protocol, 1988
—enforcement, 56-7
——reporting procedure, 57 n. 195
—penalties for violations of, 108
—sanctions—
——Bonn Declaration, 1978, 56 n. 195
——halt in air traffic, 56 n. 195
——International Federation of Airline Pilots Associations, proposals, 56 n. 195
——objections, 56 n. 195
——other aviation agreements, effect on, 56 n. 195
——third parties, effect on, 56 n. 195
——Vienna Convention on the Law of Treaties, and, 56 n. 195
International Commission of Jurists—
asylum in Latin America, 328-9
International Committee of the Red Cross—
Geneva Conventions, 1949—
—ANC declaration, 290 n. 79
refugees—
—consular protection, 181-3
International Court of Justice—
Case Concerning the United States Diplomatic and Consular Staff in Tehran, 3 n. 12, 110 n. 3, 317 n. 23, 343 n. 3
judgments—
—compliance with, 343 n. 2
—continuing effect, 344 n. 4
jurisdiction—
—exercise of—
——*Northern Cameroons* case, 344 n. 4
Legal Consequences for States of the Continued Presence of South Africa in Namibia, 293
—international organization, evidence of view of, 310 n. 30
—treaty interpretation, 293
Northern Cameroons case, 344 n. 4
ongoing dispute, during—
—*Case Concerning the United States Diplomatic and Consular Staff in Tehran*, 343 n. 3
travaux préparatoires, use of—
—*Conditions of Admission of a State to Membership in the United Nations*, 67 n. 255
—*Interpretation of the Convention of 1919 concerning the Employment of Women during the Night*, 67 n. 255
treaty interpretation—
—continuing effect, 344 n. 4
—*Legal Consequences for States of the Continued Presence of South Africa in Namibia*, 293
International Covenant on Civil and Political Rights—
extradition—
—unreasonable delay, 174
International crimes—
"adjective international criminal law", 94 n. 4
aut dedere aut judicare principle, 188-93
conventions, 93-4
—apartheid, 91 n. 53, 94 n. 2, 97, 137 n. 15
—counterfeiting, 94 n. 2, 188
—drug-trafficking, 94 n. 2, 137
—genocide, 94 n. 2, 97, 233-4
—obscene publications, 94 n. 2, 136
—torture, 94 n. 2, 139 n. 22, 145 n. 39
—war crimes, 94 n. 2
crimes against humanity. *See* Humanity, crimes against
customary law—
—piracy, 93 n. 1
—war crimes, 93 n. 1
definition, 94 n. 2
enforcement, 55-7
ILA—
—*Report of Sixty-first Conference*, 94 n. 2
individual, responsibility of, 46 n. 153, 55, 94-9
—direct, 95-9
—Geneva Conventions, 1949, 80 n. 8
—Hostages Convention, 79-80
—ILC, 96
——Draft Code of Offences against the Peace and Security of Mankind, 97-8
—International Military Tribunals, 95-7. *See also* Nuremberg Tribunal
—piracy, 95

jurisdiction, 94-5, 100
sanctions, 56-7
"substantive international criminal law", 94 n. 4
International criminal court—
　Code of Offences against the Peace and Security of Mankind, 100
　enforcement of jurisdiction, 100, 135
　First International Criminal Law Conference, 100 n. 32
　Genocide Convention, 136
　IATA, 100 n. 33
　ILA, 100 n. 32
　ILC, 100 n. 33
　League of Nations—
　　—Convention on the Establishment of an International Criminal Court, 28, 99
　objections to, 100 n. 33
　Sixth Committee, 100 n. 33
　UN Committee on International Criminal Jurisdiction, 99-100
International Federation of Airline Pilots Associations—
　sanctions—
　　—proposals for, 56 n. 56
International law—
　breach—
　　—extradition—
　　　——unreasonable delay, 174 n. 24
　codification—
　　—anti-terrorism conventions, 46-8
　　—Geneva Conventions on the Law of the Sea, 1958, 59
　　—Hostages Convention, 7
　　—ILC role, 59-60
　　—Vienna Convention on Consular Relations 1963, 59
　　—Vienna Convention on Diplomatic Relations 1961, 59
　　—Vienna Convention on the Law of Treaties 1969, 59
　compliance, 186
　development and codification—
　　—ILC: *q.v.*
　　—UN Committee for, 96
　effectiveness, 8-9
　enforcement—
　　—municipal law as instrument of, 93-5
　　——effect on international character, 95 n. 6
　evidence of—
　　—General Assembly Resolution, 96-7, 158
　　—Nuremberg Charter and Judgment, 96
　individuals, and. *See* International crimes, individual, responsibility of
　municipal law, and—
　　—incorporation doctrine, 95
　　—instrument of enforcement, 93-5
　nature of—
　　—dualist, 95 n. 6
　　—monist, 95 n. 6
　obligations under—
　　—method of meeting discretionary, 101
　　—prevention of use of territory for crimes in other States, 122-3
　　——*Corfu Channel Case*, 123 n. 15
　　——*US* v. *Arjona*, 123 n. 15
　principles of—
　　—freedom of air, 47 n. 154
　　—freedom of international communication, 47 n. 154
　sources—
　　—treaties—
　　　——limited number of signatories, 96
　subjects. *See* International crimes, individual, responsibility of
　terrorism, and. *See* Terrorism, international law, and
International Law Association—
　Committee on International Terrorism—
　　—Fourth Interim Report, 46, 47 n. 154, 124 n. 22
　　——international obligations, compliance with, 124 n. 22
　draft Terrorism Convention, 46-7
　　—principles for inclusion, 46 n. 153
　obligation to prevent acts of terrorism, 123
International Law Commission—
　codification of international law—
　　—Geneva Conventions on the Law of the Sea, 1958, 59
　　—Hostages Convention, 59-60
　　—responsibility for, 59
　　—role in, decline, 60
　　—Vienna Convention on Consular Relations 1963, 59
　　—Vienna Convention on Diplomatic Relations 1961, 59
　　—Vienna Convention on the Law of Treaties 1969, 59
　Draft Code of Offences against the Peace and Security of Mankind.

398 INDEX

International Law Commission (*cont.*)
    See Peace and Security of Mankind, ILC Draft Code of Offences against
New York Convention—
    —commentary on, 122-3, 124
    ——"attempt", 89
    ——"conspiracy", 90-1
    ——consular protection, right to, 177
    ——discrimination clause, 212
    ——human rights, 204-7
    ——judicial assistance, 250, 254, 258, 260
    ——notification of measures taken, 174-5
    ——"organization of arbitration", 343 n. 2
    ——"participation", 90
    ——prosecution, 199, 200, 201, 203
    ——State responsibility, 122-3
    —deprivation of liberty, 179
    —drafting, 33 n. 97
    —jurisdiction—
    ——priority, 164 n. 123
    —notification of measures taken, 175, 176
    —threat to commit violence, 83 n. 26
shortcomings, allegations of, 59-60
    —conservative approach, 60
    —independence from State control, 60
    —lack of technical knowledge, 60
    —slowness, 60
    —UNITAR study, 60
terrorism—
    —General Assembly consideration of—
    ——recommendation for, 33 n. 97
    —Hostages Convention, 59-60
threat as offence, 83-4
International Maritime Organization, 43 n. 145
    conventions, 52-3. See also Rome Convention, 1988; Rome Protocol, 1988
International organizations. See also *individual organizations*
    Hostages Convention—
        —target of demands—
        ——jurisdiction, 311 n. 32
International terrorism. See Terrorism
Interpol—
    exchange of information, 129 n. 36
    political crimes—
    ——outside competence, 129 n. 36
    terrorism—
    ——role in relation to, 129 n. 36
Islamic Jihad, 4, 115 n. 19
Islands—
    artificial—
    ——jurisdiction, 146 n. 47
Israel—
    Entebbe incident: *q.v.*
    Lod Airport, 32 n. 96
    positions taken—
        —"competent authorities", 200 n. 48
        —GA Res 42/159, 43 n. 145
        —rescue missions, 314, 318-19, 323
Italy—
    Achille Lauro incident—
        —domestic politics, effect on, 27
        —role, 4, 26, 116
    positions taken—
        —extradition—
        ——Hostages Convention as legal basis for, 239
        —facilitation of hostage's departure, 116
        —release of hostages—
        ——*aut dedere aut judicare*, and, 113-14

Japan—
    positions taken—
        —*aut dedere aut judicare*, 197
        —rescue missions, 319
        —"severe" penalties, 107
Jordan—
    Hostages Convention—
        —accession, 215
    positions taken—
        —extradition, refusal, 209 n. 1, 210 n. 2, 213, 215-17, 222-3
        —jurisdiction, 153 n. 81, 164
        —modification of existing treaties, 224
Judicial assistance, 245-61
    agreements. See also Judicial assistance conventions
        —dependence on, 247
        —exceptions, 261 n. 84
        —Hostages Convention, effect of, 261 n. 84
    anti-terrorism conventions, under, 54, 246
    assets—
        —immobilization or forfeit, 251
    civil and common law systems, differences, 248, 249-50
    criminal procedures—

—differences in, 249-50
customary international law, 247
development, 248-9
diplomatic channels, 247-8
discretionary nature, 247, 251-7
double jeopardy, 261 n. 84
evidence—
—surrender of objects, 252
—taking of, 249, 250, 252
—transfer of persons, 250-1, 252
—transmission of, 246-7, 250
examination of sites, 251
exchange of information, 251
Geneva Conventions, 1949
—Supplementary Protocols, 1977, 247 n. 8, 254 n. 51
Hague Convention, 246, 254, 256, 258
Hostages Convention, 246, 250-61
letters rogatory, 247
—discretionary nature, 247
location of persons, 250
Montreal Convention, 246, 254, 256, 258
municipal law, under, 247-9, 251-3, 254-5, 256, 257-8, 259-60
New York Convention, 246, 254, 258
obstacles, 249-50
ordre public, 261 n. 84
political offence exception, 253, 261 n. 84
reciprocity, 253 n. 50
Rome Convention, 246, 254, 256
scope, 246-7
searches and seizures, 251, 252
security, 253 n. 50, 261 n. 84
service of documents, 250, 252
State sovereignty, and, 245-6, 261 n. 84
subpoena, 251
Torture Convention, 254 n. 52
Judicial assistance conventions—
Asian-African Legal Consultative Committee, Draft Model, 1984, 248-9, 250 nn. 25-7, 255
Canada-USA, 1985, 249 n. 16, 250 nn. 25-8, 251 nn. 29-31, 257-8
European Convention on Mutual Assistance in Criminal Matters 1959, 246 n. 4, 247 n. 7, 248, 250-2, 255, 256, 260 n. 78, 261 nn. 83-84
Harvard Research Draft, 246, 257
Italy-USA, 1982, 246 n. 4, 247 n. 7, 249 n. 16, 250 nn. 25-8, 251 nn. 29 *and* 33-34, 256, 260 n. 80, 261 n. 84

Netherlands-USA, 1981, 248 n. 16
Scheme Relating to Mutual Assistance in Criminal Matters within the Commonwealth, 247, 248
Switzerland-USA, 1973, 248 n. 16, 261 n. 84
Turkey-USA, 1979, 248 n. 16
UK-USA (Cayman Islands), 1986, 249 n. 16
Jurisdiction. *See also under individual States*
aircraft—
—Hostages Convention, 147
—quasi-territorial, 147 n. 49
—State of registration, 138
——customary international law, 138
——Harvard Research, 138 n. 19, 147 n. 49
——State practice, 138
——Tokyo Convention, 138
airspace, 145
—Chicago Convention on International Civil Aviation 1944, 145 n. 41
aliens, over, 148-50. *See also* stateless persons, over *below*
—crimes committed abroad, 148-50
—permanent resident, 148-50
——Tokyo Convention, 148-9
bases of, 134
—expansion of, 135-6, 140-1
—Harvard Research, 134
—international organization, membership of, 141
common law/civil law dichotomy, 134-5, 147-8
continental shelf, 145-6
—customary international law, uncertainty of, 146
——municipal legislation, 146
—platforms on—
——Rome Protocol, 146
cross-border offences, 303-6
customary international law, under, 135, 137, 146, 158. *See also* Customary international law, jurisdiction
dependent or non-self-governing territories—
—GA Res 2625(XXV), 144 n. 38
—Hostages Convention—
——duty to establish, whether, 144
—Torture Convention, 145
exclusive economic zone, 145-6
—customary international law,

Jurisdication (cont.)
    uncertainty of, 146
    —municipal legislation, 146
  extraterritorial—
    —criminal legislation, 147-8
    —enforcement, 143
    ——extradition, duty to request, 143
    ——Hostages Convention, and, 143
  flag State—
    —priority, 164 n. 123
  foreign law—
    —application of, 89
  Harvard Research Draft Convention on Jurisdiction with Respect to Crime, 134, 147, 151, 152
  Hostages Convention, and. *See* Hostages Convention, Article 5
  international crimes, 94-5, 100
  international criminal tribunal, 136-7
  —Genocide Convention, 136
  multilateral conventions, 135
    —absence of provision—
    ——Abolition of Slavery and Slave Trade Convention, 135 n. 8
    ——Abolition of Slavery, Supplementary Convention, 135 n. 8
    —Apartheid Convention, 137 n. 15
    —bases, expansion of, 140-1
    ——Chicago Convention on International Civil Aviation 1944, 145 n. 41
    —Counterfeiting Currency Convention, 137
    —European Convention on the Suppression of Terrorism, 138-9
    ——universality principle, 139
    —Geneva Convention on the Continental Shelf 1958, 145 n. 42
    —Geneva Convention on the Territorial Sea and Contiguous Zone 1958, 145 n. 42
    —Geneva Conventions, 1949—
    ——universal jurisdiction, 138
    —Genocide Convention, 136
    ——international criminal tribunal, 136-7
    ——territorial principle, 136-7
    —Hague Convention, 54
    ——priority of jurisdiction, 164
    ——territorial/nationality principles, 139
    ——universality principle, 139
    —Harvard Research—
    ——aircraft, 138 n. 19, 147 n. 49
    ——bases, 134
    ——nationality principle, 147 n. 50
    ——protective principle, 151 nn. 69-71
    ——ships, 138 n. 19, 147 n. 49
    —Hostages Convention—
    ——aircraft, 147
    ——customary international law, whether, 157-8
    ——dependent or non-self-governing territories, 144
    ——extraterritorial enforcement, 143
    ——nationality principle, 147
    ——passive personality principle, 152-4
    ——priority of jurisdiction, 163-5
    ——protective principle, 152-4
    ——ships, 147
    ——stateless person, 148-50
    ——territorial/nationality principles, 139
    ——universality principle, 139, 155-8
    —Law of the Sea Convention 1982, 145 nn. 42-43
    —Montreal Convention, 54, 139
    ——priority of jurisdiction, 164
    ——territorial/nationality principles, 139
    ——universality principle, 139
    —Montreal Protocol, 54
    —municipal law, in accordance with, 136-7
    —New York Convention, 54
    ——passive personality principle, 153, 154
    ——priority of jurisdiction, 164
    ——territorial/nationality principles, 139
    ——universality principle, 139
    —object of Convention, influence of, 139-40
    —Obscene Publications Convention, 94 n. 2, 136
    ——nationality principle permitted, 136
    ——territorial principle, 136
    —Physical Protection of Nuclear Material Convention—
    ——territorial/nationality principles, 139 n. 22
    ——universality principle, 139 n. 22

—Psychotropic Substances Convention, 137 n. 14
—Rome Convention, 54
—— passive personality principle, 154
—— priority of jurisdiction, 164 n. 123
—— protective principle, 151
—— territorial/nationality principles, 139
—— territorial sea, 145 n. 41
—— universality principle, 139
—Rome Protocol, 54
—— platforms on continental shelf, 146
—Single Convention on Narcotic Drugs—
—— universality principle, 137
—Suppression of Counterfeiting Currency Convention 1929, 137
—Suppression of the Circulation of and Traffic in Obscene Publications Convention 1923, 136
—Tokyo Convention—
—— aircraft, State of registration, 138
—— passive personality principle, 154
—— permanent residents, 148-50
—Torture Convention—
—— territorial/nationality principles, 139 n. 22, 145 n. 39
—— universality principle, 139 n. 22
—universality principle—
—— limitations on, 136-7, 139
—— requirement of, 137-8
nationality principle—
—civil law States, in, 134, 147-8
—common law States, in, 147-8
—customary international law, 147
—Harvard Research, 147 n. 50
—Hostages Convention, 147
—Obscene Publications Convention, 136
offender, presence of, 54
passive personality principle, 135, 141, 151-4
—*Achille Lauro*, and, 154
—civil law States, in, 153
—common law States, in, 152, 153
—diplomats, protection of, 153
—excess of jurisdiction, whether, 152 n. 78
—Harvard Research, 152 n. 77

—Hostages Convention, 152-4
—*Lotus* case, 152 n. 79
—New York Convention, 153, 154
—objections to, 152
—protective principle, and, 152 n. 78
—Rome Convention, 154
—Tokyo Convention, 154
priority of, 163-5
—custody determining factor, 164
—extradition treaties, and, 163 n. 120
—flag State, 164 n. 123
—Hague Convention, 164
—Hostages Convention, and, 163-5
—*locus delicti*, preference for, 144
—Montreal Convention, 164
—New York Convention, 164
—Rome Convention, 164 n. 123
protective principle, 135
—customary international law, and, 151
—Harvard Research, 151 nn. 69-71
—*Institut de Droit International*, 151 n. 71
—single interested State, whether need for, 151 n. 69
—target State—
—— Hostages Convention, 150-2
—— Rome Convention, 151
quasi-territorial—
—aircraft, 147 n. 49
registration, State of, 138, 147
ships—
—Harvard Research, 138 n. 19, 147 n. 49
—Hostages Convention, 147
—quasi-territorial, 147 n. 49
Slavery Conventions, 135 n. 8
State practice—
—aircraft—
—— State of registration, 138
—— territorial, 144
stateless persons, over—
—customary international law, 149
—habitually resident—
—— Hostages Convention, 148-50
territorial/nationality principles—
—Hague Convention, 139
—Hostages Convention, 139
—Montreal Convention, 139
—New York Convention, 139

Jurisdiction (*cont.*)
—Physical Protection of Nuclear Material Convention, 139 n. 22
—Rome Convention, 139
—Torture Convention, 139 n. 22
——dependent territories, and, 145
territorial principle—
—dependent or non-self-governing territories, and, 144
—effects doctrine, 151-2
—Genocide Convention, 136-7
—Hostages Convention, 303-6
—Obscene Publications Convention, 136
—primary importance of, 134, 144
—wholly or partly on territory—
——State practice, 144
territorial sea—
—Rome Convention, 145 n. 41
treaties, under. See multilateral conventions *above*
two-tier system, 139-40
universality principle, 135
—abnormal, 155
—*aut dedere aut judicare*, 100
—Counterfeiting Currency Convention, 137
—custody of offender, based on, 135
—customary international law—
——Hostages Convention, whether, 157-8
——piracy sole "universal" offence, 135, 157
—European Convention on the Suppression of Terrorism—
——modified application, 139
—FRG, in, 135 n. 5
—Geneva Conventions, 1949, 138
—Hague Convention, 139
—hijacking as universal offence, 157. *See also* Hostages Convention *below*
——State practice, 158
—Hostages Convention—
——offender subsequently found on territory, 139, 155-8
—Montreal Convention, 139
—multilateral conventions, under, 135, 136 n. 9
——nationals of non-signatories, over, 158 n. 103
—New York Convention, 139
—"offender subsequently found on territory", over, as, 155-8

—Physical Protection of Nuclear Material Convention, 139 n. 22
—piracy, 95, 135
—Rome Convention, 139
—Single Narcotic Drugs Convention, 137
—slavery, 135 n. 6
—Torture Convention, 139 n. 22
—war crimes, 135 n. 6
war crimes—
—universality principle, 138
—victorious power, whether limited to, 138 n. 17

Kenya—
positions taken—
—*aut dedere aut judicare*, 195 n. 25
—extradition—
——Hostages Convention as basis for, 239
—GA Res 3034, 36
—Hostages Convention—
——consistency with UN Charter, 313 n. 1
Kuwait—
position taken—
—causes of terrorism, 40 n. 149
Kuwait Airways Boeing 747 incident—
Algeria, and, 115 n. 19
deal, 115 n. 19

League of Nations—
Convention on the Prevention and Punishment of Terrorism 1937, 1, 9 n. 26, 28, 99
—terrorism—
——definition, 51
Convention on the Establishment of an International Criminal Court 1937, 28, 99
Terrorism Convention 1937, 99
Lebanon, hostage-taking in, 1985-9, 4-5, 87 n. 40
British hostages, 5
deals, 4-5
demands, 4
—direct negotiation, 4
—ransom, 4
—release of prisoners, 4
France, and, 5
Hezbollah, 4, 87 n. 40
Iran, and, 4-5
—re-establishment of diplomatic relations, 5
—release of frozen assets, 5 n. 16
—repayment of loan, 5
—sale of arms to, 4-5

Islamic Jihad, 4
Israel, and, 5 n. 16
Kuwait, 5
  rescue mission, absence of, 326
  United States, 5
Legislation. *See* Municipal law *and under individual countries*
Lesotho—
  positions taken—
    —asylum, 331
    —Hostages Convention—
      ——consistency with UN Charter, 313 n. 1
    —national liberation movements, 267, 269 n. 25
Letter bombs, 57 n. 196
Letters rogatory, 246-8
Liability—
  accomplice: *q.v.*
  individual. *See* International crimes, individual, responsibility of
  State. *See* State responsibility
Libya—
  IRA—
    —supply of arms to, 19-20
  OPEC incident—
    —country of refuge, 2
  positions taken—
    —cooperation—
      ——bilateral agreements, necessity for, 128
    —"easing position of hostage"—
      ——"appropriate measures", 111 n. 7
    —Entebbe, 314 n. 4, 320
    —Hostages Convention—
      ——consistency with UN Charter, 313 n. 1
    —national liberation movements, 35 n. 109, 267
  terrorism—
    —support for, 19 n. 34
  USA—
    —bombing by, 27, 321

Malaysia—
  position taken—
    —"for the purpose of prosecution", 159
Mali—
  position taken—
    —national liberation movements, 272 n. 38
Margin of appreciation, 112
Mauritania—
  position taken—
    —Entebbe, 313 n. 2
Mediation—
  Algeria, 3
Mexico—
  positions taken—
    —asylum, 330, 331-2, 334
    —"circumstances so warrant", 169-70
    —Hostages Convention—
      ——applicability, 311 n. 32
      ——consistency with UN Charter, 314
    —jurisdiction, 157, 308
    —national liberation movements, 269 n. 25, 270-1
    —"severe" penalties, 107
    —State agents, responsibility, 80 n. 8
    —"threat", 83
Mongolia—
  position taken—
    —extradition, refusal, 214-15
Montreal Convention, 1971, 1. *See also under* Hostages Convention, *individual articles*
  adhesion to, 48
  adoption, 52
  arbitration, 343
  Bonn Declaration, 1978, extension to, 57 n. 195
  consular protection, 178
  dispute settlement procedures, 343
  extradition, 235
  judicial assistance, 246, 254, 256, 258
  jurisdiction, 54, 139
    —priority of jurisdiction, 164
    —territorial/nationality principles, 139
    —universality principle, 139
  obligations under, 54-5
  offences under, 51
  universality, 48
Montreal Protocol, 1988, 1. *See also under* Hostages Convention, *individual articles*
  adhesion to, 49
  adoption, 52
  catalyst for, 9 n. 26
  implementation, 108
  jurisdiction, 54
  obligations under, 54-5
  offences under, 52
  universality, 49
Motivation, 18-19, 30-2, 33-45, 46-8, 50, 58. *See also* Armed conflict; National liberation movements
  aut dedere aut judicare, and, 195-6
  extradition, 195-6
  hijacking, 50

Motivation (*cont.*)
  Hostages Convention, 78-9, 195-6, 268
Munich massacre—
  Black September, 32
  General Assembly, and, 32, 35-6
Municipal law—
  anti-terrorism conventions—
    —dependence on, 55-6
  extradition—
    —"discrimination clauses", 210-11
  hostage-taking, offence of, under, 77
  international law. *See* International law, municipal law, and
  treaties, and. *See* Treaties, municipal law, and
Mutual assistance. *See* Judicial assistance; Judicial assistance conventions

National liberation, wars of, 286-98
  customary international law—
    —international nature, 291-3
  Geneva Conventions, 1949, and. *See under* Geneva Conventions, 1949
  Hostages Convention, under. *See* Hostages Convention, national liberation movements
  international, whether, 288-93
National liberation movements, 14, 19, 30-2, 37-8
  anti-terrorism conventions—
    —applicability to, 48
  aut dedere aut judicare, 270-3, 348
  GA Res 34/145, 41-2
  GA Res 42/159, 43
  General Assembly, and, 41-5
  Geneva Conventions, 1949 and Additional Protocols, 1977, 264-6, 268-9, 280, 286-9, 292-8
  Hostages Convention, and, 48 n. 162, 73-4, 75, 78-9, 263-82, 286-98
  New York Convention, 48
  status, entitlement to, 295-7
Nationals—
  protection of—
    —use of force, 318, 319, 320
Negotiations—
  direct—
    —terrorists' demands for, 4
  techniques, 57-67
    —informality—
      ——advantages, 66 n. 251
Netherlands—
  law of—

—Extradition Act 1967, 211 n. 7, 238
positions taken—
  —asylum, 332, 333 n. 32
  —*aut dedere aut judicare*, 195 n. 25, 196-7
  —causes of terrorism, 32 n. 94, 40
  —extradition—
    ——Hostages Convention as basis for, 239
    ——inequality of obligations, 242
    ——refusal, 223 n. 60
  —judicial assistance agreements, 261
  —jurisdiction, 144, 153, 157, 159-61, 309
  —"other measures necessary for institution of proceedings", 173 n. 19
  —release of hostages—
    ——*aut dedere aut judicare*, and, 113, 114
  —"severe" penalties, 107
New York Convention 1973, 1, 53-4. *See also under* Hostages Convention, *individual articles and* International Law Commission
adhesion to, 48, 345 n. 7
applicability—
  —national liberation movements, 48 n. 162
arbitration, 343
arrest, 170
asylum, 332-4, 337-9, 341 n. 69
  —treaties, 340
aut dedere aut judicare, 193
conspiracy, 90-2
consular protection, 177, 178, 180
  —refugees, 180
discrimination clause, 211-12
dispute settlement, 212, 343, 345 n. 7
drafting—
  —difficulties, 48, 60 n. 210
fair treatment, 187-8
ILC commentary, 83 n. 26, 84 n. 27
judicial assistance, 246, 254, 258
jurisdiction, 54
  —passive personality principle, 153, 154
  —priority of jurisdiction, 164
  —territorial/nationality principles, 139
  —universality principle, 139
liberty of person, 169-72
national liberation movements—
  —applicability to, 48 n. 162
obligations under, 54-5

phrases—
—"all practicable measures"—
——discretionary nature, 124
—"severe penalties", 106-8
——reasons for, 106
political persecution, 235
prosecution, 199-201, 202-3
protected persons, 53-4
threat, 83-4
universality, 48
New Zealand—
criminal law—
—penalties, 105, 108
Hostages Convention—
—implementing legislation—
——Crimes (Internationally Protected Persons and Hostages) Act 1980 (No. 44). *See under* law of *below*
jurisdiction—
—stateless persons, 149 n. 62
law of—
—Aviation Crimes Act 1972, 108
—Crimes (Internationally Protected Persons and Hostages) Act 1980 (No. 44), 81 n. 15, 105, 149 n. 62, 229 n. 4
Montreal Convention—
—implementing legislation, 108
Nicaragua—
positions taken—
—asylum, 331 n. 19
—"severe" penalties, 106 n. 57
Nigeria—
positions taken—
—"easing position of hostage"—
——"appropriate measures", 111 n. 7
—Hostages Convention—
——consistency with UN Charter, 313 n. 1
—jurisdiction, 308
—national liberation movements, 267, 269 n. 25
—notification of results, 155
Nuremberg Tribunal—
Draft Code of Offences against the Peace and Security of Mankind, and, 96-9
General Assembly affirmation of Charter and Judgment, 96
governing law, 95
individual responsibility—
—crimes against peace, war crimes and crimes against humanity, 95-6, 98

Obligations. *See under* Terrorism,

conventions *and under individual conventions*
Occupation. *See also* Geneva Conventions, 1949
occupied territory—
—State terrorism in, 15
Oman—
position taken—
—national liberation movements, 31 n. 89
OPEC hostage-taking, 2
Austria, and, 2
deal, 2
demands, 2
General Assembly, and, 42
hostages, release of, 2
Iran, and, 2
Popular Front for the Liberation of Palestine, 2
Saudi Arabia, and, 2
ransom, payment of, 2
Ordre public—
judicial assistance, and, 261 n. 84
Organization of Petroleum Exporting Countries. *See* OPEC hostage-taking

Pakistan—
Karachi airport incident, 111
—rescue mission, 111
positions taken—
—conspiracy, 90 n. 49
—extradition, refusal, 213
—national liberation movements, 272 n. 38
—rescue missions, 323-4
Palestine Liberation Front—
Achille Lauro, 4, 26 n. 65, 115-16
Palestine Liberation Organization—
officials—
—diplomatic immunity, 26, 171
status, 171 n. 14
Paraguay—
position taken—
—*Ad Hoc* Committee on Terrorism, establishment, 34 n. 104
Peace and Security of Mankind, ILC Draft Code of Offences against, 96-7
codification, Nuremberg principles, as, 97
difficulties, 97-8 n. 21
formulation of principles—
—limited nature of task, 96 n. 13
implementation, 97 n. 21
individual responsibility, 96-7
—absence of penalty, and, 96 n. 13

Peace and Security (*cont.*)
responsibility under—
—individual, 98 n. 22
—State, 98 n. 22
scope, 97-8 n. 21
—aggression, 97 n. 18
—annexation of territory, 97 n. 18
—apartheid, 98 n. 25
—armed bands, incursions by, 97 n. 18
—colonialism, 98 n. 25
—complicity, 97 n. 21
—drug-trafficking, 98 n. 25
—economic aggression, 98 n. 25
—environmental damage, 98 n. 25
—fomentation of strife or terrorist activities in another State, 97 n. 18
—genocide, 97 n. 18
—inhuman acts against civilian population, 97 n. 18
—limited, 98-9
—mercenaries, use of, 98 n. 25
—nuclear weapons, use of, 98 n. 25
—piracy, 99
—violation of treaties relating to international peace and security, 97 n. 18
—war crimes, 97 nn. 18 *and* 21
Permanent Court of International Justice—
"habitual residence"—
—*Acquisition of Polish Nationality Case*, 149
Peru—
positions taken—
—asylum, 332 n. 27
—extradition, refusal, 214 n. 22
Philippines—
Hijacking Law 1971, 108
Hostages Convention—
—implementing legislation—
——absence of, 104
—obligations under—
——whether met, 104
Penal Code (Revised)—
—"kidnapping and serious illegal detention", 104
—penalties, 108
——*reclusion perpetua*, 104
——*reclusion temporal*, 104
—private individuals, limited to, 104
—"slight illegal detention", 104
—State agents under, 104
positions taken—

—extradition, refusal, 217, 218
—Hostages Convention—
——consistency with UN Charter, 314
—judicial assistance agreements, 261
—jurisdiction, 309
Piracy—
Draft Code of Offences against the Peace and Security of Mankind, 98
individual liability, 98
international crime, as—
—customary international law, 93 n. 1, 98 n. 26
obligation of State acquiring possession to return spoils, 117
threat to peace, whether, 98 n. 26
Poland—
positions taken—
—"easing position of hostage"—
——"appropriate measures", 111 n. 7
—extradition—
——place of registration, to, 191 n. 15
——refusal, 214-15, 218
—"in accordance with the laws", 201
—"severe" penalties, 107 n. 63
—US bombing of Libya, 321 n. 54
Political offences—
asylum, 335
aut dedere aut judicare, 193
extradition. *See* Extradition, political offence exception
Hostages Convention, 233-5
Interpol, and, 129 n. 36
judicial assistance, 253, 261 n. 84
Popular Front for the Liberation of Palestine (PFLP)—
Arm of the Arab Revolution—
—OPEC incident, 2
Entebbe incident, 2
Prosecution. *See also Aut dedere aut judicare*
discretion, 198-203
good faith, 199 n. 47, 202, 203
obligation—
—European Convention on the Suppression of Terrorism, 201
—Hague Convention, 198-9, 201-2
—Hostages Convention, 196-204
——extradition request, relevance, 196-8
—Montreal Convention, 201
—New York Convention,

INDEX 407

199-201, 202-3
—Rome Convention, 201
political offence exception, and, 193

Qatar—
  positions taken—
    —Entebbe, 313 n. 2
    —US bombing of Libya, 321 n. 54

Recognition—
  belligerency, 286
  Geneva Conventions, 1949, 1977 Additional Protocol I—
    —"authority representing a people", 296 n. 103
Red Cross. *See* International Committee of the Red Cross
Refugees—
  consular protection—
    —European Convention on Consular Functions, 179 n. 44
    —State of habitual residence, 179 n.44
    —UNHCR, 180
    —Vienna Convention on Consular Relations, 180 n. 47
  definition—
    —Status of Refugees Convention, 180 n. 46
    —Statute of Office of UNHCR, 180 n. 46
  European Convention on Consular Functions—
    —Protocol Concerning the Protection of Refugees—
      ——diplomatic protection, 179 n. 44
  Hostages Convention, and, 179-80
    —jurisdiction over, 149 n. 64
  non-refoulement, 211-12
  protection. *See* diplomatic protection *above*
  stateless persons, and—
    —assimilation to, 149, 179-80
    —distinction, 180
    —Statute of Office of UNHCR, 180 n. 45
  Status of Refugees Convention, 1951—
    —*non-refoulement*, 211-12, 218 n. 42
    —refugee, definition, 180
  UN Conference on Territorial Asylum, 220 n. 51
  Vienna Convention on Consular Relations—
    —protection, 180 n. 47
Reprisals—

US bombing of Libya—
  —justification, 321
  —legitimacy, 321
Rescue missions. *See under* Hostage-taking
Romania—
  positions taken—
    —asylum, 333 n. 30
    —extradition, refusal, 214-15, 220
Rome Convention, 1988, 1-2. *See also under* Hostages Convention, *individual articles*
  accomplice, 9 n. 26
  Achille Lauro, and, 9 n. 26
  adhesion to, 49
  adoption, 52-3
  arbitration, 343
  consular protection, 178
  dispute settlement procedures, 343
  fair treatment, 187-8
  judicial assistance, 246, 254, 256
  jurisdiction, 54
    —passive personality principle, 154
    —priority of jurisdiction, 164 n. 123
    —protective principle, 151
    —territorial/nationality principles, 139
    —territorial sea, 145 n. 41
    —universality principle, 139
  obligations under, 54-5
    —avoidance of undue delay to ship, crew, passengers or cargo, 110
  offences under, 53
  prosecution, 201
Rome Protocol, 1988, 2
  adhesion to, 49
  adoption, 53
  continental shelf—
    —platforms on, 146
  jurisdiction, 54
    —platforms on continental shelf, 146
  offences under, 53

Safe-havens. *See also* Asylum; *Aut dedere aut judicare*
  cause of terrorism, 41 n. 140
Sanctions—
  anti-terrorism conventions, and, 56 n. 195
  Security Council, sole competence, 56 n. 195
Saudi Arabia—
  embassy in Sudan, 47 n. 156

INDEX

Saudi Arabia (*cont.*)
  Lebanon, hostages in—
    —target of demands, 4
  OPEC incident—
    —ransom, 2
  position taken—
    —General Assembly discussion of terrorism, 33-4
Security Council—
  competence, 38
    —sanctions, 56 n. 195
  Entebbe, 313
  Resolutions—
    —457, 3 n. 12
  sanctions, 56 n. 195
  US bombing of Libya, 321
Self-defence—
  use of force—
    —rescue missions, 313-26
    —*The Caroline*, 318-19
Slavery—
  Convention for the Abolition of Slavery and the Slave Trade 1927, 135 n. 8
  international crime, 135
  Supplementary Convention on the Abolition of Slavery 1956, 135 n. 8
Sovereignty. *See* State sovereignty
Spain—
  criminal law—
    —penalties—
      ——Organic Law of 26 December 1984, 105
      ——Penal Code, 105
  Hostages Convention—
    —implementing legislation—
      ——Organic Law of 26 December 1984, 105
  kidnapping, 105
  Penal Code—
    —kidnapping, 105
  positions taken—
    —extraditable offences, 237
    —extradition—
      ——Hostages Convention as legal basis for, 239
State—
  agent of—
    —liability—
      ——Hostages Convention, 79-80
      ——Philippines law, 104
  sovereign will—
    —multilateral treaties, modification of, and, 324-5
State practice—
  jurisdiction—
    —aircraft—
      ——State of registration, 138
      —territorial, 144
  treaty interpretation, and, 115 n. 19
State responsibility—
  aliens, protection in terrorist attack, 123 n. 15
  Draft Code of Offences against the Peace and Security of Mankind, 98 n. 22
  hostage-taking, 79-80
  territory, prevention of misuse of, 123
    —*Corfu Channel* case, 123 n. 15
    —*US* v. *Arjona*, 123 n. 15
  use of territory contrary to rights of other States, 122-3
State security—
  judicial assistance, and, 253 n. 50, 261 n. 84
State sovereignty—
  extradition, and, 214
  judicial assistance, and, 245-6, 261 n. 84
  treaty modification, and, 324-5
State terrorism. *See under* Terrorism
State-controlled terrorism. *See under* Terrorism
Stateless persons—
  consular protection, 179-80
  de jure—
    —assimilation of *de facto*, 179
  definition, 149, 179
  Hostages Convention, and, 148
    —jurisdiction—
      ——habitual residence as basis, 148-50
  jurisdiction over—
    —customary international law, 149
    —Hostages Convention, 148-50
  protection. *See* consular protection *above*
  refugees: *q.v.*
  Status of Stateless Persons Convention, 1954, 179
Sudan—
  Saudi-Arabian embassy in, incident involving, 47 n. 156
Sweden—
  criminal law—
    —attempt, 90 n. 47
  Hostages Convention—
    —implementing legislation—
      ——absence of, 104-5
    —obligations under—
      ——analogous offence technique, 104
  jurisdiction—

—assimilation of *de facto*, 179
definition, 149, 179
Hostages Convention, and, 148
—jurisdiction—
——habitual residence as basis, 148-50
jurisdiction over—
—customary international law, 149
—Hostages Convention, 148-50
protection. *See* consular protection *above*
refugees: *q.v.*
Status of Stateless Persons Convention, 1954, 149 n. 63, 179 n. 42, 180 n. 46
Sudan—
Saudi-Arabian embassy in, incident involving, 47 n. 156
Sweden—
criminal law—
—attempt, 90 n. 47
Hostages Convention—
—implementing legislation—
——absence of, 104-5
—obligations under—
——analogous offence technique, 104
jurisdiction—
—aliens—
——crimes committed abroad, 148
—protective principle, 151 n. 70
law of—
—Extradition Act 1957, 211 n. 7, 241
—Penal Code—
——attempt, 90 n. 47
——Chapter 2(2), 148 n. 57, 151 n. 70
——Chapter 4(1), 77 n. 1, 231
——kidnapping, 77 n. 1, 104-5
——penalties, 105
positions taken—
—jurisdiction, 153 n. 84
—national liberation movements, 268
Syria—
El Al flight from Heathrow, 1986—
—attempted sabotage, 20
FRG—
—expulsion of diplomats by, 20 n. 36
Lebanon, hostage-taking in, and, 4
positions taken—
—extradition, refusal, 213
—General Assembly, discussion of terrorism, 33

—Hostages Convention—
——consistency with UN Charter, 315
—human rights provisions, 207
—national liberation movements, 43-4, 45, 267
terrorism—
—State agents, by, 21
—support for, 20 n. 34
terrorist organizations, links with, 4
UK—
—diplomatic relations, breaking-off, 20 n. 36, 27
West Berlin bombing, 20 n. 36

Tanzania—
positions taken—
—*Ad Hoc* Committee on Terrorism, establishment of, 36 n. 112
—*aut dedere aut judicare*, 195 n. 25
—causes of terrorism, 40 n. 137
—Entebbe, 320
—extradition—
——Hostages Convention as basis for, 239
—"for the purpose of prosecution", 159
—Hostages Convention—
——consistency with UN Charter, 313-14
—national liberation movements, 267, 269 n. 25, 272 n. 38
Territory—
misuse of—
—State responsibility to avoid, 123 n. 15
——ILA, Report of Sixty-First Conference, 123 n. 17
——ILC commentary on New York Convention, 122-3
Terrorism—
banning of terrorist organizations, 126-7
Bonn Declaration, 1978: *q.v.*
causes, 38-9, 41-2
—aggression, 41 n. 140
—*apartheid*, 38
—colonialism, 38, 41, 43
—exploitation, 38, 41
—GA Res, 31-2
—human rights violations, 41, 43
—occupation, 38
—poverty, 38, 41, 43
—racism, 38, 41, 43
—safe-havens, granting of, 41 n. 140
—State-sponsorship of terrorism, 41 n. 140

Terrorism (*cont.*)
  —UN *Ad Hoc* Committee on International Terrorism, 37-9, 40-1
  —unjust economic order, 41
colonialism as, 33, 41 n. 141
condemnation of—
  —General Assembly, 41-5
  ——reasons for, 45
conventions, 6-7, 46-57. *See also* European Convention on the Suppression of Terrorism 1977; Hague Convention 1970; Hostages Convention 1979; League of Nations, Convention on the Establishment of an International Criminal Court, 1937; League of Nations, Convention on the Prevention and Punishment of Terrorism, 1937; Montreal Convention, 1971; Montreal Protocol, 1988; New York Convention, 1973; Organization of American States, Convention to Prevent and Punish Acts of Terrorism 1971; Rome Convention 1988; Rome Protocol 1988; Tokyo Convention 1963
  —adhesion to, 48-9
  —applicability—
  ——national liberation movements, 48
  —codification of international law, as, 47-8
  —comprehensive—
  ——impediments to, 46
  —consensus—
  ——adoption by, 49
  ——differences between, 55 n. 191
  —enforceability, 55, 56-7
  —enumerative approach, 49-50
  ——criticisms of, 50-1
  —ILA draft, 46 n. 153
  ——principles for inclusion, 46 n. 153
  —jurisdiction provisions, 139-40
  —letter bombs, 57 n. 196
  —liability—
  ——individual, 46 n. 153, 55
  ——international law, under, 55
  —motivation, 47-8, 50
  —municipal law, dependence on, 55
  —obligations—
  ——*aut dedere aut judicare*, 54
  ——establishment of jurisdiction, 54
  ——extraditability of offences, 55
  ——judicial assistance, 54
  ——listed offences to be made punishable, 54
  ——steps to prevent offences, 54
  —piecemeal approach, 46-8
  ——reasons for, 47-8
  —"political offence exception", 234-7
  ——reservations, 235
  —principles of—
  ——*aut dedere aut judicare*, 46 n. 153, 48, 49, 54
  ——individual liability, 46 n. 153
  ——motive, irrelevance, 46 n. 153
  ——State responsibility, prohibition, 46 n. 153
  —reporting procedures, 57 n. 195
  —sanctions, 56-7
  —shortcomings, 56-7
  ——enforcement machinery, absence, 56
  —terrorism—
  ——avoidance of definition, 51
  —universality, 48-9
  —US draft. *See under* General Assembly Sixth Committee
  —value, 56
cooperative measures against, 129-31
  —*aut dedere aut judicare*, 42
  —"Berner Club", 130
  —bilateral arrangements, 131
  —Council of Europe, 131
  —diplomatic missions, increased control of, 131
  —European Communities, 130
  —implementation of anti-terrorism conventions, 42
  —League of Nations, 28-9
  —liberty of person, and, 26
  —NATO, 131
  —obstacles, 9, 58
  ——consensus, absence of, 28-45
  ——lack of political will, 45
  —post-World War II, 29-45
  —prevention of preparatory measures, 42
  —pre-World War II, 28-9
  ——International Conferences for the Unification of Penal law, 28
  ——League of Nations, 28-9
  —sanctions against States involved in, 131
  —TREVI, 130
  —US Anti-Terrorism Assistance Program, 130-1

for, 17-18, 50-1
—"terror", 13 n. 3, 14 n. 11
—threat or use of violence, 13
—US State Department, 18-19
effectiveness, 24
effects, 23-8
  —inter-State relations, on, 26-7
  ——*Achille Lauro*, 26-7
  ——UK-Syria, 27
  ——US-Libya, 27
elements. See definition *above*
foreign policy, as arm of, 45
Hostages Convention—
  —element in, 61 n. 213, 75
incidents—
  —*Achille Lauro*, 1985: *q.v.*
  —airports, at—
  ——Frankfurt, 1985, 9 n. 26
  ——Lod, 1972, 32 n. 96
  ——Rome, 1985, 26
  ——Tokyo 1985, 9 n. 26
  ——Vienna, 1985 9 n. 26
  —Entebbe, 1976: *q.v.*
  —Hamadeh (TWA airliner), 1985, 87 n. 40
  —Kuwaiti Airlines Boeing 747, 1988, 115 n. 19
  —Larnaca, 1978, 65
  ——rescue mission, 319
  —Lebanon, in, 1985-9. See Lebanon, hostage-taking in
  —Mogadishu, 1977, 65
  ——rescue mission, 317 n. 21
  —Munich massacre, 1972: *q.v.*
  —OPEC, 1975: *q.v.*
  —Stockholm, FRG Embassy in, 57 n. 196
  ——Holger Meins Kommando, 57 n. 196
  —Sudan—
  ——Saudi-Arabian embassy in, 47 n. 151
  —United States hostages in Tehran, 1979: *q.v.*
increase, 25
international, 22-3
  —anti-terrorism conventions, 23
  —definition, 22-3
  ——International Law Association, 22 n. 47
  ——US Draft Convention, 34
  ——US State Department, 22
international law, and, 8-9
  —codification, 46-8
International Law Commission, 30
jurisdiction: *q.v.*
legitimacy, 30-2. See also motivation *and* national liberation movements *below*
  —New York Convention, 48 n. 162
  —UN Secretariat, 37 n. 121
letter bombs, 57 n. 196
liability—
  —individual, 46 n. 153
motivation. See also Motivation
  —relevance, 18-19, 30-2, 33-45, 46 n. 153, 47-8, 50, 58
  ——UN Secretariat, 37 n. 121
national liberation movements, and, 14, 19, 30-2. See also National liberation movements
  —anti-terrorism conventions—
  ——applicability to, 48
  —General Assembly, and, 32-45
  —UN *Ad Hoc* Committee on International Terrorism, 36-9
  —UN Sixth Committee, 34-6
nature—
  —act—
  ——relevance of, 50
  —change, 25 n. 61
political connotations, 13-14
  —Geneva Declaration on Terrorism, 1987, 14 n. 9
obligations respecting—
  —conduct of, 29, 30
  —encouragement of, 29, 30
  —prevention, 122-3
  —support of, 29, 30
reasons for, 27
State, 9, 14, 15-17, 44, 45
  —definition, 15
  ——coercive diplomacy, 16
  ——Geneva Declaration on Terrorism, 16 n. 19
  —ILA draft, 46 n. 153
  ——UN *Ad Hoc* Committee on International Terrorism, 16
  —individual terrorism, inter-relationship, 16-17
  —Jacobin terror, 15
  —Latin America, in, 15
  —military activity, 16
  —Nazi, 15, 16-17
  —nuclear deterrence, 15
  —own population, against, 15
  —Pol Pot, 15, 17
  —purpose, 15
  —Stalinist, 15
  —UN *Ad Hoc* Committee on International Terrorism, 38-9
State-sponsored, 9, 19-22
  —effects of, 19 n. 34
  —France, and—
  ——*Rainbow Warrior*, 21

Terrorism (cont.)
—conduct of, 29, 30
—encouragement of, 29, 30
—prevention, 122-3
—support of, 29, 30
reasons for, 27
State, 9, 14, 15-17, 44, 45
—definition, 15
——coercive diplomacy, 16
——Geneva Declaration on Terrorism, 16 n. 19
—ILA draft, 46 n. 153
——UN *Ad Hoc* Committee on International Terrorism, 16
—individual terrorism, inter-relationship, 16-17
—Jacobin terror, 15
—Latin America, in, 15
—military activity, 16
—Nazi, 15, 16-17
—nuclear deterrence, 15
—own population, against, 15
—Pol Pot, 15, 17
—purpose, 15
—Stalinist, 15
—UN *Ad Hoc* Committee on International Terrorism, 38-9
State-sponsored, 9, 19-22
—effects of, 19 n. 34
—France, and—
——*Rainbow Warrior*, 21
—GA Res—
——2625 (XXV), 20
——3314 (XXIX), 20
—Iran, 21
——US hostages in Tehran, 21
—Libya, and, 21
—IRA, support for, 19-20
—*locus*, 21
—pre-World War II, 19 n. 33
—Stalin, and, 20
—Syria—
——sabotage of El Al flight, 1986, 20
State responsibility, and, 123
suppression of—
—dependence on municipal law, 95
types, 9
—distinction, 21-2
——nature of act as determining factor, 21 n. 43
United Nations, and, 9
—*Ad Hoc* Committee on International Terrorism. *See* United Nations *Ad Hoc* Committee on International Terrorism

—General Assembly. *See* General Assembly
—ILC. *See* International Law Commission
—Sixth Committee. *See* General Assembly Sixth Committee Committee
Threat—
difficulty of establishing, 83-4
offence, whether—
—Hague Convention, 83
—Hostages Convention, 83-4
—Montreal Convention, 83
—New York Convention, 83-4
Tokyo Convention, 1963, 1, 51-2
aircraft—
—crimes on board—
——jurisdiction, establishment of, 51
—customs, 51
—jurisdiction—
——State of registration, 51
—military, 51
—police, 51
extradition—
—place of crime, 51
jurisdiction—
—obligation to establish, 51
—State of registration, 51, 138
obligations, 51-2
—*aut dedere aut judicare*, 51-2
—establishment of jurisdiction, 51
scope—
—civil aircraft, limitation to, 51
—limited, 51
Torture—
Convention for the Suppression of Torture and Other Cruel and Inhuman or Degrading Treatment or Punishment 1984, 229 n. 5
—*aut dedere aut judicare*, 189-90 n. 9
—judicial assistance, 254 n. 52
—jurisdiction, 139 n. 22, 145 n. 39
Travaux préparatoires, 10, 65-7, 113-14, 164, 169, 198, 228, 233, 254, 339 *and passim*
Hostages Convention, 65-6
treaty interpretation, use in—
—comparable treaties, and, 67
—confirmation of plain text, 67 n. 255
——ICJ, 67 n. 255
——international tribunals, 67 n. 255
——Vienna Convention on the Law of Treaties, 66-7

—Vienna Convention on the Law of Treaties, 66-7
Treaties. *See also* Conventions; Treaty interpretation; Vienna Convention on the Law of Treaties
compliance, 186
customary international law—
—creation by, 291-3
—persistent objection, 291, 292
denunciation, 346
derogation from—
—European Convention for the Protection of Human Rights—
——extent of discretion, 112 n. 8
enforcement, 278 n. 50
extradition. *See* Extradition conventions
implementing legislation—
—correspondence of language
multilateral. *See also* Conventions; Extradition treaties; Judicial assistance conventions
—customary international law, and, 291-3
multilingual—
—drafting, 7-8
—flexibility of language, need for, 81
municipal law, and—
—constitutional limitations—
——Convention on Psychotropic Substances, 137 n. 15
——Single Convention on Narcotic Drugs, 137 n. 15
—provisions subject to—
——Apartheid Convention, 137 n. 15
——Convention on Psychotropic Substances, 137 n. 15
——Single Convention on Narcotic Drugs, 137 n. 15
obligations—
—duty to comply—
——good faith, 345 n. 5
pacta sunt servanda, 337 n. 52
reservations—
—political offences, extradition for, 235
third parties—
—imposition of obligations, 157
violations—
—good faith, whether defence, 112 n. 8
—penalties established by States for, 106-8
Treaty interpretation. *See also* Vienna Convention on the Law of Treaties

aids—
—preamble, 71-2
applicable law, 10
case, relevance, 273 n. 41
context, 292
—preamble as part of, 72
hierarchy of articles, 113-14
object and purpose, 71, 113, 292
ordinary meaning. *See* plain meaning *below*
phrases—
—"conventions", 273 n. 41
—"Powers", 287
plain meaning, 66-7, 113
subsequent practice, 115 n. 19, 292
—*Legal Consequences for States of the Continued Presence of South Africa in Namibia*, 293
teleological, 113
travaux préparatoires: *q.v.*
TREVI, 130
Tribunals, international—
"permanent residence"—
—*Interpretation of Minorities Treaty*, 149-50
travaux préparatoires, use of, 67 n. 255
Tunisia—
positions taken—
—extradition—
——Hostages Convention as basis for, 239

Uganda—
OPEC incident, 3
positions taken—
—*aut dedere aut judicare*, 198
—extradition—
——Hostages Convention as basis for, 239
——refusal, 214-15
—national liberation movements, 35 n. 109
—rescue mission, 320
Ukrainian SSR—
position taken—
—extradition, refusal, 214-15
Union of Soviet Socialist Republics—
positions taken—
—*Ad Hoc* Committee on Terrorism, establishment, 34
—asylum, 333
——treaties, 338 n. 58
—easing hostage's position, 109 n. 1
—extradition—
——Hostages Convention as basis for, 240
——inequality of obligations, 242

414 INDEX

United Kingdon (*cont.*)
  Hague Convention—
    ——implementing legislation, 108
    ——Hijacking Act 1971, 108
  Hostages Convention—
    ——implementing legislation, 78 n. 2
    ——House of Commons debate, 81, 194
    ——Taking of Hostages Act 1982. *See under* law of *below*
  judicial assistance, 247 nn. 7-8, 249 n. 18, 252, 253, 258
  —political offences, and, 253
  —State security, and, 253
  jurisdiction—
    —aircraft—
      ——State of registration, 138 n. 22
    —continental shelf—
      ——installations, 146
    —nationality principle, 148
    —passive personality principle, 154
    —permanent residents, 148
    —protective principle, 151 n. 70
    ——*Joyce* v. *DPP*, 151 n. 70
    —stateless persons, 149
    —territorial—
      ——exceptions, 148
    —universal, 155-6
  kidnapping, 77 n. 1
  law of—
    —Accessories and Abettors Act 1861, 91 n. 54, 103
    —Continental Shelf Act 1964, 146
    —criminal. *See* criminal law *above*
    —Criminal Attempts Act 1981, 89 n. 47, 91 n. 51, 103
    —Criminal Law Act 1977—
      ——Section 1, 91 nn. 51 *and* 54
    —Evidence (Proceedings in Other Jurisdictions) Act, 252, 253, 258
    —Exchange Control Act 1947, 148
    —Extradition Act 1870, 230 n. 8, 238
    —Extradition Act 1873, 252, 253, 258
    —Fugitive Offenders Act 1967, 229 n. 4, 230 n. 8
    —Hijacking Act 1971, 108
    —Interpretation Act 1978, 86 n. 36
    —Offences against the Person Act 1861, 148 n. 53
    —Prevention of Terrorism (Temporary Provisions) Act 1984, 23 n. 53, 125-6
    —Protection of Aircraft Act 1973, 108
    —Taking of Hostages Act 1982, 81, 86, 88, 103, 148, 149 n. 62, 154, 155, 229 n. 4, 243 n. 63
      ——Parliamentary debate, 78 n. 3, 81, 155-6, 162-3
      ——penalties, 108
      ——private acts under, 78 n. 3
    —Theft Act 1968, 304
    —Tokyo Convention Act 1967, 138 n. 22
Lebanon, hostages in—
  —Iran, and, 5 n. 16
Montreal Convention—
  —implementing legislation—
    ——Protection of Aircraft Act 1973, 108
offence—
  —place of—
    ——*R* v. *Owen*, 304 n. 11
    ——Theft Act 1968, 304
    ——*Treacy* v. *DPP*, 304-5
positions taken—
  —*Ad Hoc* Committee on International Terrorism, establishment, 34 n. 104
  —*aut dedere aut judicare*, 195, 197
  —causes of terrorism, 40
  —"circumstances so warrant", 169
  —"easing position of hostage"—
    ——"appropriate measures", 111 n. 7
  —Entebbe, 319
  —extradition—
    ——Hostages Convention as legal basis for, 239, 240
  —"for the purpose of prosecution", 199
  —jurisdiction, 144, 153 n. 81, 160 n. 105, 309
  —"other measures necessary for institution of proceedings", 173 n. 19
  —prompt return of object, 118
  —"severe" penalties, 107
  —US bombing of Libya, 321 n. 54
Syria—
  —diplomatic relations, breaking-off, 27
terrorism—
  —El Al aircraft, sabotage of, 27
  —Lebanon, hostages in, 5
  —legislation, 23
treaties—

—implementing legislation—
——necessity for, 103 n. 40
—unincorporated—
——effect, 103 n. 40
United Nations—
Charter—
—Article 2(4)—
——*Achille Lauro*, 322
——rescue missions, and, 318, 320, 322
—Article 51—
——reprisals, and, 321
——rescue missions, and, 318
—Hostages Convention—
——consistency with, 313-26
——Entebbe, and, 313-12
Declaration on Principles of International Law concerning Friendly Relations and Cooperation among States. *See* GA Res 2625 (XXV)
Economic and Social Council, 38 n. 129
General Assembly: *q.v.*
Human Rights Committee, 38 n. 129
purposes and principles—
—hostage-taking, and
—Hostages Convention, and
Secretariat—
—violence, legitimacy, 37
Security Council: *q.v.*
specialized agencies. *See* International Civil Aviation Organization; International Maritime Organization
terrorism, and, 1, 9, 23
—Conventions regarding, 53-4
Universal Declaration of Human Rights: *q.v.*
United Nations *Ad Hoc* Committee on International Terrorism, 36-9, 40-2
competence, 38 n. 129
—Economic and Social Council, 38 n. 129
—Human Rights Committee, 38 n. 129
—Security Council, and, 38 n. 129
Hostages Committee—
—interaction with, 61 n. 213
Hostages Convention, 60-1
mandate—
—GA Res 3034, 36-7
national liberation movements, 37-8
non-aligned group proposals, 37 n. 120
recommendations, 40-1
—absence, 39

——reasons for, 37-9
reports—
—1973, 36, 39
—1979, 40-1
——delayed consideration, 61 n. 213
resumption of work, 40, 61
sub-committees—
—definition of terrorism, 37
—measures to prevent, 37
—study of underlying causes, 37
terrorism—
—causes, 38-9, 41-2
——aggression, 41 n. 140
——*apartheid*, 38
——colonialism, 38, 41, 43
——exploitation, 38, 41
——human rights violations, 41, 43
——occupation, 38
——poverty, 38, 41 n. 140
——racism, 38, 41, 43
——unjust economic order, 41
—definition, 37-8
—motivation, relevance, 37-8
—national liberation movements, and, 37-8
—State terrorism, 38
United Nations High Commissioner for Refugees—
refugees—
—protection of, 180
Statute of Office of, 180 nn. 45-46
United States. *See also* United States hostages in Tehran, seizure of
Achille Lauro: *q.v.*
Anti-Terrorism Assistance Program, 130-1
criminal law—
—penalties, 108
criminal procedure—
—Federal Rules of, 174 n. 25
diplomatic relations—
—breaking-off—
——Iran, 3
——Libya, 27
expulsion—
—Iranians, of, 3
extradition, 230, 238
—*Achille Lauro*, 26-7
—Italy, from, 26-7
—territorial State, to, 194
—treaties. *See* Extradition treaties
—Yugoslavia, from, 26
Foreign Relations, Senate Committee on—
—Report on the International Convention against the Taking

United States (*cont.*)
    of Hostages, 55 n. 194
    Hague Convention—
    —implementing legislation, 108
    Hostages Convention—
    —implementing legislation, 103-4, 194
    ——Act for the Prevention and Punishment of the Crime of Hostage-taking. *See under* law of *below*
    ——hearings before the Subcommittee on Security and Terrorism, 85-6
    ——necessity for, 102 n. 38, 104 n. 43
    ——"third parties", 85-6
Iran—
  —diplomatic relations, breaking-off, 3
judicial assistance, 247 n. 10, 248-50, 252, 253, 256, 258, 260 nn. 77 *and* 80
  —*John Deere Ltd.* v. *Sperry Corp.*, 247 n. 10
jurisdiction—
  —artificial islands, 146 n. 47
  —continental shelf—
  ——substructures, 146 n. 47
  —passive personality principle, 154
  —stateless persons, 149
  —territorial, 144 n. 37
  ——exceptions, 148 n. 53
  —terrorist offences, 23 n. 49, 153 n. 83
  —universal, 155
kidnapping, 102 n. 38
law of—
  —Act for the Prevention and Punishment of the Crime of Hostage-taking, 78 n. 3. *See also* law of, 18 USC 1203 *below*
  ——private acts under, 78
  —Act to Combat International Terrorism 1984, 23
  —anti-terrorism legislation, 23
  —"attempt"—
  ——"substantial step" test, 89 n. 47
  —Constitution—
  ——Fourth Amendment, 170
  —Omnibus Diplomatic Security and Antiterrorism Act 1986, 154
  —18 USC 5, 144 n. 37
  —18 USC 32, 108
  —18 USC 1201, 102 n. 38
  —18 USC 1203, 81 n. 15, 88, 104 n. 43, 148 n. 54, 149 n. 62, 231 n. 13
  —18 USC 1331, 146 n. 47
  —18 USC 1696, 252, 253
  —18 USC 1782, 249 n. 22, 250 n. 27, 252, 253, 260 nn. 77 *and* 80
  —18 USC 1963, 117 n. 30
  —18 USC 2331, 154 n. 87
  —18 USC 3181, 238
  —18 USC 3184, 238
  —49 USC 1472, 108
Lebanon, hostages in, 4-5
letters rogatory, 247 nn. 7 *and* 10
liberty of person, 170
Libya—
  —bombing, 27, 321
  —diplomatic relations, breaking-off, 27
Montreal Convention—
  —implementing legislation, 108
Office of Counter-Terrorism, 23
  —Ambassador-at-large for Counter-Terrorism, 23
positions taken—
  —*Achille Lauro*, 322
  —*Ad Hoc* Committee on Terrorism, establishment, 34 n. 104
  —asylum, 330
  ——treaties, 337 n. 57, 341 n. 68
  —*aut dedere aut judicare*, 197, 198
  —bombing of Libya, 321 n. 54
  —causes of terrorism, 40
  —"circumstances so warrant", 169
  —extradition—
  ——Hostages Convention as legal basis for, 239
  ——place of registration, to, 191 n. 15
  ——refusal, 212 n. 14
  —GA Res 42/159, 43 n. 145
  —Hostages Convention—
  ——applicability, 311 n. 33
  ——consistency with UN Charter, 314
  —jurisdiction, 153 n. 84, 157 n. 97, 160 n. 105
  —national liberation movements, 35 n. 109, 268, 269, 271 n. 34, 291, 309 n. 25
  —"severe" penalties, 107 n. 62
  —supplementary agreements, necessity for, 119, 128
racketeering—
  —obligation to return spoils, 117
terrorism. *See also* United States hostages in Tehran

—*Achille Lauro*, 322
—*Ad Hoc* Committee on Terrorism, establishment, 34 n. 104
—asylum, 330
——treaties, 337 n. 57, 341 n. 68
—*aut dedere aut judicare*, 197, 198
—bombing of Libya, 321 n. 54
—causes of terrorism, 40
—"circumstances so warrant", 169
—extradition—
——Hostages Convention as legal basis for, 239
——place of registration, to, 191 n. 15
——refusal, 212 n. 14
—GA Res 42/159, 43 n. 145
—Hostages Convention—
——applicability, 311 n. 33
——consistency with UN Charter, 314
—jurisdiction, 153 n. 84, 157 n. 97, 160 n. 105
—national liberation movements, 35 n. 109, 268, 269, 271 n. 34, 291, 309 n. 25
—"severe" penalties, 107 n. 62
—supplementary agreements, necessity for, 119, 128
racketeering—
—obligation to return spoils, 117
terrorism. *See also* United States hostages in Tehran
—*Achille Lauro*, 4, 26-7, 115-16
—definition, 18-19, 22
—draft Convention for Prevention and Punishment of. *See under* General Assembly Sixth Committee
—jurisdiction, 23 n. 49
—legislation, 23
—Office of Counter-Terrorism, 23
——Ambassador-at-large for Counter-Terrorism, 23
—reprisals, 23
—statistics, 25 n. 62
treaties—
——non-self-executing—
———Hostages Convention, 102 n. 38
———*Over the Top* case, 102 n. 43
——treaties defining crimes, 102 n. 43
United States hostages in Tehran, 1979, 3
—Algeria, and, 3
—*Case concerning the United States*

Diplomatic and Consular Staff in Tehran, 3 n. 12
—demands, 3
—diplomatic relations, breaking-off, 3
—Hostages Convention, and, 65
—release of hostages, 3
—reprisals—
——diplomatic relations, breaking-off, 3
——economic sanctions, 3
——expulsion, 3
——freezing of assets, 3
—rescue mission, 3
Universal Declaration of Human Rights, 205, 206
asylum, 328 n. 1
Universal Postal Union, 9 n. 26, 43 n. 145
Uruguay—
positions taken—
—asylum, 333 n. 31
—extradition, refusal, 214 n. 22
—General Assembly postponement of discussion of terrorism, 39

Venezuela—
positions taken—
—asylum, 331, 332, 333-4
—national liberation movements, 39 n. 132
Vienna Convention on Consular Relations 1963, 178
Article 31, 111 n. 5
Article 36(1), 177
Article 36(2), 181
codification, as, 59, 60 n. 210
inviolability of premises, 111 n. 5
refugees, protection of, 180 n. 47
Vienna Convention on Diplomatic Relations 1961—
Article 22, 111 n. 5, 336 n. 51
Article 29, 110 n. 3
Article 31, 171 n. 14
Article 40, n. 14
codification, as, 59, 60 n. 210
inviolability of premises, 111 n. 5
Vienna Convention on the Law of Treaties 1969, 353
anti-terrorism conventions—
—sanctions under, 56 n. 195
Article 26, 337 n. 52, 345 n. 5
Article 30, 225
Article 31(1), 66 n. 254, 71, 113 n. 10
Article 31(2), 71
Article 31(3), 115 n. 19

Words and phrases (*cont.*)
   jus cogens, 190   *levée en masse*, 285
   modus procendi, 260
   non bis in idem, 205 n. 70
   non-refoulement. See under Aliens
   ordre public, 261 n. 84
   pacta sunt servanda, 337 n. 52
   pirata non mutat dominium, 117 n. 31
   post factum, 119
   prima facie, 202, 232
   reclusion perpetua, 104
   reclusion temporal, 104
   sine qua non, 128
   status quo ante, 109, 117, 118
   travaux préparatoires: *q.v.*
World Tourism Organization, 43 n. 145

Yemen—
   position taken—
     —national liberation movements, 31 n. 90, 264 n. 4, 268
Yugoslavia—

Achille Lauro—
   —refusal to hold for extradition, 26 n. 65
extradition agreements. See Extradition treaties
PLO—
   —officials—
     ——diplomatic immunity, 26 n. 65
positions taken—
   —"all practicable measures", 124
   —easing hostage's position, 109 n. 1
   —Entebbe, 314 n. 4
   —GA Res 3034, 36
   —prevention of hostage-taking, 119

Zambia—
   position taken—
     —extradition—
       ——Hostages Convention as basis for, 239